Techniques and Guidelines for Social Work Practice

Techniques and Guidelines for Social Work Practice

Second Edition

Bradford W. Sheafor
Colorado State University

Charles R. Horejsi
The University of Montana

Gloria A. Horejsi
Community Medical Center
Missoula, Montana

Allyn and Bacon

Boston   London   Toronto   Sydney   Tokyo   Singapore

Series Editor: *Karen Hanson*
Series Editorial Assistant: *Laurie Frankenthaler*
Production Administrator: *Annette Joseph*
Production Coordinator: *Susan Freese*
Editorial-Production Service: *TKM Productions*
Text Designer: *Denise Hoffman, Glenview Studios*
Manufacturing Buyer: *Megan Cochran*
Cover Administrator: *Linda K. Dickinson*
Cover Designer: *Suzanne Harbison*

This textbook is printed on
recycled, acid-free paper.

Library of Congress Cataloging-in-Publication Data
Sheafor, Bradford W.
    Techniques and guidelines for social work practice / Bradford W.
Sheafor, Charles R. Horejsi, Gloria A. Horejsi. — 2nd ed.
      p.   cm.
    Includes bibliographical references and index.
    ISBN 0–205–12768–1
    1. Social service—United States. I. Horejsi, Charles R.
II. Horejsi, Gloria A.   III. Title.
HV91.S48   1990
361.3′2—dc20   90–42748
                                               CIP

Printed in the United States of America

10 9 8 7 6 5 4 3 2 1   95 94 93 92 91 90

Permissions: Various citations from Fisher (1978) are reprinted with permission of McGraw-Hill, Inc.

To the next generation of social workers
who have chosen to devote their time and talents to
the service of others and the struggle for social justice

and

to our families
Nadine, Laura, Brandon, Perry, Christopher,
Angela, Martin, and Katherine
for their love and support

Contents

III.   Techniques and Guidelines for Direct Service   169

Chapter 9   Intake and Engagement   171

Chapter 10   Data Collection and Assessment   211

Chapter 15 The Community Context of Practice 468

Preface

The quality of life in the United States is significantly influenced by the services performed by social workers. Working in courts, schools, hospitals, businesses, private practice, and a myriad of social agencies, social workers help people and the society in which they live change—to solve problems or enhance social functioning. In addition to services given directly to individuals and families, the very nature of social work requires that issues of social betterment and social justice that affect both clients and the general public be addressed. Indirectly, the whole society—including its economy—benefits from the social worker's activity, because improving the quality of life for an individual, family or other household, group, organization, and/or community will ultimately impact the general society, as well.

The first part of this book is concerned with identifying and describing the fundamentals of social work practice. We included this material because we believe that the proper application of all practice tools is dependent on and directly related to the social worker's values, knowledge base, professional background, and certain other personal characteristics and life experiences. The application of practice techniques outside that context not only limits their usefulness but, more importantly, could harm clients.

Most of this book is devoted to presenting techniques and guidelines that expand the repertoire of practice tools available to the social worker. The mastery of a range of such techniques and guidelines is necessary for effectively serving people in need of social work services. This material is presented in handbook form to make it readily accessible to the practitioner, but we anticipate that the examples contained in this text will stimulate the reader to invent new techniques and additional guidelines for practice.

We wish to emphasize the importance of consciously choosing practice tools in a manner compatible with the practice theory that has been selected to guide and inform a particular intervention. It is our belief that practice should begin "where the client is." That is, the social worker should select a guiding conceptual framework that fits the unique situation of the individual, family, group, organization, or community being served and then choose the specific techniques and practice guidelines that implement that broader framework. The handbook format of this book is intended to facilitate the latter step in the change process.

In the Foreword to the first edition of this book (1988), Barbara Solomon clearly articulated both the dangers and advantages of the emphasis we have placed on describing techniques and guidelines for social work practice:

> This handbook format is likely to draw criticism from certain sections of the social work community. For example, there will be those who argue that it is impossible to disconnect a practice intervention from its theoretical framework. Moreover, it is the utilization of theory to determine practice that distinguishes the professional from the technician. However, our theoretical framework may provide insights as to how a problem develops and even in general terms what we ought to do to resolve it, but rarely will it specify our actions. An ecological systems frame of reference, for example, might dictate that a particular client should be referred to a community resource. It will not, however, specify *how* the referral should be made. Furthermore, no theoretical orientation goes so far as to point out the most effective ways for the social worker to utilize the telephone, testify in court, write a report, use supervision, or engage in many of the activities often considered essential to the social work change process and, therefore, included in the handbook. (p. ix)

This book, then, addresses specific actions that a social worker might take to serve his or her clients most effectively or to change social institutions that affect those clients.

Plan for the Text

Although the reader may already have developed a professional orientation, Part I, "A Framework for Social Work Practice," reviews several important background characteristics a social worker must possess, including:

1. A clear conception of the domain of social work and the competencies the social worker is expected to bring to the change process
2. The native talents or artistic abilities necessary for perceptively entering the interpersonal relations that are at the heart of practice
3. An ability to draw upon and apply the science of social work, the profession's knowledge base, and its ethical principles
4. A clear understanding of the varied roles performed by social workers in delivering human services and the specific functions associated with these roles
5. The ability to apply the fundamental practice principles that have evolved in social work
6. Skill in performing the important activity of guiding the process of change

Part II, "Techniques Common to All Social Work Practice," identifies techniques and guidelines that strengthen the ability of the social worker in these fundamental aspects of professional competence. Social work practice can take many different forms, ranging from counseling individuals to working with committees. Yet a number of fundamental skills are required for all social work practice.

1. The social worker must have the interpersonal competence to carry out effective communication and engage in a set of basic helping activities.
2. The social worker must be skilled at case management (i.e., organizing the delivery of services and resources needed in a specific case) and able to effectively manage his or her own workload in order to maximize the quality of services.
3. The social worker must be able to maintain a pattern of personal and professional growth and development that keeps him or her current, enriched, and energized to carry out practice.

Part III, "Techniques and Guidelines for Direct Service," focuses on a number of practice tools for working with clients who are direct recipients of the social worker's service; each chapter addresses a specific phase of the change process. For the social worker who finds that he or she is stuck at one phase of helping a client or group of clients, the chapter relating to that phase provides a range of suggestions that may help the worker move forward. The techniques and guidelines included here are not exhaustive, but a sufficient range has been selected, such that one or more should either directly apply to the situation or suggest ideas that might help the worker create other approaches. The worker should approach these techniques with the anticipation of both adopting and adapting them for practice.

For the social worker engaged in service activities in behalf of clients, Part IV, "Techniques and Guidelines for Indirect Practice," offers suggestions for practice activities when working in or among organizations or the community at large. Although the social work literature is less extensive and less specific regarding practice at this level, tools have been developed and are reported in this section.

Definition of Terms

Writing about social work practice inherently presents some language problems between authors and readers. One has to read only a few social work texts or articles to become at least a little confused with the terminology used to describe practice. Perhaps that is to be expected in a relatively new profession, especially one like social work, which focuses on complex and dynamic human and social interactions. This book cannot overcome these long-standing problems of terminology, nor can it present definitions that will be acceptable to every reader. Yet the ideas presented here will be more readily understood if we make the meanings of three frequently used terms more explicit.

The reader should be alert to the term **client.** Common usage implies a narrow view of an individual person who is the consumer of services. As used here, the term has a broader connotation. The client of the social worker providing services at the interface of person and environment may be an individual or a family, small group, committee, organization, neighborhood, community, or other social structure. Throughout the book, the term *client* is occasionally expanded to mention *clients, client groups,* or *client system,* reminding the reader that the narrow definition of client is not intended.

A **technique** is viewed as a relatively brief, circumscribed, goal-oriented behavior performed in a practice situation by the social worker. It is a planned action deliberately taken by the practitioner. The application of a simple technique (e.g., using an "I-message") may take only a minute; more complex techniques (e.g., family sculpting) may require an hour or more.

Guidelines, by comparison, are a set of directions intended to influence the social worker's professional behavior and decisions. Guidelines are essentially lists of dos and don'ts. They might be used when working with a specific type of client (e.g., an elderly or dangerous client), when performing certain activities (e.g., making a referral or planning a meeting), or when carrying out workload management tasks (e.g., recording or writing reports).

In addition to techniques and guidelines used by the worker, practice theory and assumptions about human behavior and the change process are necessary in helping the social worker understand the client and his or her situation. Interestingly, however, many practitioners use many of the same techniques and guidelines regardless of the practice theory, model, or approach they purport to follow. In other words, differences in theoretical orientations often are not readily evident at the level of worker behavior.

Although the client is indirectly affected by the social worker's theoretical knowledge, he or she is most directly influenced by what the worker actually does or, more accurately, by what the client *perceives* the worker does. Fischer (1978) makes a useful distinction between *knowing* and *doing,* between the worker's *thought* and the worker's *behavior:*

> In the context of the worker's relationships with the client . . . "something" has to be done by the worker. The worker obviously does not "do" a theory. A theory, a complex set of ideas, observations, facts, etc., in itself cannot be applied to a person. There must be some way of translating the theory, or a principle of the theory into action. The technique is that translation, that application in action. The technique or procedure of helping is merely the way the worker attempts to use some principles, or use the theory to make it "come alive" in application with clients. (p. 60)

Thus, it is through applying techniques that the worker directly interfaces with the client or client group. Although much of the attention devoted to knowledge building in social work has addressed the further development of theory, it is also important for social workers to turn their attention to the development, description, and dissemination of knowledge regarding the techniques and guidelines that enhance social work practice. Epstein (1980) comments that "the search for grand theory does not seem to be urgent. Much more urgent and badly needed are frameworks to guide practice. This means techniques" (p. 138).

Others have also urged the profession to give more attention to its techniques. In describing what he terms as a "revolution" in social work, Fischer (1981) explains:

The new form of practice must rely less on utilizing traditional *theories* than on developing or utilizing specific interventive techniques.... The major alternative to traditional practice grounded in particular theories is the development of an eclectic approach to practice made up of a variety of empirically derived and validated principles and procedures.... Thus practitioners can have available to them a body of specific techniques to apply with their clients, based on a careful assessment of the client, situation, and problem. (p. 203)

Because other texts have focused mostly on theory and because the profession and its educational programs need to give greater attention to the "what" and the "how" of practice, we have prepared this text to begin filling the void by collecting, analyzing, developing, and transmitting practice techniques and guidelines. We hope this effort will further stimulate social workers to examine their practice at this very concrete level and to describe and share the techniques and guidelines that contribute to successful intervention with clients and client groups.

Acknowledgments

We would like to recognize a number of people who have contributed to the revisions presented in this second edition.

Many professional colleagues have graciously given their time and expertise to offer constructive criticisms on various sections of this book. A special thank you is extended to:

- Mona Schatz, D.S.W. (social work roles and functions)
- Michael Silverglat, M.D., and Terri Loftus, B.S.W./L.P.N. (psychotropic medication)
- Robert Deaton, Ed.D. (suicide)
- Dan Morgan, M.S.W., George Galinkin, M.S.W., Cindy Bartling, M.S.W., and Colleen Lippke, M.S.W. (children and adolescents)
- Richard Shields, M.S.W., Deborah Nelles, M.A., Jo Ann Blake, M.A., Ted Lewis, and Lloyd Barron, B.S.W. (chemical dependency)
- Mary Birch, M.S.W. (small groups)
- Cindy Garthwait, M.S.W. (working with the elderly)
- Charlotte Booth, M.S.W. (hard-to-reach clients)
- Jon Bertsche, M.S.W. (evaluation and informal resources)
- Barbara W. Shank, M.S.W. (sexual harassment)
- Tom Roy, M.A., and Frank Clark, Ph.D. (advocacy, assessment, and evaluation)
- John Spores, Ph.D. (cross-cultural interaction)
- Kathleen Gallacher, M.A. (child development)
- Peter Pecora, Ph.D. (evaluation)
- Elizabeth Tracy, Ph.D., and James Whittaker, Ph.D. (social support assessment)
- Angeline Barretta-Herman, M.S.W./M.B.A. (team meetings)

In addition, we wish to acknowledge those individuals who reviewed the book at various stages for Allyn and Bacon:

- John Burdick, Winona State University
- Kay Van Buskirk, Mankato State University
- Larry Lister, University of Hawaii at Manoa
- Sol Spector, California State University at Sacramento

Finally, we are especially indebted to Bernadette Lahr, Emily Rinehart, and Pat Cross for the many hours they spent typing draft materials and parts of the final manuscript.

B. W. S.
C. R. H.
G. A. H.

Selected Bibliography

Barker, Robert. *The Social Work Dictionary.* Silver Spring, Md.: NASW, 1987.

Corey, Gerald, Marianne Schneider Corey, Patrick J. Callanan, and J. Michael Russell. *Group Techniques,* rev. ed. Pacific Grove, Calif.: 1988.

Epstein, Laura. *Helping People: The Task-Centered Approach.* St. Louis: C. V. Mosby, 1980.

Fischer, Joel. *Effective Casework Practice: An Eclectic Approach.* New York: McGraw-Hill, 1978.

———. "The Social Work Revolution." *Social Work* 26 (May 1981): 199–207.

Techniques and Guidelines for Social Work Practice

A Framework for Social Work Practice

I.

Social work is an essential profession in our complex and rapidly changing society. But it is an often misunderstood profession, as well, in part, because it cannot be easily described or explained. It is a profession characterized by variety and diversity. Social workers engage in a wide range of activities within many types of settings. Some work intensely with individuals and families, while others work with small groups; still others work with organizations and whole communities. Some deal primarily with children; others, with elderly persons. Some are counselors and psychotherapists; others are program planners, administrators, and fundraisers. Some are concerned with the problem of family violence; others, with the problem of how to provide medical care to the poor. This variety is what makes social work challenging and stimulating. But it is because of this diversity of clients and activities that it is so difficult to answer the simple question, What is social work?

One could ask five social workers this question and get at least as many answers. Typically, it would be at only very abstract levels that the answers would reflect the commonality that allows these individuals to practice under the rubric of a single profession—social work. They might agree on the broad purposes of the profession and be supportive of the Code of Ethics; they perhaps would hold certain values in common and share much of the profession's knowledge base. But it is likely that they would differ a great deal in their day-to-day activities and the techniques they use in their work.

The problem of defining social work in a manner that encompasses the wide range of activities in which social workers engage has plagued the profession throughout its first century of development. And it is unlikely this definitional problem will be resolved in the near future. In this book, and particularly in Part I, the authors present a perspective on social work and describe the context in which they assume the techniques and guidelines included in the remainder of the book will be applied. Part I reflects one conception of this

1

*profession. The authors' perspective of social work is made explicit in the fol-
lowing three-part definition of a social worker. A social worker*

1. *has recognized professional preparation (i.e., knowledge, ethics, and competencies);*
2. *is sanctioned by society to provide specific services targeted primarily at
   helping vulnerable populations (e.g., children, the aged, the poor, minorities, women, families) engage in efforts to change themselves, the people
   around them, or social institutions; and*
3. *has the purpose of helping others meet social needs or eliminate difficulties so that they might make maximum use of their abilities to lead full
   and satisfying lives and contribute fully to society.*

*To carry out the responsibilities identified in the above definition, the so-
cial worker must function within the profession's domain. Chapter 1, "Practice
within the Social Work Domain," elaborates the authors' definition of social
work and presents its central mission as helping people change so that they fit
more comfortably within their worlds—or, conversely, helping the world
change to be more supportive of the person. This help is provided through
social programs that include making tangible social provisions available to
people in need, offering intangible social services such as counseling or treatment, and engaging in social change activities.*

*As the primary helping profession providing human services, social work is
responsible for implementing society's commitment to help people who are
experiencing social needs. Sanction to provide services is expressed through
the creation of social agencies, both governmental and voluntary, and support for a variety of social programs. Although the private practice of social
work is growing and is viewed as an appropriate medium for providing services, social work practice is most commonly conducted under the sponsorship of a social agency or similar organization, which can have profound
influence on the social worker's practice.*

*Throughout its history, social work has been described as both an art and
a science. Chapter 2, "Art and Science in Social Work Practice," provides a
description of worker personality characteristics that contribute to high-quality
practice and identifies the primary knowledge required of beginning-level social workers. Although there have been consistent efforts throughout the
emergence of this profession to identify and develop its scientific base, during
the last half century, little attention has been given to the artistic or individual
human traits that are prerequisite to effective practice. While social work
practice requires certain learned behaviors and is enhanced by a growing
body of techniques and guidelines upon which the social worker can draw,
there is no substitute for these inherent individual capacities.*

*However, the effective social worker cannot operate only on the basis of
his or her artistic talents. The science of social work requires the social worker
to possess knowledge that is gained through experience and/or obtained
from research and theories. The knowledge required of the social worker includes understanding people and their behavior (both individually and as*

they play out their lives in families, groups, organizations, and communities), being cognizant of social work practices that can be applied in helping situations, and attaining the necessary information to function as a responsible member of the social work profession.

The art and science possessed by the individual social worker blend in daily practice. The social worker must match his or her unique abilities with the roles to be performed in helping clients. In Chapter 3, "The Roles and Functions of Social Workers," attention turns to what social workers do in their practice. When providing human services, social workers perform a variety of helping roles that might include everything from advocating for clients or client groups, to providing individual or family counseling or therapy, to administering a social agency or supervising a less experienced colleague. The skillful performance of one's practice roles is essential for bringing the resources of the community (i.e., worker, agency, and programs) to bear on meeting the clients' needs.

A number of fundamental practice principles have evolved as social workers have conducted their practice. To many social workers, the phrases used to communicate these principles have become clichés: "Begin where the client is," "Help the client help himself (or herself)," "Guide the process, not the client." The casual use of these phrases too often masks their importance. Chapter 4, "The Principles of Social Work Practice," identifies eighteen basic principles that should guide the social worker's practice. These principles provide the bottom line for consistently offering appropriate and effective services to clients.

Finally, the social worker must guide the change process so that clients can become appropriately involved in this activity, make an informed assessment of the change that is required, carefully plan a strategy to achieve that change, carry out that change effort, evaluate the success of that activity, and terminate the service. Chapter 5, "The Change Process in Social Work Practice," outlines the essentials of the change process and its importance in successful practice.

In summary, Part I examines five essential dimensions of social work (i.e., domain, art and science, roles and functions, principles, and process), but does not develop them in depth. The intent of these chapters is to provide a reminder that the application of the techniques and guidelines that constitute the remainder of the book must be carefully selected and applied as part of a complex change process.

Practice within the Social Work Domain

1

When a person sets out to help people, and especially those who are most vulnerable to social problems, the responsibility must be taken seriously. Social workers can and do damage clients when they are not well prepared and when they conduct their practice outside the competence and ethics of their profession. It is the responsibility of each social worker to prepare himself or herself through professional education and continued professional development to give clients the highest quality of service possible.

It is useful for the social worker to examine periodically the domain of social work (i.e., to review its purpose, scope, and sanction to perform its services). Such an examination is useful for the student or the new social worker because educational programs divide the study of social work into units, or courses, as a means of focusing on particular aspects of practice for intensive study. Thus, it is helpful from time to time to take a comprehensive view of social work to help integrate knowledge gained from that study. For the experienced practitioner, working in a single agency or with the specialized approaches typically used in private practice necessarily narrows one's perception of social work. Taking the time to stand back from one's daily routine to view the profession as a whole may strengthen the practitioner's identification with social work and increase his or her appreciation of the varied and creative approaches that are available for use.

The new social worker often struggles to identify what competencies he or she should bring to the practice setting. In multidiscipline settings, the problem is compounded, as there is overlap in the contributions that the different disciplines have to offer. At times, the social worker is tempted to take on the characteristics of another discipline (i.e., "professional drift") and begin to mimic the work of that profession. If the agency and clients are to benefit from the unique perspective that social work brings to professional helping and if the social worker is to use the knowledge, values, and skills that he or she has developed through professional preparation, it is essential to have a clear understanding of the domain of social work. The remainder of this chapter addresses the purpose, scope, and sources of sanction that serve to define the domain of social work.

What is social work practice? In its most elementary form, it is a process whereby people with social needs engage with social workers in a process that results in social change. That change may include individual change, change within a social organization (family, group, organization, community, or the larger society), or a combination of these.

A common image of social work practice is that of a social worker and client engaged in a face-to-face discussion of some problem or situation. Although such meetings frequently occur in practice, this image reflects only one kind of practice activity, and even in this activity, the worker-client conversation is only one component of the professional relationship. In all types of practice activities, much that is happening is not readily observable. Furthermore, practice behaviors are influenced by the social worker's personal and professional knowledge and values; the employing agency's established requirements for the conduct of practice; the quality and funding level of the social programs intended to help persons in need; and, in fact, the general condition of the nation and the world.

Figure 1.1 presents a model of the factors that influence social work practice. The model focuses on the place where the lives of clients and workers overlap, that is, engaging in a *process of social change.* The client brings the *problem* to be solved or the *situation* to be improved as a result of the change activity. Sometimes the client voluntarily seeks to help with this change, but on other occasions, the change activity is forced by a spouse, a school, a court, the police, or others.

The change process involves several phases of activity in which the client and social worker move from a decision to initiate service, through the change activity, to an evaluation of the success of the change effort and a decision to terminate the helping activity (see Chapter 5). Although the social worker is expected to guide this process, the client must ultimately make decisions about how he or she (or that family, group, organization, or community) will change behaviors or utilize resources to deal with the situation. In addition to the ability to perform the tasks necessary to lead clients through the change process, the social worker's primary contribution is applying his or her skill in the selection and use of available *techniques and guidelines* for helping clients achieve the desired change.

"The Client" side of Figure 1.1 indicates that the problem, interpersonal functioning, or social situation the client seeks to change is assumed to be the product of a combination of personal and environmental factors. After all, the uniqueness of social work among the helping professions is its mission to facilitate change in the interactions between people and the world around them. Each client has *personal characteristics* that may have contributed to the situation being addressed. Whether the client is an individual, family, or some larger social structure, it is the special needs, wants, capacities, knowledge, beliefs, physical characteristics, and life experiences of the client that make every situation unique.

Figure 1.1   An Integrative View of Social Work Practice

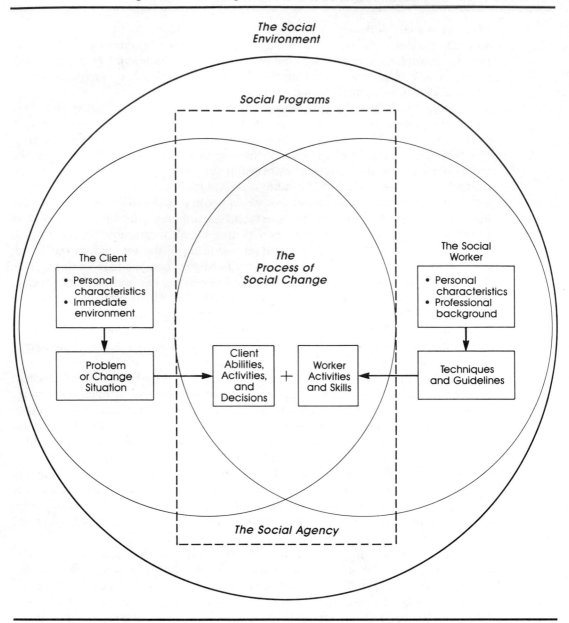

The Social
Environment

Social Programs

The Client

- Personal
  characteristics
- Immediate
  environment

Problem
or Change
Situation

The
Process of
Social Change

Client
Abilities,
Activities,
and
Decisions

+

Worker
Activities
and Skills

The Social
Worker

- Personal
  characteristics
- Professional
  background

Techniques
and Guidelines

The Social Agency

Moreover, clients do not exist in isolation. They have an ***immediate environment*** that also influences the situation. This immediate environment might include friends, family, school personnel, employers, natural helpers, neighborhood or community groups, or even other professional helpers, to mention a few. Because environmental influences have contributed to the need for change and can also be a part of the solution, people in the immediate environment must be kept in the foreground as possible targets and resources for the change activity.

"The Social Worker" side of Figure 1.1 suggests that the worker brings both personal characteristics and professional background to the change process. The **personal characteristics** reflect such important factors as one's unique *life experience* and especially the social worker's *artistic talents* (see Chapter 2), as they apply to social work practice. In addition, the general knowledge of the human condition that the social worker has acquired, as well as his or her particular belief system, are also part of the individual uniqueness that is introduced into the helping process. Finally, social workers bring a perspective from their own racial or ethnic background, gender, age, culture, sexual orientation, and the like that affects how they relate to and are viewed by their clients.

At the same time, the practitioner brings the special contribution of a **professional background** in social work, which differentiates the social worker from friends, family, or other natural helpers that may have attempted to help the client deal with the situation requiring change. What is the social worker's professional background? First, the social worker brings professional expertise to tasks that are performed within the *domain*, or territory, of social work. That territory is defined by social work's purpose, its scope of responsibility among the helping professions, the areas of service the public has sanctioned it to provide, and the functions performed by social workers when participating in a change process. (Domain will be discussed more fully later in this chapter.)

Second, social work is both an *art* and a *science.* Through ongoing practice experience, the social worker is able to develop a practice wisdom and recognize how his or her personal characteristics and style can be effectively used to help clients. The talents of the individual social worker, as well as the specialized professional knowledge and a generally accepted set of values and ethical behaviors, should guide the thoughts and actions of the social worker. Chapter 2 contains a general description of necessary native abilities, as well as professional knowledge and value positions that are especially relevant to social work practice.

Third, as social workers carry out their professional responsibilities, they must effectively perform the appropriate *helping roles.* As Chapter 3 describes more fully, social workers must be prepared to perform practice tasks or functions ranging from linking clients to appropriate resources in the community, to assessing and providing direct services, to planning and conducting social change efforts.

Finally, as social workers have interacted with clients, they have informally tested the general applicability of their approach to providing human services, largely through trial and error. Some of the tried-and-true guidelines for practice have been reduced to a group of *practice principles* that serve as the most fundamental directives to successful practice (see Chapter 4). Armed with a thorough understanding of these principles and an ability to guide the *change process* (see Chapter 5), the social worker, at best, maximizes the chance of successful change and, at worst, minimizes the risk of harm to the client.

It is important to recognize that social work practice takes place within a **social environment.** An environment that supports quality living for all people benefits the more secure as well as the more vulnerable members of that society. A nation or world that is committed to the health, safety, and welfare of all people creates a positive social environment. Yet every social worker knows that Utopia has not yet arrived and that our society has had an ambivalent and transient commitment to improving the quality of life for all its citizens.

The degree of commitment that society has for the well-being of its members directly affects social work practice. While the willingness to act on its commitment to human welfare varies in different societies (and even different regions, states, and communities), ultimately, there is some expression of responsibility for caring for those people whose needs are not met through family, friends, and other social institutions.

Thus, through its legislative and other decision-making bodies, society decides it will create **social programs** to help those in need. These programs, as reflected in Figure 1.1, take three distinct forms. *Social provisions* involve giving tangible goods (such as money, food, clothing, and housing) to persons in need. *Social services* include intangible services (such as counseling, therapy, and group interaction experiences) intended to help people resolve problems with social functioning. Finally, *social action* programs are concerned with changing the social environment to make it more responsive to other people's needs.

The philosophy on which these programs are based has a significant impact on how the social worker functions. The dominant philosophy in the United States contends that these programs should be residual or a "safety net" that is available only to people who are in need because of the failure of the individual, family, or economy to provide adequately. In other words, social programs should exist only to help people solve problems. This view fails to appreciate the potential for enhancing the quality of life when no defined problem exists. A second philosophy (the institutional conception), which considers social programs to be first-line functions of society (like education and recreation), is receiving increased recognition. This view avoids forcing the client to identify a problem or admit to some failure in order to benefit from human services (Wilensky and Lebeaux 1965, 138–40).

Social programs are typically offered through a **social agency** and are based on a mixture of residual and institutional philosophies. As suggested in Figure 1.1, the client and social worker temporarily interact under the aegis of the social agency to engage in a change process that does not (or should not) compromise the autonomy or freedom of either individual in other aspects of his or her life. The basic functions of the agency are to *administer social programs* needed by clients and to *monitor the quality* of the helping process to assure its viability. To perform these functions, the agency must secure money, staff, and other resources; determine which people in the community are eligible for its services; and maintain an administrative structure that will meet targeted social needs in an efficient and effective manner.

A social agency might be a welfare office, mental health center, school, hospital, neighborhood recreation center, or any of a number of differing organizational structures. It may be a public agency supported by tax funds and governed by a governmental body or a private agency operating under the auspices of a volunteer board and supported primarily by fees and voluntary contributions. The most important ingredient of a social agency is people. Receptionists, typists, custodians, administrators, and service providers all must work together to deliver successful social programs. Often, several helping professions are employed by the same agency and each brings its own perspective on helping—as well as the special competencies appropriate to the domain of that profession. To maximize the quality of services given, the social worker must recognize and function within the domain of his or her profession.

The Social Work Domain

A profession's *domain* is its territory or its sphere of interest and legitimate functioning. Among all helping professions, social work stands out as the one that is particularly concerned about the social aspects of life and human problems. For example, take the case of Mrs. S, who displays signs of depression. Certainly, the social worker is concerned about her depressed mood and her troubled thoughts and feelings. However, the worker's primary attention is focused on how feeling depressed is affecting Mrs. S's functioning as a wife, a mother, and an employee and how these social roles and responsibilities are in turn related to her feelings of depression. The attention given to the social aspects of Mrs. S's problem identifies a core feature of social work—a focus on the human interaction, or *social functioning*, dimensions of the situation.

Part of the name of the profession was derived from this emphasis on the social dimensions of human problems. The word *social* refers to relationships among people and the interactions of people living with each other in a community and societal context. Thus, the primary concern of social workers is with human interaction.

The word *work* was also placed in the title for a reason. It is attributed to Jeffrey Brackett, who successfully argued for adopting the name *social work* in the early 1900s. Brackett, initially an influential volunteer in the Baltimore Charity Organization Society, served nearly thirty years on the Massachusetts State Board of Charities and later became the first director of what is now known as the Simmons College School of Social Work. Brackett argued that the word *social* should be part of this developing profession's title because it depicts the social forces that shape people's lives. He added *work* as a reaction to what he considered was misguided and self-serving philanthropic activity. Brackett was particularly concerned about those individuals who engaged in "slumming" as recreational activity. He felt that including the word *work* in the profession's title emphasized that the activities were to be orderly, responsible, and disciplined—not something to be engaged in by the curious or whimsical.

While Brackett did not select a name that generates strong public appeal and is perhaps a title that most social workers have wished to change at some time, it has helped to identify the profession's domain. It is an accurate title for a profession that addresses social concerns in a disciplined manner. During the years since Brackett convinced social workers to accept this title, the domain of social work has been greatly clarified. Three factors—purpose, scope, and sanction—help identify the domain of social work and differentiate it from other helping professions.

Purpose

Social work practice should always be viewed as helping people bring about change in relation to other individuals, groups, organizations, or social systems. Change efforts usually are directed at solving problems, but they might also include helping a person accept a situation that cannot be changed. The person who is frustrated by a physical disability, for example, may not find a cure for that condition, yet changing his or her attitude toward the disability may dramatically lessen the degree to which it is allowed to be a handicap in his or her life. Thus, helping people change attitudes and behaviors is central to the purpose of social work.

The social worker is most often asked to provide service when a problem in social functioning must be resolved. These problems occur when there is a so-called lack of fit between the client and the client's immediate environment. Social functioning, then, refers to the match or balance between the needs and capacities of the person and the opportunities and demands of his or her social environment. Social functioning can be viewed as a sphere in which the person's needs, wants, capacities, and beliefs meet and interact with the demands and expectations of other people and social systems. In short, social workers help people change in order to solve problems in their social functioning.

However, change that enhances social functioning even when no problem has been identified is equally valid for the social worker. The parents who want to improve their childrearing skills when their children have not displayed any specific difficulties are just as appropriate clients for social work services as the parents who are referred to the worker by the school or juvenile court because their child is in trouble. Social work seeks to help all people change in order to *enhance their social functioning* and/or *resolve problems in social functioning.*

The social worker's client may be an individual, family, group, organization, or community. Even though the social worker may specialize in working primarily with certain client systems, such as individuals and families, it is necessary that he or she be able to work with systems of all sizes. The term *direct service* refers to practice that involves face-to-face contact with persons experiencing a need or problem, whereas the term *indirect service* is used to describe work that focuses on changing organizations, communities, and society in order to improve the resources, opportunities, and overall quality of life available to persons with needs and problems. No matter on which side of the person/environment boundary the social worker focuses his or her efforts, the purpose is to help people and social institutions change in order to solve problems and/or enhance social functioning.

Social work's mission, then, is to serve all people who want to improve their social functioning—the poor and the rich, majority and minority groups, men and women, the able and the disabled, the young and the old. However, throughout its history, social work has devoted its primary attention to people who are most vulnerable to problems with social functioning. The Council on Social Work Education's "Curriculum Policy Statement" (1984), which serves as a basis for the accreditation of social work education programs, clearly identifies this commitment: "The fundamental objects of social work concern are the relationships between individuals and between individuals and social institutions. Historically, social work has contributed to the development of these relationships in such a way as to promote social and economic justice and protect the opportunities for all people to live with dignity and freedom" (Appendix 1, p. 2, #4.2).

A conception of purpose has been emerging from social work's beginnings nearly a century ago. It can be summarized as follows: *The purpose of social work is to provide services directly to individuals, families, households, and groups to help them cope with unchangeable social problems, reduce or eliminate those problems that can be changed, or experience growth in those areas where enhancement of social functioning is desired. Of equal importance is the activity of the social worker to influence groups, organizations, communities, and even society to provide helpful social programs and create an environment that is conducive to satisfying and productive lives for all people.*

Scope

The scope of the social work profession is broad, since its purpose is to help people interact more effectively with the world around them. The social worker is concerned about the interactional and relational aspects of human problems—about what is going on among people and between people and their social environment.

This concern leads to a contextual or ecological focus in social work practice that distinguishes it from other helping professions. The physician, psychologist, nurse, or teacher is primarily concerned about what is happening within or inside the individual. The lawyer or city planner is primarily concerned with matters that are external to the individual (i.e., the legal system or the growth and development of cities). While these professions are interested in the social interactions between people and their environments, that is not their primary concern. By contrast, social work is primarily concerned about the interactions among people and between people, their communities, and society.

The activity of the social worker is sometimes described as "boundary work," meaning that the focus is on the interaction and overlap of one system with others. It is this dual focus on person and environment, with the emphasis placed on interactions and transactions between them, that sets social work apart from other helping disciplines. Minahan (1981) helpfully describes the scope of social work:

> Social workers focus on person-and-environment in interaction. To carry out their purpose, they work with people to achieve the following objectives:
>
> ▪ Help people enlarge their competence and increase their problem-solving abilities.

- Help people obtain resources.
- Make organizations responsive to people.
- Facilitate interaction between individuals and others in their environment.
- Influence interactions between organizations and institutions.
- Influence social and environmental policy.

To achieve these objectives, social workers work with other people. At different times, the target of change varies—it may be the client, others in the environment, or both. (p. 6)

Sanction

The domain that social work can claim is influenced by the willingness of society to sanction it to perform its services. *Sanction* refers to the authorization, approval, or permission needed to perform certain actions. Professional sanction reflects the right or authority given to the worker to provide human services. Four sources of sanction for social work activities include (1) local and federal governments, (2) legally incorporated private agencies, (3) the social work profession, and (4) the clients or consumers of social work services.

The government authorizes the actions of social workers through legislation that creates social programs, through the allocation of funds for social work activities, through the licensing of organizations (e.g., licensed child-placing agencies) that employ social workers, and in most states through licensing individual practitioners. In addition, many government agencies sanction social work by hiring social workers to provide services or by purchasing services from those who are in private practice or employed elsewhere.

Private agencies sanction social work practice in much the same way. Many agencies define their purpose as providing the services that social workers are equipped to offer, soliciting funds from the community to support the delivery of those services, and hiring social workers to do the job. In a sense, they convince the community of the need for social work, and the community, in turn, sanctions social workers to perform these tasks.

In return for the sanction to practice granted by society, social workers are obliged to provide high-quality services and to protect clients from possible abuse by a professional monopoly that the sanction creates. The profession, acting through the National Association of Social Workers (NASW), sanctions the practice of individual social workers by requiring adherence to its **Code of Ethics**, offering certification (i.e., the Academy of Certified Baccalaureate Social Workers, the Academy of Certified Social Workers, and the Diplomate in Clinical Social Work), and providing education of the membership through its publications and conferences.

The true test of public sanction for social work practice, however, is the willingness of clients to use the services of social workers. Social workers simply must demonstrate on a daily basis that they are committed to providing high-quality services to their clients and that they conduct their practice in an ethical fashion that protects clients' rights and privacy.

Conclusion

The extensive knowledge base and complexity of social work practice is often not fully appreciated by either the clients of social workers or the general public. It is essential, however, that the social worker possess the substantial background knowledge and skills required to effectively meet human needs and help people improve their social functioning. The competent social worker must make a life-time commitment to adding to his or her knowledge base, increasing understanding of both the profession's and one's own beliefs and values, gaining insights from personal and practice experiences, and extending and updating knowledge of the human service delivery system.

The broad focus of social work on person/environment interaction frequently places the social worker at boundary points between social work and other professions. Social workers who drift into the domains of other professions risk operating beyond their own abilities and professional and/or legal sanction. That jeopardizes the quality of service that the client receives and prohibits him or her from having access to the special perspectives that social work brings to the change process. However, if social workers are too rigid or too permissive about their own domain, they may limit client access to other professionals who may be more competent in areas of overlap between the professions. Here, the social worker's understanding of the domain of social work and his or her skill in interprofessional collaboration become important tools for maintaining effective social work practice.

Selected Bibliography

Council on Social Work Education. "Curriculum Policy Statement," *Handbook of Accreditation Standards and Procedures.* Rev. ed. New York: CSWE, 1984.

Minahan, Anne. "Purpose and Objectives of Social Work Revisited." *Social Work* 26 (January 1981): 5–6.

Wilensky, Harold L., and Charles N. Lebeaux. *Industrial Society and Social Welfare.* New York: The Free Press, 1965.

The Art and Science of Social Work

2

Ralph W. Tyler, an expert on education for the professions, wrote that "professional activity involves complex tasks which are performed by the artistic application of major principles and concepts rather than by routine operations and skills" (1952, 55). The practice of social work is far from routine. It must be conducted with the best knowledge and skill available, as well as with insightful sensitivity to the client(s) and community, if social functioning is to be improved.

As indicated in Chapter 1, among the personal characteristics a social worker brings to the change process is the art or native abilities required for facilitating the change process. Although one's art can be enhanced through professional education, it cannot be taught—at least not through traditional educational approaches. One must bring those artistic abilities to the profession. However, from professional preparation and practice experience, the social worker can learn the science of social work. It is the blend of one's art and science that shapes the social worker's individual professional style.

What is the difference between art and science? "Art always relates to something to be done, science to something to be known" *(Funk and Wagnalls* 1963, s.v. "science"). When applied to social work practice, the artistic factors are concerned with how the social worker interacts with clients, other people, and social institutions, whereas the science is concerned with the knowledge the social worker brings to the change process.

Artistic Factors in Social Work

Art is defined as "a specific skill in adept performance, conceived as requiring the exercise of intuitive faculties that cannot be learned solely by study" *(American Heritage Dictionary* 1978, s.v. "art"). One need not look far to observe successful helpers who rely primarily on their artistic abilities. Good natural helpers, volunteers, and "untrained" human service providers demonstrate daily that even without any formal education they can be helpful to people in need.

14

Similarly, it is not uncommon to see people who have extensive knowledge, but lack the necessary artistic ability, fail in their efforts to serve clients. Native artistic ability, when used in a disciplined way, is a prerequisite to successful practice.

As social work sought to increase its credibility among the professions, the artistic characteristics of the social worker were treated as relatively unimportant. Bowers (1950, 111–13), for example, reviewed thirty-four definitions of social work that had appeared in social work literature between 1915 and 1947. Of the seventeen that appeared before 1930, more than half used the term *art* as part of the definition, whereas only one of the post-1930 definitions used that concept. Subsequent definitions of social work have also typically failed to recognize the intuitive features of the social worker's helping activity. However, when one examines the nature of social work practice—whether providing individual services or promoting the development of social policies—it is clear that personal characteristics of the social worker have substantial influence on the outcome of the helping activity.

What factors comprise the art of social work? Building effective helping relationships, approaching practice situations creatively, applying personal energy to activate the helping process, using sound judgment, as well as understanding one's personal value system and controlling for its impact on clients are essential artistic capacities required of the social worker.

Relationship

Perhaps the most fundamental tool of the social worker's trade is the use of a positive *relationship* to help people become open to change and actively engage in the change process. In many situations, this is a necessary precondition to effective work with individuals, families, or groups of clients. An emotional bond of trust and concern simply must exist before most people are willing to risk that difficult human experience—change.

The qualities of relationship are elusive. What makes it possible for a stranger to somehow enter the life of an individual or group and establish a bond that allows them to work on changing situations that previously had been resistant to change? Why are clients willing to share very personal and confidential information about themselves and others as they engage in a change process? What motivates groups of people to form committees and take action to change a social condition with a social worker present when they failed to mobilize their resources before the helper was involved?

In his critical analysis of casework practice, Joel Fischer (1978) neatly summarized the state-of-the-art knowledge regarding relationship:

> One of the continuing debates in casework and related fields is between those
> schools of thought which believe that changes in the client are brought about by the
> professional's use of techniques and those which believe that . . . personality
> qualities of the worker . . . [are] responsible for the effects of interpersonal
> encounters. As research accumulates, it increasingly appears that "personality" and

"techniques" both can have measurable, beneficial effects on other human beings. However, to date, only selected personality characteristics, or interpersonal skills of helping people, have been identified as related to successful outcome ... —empathy, nonpossessive warmth, genuineness. (p. 191)

Empathy. *Empathy* is best described as taking on the perspective of another person or "getting into someone else's head" to view the situation as he or she does. Although one never fully appreciates the viewpoint of another person, the social worker needs to get as close to that understanding as possible. To understand the fear and anger of a battered wife, to be sensitive to the guilt of an abusive parent, to appreciate the difficulty of the silent teenager risking criticism by peers for speaking up in a group, or even to hear out the frustrations of an overworked staff member requires empathy. It is an ability that is critical to all social workers—from caseworker to administrator.

Carl Rogers (1982), who has perhaps made the most substantial contribution to our understanding of empathy, identified the factors that make empathic listening an effective helping tool and has described empathy in the following manner:

It means entering the private perceptual world of the other and becoming thoroughly at home in it. It involves being sensitive, moment to moment, to the changing felt meanings which flow in this other person, to the fear or rage or tenderness or confusion or whatever, that he/she is experiencing. It means temporarily living in his/her life, moving about in it delicately without making judgments, sensing meanings of which he/she is scarcely aware. (p. 31)

Empathy, however, is a dynamic quality. Some people display greater amounts of empathy than others, and, certainly, a social worker cannot always maintain the same level of empathy for all clients or for the same clients at all times. It is difficult to live temporarily in another person's world. And sometimes, even the most empathic person does not have the energy to make this effort.

Warmth. *Warmth* is a characteristic that communicates respect, concern, and interest in the well-being of the client or client group. Expressions of warmth, whether made verbally or nonverbally, reflect the worker's understanding and caring about the client. For example, when meeting with a group of adults who are mentally retarded, the social worker may be communicating concern over the problems these individuals face living in a world of more intellectually able people and, at the same time, letting them know that they are important as individuals to the worker.

Warmth is not just saying "I care," although at times that is important. Warmth is transmitted in many direct and indirect forms of communication—from a reassuring smile to an offer to give explicit help. Warmth is a very individual human quality that is expressed differently by each person.

Genuineness. Closely linked to expressions of warmth and empathy is *genuineness.* The social worker may know the correct statement to make or the proper action to recommend, but the client will find that statement or recommendation of little value unless he or she feels the worker is honestly concerned. Trite as it may sound, the social worker must truly like working with people and gain personal satisfaction from the experience of being a social worker.

Clients occasionally approach the helping process feeling that professional helpers have little genuine interest or concern for clients, that they are providing service only because it is the job they are paid to perform. Contrived expressions of interest in clients' well-being are quickly detected. The social worker simply must bring a fundamental caring about the well-being of others to the helping situation.

These three factors—empathy, warmth, and genuineness—are interpersonal characteristics that are fundamental to the social worker's success in developing effective relationships. Like other artistic characteristics, they can be enhanced through education and training activities, but unless they are innate to the individual, little can be done to develop these qualities. (See Technique 6.1 for additional information on these qualities.)

Creativity

Creativity is another attribute of the effective social worker. Heus and Pincus (1986), for example, effectively argue that "the creative generalist is better prepared [than the specialist] to confront the challenges facing social work" (p. 10). Social work deals with constantly changing people and constantly changing situations. So-called textbook answers are strained by unique human conditions. And agency regulations are, at best, designed for the typical client and require creative adaptation to unique human needs.

Creative thinking is characterized by the disciplined integration of information with original ideas. Parnes (1967) describes creative thinking as "the association of thoughts, facts, ideas, etc., into a new and relevant configuration, one that has meaning beyond the sum of the parts" (p. 14). Two essential components of creative thinking are imagination and flexible persistence.

Imagination. *Imagination* is required at a number of points in social work practice. For instance, the social worker must employ an imaginative approach in the search for alternative solutions. A creative social worker helps clients examine a variety of ways to solve any problem. The unimaginative or rigid social worker sees only one or two options—or perhaps none at all.

For example, an agency board attempting to provide the physically handicapped with more access to public facilities might think only of encouraging merchants or the city parking control office to create additional restricted spaces for handicapped persons. On the other hand, the imaginative social worker might identify many other ways to resolve the problem. The number of existing spaces may be adequate; perhaps more effective enforcement of parking restrictions is a better solution. Another option might be to deputize handicapped persons to ticket unauthorized automobiles when they find them in spaces reserved for handicapped parking. Public education, improving public transportation, or providing increased transportation services from human service agencies may all be viable alternatives that the imaginative social worker might encourage the board to examine.

Another area in which the social worker must be imaginative is in interpreting and implementing agency policies and procedures. Policies are created to serve the typical, yet the human condition is of infinite variety. Although the social worker cannot ethically (or legally) ignore or subvert agency policy, the effective worker must find ways to adapt policy to meet unique client needs. The social worker who is bound by a literal interpretation of "The Manual" is simply not able to make the system work for all clients.

Flexible Persistence. *Flexibility* is another dimension of creativity important to the process of change. Planning and implementing a change effort requires an ability to understand the situation from the perspective of all those affected by the change. The social worker making a foster home placement, for example, must have the flexibility to appreciate the often competing perspectives of biological parents, foster parents, the child, the court, the agency, and even the neighborhood. To rigidly align oneself with any of the affected parties limits the social worker's ability to help resolve problems and conflicts.

Social work practice also requires that the social worker be flexible in relating to clients. At times, a social worker needs to be warm and supportive; at other times, it is necessary to challenge the client. And at still other times, the social worker must be directive or make use of legitimate authority. The effective social worker must be able to judge when it is appropriate to assume these alternate roles.

In addition to being flexible, the creative social worker must possess the trait of *persistence* (Gelfand, 1988). Flexibility without the hard work and discipline to translate one's creative ideas into feasible actions is of little value to clients. The term *flexible persistence* was coined by McMullan (1976) to emphasize the need for both flexibility and persistence in the creative problem-solving process.

Energy

Energy may be defined as "the power by which anything acts effectively to move or change other things or accomplish any result" (*Funk and Wagnalls* 1963, s.v. "energy"). The social worker should bring such power to the helping process to activate the client or client group to change themselves, their environment, or both. As used here, energy is a quality that transmits hope and confidence to clients that desirable change can occur through the change process. The ability to energize the change activity is a characteristic that the worker brings and, as such, is another aspect of the art of helping.

People who seek the help of social workers are often frustrated and defeated by prior unsuccessful helping experiences. Quite often, existing natural helping systems such as family, friends, and neighbors have attempted to bring about the desired change, but these well-intentioned efforts have not succeeded. The social worker must communicate a spirit of hopefulness to energize the process.

One need not assume the posture of an effervescent cheerleader to communicate energy to clients or client groups. To reflect a realistic hopefulness or even a quiet confidence that the situation can be improved is an important beginning. For example, the aged person who is frustrated by increasing problems of living alone can be encouraged by the social worker who communicates the view that nursing home care may be only one alternative and that, with careful planning and the use of other supportive services, he or she may be able to continue living at home for some time.

Energy must be translated into activity. Communicating hopefulness without supportive action is of limited value. The willingness of the social worker to commit time and energy to the change process can encourage clients to also invest themselves in that activity. For example, a group of renters, frustrated by the failure of landlords to provide housing free of rats and insects, can be energized by the social worker who offers to help plan a meeting between tenants, landlords, and the local health department.

Judgment

Another characteristic of the competent professional is *sound judgment*. The nature of the helping services and uniqueness of individual human situations requires that social workers make a number of judgments, including assessing client situations, providing alternative solutions, helping plan and conduct change activities, and deciding when to terminate services. However, the helping process also involves making judgments about when the services needed are beyond the capacities of the social worker. While professional judgments should be based on the best available knowledge and cognizant of the relevant values, ultimately, they must depend on the clear and reasoned thinking of the social worker.

We often use the qualifier *mature* to describe the effective social worker. A review of several definitions indicates two perceptions of maturity that often become mixed in our thinking. One definition relates to having "ripened" or "reached an advanced stage of growth." The second relates to "the use of careful and wise consideration to arrive at judgments." Too often, we assume that these concepts of maturity are correlated—that chronologically mature people make mature judgments. Certainly, one's life experience presents a number of opportunities to gain helpful insights on which to base those judgments. If one learns from those experiences, then age and maturity are surely associated. However, many of us are slow learners of the lessons of life, and they may have contributed little to our ability to make sound judgments. It is not uncommon for a young and inexperienced person who is thoughtful and insightful to arrive at judgments that are just as valid as those of older and more experienced people.

Similarly, the experience of providing human services over time affords the opportunity to test and refine one's ability to understand complex situations and thus develop practice wisdom. Although experience presents an opportunity to gain practice wisdom, it does not assure that the social worker will gain helpful insights from repeated practice activities. The social worker must be analytical and open to learning from both the successes and failures experienced in providing services.

Personal Values

Personal values create a dilemma for the social worker. The reasons for entering social work are varied, but the fundamental motive in selecting such a career is typically one's altruistic orientation. When a person makes the decision to use himself or herself as an instrument for change, there is usually some notion in that person's mind about what constitutes a good quality of life for people. In other words, social workers want to make things "right."

The problem comes in determining what is "right." The social worker's view of the "right" outcome may be very different than the clients' perspective, and that may differ from the perspective of the human service agency where services are provided or the community that sanctions the services in the first place. Is it "right" to encourage a single mother to find employment that necessitates leaving her children in daycare? Is it "right" to refer a woman to an abortion clinic? Is it "right" to withhold financial assistance from a client who has violated an agency rule by not reporting the income from a part-time job? Is it "right" to remove a child from his birth parents when a neighbor makes a yet unsubstantiated accusation of child abuse? Is it "right" to force homeless people to reside in shelters against their will? Whose "right" is right?

Values are most simply defined as one's belief about how things ought to be (i.e., what is "right"). Strong feelings and emotions are often attached to these beliefs. One's basic values are somewhat stable, but they do change over time. Value dilemmas, which result from conflicting values, must be resolved when taking action. Given that values do not provide absolute guides to behavior, is it appropriate to expect the client to conform to what the social worker considers right? Logic would answer "no," but clients often feel pressured to agree with their social workers.

If a social worker accepts the principle of maximizing clients' self-determination (see Principle 13 in Chapter 4), he or she must be prepared to suspend his or her own values to allow the clients to move toward outcomes that they believe are most desirable. Suspending one's values does not mean that the social worker must be valueless. Rather, it means that outside of values that are expressed in the law, the social worker should hold his or her personal beliefs about what is "right" in abeyance in favor of allowing the clients to achieve what they believe is best for them and their unique life situations.

Prerequisite to the ability to suspend one's values is the social worker's knowledge of his or her belief system. The social worker should regularly work toward increased understanding and self-awareness. As new situations arise, it is important for the social worker to consider what he or she believes about that situation, and why. It is useful to discuss these values with family, friends, and colleagues to obtain alternate views or refinements to one's thinking. By fully understanding one's own belief system, it is then more possible to avoid inadvertently and inappropriately imposing one's personal values on clients.

The social worker's personal values must be, for the most part, compatible with the values of the social work profession. If these two value systems are incompatible, one of two things is likely to happen: (1) the worker goes through the motions of being a social worker but his or her heart is not in it and practice behaviors are not genuine (which soon becomes apparent to both clients and colleagues); or (2) the worker will reject the profession's values and principles as a guiding force and respond to clients entirely on the basis of personal beliefs and values.

What are the professional values that characterize social work? In what is perhaps the most thorough study of social work values to date, Ann A. Abbott (1988) distilled four basic social work values that became evident from a content analysis of the NASW public social policy statements (NASW 1988), the NASW "Code of Ethics" (NASW 1980), and the Council on Social Work Education's "Curriculum Policy Statement" (CSWE, 1984). These values were:

1. *Respect for Basic Rights.* This value reflects the belief that all people should have equal access to resources and services that will help them accomplish their goals in life, prevent or alleviate problems, and realize their full potential as human beings.
2. *A Sense of Social Responsibility.* Here, the emphasis is on making social institutions such as the family, education, government, and social welfare humane and responsive to human needs.
3. *Commitment to Individual Freedom.* Social work's emphasis is on appreciating human diversity and respecting the right of people to make their life choices.
4. *Support for Self-Determination.* This value supports the right for people to make their own choices. It also seeks to empower people who do not have freedom to make their own life choices to do so whenever possible.

Since much of social work involves the use of practice interventions that have implicit value dimensions or are selected on the basis of value considerations, it behooves the social worker to examine his or her own congruence with these basic social work values.

Scientific Factors in Social Work

If the social worker possesses appropriate artistic characteristics, the quality of his or her work can be strengthened by adding the available science to the repertoire of knowledge, values, and skills used to serve clients. In other words, the social worker must use both the heart and the head when providing services—the art and the science.

What is the scientific component of social work? Two meanings of the word *science* appear in the dictionary: (1) "Knowledge covering general truths or the operation of general laws especially as obtained and tested through scientific method" and (2) "Possession of knowledge as distinguished from ignorance or misunderstanding, . . . knowledge attained through study or practice" (*Webster's,* s.v. "science").

The first definition represents a view of science commonly held in the United States. It argues that the only valid or trustworthy knowledge is that which may be derived from the rigid application of certain principles, including the painstaking definition and isolation of the problem under study, formulating hypotheses to be tested, following an established study of protocol or methodology, using control and experimental groups for comparison, measuring with valid and reliable instruments all cases or a sampling of cases representing the phenomena under study, and submitting the research findings to scrutiny by professional peers so they can replicate the study and either support or repudiate the findings. Clearly, this approach has been successful in furthering the development of the "hard" sciences such as physics and chemistry.

For social work, as well as for all of the social and behavioral sciences, the rigorous application of the scientific method is difficult; perhaps that is why they are termed the "soft" sciences. Social problems cannot easily be quantified and are frequently of such a nature (e.g., child abuse or spouse battering) that it would not be appropriate to create problem situations or withhold intervention for experimental purposes. In addition, human subjects are often not available for controlled study, confidentiality prohibits some studies, and sufficient identical items do not exist to accumulate adequate samples for scientific testing. Although studies based on the scientific method occasionally appear in the social work literature, the profession can claim a scientific component only because much of its knowledge fits the second definition of science—knowledge derived from study and practice.

By accepting this second definition of science, it is possible to define as science the full range of knowledge used by a social worker, including his or her *hunches* about a practice situation, *practice wisdom* that is rooted in experience, the use of *concepts* to guide assessment and intervention activities, the application of *precepts* such as the ethical and practice principles that guide the social worker's decisions and actions, and the utilization of *theories* and *practice models* that help to explain human behavior and the change process. In addition, social workers need to draw on any relevant *facts* established through research and data collection techniques. Each of these forms of knowledge is valid and valuable.

Given the enormity of the materials that make up the scientific base of social work, a comprehensive recitation of the science of social work would extend well beyond a book or even multiple volumes of material. In this chapter, the intention is only to identify the general clusters of knowledge that make up this base.

Figure 2.1 suggests that social workers should be knowledgeable in regard to existing social conditions, relevant social phenomena, the range of social programs, and the social work profession; his or her own unique mix of art, science, and professional style; and the competencies required for social work practice.

Social Conditions

The social worker must be aware of the many social factors that affect the quality of life for people being served. These social conditions range from events and atti-

Figure 2.1   Science for Social Work

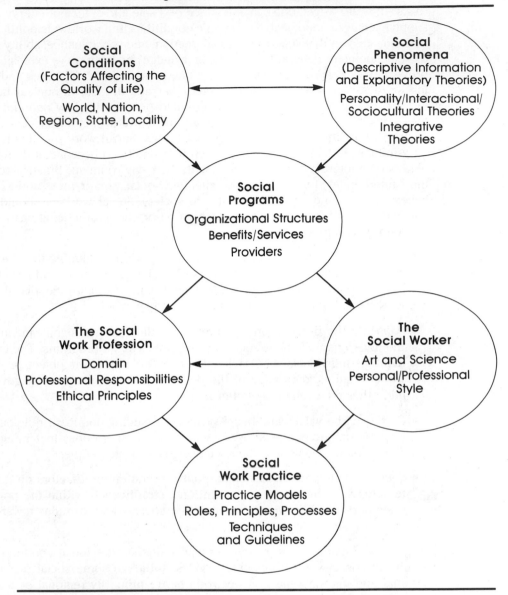

tudes occurring at an international level to those occurring in the locality where practice takes place. The interdependence of people at these several levels is an inescapable fact of life.

Because social work is concerned primarily with the interdependence between people and environment, it requires a *world view*. The social worker should be generally knowledgeable of factors that work independently or in combination to affect the quality of life on this planet, such as the ecology of the world (e.g., air, water, vegetation); maintenance of a safe and sufficient energy and food supply; achievement of stable economic conditions and worldwide political conditions throughout that support personal freedom and social justice; ability to wisely use developments generating from the knowledge and technology explosions to improve human welfare; success in controlling communicable illnesses and promoting wellness; and creating a world free of war and the fear of nuclear holocaust.

World events, however, may be modified or intensified by *national perspectives.* Unique economic, political, social, and cultural factors affect a country's desire and ability to deal with social conditions. Social work practice is particularly influenced by the country in which it is practiced because of its mission to help people interact more effectively with their environment. When practicing in the United States, for example, the effective social worker must understand the beliefs, values, and organization of U.S. society. Social workers should be well informed about how the country in which he or she is practicing has addressed the following factors:

- *Economic.* The production of goods and services, including the use of natural resources, impacts most aspects of society, influencing industrial/technological/urban development, employment patterns, and the distribution of wealth (and poverty) throughout the country.

- *Political.* The distribution of power and influence has significant impact on the decisions that shape social welfare policies and programs. The empowerment of individuals who lack influence (an important objective of social work) requires knowledge of the decision-making processes of government and other politically oriented groups.

- *Cultural.* The values and belief systems (including dominant religious beliefs and the unique perspective of racial and ethnic groups) that influence the aspiration of people and the society's goals for its people.

- *Social.* The impact of economic, political, and cultural factors on human interactions, including social institutions, stratification within the population, roles performed by various members of society, and attitudes toward others based on social class, ethnicity, gender, and age.

Regional and state characteristics also influence the social conditions under which the social worker provides services. Although some social problems are national and international in scope, others are primarily regional or a result of characteristics of individual states. For example, unemployment caused by fluxuating oil prices has been most seriously experienced in Oklahoma, Texas, Louisiana, and Alaska, whereas the success of Japanese automobiles has severely damaged the economy of Michigan. Both events increased the incidence of poverty in those states. On a regional basis, the closing of mines in Appalachia aggravated the most serious problems of poverty in the United States, and drought conditions and the farm crisis affected people in the Midwest much more than other regions of the country.

Finally, some social conditions impact *local communities* but not whole states or regional areas. The well-publicized crime rate in Washington, D.C., and the high incidence of juvenile gang activity in Los Angeles have dramatically affected those cities, whereas towns just a few miles away are relatively free of those problems. Rural areas also experience locality-relevant social problems due to factors such as a decline in timber prices in Montana or the closing of a small town's single industry in Kansas.

Social Phenomena

Due to the breadth of social work, it is necessary for the social worker to possess a knowledge base consisting of wide-ranging descriptive information and numerous explanatory theories. Psychology, sociology, political science, economics, and anthropology all provide important theoretical content for the social worker. The ability to consume and integrate knowledge from these disciplines strengthens the scientific basis of the social worker's practice.

De Hoyos (1989) suggests that the social phenomena that most directly concern social workers can be divided into three levels or systems: the personality systems, interactional systems, and sociocultural systems. It is important for the social worker to have basic information about the *personality systems* in order to understand the individuals involved. Knowledge of individual physical and psychological factors, growth and development patterns, and both normal and abnormal social functioning is essential. For example, De Hoyos identifies the major personality theories with which the social worker should be knowledgeable as Freudian and Neo-Freudian theories, cognitive theory, humanism, and behaviorism.

At the *interactional systems* level, the social worker must understand families or households and the functioning of various kinds of groups. The family has long been a central intervention point for social workers, and knowledge of the nuclear and extended family is critically important. However, with the increase of nontraditional family structures, understanding alternate living and intimacy patterns has become important for the social worker. Further, a considerable amount of practice takes place with small groups of people, including task groups, therapeutic groups, and committees. The social worker needs to have a thorough understanding of communications theory, family development theory, and group structure and processes as a foundation for intervening at the interactional systems level.

Social workers devote considerable energy to working with problematic social structures and addressing cross-cultural problems. Thus, knowledge of *sociocultural system* issues and their causes is essential. Most social work practice takes place under the auspices of a formal organization such as a social agency, school, hospital, or correctional facility. To work effectively within these organizations, a social worker must have knowledge of theories that explains organizational development, structure, and operation. People are also influenced by the communities in which they live. To understand and address local issues, the social worker must be familiar with government structures, community decision-making theory, conflict theory, and community change theory. In addition, he or she needs an understanding of public attitudes related to cultural diversity, racism, gender roles, aging, sexual preference, handicapping conditions, and other sociocultural factors that shape the environment in which people live.

In dealing with people interacting with their environments, the social worker also needs to be familiar with integrative theory to understand the connections between these system levels (i.e., personality, interactional, sociocultural levels). Two integrative theories are prevalent in social work today: general systems theory and ecological theory (or, more accurately, the ecosystems perspective derived from ecological theory).

General systems theory suggests that all life can be viewed as a series of interrelated systems. Thus, the social worker identifies the primary system of attention (i.e., focal system) for a specific practice situation, determines what components (i.e., people and tangible resources) are included in that system, and examines the relationships and processes of interaction among the components. Subsystems internal to the focal system (e.g., husband-wife, parent-child) may then be identified and the impact of their functioning on the system understood. In addition, the systems perspective allows the social worker to determine the impact of the system on one or more larger "suprasystems" and the immediate environment as well as attending to the impact of those larger units on the focal system. Although a number of other concepts incorporated within general systems theory are useful tools for the analysis of practice situations, the compatibility of the perspective with the focus of social work on the transactions between people and their environment makes it a particularly valuable integrative theory.

Another integrative framework, the *ecosystems perspective,* increasingly used in social work is what Whittaker and Tracy (1989) term "the ecological paradigm." It is attractive to many social workers because it keeps the helping process focused on the dynamic interaction between the person and his or her immediate and relevant environment (i.e., person-in-environment). Building on systems concepts and ecological theory, the ecosystems perspective helps to place the situation of the client or client group into context where the influence of various systems on each other can be understood. The concept recognizes that each living thing, directly or indirectly, exchanges energy and materials with all other living creatures and also with the nonliving environment. Its emphasis on independence and interrelatedness has attracted social workers to ecology in search of concepts and models.

Ecological thinking keeps one from viewing only the personality or only the environment as a primary cause of problems in social dysfunctioning. According to Germain and Gitterman (1987):

> People's needs and predicaments are viewed as outcomes of people:environment exchanges, not as products of personality or environment alone. (There is a notable exception, however, in that certain plights may be created by environmental-societal processes alone, affecting segments of a population or an entire population.) As important as personality is, so too is the environment and so too are their exchanges. (p. 489)

Thus, one is reminded to consider always the person, his or her environment, and the nature of the exchanges between person and environment. Ecological thinking also stresses the multitude of factors that make up our environment and directly or indirectly affect our ability to adapt and cope with change. In applying ecosystem concepts to human development, Bronfenbrenner (1979) proposed that a child's environment or ecosystem consists of four levels:

- *Microsystems.* The child's closest and most intimate relationships such as those with parents, siblings, family members, teachers, playmates, and so on. An adult's microsystem would usually include certain persons at work.

- *Mesosystem.* The less personal parts of the environment, including persons living in the neighborhood, relatives that are seen infrequently, peer group, fellow members of the church, and so on.

- *Esosystems.* Those parts of the environment that the individual does not participate in actively, including such groups as school boards, city councils, legislatures, union leadership, and so on.

- *Macrosystems* Broad economic, cultural, and social patterns and belief systems.

General systems theory and the ecosystems perspective serve as examples of two important integrative theories that help social workers to connect the various pieces of life that they might find in any practice situation. Mastery of one or more such integrative theories is important for understanding the social phenomena that social workers must address.

Social Programs

When social conditions exist that are perceived as either harmful to the person affected or a threat to the community or the society as a whole, social programs may be created to help those in need or to address the threatening problem. Conceptually, social programs consist of three major elements: organizational structure, benefits or services, and providers.

Social programs must be delivered to people through some form of *organizational structure.* No matter what type of human service is provided, there must be a method of organization that determines who is eligible for the benefit or service, how much will be given at what cost, how it will be provided, and who will give the service. As a profession with only a relatively small (12 percent) private practice component, most social workers work from an organizational base and must be knowledgeable about providing professional services within the context of formal organizations.

As described in Chapter 1, the *benefits and services* incorporated in social programs can take three forms. They might be tangible *social provisions* such as money, food, housing, and clothing. They sometimes are *social services* such as counseling and therapeutic interventions. At still other times they involve *social action* activities in which there is an effort to change the human service delivery system or other aspects of the society to make it more humane and responsive to human needs. These programs are established by government or voluntary social agencies. The social worker must not only be familiar with the programs offered by his or her employing agency but must also be knowledgeable of other programs to which clients might appropriately be referred.

Finally, social programs require *providers* to actually reach the clients. Providers may be volunteers but most frequently are paid professionals and support staff who make it possible for clients to receive benefits or services. Social work is only one of the professions that deliver social programs. Teachers, psychologists, physicians, nurses, occupational therapists, and others provide a wide array of human services. Each has its own focus but there are obvious areas of overlap. Understanding the competences of each related profession, as well as the dynamics of interprofessional cooperation, are important aspects of the social worker's knowledge.

The Social Work Profession

The social worker must understand that the special contribution social work brings to the helping process is that of helping people interact more effectively with some part of their environment or, conversely, changing some part of that environment to more effectively support the individual. The purpose and goals of the social work profession, as well as the activities of the individual social worker, must be appropriate to its *domain.* (See Chapter 1 for a discussion of social work domain.)

The social worker also needs to understand the functions professions perform in Western societies and the benefits, as well as the *professional responsibilities,* that accrue from this status. Society grants professions the authority to provide the specific services that fall within their domain. In essence, a monopoly is given to a profession to determine the qualifications of its members (e.g., educational and experiential prerequisites for memberships). In return, the profession is charged with monitoring its members to protect the public against abuses of that monopoly.

Social workers have been ambivalent about professionalizing their discipline. Throughout this century, they have devoted considerable effort to identifying their knowledge base, creating professional organizations, staking out their domain, specifying criteria for becoming a recognized social worker, and taking other steps to become a valued profession. At the same time, they have been uncomfortable about the inherent elitism that characterizes any profession. In the United States, social workers have struggled with the conflict between assuring quality services to clients and keeping access to the profession open to as many people as possible. Where this was once a profession that recognized only people with a master's degree in social work, in the past two decades, it has opened its membership to many more people by admitting persons with undergraduate social work education to the membership of the National Association of Social Workers (NASW). Because two years of graduate study is no longer required for the beginning-level social worker, substantially greater numbers of minority group members and people from economically deprived backgrounds have entered social work and now have the opportunity to contribute their talents.

Professional standards, as defined by the NASW, represent an important feature that has emerged from the professionalization of social work. These standards help both the consumers of social work practice (agencies and the general public) and prospective social workers by designating the necessary professional preparation for performing various practice activities and specifying desirable personnel standards for organizations that employ social workers. This classification system identifies the requisite educational and experiential preparation at four levels:

1. *Basic professional.* Requires a baccalaureate degree from a social work program accredited by the Council on Social Work Education (CSWE).
2. *Specialized professional.* Requires a master's degree from a social work program accredited by CSWE.
3. *Independent professional.* Requires an Accredited MSW and at least two years of post-master's experience under appropriate professional supervision.
4. *Advanced professional.* Requires special theoretical, practice, administrative or policy proficiency or ability to conduct advanced research or studies in social welfare; usually demonstrated through a doctoral degree in social work or closely related social science discipline. (NASW 1981, 9)

In its complete form, this classification plan elaborates the knowledge and skill the social worker at each level should possess, the kind of professional responsibilities that might appropriately be undertaken, and the variations in the difficulty of practice activities due to the complexity of the situation, vulnerability of the client, and potential consequences of the practice activity.

A second set of professional standards has been developed by the NASW (1971) to guide social agencies in establishing personnel practices that support good social work practice. The guidelines include such items as personnel selection, staff development, worker evaluation, promotion, fringe benefits, and termination of employment. An agency that does not follow these guidelines may be the subject of a complaint and, if found to be in violation after a thorough process of investigation by the local NASW chapter and the National Committee on Inquiry, may be placed on the NASW's published list of agencies that have failed to operate in compliance with these standards.

The final cluster of professional knowledge required of the social worker is a thorough understanding of the *ethical principles* that guide the practice of social work. Ethics are concerned with what is morally right or, in a profession, what is the correct course of professional action (Loewenberg and Dolgoff 1988, 3). Perhaps no single document is more important to the practice of social work than the NASW *Code of Ethics* (1980), which specifies the fundamental ethical behaviors expected of the social worker. (The *Code of Ethics* can be found in Appendix 8.1 of this book.)

When a social worker joins the NASW, he or she pledges to practice within social work's ethical principles. As part of its professional monitoring responsibility, the NASW depends on the *Code of Ethics* as the standard for determining if charges of unethical social practice have a justifiable basis. If such accusations are made about an individual social worker, the local NASW chapter and the National Committee on Inquiry of the NASW serve to review the complaint.

For the social worker, ethical decisions are not always as clear cut as the *Code of Ethics* would suggest. Practice situations often present issues involving a choice between two or more ethical obligations. For instance, should a social worker protect client confidentiality at the risk of the safety of the client or others? Or how does a social worker deal with a needy client who fails to report sources of income in order to become eligible for public assistance or subsidized housing? To help in sorting out such issues, guidelines for making ethical decisions are included in Technique 8.7 of this book.

The Social Worker

In the final analysis, it is the social worker himself or herself that is the instrument of social work practice. The culmination of the social worker's *art and science* is expressed through that person's individual style. A person's style reflects how his or her individual uniqueness is translated into practice behaviors. It is the "outward and visible sign" of one's inner self. The social worker's *style*—how he or she relates to clients, uses creativity, transmits energy, makes mature judgments, and applies the science of social work—is communicated through interaction with the client.

Lewis (1982) notes that "a theory of practice cannot be complete unless it accounts for style" (p. 147). Although largely ignored in the social work literature, style is the most apparent personal characteristic to the client or group being served. It can immediately open up the helping process or, just as quickly, close it down.

People reveal a great deal about themselves through their personal style. Clothing, hairstyles, patterns of speech and posture, the decor in homes and offices, and hundreds of other subtle and not so subtle behaviors send important messages about who people are, what they believe, and even what they think of themselves.

One's style must be appropriate for both the situation and the person. For example, the social worker's mode of dress, one expression of style, illustrates the point. The clean-shaven social worker dressed in a three-piece suit will surely have difficulty establishing rapport with a group of street people, yet he may be highly effective in influencing a city council to create needed services for those same people. Similarly, the protective services worker may quite appropriately dress informally when working with children and families but should dress much more formally when making a court appearance in their behalf.

"Know thyself" is an important admonition for the social worker. Continuing introspection helps the social worker stay tuned to changes in personal style that may affect his or her ability to develop positive relationships with clients. Yet, knowing oneself is never easy. It is helpful for the social worker to step back periodically and gain a perception of how others perceive his or her style. Clues from clients, family, friends, colleagues, and supervisors can prove helpful in making these assessments.

A social worker's practice style emerges as he or she balances individuality with the behaviors required for professional practice. Inherent in professional socialization is pressure to conform and perform in particular ways. It moves members of a profession toward a sameness that, although desirable in many respects, must be weighed against the importance of preserving one's uniqueness. The continuing effort to resolve the competing expectations of profession, agency, and clients with one's individuality is an issue for every social worker. The social worker must ask, How far am I willing to compromise my individuality in order to effectively serve my clients and meet agency expectations? Within the broad parameters of "being yourself," one has considerable latitude. In fact, the social work profession is enriched by the varied styles and abilities of its members.

Social Work Practice

Finally, the science of social work entails knowledge related to how one directly interacts with clients or indirectly works in behalf of clients by seeking to improve human services or change social conditions. An essential element of practice knowledge is familiarity with various *practice models* or approaches. The 1987 edition of the *Encyclopedia of Social Work* includes summary descriptions of more than twenty practice approaches a social worker might use. It is beyond the scope of this chapter to describe each practice model or approach used by social workers. However, it is useful to review the following listing from the *Encylcopedia:* advocacy, behavioral approach, case management, cognitive therapy, community-based social action, community development, crisis intervention, ecological perspective, ethnic–sensitive practice, existential approach, family practice, feminist social work, generalist perspective, gestalt therapy, political action, practice with groups, primary prevention, psychosocial approach, radical social work, social planning, task-centered approach, and transactional analysis. The list is far from exhaustive, but suggests the importance of the social worker developing a repertoire of intervention approaches that can be used in practice situations.

Social workers also need knowledge of a range of *practice roles* performed by social workers, the fundamental *practice principles* that have proven to be successful guides to practice over time, and the *change process* that social workers should lead as clients are served. The three essential practice elements are described more fully in Chapters 3, 4, and 5.

Conclusion

In order to perform social work practice activities effectively, it is essential that the social worker uses a combination of art and science. The social worker brings intangible factors to the practice situation that make a difference in practice outcomes—the art encompassed in building relationships, creative thinking, creatively communicating energy, using sound professional judgment, and committing to appropriate values. At the same time, the effective social worker must combine his or her artistic abilities with the profession's science. Without art, the science is of little value in social work practice. But without the science, the art is of limited effectiveness.

The science of social work includes several sets of knowledge. It is essential that the social worker be knowledgeable about the social conditions that affect the quality of life, the social phenomena (i.e., people and social structures) with which they work, the social programs they deliver, the requirements of their profession, their own strengths and limitations, as well as the fundamental models, roles, principles, processes, and techniques and guidelines required for practice interventions. To acquire and remain up to date on the requisite science of social work, the worker not only needs to complete professional education but must also continually seek to expand his or her knowledge base by regularly reading the social work literature, attending seminars and workshops, or enrolling in formal coursework. In addition, the social worker must help the profession expand its scientific base by presenting papers at conferences, contributing to the literature, and conducting research on the effectiveness of practice activities.

Selected Bibliography

Abbott, Ann A. *Professional Choices: Values at Work.* Silver Spring, Md.: National Association of Social Workers, 1988.

American Heritage Dictionary of the English Language. New College Edition. Boston: Houghton Mifflin, 1978.

Bowers, Swithun. "The Nature and Definition of Social Casework." In *Principles and Techniques of Social Casework,* edited by C. Kaslus. New York: Family Service Association of America, 1950.

Bronfenbrenner, Urie. *The Ecology of Human Development.* Cambridge, Mass: Harvard University Press, 1979.

Brown, Lester R. et al. *State of the World 1989: A Worldwatch Institute Report on Progress Toward a Sustainable Society.* New York: W. W. Norton, 1989.

Council on Social Work Education. "Curriculum Policy Statement," *Handbook of Accreditation Standards and Procedures.* Rev. ed. New York: CSWE, 1984.

De Hoyos, Genevieve. "Person-in-Environment: A Tri-Level Practice Model." *Social Casework* 70 (March 1989): 131–38.

Fischer, Joel. *Effective Casework Practice: An Eclectic Approach.* New York: McGraw-Hill, 1978.

Funk and Wagnalls New Standard Dictionary of the English Language. New York: Funk and Wagnalls, 1963.

Gelfand, Bernard. *The Creative Practitioner: Creative Theory and Method for the Helping Services.* New York: Haworth, 1988.

Germain, Carel B., and Alex Gitterman. "Ecological Perspective." In *Encyclopedia of Social Work,* 18th ed., edited by Anne Minahan. Silver Spring, Md.: National Association of Social Workers, 1987, pp. 484–99.

Heus, Michael, and Allen Pincus. *The Creative Generalist: A Guide to Social Work Practice.* Barneveld, Wisc.: Micamar, 1986.

Lewis, Harold. *The Intellectual Base of Social Work Practice.* New York: Haworth, 1982.

Loewenberg, Frank, and Ralph Dolgoff. *Ethical Decisions for Social Work Practice.* 3rd ed. Itasca, Ill.: F. E. Peacock, 1988.

McMullan, W. E. "Creative Individuals: Paradoxical Personages." *Journal of Creative Behavior* 10 (Fourth Quarter, 1976): 265–75.

Minahan, Anne, ed. *Encyclopedia of Social Work.* 18th ed. Silver Spring, Md.: National Association of Social Workers, 1987.

Morales, Armando, and Bradford W. Sheafor. *Social Work: A Profession of Many Faces.* 5th ed. Boston: Allyn and Bacon, 1989.

National Association of Social Workers. *Code of Ethics,* Policy Statement #1. Silver Spring, Md.: NASW, 1980.

_____. *NASW Standards for the Classification of Social Work Practice,* Policy Statement #4. Washington, D.C.: NASW, 1981.

_____. *NASW Standards for Social Work Personnel Policies,* Policy Statement #2. Washington, D.C.: NASW, 1971.

_____. *Social Work Speaks: NASW Policy Statements.* Silver Spring, Md.: NASW, 1988.

Parnes, S. J., R. Noller, and A. Biondi. *A Guide to Creative Action.* New York: Charles Scribner's Sons, 1967.

Perlman, Helen Harris. *Relationship: The Heart of Helping People.* Chicago: University of Chicago Press, 1979.

Rogers, Carl R. "Empathic: An Unappreciated Way of Being." In *Things That Matter: Influences on Helping Relationships,* edited by Hiasaura Rubenstein and Mary Henry Bloch. New York: Macmillan, 1982.

Schacter, Burt. "Growing Up under the Mushroom Cloud." *Social Work* 31 (May–June 1986): 187–92.

Tyler Ralph W., "Distinctive Attributes of Education for the Professions." *Social Work Journal* 33 (January 1952): 55–62.

Whittaker, James, and Elizabeth Tracy. *Social Treatment.* 2nd ed. New York: Adline DeGruyter, 1989.

The Roles and Functions of Social Workers

3

When social workers engage in practice, they provide a wide range of services to people in need. Although other professionals or volunteers may share in the effort to make these services available to clients or client groups, the social worker must be especially prepared to perform the particular practice roles associated with the social work profession.

A role, according to *The Social Work Dictionary* (1987, s.v. "role"), is a "culturally determined pattern of behavior that is prescribed for a person who occupies a specific status." Thus, role behavior is linked to the position one holds rather than to the individual who holds the position (i.e., to the social work profession rather than to the social worker). How one performs that role is highly individual and depends on the unique mix of art and science the social worker brings to the helping situation.

To carry out the various social work roles, a variety of job functions must be performed. A *job function* can best be defined as an assigned duty, task, or activity associated with a specific occupational role. Thus, one can engage in social work practice most effectively by understanding the roles typically performed by social workers and mastering the role functions or activities each social worker is expected to perform. The emphasis a social worker places on each role or function embedded in that role will, of course, vary depending on one's field of practice, methodological orientation, and the duties assigned to the social worker's position within his or her agency.

Defining Professional Roles

The roles of the many helping professions (e.g., physical therapy, nursing, counseling, etc.) are defined by social norms, the types of services each profession provides, and the administrative regulations or laws that sanction their activity. The domain of social work among the various professions further shapes the roles each social worker is expected to perform. Although individuals may have capacities that extend beyond their usual professional roles, each member of this profession must be prepared to at least carry out the roles assigned to social work.

This chapter describes nine roles and thirty-eight functions expected of social workers. It reflects a synthesis of roles and functions described in the social work literature where (1) authors conceptually describe these factors as they have observed them in social work practice or (2) job factoring research has been performed to statistically determine the clusters of activity in which social workers typically engage. It should be recognized that when carrying out the duties of any position, the social worker may perform as few as one role but is more likely to engage in several. In the performance of any practice role, the use of several distinct functions may be required. Similarly, a specific function or activity may be used in the performance of more than one practice role. For example, one might engage in an assessment of a client's situation, both in the role of a broker of human services and as a counselor or clinician serving that client. In the following pages, however, each function is described only once.

1. Human Services Broker

Purpose. To link clients to appropriate human services and other resources.

Description. Social work's particular emphasis among the helping professions is to assist people in relating more effectively to their social environment. That places the social worker in the position of being the primary professional person to facilitate linkage between client needs and community resources. Like a real estate or insurance broker, the social worker identifies client needs and helps them gain access to appropriate resources. At times the social worker provides that resource or service himself or herself, at other times the clients should be connected with someone else in the agency who may be able to provide some or all of the services needed, and at still other times clients should be referred to other professionals or community agencies to meet the identified needs.

As a human services broker, the social worker must be knowledgeable about the various resources available and must maintain an up-to-date assessment of the strengths, limitations, and processes for accessing those resources. As noted in Chapter 1, the resources may include social provisions (e.g., money, food, clothing, and housing) and/or social services (e.g., counseling, therapy, group interaction experiences, and rehabilitative services).

Functions

Client Situation Assessment. The first step in effective brokering is to understand thoroughly and accurately the needs and abilities of the client or clients. Connaway and Gentry (1988, 62–64) suggest that the social worker should be skilled at assessing such factors as the clients' vulnerability, culture and resources, verbal ability, appearance, stability, self-respect, intelligence, and commitment to change.

Resource Assessment. The social worker must accurately assess the various resources available to meet client needs. For his or her own agency, as well as for other community agencies, the social worker must be familiar with the programs offered, the quality of staff, the general eligibility requirements, and the costs of those services. The social worker must also know the best way to help clients gain access to those resources.

Information Giving. At times brokering requires the transmittal of information to clients or community groups. As a repository of knowledge about the service delivery system, the social worker helps others by sharing his or her knowledge of resources. At other times the social worker may call to the attention of the general public information about the community services being provided and gaps between services and needs.

Referral. The social worker may identify a "fit" or "match" between client needs and a natural helper, agency, or other community resource that would make it desirable to refer clients to one or more of these sources of help. Effective referral requires that the social worker make a judgment regarding the motivation and ability of the clients to follow through and the receptivity of the resource to accept the client for service. Depending on these two factors, the social worker will be more or less active in the referral process.

Client Advocacy. When resources are not responsive to client requests for service, the social worker might perform the function of advocating with or in behalf of the clients. The social worker might use techniques of negotiation, mediation, or more aggressive strategies to help secure needed client services.

Service System Linkage. Finally, brokering requires that the social worker facilitate continuing interaction between various segments of the human service delivery system. To strengthen the linkage among these segments, the social worker may engage in such activities as networking to establish communication channels between the various agencies, negotiating resource sharing, and/or participating in interagency information exchange and coordination activities.

2. Social and Adaptive Skills Teacher

Purpose. To prepare clients with skills to prevent difficult life situations or enhance their social functioning.

Description. Much of social work practice involves teaching clients or client groups to deal with troublesome life situations or to anticipate and prevent crises in their lives. Some of the knowledge the social worker gains through professional education and experience is transferred to the client during the helping process. The transmission of this knowledge is empowering to clients. In the *Social Work Dictionary,* Barker (1987, s.v. "educator role") defines this role as "the responsibility to teach clients necessary adaptive skills. This is done by providing relevant information in a way that is understandable to the client, offering advice and suggestions, identifying alternatives and their probable consequences, modeling behaviors, teaching problem-solving techniques, and clarifying perceptions."

A fundamental purpose of social work practice is to help clients change unproductive and ineffective behavior. Teaching clients to adhere to the various rules or laws and norms of society, develop social skills and living skills, learn more effective methods of role functioning, and gain insights into their own behaviors is one approach to achieving that purpose. The teaching of skills or specialized knowledge may occur informally in the course of interaction with clients or may take place in more formal educational activities such as brief courses in family budgeting, volunteer orientation and training, or parent effectiveness training. The method selected requires professional judgment based on an assessment of the readiness and ability of the clients to acquire this knowledge.

Functions

Teach Social and Daily Living Skills. Social workers are often called on to help clients learn how to perform particular tasks in their lives more effectively. Teaching skills in budgeting and money management, use of public transportation, orientation to new living arrangements, personal care and hygiene, and developing effective communication skills are examples of activities regularly engaged in by social workers (Teare, Sheafor, and Gauthier 1987).

Facilitate Behavior Change. At times the practice of social work requires helping clients learn new or more acceptable behaviors. The social worker may use intervention approaches such as role modeling, value clarification, and/or behavior modification techniques in teaching clients more effective interpersonal behaviors. When dealing with larger social structures, the social worker may, for example, educate a board of directors about the impact of an emerging social issue on the clients of an agency or urge a client advocacy group to reexamine a change strategy that is failing.

Primary Prevention. Soby (1977,7) reminds us that a purpose of the teaching role is preventing repeated or more serious problems from emerging. She comments that social workers are "more practiced at picking up the pieces than in preventing something from happening, . . . (but they) are now adapting their practice to include primary prevention." Examples include premarital counseling, providing family planning information, and group instruction related to parenting skills.

3. Counselor/Clinician

Purpose. To help clients change their social functioning by gaining insight into their attitudes, feelings, and coping behaviors related to problematic social situations or aspects of functioning in which they desire personal growth.

Description. Perhaps the most visible social work role is that of counselor or clinician. The *NASW Guidelines for the Selection and Use of Social Workers* (1981) captures the substance of the counselor/clinician role:

> The direct personal engagement with an individual, group or family for the purpose of systematically impacting the interpersonal and/or intrapsychic functioning of the client in order to resolve, contain, or provide symptomatic relief of a developmental, behavioral, interpersonal and/or situational problem . . . (and promoting) human growth in individuals, group members and families who are defined as having developmental, interpersonal or situational problems. (p. 36)

In short, the social worker assists the clients in taking actions that will alter their responses to stresses created by special interaction and social conditions.

In order to perform this role, the social worker needs a basic knowledge of human behavior and an understanding of the impact of the social environment upon people, an ability to assess client needs and make accurate judgments about interventions that will help clients deal with these stresses, skill in applying appropriate intervention techniques, and ability to guide clients through the change process.

Functions

Psychosocial Assessment and Diagnosis. Assessment is a prerequisite to any intervention effort. The clients' situations must be thoroughly understood, their eligibility for service determined, and their capacities for change assessed. The *NASW Guidelines for the Selection and Use of Social Workers* (1981, 15) describe the typical assessment activities as "intake, interviewing, social history preparation, and the development of a plan for service." The social worker accurately observes verbal and nonverbal behavior and identifies factors in the clients' social situation that affect their social functioning. Once the situation has been assessed, the social worker formulates a diagnosis, using a conceptual framework to organize the information in a way that promotes an understanding of both the clients and the social environment and yields a workable intervention plan.

Ongoing Stabilizing Care. The counselor/clinician role does not always involve efforts to change the client or social situation. Sometimes the appropriate service involves providing support or care on an extended or continuing basis. For example, counseling with disabled, aged, or terminally ill people or their families may involve efforts to increase their choices and most comfortably deal with difficult life situations.

Social Treatment. Social workers often work with clients in a effort to help them resolve situational problems they experience or to "remedy, cure, or abate some disease, diability, or problem" (*The Social Work Dictionary,* Barker 1987, s.v. "therapy"). This function involves such activities as helping clients understand the emotional relationships among the relevant persons and social groups, supporting client efforts to adjust social relationships, engaging the clients in the problem-solving or interpersonal change efforts, and mediating differences or conflicts between individuals and/or between individuals and social institutions. Problem-solving and therapeutic activities may involve individual, family, or group approaches to intervention.

Practice Research. Although research should be part of the social worker's performance of every practice role, it is especially important for the counselor/clinician. Practice research at this direct service level takes two forms. First, the social worker should consistently examine his or her own performance to assess the effectiveness of the interventions selected. In this way the social worker can be accountable to clients, the employing agency, the general public, and the social work profession. Second, the social worker should collect data and assess his or her practice experiences to detect emerging community and broader social problems that might be addressed by new or revised services and public policies.

4. Case Manager

Purpose. To achieve continuity of service to individuals and families through the ongoing process of connecting clients to appropriate services, coordinating the utilization of those services, and ensuring that clients receive necessary services.

Description. The human services delivery system is very complex and difficult for clients to negotiate—particularly for clients who have long-term care needs. An important role of social workers is to help people locate and gain access to services that can meet their needs and, when necessary, to serve as a champion for the clients' rights. When multiple services are required, the social worker as case manager may serve in the capacity of coordinating the service delivery to a client by planning and scheduling the various contacts with the service agencies. The social worker in this capacity becomes a liaison between the client and the network of human services.

The *NASW Guidelines for the Selection and Use of Social Workers* (1981) describes the case manager role in the following manner:

> The activity of developing, implementing and monitoring a social service plan to meet the needs of an individual or family. It involves conceptualizing the client system in its social environment(s); identifying, providing or referring to other social services, legal services, health services, etc.; involving the client in the solution to the problem and coordinating and monitoring progress made toward resolution of the problem(s); representing or advocating on behalf of the client with other service providers to assure that needed services are given. (p. 7)

In performing the case manager role, the social worker must be skilled in the use of both therapeutic and managerial techniques (Weissman, Epstein, and Savage 1983, 76). The work involves the interpersonal skills in helping clients formulate goals for service, gain access to those services, and follow-up to ensure that those services continue to be appropriate and available. At the same time, the social worker carries out the managerial activity of working within the delivery system to coordinate the services and facilitate interagency cooperation.

Functions. Christine Rich (date unknown, 5) has identified five core functions of case managers.

Case Assessment. As in other social work roles, the social worker must make an accurate assessment of the situation experienced by the client or family. This involves gathering information and formulating an assessment of the client and the relevant environment(s).

Service/Treatment Planning. With the clients and other relevant actors, the social worker can help to identify the various services that can be accessed to meet client needs. Bertsche and Horejsi (1980, 96) describe these tasks as the work

---

necessary to "assemble and guide group discussions and decision-making sessions among relevant professions and program representatives, the client and his or her family, and significant others to formulate goals and design an integrated intervention plan." It is, perhaps, the involvement of representatives of the service delivery system and the family members in the planning process that most clearly distinguishes the case management role from other social work practice roles.

Linkage with Requisite Services. As in the broker role, the case manager must connect clients with the appropriate human service resources. The role differs, however, by the fact that the social worker remains an active participant in the delivery of services to the individual or family. As opposed to "referring out" the clients, the case manager places emphasis on coordinating the clients' use of other resources.

Monitoring of Service Delivery. When a client is a recipient of services from an array of human service agencies and professionals, the case manager follows-up or maintains contact with the referral source to ensure that the needed services are actually received. Bertsche and Horejsi identify seven basic tasks associated with this function:

1. Monitor adherence to the plan and manage the flow of accurate information within the action system to maintain a goal orientation and coordination momentum.
2. Provide "follow-along" to the client and his or her family to speed identification of unexpected problems in service delivery and to serve as a general troubleshooter on behalf of the client.
3. Provide counseling and information to help the client and his or her family in situations of crisis and conflict with service providers.
4. Provide ongoing emotional support to the client and his or her family so they can cope better with problems and utilize professionals and complex services.
5. Complete the necessary paperwork to maintain documentation of client progress and adherence to the plan by all concerned.
6. Act as a liaison between the client and his or her family and all relevant professionals, programs, and informal resources involved in the overall intervention plan to help the client make his or her preferences known and secure needed services.
7. Act as a liaison between programs, providing services to the client to ensure the smooth flow of information and minimize conflict between subsystems. (pp. 96–97)

Case Advocacy. When needed assistance is not forthcoming, it is the function of the case manager to advocate on behalf of the client(s) to negotiate the complex rules and regulations of human service agencies. It is the social worker's responsibility to assist clients in securing services and resources that are rightfully theirs. This may involve forcefully negotiating with other professionals and agencies to assure access to these resources.

5. Workload Manager

Purpose. To manage one's own workload to most efficiently provide client services and be responsible to the employing organization.

Description. Social workers must simultaneously seek to secure the social resources or provide the services needed by clients and to adhere to the management requirements of the employing social agency. In other words, they must balance efficiency and effectiveness.

Although the emphasis on accountability to the funding sources for human services has increased in recent years, social workers have been responsible throughout their history for maximizing the services provided with scarce resources. They simply must be effective in managing the typically heavy workloads they carry. Part of workload management revolves around how they organize their efforts to maximize the services they provide. Another part is concerned with the manner in which they supply information and participate in the operation of their employing agency.

Functions

Service Planning. The ability to organize practice activities efficiently is an essential part of maximizing the services that a social worker can deliver. Service planning involves assessing one's own workload and establishing plans for accomplishing that work in the most efficient and effective way possible. Priorities must be established, sequence of work activity set, and realistic amounts of time allotted to the accomplishment of each activity.

Time Management. The ability to manage time effectively is also essential for the social worker. Since few social agencies are adequately staffed, social workers typically carry very heavy workloads. If the social worker is to give each client and all of the service activities proper attention, priorities for the use of one's time must be set and the working hours carefully allocated to accomplish the tasks at hand.

Quality Assurance Monitoring. Social workers must be responsible for assuring that the services provided are of sufficient quality. As part of the workload management, the social worker must regularly evaluate the effectiveness of his or her own service provision. Frequently he or she is also involved in the assessment of services provided by colleagues. These activities might include "reviewing agency records, conducting job performance evaluations ..., and holding performance review conferences" with colleagues or volunteers (Teare, Sheafor, and Gauthier 1987).

Information Processing. The social worker is responsible for processing information that facilitates the functioning of the employing agency. Data must be provided to document service provision, papers must be completed to secure client resources, case records must be maintained, and various expenses must be documented. In addition, effective organizations require coordination among the staff members. Information about agency regulations and procedures must be understood by all; this requires the preparation and reviewing of memoranda, attendance at staff meetings, and other activities that facilitate intraagency communication.

6. Staff Developer

Purpose. To facilitate the professional development of agency staff members through training, supervision, consultation, and personnel management.

Description. Social workers often serve in middle-management positions in human service agencies. In that capacity they devote a part of their energies to the enhancement of the functioning of the agency staff. At times that might involve working with secretaries, receptionists, volunteers, and other persons who perform important activities, but most often the staff developer role centers on maximizing the effectiveness of professional helpers.

The staff development role requires many of the skills used in the teacher role because the social worker again transmits information to others. In this case, however, the knowledge is transmitted to peers for the purpose of helping them perform more effectively. Staff development is predicated on accurate assessment of the training needs. That training may take the form of individualized instruction such as supervision and consultation and/or may include conducting or participating in training sessions.

Functions

Employee Orientation and Training. Carefully planned job training and orientation to the agency and the specific job assignments must be provided. As much as possible, that orientation should be individualized to meet the learning needs of each worker, which inherently requires ongoing involvement in the evaluation of the worker's competencies. Among the tasks typically required to perform this function are "specifying job expectations, orienting workers to the organizational policies and procedures, reviewing case records, and evaluating job performance" (Teare 1984).

Personnel Management. Personnel management activities may range from the selection of new employees to the termination of employment. Many of these middle-management activities have an effect on the professional development of other workers. For example, the selection of case assignments not only involves judgments about the worker's capacities but also involves assisting in the training and development of the worker by allowing for new and challenging professional experiences. In addition, the staff development role may call for the social worker to allocate funds for attendance at workshops or conferences where the knowledge and skills of the worker can be increased.

Supervision. Professional supervision involves directing the activities of other staff members to enhance the quality of services they provide and assure that agency rules and regulations are followed. Supervision involves such tasks as overseeing staff activities, monitoring case assignments and services, developing performance standards, and negotiating changes to accommodate better the needs and interests of clients (*NASW Guidelines* 1981, 15).

Consultation. Consultation is "the activity in which knowledge, experience, skills and professional attitudes are transmitted through a relationship" that is somewhat equal between the consultant and the person receiving the consultation (*NASW Standards* 1981, 61). As compared to supervision where the function is assigned as a part of the administrative hierarchy of the agency, consultation is given on a peer level—from one professional to another. As an equal, the consultee has the freedom either to use or not use the advice offered by the consultant. Consultation is focused on the learning needs of the worker (as opposed to supervision that is primarily concerned with programmatic needs of the agency) and, as such, is a learning tool that fits the professional model of worker growth and development.

7. Administrator

Purpose. To plan, develop, and implement policies, services, and programs in a human service organization.

Description. In the administrator role, the social worker assumes responsibilities for implementing the policies and programs of a social agency. When performing this role, the social worker might be the chief administrative officer, or one's administrative role may be only one of several roles the social worker has as part of his or her responsibilities. The *Social Work Dictionary* (Barker 1987, s.v. "administration in social work") defines *administration* as "the coordinated totality of activities in a social welfare organization that is necessary for transforming policies into services; also, a method of practice used to plan, assign, coordinate, evaluate, and mediate the interdependent tasks, functions, personnel, and activities that are called upon to achieve specified organizational goals."

The administrator must implement policies, programs, or laws made by others. Agency boards or elected officials typically establish the major guidelines and allocate the funds required to operate the human service agency. Normally, either a volunteer agency board or a governing board appointed by a legislative body then appoints the chief administrative officer (or executive director) to administer the organization. Securing staff, establishing operating procedures, managing the operations of the agency, developing and evaluating the services, and maintaining liaison with the board are the primary responsibilities of the administrator. Depending on the size and complexity of the organization, the executive director may perform all or some of the administrative functions, but he or she must ultimately be accountable for their quality.

Functions
Management. The management function calls for the administrator to maintain oversight of the operations of a facility, a program, a service unit, and/or the entire organization. Management includes such responsibilities as facilitating the work of the agency board, recruiting and selecting staff, directing and coordinating staff activities, developing and setting priorities, analyzing the organizational structure, promoting professional standards within the organization, adjudicating employee conflicts, and obtaining the necessary resources to operate the organization (*NASW Standards* 1981, 4). In addition, management involves budgeting,

documenting the use of resources, and arranging for the care and maintainence of buildings and equipment.

Internal and External Coordination. A primary task of the administrator is to co-ordinate the work of the agency. Internally, this role involves developing plans for implementing the agency's programs in an efficient and effective manner. Often that requires negotiating among several units or programs that are a part of the total agency operation and working with staff to assure that new programs are integrated into the agency's functioning. The administrator also serves as the primary representative of the agency with external constituencies. One job analysis study identified these external tasks as "serving as a buffer to protect staff from external pressures, negotiating with consumers, and interpreting programs to the community in order to maintain viability" (Teare, Sheafor, and Gauthier 1987). Thus, the administrator is engaged in external work not only with the governing board but also as a key figure in the agency's public relations and communication with consumers, other social agencies, and the general public.

Policy and Program Development. The effective administrator is proactive. Although considerable time and energy must be devoted to maintaining established programs, an administrator should regularly assess the need for new or different services through such devices as conducting a needs assessment (see Technique 14.11), being knowledgeable about emerging social trends, generating alternative policy goals for the governing body to consider, and translating new program or policy goals adopted by the governing board into services.

Program Evaluation. Finally, the administrator is responsible for quality control. He or she must oversee the monitoring and evaluation of the agency's programs. The administrator must establish systems for collecting data to document and assess the success of the programs in meeting the agency's objectives for client service. Schneiderman (1974) notes that "each client contact (should be) viewed . . . not only as an opportunity for service, but as an opportunity to document the adequacy of existing policies and programs for such populations groups" (p. 367). In addition, as Teare's (1984) research indicates, the administrator must "carry out activities associated with the assurance of compliance with organizational, professional, state, or federal regulations or standards." Program evaluation, then, is concerned with both program development and program compliance.

8. Social Change Agent

Purpose. To participate in the identification of community problems and/or areas where the quality of life can be enhanced, and to mobilize interest groups to advocate for change or the development of new resources.

Description. Social work's dual focus on both the person and environment requires that the social worker be prepared to facilitate change in neighborhoods, communities, or larger social structures. The role of social change agent has been a part of social work since its beginnings in the late 1800s. Its inclusion in the social worker's repertoire of practice roles has been a key factor that distinguishes social work from the many other helping professions.

The Social Work Dictionary (Barker 1987, s.v. "social action") defines the social change agent role as "a coordinated effort to achieve institutional change in order to meet a need, solve a social problem, correct an injustice, or enhance the quality of human life."

When working directly with clients, social workers are in an exceptionally good position to recognize social problems that are contributing to the social needs of people who use human services. The social worker must take responsibility for assuring that resources are available to meet those needs and/or stimulating action by others to eliminate those problems. Social change typically does not occur rapidly or easily, and the authority to make the necessary decisions to achieve change is rarely held by social workers. Rather, social change typically requires political skill in stimulating concerned and influential groups to address the problems.

Functions

Social Problem or Policy Analysis. A first step in the resolution of social problems and/or the creation or revision of social policies is to understand thoroughly the nature of the problem. Social trends must be analyzed, data collected and synthesized, and accurate assessment of the implications of the data recorded. Without this background work, subsequent change efforts have little chance of success. The *NASW Standards* (1981, 16) identify the tasks involved in such analysis as (1) developing criteria for the analysis, (2) ascertaining the impact of the policy on clients and social problems, and (3) analyzing community values and beliefs that affect the issue.

Mobilization of Community Concern. Translating one's understanding of policies and problems into social change efforts requires mobilizing and energizing concerned individuals, groups, and organizations to seek the desired change. This might involve facilitating the efforts of clients, special interest groups, human service organizations, and/or other citizen groups to address the problem. This mobilization for action might involve initiating the change effort by assembling interested parties and presenting a preliminary analysis of the situation, helping the group expand their understanding of the issues involved and identify goals they would hope to achieve, aiding in the consideration and selection of change strategies, identifying the decision makers who can effect the desired change, and planning and/or carrying out the interventions to affect the actions the decision makers select.

Class Advocacy. As a social change agent, the social worker often serves as an advocate for groups of clients that experience a common problem or that are concerned with the same issue. Typically, class advocacy entails action intended to remove obstacles or barriers that prohibit groups of people from realizing their civil rights or receiving entitlements or benefits due them. Weissman, Epstein, and Savage (1983) provide examples of a social worker's class advocacy including "working on behalf of disadvantaged minorities, the poor, and the handicapped ... to obtain changes in the interpretation of rules, services to which clients are entitled, ... and reforms in laws and programs structures" (p. 141).

Social Resource Development. The social change agent might also work toward the development of resources needed to enhance the quality of life of clients or to prevent social problems from occurring. The *NASW Guidelines* (1981) describe *resource development* as "the activity of creating new resources where they do not exist, extending or improving existing resources, planning and allocation of available resources in order to avoid unnecessary duplication of human services in order to increase the effectiveness and efficiency of services offered by a unit, an agency, or a group of agencies" (p. 27). This activity may involve engaging in political action such as lobbying and providing expert testimony to legislative committees, or more informal interaction with relevant decision makers to inform them of the need for these social resources.

9. Professional

Purpose. To engage in competent and ethical social work practice and to contribute to the development of the social work profession.

Description. A final role expected of the social worker is that of functioning as a professional. It is incumbent on the social worker to practice in a manner that reflects the highest professional standards. Clients and community groups have given sanction to social workers to perform certain helping roles. Social workers in turn become responsible for demonstrating that such confidence is appropriately placed by conducting their practice as competently and ethically as possible. The social worker must constantly seek to develop his or her knowledge and skills and to examine regularly his or her practice to improve the quality of services offered.

In addition, as one who benefits from professional status, the social worker should actively engage in the further enhancement and strengthening of the social work profession. Active participation in professional activities at the local, state, and national levels is an essential component of the social worker's professional role.

Functions
Self-Assessment. The autonomy required for individual decisions regarding how one conducts professional practice carries with it the responsibility for ongoing self-assessment. It is noteworthy that each of the job-factoring studies of social workers reported previously (Teare 1984; Sheafor, Teare, Hancock, and Gauthier 1985; and Teare, Sheafor, and Gauthier 1987) found that social workers, serving in all capacities from frontline service provision capacities to agency administration, regularly engage in tasks related to assessing their own professional performance.

Personal/Professional Development. The corollary to self-assessment is further development of oneself in areas where there are limitations and/or opportunity to further build one's strengths through ongoing enhancement of knowledge, values, and skills. In his job analysis study of MSW social workers, Teare (1984) found that they

> engage in activities designed to assess the effectiveness of (their own) functioning, keep informed, and improve . . . skills. Emphasis is placed on the development of insight into the adequacy of one's personal and professional performance. Tasks include reading journals and other professional literature, attending workshops, planning personal time, and having work-related discussions with colleagues and supervisors. (pages not numbered)

Enhancement of the Social Work Profession. The activities of social workers should also involve contributing to the growth and development of the social work profession and the expansion of its knowledge base. Maintaining membership in the National Association of Social Workers (NASW) and contributing time and energy to the efforts of NASW to strengthen the quality of professional practice, protect the domain of social work, and support legislative initiatives are obligations of each social worker. In addition, social workers should actively contribute the knowledge gained from their practice or research efforts to their collegues through presentations at professional conferences and to the body of professional literature through professional writing.

Conclusion

The social work literature reflects surprisingly little attention to identifying and defining the roles social workers are expected to perform. Where there has been attention to role definition, the approaches have ranged from the efforts of experienced social workers to describe what they have observed in practice to research-based job-factoring approaches. Given the vastly different approaches to discerning social work role performance, it is understandable that a generally accepted listing of social work roles has yet to evolve. This chapter represents an effort to present a set of role descriptions that incorporates understanding gained from a synthesis of both the observational and job-factoring approaches.

The range of practice roles performed by the social worker is indeed large and varied. Although one's personal preferences or job duties may promote more specialized practice using a limited number of these roles, the effective social worker must master at least the basic elements of each. The generalist social worker, in particular, must continually seek to expand his or her competence in performing all practice roles.

To enhance role performance, the social worker must master the functions or activities associated with each role. In addition to learning the techniques required to carry out each job function, the social worker must consider how to bring his or her unique art and science to the application of these techniques in practice situations. How does one perform these roles in a manner that is of maximum benefit to the clients? One ingredient is to follow the practice principles that have evolved throughout social work's history; another is to guide clients carefully through the phases of a planned change process. The basic social work practice principles are discussed in Chapter 4 and the key elements of a planned change process are described in Chapter 5.

Selected Bibliography

Barker, Robert L. *The Social Work Dictionary.* Silver Spring, Md.: NASW, 1987.

Bertsche, Anne Vandeberg, and Charles R. Horejsi. "Coordination of Client Services. "*Social Work* 25 (March 1980): 94–98.

Connaway, Ronda S., and Martha E. Gentry. *Social Work Practice.* Englewood Cliffs, N.J.: Prentice-Hall, 1988.

National Association of Social Workers. *Guidelines for the Selection and Use of Social Workers.* Silver Spring, Md.: NASW, 1981.

———. *NASW Standards for the Classification of Social Work Practice,* Policy Statement #4. Silver Spring, Md.: NASW, 1981.

Rich, Christine. "Overview of Case Management." (Mimeographed materials. Source unknown.)

Schneiderman, Leonard. "Social Welfare, Social Functioning, and Social Work: An Effort at Integration." In *The Practice of Social Work,* 2nd ed., edited by Robert W. Klenk and Robert M. Ryan. Belmont, Calif.: Wadsworth, 1974.

Sheafor, Bradford W., Robert J. Teare, Mervin W. Hancock, and Thomas P. Gauthier. "Curriculum Development Through Content Analysis: A New Zealand Experience." *Journal of Social Work Education* 21 (Fall 1985): 113–24.

Soby, Francine, ed. *Changing Roles in Social Work Practice.* Philadelphia: Temple University Press, 1977.

Teare, Robert J. "Validation of the ACSW Examination: Status Report to the National Association of Social Workers." (Photocopy materials. The University of Alabama School of Social Work, 1984.)

Teare, Robert J., Bradford W. Sheafor, and Thomas P. Gauthier. "Establishing the Content Validity of Social Work Credentials." (Photocopy materials accompanying a paper presented at the 33rd Annual Program Meeting of the Council on Social Work Education, St. Louis, Mo., March 9, 1987.)

Weissman, Harold, Irwin Epstein, and Andrea Savage. *Agency-Based Social Work: Neglected Aspects of Clinical Practice.* Philadelphia: Temple University Press, 1983.

The Principles of Social Work Practice

4

As the social worker gains experience in performing the expected practice roles, his or her abilities in the art and science of social work begin to merge. The novice gradually becomes more comfortable in using his or her native talents in practice activities, and the information learned in the classroom takes on new significance. Formal education, and particularly professional education, is intended to help the student acquire the most critical and fundamental knowledge and skill needed for practice. However, increased practice wisdom, gained from experience and a growing knowledge base attained from the professional literature, should continue to increase the social worker's competence throughout his or her career.

One important step in the merging of art and science occurs when the social worker begins to "own" the practice principles. These principles are often expressed as clichés—"Start where the client is" or "Accept the client as he or she is"—making them appear deceptively simple. Perhaps this has been a factor in social work diverting its attention from these principles to matters that are supposedly more scientific. These principles often seem so obvious to the experienced social worker that instructors and supervisors sometimes fail to consciously teach them as part of the new worker's socialization to the profession.

Alfred Whitehead (1929), an expert in higher education, placed the importance of a student learning such principles in context by noting that "the function of a university is to enable the student to shed details in favor of principles" (p. 42). Social work education, too, should make a concerted effort to assure that every student understands the principles that guide professional practice. These tenets have been the folklore of the profession, which has been passed from supervisor to worker—from one generation to the next. They require formal study, careful explication, and planful transmission to new members of the profession.

A *principle* is defined as "a basic truth, law, or assumption" (*American Heritage Dictionary,* 1st ed., s.v. "principle"). The concept of a *law* may be too strong for the practice principles used in social work. More accurately, they should be viewed as fundamental guidelines for practice decisions and actions. The ability to use good judgment in applying these principles is part of the social worker's art. Siporin (1975) comments, "Practice principles are not rules to be obeyed implicitly or immediately. A professional is supposed to know when, how, and to what extent exceptions to rules can be made. . . . But there is a professional obligation to act as much as possible in accord with professional practice principles" (p. 113). Practice principles, then, are a combination of knowledge, ethical prescriptions, practice wisdom, and common sense. They draw together the art and science of social work.

For the student or the new social worker, it is often difficult to identify clearly these practice principles, as they seldom are given much attention in the literature. This chapter attempts to overcome that gap in the literature by presenting a synopsis of eighteen basic practice principles. They are arranged according to those that relate directly to the individual social worker and those that relate to the social worker in interaction with a client or client group. The reader is reminded that these principles apply across the several levels of clientele. For example, the worker should seek to "maximize client participation" whether serving an individual, family or household, group, organization, or community.

Principles Focused on the Social Worker

1. The Social Worker Should Practice Social Work

This fundamental principle seems so obvious that it appears trite. We expect the teacher to teach, the physician to practice medicine, and the social worker to practice within the boundaries of the social work profession. Yet it is not uncommon to find each of these professions extending into the domain of others. This principle simply admonishes the social worker to do what he or she is sanctioned and trained to do.

As discussed in Chapter 1, social work is sanctioned to help improve the interaction between people and their environments. The requisite educational preparation equips the social worker with the basic knowledge, values, and skills to work at the interface of person and environment, which is the social work domain. In 1954, Rawley formulated a set of principles of social casework in which he noted that social workers should be guided by the fact that "both internal and external factors affect an individual's adjustment . . . [and that] there is an interaction between these two forces" (1954, 154). The subsequent "Working Definition of Social Work Practice" (Bartlett 1958, 3–9) and continuing efforts to define social work have increasingly focused on "person and environment interaction" as the unique contribution of social work among the helping professions. The social worker is not sanctioned to be either a cut-rate psychiatrist, at one extreme, or a humanistic environmental planner at the other.

Due to the inevitable lack of clarity and areas of overlap, the "turf" problems among the disciplines are difficult enough when each practices within professional boundaries. Such problems are magnified when a member of one discipline strays into another discipline's area of operation. Ethical practice requires that the social worker function within his or her professional expertise. Although individual social workers may have special talents that exceed the professional domain, they do not have license to offer services that exceed the sanction given to the profession. More importantly, the social worker who drifts from the profession's area of service deprives clients of the important perspective social work brings to helping people change.

2. The Social Worker Should Engage in Conscious Use of Self

The social worker must be conscious and planful in applying his or her practice competencies. The primary tool of the social worker's trade is self. Thus, the social worker must possess self-knowledge and self-awareness of preferences, prejudices, strengths, and limitations (Siporin 1975, 78).

The ability to build and sustain productive helping relationships is basic to social work practice. Relationship requires that the social worker reveal personal thoughts, perceptions, and reactions. Whether working with an individual, group, or community, the social worker must be "sufficiently conscious of responses to a client to separate out what goes on in the relationship that is professionally motivated—that is, aimed at helping the client—and personally motivated—that is, aimed at fulfilling the worker's own personal drives" (Friedlander 1958, 88). This self-awareness requires a continuing openness to evaluation and self-criticism. The social worker must be able to stand back from his or her own practice and critically and nondefensively observe how that professional self is functioning.

3. The Social Worker Should Maintain Professional Objectivity

By the time most clients come into contact with a professional helper, they have attempted to resolve the situation themselves—by either personally working through the situation or getting assistance from family, friends, or other natural helpers. Often, these helping efforts are thwarted by high levels of emotion that preclude clear understanding and response to the situation. As opposed to the natural helper, the professional adds a new dimension to the client or client group by operating with a degree of emotional neutrality.

Maintaining this neutrality without appearing unconcerned or uncaring is a delicate balancing act for the social worker. The worker who becomes too identified with the client's situation can lose perspective and objectivity. At the other extreme, the worker who appears disinterested fails to energize clients, at best, and, at worst, discourages clients from committing the emotional energy necessary to achieve change. Biestek (1957, 48–50) suggests that the social worker can maintain this balance through a "controlled emotional involvement" in the practice situation.

Further, this professional objectivity becomes personally important to the social worker's mental health. An emotional detachment is needed, allowing the worker to set aside the troubles of clients and the society—to partialize the professional and personal aspects of one's life—in order to maintain an independent perspective and to refresh oneself for the ongoing practice responsibilities. Professional objectivity is, perhaps, the best antidote to worker burnout.

4. The Social Worker Should Respect Human Diversity

The practice of social work involves activity with and in behalf of people from virtually all walks of life, most racial and ethnic backgrounds, a variety of cultures, a range of physical and intellectual handicaps, and various genders, sexual preferences, and ages. The social worker should understand and respect these and other human uniquenesses. To the social worker, difference brings richness to the quality of life. Failure to appreciate difference creates barriers to helping.

Human diversity is expressed in the behavior of individuals, families, communities, and even societies. What may appear to be deviance or unusual behavior from the social worker's own set of values or life experiences may be quite appropriate behavior given a different set of individual and social experiences. Respect for these varied perceptions of life is important to effective social work practice. Baer (1979) identifies some of the analytical tasks required to implement this principle. She notes that the social worker must be continually involved in

> studying the heritage, culture, and lifestyle of individuals and groups; analyzing values held and ways in which individual and group differences are expressed; assessing own strengths as well as "blind spots," prejudices, and intolerances, and developing plans to deal with them when they interfere with professional functioning; identifying uniqueness, strengths, and other resources emerging from assessment of individual and group diversity, and developing plans to utilize and maximize them in the development and implementation of an intervention plan. (p. 149)

5. The Social Worker Should Seek Personal and Professional Growth

Social work is a contemporary discipline. The very nature of helping people interact more effectively with their environments requires that the social worker be in tune with the world. One cannot be empathic and creative in working with a wide range of clients while holding a narrow and uninformed view of life. The social worker must continuously seek growth and development—both personally and professionally.

The rapid growth and change in the knowledge relevant to social work requires constant updating. New concepts, theories, and intervention techniques regularly appear in the social work literature or are presented at workshops or conferences. To bring the best possible service to clients or client groups, the social worker must be current with the professional information. However, the person who becomes immersed in social work to the exclusion of other experiences and perspectives on life limits his or her ability to be helpful. To appreciate the infinite variety of the human condition, one must understand life from various orientations. Knowledge gained from history, literature, science, the arts, and interaction with a range of people in one's daily life is vital to the continuing development of the social worker.

Principles that Guide Practice Activities

In addition to the principles related to the social worker's own approach and preparation for practice, a number of principles are concerned with the social worker's intervention with individual clients and client groups.

6. The Social Worker Should Engage in Conscious Knowledge- and Value-Guided Practice

Clients are not well served unless the social worker brings the latest and most appropriate knowledge to the helping process. At the same time, it is critical that the social worker is able to consciously recognize value issues that arise in practice and help individuals or groups of clients understand their implications. In her important book, *The Common Base of Social Work Practice,* Bartlett (1970) sufficiently identified the centrality of this principle in social work practice: "It is through the conscious action of the social worker, who selects what is relevant for the particular situation before him, that the appropriate knowledge and values become integrated with the intervention" (p. 78).

The social worker must regularly ask, What knowledge can I bring to this situation? Although knowledge derived from life and practice experiences are valuable, the social worker should also seek out and provide the most advanced theoretical knowledge and most fully tested knowledge available. Like Garvin and Glasser (1974), who make a strong call for an "empirical basis of practice . . . principles to be derived scientifically" (p. 38) when working with groups, Arthur Dunham (1969) notes that, when working with communities, "social welfare programs should be the product of careful planning, on the basis of ascertained facts, rather than an expression of guesswork, 'hunches,' or mere trial and error" (p. 421). At all levels of social work practice, the effective social worker must consciously build on existing knowledge and add to that knowledge base when possible.

The social worker must also recognize that beliefs are powerful guidelines to action. If clients are to change themselves or their situations, they must understand their own values and how they impinge on, and are impinged upon, by people in their immediate environment. In a practice situation, several important values may be in conflict. Much of effective social work practice involves efforts to clarify these values and help clients assess the relative importance of one value as opposed to others in the situation. Baer (1979, 151) also notes that, in every intervention effort, the social worker "should recognize that there are ethical issues involved in the effort that should be identified and assessed against the stated ethics of the profession." Value and ethical issues are too important to be left to chance. They must be consciously attended to in the practice of social work.

7. The Social Worker Should Be Concerned with the Whole Person

Most professions focus on only one dimension of the human condition. Physicians are primarily interested in physical well-being, teachers focus on intellectual development, and psychologists are concerned with emotional and cognitive processes. Social work, however, is unique among the professions because of its concern for the whole person—biological, psychological, social, and spiritual. For the social worker, practice activities rarely relate to a single factor. The helping process must be approached from the perspective of assessing and intervening with a number of interrelated factors.

Concern for the whole person requires simultaneous attention to at least three factors. First, the social worker must be concerned with the well-being of the client and the many other people that are affected by the practice activity (i.e., the person's impinging environment) (Cohen 1959, 139–40). Second, the social worker must attend to both the immediate problem and the underlying factors that may have contributed to the situation; the social worker must relate to both symptoms and causes of client problems. Finally, while the social worker must be concerned with the situation that brought the client to service, the long-range implications of the change must also be considered. The "whole person" includes the client's past, present, and future.

8. The Social Worker Should Treat the Client with Dignity

Philosophically, the social worker must accept the proposition that each person or group deserves to be treated with dignity. The goal of social work is to help people change; it is not intended to punish or condemn. Therefore, it is necessary to accept clients as valued people simply because of their humanity and to avoid making judgments of worth based on personal or dominant societal values.

Acceptance does not imply approval of all the client's actions. The phrase "accept the client as he or she is" encourages the social worker to approach clients as people who deserve respect. Biestek (1957) identifies acceptance of clients as occurring when the worker "perceives the client as he really is, including his strengths and weaknesses, his congenial and uncongenial qualities, his positive and negative feelings, his constructive and destructive attitudes and behavior, maintaining all the time a sense of the client's innate dignity and personal worth" (p. 72).

Groups of clients, too, must be accepted by the social worker and approached with dignity. One need not personally like the individual or group member, but the social worker must approach each client with an attitude of respect—the basis for a meaningful helping relationship that can support and encourage change.

Communicating acceptance requires that the social worker avoid assigning guilt or innocence to clients. This nonjudgmental attitude helps individual clients or client groups focus on their strengths by minimizing the fear of being judged negatively or inaccurately by others (Biestek 1957, 89–91). It frees up the helping relationship for positive action. At the same time, the failure to adopt a nonjudgmental approach contributes to stereotyping clients and, therefore, failure to individualize their situations. Treating the client with dignity helps avoid the inappropriate intrusion of the social worker's biases into the clients' lives.

9. The Social Worker Should Individualize the Client

"Starting where the client is" is frequently the first practice principle to which the new social worker is introduced. From the first day in the first social work class, the student can expect to be taught in a variety of ways that no two people are exactly alike, and, therefore, the social worker must treat each as being unique (Rawley 1954, 155). This continuing effort to individualize requires a conscious effort to understand as fully as possible the specialness of each individual, family group, or community with which the social worker is involved. Biestek (1957) notes that "individualization is based on the right of human beings to be individuals and to be treated not just as *a* human being, but as *this* human being with his personal differences" (p. 25).

The social work literature is replete with references to the importance of treating each client or client group as being unique. Goldstein (1983) traces this principle through social work's history from Mary Richmond to the work of Gordon Hamilton, Helen Harris Perlman, and Carel Germain and Alex Gitterman (pp. 267–68). Dunham (1969) translates it to the community level by suggesting that any local community social welfare program should be based on the unique needs of the people in that community, and the citizens should participate in the development of its programs so that they will, in fact, be adapted to their special situation (p. 417).

The social worker must appreciate the unique nature of each change situation, each client or group of clients, as well as the ability of clients to successfully use selected intervention strategies. Individualization allows the social worker to make judgments about where and how to begin while, at the same time, communicating respect for the specialness of the people that he or she is serving.

10. The Social Worker Should Lend Vision to the Client

A central feature of professional helping is to bring new understanding and different approaches to old problems. If an individual or group is to invest in the

---

difficult process of changing an existing behavioral pattern, they must be convinced that improvement is possible. The social worker must introduce a sense of hopefulness and offer a vision that suggests new and creative ways to deal with the situation.

Anderson (1981), building on the work of William Swartz, identifies four activities used to operationalize this practice principle: "(1) the revelation of faith in the individual's dignity and power to act on his or her own behalf; (2) the revelation of the worker's own investment in the transactions between people and their social systems; (3) the trust in the power of human relations for synergistic growth; and (4) the encouragement of synergistic growth in the individual's specific situation" (p. 61).

While offering new perspectives, encouragement, support, and techniques for change, the social worker must also be honest about limits. Clients are not helped by projecting unrealistic outcomes for the helping process. Rather, the tempered infusion of energy and vision allows the client or client group to make progress toward achieving more desirable social outcomes.

11. The Social Worker Should Build on Client Strengths

Professions are organized around meeting specific physical, psychological, and social needs. They typically have become problem focused and devote considerable effort to identifying what is wrong with a situation and the limitations of a client or client group. It is not uncommon to observe an interdisciplinary staffing in which the client assessment reveals that, when the various disciplines combine their evaluations, the client is more than 100 percent disabled—yet no one has addressed the client's abilities.

For the social worker, it is the abilities and potentials of the client that are most important in helping bring about change. Since change in social functioning must be largely self-induced, it is important that the social worker help clients recognize and utilize their strengths. The emphasis on maximizing client strengths helps change the tone of the helping relationship from one of gloom over problems and pathology to one of optimism that good use of existing abilities can lead to improvement. Thus, the social worker should carefully assess the strengths as well as the limitations of the client.

12. The Social Worker Should Maximize Client Participation

"Help the client help himself or herself" is something the social work student can expect to hear on the first day of field instruction. At the community level, Dunham (1969) has formulated this principle by noting that "so far as possible, every social welfare program should enlist active and vital participation and leadership" (p. 85). Friedlander (1958) states the parallel when working with individuals and families: "If a client is to be helped to extricate himself from a stressful situation and to regain a personal-social balance that is satisfying and enduring, he must be involved as an active participant in the corrective activities of the case-work method itself" (p. 85). In short, the social worker should "do *with* the client and not *to* or *for* the client." It does little good for the social worker to construct a sophisticated diagnosis of a client's situation if that client does not understand or accept those conclusions. Meaningful change will only occur when those who must change clearly understand their situation and are willing and able to take action.

The change process is most effective when developed with the active participation of the clients (Smalley 1967, 175–76). As opposed to the attorney, who single-handedly develops and presents a case for the client, or the physician, who injects the patient with a chemical that can cure an illness with minimal patient involvement, the social worker must assume a very different posture. The social worker must view himself or herself as a collaborator and facilitator. Although situations do arise in which a social worker must act in behalf of clients who are unwilling or unable to participate in this change process, the social worker should always seek to maximize their involvement.

Consistent with the principle is the growing recognition in social work that one of the most important functions of the social worker may be the empowerment of oppressed people to participate in the decisions that impact their lives. Solomon (1976) suggests four goals for a social worker who seeks to empower clients to become more in control over the factors that impact their lives. She suggests activities should be directed toward:

> 1. Helping the client perceive himself or herself as casual agent in achieving a solution to his (or her) problem or problems.
> 2. Helping the client to perceive the social worker as having knowledge and skills which he (or she) can use.
> 3. Helping the client to perceive the social worker as peer collaborator or partner in the problem-solving effort.
> 4. Helping the social worker to perceive the "power structure" as multipolar, demonstrating varying degrees of commitment to the status quo and therefore open to influence. (p. 26)

13. The Social Worker Should Maximize Client Self-Determination

The instruction to "guide the helping process—not the client" captures another important practice principle. This principle places the decisions that affect the lives of clients in their own hands. It maintains that those who must ultimately live with the outcomes of decisions should have the freedom to make the decisions. The job of the social worker is to help clients explore alternatives and implications but not to prescribe their final choices.

Biestek and Gehrig (1978) summarize the major themes in this principle as it applies to working with individuals and families:

> 1. The client has a right and a need to be free in making his own decisions and choices.
> 2. This right to freedom, however, is limited by the client's capacity, by law and authority, by written community standards, and by the function of the agency.

3. The caseworker has a corresponding duty to respect this right, in theory and practice, by refraining from any direct or indirect interference with it, and by positively helping the client to exercise that right. (p. 75)

Although emphasizing the negative side of this principle, Dunham (1969) captures a similar theme for social workers serving at the community practice level: "Invoking the application of authority or compulsion may sometimes be necessary in community organization, but it should be used as little as possible, for as short a time as possible, and only as last resort" (p. 419).

The principle of self-determination must be qualified in its application. The principle assumes that the client is able to make appropriate decisions in relation to self and others. Sometimes, that is not a valid assumption. Clients occasionally do not understand the consequences of an action or lack the capacity or the emotional stability to make sound judgments and, therefore, may make choices that are harmful to themselves, to other individuals, or to society. At times, the social worker must temporarily take on the decision-making role for these clients. This may involve persuading them to take or not take a particular action, using authority or power that the social worker's position might command, or, in the most extreme situations, it might require calling for the assistance of the police or other authorities.

The social worker should reluctantly assume the responsibility for making decisions in behalf of clients and then only after careful review of the situation and always with the intent of returning that responsibility to the client as soon as possible. In the final analysis, the social worker should attempt to maximize the client's ability to determine his or her own destiny.

14. The Social Worker Should Help the Client Learn Self-Directed Problem-Solving Skills

All social workers have heard their professional activity described as the "process of helping people help themselves." Perhaps this should be extended to "helping people help themselves *now and also in the future.*"

Many of us have had the experience of being pleased with a loss of weight only to discover a few months later that we had slipped back into the old eating patterns and regained all the lost pounds. Similarly, the changes in social functioning made by a client with the assistance of a professional helper can come unraveled unless the client is prepared to sustain that change over time. Hopefully, the client can be prepared to cope successfully with inevitable problems and difficulties of the future and engage in self-directed problem solving without needing to return to the social worker or agency for additional assistance.

Ideally, what the client learns during his or her interaction with the social worker can be applied to additional concerns in day-to-day living—at present and in the future. Vinter (1974) labels this the *requirement of transferability.* He contends that the "gains achieved by clients within the treatment process must be transferrable beyond this process" (p. 14). The admonition "Don't do for the client what the client can do for himself or herself" captures this principle of helping clients become independent and self-reliant. Only then can they learn to trust and depend on their inner strengths and on conventional and informal resources to which they have easy access.

An important aspect of preparing a client for the future is to teach him or her how to identify and make use of the informal resources and natural helpers to be found in the immediate environment. Such resources include family members, relatives, friend, service clubs, and church or synagogue groups.

15. The Social Worker Should Protect Client Confidentiality

Although all social work practice activities do not deal with confidential material, the helping process frequently involves working with sensitive information. Individuals and families seeking help from a social worker often discuss very personal and private aspects of their lives. In groups, clients might also reveal secrets and self-perceptions that could be embarrassing or damaging if made public. The community worker, too, encounters instances when sensitive information about individuals, agencies, and organizations that must be treated as confidential. All social workers, therefore, must make judgments about what information should or should not be shared and provide guidance to others about maintaining appropriate confidentiality.

Wilson (1978) identifies two forms of confidentiality: absolute and relative (pp. 2–4). *Absolute confidentiality* refers to a situation when information can be imparted by the client and never goes beyond the social worker. That type of confidentiality is quite rare in social work practice. It is only under the protection of some state licensing statutes that there is a legal right of privileged communication. Most social work practice involves *relative confidentiality,* meaning that the most the social worker can promise is to act responsibly and within the profession's *Code of Ethics,* and existing laws and agency policy.

The degree of confidentiality that can be given a client will, of course, depend on the nature of the agency setting, the state and federal laws and regulations that govern its operation, and the existence of other legal requirement such as the mandated reporting of child abuse. In correctional programs (e.g., prison, parole, probation), the client can expect little confidentiality. On the other hand, a client receiving social services within a hospital setting will have a much higher level of protection; but even here, a client's records might be reviewed by nonhospital personnel such as insurance companies, Medicaid or Medicare authorities, worker's compensation officials, and other third parties who have legal authority or authorization to review the patient records for purposes of quality control. Clients should be advised of the limits of the confidentiality the social worker can guarantee.

The social worker must be especially thoughtful and prudent regarding decisions as to the information placed in the agency's permanent records. In addition, care must be taken in preparing the clerical staff to respect the confidential nature of the materials they may type, file, or inadvertently overhear. To protect confidential information, social workers must carefully plan the location and cautiously select the content for professional consultation or materials reviewed in case conferences. Further, clearly separating one's personal life and work life is especially important in protecting against breaches of confidentiality that might accrue from discussing work experiences with family and friends. (Additional information on the handling of confidential information is provided in Chapter 9.)

16. The Social Worker Should Adhere to the Philosophy of Normalization

Many social work clients have significant mental and physical disabilities. Because of these limitations, they often experience discrimination and social isolation. The philosophy of **normalization** is a powerful force in efforts to minimize isolation and integrate persons with handicaps into the life of the community and to ensure that their life resembles that of the so-called normal person as much as possible. This philosophy originated in the field of mental retardation but has gradually spread to other areas of service to groups such as the elderly, the physically disabled, and the seriously mentally ill.

The National Association for Retarded Citizens (October 1973) defines *normalization* as follows: "The concept of helping the developmentally disabled persons to obtain an existence as close to the normal as possible, making available to them patterns and conditions of everyday life that are as close as possible to the norms and patterns of the mainstream of society. Specifically, the use of means that are as culturally normative as possible to elicit and maintain behavior that is as culturally normative as possible" (p. 72).

The term *normative* in this definition can be equated with *typical* or *conventional.* This means, for example, that a person who is mentally retarded should, to the greatest extent possible, live in typical or conventional homes in ordinary neighborhoods and communities. Also, his or her work, recreation, religious participation, clothing, transportation, and daily activities should be as conventional as possible. Likewise, the individual should be able to receive educational, medical, and social services in ways and in an environment that closely resembles how other citizens utilize these formal resources.

Horejsi (1979) describes the behavioral rationale for seeking to normalize the life of persons with severe handicaps: "The principle of normalization rests on the assumption that adaptive or socially acceptable behavior is learned and maintained because the individual has been given an opportunity to behave in conventional ways and that such behavior has been reinforced. Moreover, appropriate behavior is more likely to be emitted and reinforced in a normal environment" (p. 45). The theoretical underpinnings of the normalization philosophy are rooted in learning theory, especially concepts of modeling and imitation. More importantly, it is a philosophy that recognizes the dignity and worth of all people, regardless of appearance or physical or mental limitation.

17. The Social Worker Should Continuously Evaluate the Progress of the Change Process

The practice of social work is far from an exact science. It involves working with changing people and changing situations. The objectives of helping activities, therefore, must be clearly delineated and regularly reviewed to be certain that they maintain relevance to the client's needs. It is not enough to set the course of an intervention strategy and assume that the desired outcome will be achieved. Rather, a continuous monitoring and evaluation of the change process by both the social worker and client is necessary. Anderson (1981) reinforces the need for regular evaluation of practice activities and comments that effective social work practice "requires mutual periodic reviews of the selected goals and targets, the method and skills used to achieve those goals, and the outcomes of the mutual work" (p. 64).

To achieve a continuous evaluation, both the worker and the client or client group must regularly collect and record data that are indicators of change and these data must be reviewed and analyzed. If the desired change is not occurring, the worker is obligated to try another approach or redesign the intervention. An ongoing evaluation of progress is a central feature of effective social work.

18. The Social Worker Should Be Accountable to the Client, Agency, Community, and Social Work Profession

One factor that complicates practice is that the social worker must be accountable to a number of parties. Where practitioners in some disciplines might feel that they are accountable only to the client, the social worker—working at the interface of person and environment—faces multiple sources of accountability.

Clearly, the social worker must be accountable to those individuals, families, and groups he or she directly serves. The social worker's activities must be competently and ethically completed in an appropriate and timely fashion. Social workers are obligated to give their best services to all clients at all times. In addition, since most social workers are employed in a social agency or are part of a private practice group, they are responsible for carrying out the programs and procedures of that organization. The reputation and success of any human service organization ultimately rests with the quality of services provided. For the organization to be accountable to its public, the workers must be accountable to the organization for the quality of their service.

The act of granting a professional monopoly demands that the members of the profession also be accountable to the community. For social workers in many states, this accountability is formalized through licensing. For others, the accountability is less structured but nevertheless expected.

As clearly stated in the NASW *Code of Ethics* (see Technique 8.7 and Appendix 8.1), the social work profession expects accountability to clients, colleagues, employers, the profession, and society. At times, practice situations place the individual worker in a position that makes it impossible to be fully accountable to all audiences. To which audience is the social worker primarily accountable?

Adopting the principle of maximizing accountability to these several audiences does not resolve the ethical dilemmas that inevitably occur in social work practice. In the final analysis, the social worker must examine those situations where these conflicts occur and arrive at a personal judgment regarding one's primary source of accountability.

Conclusion

The new social worker is often inundated with information that reveals, in bits and pieces, the knowledge and values that guide social work practice. Some of this information is formally taught in planned classroom and field experiences in both baccalaureate and master's degree programs in social work, while other information is transmitted more subtly. It is, at times, difficult for the worker to sort through this information to identify that which is fundamental to social work.

Practice principles reflect that combination of values and knowledge that should underlay the practice of social work. If all else fails, the worker cannot go too far wrong if operating within these principles. They might be viewed as a fail-safe mechanism in social work practice. The eighteen principles identified in this chapter represent the authors' effort to ferret out such principles from the social work literature. With these principles firmly in mind, the social worker is prepared to engage the client in a change process and to identify and select the most appropriate techniques for addressing the problems or enhancement needs of the client.

Selected Bibliography

The American Heritage Dictionary of the English Language, 1st ed., edited by William Morris. Boston: Houghton Mifflin, 1978.

Anderson, Joseph. *Social Work Methods and Processes*. Belmont, Calif.: Wadsworth, 1981.

Baer, Betty. "Social Work Practice." In *Educating the Baccalaureate Social Worker: A Curriculum Development Resource Guide*. Vol. 2, edited by Betty Baer and Ronald Federico. Cambridge, Mass.: Ballinger, 1979.

Barlett, Harriett M. *The Common Base of Social Work Practice*. New York: Columbia University Press, 1970.

――――. "Toward Clarification and Improvement of Social Work Practice." *Social Work 3* (April 1958): 3–9.

Biestek, Felix P. *The Casework Relationship*. Chicago: Loyola University Press, 1957.

Biestek, Felix P., and Clyde C. Gehrig. *Client Self-Determination in Social Work: A Fifty-Year History*. Chicago: University of Chicago Press, 1978.

Cohen, Nathan E. "Reversing the Process of Social Disorganization." In *Issues in American Social Work*, edited by Alfred J. Kahn. New York: Columbia University Press, 1959.

Dunham, Arthur, *Community Welfare Organization: Principles and Practices*. New York: Crowell, 1969.

Freedberg, Sharon. "Self-Determination: Historical Perspectives and Effects on Current Practice." *Social Work* 34 (January 1989): 33–38.

Friedlander, Walter E., ed. *Concepts and Methods of Social Work*. Englewood Cliffs, N.J.: Prentice-Hall, 1958.

Garvin, Charles D., and Paul H. Glasser. "Social Group Work: The Preventive and Rehabilitative Approach." In *Individual Change Through Small Groups,* edited by Paul Glasser, Rosemary Sarri, and Robert Vinter. New York: The Free Press, 1974.

Goldstein, Howard. "Starting Where the Client Is." *Social Casework* 64 (May 1983): 267–75.

Horejsi, Charles R. "Applications of the Normalization Principle in the Human Services: Implications for Social Work Education." *Journal of Education for Social Work* 15 (Winter 1979): 44–50.

National Association for Retarded Citizens. *The Right to Choose.* Arlington, Tex.: NARC, 1973.

Rawley, Callman. "A Sampling of Expert Opinion on Some Principles of Casework." *Social Casework* 35 (April 1954): 154–58.

Schwartz, Gerald. "Confidentiality Revisited." *Social Work* 34 (May 1989): 223–26.

Siporin, Max. *Introduction to Social Work Practice.* New York: Macmillan, 1975.

Smalley, Ruth. *Theory for Social Work Practice.* New York: Columbia University Press, 1967.

Soloman, Barbara. *Black Empowerment: Social Work in Oppressed Communities.* New York: Columbia University Pres, 1976.

Vinter, Robert. "Components of Social Work Practice." In *Individual Change Through Small Groups,* edited by Paul Glasser, Rosemary Sarri, and Robert Vinter. New York: The Free Press, 1974.

Weick, Ann, Charles Rapp, W. Patrick Sullivan, and Walter Kisthardt. "A Strengths Perspective for Social Work Practice." *Social Work* 34 (July 1989): 350–56.

Whitehead, Alfred N. *The Aims of Education and Other Essays.* New York: The Free Press, 1929.

Wilson, Suanna J. *Confidentiality in Social Work: Issues and Principles.* New York: The Free Press, 1978.

The Change Process in Social Work Practice 5

The traditional view of professional helping emphasizes the importance of the helper studying the problem presented by the patient or client, making a diagnosis of the situation, and treating that client to cure the problem. One of the principles of social work, however, is to empower clients to become active participants and decision makers in all phases of their lives. When empowerment is incorporated into professional helping, clients can no longer act as the uniformed subjects of clinical tests or passively accept the helper's prescribed remedy. They must actively review, analyze, decide, plan, act, and evaluate for themselves throughout the entire process.

For the person who gains satisfaction from controlling the behaviors of others or having the power to determine the outcome of events in another person's life, empowering clients may prove frustrating. Outcomes that appear best to the social worker may not be judged as at all desirable by the individual, family, or group of people that the social worker is serving. In the final analysis, the social worker cannot administer a cure for a social problem or change the client. At best, the social worker can guide the client through a series of activities to bring about a desired change. The primary functions of the social worker, then, are (1) attending to the process and (2) involving clients in analysis, decisions, and action that will help them and/or their environments change.

Understanding the Change Process

As a member of a profession concerned with helping people change in relation to some aspect of their environment, it is important that the social worker be knowledgeable about the concept of *change* and the *process* by which change occurs.

Change

One of the reasons that social work exists is that the world is so dynamic. People and the social systems of which they are a part require the services of a social worker when they have not been able to interact in a favorable way with their changing environments. Or conversely, help may be needed when people have changed more rapidly than their environments. Some social workers begin the change process by working with individuals, groups, and families (i.e., direct services), while others begin by working with larger social structures such as organizations, communities, and social policy-making bodies at even higher levels (i.e., indirect services). In every case, the social worker is involved in some form of change.

Brill (1990) summarizes some attributes of change for both individuals and social systems:

1. People change as a result of rational decisions in order to provide greater self-fulfillment and to avoid pain and discomfort.
2. People change when they learn, through facing and accepting the logical and inevitable consequences of their own behavior, that what they are doing is not really meeting their needs in a satisfactory and constructive way of contributing to their happiness and well-being.
3. People change through the development of relationships in which emotional needs are more adequately met and defenses accordingly need not be so rigid and constraining.
4. People change when, as a result of learning different ways of behaving, they provoke different responses from other people which in turn push them to respond differently.
5. People change when they are required to adapt to changing demands of the social system of which they are a part.
6. People change when they have hope of reward for the risk they are taking in upsetting the status quo.
7. Systems change when there is change within the parts that comprise them and when provision is made for the utilization of new input. (p. 123)

Thus, people are motivated to change for a variety of reasons: to avoid pain or punishment, to reduce dissatisfaction, to improve functioning, or to achieve some desired reward. In all cases, change means new patterns of functioning, new ways of relating to others, and a certain degree of disruption to one's life. While one part of the human personality desires and seeks change, there is a counterforce that desires stability and resists change. Change is risky. One cannot be sure of the impact a change will have. Even the most elementary knowledge of social systems theory makes the social worker aware of the so-called ripple effect of change: change in one system inevitably affects others.

The social worker must constantly be aware of the inherent ambivalence experienced by clients and client groups in the process of change. Ultimately, however, the client must determine if the potential reward that could accrue indeed justifies the risks and disruptions to one's life that are certain to occur.

Process

Successful practice requires discipline. The disciplined application of tested practice techniques and guidelines improves the chances of success. However, in

---

order for these techniques to have maximum effectiveness, they must be used *with* careful attention to process.

Process is defined as a "progressively continuing operation that consists of a series of controlled actions or movements systematically directed toward a particular result or end" (*Webster's*, 3rd ed., s.v. "process"). In applying this concept to working with people, Satir (1983) notes three important characteristics of process:

1. Process implies movement. It is dynamic, not static.
2. Process focuses not on the activity *per se,* but on the carrying on of that activity.
3. Process is more a matter of "how" than of "what"; form and content (in this book, "techniques and guidelines") are more matters of "what" than of "how." (p. 229)

The social worker must address specific matters at each phase of the change process. Laypersons or inexperienced professionals, for example, often move too quickly through the initial phases of the process with the understandable desire to get on with action that will bring about change. Impatience with the initial phase of the process is frequently a reason that natural helping systems have failed and clients require professional service to resolve a problem. Professional helping requires patience and discipline in moving through the process of change to assure that careful attention is given to each phase.

The term *phase* requires special note. A phase is part of a cycle of events to which particular attention is given at one point in time. In reality, all parts of the cycle occur simultaneously, but the social worker directs primary attention to specific activities at particular times. "Unlike infancy and adolescence, they are not stages through which one passes never to return; rather, these phases are often overlapping and circular in nature" (Sheafor and Landon 1987, 660–69). Thus, the phases must be viewed as guides to the changing focus of activity in the helping process.

An Overview of the Change Process

Descriptions of the change process have been a part of the social work literature throughout the development of this profession. In her classic book *Social Diagnosis* (1917), Mary Richmond discusses the "nature of social evidence" and the interpretation of data leading to the "social diagnosis" (pp. 38–50, 342–63). Forty years later, the work of Helen Harris Perlman echoed the same theme when describing the problem-solving process. In *Social Casework* (1957, 88-95), she described the process as (1) beginning with study that would ascertain and clarify the facts of the problem, followed by (2) diagnosis where the facts would be analyzed, and concluding with (3) treatment that involves making some choice or decision to resolve the problem. In subsequent years, this basic study-diagnosis-treatment process has been expanded, described in more detail, and applied to a range of helping approaches, from work with individuals to communities—and even to practice research. Yet the basic elements continue to be valid.

Careful analysis of the descriptions of the change processes that appear in the social work literature today indicates that while different authors use varied terminology and differentially emphasize activities to be accomplished at each phase of the process, the general pattern practice is quite similar, whether the social worker is engaged in direct practice, community or organizational change, or research.

Phases of the Change Process

In this book, the change process is segmented into five phases:

Phase I   Intake and Engagement
Phase II Data Collection and Assessment
Phase III Planning and Contracting
Phase IV Intervention and Monitoring
Phase V   Evaluation and Termination

These labels identify the primary tasks that must be completed in each phase. The reader is reminded that, regardless of where one is in the process, tasks identified as the primary focus in another phase might also be addressed. For example, the social worker never fully completes the task of engaging the client and is constantly acquiring new data, assessing the situation, and evaluating the success of the plan of action. In one sense, any effort to define the phases of change is artificial. Yet, recognizing that limitation, it nevertheless provides a helpful guide to practice.

The practice techniques and guidelines presented in Part III of this book are organized to reflect this change model. For the social worker engaged in direct practice, it is anticipated that this organization will make the techniques and guidelines readily accessible. By simply selecting the chapter appropriate to where a particular case situation might be in the change process, it is possible to find a collection of potentially useful practice techniques and guidelines.

Phase I. Intake and Engagement

The manner in which the helping process begins is important. Professional helpers are often suspect when helping is initiated. Clients wonder:

- Will they really care about me?
- Will I be treated with respect?
- Are they only interested in me because they are paid to perform this job?
- Is my problem worth taking their time or resources?
- Will they be competent to deal with this matter?
- Will this group or committee really be interested in my concerns or want to hear what I have to say about this matter?

Preintake Considerations. A crucial point in successful helping occurs even before the change process is begun. Typically, the client has had a history of efforts to get assistance from family, friends, or even other professional sources. Siporin (1975) notes that "people apply for social work help after failing in self-help efforts or after finding their life tasks beyond their capabilities or resources" (p. 193). By the time they reach the social worker, people are often discouraged or problems have compounded to the point that it seems doubtful the problem will ever be solved. The client's motivation to become involved in the helping process may depend on the nature of that prior problem-solving experience.

It is important that the client's first experience with the agency be conducive to developing a positive attitude about the service to be given. How the telephone is answered, how appointments are scheduled, how the receptionist greets people, and how comfortable the reception area is all influence the initiation of service. While the creation of a favorable environment is the primary responsibility of agency administrators, it must also be monitored by the direct service workers as a means of assuring that their practice has the maximum chance of success.

The social worker's preparation for the first meeting is also important. Attending to the aesthetics of an office, preparing a meeting room, and becoming familiar with any preexisting knowledge of the client or situation are preintake activities that can influence the client's readiness to engage in change-producing activity. The initial impression made by the social worker also sets a tone for the working relationship and must be carefully considered, as do the social worker's manner of dress, grooming, and attentiveness. In addition, the social worker must quickly transmit a positive attitude that lets the client know that professional help can make a difference and that he or she is prepared to help that client.

Engagement. The social provisions that a social worker may administer (e.g., financial assistance, food stamps, housing) are essential if some clients are to begin to change their social functioning; however, the primary tool of the social worker is the relationship that is established with the client. Many of the barriers to establishing a productive working relationship are removed when the client is voluntary (i.e., has elected to seek this help). In these situations, the client has demonstrated at least some motivation to change. However, a large part of the clients served by social workers are there involuntarily. They may have been pressured by spouses, friends, schools, courts, or other social agencies to seek this service in order to avoid punishment or receive some benefit. Dealing with the resistance to service that the involuntary client typically brings to the helping process is the first test of the social worker's ability to help (see Technique 9.7.).

During engagement, perhaps more than at any other phase of the helping process, the artistic aspects of social work practice are essential. The social worker's ability to establish working relationships reflecting empathy, warmth, and genuineness; the ability to infuse the activity with energy; and the demonstration of mature judgment helps build the necessary trust and confidence of clients. Certainly, special attention should be given to engaging the client in the initial stages of the helping process, but it may take some time for the client to become fully involved.

Intake. Engagement focuses on the interpersonal relationships between the clients and the social worker; intake involves discrete actions and decisions. First, the client and social worker must clarify the purpose for seeking help and discuss expectations of the helping process. Second, the situation must be appraised, if only initially; the worker must engage the client in sufficient discussion of the issues to arrive at a tentative agreement on the change that will be addressed. Third, the match between client and the agency must be assessed, which involves a review of the fit of the client's needs with the agency's eligibility requirements and resources.

At this point, a decision must be made. The service may be terminated, the client may be referred elsewhere for service, or service may be continued and the next phase of the helping process begun.

The decision to discontinue service may be made if it is determined that the matter cannot be resolved by the provision of service or if the client is not sufficiently motivated to invest the time, energy, or resources necessary. In either case, it is important that the social worker leave the door open for the client to return should the client's motivation change or should help be needed with another matter.

The decision to refer the client elsewhere may be made for a variety of reasons, as identified by Epstein (1988):

1. Lack of sufficient staff
2. Lack of staff with necessary skills
3. Clients or their problems are outside the normal and usual mission or function of the agency
4. Presumed superiority of the quality of some other agency's resources
5. Presumed quantity of services available in another agency
6. Assumption that another agency has been vested with responsibility for certain classes of clients or problems (pp. 87–88)

Because he or she works at the interface of person and environment, the social worker has a special responsibility to help clients gain access to other services, whether offered by the worker's own agency or available elsewhere in the community. In the role of a human services broker, the social worker must be thoroughly familiar with the resources available to meet a wide range of human needs.

If the decision is to continue service, the process of role induction is begun. This involves clearly defining the roles and expectations of both the worker and the client. Goldstein (1973, 191) notes that role induction must be conducted with clarity, perceptiveness, and specificity because it establishes the pattern for subsequent interaction and negotiation. Before the process moves on to placing greater attention on collecting data and assessing the situation in depth, the client should complete a thorough orientation to the roles and expectations of the social worker and the agency. And simultaneously, the social worker should be well-oriented to the needs and abilities of the client or group of clients to be served.

Phase II. Data Collection and Assessment

This phase of the change process is primarily concerned with understanding the situation confronted by the client and making judgments regarding the probable reasons for the needed change. The worker and client must have sufficient background information to place the situation into context, be familiar with the issues of immediate concern, and formulate a sound basis for embarking on the next phase—planning the action to bring about change.

Data Collection. One of the social worker's central roles is to direct a thorough investigation of the situation. The client will be expected to participate in this investigation, but the worker must help identify the type of information to be collected and guide the process of determining how those data will be gathered. At times, the client will collect information and present it to the worker; at other times, the worker and client will work together to retrieve and compile necessary data; and still at other times, the worker will act independently to secure relevant information.

The intent of this investigation is to arrive at a clear description of the situation being addressed, including events, facts, concerns, and reactions. At this point, it is essential that the situation is individualized and that the uniquenesses as well as the commonalities with similar situations the worker or clients may have experienced are understood. However, the worker must be cautious that data collection does not become an excuse for inaction. Due to the complexities of the human condition, it is possible to collect substantial amounts of information. To be useful, the search must be limited to collecting only that information that is relevant to understanding the situation.

The types of data required vary according to the kind of situation being addressed and the client system involved (i.e., individual, group, family, organization, or community). In general terms, this information might be historical, demographic, financial, physical, emotional, cultural, or a combination of these. The sources of these data might be the client, significant people in the client's life, or records, tests, reports, studies, or evaluations that may already be available (Brill 1990, 127–29).

The social worker must be resourceful in selecting techniques for gathering data. These techniques involve questioning, observation, use of existing material, and the collection of new data relevant to the practice situation. Regardless of the technique used, it is important that the information collected be carefully validated; when impressionistic data are used, they should be clearly recognized as such.

Assessment. Data collection leads to analysis. It is essential that the client or client group shares in making this analysis because the ultimate success of the helping process will depend on the client's comprehension of the situation and clarity about the purpose of the intervention. While the social worker may arrive at his or her own conclusions or diagnosis of the situation, assessment must involve sharing interpretations of the data with clients and modifying these views in light of the client's own perceptions. Perhaps more than at any other time in the helping process, the social worker must strive to communicate in clear, concise language and avoid the temptation to use diagnostic labels and professional jargon.

Assessment is accurately described as "the logical process by means of which we reason from the facts or particulars in a given situation to tentative conclusions regarding their meaning" (Powers, Meenaghan, and Toomey 1985, 25). In short, the information is organized in order to make sense of it. The social worker is obliged to bring the best knowledge available to this activity, both in fitting the information to the best explanatory theories and through the use of wisdom gained from experience in social work practice. At the same time, the analysis of social situations is inevitably influenced by value choices. Making the values issues explicit from the vantage point of the client, relevant others, and the worker and understood by the affected persons is a critical part of assessing a situation.

Effective practice involves developing alternative assessments. The social worker and client who limit the assessment of a situation to a single explanation often miss the richness of understanding that can accrue from several differing perceptions. A goal in each case should be to generate several plausible explanations and subsequently determine which one provides the most useful explanation on which to proceed. It is here that interaction between data collection and assessment might again occur. As differing explanations are compared, more focused data collection may be required. And upon attaining that information, a hypothesis regarding the situation can be generated. In essence, the remainder of the helping process involves confirming or disproving that hypothesis.

In addition to assessing the situation that the change activity is intended to address, the social worker must also assess the client's strengths and limitations in being able to engage in the possible change strategies. Assessment of the client's motivation is essential. Is the client experiencing serious discomfort from the situation? Does the client have the needed time and energy? Does he or she actually expect that changing would make a significant difference in the situation?

The social worker must also make a realistic appraisal of the possibility of achieving sufficient change to reduce or resolve the problems. Is this an appropriate time to engage in the change process? Is the change effort likely to be successful?

Finally, the social worker must assess the degree to which the client and affected persons have the capacity to successfully engage in a process that will achieve the desired change. To what extent are the necessary resources available, or are relevant others willing to participate in this change activity?

Phase III. Planning and Contracting

Based on the assessment of the situation, the phase of the change process that emphasizes the specification of goals, consideration of various action strategies, selection of a rational action plan, and the development of a formal or informal contract for initiating the change activity can be begun. Again, it is essential that the client or client group is actively involved in this activity. Involving the client in this phase is an important part of motivating him or her to action. The worker's sensitivity to the client's goals and abilities and the infusion of enthusiasm over the possibility of designing a plan to achieve the desired change are significant factors in accomplishing a successful outcome.

Planning. The development of an action plan is the bridge between the assessment and the actual intervention. Clients often want to short-cut this activity and get on with change. The social worker must insist that this phase be carried out with discipline and thoroughness.

Planning begins with specifying exactly what the client hopes to achieve. Clarification of the desired outcome at this point helps the worker and client remain focused on the goal during the helping process and avoid being sidetracked onto irrelevant tasks. The goal-setting activity should consider the impact of the desired change on the client, his or her immediate environment, and society in general.

However, the specification of long-range goals does not substitute for the establishment of short-term or working objectives. These objectives should be expressed in terms of specific behaviors to be achieved, specific resources to be made available, or specific policies to be adopted. The objectives should be concrete, attainable, and measurable.

Once goals and objectives have been established, the client and social worker can begin to consider alternative strategies to attain them. This places a special demand on the creativity of the social worker and the willingness of the client or client group to consider the advantages and disadvantages of alternative courses of action. It is essential that a wide range of action plans be considered and that the social worker is flexible in adapting to the needs and interests of the client. The range of possible strategies is limited only by the creativity of the client and social worker.

Each potentially feasible action plan must be evaluated. What can be predicted about its helpful and harmful impact on the client and others? What resources would be required to carry it out? What would be the demands on client, worker, and agency? Is there sufficient client and worker competence to successfully implement this plan? Can it be carried out in a realistic time frame? Do the possible gains sufficiently move toward the long-range goal of the client and outweigh any anticipated losses that may result?

After careful examination of the various strategies, the worker and client must finally select and develop in detail the plan they will follow. While this game plan must be used flexibly, each action to be taken must be carefully identified and the reasons for engaging in that action must be understood. It is helpful to design the plan so that some success can be achieved early in the process, such that the client can be rewarded with a sense of accomplishment.

Contracting. When an action plan has been agreed upon, commitment must be made to its implementation. The worker and client must arrive at a contract to fulfill that commitment. Barker (1987) defines a *social work contract* as "a written, oral, or implied agreement between the client and the social worker as to the goals, methods, timetables, and mutual obligations to be fulfilled during the intervention process" (p. 33).

In recent years, formal contracts have been used increasingly to clearly specify the elements of that agreement. Formalization of the contract in writing has consistently been found to strengthen the helping process. Its explicitness helps identify points of agreement and disagreement between worker and client; it serves as a basis for providing accountability to client and agency; and it can be an effective tool in facilitating the transfer of cases to another social worker, should that become necessary. The most serious limitation of formal contracts, however, may lie in their unintended use in potential litigation and agency personnel decisions (Epstein, 1988, 147).

The basic elements of a contract are similar, even though the language and format may vary, when working at the individual, family, group, organization, or community levels. Although discussing only direct practice, Epstein (1988) delineated the elements to be specified in a contract:

1. Major priority problems (three at most)
2. Specific goals
3. Client tasks: activities the client will undertake
4. Practitioner tasks: activities the practitioner will undertake
5. Duration of intervention: approximately how long the process is to last
6. Scheduling of interventions
7. Scheduling of interviews
8. Participants: who will take part
9. Location: where the sessions will occur (p. 149)

The completion of a contract signifies the end of this phase of the change process. It must be recognized, however, that even the most carefully developed plan of action may not be sufficient when the implementation is attempted. The worker and client must always be open to renegotiating the contract in light of the experience of actually working to achieve change.

Phase IV. Intervention and Monitoring

The intervention and monitoring phase is the point at which the focus of the change process turns to action. The plan designed to change the behavior and/or situation that concerns the client or client group can now be implemented. The social worker is responsible for carrying out his or her part of the plan, helping the client perform the agreed upon tasks, bringing necessary resources to bear on the situation, monitoring the progress of the change activity, and helping to stabilize positive changes that occur.

Intervention. Whether the client is an individual, family, or group, the fundamental role of the social worker is to help the client achieve change. Siporin (1975) indicates that "the basic intervention in helping people is to influence them, arouse their wills, and move them to choose and to act so as to accomplish change in their behavior, in their life situations, and in their relationships with their environment. It is essentially the client who learns, relates, resolves his problems, and fulfills himself" (p. 293).

The knowledge and skills that the social worker needs to carry out this phase of the change process are the subject of a major part of the social work literature; full recitation of the factors involved is beyond the scope of this book. However, a review of the purpose of actions taken by social workers and the models of practice they most commonly use helps place the techniques and guidelines presented in Chapter 12 into context.

The *actions* taken by social workers can be grouped into two categories: (1) those that directly involve clients (*direct services*) and (2) those taken on behalf of clients *(indirect services)*. Johnson (1989) provides a useful summary of the purpose of actions typically undertaken with clients:

1. action taken to enable development of relationships
2. action taken to enable development of understanding of persons in situations
3. action taken in the planning process
4. action taken to enable the client to know and use resources available
5. action taken in crisis situations
6. action taken to support the social functioning of clients
7. action taken that uses activity with clients as the basis of help
8. action taken to mediate the social functioning of clients and others
9. action taken in using a clinical model of social work (p. 308)

In relation to the indirect services that social workers perform for clients, Johnson (1989) further identifies the following:

1. action relative to coordination of services
2. action for program planning and development
3. action designed to manipulate the environment
4. action taken to change organizations
5. cause advocacy action (p. 351)

The *models of practice* adopted by social workers vary according to the needs of the client, the agency setting, the nature of the situation, and the ability of the social worker to use a specific model effectively. Basically, a model of practice is a conceptual framework. Visualize a house under construction, one that is framed in. It consists of only a foundation and the wooden 2 × 4 framework. There are no walls, doors, windows, or a roof, only the outlined structure of the house. The conceptual frameworks used in social work practice are something like that wooden framework, except they are constructed of ideas, principles, and assumptions. They provide the worker with only a basic outline of what to do. The worker must fill in the specifics, which will differ, depending upon the client's problems, personality and relationship factors, and the worker's own style.

The *Encyclopedia of Social Work* (Minahan 1987) provides descriptions of several approaches or models commonly used by social workers. Among those used in work with individuals, families, and small groups are, for example, the behavioral, existential, family, feminist, psychosocial, task-centered, and trans-actional analysis approaches to practice. Zastrow (1985) further identifies a number of direct service practice models from which social workers have borrowed concepts and techniques, including psychoanalysis, client-centered, gestalt, play therapy, transactional analysis, reality therapy, rational-emotive, and psychodrama. Many of these direct service models have much in common and the differences that do occur are often more in emphasis than in basic or core principles.

The indirect service models include community organization, financial and personnel management, policy analysis, program evaluation, social action, social and health planning, and supervision (Minahan 1987). Whether using direct or indirect practice approaches, it is critical that the social worker select and skillfully apply the most effective intervention methods and techniques to help the client accomplish the desired change.

Thus, when we speak of social work intervention, we refer to actions by a social worker designed to interfere with or modify an existing behavior pattern or situation deemed harmful to the client. It is also helpful to view intervention against a backdrop of three levels of prevention: primary, secondary, and tertiary. When applied to the problem of child abuse, for example, we have:

1. *Primary Prevention.* Actions taken to prevent the development of those situations or conditions that give rise to the problem of child abuse and neglect.
2. *Secondary Prevention.* Early detection of a developing problem so it can be addressed in its early stages when it is most easily "treated" and before it becomes a serious problem.
3. *Tertiary Prevention.* Treatment of an already serious problem in order to keep it from having an even more drastic and far-reaching impact on child and family.

Since an action taken to prevent a problem is, in reality, an intervention, social work practice can be viewed as involving primary, secondary, and tertiary intervention.

Monitoring. As the interventive activities unfold, the social worker is responsible for keeping track of that activity and continuously evaluating the success of those actions in achieving the objectives of the intervention. This ongoing evaluation is an "assessment of the validity, accuracy, and efficacy of each step of the helping process as it occurs" (Wood 1978, 454). Depending on the degree of success in implementing the plan, the intervention might be continued, corrective action might be taken to overcome blockage to some aspect of the plan, or the plan could be aborted and a new contract negotiated.

It is important that the worker and client approach the intervention phases flexibly, recognizing that there are many routes to achieving change. While the carefully developed plan deserves a serious effort at implementation, the commitment to that plan must not be so rigid that it cannot be revised to maintain progress toward the long-range goal of the change activity.

Stabilizing. Finally, when change occurs, various systems are in a state of disruption. Thus, the new behavior, attitude, method of operation, or policy must be incorporated into the normal pattern of operation when the change activity is completed. The social worker must ensure that the change becomes more than a temporary accommodation to the interventive activities and is institutionalized as part of the ongoing method of functioning for the client and/or the relevant environment.

Phase V. Termination and Evaluation

The final phase of the change process is concerned with the termination of service to the client and the formal evaluation of the effort. The evaluation has implications for both administrative decisions and upgrading the quality of professional practice.

Termination. Every helping relationship must terminate. Counseling must end, and groups or committees must eventually be disbanded. While termination is inevitable, the attention given to it by the worker and client is important to the success of the change process. It is a particularly important consideration when providing direct services, although work with agency and community groups should be discontinued in a manner that will maintain the interest and commitment of those who may later become involved in related issues.

There are two points of view regarding the significance of termination to individual clients. One perspective holds that, when client and worker engage in change activity, meaningful relationships are formed and strong emotional bonds develop. Sensitive issues are addressed, painful change occurs, dependency develops, and thus, when the helping relationship is severed, the client experiences a sense of loss. Feelings of anger and rejection may contribute to regression from the progress that has been made. Thus, the social worker must be sensitive to the negative feelings that may result when service is discontinued.

A second viewpoint is that social workers and other helping people tend to overdramatize their impact on clients; while termination may occasionally be traumatic for clients, it is usually not such an intensive experience that it has a serious negative impact. For example, Epstein (1988) notes, "It is a rare client indeed who truly becomes unhappy or is set adrift when termination occurs. Practitioners tend to overestimate the value they have for a client's well-being. The rewards of termination to a client are great: more money in the pocket (if the client is paying a fee), more time, freedom from the practioner's influence and surveillance, and greater independence" (p. 215).

Certainly, both perspectives have some merit. In either case, the worker must be sensitive to how the termination occurs. It should be anticipated throughout the change process and be treated matter of factly. A gradual reduction of activity helps avoid feelings of rejection when there is unfinished business between the worker and client. Given an opportunity to anticipate the end, it is possible for the client to appropriately disengage from the relationship.

Occasionally, service will terminate unexpectedly, at a time other than that planned by the worker and client. For example, various external factors may make it necessary for the client or worker to discontinue, the worker may accept employment elsewhere, the work may be blocked by a problem in the worker-client relationship and a transfer of the case may be best for the client, or specialized services may be needed from another social worker, professional, or agency. In these cases, it is important that the worker maintain positive relations, keeping the door open to further service, should the client need it.

Evaluation. As opposed to the ongoing monitoring that occurs throughout the helping process, a final evaluation of the helping activity is important both for the agency and the social worker. Kettner, Daley, and Nichols (1985) summarize the purpose of this final evaluation: "The purpose of evaluation is to provide information to make the change episode effective and efficient. While monitoring keeps track of the completion of activities and outcomes, evaluation places a value on their usefulness. Evaluation responds to the question 'Is the process effective?' and 'Is the change effort making a difference in the situation it was designed to address?' " (p. 30).

From the perspective of the agency, this final evaluation is a significant part of its effort to be accountable. The agency should be concerned with the staff's effectiveness in providing services. Measuring the success of interventive efforts is difficult, as valid cause and effect is not easily determined in the relatively uncontrolled environment of human life. Yet the ability of the agency to assess the effect of service on clients' lives is essential if support for the agency is to be maintained. Thus, procedures for making a cost-effectiveness appraisal of the helping activity is commonplace in social agencies.

The social worker, too, is ethically obliged to be accountable to clients and provide the best services possible. It is important to engage clients in a final review of the process, encouraging them to judge the success of the experience from their vantage point and help the worker assess the adequacy of his or her performance. From this information, the worker can make a self-evaluation or seek consultation that will help improve performance in other situations. The social worker's openness to this evaluation is a key to ongoing professional development.

Conclusion

Like other central themes that are essential to high-quality social work practice, the importance of giving attention to the change process has been reported in the literature to the point that it often appears trite. Yet guiding the change process is such a fundamental part of serving clients that it simply must be addressed in any book on social work practice. The social worker should know this process so thoroughly that it becomes second nature. For the new social worker, it is useful to periodically review descriptions of the several phases to be certain that he or she is not developing any habits that omit important aspects of this process. Even the experienced social worker should periodically review his or her practice to determine if patterns may have developed that fail to give sufficient attention to all phases of the change process.

Selected Bibliography

Barker, Robert. *The Social Work Dictionary.* Silver Spring, Md.: NASW, 1987.

Brill, Naomi I. *Working With People: The Helping Process.* 4th ed. New York: Longman, 1990.

Epstein, Laura. *Helping People: The Task-Centered Aproach.* 2nd ed. Columbus, Ohio: Merrill, 1988.

Goldstein, Howard. *Social Work Practice: A Unitary Approach.* Columbia: University of South Carolina Press, 1973.

Johnson, Louise C. *Social Work Practice: A Generalist Approach.* 3rd ed. Boston: Allyn and Bacon, 1989.

Kettner, Peter, John M. Daley, and Ann Weaver Nichols. *Initiating Change in Organizations and Communities.* Monterey, Calif.: Brooks/Cole, 1985.

Minahan, Anne, ed. *Encyclopedia of Social Work.* 18th ed. Silver Spring, Md.: NASW, 1987.

Perlman, Helen Harris. *Social Casework: A Problem-Solving Process.* Chicago: University of Chicago Press, 1957.

Powers, Gerald T., Thomas M. Meenaghan, and Beverly G. Toomey, *Practice Focused Research: Integrating Human Service Practice and Research.* Englewood Cliffs, N.J.: Prentice-Hall, 1985.

Richmond, Mary E. *Social Diagnosis.* New York: Russell Sage Foundation, 1917.

Satir, Virginia. *Conjoint Family Therapy.* 3rd ed. Palo Alto, Calif.: Science and Behavior Books, 1983.

Sheafor, Bradford W., and Pamela S. Landon. "Generalist Perspective." In *Encyclopedia of Social Work,* 18th ed., edited by Anne Minahan. Silver Spring, Md.: NASW, 1987.

Siporin, Max. *Introduction to Social Work Practice.* New York: Macmillan, 1975.

Webster's Third New International Dictionary. Springfield, Mass.: Merriam, 1966.

Wood, Katherine M. "Casework Effectiveness: A New Look at the Research Evidence." *Social Work 23* (November 1978): 437–58.

Zastrow, Charles. *The Practice of Social Work.* 2nd ed. Homewood, Ill.: The Dorsey Press, 1985.

Techniques Common to All Social Work Practice

II.

The three chapters in Part II focus on techniques and guidelines basic to social work practice, regardless of agency setting or type of client served. In every practice setting, the social worker must be a skillful communicator, be able to develop relationships, know how to manage a workload, cope with job-related pressures, and continue to learn and grow as a professional person.

Chapter 6, "Basic Communication and Helping Skills," presents information on effective communication and relationship building. The chapter lays a foundation for understanding and applying the more specialized practice techniques and guidelines discussed in Parts III and IV. While the examples used to illustrate these basic skills are drawn from direct service, most can and are applied in administrative, community organization, and social planning activities. Chapter 6 draws heavily on Lawrence Shulman's useful conceptualization of twenty-seven basic helping skills used by social workers. In addition, the reader is reminded of the importance of nonverbal communication and offered a review of the techniques of active listening and the "I-message" that is so useful in dealing with interpersonal conflict. It is assumed that those using this book have been exposed to the ideas in this chapter; however, the authors' experience with practicum students suggests that readers will appreciate this concise review.

Chapter 7, "Workload and Caseload Management," is especially important to the worker who is going into a social agency for the first time. Few new workers are adequately prepared to cope with the time pressures and paperwork they encounter. This chapter provides practical guidance on such things as time management, how to write reports, and how to maintain records. The worker's ability to master these tasks often determines whether an individual can make it in social work.

Chapter 8, "Personal and Professional Development," recognizes the importance of the social worker being able to handle job-related pressures and dilemmas while continuing to acquire new knowledge and professional skills. The day-to-day struggles of the practicing social worker are frequently overlooked by agency administrators, program planners, and sometimes even supervisors. Consequently, many workers get little or no guidance on how to survive and grow as a professional person.

Basic Communication and Helping Skills   6

Introduction

This chapter presents what might be called "the basics" of social work communication and relationship. The focus is on generic communication and helping skills—namely, those used with all clients, whether the client is an individual, a family, a small group, an organization, or a community.

The specific purpose of a professional interaction will determine the type of relationship the worker attempts to develop and the types of messages communicated to the client. In general, the social worker providing direct services attempts to develop a professional relationship that has attributes known to positively affect the outcome of the helping process. These include empathy, warmth, and genuineness. The worker in the indirect service area places relatively more emphasis on precision, clarity, and goal directness. This is not to say, however, that the factors of empathy, warmth, and genuineness are not important in the relationships of the indirect service worker. Rather, it is a matter of emphasis.

Essentially, communication is a process wherein one individual conveys information—either intentionally or unintentionally—to another person. It occurs when one person attaches meaning to the verbal or nonverbal behavior of another. Communication is a form of behavior, but not all human behavior is communication; it all depends on whether a person perceives a message in the words or behavior of another. Communication is primarily a receiver phenomenon; regardless of what one says in words or intends to communicate, it is the person on the receiving end that assigns meaning to those words and body movements.

We must be constantly aware of the complexity and inherent limitations of communication. Lingren (1986) reminds us that:

1. A word or symbol is not the thing it represents—it is an abstraction; hence, it should not be confused with the thing it represents (e.g., a man's I.Q. is not his intelligence).
2. No two people, events, ideas, places, or things are identical; hence, our predictions, generalities, and systems of classification are limited. . . .

3. Words and symbols have both denotative and connotative aspects, and no single word, event, or symbol will be interpreted the same way by different persons ... (e.g., not everyone is depressed at becoming unemployed). (p. 9)

Also, we need to remember that one's own experience and background act as a filter that causes each of us to perceive things in a unique way. Morain (1986) explains:

All living things ... separate out from their environment what is useful to them. As humans, our senses abstract only limited aspects of the dynamic, process world, ... of which we are a part. Our perceptions are not identical to the processes going on inside and outside our skins and are, to a surprising extent, personal. On a walk in the country those who are colorblind or trained in botany perceive differently from people without such limitations or backgrounds. Our different experiences, skills, and cultures give us individuality and contribute to our different perceptions and evaluations. (p. xii)

Communication depends on the proper functioning of the senses (e.g., vision, hearing, touch, etc.) and the complex cognitive activities of the brain, which include: *attention* (focusing on certain stimuli while disregarding others); *perception* (using attention, pattern recognition, and sensory memory to interpret stimuli picked up by our senses); *memory* (retaining information over time); *language* (interpreting, expressing, and remembering verbal and written words and symbols); *conceptualization* (organizing information and ideas into categories); *reasoning* (drawing conclusions from information); and *decision making* (making choices based on an anticipation of future events). These cognitive processes are interrelated and overlapping. If the senses are impaired or if the brain has been damaged, the ability to communicate will be limited to some degree. Common causes of brain damage are strokes, trauma, chemical intoxication, tumors, and dementia-type illnesses such as Alzheimer's disease.

The capacity to send and receive messages accurately can also be distorted by one's emotional state and social expectations. In general, we "hear" what we want to hear, hear what we have learned to expect, and hear what serves our self-interest at the moment. In other words, we often distort messages in order to avoid discomfort and to meet our emotional needs. For example, often we do not really hear bad news. Also, individuals with certain personality disorders characteristically distort messages in a self-serving fashion. In addition, situational and social-interactional factors have a powerful influence on how words and gestures are interpreted. How, when, and where a message is sent are usually as important as the literal meaning or the words used.

The lack of clear communication is a common cause of problems within families, organizations, and other social systems. In general, communication problems develop when

- We speak for others rather than let them speak for themselves.
- We let our prejudices and stereotypes affect what we hear and what we say.

- We do not take the time to listen and understand what the other person is trying to say.
- We keep things to ourselves because we think others will disapprove of what we really believe and feel.
- We make no attempt to communicate because we assume others already know how we feel and what we think.
- We are afraid to take the risks that are necessary to communicate honestly and openly with others.
- We discourage or suppress communication by ordering, threatening, preaching, judging, blaming, or humoring.
- Negative feelings about ourselves (low self-esteem) cause us to conclude that we have nothing to say and that no one wants to listen to us.

This chapter begins by reviewing the characteristics of a helping relationship. Because Lawrence Shulman's research on the helping activities of social workers has yielded a useful conceptualization of the helping process, descriptions of his twenty-seven basic helping skills have been included. Also included in this chapter is information on active listening, asking questions, the "I-message," nonverbal communication, and how to respond to defensiveness.

Selected Bibliography

Lingren, Henry. "General Semantics: A Tool for the Counselor." *Enriching Professional Skills Through General Semantics,* edited by Mary Morain. San Francisco: International Society for General Semantics, 1986.

Morain, Mary. "For the Newcomer to General Semantics." *Enriching Professional Skills Through General Semantics,* edited by Mary Morain. San Francisco: International Society for General Semantics, 1986.

Nunnally, Elam, and Caryl Moy. *Communication Basics for Human Service Professionals.* Newbury Park, Calif.: Sage, 1989.

6.1   *Creating an Effective Helping Relationship*

Purpose: To develop a helping relationship with a client.

Discussion: At the very heart of an effective helping relationship is human caring. A social worker must genuinely care about his or her clients. Clients want a social worker to be knowledgeable but they do not pay attention to how much the worker knows until they know how much he or she cares.

Goldstein (1975) explains that "most psychotherapists and psychotherapy researchers view a positive relationship between helper and client as necessary, but not sufficient for client change. Without such a relationship, change is very unlikely. With it, the foundation exists for other more specific change procedures... to yield their intended effects." (p. 71)

Some type of relationship will develop whenever a social worker and client interact. However, the relationship may be either a positive or negative one, depending on the worker's behavior and the client's perceptions. Obviously, one can control only one's actions; it is impossible to control the perceptions of the client. Thus, the social worker cannot *make* a good relationship happen. At most, he or she can attempt to become the type of person that most clients find helpful and do those things that increase the possibility that a positive relationship will develop.

Extensive research has been conducted on the so-called core conditions of the helping relationship. These include empathy, positive regard, warmth, and genuineness. ***Empathy*** is the ability to understand accurately the experiences and feelings of another person. It is sometimes described as the ability to step into someone's shoes and see and feel life as that individual does. The truly empathetic worker is able to sense the meaning and the significance of a client's experience. Empathy is conveyed primarily through active listening, by giving undivided attention to the client, and by being sensitive to nonverbal cues that indicate how the client is feeling. It is important to make frequent use of paraphrasing and reflection in order for the social worker to understand what the client is saying and feeling. Fischer (1978) explains, "This active process not only provides the framework for the moment-to-moment contact necessary for accurate empathy, but ensures the errors in the worker's perception or understanding of what the client has communicated will be quickly recognized" (p. 192).

Essentially, ***positive regard*** means believing that all clients are persons of value and treating them with dignity regardless of appearance, behavior, or life circumstances. This does not mean that the social worker must accept or approve of destructive behaviors, but rather that the client is seen as a person of inherent worth. Our tendency to judge is a major barrier to effective communication; it is strongest when our feelings and emotions are stirred. When we judge, we are usually looking at a situation from our point of view rather than the client's. Communication can be improved with clients by maintaining a *nonjudgmental attitude,* which Cormier and Cormier (1985) define as "capacity to suspend judgment of the client's actions or motives and to avoid condemning or condoning the client's thoughts, feelings or actions" (p. 31).

The core condition of ***warmth*** exists when the social worker treats clients in a way that makes them feel safe, accepted, and understood. Goldstein (1975) has observed that without warmth, the professional may be "technically correct but therapeutically impotent" (p. 34). Warmth is expressed in a smile, a soft and soothing voice, a relaxed but interested posture, eye contact, and gestures that convey openness.

Genuineness means being one's self and being real. Fisher (1978) explains:

Genuineness may be best understood as the absence of phoniness, as nondefensiveness, as congruence, and as spontaneity. In fact, it would be difficult to conceive of the meaningful communication of empathy and warmth by someone who was not at least minimally "real." . . .

Genuineness is not synonymous with being totally honest. Workers need not disclose their total selves; but whatever they do reveal should be a real aspect of themselves, not a response growing out of defensiveness or a merely 'professional' response that has been learned and repeated. . . . This, again, does not mean that workers cannot 'have' negative or defensive responses. Rather, and this is crucial to the concept of genuineness, if workers do have such responses, they do not employ them in ways that will be destructive to their clients. (p. 199)

Those who are new to social work sometimes worry that they cannot simultaneously behave in a professional manner and be truly genuine in their relationships with clients. We would argue that being professional has nothing to do with "playing the role" or trying to imitate some idealized or stereotyped image of a professional person. A true professional is knowledgeable, self-disciplined, responsible, ethical, and, most of all, effective. There is no conflict between these qualities and being genuine.

Much of the research on helping relationships has been conducted outside the field of social work, but those research findings are consistent with ones that emerged from social work research, such as the extensive study by Shulman (1979). Fischer (1981) concludes that the core conditions of empathy, positive regard, warmth, and genuineness are clearly relevant to social work: "They constitute the essential skills involving relationships and therapeutic interviewing that are the heart of practice" (p. 204). Maluccio (1979) used in-depth interviewing to secure clients' opinions about social workers and his data also underscore the importance of these core conditions. However, three additional worker qualities emerged from his study: *concreteness* (ability to communicate thoughts and ideas clearly and specifically), *competence* (proficiency in carrying out professional tasks and activities), and *objectivity* (being unbiased and able to appreciate differing points of view).

Maluccio (1979) states that, from the client's perspective, an ideal social worker is "warm, accepting, understanding, involved, natural, genuine, competent, objective and able to share of himself or herself with the client" (p. 125). After reviewing current research on the helping relationship and studies of intervention outcome, Fischer (1978) concludes that the effective social worker is

deeply involved, deeply personal, deeply caring. Effective caseworkers are *real* people, unafraid of their own experiences, trusting those experiences, knowing who they are, and offering every client all they are. Effective caseworkers are not afraid of emotions, their own or their client's; they are not afraid to *feel* or express those feelings. And when they express feelings, they do so in a way that is constructive for others. Effective caseworkers are both secure and competent enough to recognize that one can be deeply involved with the problems of others, yet retain the objectivity necessary for appropriate selection and use procedures that will be facilitative for clients. (p. 213)

The term *structuring* refers to the use of various interpersonal arrangements (e.g., worker-client matching) and symbols (e.g., worker dress and office environment) to enhance relationship building. We know, for example, that a client is most likely to be influenced by someone to whom he or she is attracted. We are usually attracted to those who have beliefs, backgrounds, interests, and a lifestyle similar to our own. Maluccio (1979) found that, "in general, clients felt more positively and were more satisfied with the service and its outcome the closer they were to their workers in respect to characteristics such as age, family status and sex" (p. 183). It follows, therefore, that a social worker who wants to increase his or her attractiveness to a client should look for similarities and mention them to the client. For example, the worker might point out that he or she and the client both have children of about the same age or both have an interest in the same type of music. It should be noted, however, that a study by Beck (1988) found that client-worker matching by sex, age, marital status, race, parenthood, and socioeconomic status had little or no effect on client outcome. Some of Beck's research findings suggested that differences in the life experience of the counselor and client had a positive effect on outcome.

Research findings tell us that *expertness*—or at least the appearance of expertness—can have a significant positive impact on the initial phases of the helping process. According to Cormier and Cormier (1985) and Goldstein (1975), such things as certificates and diplomas on the wall, type of agency setting, office size, proper use of language, and clothing style can increase the client's respect for the helper and result in the client being more open to influence. Clearly one must be alert to the importance of such factors, but the social worker should remember that clients, like all people, make deliberate decisions about whose influence they accept and whose they reject. Moreover, one's "expertness" is often measured in ways other than counting college degrees and credentials. For example, in discussing social work with the black family, Hartman (1985) explains:

> A professional is assessed, not by status or role or degree, but in terms of who she is; what she has done; what her life experience has been; whom she knows; and who knows her. Asking personal questions is usually a Black person's way of credentialing a worker, whereas most social workers are taught to avoid giving personal information and to turn questions back to clients: a clear example of dissonance between white worker and Black client. (p. 106)

One's waiting room and office can also have a significant impact on clients, either positive or negative. For example, if a client must talk with the social worker in a space that lacks privacy and comfort, respect for the worker is greatly diminished. It is very important to give careful attention to making offices and meeting rooms as comfortable and dignified as possible.

Selected Bibliography

Beck, Dorothy Fahs. *Counselor Characteristics: How They Affect Outcomes.* Milwaukee: Family Service of America, 1988.

Cormier, William, and L. Sherilyn Cormier. *Interviewing Strategies for Helpers.* 2nd ed. Monterey: Brooks/Cole, 1985.

Fischer, Joel. *Effective Casework Practice: An Eclectic Approach.* New York: McGraw-Hill, 1978.

———. "The Social Work Revolution." *Social Work* 26 (May 1981): 199–207.

Goldstein, Arnold. "Relationship Enhancement Methods." In *Helping People Change: A Textbook of Methods,* edited by Frederick Kanfer and Arnold Goldstein. New York: Pergamon Press, 1975.

Hartman, Ann. "Summing Up." In *Empowering the Black Family,* edited by Sylvia Sims, Ann Hartman, and Ellen Saalberg. Ann Arbor: University of Michigan, School of Social Work, 1985.

Maluccio, Anthony. *Learning from Clients: Interpersonal Helping as Viewed by Clients and Social Workers.* New York: The Free Press, 1979.

Shulman, Lawrence. *The Skills of Helping: Individuals and Groups.* Itasca, Ill.: F. E. Peacock, 1979.

6.2 Shulman's Twenty-Seven Basic Helping Skills

Purpose: To understand and utilize basic helping skills in social work practice.

Discussion: One of the most intensive studies of helping skills in social work practice was conducted by Lawrence Shulman (1977, 1979). His four-year research effort was rooted in the conceptual framework known as the "mediating model," developed by William Schwartz (1961). Shulman's research data were drawn from videotapes of individual and family counseling sessions and group sessions with a wide variety of clients in several social agencies. The clients included unmarried parents, adolescents and younger children in foster care, foster parents, adopting parents, and dysfunctional families. Twenty-seven basic communication, relationship-building, and problem-solving skills were identified and conceptualized:

1. clarifying purpose
2. clarifying role
3. encouraging the client's feedback on purpose
4. displaying belief in the potential of the work
5. reaching for between-session data
6. moving from the general to the specific
7. reaching inside the silences
8. understanding the client's feelings
9. putting the client's feelings into words
10. connecting feelings to work
11. displaying feelings openly
12. sharing personal thoughts and feelings
13. supporting the client's strengths
14. partializing the client's concerns
15. holding to focus
16. checking for artificial consensus
17. pointing out the illusion of work
18. supporting the client in taboo areas
19. identifying affective obstacles to work
20. dealing with the authority theme
21. providing data
22. viewing system people in new ways
23. contacting system people directly
24. pointing out endings
25. sharing ending feelings
26. asking for a review of learning
27. reaching for ending feelings*

*Reprinted with the permission of the Council on Social Work Education.

Shulman and Schwartz suggest that a worker's utilization of techniques or specific skills must be understood against a backdrop of time and four phases in the helping process: (1) the tuning-in phase, (2) the beginning phase, (3) the work phase, and (4) the ending or transition phase. The twenty-seven skills are described briefly in the following sections. Each is presented after a brief explanation of the phase in which it is most likely to be utilized.

The Tuning-In Phase

The *tuning-in phase* occurs prior to the first meeting between social worker and client. According to Shulman (1981, 8), during this phase the worker attempts to develop a "preliminary empathy" by trying to imagine feelings the client may have as he or she thinks about going to the agency and discussing personal matters with a stranger. By tuning into how the client might be feeling, the worker can prepare to address the client's initial responses and ease the entry into the helping relationship. Shulman does not identify any specific skills with the tuning-in phase.

The Beginning Phase

In this book, the *beginning phase* is termed *intake and engagement* (see Chapter 9). During this phase the worker must explain and clarify his or her purpose and role and the services provided by the agency. It is during this phase that client and worker must reach a tentative agreement or a "working contract" that will guide initial efforts to address the client's need or problem. Four skills are used to engage and orient the client to the helping process and minimize testing and resistance: (1) clarifying purpose, (2) clarifying role, (3) encouraging the client's feedback on purpose, and (4) displaying belief in the potential of the work.

Clarifying purpose refers to a simple, nonjargonized statement by the worker regarding the general purpose of the worker-client meeting. A clear statement of purpose serves to define expectations. For example:

> *Worker:* I am really glad you were able to come in today. As you know, your wife first came to the agency about three weeks ago. She expressed concern about your marriage. I would like to get your perspective on this matter and find out if you believe there are problems in the marriage, and, if so, what you think they are.

When the contact is initiated by the client, the worker should encourage the client to express in his or her own words the reason for requesting the interview. The social worker must never assume that he or she knows what is on the client's mind. If the client has a hard time explaining his or her purpose, the worker should ask questions about circumstances that led to the request for an interview and what the client hopes will come from the meeting.

When the social worker initiates the contact, he or she should explain why. The explanation should be clear, direct, and to the point.

> *Good Explanation:* I need to talk with you about your son, John. He has missed fourteen out of the last twenty school days. This is a serious problem.

Bad Explanation: Hi there. I know your son, John. I was just in the neigh-borhood and I thought I would stop by to chat. How are things going?

The skill of **clarifying role** refers to a statement by the worker designed to give the client a beginning idea of how the worker might be able to help. The statement should be directly related to the client's presenting problem. For example:

Worker: As you get ready to leave this hospital, it's important to anticipate the problems you will face and figure out how to deal with them. Basically, that is why I want to spend time with you. I will be trying to get your ideas on the problems you face. I will share my ideas, as well. Between the two of us, I hope we can come up with ideas that will minimize the difficulties you will have when you go back home.

The skill of **encouraging the client's feedback on purpose** refers to statements that encourage the client to respond to the worker's explanation of why the worker and client are meeting. This gives the client an opportunity to voice differences in expectation. Consider these two examples:

Worker: What are your reactions to what I have said about this meeting? Do you see things differently?

or

Worker: It's quite possible you and I have different ideas about why we are talking today. I want to know if you were expecting something else.

Displaying belief in the potential of the work refers to worker statements intended to convey the worker's belief that professional intervention can be helpful. It is an offer of realistic hope to the client. For example:

Worker: The problems you have described are serious, and I can under-stand why you feel overwhelmed. But I think we can successfully deal with some of these problems if we work together and start chipping away at the problems one at time. It won't be easy, but I think we can make some progress over the next few weeks.

The Work Phase

Shulman calls the third phase of the helping the **work phase.** The beginning phase is guided by only a tentative agreement as to the purpose, but as the re-lationship deepens and the client feels more comfortable, more concerns are re-vealed, the nature of the client's problem is clarified, and the helping process takes on a more definite focus. Twenty of Shulman's twenty-seven skills are used predominately during the work phase.

Each session with the client has three time phases—getting started, the session's work, and the drawing to a close. At the beginning of each session, the worker must provide an opportunity for what Shulman (1981, 12) terms *sessional contracting.* Even when there has been a prior agreement on how the session will be used, it is important to check again for consensus. Quite possibly some change in the client's situation has altered the client's sense of priorities. The skill of **reaching for between-session data** is used to initiate sessional contracting. Essentially, this is asking the client to bring the worker up to date and allowing the client to determine the content of the session, even if it is somewhat different than what was planned in the previous meeting. It can be viewed as an attempt to adhere to the principle of "starting where the client is at." For example:

> *Worker:* You will recall that last week we agreed to spend this session talking about your reluctance to visit your children in foster care. Do you think that is how we should spend our time today, or has some more pressing concern come up?

During the helping process, the social worker encourages the client to expand and elaborate on his or her concerns. Two specific skills are used: (1) moving from the general to the specific and (2) reaching inside the silences.

Moving from the general to the specific refers to helping the client express his or her concerns in a more precise and focused manner. For example:

> *Client:* Things are really a mess at home.
> *Worker:* I'm not sure what you mean by "a mess." What exactly happened?
> *Client:* We were eating when Dad came home from work. He was drunk and ended up hitting Mom.
> *Worker:* What did you do when all this was happening?

The skill of **reaching inside the silences** refers to efforts by the worker to explore the meaning of the client's silence. Silence can be a critical moment in client-worker communication. Silence is a behavior. It has meaning, and sometimes it is important to discover that meaning. For example:

> *Client:* (thoughtful silence)
> *Worker:* You appear to be puzzling over something. Can you tell me what you are thinking about?
>
> *or*
>
> *Client:* (thoughtful silence)
> *Worker:* Our discussion about your mother's illness seems to be pretty hard on you. Did I ask you to talk about something that is just too painful to discuss?

A brief silence is best responded to with silence. If the silence is a long one, the worker should attempt to "reach inside." An error commonly made by beginning workers is to respond to silence with a change of topics. This happens because the worker becomes nervous when the client is silent. Don't be afraid of silence.

Throughout the helping process, the social worker must look for ways of demonstrating empathy for the client. Three techniques or skills are commonly used to demonstrate empathy: (1) understanding the client's feelings, (2) putting the client's feelings into words, and (3) connecting feelings to work.

Understanding the client's feelings refers to verbal and nonverbal communication aimed at demonstrating that the social worker comprehends and can identify with the client's thoughts and feelings. Shulman (1979) explains that this skill "involves indicating through words, gestures, expression, physical posture or touch the worker's comprehension of the expressed affect" (p. 55). For example:

Client: Having to place Mary in foster care is one of the most difficult decisions I have ever made.

Worker: It must be hard to make a decision that is going to be very upsetting to Mary. It seems like this is tearing you apart inside.

The skill of *putting the client's feelings into words* refers to the worker's articulation of what the client is feeling but has stopped just short of expressing in words. For example:

Worker: How did the visit with your mother go?

Client: OK I guess, but I don't know if I can take this much longer.

Worker: Watching your mother die is putting you under a lot of stress. It sounds like you hope death will come soon, but I expect that such a thought makes you feel guilty.

Using this skill gives the client a gentle and supportive invitation to express what he or she is feeling at the moment. Here is another example:

Worker: Do you have any other questions about adoption, especially about the fact that there are very few infants available for adoption but quite a few older children who need adoptive homes?

Client: No, I don't think so. You explained it pretty well. I guess it's just a lot different than I expected.

Worker: I have the impression you were disappointed with what I had to say. You looked quite sad and hurt. Can you tell me how you are feeling?

Encouraging a client to express feelings is appropriate and useful only when those feelings are directly related to the overall goals of professional intervention.

The skill of *connecting feelings to work* refers to communication that helps the client make a connection between feelings, behavior, and the agreed-upon objectives of intervention. For example:

Client: I know I said I wanted to visit my kids more often, but I have just been too busy at work to get away for a visit.

Worker: I know you are a hard worker and that your job demands much of your time, but I suspect the anger and guilt you feel about your divorce is also causing you to avoid visiting your kids. Perhaps you need to come to terms with those feelings.

An effective worker must be genuine; he or she must be a real and caring person. If the worker appears artificial, the client will either withdraw from the relationship or engage in testing to break through the worker's facade. Three skills are often used by the worker to display the quality of genuineness: (1) displaying feelings openly, (2) sharing personal thoughts and feelings, and (3) supporting the client's strengths.

Displaying feelings openly refers to honest expressions of feelings by the worker. These feelings can be either positive or negative, as shown in these two examples:

> *Worker:* I feel anger inside when I think about all the time we spent looking for your job and now, after just one week, you are talking about quitting.
>
> *or*
>
> *Worker:* I really feel good about what you have done. I guess I feel proud that I had something to do with you getting that job.

It is important to note that when we speak about the worker's expression of feelings, we are referring to the sharing of feeling only in relation to the client's problem or to the client-worker interaction. It is usually inappropriate for the worker to express feelings about his or her own personal problems.

The skill of displaying feelings openly focuses on feelings toward the client's problem or situation. The skill called *sharing personal thoughts and feelings* relates to the worker's own behavior. For example:

> *Worker:* I am sorry about how I reacted on the phone. I guess you noticed that I have some trouble when we talk about your mother's death. There is something about that that touches me deeply.

The worker also displays genuineness and concern when he or she makes statements of honest belief in the client's ability to deal with his or her problem. The skill of *supporting the client's strengths* refers to the expression of confidence in the client's ability to accomplish some task or cope with a difficult situation. Here are two examples:

> *Worker:* I know it is going to be difficult for you to visit the kids in their foster home, but it is important to them, and I think you can handle it.
>
> *or*
>
> *Worker:* You faced this problem in the past, and somehow you weathered the storm. It's going to be painful, and I know you wish you could just run away from the whole thing, but I really believe you can deal with it without going to pieces.

Effective helping involves much more than understanding the client's problem or situation. The client needs to be helped to make decisions and take action. Realistic, gentle, and supportive demands for action are necessary. Even a client who is highly motivated to make change feels an inner resistance to changing a familiar pattern. Change usually involves having to reexamine one's assumptions and reevaluate past behavior. This can be painful. Change also involves trying out new behaviors and completing unfamiliar tasks. This involves risk taking. It is important to recognize that a degree of fear, ambivalence, and resistance is a normal reaction to change. In fact, a lack of ambivalence and resistance may indicate that what looks to be a client's effort to change is only an illusion. Shulman (1981)* explains that

> the worker must make a consistent demand for work. The demand may be expressed in many ways, but it is generally experienced by the client as the worker saying: "I mean business." It is a critical skill because it conveys to the client the worker's belief in the client's strength and the worker's willingness to deal with even the toughest problems and feelings faced by the client. It is precisely this additional pull that clients need at that moment to mobilize their strength and to take their next steps. . . .
>
> The demand for work needs to be linked closely to the empathic skills mentioned earlier. A worker who is demanding, but not empathic, will be seen by the client as rejecting. On the other hand, the worker who is empathic but makes no demand, will appear to the client as easy to put off. It is critical synthesis of these two behaviors that will lead to effective work. (p. 20)

Four skills are used by the worker to make a *demand for work:* (1) partializing the client's concerns, (2) holding to focus, (3) checking for artificial consensus, and (4) pointing out the illusion of work.

The skill of **partializing the client's concerns** refers to breaking down a seemingly insolvable problem into smaller, more manageable components. Clients often feel overwhelmed, immobilized, or helpless when faced with large, complex problems. When a problem is broken down into several smaller concerns, it seems less frightening, and the client is better able to focus on a solution. For example:

> *Client:* I cannot believe what is happening. First, Jimmy cut his head and I took him to the hospital. That crazy doctor notified child protective services and accused me of abusing Jimmy. Then my oldest son got into a shouting match with the landlord, and the landlord has asked me to find another apartment. I cannot afford a lawyer, my child support check is late, and on top of everything else, our car won't start. Things are so screwed up I cannot even think straight. All of a sudden the whole world has caved in on me.
>
> *Worker:* You do indeed have some problems. But I think we better talk about them one at a time. Otherwise, we will get confused and feel even more frustrated. Let's first focus on the child abuse report. We will return to the other problems later. First, tell me more about Jimmy's injury and the abuse report. For now, let's only talk about that problem, OK?

The skill termed **holding to focus** is an attempt to keep the client's thoughts focused on a specific concern or task. This is especially important if the client tends to ramble or wants to avoid work on a relevant concern. Holding to focus is illustrated in this example:

* Excerpts from Shulman (1981) are reprinted with the permission of the Council on Social Work Education.

Worker: Because you were saying last week that your boss threatened to fire you, I think we better focus on that problem.

Client: Yeah. I guess so. I really wish I could get a transfer. But the company has such old-fashioned views on things like that. I'm surprised they make any money at all. With the economy the way it is, you would think they would change the whole operation. They are just not prepared for competition from Japanese industry. I recently read an article on Japanese management and . . .

Worker: I think we better come back to the conflict between you and your supervisor. You have lost a couple of other jobs because of conflict. I know you need this job, so I think we better figure out a way of dealing with the problem between you and your supervisor.

The skill of **checking for artificial consensus** refers to flushing out a client's feelings of ambivalence. Often clients agree to take an action without being fully aware of the resistance they will feel later. For example:

Worker: I certainly agree that you should talk to your math teacher about your failing grade. That needs to be done. But I also know you have always felt intimidated by that teacher. Don't you think this is going to be a very rough thing for you to do?

The skill of **pointing out the illusion of work** is a type of confrontation aimed at showing the client that his or her verbalizations and actions regarding the present problem are, in reality, a form of resistance that results in avoiding significant work on the problem. Real work on a personal problem is painful; it is a struggle. Thus, the helping process and the content of the client-worker communications are almost always emotionally charged. If, over a period of several sessions, there is little or no affectively charged discussion and no significant change in the client's behavior or situation, it is likely that the client's participation is only an illusion of work.

The next example illustrates pointing out the illusion of work during a marriage counseling session:

Worker: There is something that concerns me. When you two first came to the agency a few weeks ago, you requested help with your marriage. We have met three times. However, both of you have spent most of our time together talking about your jobs, your kids, and your wish for a new house. I know there have been times when you have been close to divorce. Yet you seem to be avoiding a discussion about your marriage relationship. I know that's difficult, and I can understand your wish to avoid talking about it, but that is why we are meeting. It may be painful, but unless we focus on the marriage, we are not going to get anywhere. If you are really concerned about your marriage, then let's talk about your marriage.

Obstacles of an interpersonal nature almost always emerge in an intense helping relationship. For example, the client may want to avoid discussing important but highly charged topics such as feelings of dependency, sexual behavior, or management of money. Many clients have had prior difficulties with authority figures and view the worker as an authority. The client's feelings toward the worker—whether positive or negative—may block communication. The dynamics of *transference* and *countertransference* may also significantly affect the relationship. These obstacles need to be recognized and addressed head on. They must be discussed openly, so they will no longer impede the helping process. Shulman describes three skills for dealing with obstacles: (1) supporting the client in taboo areas, (2) identifying affective obstacles to work, and (3) dealing with the authority theme.

Supporting the clients in taboo areas refers to worker communication designed to assist the client in discussing sensitive topics. For example:

Client: I always feel nervous when I get to the topic of sex. It's hard for me to talk about it because of the way I was raised.

Worker: You are not alone. Many of us were raised the same way. But I want you to try. You and your husband need to learn to express your thoughts about your sexual relationship. That area in your marriage is causing you some real problems. It's difficult to discuss, but let's keep at it.

Many times, a client's feelings will block discussion of an important issue, and he or she may not even be aware of what is happening. The skill of ***identifying affective obstacles to work*** refers to messages aimed at elevating the client's awareness of the blockage. For example:

Worker: I have noticed something, and I think we need to talk about it. We started meeting together because you wanted some help in learning how to handle your children. Yet each time I ask about Jimmy, you get tense and start talking about the older children. What is it about your relationship with Jimmy that makes you so uncomfortable?

There are times when the client has a negative reaction to the worker. Problems in the working relationship should be discussed openly and honestly by one another. Clients are often reluctant to voice criticism of the worker. All too often, they simply withdraw from the helping process rather than confront the worker. The skill of ***dealing with the authority theme*** refers to worker communications that invite and assist the client to express complaints about the worker or the helping process. Consider this illustration:

Client: I think things are a lot better now at home. I don't think we need to set up another meeting.

Worker: I hope things are better, but I think something else is going on here. Last week, I offered you some advice. I have been thinking about that. I think I was wrong in telling you what to do. In fact, I think I made you angry, even though you didn't show it. How about it? Can we talk about your feelings toward my advice?

An important but complex social work activity is providing clients with the information they need to consider as they make decisions and plans. Shulman (1981, 23) terms this skill *providing data.* As used in this context, data refer to the facts, beliefs, and values that the worker has acquired as a result of professional training and life experience. Many clients look to their social worker as a knowledgeable person and expect to hear what the worker has to say. They often expect workers to give advice and guidance; if the worker withholds opinions, the client may conclude that the worker does not really care. This situation places workers in an awkward position because they know the pitfalls of giving advice and want to avoid imposing their values on the client. In discussing this dilemma, Shulman (1981) explains that

> the worker's concern about providing data is a real one. It would not be helpful for the client simply to substitute the worker's sense of reality for his or her own. Therefore Schwartz placed a number of qualifications on the sharing of data. First, the worker needs to share ideas in such a way that they are open to challenge. If the ideas do not ring true to the client they should not be accepted. If the client tends to accept the worker's perceptions uncritically, real learning may not take place. The worker needs to point this out to the client and develop the client's ability to challenge the worker's perceptions and to use only what makes sense. Rather than using "expertise" to convince a client, a worker needs to help the client see the data as a contribution to the client's work, rather than as an answer to the client's problems.
>
> A second qualification is that the data provided must be related to the client's current theme of concern. Workers must resist the temptation to teach the client something the client may need in the future, or that the worker feels is important. Unless data are relevant to a current piece of work, they will represent the worker's effort to "change" the client and will be perceived as unhelpful. (pp. 23–24)

The next example illustrates worker communications aimed at providing data:

> *Worker:* You are really having a difficult time deciding if you should get married or not. I think I have learned one thing about making big decisions in my own life. If the decision is a big one with long-term consequences and if I have some real doubts about it, I know I should delay making a decision until I am more sure about what to do. What is your reaction to the idea of waiting a couple of months before you decide?

(Additional information on giving advice and direction can be found in Chapter 12.)

It is said that "no man is an island." Each of us affects and is affected by other individuals, our family, groups, and organizations. This point of view is at the heart of the systems and ecological perspectives in social work. Work with clients often centers on helping them deal more effectively with other family members, people at work, school, social agencies, and other social systems. These relationships are complex, and both the client and the system may erect blocks to effective interaction, such as fear, prejudice, and distorted perceptions. The worker must be prepared to help the client examine these relationships, clarify perceptions, uncover alternative interpretations of reality, and learn how to gain access to and negotiate those systems needed for fulfillment and problem solving.

The skill of *viewing system people in new ways* refers to communication designed to modify how the client perceives the actions of another. This skill is similar to the technique of *reframing* described in Chapter 12. For example:

Client: I wish Dad would get off my back. I am tired of hearing that I should get a job.

Worker: I know that bothers you. I also know your Dad has a hard time showing affection, and I know he wants you to end up with a better job than he has. Maybe what seems like a hassle is really your Dad's way of caring for you and trying to help you prepare for the future. Maybe it is his way of expressing love.

The skill of *contacting system people directly* refers to efforts by the worker to establish communication between the client and those people with whom he or she needs to communicate. For example:

Worker: This is the third time you have told me that you haven't been able to tell your doctor about your concerns. Suppose I give her a call and explain that I know you have something to talk to her about. I think that might cause her to spend more time with you when she visits you in the hospital tomorrow.

The Ending and Transition Phase

The client-social worker relationship may end either because their work together is finished or because the social worker must transfer the client to another worker. The *ending phase* can be difficult because it involves separation and loss. Because many clients have experienced so many losses during their lives, the ending phase can be particularly painful because it reactivates the feelings attached to prior losses. These feelings must be addressed directly by the worker. Shulman (1981) explains that

> because of the general reluctance to face endings, both on the part of the worker and the client, endings often are handled too quickly, without an opportunity for the client and worker to deal with the complex feelings involved. . . . Since the client needs time to deal with the ending, encompass it, and not experience it as a sharp rejection by the worker, it is important for the worker to point out the ending well in advance in order to allow the process to become established. . . . It is only when workers can come to grips with their own feelings that they can begin to help the client in this important phase. (pp. 26–27)

Four of the twenty-seven skills identified by Shulman are used during the ending or transition phase of the helping process. The skill of *pointing out endings* is designed to remind the client of the ending so the best possible use can be made of the remaining time. For example:

Worker: Before we get started today, I want to remind you that when we began meeting a month ago, we agreed to meet for a total of eight times. We have three sessions left. If we are to stick to our agreement, we need to make sure that those three sessions focus on your high-priority concerns.

The worker can help the client deal with the emotional aspects of separation by voicing his or her feelings about termination. This skill is termed *sharing ending feelings.* For example:

> *Worker:* I have been thinking about our relationship. Since you came to this hospital last September, we have been through a lot together. I am glad you are going home, but I want you to know that I will miss you.

The review of what the client and worker have done together to address the client's concerns is an important element in termination. Worker communication designed to prompt such a review is called *asking for a review of learning.* Here is an example:

> *Worker:* Altogether, we have been meeting for about four months. A lot has happened since you were reported for child abuse. You have made some real positive changes in how you deal with your son, Michael. What has been helpful to you? What have you learned from this whole experience?

It is important to help the client express his or her feelings about termination. These feelings may be positive or negative or a mix of both. The skill of *reaching for ending feelings* refers to worker communication that helps the client articulate his or her feelings. For example:

> *Worker:* I know you are pleased about getting off probation. You are no longer required to see me. But I also sense that you have mixed feelings about our weekly meetings coming to an end. I wonder if it will be difficult for you to say good-bye. How about that?

This section has provided an overview of the basic helping skills identified by Shulman. The reader is reminded that other researchers attach different terms to many of these skills. Regardless of label, the skills described by Shulman can be properly viewed as basic and essential in the helping process.

Selected Bibliography

Schwartz, William. "On the Use of Groups in Social Work Practice." In *The Practice of Group Work,* edited by William Schwartz and Serapio Zalba. New York: Columbia University Press, 1971.

———. "The Social Worker in the Group." In *New Perspectives on Services to Groups: Theory, Organization, Practice.* New York: NASW, 1961.

Shulman, Lawrence. *Identifying, Measuring and Teaching Helping Skills.* New York: Council on Social Work Education, 1981.

———. *The Skills of Helping: Individuals and Groups.* Itasca, Ill.: F. E. Peacock, 1979. (2nd ed., 1984)

———. *Social Work with Groups: The Mediating Model.* New York: Council on Social Work Education, 1968.

———. *A Study of the Helping Process.* Vancouver: University of British Columbia, Social Work Department, 1977.

6.3　Nonverbal Communication

Purpose:　To understand and use nonverbal messages.

Discussion:　About 90 percent of human communication is nonverbal. Some researchers suggest that about 50 percent of every message we send to another person is sent by facial expression alone, especially through the eyes, and about 30 percent is expressed by voice tone, pitch, and resonance. It is by paying careful attention to the client's nonverbal communication that the social worker can determine how he or she is being perceived by the client. Observing nonverbal behavior also tells the worker if what the client is saying in words reflects inner thoughts and feelings.

Eye contact is a powerful means of communication. Eyes reveal much about our emotional state and have been called the "windows of our heart." Eye contact usually indicates a willingness to engage in communication and is an indicator of sensitivity and understanding. A lack of eye contact is often interpreted as a lack of interest or lack of sincerity. It is important to maintain eye contact with your client; however, glaring and staring are taken as rudeness and anger. Also remember that intense eye contact is not an acceptable behavior within some ethnic groups.

Tone of voice reveals feelings. A loud, forceful tone suggests aggressiveness, control, and strength. A meek, scarcely audible tone suggests withdrawal, fear, and weakness. A monotonous or flat voice suggests a lack of interest.

Facial expressions—such as smiles, frowning, nodding the head, shaking the head, lip quivering, and blushing—send messages to the observer. Quite often, facial expressions reveal that the person is saying one thing but thinking or feeling another. And it is often facial expressions that reveal a worker's disapproval of a client, even when the worker is trying hard to be nonjudgmental.

Arm and hand movements frequently communicate strong but unexpressed emotions. Crossed legs, arms folded across the chest, and body rigidity usually suggest defensiveness, while arms and hands at the body's side or in an outreached position suggest openness to others. Clenched fists indicate anger or anxiety. Fidgety movements, toe and finger tapping, leg bouncing, and similar movements suggest impatience, nervousness, or preoccupation.

Body positioning conveys various attitudes and intentions. It is best to face the client at a ninety degree angle, since this suggests both safety and openness. Facing the client directly may communicate aggressiveness. A desk separating the client and worker inhibits closeness and openness and also suggests the worker is in a superior position. Leaning slightly toward the client communicates interest and acceptance. Physical closeness invites trust and involvement, but being too close is threatening. Each client has his or her own sense of personal space. The worker can avoid invading this space by reading the client's body movements and adjusting his or her chair to accommodate the client's preferences.

Dress and appearance are important forms of nonverbal communication. The worker must give special attention to his or her own clothing and hairstyle. Dress that would be appropriate in an agency serving young people may be inappropriate in a hospital or court setting. Likewise, dress that is acceptable to adolescent clients may be offensive to elderly clients. Some agencies have established dress codes. The new worker should consult his or her supervisor for guidance on selecting appropriate dress.

Selected Bibliography

Cormier, William, and L. Sherilyn Cormier. *Interviewing Strategies for Helpers.* 2nd ed. Monterey, Calif.: Brooks/Cole, 1985.

Kadushin, Alfred. *The Social Work Interview.* 2nd ed. New York: Columbia University Press, 1983.

Knapp, Mark. *Essentials of Nonverbal Communication.* New York: Holt, Rinehart & Winston, 1980.

6.4   *Active Listening*

Purpose: To encourage client communication by using the techniques of clarification, paraphrase, reflection, and summarization.

Discussion: Listening does not come naturally to most people; it is a skill that must be developed. The social worker must be an active listener. In active listening, the worker attends to the client's verbal as well as nonverbal messages and reflects what has been heard back to the client so that the client knows his or her message has been accurately understood. When engaged in active listening, the social worker

- Pays attention to the client's underlying feelings—rather than just the literal meaning of the client's words.
- Uses a clear, calm, and interested tone of voice.
- Uses body language that communicates attentiveness (e.g., eye contact, leaning forward slightly) and uses gestures that demonstrate openness and concern.
- Asks questions that expand and clarify what is being said by the client.
- Speaks in order to better understand the client, not just to make a point.
- Reflects perceptions of what the client is saying back to the client. By doing this, the worker gives the client concrete evidence that the message has been received correctly or provides the client with an opportunity to correct the message if it was misunderstood.

The technique of *clarification* refers to asking a question designed to encourage a client to become more explicit and/or to verify the worker's understanding of what the client has said. Clarification questions usually begin with "Are you saying that . . . " or "Do you mean that . . . " and end with a rephrasing of the client's words. For example:

Client: Things are really a disaster. I thought I could get things squared away, but it doesn't look like that will be possible.

Worker: Are you saying that things are changing more slowly than you expected or that your situation is now worse than before?

The skilled social worker listens to both the literal meaning of a message and the affective component. The components are, of course, interrelated because the affect is often a response to the content. The *paraphrase* is a rephrasing of the content of the client's statement; the technique of *reflection* of feeling is a rephrasing of the affective component of the message. The use of paraphrase and reflection frequently overlap; in fact, some authors do not distinguish between the two. Also, it is important to note that reflection is very similar to the emphatic techniques of responding to feeling and putting a client's feelings into words. (See Technique 6.2.) Examples of paraphrase and reflection responses are as follows:

Client: That guy down at the employment office is a real sleazeball. How does he get away with treating people like that? I feel three inches tall when I go down there.

Worker: (paraphrase) The man at the employment office upsets you, treats you badly, and makes you feel put down.

or

Worker: (reflection of feeling) You feel embarrassed and humiliated at the employment office. Is that right?

Summarization refers to an extension of paraphrase and reflection to one or more themes that run through the client's statements. It is a pulling together of the content and affective components of several messages. For example, a worker might use summarization to draw together the key affective and content elements of what was discussed during the previous ten minutes. Here is an example of a summarization by a worker:

Worker: From what you are saying, I am hearing a number of things. You are desperate for a job and feel a mix of anger and depression because you haven't found one yet. You have been going to the employment office but that adds to your feelings of frustration. On top of that, you are feeling deep regret for having dropped out of high school.

Selected Bibliography

Carkhuff, Robert. *The Art of Helping.* 6th ed. Amherst, Mass.: Human Resource Development Press, Inc., 1987.

Cormier, William, and L. Sherilyn Cormier. *Interviewing Strategies for Helpers.* 2nd ed. Monterey, Calif.: Brooks/Cole, 1985.

Dillard, John, and Robert Reilly, eds. *Systematic Interviewing.* Columbus, Ohio: Merrill, 1988.

6.5   Questioning

Purpose: To obtain needed information and assist the client in expressing thoughts and feelings about his or her problem or situation.

Discussion: To learn about a client and his or her situation, the social worker must ask questions. Students and inexperienced workers often have difficulty in their use of questioning techniques. In particular, they tend to use too many closed-ended questions and "why" questions, they stack questions, and they ask leading questions.

A question such as "What are the names of your children?" is termed a **closed-ended question;** it limits how the client can respond. By contrast, an **open-ended question,** such as "Tell me about your children," gives the client an opportunity to say whatever he or she thinks is important. Open-ended questioning allows the client to move the conversation to topics of his or her choosing. Thus, responses to open-ended questions are likely to reveal the client's real concerns and feelings.

During counseling sessions, the worker will use mostly open-ended questions. However, open-ended questions vary in the amount of direction they provide. The three questions that follow are open-ended, but some are more open than others.

"Tell me about your job."

"What do you like and what do you dislike about your job?"

"I don't understand the nature of your job. What are some examples of the tasks and responsibilities that are part of your job?"

Closed-ended questioning is appropriate when the worker needs specific data about the client and his or her situation or when the client is so confused or overwhelmed that structure is needed to maintain a focus.

The phrase *stacking questions* refers to asking several questions at once. Consider this example:

> *Worker:* So, you are interested in adoption. How long have you been thinking about adoption? Have you known others who have adopted? Are you thinking about an infant? Have you thought much about an older child or one that has a handicap?

Stacked questions are confusing to clients. It is best to ask questions one at a time.

Leading questions are those that directly or indirectly push or pull the client toward a certain response; for example, "Didn't you think that was wrong?" or

"I'm sure you explained why you missed work?" A leading question may prompt the client to lie rather than suffer embarrassment or disappoint the worker. Leading questions often reveal judgmentalness and they can be insulting to clients.

Another common error is to ask too many *"why" questions;* for example, "Why do you get so angry when Johnny spills food at the table?" Essentially, "why" questions ask the client to justify his or her behavior and this tends to produce defensiveness. Moreover, many people simply do not know the "whys" of their behavior so, when asked, they simply speculate or give a socially acceptable answer. Instead of using "why" questions, use questions that focus on the what, where, and when of behavior.

Selected Bibliography

Dillard, John, and Robert Reilly. *Systematic Interviewing: Communication Skills for Professional Effectiveness.* Columbus, Ohio: Merrill, 1988.
Ivey, Allen. *Intentional Interviewing and Counseling.* Monterey, Calif.: Brooks/Cole, 1983.
Kadushin, Alfred. *The Social Work Interview.* 2nd ed. New York: Columbia University Press, 1983.

6.6 *The "I-Message"*

Purpose: To send a clear and direct message.

Discussion: The term *"I-message"* refers to a type of message composition designed to increase the effectiveness of communication. This particular structure makes it possible to send a clear, direct message and reduce the chance that the person receiving the message will be put on the defensive. The "I-message" is especially useful in situations of interpersonal confrontation and conflict because it allows the sender to express disappointment, anger, or frustration while minimizing the chance that the discussion will turn into a fruitless argument.

All too often, the messages we send to others are what might be called "You-messages"; for example, "You should clean up your room," "You need to have more confidence in yourself," or "You are driving me crazy." Such messages, even when well intended, cause the person on the receiving end to feel put down or guilty. The purpose of a "You-message" may be to bring about a needed change in the behavior of another, but it usually ends up creating added resistance to change. Other forms of the "You-message" are orders and commands (e.g., "Stop doing that!"), blaming or name-calling statements (e.g., "You are acting like a baby"), and statements that give solutions (e.g., "You better forget that idea and take my advice"). Perhaps the most irritating form of the "You-message" is the "if-then threat" (e.g., "If you don't . . . , then I will. . . .").

In contrast to the "You-message," which usually blocks real communication, the "I-message" allows the person bothered by the behavior of another to describe in a noncritical or nonaccusatory manner, the impact the behavior is having, while leaving the responsibility for modifying the behavior with the person exhibiting the troublesome behavior. In effect, the "I-message" allows the sender to say, "This is my concern, this is how it bothers me, this is how I feel." The "I-message" does not accuse or blame; instead, it says implicitly, "I trust you to decide what change in your behavior is necessary." An "I-message" consists of three parts:

1. A brief, clear description of a *specific behavior*
2. The *resulting feeling* experienced because of that specific behavior
3. A description of the *tangible impact* the behavior has had

For example, a social worker using an "I-message" might say to a client:

> *Worker:* When you did not show up for our scheduled appointment (specific behavior), I felt upset and put down (feeling) because I don't like having to wait around and because it disrupts my work schedule (tangible impact).

The "I-message" is a basic communication technique that has wide applicability. The typical social worker will use it many times each day with clients and other professionals. Also, it can be taught to clients as a method of helping them deal with common interpersonal problems, such as those that occur between parent and child, husband and wife, and so on.

Selected Bibliography

Gordon, Thomas. *Parent Effectiveness Training.* New York: Peter Wyden, 1973.
Stayhorn, Joseph. *Talking It Out.* Champaign, Ill: Research Press, 1977.
Zastrow, Charles. *The Practice of Social Work.* 2nd ed. Homewood, Ill.: Dorsey Press, 1985.

6.7   *Responding to Defensive Communication*

Purpose: To reduce the client's defensiveness.

Discussion: The social worker needs to be skilled in reducing a client's need to be defensive and guarded. Schlosberg and Kagan (1988, 7) identify a number of common defensive maneuvers used by clients: "We do not have a problem" (denial); "It's all John's fault" (blaming); "She can't help it, she's retarded" (labeling); "If I get one more pressure, I'll go crazy" (being fragile); "My husband couldn't come today!" (avoidance); "Johnny was in another fight and I must talk about it!" (using crisis or distraction); and "What's the use, nothing will ever change" (helplessness). In addition, some clients use their physical environment (e.g., drawn shades, mean dogs, terrible smells) and even their style of dress as a means of intimidation and keeping people at a distance. Still others use cursing, aggression, and threats.

Often the client is defensive before he or she even meets the social worker, but sometimes the worker's behavior or personal style can add to the problem. Worker behaviors that increase client defensiveness include appearing rushed, being brusque or insensitive to a client's feelings, making judgmental statements, using jargon or quoting agency rules and policy without explanation, failing to identify yourself and your role clearly, calling an adult by his or her first name without permission, being authoritarian, and creating long waits and delays. By following several guidelines, the social worker can reduce a client's defensiveness.

1. Remember that defensiveness in interpersonal relationships is an attempt to protect oneself from real or imagined danger. Within a context of social service delivery, the dangers or threats perceived by clients are those of embarrassment, humiliation, loss of control over one's life, loss of privacy, or failure to receive an expected social provision. Thus, do not respond to the defensive behavior as such but rather focus on what might be your client's underlying fear. Determine what is causing your client to feel threatened and try to remove that cause. Acknowledge those aspects of the situation that may cause your client to feel awkward, threatened, or humiliated (e.g., "I know it can be embarrassing to have to ask for financial assistance"). Use a generous amount of active listening (see Technique 6.4) and make it as easy as possible for your client to verbalize those feelings, but do not pressure him or her to do so.

2. Expand your tolerance of annoying defensive behavior by understanding that the behavior may have served a functional purpose in the past. If the client's defensiveness is a long-term pattern rather than situational behavior, hypothesize how it may have protected the client from pain associated with some fundamental disruption (e.g., rejection by a parent, breakup of one's family, or separation from loved ones) or a frightening event (e.g., major personal problem, a disability, or a life-threatening illness). Patterns of defensiveness often develop in response to such fear and pain. Your gut reactions to the client will often provide clues as to the function served by the defensiveness. For example, if you feel a strong desire to walk away from the client, the client's defensiveness may serve as protection against interference by outsiders. If the client's sad and helpless behavior makes you feel sorry and want to protect the client, this defensive pattern may help the client avoid a frightening responsibility (See Chapter 10 for discussion of ego defense mechanisms.)

3. If your client exhibits a positive or nondefensive behavior, respond with reinforcement and use the technique of **mirroring.** This technique is similar to *pacing,* which Cormier and Cormier (1985) describe as "simply moving as the client moves or matching the client's non-verbal behavior without mimicking the client or doing it so deliberately that the client becomes aware of it" (p. 23). In other words, follow a nondefensive conversational exchange with a vocal tone and cadence, posture, and nonverbal behavior that mirrors or imitates the client's verbal and nonverbal behavior. On the other hand, if your client assumes a defensive posture or tone of voice, respond with exactly the opposite (e.g., an open, nondefensive posture and a soft comforting tone of voice). If your client's

---

conversation speeds up as a result of anxiety or anger, respond with a slow and nurturing manner; this usually has a calming effect on the client.

4. To the extent possible, use words and phrases that match your client's dominant mode of receiving information. The three basic modes are visual, auditory, and touch. A client reveals his or her dominant mode in the frequent use of certain predicates in phrases such as "I see what you mean" (visual), "I hear what you are saying" (auditory), or "That idea is beyond my reach" (touch). If you can identify your client's dominant mode, try to mirror or match your phrases to your client's mode; for example, "Do you have a clear picture of what I am suggesting?" (visual), "Does this plan sound ok to you?" (auditory), or "I don't think this plan is going to hurt you—do you feel the same way?" (touch).

5. Whenever possible, give your client opportunities to make choices and remain in control of what is happening in his or her life. Use words like *we, us, together,* and *it will be your decision;* these imply cooperation, respect, and choice.

6. Consider using the technique of ***joining the resistance*** by aligning yourself with the client's feelings; for example, "After such a long wait, you deserve to be angry. I would be angry also." Such an alignment with the client's emotions and hurt feelings reduces resistance by removing the client's need to keep defenses up and it gives the client permission to vent pent-up feelings.

7. Do not label or categorize your client (e.g., "All Medicaid recipients have to fill out this form"). People quickly become defensive when they experience a loss of individuality. Also, do not embarrass or back your client into a corner, either physically or figuratively. Arrange your office and your own seating position so your client does not feel trapped. Allow your client to save face in embarrassing situations.

8. A defensive or resistant individual may attempt a number of maneuvers to block a worker's engagement efforts. In situations where it is critically important to engage the resistant client (e.g., in cases of child abuse), you will need to be assertive and deal directly with the issue. For example, if your client is silent, you might say something like, "I can see you do not want to talk to me about how your child was injured, but I am going to stay here until we have discussed it." If your client appears overly agreeable to what you have said, you could say, "I certainly hope you will take the actions you have promised, but how will I know that you have followed through on those plans?" Some defensive clients attempt to divert attention away from the real issue. When that happens, you might say, "I can sense you do not want to focus on the child abuse report, but that is why I am here and we have to get back to that topic." If your client attempts to avoid the central issue by talking about secondary concerns, you may need to take control by saying something like, "You have mentioned at least five other problems and I can understand that they are of concern to you, but we have to come back to the question of how Jimmy got those bruises—that must be the primary focus of this interview." Sometimes clients attempt to defend themselves by trying to make the worker feel guilty. When that happens, you may need to say, "I know you are upset and I don't like to see people cry, but your child has been seriously injured and it is my job to find out what happened. Take a few minutes to compose yourself and then we must get to the bottom of this. If you cannot talk to me I will ask someone from the prosecutor's office to speak with you." If your client verbally or physically threatens you, you will need to say something like, "I have no intention of harming you. I will not argue with you and I cannot continue the interview under these conditions. If you are too angry to talk now, I will come back this afternoon with a police officer. Do you prefer to talk now or later?" (See Chapter 9 for discussions of "Dangerous Client" and "Involuntary Client.")

9. If your client uses obscene or abusive language, remain calm and do not respond in ways that might reinforce the behavior (e.g., shock, attention, etc.). Respond immediately with verbal and nonverbal attention and reinforcement to any part of the client's communication that is appropriate and constructive.

10. If the client persists in verbal attacks, consider using the technique termed *"fogging."* This name comes from the notion that rocks thrown into a fog bank have no effect. If the person under verbal attack can mentally and emotionally behave like the fog, the verbal "rocks" have no impact and, hopefully, the attacker will soon abandon his or her efforts to cause discomfort. This technique works because the person under attack offers no resistance and avoids responding with either anger or defensiveness and because it calmly acknowledges that the angry person may have a point and is possibly accurate in his or her criticism and judgments. For example:

Angry Client:	"All you ever do is talk!"
Worker:	"You're right. I do talk a lot."
Angry Client:	"If you would pay attention to what I have been saying you wouldn't have to ask these dumb questions!"
Worker:	"That may be true. I could be more attentive to what you say."
Angry Client:	"You are just like all the other lazy government employees and state social workers! You are always telling people what to do and butting into things that are none of your damn business."
Worker:	"I am a state employee. It does make sense that all state employees would do their job in similar ways."

Selected Bibliography

Cormier, William and Sherilyn Cormier. *Interviewing Strategies for Helpers.* 2nd ed. Monterey, Calif.: Brooks/Cole, 1985.

Rooney, Ronald. "Socialization Strategies for Involuntary Clients." *Social Casework* 69, No. 3 (March 1988): 131–40.

Schlosberg, Shirley, and Richard Kagan. "Practice Strategies for Engaging Chronic Multiproblem Families." *Social Casework* 69, No. 1 (January 1988): 3–9.

Workload and Caseload Management

7

Introduction

The new social worker learns quickly that there is not enough time to do all that needs to be done. Faced with that reality, the worker must make the best possible use of limited time and focus on matters of highest priority. Time and workload management skills are essential. Paperwork and recordkeeping consume much of a social worker's time. Most workers dislike these tasks, but recordkeeping is an essential component of service provision. As Kagle (1984) notes, the "social work record is, above all, a record of service; therefore, the essential function of the record is to document the bases, substance, and consequences of professional decisions and actions" (p. 14).

Given the fact that paperwork is necessary and unavoidable, we include in this chapter items related to report and letter writing and recordkeeping. Also included are guidelines and techniques that can help workers increase their efficiency on the job: time management, using a telephone and dictating machine, planning effective meetings, and refusing and accepting added workload. The chapter ends with a section on testifying in court. With increasing frequency, social workers in all fields are called to be witnesses in court proceedings; workers in child and adult protective services make frequent court appearances. The new worker, and even the practicum student, need to prepare for this inevitable experience.

Selected Bibliography

Kagle, Jill. *Social Work Records.* Homewood, Ill.: Dorsey Press, 1984.
Lauffer, Armand. *Working in Social Work.* Newbury Park, Calif.: Sage, 1987.

7.1 *Managing Time at Work*

Purpose: To make the best possible use of limited time.

Discussion: Nearly every social worker is faced with the problem of having too much work and too little time. Thus, the worker must use basic time management skills as a way of increasing efficiency on the job. Consider these guidelines:

1. Come to terms with your "inner rebellion" toward the use of time management principles. Do not hide behind the claim that you are too busy to get organized, and do not mistake motion for work. Some people appear extremely busy because they are always in motion. But activity does not always mean that something is being accomplished. Clear goals and an understanding of the tasks to be achieved must precede the activity.

2. Understand your job description. If your assignments and responsibilities are not clear, discuss them with your supervisor or administrative superiors. Find out what tasks and assignments are of highest and lowest priority within the agency. Unless you are clear about what you need to do, you cannot figure out ways to do it effectively and efficiently.

3. Plan your work and set priorities. Every hour spent in planning can save three or four hours in execution of a major activity. Take fifteen minutes at the end of each day to write down exactly what you plan to accomplish the next day. Prioritize this list of tasks by using, for example, the *ABC Priority System* (Lakein, 1973). Write an *A* next to those tasks that are most important and have the highest priority. Assign a *B* to those of intermediate value and a *C* to those of lowest priority. Next, prioritize each *A* task in order of importance, labeling them *A-1, A-2, A-3,* and so on. The *B*s can be labeled in the same way: *B-1, B-2,* and so on. At the beginning of the working day, start at once on task *A-1* and stay with it until it is completed. Then move to *A-2* and on down the list.

A less complex approach to setting priorities is to classify all tasks into three categories: (a) tasks that must be completed today, (b) tasks that should be started today, and (c) those that can wait a few days. No matter what approach you use, it is important to realize that priorities may change over the course of a day or week. Thus, it is necessary to continually review and revise your priorities. Also, cultivate equanimity about priority setting. If a task you thought was a low priority suddenly becomes a pressing high-priority task, do not chastise yourself for poor planning. Accept such shifts as being unavoidable, but do not abandon priority setting as a daily activity.

4. Use "to-do" lists. Good managers of time use a *"things-to-do" checklist* that they always carry with them. The list should include an estimate of how long it will take to complete each item on the list, so adequate time can be budgeted for tasks of highest priority. When developing a "to-do" list, it is important to anticipate future deadlines and begin tasks early enough to meet them. It is usually best to tackle lengthy tasks before those that can be done in a short time. It is also best to schedule work on the most difficult tasks when your energy level is highest (e.g., first thing in the morning). Save some time at the end of each day for clearing your desk, taking care of last-minute letters, and starting your "things-to-do" list for the next day.

5. Plan for the unexpected. Allow time in your schedule for emergencies. Remember Murphy's Laws: "Nothing is as simple as it seems," "Everything will take longer than you think," and "If anything can go wrong, it will." Try to schedule at least one hour of unplanned time each day to deal with unanticipated tasks.

6. Reduce interruptions to a minimum. Granted, some interruption of your work is inevitable. When you are interrupted, maintain control of the situation by giving the interruption full attention, avoiding irritation, and, where appropriate, setting a time limit on the interruption. Drop-in clients are often less of a problem than staff who interrupt other workers. Being able to say "no" to the question "Do you have a minute?" is an important time management skill. Closing your office door or standing up to converse with someone who just stopped by your office can help control unnecessary interruptions.

7. Learn to make decisions without procrastination. Some workers are afraid of making mistakes; as a result, they delay making decisions. Setting a limit on the time to be spent prior to making a difficult decision can reduce procrastination. Some workers avoid making decisions because they cannot arrive at a perfect solution. There are few if any perfect solutions in the real world of social work practice. One must strive for *excellence;* striving for *perfection* will result only in frustration, stress, and the loss of valuable time. Remember that everyone makes mistakes. When you make a mistake, learn from it; don't waste time brooding over it. A "good" mistake is one from which you learn and do not repeat. A "bad" mistake is one you will repeat again.

8. Keep your copy of your agency's policy and procedure manual up to date and close at hand. As changes occur, insert the new pages and discard the old. Much time can be lost in fervid search for manual information or when you erroneously follow an outdated procedure.

9. Develop a *tickler file* to keep track of deadlines for submitting monthly reports and other tasks that must be completed according to a schedule. A tickler file can be as simple as notations on a calendar of things to be done on certain dates or a more complex system, such as a desktop file or computerized calendar.

10. Develop a desktop system for the rapid retrieval of frequently used information, telephone numbers, and addresses. Since social workers deal with a large number of people other than clients (e.g., doctors, lawyers, other social workers, etc.), some type of resource file is needed. As you learn about new programs and services and meet human service personnel, place their names, phone numbers, and other relevant data in a file for future reference.

11. When appropriate, delegate a task to staff at the next-lowest level within the organization (e.g., a secretary, case aide, or paraprofessional). However, you must be careful not to overburden others, or give them assignments they are not prepared to carry out.

12. Limit the time spent in meetings. The following suggestions are helpful:
  ▪ Consider alternatives to a meeting (e.g., conference phone calls).

- Choose an appropriate and convenient time and location for the meeting.
- Attend only for the time needed to make your contribution.
- Define the purpose clearly before scheduling the meeting so everyone understands why he or she is attending and can properly prepare.
- Prepare an agenda and follow it. Start on time; end on time. Control interruptions. Stay on task; accomplish the purpose of the meeting.
- Evaluate the success of the meeting and agree on necessary changes in future meetings.

(See Chapter 15 for additional guidelines on planning an effective meeting.)

13. To the extent possible, structure your day by using scheduled appointments for interviews with clients, collateral contacts (contacts with other service providers), and the like. Reduce travel time by scheduling all meetings in a given locality for the same day.

14. Organize your desk and eliminate clutter in your workspace. Keep those things you are working on in front of you, but clear your desk of materials related to other tasks. This will help keep your attention on the task at hand.

15. The most important rule in managing paperwork is to handle each paper only once. If you pick up a letter, report, or request, take the action required or throw it away if no action is necessary. Do not set it aside; do not let papers pile up on your desk.

16. Learn to use a word processor and/or dictating equipment to prepare letters and reports. (See Technique 7.4.) Also learn to use your agency's computer so you can quickly and accurately input and retrieve data.

17. Secure needed training. If lack of skill or knowledge is slowing you down or causing you to make mistakes, request appropriate training or consultation.

18. Develop a workable recording and notetaking system. Ask experienced workers to help you develop an effective and efficient system of keeping notes and records. (See Techniques 7.7 and 7.8.)

19. Practice clear communication. Much time is wasted trying to deal with problems that arise from simple misunderstandings caused by poor communication. Learn to use the telephone effectively and efficiently. Poor telephone communication technique causes confusion and wastes time. (See Technique 7.5.)

20. Reward yourself. Find ways of celebrating even small accomplishments. It may be as simple as putting a line through an item on your "things-to-do" list or giving yourself a piece of gum. These little actions underscore the accomplishment and give you a feeling that progress has been made.

21. Take breaks from your periods of intense work. Briefly switching to a different type of activity counteracts boredom. If you have been sitting, take a brief walk; if you have been reading, do something with your hands; if you have been writing, switch to reading tasks.

22. Concentrate on your work. Focus your energy on the task at hand. Focus on one thing at a time until you either complete the task or reach a preset time limit for that activity. Avoid jumping from task to task without completing one.

23. Separate your work from other parts of your life. Do not let your work interfere with your family and social life, and do not let your personal life interfere with the time spent at work. Try to keep the two separate; allow one to provide a break from the other so each day has variety.

24. Do your own work. Do not do someone else's work. Nothing reduces your energy or motivation more quickly than trying to compensate for someone else's incompetence. This does not preclude helping others on occasion but do not make a habit of rescuing others.

25. Keep track of how you spend each day. Once you have this information, analyze it and identify those areas that need special attention and those areas in which you can make time-saving changes.

Selected Bibliography

Bowman, Mimmie, and Mitzi Jones. *Caseload Management.* Knoxville: Office of Continuing Social Work Education, University of Tennessee, 1983.
Ferner, Jack. *Successful Time Management.* New York: Wiley, 1980.
Grossman, Lee. *Fat Paper: Diets for Trimming Paperwork.* New York: McGraw-Hill, 1976.
Laken, Alan. *How to Get Control of Your Time and Your Life.* New York: New American Library, 1973. (Signet Book)

7.2   *Report Writing*

Purpose: To prepare a clear and useful professional report.

Discussion: A social worker must prepare many reports. Reports that are inaccurate, incomplete, or unclear create misunderstanding, antagonism, and costly errors. Like other work-related activities, the skill of report writing can be developed. A number of guidelines can improve the quality of professional reports.

1. A report is always addressed to someone; thus, it is important to analyze the report's audience and determine what information they really need. Determine whether the report you prepare may be passed on to other organizations and possible clients. Keep the reader or readers in mind as you write.

2. Decide whether a formal report or just a memo is required. A formal report usually follows the format prescribed by the agency. A copy of a report—one judged by others in the agency as a good model—can be used as your guide. A memo may contain abbreviations, first names, and jargon, but such shorthand should be avoided in a formal report.

3. Before you begin to write, organize the information to be presented in a logical structure. Construct an outline. If you present your ideas in an orderly way, the reader will be more likely to understand you. Make it a habit to always think about how the reader will interpret your words and perhaps misinterpret what you have written.

4. Two or three drafts or revisions may be needed before the final version is produced. Ask your peers to review your early drafts. If they are not sure of what you are trying to say, you can be certain that the intended reader will not understand either. Also read the drafts aloud; if it doesn't sound right, revise it.

5. Use language that is simple and clear. Select your words carefully, using only those your reader will understand. Avoid using words that have different meaning in different contexts. Also avoid using slang or phrases that might offend the reader. For example, consider the following series of words:

- inebriated, intoxicated, drunk, pickled
- portly, stout, obese, fat
- firm, obstinate, stubborn, pig-headed

Each of the words in a given series has the same basic meaning, but each strikes you in a slightly different way. Thus, word connotation—the emotion or attitude the word implies—must be considered, as well as the word's denotation or definition.

6. Do not use "weasel words"—words or phrases that let the writer avoid responsibility for his or her statements. The result is indirect and wishy-washy language, such as: "It would appear that...," "There may be a tendency toward...," "It seems as though...," "There is some reason for believing that...," or "I feel there might be...." The weasel words *feel* and *seems* appear frequently in social work reports. Instead of saying, "I feel placement is necessary...," it would be better to say, "I believe placement is necessary...." Wishy-washy language gives the reader the impression that the report writer is insecure or unsure of what he or she is talking about. This, in turn, causes the reader to doubt the validity of the report and question the worker's competence. Avoid this by being direct in both writing and speech.

7. Avoid hackneyed expressions such as: "It certainly merits study...," "The matter is receiving our closest attention...," "We will explore every avenue...," or "Naturally, the child's interest is our concern...." The use of trite words and phrases suggests that the writer is insincere or responding as a mere formality. Be specific about what you think and what action will be taken.

8. Use the number of words necessary but no more than that. Wordiness lessens the force of expression and distracts the reader from the very point you want to make. Also avoid redundant phrases, such as: "first beginnings," "the present time," "join together," or "point in time."

9. Keep your sentences short, usually twenty words or less. Most often, the straightforward subject-verb-object sentence is the best arrangement because it is quickly read and seldom misunderstood. Consider these two sentences:

- After much discussion, not all of which was productive, a foster home placement—the agreed-upon arrangement—was made for the child.
- The child was placed in a foster home.

Although both sentences say essentially the same thing, the second sentence is easier to read and understand. It is short and follows the subject-verb-object structure.

10. Use active verbs whenever possible. The passive voice adds unnecessary words, weakens the statement, and makes the meaning less clear. For example, "Don hit John" has a clearer, stronger impact than "John was hit by Don."

11. Give special attention to paragraph construction. Each paragraph should focus on a single idea. It should begin with a topic sentence, which introduces the central idea. That idea is then explained by supporting details, presented in additional sentences. The paragraph ends with a summary sentence. Thus, by reading only the first and last sentences of a paragraph, the reader should be able to pick up much of what you are trying to communicate. The outline for a good paragraph is as follows:

- In the first sentence, state the central point of the paragraph.
- If necessary, restate the central point in other words or provide additional clarification.
- Present evidence or background supporting the central point, including examples, where appropriate. Draw conclusions.
- Finally, draw the paragraph to a close, summarizing the key point in a single sentence.

In general, a page of typewritten copy should contain two or three paragraphs. If there is only one paragraph per page, it indicates that too many ideas have been crammed into a single paragraph.

12. Use the dictionary on a regular basis to determine the exact meaning of a word, the correct spelling of a word, whether or not a word should be capitalized, correct word forms for different parts of speech, how a word should be divided at the end of a line, correct punctuation (i.e., hyphens, apostrophes, accents), and whether a hyphen should be used in a compound word. Most dictionaries contain a section listing the basic rules of pronunciation, capitalization, and spelling; some also contain information on grammar. A thesaurus, which contains synonyms and antonyms, will help the writer add variety and freshness in word selection.

In recent years, the word processor has dramatically changed the tasks of writing and editing. Computer programs now include a thesaurus, spelling checks, and even grammar checks. Because writing is so much a part of social work practice, all social workers should learn to use a word processor.

Selected Bibliography

Crews, Frederick. *The Random House Handbook.* 5th ed. New York: Random House, 1988.

Houp, Kenneth, and Thomas Pearsall. *Reporting Technical Information.* 6th ed. New York: Macmillan, 1988.

Strumpf, Michael, and Auriel Douglas. *Painless, Perfect Grammar.* New York: Monarch Press, 1985.

Purpose: To communicate ideas and information clearly and concisely in letters.

Discussion: Most of the principles that guide report writing (see Technique 7.2) also apply to letter writing. In addition, the following guidelines will improve correspondence. Several are based on suggestions made by Fear (1977, 126).

1. Plan carefully before you write even the shortest letter. If it is worth doing, it should be done well because your image as a professional person is shaped by the appearance of your letter.

2. Revise and polish all drafts of letters and proofread the final version. All letters to other agencies and professionals should be typed on letterhead stationery. Ordinarily, letters to a client should also be typed. If you know the client well, short notes may be handwritten.

3. A copy of all letters and notes should be retained for agency files.

4. Always use proper titles, such as "Mr.," "Mrs.," "Miss," "Ms.," "Dr.," "Rev.," and so on. The use of "Ms." is appropriate when a woman's marital status is unknown. First names should be used only when addressing children or clients' with whom you have a close relationship.

5. Develop several model or sample letters based on situations commonly encountered in your agency. Use these as a starting point when preparing new letters.

6. Remember that a professional letter will have at least the following parts: letterhead, date, inside address, reference line or subject line, salutation, body, complimentary close, typed signature, and written signature. When appropriate, there should also be an enclosure notation ("enc.") and a carbon copy notation ("cc") which names others receiving the letter.

7. In some letters, you will be complaining or making demands. However, you can usually make your point clearly and emphatically without being aggressive. On the other hand, do not go to the other extreme by humbling yourself or avoiding an important issue. By doing so, you risk being considered a pushover. Write with enough authority that you are taken seriously.

8. Humanize and personalize your letters, especially those to clients. The recipient of your letter should feel that he or she is dealing with a real person, not an impersonal representative of an organization.

9. When writing to people in important positions, be careful not to be too friendly. Use a businesslike tone. Be pleasant but not folksy.

10. Many readers of letters object to what they term the "I" point of view. This occurs when the writer constantly refers to himself or herself, especially by beginning sentences with "I." Employing an "I" two or three times in an ordinary letter will not hurt; even starting an occasional sentence with it is all right, but do not overdo it.

11. Do not include material that would violate confidentiality or prove embarrassing if read by persons other than the intended recipient of the letter. Be alert to the fact that an agency's name and address on an envelope may reveal the client's involvement with an agency.

Selected Bibliography

Fear, David. *Technical Communication,* Glenview, Ill.: Scott, Foresman, 1977.

Houp, Kenneth, and Thomas Pearsall. *Reporting Technical Information.* 6th ed. New York: Macmillan, 1988.

Wilson, Suanna. *Recording: Guidelines for Social Workers.* New York: The Free Press, 1980.

7.4   *Using a Dictating Machine*

Purpose: To reduce time needed to prepare letters and reports.

Discussion: Social workers prepare numerous reports and write many letters. Studies suggest that the skillful use of a dictating machine can cut writing time in half. We offer here a number of suggestions for efficient and effective dictation. Many are based on guidelines developed by Harris (1976).

Preparation

1. Select a comfortable and convenient location for dictating. Arrange to use a comfortable chair and a large table top so you can spread out your notes for easy scanning.

2. Set aside time each day for dictation. Keep interruptions to a minimum.

3. Arrange all the information and background materials in the order in which they will be needed.

4. Select a number of headings under which the content will be presented. A report with several headings facilitates comprehension by the reader.

5. Prepare a rough outline using the headings you've selected. Give special attention to the sequence of topics you want to address.

6. Visualize the person(s) who will be reading your report or letter. Consider their needs when organizing your report.

7. Visualize the typist who must listen to your voice and understand your recorded message and instructions.

Using the Machine

8. If you feel awkward using the machine, consider saying each sentence aloud before dictating into the recorder.

9. Dictate in a natural tone of voice, being careful to enunciate clearly.

10. Talk at a steady pace but at a slightly slower rate than usual. Keep your sentences short and to the point.

11. It is easier to talk than to write. Thus, when using a dictating machine, there is the danger of producing an unnecessarily long report. Follow your outline and be concise.

12. Spell any words that sound similar to other words, as well as any uncommon or confusing names. Dictate figures by digits (e.g., refer to 11,065 as "one, one, zero, six, five"). Dictate only periods, paragraphs, and unusual punctuation; the transcriber will usually take care of other punctuation.

13. Play back the tape to be sure it reflects your intended message. Remember, the initial dictation is only a rough draft. Once the ideas have been put in writing, it will be easier to revise and fill in the gaps.

14. Edit the dictated draft carefully. Be sure to check for any errors and clarify and tighten up the ideas expressed.

15. Proofread all dictated material before signing it. Errors can easily be introduced into dictated reports.

Selected Bibliography

Harris, Linda. *Support Skills for Direct Service Workers: Managing Your Job.* Minneapolis: Minnesota Resource Center for Social Work Education, 1976.
Wilson, Suanna. *Recording: Guidelines for Social Workers.* New York: The Free Press, 1976.

7.5   *Effective Telephone Communications*

Purpose: To communicate clearly and concisely when using the telephone.

Discussion: Many important social work transactions occur over the telephone, making this a frequently used tool in social work practice. Skillful use of the telephone can contribute to the social worker's effectiveness. However, it is important to remember that the telephone is not always the most efficient or effective method of communication. Harris (1976, 39) identifies the following disadvantages of the telephone:

1. The person you are calling may not be in when you call.
2. You may not be available when that person returns your call.
3. Verbal phone communication can be easily misunderstood.
4. Facts communicated orally generally won't be retained accurately for more than a few days.
5. Unless you have jotted down your ideas prior to the conversation, it is easy to forget some of the key elements you want to discuss.

The telephone should be used when a quick response is needed and the matter under discussion is relatively uncomplicated. It is important to remember that a phone call does not establish a permanent record of the transaction. A letter or memo may be preferred when time is not critical, when a record must be established, or when the message involves many details.

The following guidelines will help improve telephone use; several are adapted from those offered by Harris (1976).

1. The task of communicating over the telephone has to be accomplished by your voice. The person to whom you are speaking does not have the advantage of being able to observe your body language. Take care to enunciate distinctly. Use a normal speaking voice, since a loud voice can be disagreeably penetrating. The limited tonal range of the telephone can make a high-pitched voice sound screechy, so speak in as low a pitch as possible to produce a more pleasant sound.

2. Jot down the major points you wish to cover before placing the call.

3. When making and receiving calls, always fully identify yourself by name, organization, and department.

4. Take notes while you are on the phone. Depending on the nature of the call, it may be appropriate to review the information relayed to make sure you have understood everything accurately. In addition, summarize your purpose for calling before saying good-bye.

5. If the person on the other end is talking at some length, interject a brief comment at intervals: "Yes, I see" or "I understand." This lets the other person know that you are still listening. If your caller gets sidetracked on trivia steer him or her back to the main subject of the call.

6. Whenever possible, answer the telephone on the first or second ring—and immediately respond to the caller. Do not just pick up the receiver and hold it while you finish a conversation in your office.

7. If you are unable to reach the person with whom you need to speak, always leave a message that you called. But keep the message short (e.g., your name, phone number, and reason for calling) and assume there is a good chance that the message will get garbled. If you must leave a long message or fear that your message was misunderstood, ask the person taking your message to repeat it back to you.

8. If the person you are calling is not in his or her office, suggest a specific time for the person to return your call, or find out what time you can call again. You will probably save time by calling back yourself, rather than waiting for your call to be returned.

9. When you leave your office, always tell the secretary or someone near the phone where you can be reached or when you will be back. If possible, establish a regular time to make and receive telephone calls: first thing in the morning, after lunch, or some other convenient time.

10. When transferring calls to other lines, let callers know what you are doing; tell them the name and title of the person to whom they will be speaking, and why you are passing their call on. Similarly, when you must leave the phone, explain why: "Please hold on for a few seconds while I get that file." Unless you are sure you will be away for only a few moments, tell your caller that you will call back. If you have left the phone, alert your caller to your return before resuming the conversation: "Hello" or "Thanks for waiting" or "I have that file now."

Selected Bibliography

Harris, Linda. *Support Skills for Direct Service Workers: Managing Your Job.* Minneapolis: Minnesota Resource Center for Social Work Education, 1976.

7.6 Controlling Workload

Purpose: To manage workload by refusing and accepting additional work assignments.

Discussion: Tight budgets generally leave most social agencies short of needed staff. Given the excessive demands placed on a social worker, the worker must view his or her time as a limited resource. (See Technique 7.1.) If the worker does not or cannot control workload, he or she will be spread too thin and effectiveness will diminish. Broadly speaking, there are only a couple ways to control an ever-growing workload—you can either say no to additional work assignments or you can ask other staff for their assistance.

Saying no is difficult for most people. When someone asks you to take on additional work, it may seem easier to say yes in order to avoid conflict or feeling guilty. Nevertheless, you must take responsibility for managing your workload and this requires saying no to some requests. Follow these guidelines:

1. Decide if the proposed assignment or request for your time is reasonable, given your job description and current workload. Ask yourself: Is this a matter of high priority? Am I responsible for this matter or is someone else? If I say yes, will I soon regret it and feel angry and put upon? Am I tempted to say yes mainly because I want to avoid a conflict or the appearance of selfishness?

2. If you have doubts about whether the request is reasonable, obtain more information before saying yes or no. If still in doubt, ask for time to think about the request, and set a deadline for making the decision (e.g., "I'll let you know in a half hour").

3. If you decide that you must refuse, say no firmly and calmly. If may be appropriate to give a honest and straightforward explanation of why you must say no. But say no without saying "I'm sorry" or offering excuses and rationalizations. If you have a good reason for refusing the request, there is no need to apologize or feel guilty.

As previously suggested, it is difficult for many people to say no, even when there is good reason for doing so. It is also often difficult to accept a refusal from someone who has decided he or she must say no to your request for assistance. Whenever you ask others for assistance, explain why you think it is an important and reasonable request and why you are asking them to take on the task. If your request is refused, adhere to three guidelines:

1. Accept the answer graciously. Do not put pressure on the person, and do not make the individual feel guilty for having refused.
2. Be pleasant and appreciative. Respond with something like, "That's OK; thank you for your consideration."
3. If appropriate, ask if your request might be acceptable under other circumstances, such as at a later time or date.

It is important to note that this brief discussion of refusing and accepting additional assignments presumes a situation in which there is room to negotiate. Such a situation does not always exist. Within an agency, a supervisor or administrator has the legitimate authority to assign additional tasks, even when the individual knows you are already overloaded. In other words, a worker does not always have the freedom to refuse.

Selected Bibliography

Alberti, Robert, and Michael Emmons. *Your Perfect Right.* 5th ed. San Luis Obispo, Calif.: Impact, 1986.

Jakubowski, Patricia, and Arthur Lange. *The Assertive Option.* Champaign, Ill.: Research Press, 1978.

7.7 *Maintaining Casenotes for Narrative Recording*

Purpose: To improve efficiency in creating narrative case recordings.

Discussion: Each social agency develops its own standards for recordkeeping. What is recorded and the format used will depend on factors such as the agency's mission, relevant state and federal laws and regulations, type of service provided, and who has access to the records.

Narrative recording is still a common style of recording in direct service agencies, even though many agencies are moving toward computer-assisted systems, problem-oriented recording, and other structured formats. The narrative record remains popular because it is flexible—anything deemed important can be written into the record. The major disadvantage is that it is a very time-consuming and costly method. Because workers seldom have the time needed to maintain an up-to-date narrative, these records are seldom current, which, of course, negates the purpose of recordkeeping. Another disadvantage is that the narrative does not lend itself to the easy retrieval of information; individuals looking for specific information may have to read a dozen or more pages before they find what they are looking for. Also, because narrative records tend to grow so large, storage is a problem. Kagle (1984) observes that

> these problems have led some agencies to eliminate the use of narrative records entirely. Many agencies, though, cannot or do not wish to take such a step. Their goal should be to maximize the assets of narrative records while minimizing their limitations. Agencies can achieve this goal by
>
> - Limiting the use of narrative records to complex, individualized services; using structured forms for short-term or routine services.
> - Limiting narrative recording to those elements of the record which focus upon individualization; using forms, lists, or outlines for systematic or typical information.
> - Establishing guidelines for what to include in the narrative; these guidelines might suggest relevant topics for records of different client groups, service programs, and practice modalities.
> - Establishing guidelines for what to exclude from the narrative, especially: content that is documented elsewhere, content that needs to be readily accessible, and content that could be sufficiently documented using a more efficient style. (p. 43)

Two steps are involved in the creation of a narrative record: (1) the worker creates many handwritten notes and then, at a later date (sometimes weeks or even months later), (2) the worker reviews these notes and dictates a summarization of his or her work with the client. The handwritten notes record the many and varied day-to-day or hour-by-hour actions and activities related to a specific case (e.g., "Mr. Smith, Johnny B's teacher, called to say..."). Notes help the worker keep track of what is happening. Some of these handwritten notes are self-messages or reminders that a specific task should be undertaken (e.g., "Contact Mrs. Jones's attorney before next Friday and request..."). Thus, many notes have meaning only to the worker.

In order for the worker to do the summary dictation as efficiency as possible, he or she must develop a system of notetaking that (1) keeps all casenotes in one place so this information is always at hand, (2) maintains a chronological record of activities, and (3) facilitates summarization. One such method is to utilize a loose-leaf notebook filled with sheets of paper specifically designed for brief handwritten and chronological entries. Each sheet can be constructed to facilitate the recording of statistics kept by the agency (e.g., number of office interviews). Figure 7.1 is a sample sheet with several typical entries. This method maintains all the notes in one place and allows for quick review and update of what has happened and what should be done. Such a method is especially important when the worker has a large caseload. Without a good notekeeping system, it is impossible to remember the details of a situation. All of the notesheets are kept in one place and used as a basis for the periodic (e.g., once a month or bimonthly) dictation of a summary entry into the agency record.

Selected Bibliography

Kagle, Jill. *Social Work Records.* Homewood, Ill.: Dorsey Press, 1984.
Wilson Suanna. *Recording: Guidelines for Social Workers.* New York: The Free Press, 1980.

Figure 7.1   Sample Recording of Casenotes

Client _Jimmy Jones_	Case Number _321_	Cross Reference _L. Smith Fosterhome_

Type of contact										Date			Notes
Client (child)	Client (adult)	Foster parent	Collateral	Other	Office	Out-of-Office	Telephone	Letter	Other		Time spent	To Do	
	✓						✓			Jan 27			Mrs. Smith called to say Jimmy ran away. He did not come home from school. She will call his friends and will inform Jimmy's probation officer. (Leland Green)
	✓						✓			1/28			I called Mrs. S. still no word on Jimmy. Police have been informed.
		✓					✓			•••			Learned from L. Green that Jimmy was picked up. No charges.
✓	✓					✓				•••			Jimmy returned to Smith home. Jimmy having trouble in school. Failing math. Picked on by other kids. Wants to quit school. (set up meeting with math teacher + school counselor. Is tutor possible?)
	✓						✓			1/29			Mr. + Mrs. Smith and I will meet at school for conference, 4 pm today. Room 104
✓							✓			1/29			Spent hr. with Jimmy. He is angry with math teacher. Feels he is not treated fair because he is "foster kid." Also upset because mother forgot his birthday. "She is probably drunk again." He cried as he talked about mother. He cares for her and worries about her but "hates her when she drinks." He wants to visit older sister, Mary. "Mary helps me understand Mother." (arrange meeting between Jimmy and Mary.)

7.8   *Problem-Oriented Recording (POR) and the SOAP Format*

Purpose: To facilitate concise recordkeeping that focuses on the client's problem and the professional interventions to deal with that problem.

Discussion: *POR,* which stands for *Problem-Oriented Recording,* is a method of recordkeeping. It is widely used in hospitals and medical programs. Its use has also spread to many social agencies. The **SOAP** format is a simple conceptual framework for recording the essential information used in assessing a specific problem and formulating an action plan.

In commenting on the use of POR in social work, Kane (1974) notes that the system "provides a framework of organization that permits even long records to become coherent, usable and goal oriented" (p. 413). The system can be used in work with individuals, groups, communities, and in all fields of social work practice. POR has a number of advantages:

- It permits the worker, agency supervisor, outside consultants, or researchers to review the way in which a particular problem was approached by the worker or agency.
- It displays the multiplicity and interrelatedness of problems experienced by a client, yet it permits focused attention on each specific problem.
- It promotes case coordination and teamwork because it facilitates interprofessional communication and clarity of direction.
- It provides continuity of professional attention on specific problems, even when there is personnel turnover in the agency.
- It provides a mechanism for follow-up and the monitoring of progress toward problem resolution. A review of a problem-oriented record will quickly reveal inaction or actions unrelated to the client's problem.
- It encourages concise recording. Because specific problems are kept in focus, irrelevant information is kept out of the record.

POR consists of four components, which are related to the basic steps of the problem-solving process: (1) establishment of a data base; (2) listing of specific problems, each of which is assigned a number; (3) development of an action plan to address each problem; and (4) implementation of the plan

The data base consists primarily of the information collected during the intake phase and includes demographic characteristics and a description of the problem that brought the client to the agency. Much of the data base appears on the record facesheet or in the social history. This data should be systematically collected, organized, or recorded, for it provides a foundation for identifying and conceptualizing the client's problems and gives rise to a preliminary problem list.

A problem can be anything of concern to the client, the social worker, or both. All problems become part of the problem list. Each problem is assigned a number and described in behavioral language. Diagnostic labels and jargon should be avoided, if possible. All too often, diagnostic labels mean different things to different professionals and usually mean little to the client. The words used to describe the problem should be clear to all persons using the record, including the client. This, of course, promotes interprofessional communication and teamwork as well as reduces the chance of persons working at cross purposes.

The problem list serves to focus case planning and intervention. What the social worker does should be logically related to a specific problem in the list. As problems are resolved, they are removed from the list. However, the resolved problem's number is not reassigned; each number is used only once. Thus, the intervention and progress on a specific problem can be traced throughout the case record. In a sense, the numbering system serves as a auditor's trail. It is important that the problem list be a separate and distinct page in the case record. This makes it easy for the user to find the list and provides a ready reference point for a quick review of progress and planning.

Figure 7.2 Problem List for the Brown Family

Problem Number	Problem	Date	Inactive or Resolved Problem	Date Resolved
1.	Crowded housing	4/10		
2.	Short of food money	4/10	Client enrolled in food stamp program	4/20
3.	Johnny (age 8) needs glasses	4/15	New prescription issued by Dr. Green at Clinic	4/25
4.	Ann (age 10) failing in school	4/28		

Figure 7.2 is a sample problem list for Mrs. Brown, a mother of three, who was reported to a protective services agency for child neglect. Note that each numbered problem is dated according to when the problem was first identified. If additional problems were identified in the Brown case, they would be added to the list. Figure 7.2 shows that problems 2 and 3 have been resolved, but problems 1 and 4 continue to receive the worker's attention.

Some agencies have adopted the concept of a master problem list, which utilizes a standard problem nomenclature and numbering system. For example, the number 15 might be assigned to the problem of unsafe housing. This uniformity of problem numbering facilitates research on the type of problems brought to an agency.

POR requires some type of action or response to each item on the problem list. Basically, three actions are possible: (1) intervention, (2) secure additional information in order to more fully understand the problem, or (3) do nothing except monitor the situation and wait for further developments. The social worker records the action in the main body of the case record but is careful to utilize the problem number to reference the action to a specific problem.

When professional intervention rather than additional data collection or monitoring is required, it is helpful to use the SOAP format to describe this action. The acronym SOAP can be explained as follows:

S: *Subjective information* refers to how the client feels or perceives the situation. It is derived from client self-report. By definition, subjective information does not lend itself to independent or external validation.

O: *Objective information* includes that which has been obtained by way of direct observation by professionals, clinical examinations, systematic data collection, and the like. As compared to subjective information, this category of information can be independently verified by others.

Figure 7.3 Sample SOAP Entry

Subjective: Mrs. Brown states she worries about children's diet. The children complain of being hungry and to her embarrassment they have asked neighbors for food. Since Mrs. B grew up on welfare, she has vowed "never to go on the dole." She says she is in a "panic" about the thought of losing her children.

Objective: Her part-time job earns $105 take-home pay per week. Rent is $250 per month. It is hard to follow Mrs. Brown in conversation; she jumps from topic to topic. Agency records indicate that she was herself neglected as a child and placed in foster care for two years.

Assessment: Family clearly does not have enough money for food. Mrs. Brown is probably eligible for food stamps. Much of her disorganization is due to her anxiety about losing children to foster care, which is, in turn, related to her own experience in foster care. She fears that accepting welfare will label her a "bad parent."

Plan: Need to support Mrs. Brown's application for food stamps and show her that application is a way to be a "good mother" under these very trying circumstances. Need to assure her that agency has no plans to place her children. Begin long-term effort to help Mrs. B find higher-paying job. Plan to complete food stamp application by 5/25.

A: *Assessment* refers to the professional's conceptualization or conclusions derived from reviewing the subjective and objective information.

P: The *Plan* spells out how the professional intends to resolve the specific problem.

One advantage of the SOAP format is that it forces the social worker to make a clear connection between what is known about the problem and the plan for resolving the problem. It should be noted that POR requires the use of the SOAP format; however, the SOAP format can be used apart from the POR system.

Figure 7.3 is a SOAP entry related to problem 2 (lack of money for food) in the Brown case (Figure 7.2). Note the deadline set for making the application. It is important to set a deadline for accomplishing a particular task; this encourages implementation and counteracts the tendency to delay or avoid taking action.

Once the plan has been formulated, intervention follows. An advantage of POR is that its structure and especially the numbered problem list make it easy to monitor intervention. This counteracts the tendency of some professionals to formulate good plans but not follow through on implementation. Clients are only helped by *action,* not by *plans,* no matter how logical or well written.

Selected Bibliography

Burrill, George. "The Problem-Oriented Log in Social Casework." *Social Work* 21 (January 1976): 67.

Hartman, Barbara L., and Jane M. Wickey. "The Person-Oriented Record in Treatment." *Social Work* 23 (July 1978): 296–99.

Kane, Rosalie A. "Look to the Record." *Social Work* 19 (July 1974): 412–19.

Schmitt, Barton. "The Problem-Oriented Record and Team Reports." In *Child Protection Team Handbook,* edited by B. Schmitt, pp. 175–85. New York: Garland STPM Press, 1978.

7.9   Process Recording

Purpose: To establish a record of the social worker's practice so the process of helping and client-worker interaction can be studied.

Discussion: Process recording is a very detailed form of case recording often used to assist students and new workers in learning basic practice skills. It is used when a worker is having some unusual problems with a client and wants to create a written record that can be examined by his or her peers, supervisor, or consultant as a basis for making suggestions on how the worker might overcome the problems. According to Wilson (1980), a process recording usually contains

1. names of worker, clients, and others involved in the session
2. a word-for-word, "blow-by-blow" description of what happened, to the extent that it can be remembered
3. the worker's observations of nonverbal communications
4. the worker's own emotional reactions or feelings during the session
5. the worker's assessment of what happened and why
6. a diagnostic summary that pulls together in one paragraph the worker's thoughts on the session
7. a brief statement that outlines the plan for further contact with the client.

Dwyer and Urbanowski (1965) suggest that a student's process recording should consist of six major components:

1. *Purpose of interview.* The social worker should formulate a statement of purpose that is clear, concise and specific.
2. *Observations.* The social worker should state general impressions of the physical and emotional climate at the outset of the interview and its impact on the client.
3. *Content.* One section of the recording should be devoted to the actual description of the interview, its length, depending upon the person's stage of development, and learning patterns. The content section should include:
   a. A description of how the interview began.
   b. Pertinent factual information and responses to it by both the client and student.
   c. A description of the feeling content of the interview on the part of both student and client.
   d. Notes on the client's preparation for the next interview and on how the interview ended.

4. *Impressions.* This part should include impressions based on facts. This process gradually develops into diagnostic thinking as one begins to integrate course content and to gain understanding of the interaction between oneself and the client.

5. *Worker's role.* This section highlights activity in the interview and reflects use of social work skills and techniques one has acquired.

6. *Plan.* The worker should make a brief statement of plans for the next interview and record thoughts about some long-range goals for this client. (pp. 285–86)

Properly used, a process recording is an excellent teaching tool, primarily because it forces the writer to analyze carefully his or her practice behavior and decisions. A major disadvantage is that it requires a great deal of time to prepare a process record. Many experienced social workers recommend the process recording of at least one case in their caseload. A careful and detailed study of even one case can provide valuable feedback for skill development and increase self-awareness.

Audio- or videotape recordings are, in many respects, superior to process recording as a teaching tool. However, many agencies do not have video equipment; even if they do, it often requires that the interview take place in a studio atmosphere in order to escape background noise and interruptions. It is usually not feasible to videorecord a meeting in the client's home. The new compact and relatively inexpensive camcorders may expand opportunities for students and workers to study their own performance. Although the audiotaping of an interview can be useful, listening to a tape is tedious and voices may not be clear. The preparation of a written process recording has the advantage of forcing the worker to organize his or her thoughts and observations carefully; this is not required in electronic recordings.

Selected Bibliography

Dwyer, Margaret, and Martha Urbanowski. "Student Process Recording: A Plea for Structure." *Social Casework* 46 (May 1965): 283–86.

Urbanowski, Martha, and Margaret Dwyer. *Learning Through Field Instruction.* Milwaukee: Family Service America, 1988.

Wilson, Suanna. *Recording: Guidelines for Social Workers.* New York: The Free Press, 1980.

7.10 *Testifying in Court*

Purpose: To prepare for a court appearance as a witness.

Discussion: Social workers employed in child protective services, probation, and parole settings make frequent appearances in court. Sooner or later, however, nearly every social worker—regardless of agency setting—will face serving as a witness. A number of guidelines can help the worker perform effectively on the witness stand; several of these are based on guidelines presented by Downs and Taylor (1978).

1. Prepare for the court appearance. Consult with the attorney who will call you as a witness and find out the type of questions he or she will ask and also the questions you are likely to be asked by the attorney who will cross-examine you.

2. Inform the attorney representing the side for which you are testifying of any problems or weaknesses in your testimony. He or she should know of these problems before you get on the witness stand. Of course, you should not voluntarily share this information with the opposing attorney.

3. Be prepared to tell the truth, regardless of how you think it will affect the case. Remember that you will be under oath. You must tell the truth, even if you know it will help the other side. Any exaggeration, speculation, or departure from facts will be uncovered and your credibility as a witness (and a social worker) will suffer dramatically.

4. Your appearance and demeanor as a witness are critical. You should be neat, clean, and dressed to reflect the solemnity of the courtroom. When seated in the witness chair, you should appear dignified, interested, attentive, and courteous. Maintain this attitude throughout the testimony.

5. Your testimony will probably fall into one or more of three categories:
a. *Personal observations.* Prepare to testify from memory with little, if any, reference to your notes. If your observations occurred over a long period of time, you can prepare a chronology of events, which can be used to refresh your memory and keep your thoughts and recollections organized. The opposing counsel and judge will probably look at your list, but it will not usually be introduced as evidence unless if differs from your oral testimony. Memorize the facts, but avoid sounding as though you are giving a recitation.
b. *Expert conclusions.* An individual who is qualified or designated by the court as an expert witness is permitted to offer professional opinions as to the meaning of facts and observations. All other witnesses must confine their testimony to facts and observations. Opposing attorneys often argue over whether a person should be qualified as an expert. If an attorney plans to qualify you as an expert witness, be prepared to explain:
   - Your professional qualifications (e.g., degrees, experience, special training, publications, membership in professional associations, etc.)
   - The theories and principles you used in forming your opinion and the competing theories and approaches you decided not to use
   - Your mode of practice and how it is similar to or different from that of other social workers or professionals in your field
   - The opinions you formed and why (the major portion of your testimony as an expert)
c. *Reading reports.* Portions of your case record may be admitted into evidence. If so, you may be asked to read aloud portions of the record. Prepare by being thoroughly familiar with the content and organization of the record. Make sure you can read any handwritten parts and doublecheck the contents to see if any correspondence or notes have been omitted. You should be able to explain the method for producing, transcribing, and processing a case file in your office.

6. When testifying, speak slowly, loudly, and clearly. If your testimony is not heard and understood, it will be worthless. Avoid using slang and social work jargon. Much of the jargon used by social workers is incomprehensible to judges, attorneys, and juries.

7. Listen carefully to the questions you are asked. If you do not understand a question, ask that it be repeated, rephrased, or explained. If you do not know the answer, say so. Never speculate or guess. Answer only the question that is asked. Answer questions in a positive and confident manner. Wishy-washy phrases like "I feel," "to the best of my recollection," or "I guess" weaken the impact of your testimony.

8. If an objection is made by the opposing attorney during the course of your testimony, stop speaking immediately. If the judge overrules the objection, you will be permitted to answer the question. If the objection is sustained you will not be permitted to answer the question and a new question will be asked.

9. When being cross-examined by the opposing attorney, keep in mind that he or she is not your friend. Even a supposedly friendly cross-examiner is looking for ways to trip you up and discredit your testimony. Do not volunteer information that is not asked for. Doing so provides the cross-examiner with additional opportunities to confuse you. Do not explain why you know something unless you are asked. And finally, remember that the attorney offering your testimony has a chance to follow-up and ask additional questions after the other attorney's cross-examination. This may help clear up any problems in your testimony.

10. Many times, cross-examiners ask compound questions. When responding to a compound question, divide it into sections and then answer each part. Do not answer a partially untrue question with a simple yes or no, because the attorney may cut you short and not allow you to complete your response, thus giving an erroneous impression of your actions or beliefs.

11. When being cross-examined, do not lose your temper at questions you consider impertinent or offensive. Exercise absolute self-control. If you maintain your composure, you will be less likely to become confused and inconsistent. Outbursts of anger do not enhance witness credibility. If the questioning is truly improper, your attorney will object. Pause long enough before answering an improper question to allow the objection to be made, but don't pause so long that you appear hesitant or unsure. All questions should be handled with tact and truth. Fortunately, judges are familiar with the histrionics of some trial attorneys and are rarely impressed by them.

12. Do not get caught in the "yes-or-no" trap. If, on cross-examination, the opposing attorney asks a question and ends it with "Answer yes or no," don't feel obliged to do so if you believe such an answer will be misleading. Instead, begin your answer with "Well, that needs explaining." The attorney may object and the judge may require you to give a yes or no answer, but the jury will understand your position and look forward to your explanation when your attorney clarifies the situation on redirect examination.

13. Often, a witness will be asked a question regarding sympathy for one side or the other in the case. If asked, admit your beliefs or sympathies honestly. It is absurd to deny an obvious sympathy, and an honest admission of favoritism will not discredit a witness.

Selected Bibliography

Brieland, Donald, and John Lemmon. *Social Work and the Law.* 2nd ed. St. Paul: West, 1985.

Caulfield, Barbara, and Robert Horowitz. *Child Abuse and the Law: A Legal Primer for Social Workers.* 2nd ed. Chicago: National Committee for Prevention of Child Abuse, 1987.

Downs, Susan, and Catherine Taylor, eds. *Permanent Planning in Foster Care: Resources for Training.* Portland, Ore.: Regional Institute for Human Services, 1978.

Haralambi, Ann, and Donna Rosenberg. "The Expert Witness: Social Work, Medical, Psychiatric." In *The New Child Protection Team Handbook,* edited by Donald Bross et al., pp. 396–413. New York: Garland, 1988.

Personal and Professional Development

8

Introduction

Social work is a difficult and demanding profession, but it can be a rewarding one. The rewards are mostly intrinsic. By selecting social work as a career, one is virtually assured of never attaining wealth, power, or prestige. For social work is committed to a set of values and actions that are not reinforced by our economic system. Compared to many other professions, social work occupies a relatively low status. Gordon Allport, a respected social psychologist, once observed that the low status given social work in the United States may be due to the emphasis social workers place on compassion, cooperation, and mutual respect in a society that values competition and aggressiveness. To be happy and satisfied with this relatively low status and limited financial remuneration, the social worker must believe deeply in the profession's mission and be committed to its core values, especially its recognition that all individuals are persons of worth and dignity. The social worker must care deeply about the pains and troubles of all people, but especially his or her clients. No one needs to feel apologetic for being a social worker; the professions' goals, values, and history reflect that which is most noble about humankind.

From its beginnings, the social work profession has demonstrated special concern for those who are powerless, stigmatized, and devalued by wider society—those who the more powerful would like to avoid and ignore. Because social workers are in a position to see so many people in need and see the inadequacy of our professional, agency, and societal resources, they frequently suffer the anguish of knowing that no matter how hard they work, their efforts will fall short of the mark. This is a frustration with which the social worker must learn to live.

Because many clients are economically poor, few are in a position to directly pay for services. For this reason, most social workers are employed by governmental or nonprofit agencies; relatively few are in private practice. This means that most workers find themselves in resource-poor organizations—ones

131

with few "perks" for employees and limited opportunities for continuing education and in-service training.

Becoming a knowledgeable and skillful social worker who is deeply committed to social work values is a life-long endeavor, requiring a great deal of effort. This chapter provides the student and the new worker with guidance aimed at helping them develop their skills, cope with work-related frustrations, and truly appreciate the nobility of the social work profession. Specifically, this chapter offers guidance on using supervision, making a presentation, writing an article, building a library, coping with bureaucracy, coping with job-related stress, developing self-awareness, making ethical decisions, avoiding malpractice suits, and dealing with sexual harassment.

Selected Bibliography

Frey, Louise, and Golda Edinburg. "Professional Growth Through Continuing Education." *Handbook of Clinical Social Work,* edited by Aaron Rosenblatt and Diana Waldfogel. San Francisco: Jossey-Bass, 1983.

Hopps, June, Gary Pinderhughes, and Elaine Pinderhughes. "Profession of Social Work: Contemporary Characteristics." *Encyclopedia of Social Work,* Vol. 2, 18th ed., edited by Ann Minahan, pp. 351–66. Silver Spring, Md.: National Association of Social Workers, 1987.

Lauffer, Armand. *Working in Social Work.* Newbury Park, Calif.: Sage, 1987.

8.1	*Using Agency Supervision*

Purpose: To obtain knowledge and learn skills through guidance provided by the agency supervisor.

Discussion: In order for a social worker to learn job-related tasks and procedures and develop as a skilled professional, he or she must make appropriate and effective use of supervision. The term *supervision* is rooted in a Latin word that means "to look over." Modern supervisory practice places less emphasize on a supervisor as an overseer or inspector and more emphasis on a supervisor as a skilled master of work to be done, a leader, and a teacher.

An agency, its workers, supervisors, and administrators, exist for the purpose of providing quality service to clients. All other functions and activities must be viewed as the means of accomplishing that end. The supervisor serves the clients through the work of line workers or supervisees. Above all else, a supervisor must be accountable to clients. The quality of service provided to a client is the ultimate test of a supervisor's performance. Kadushin (1985) explains that "the ultimate objective of supervision is to offer the agency's service to the client in the most efficient and effective manner possible. It is toward that aim that the supervisor administratively integrates and coordinates the supervisee's work with others in the agency, educates the workers to a more skillful performance in their tasks, and supports and sustains the workers in motivated performance of these tasks" (pp. 21–22).

There are three major functions or components of supervisory practice: (1) the administrative function, (2) the supportive function, and (3) the educational function. In describing the *administrative component,* Kadushin (1985) states that "the supervisor is a link in the chain of administration—the administrator who is in direct contact with the worker. As an administrator, the supervisor has responsibility for agency management, and specific, clearly defined, administrative-managerial functions are assigned to her" (p. 48). A supervisor must attend to the management and administrative functions of directing, coordinating, and evaluating the performance of workers.

Austin (1981) explains that *supportive supervision* involves activities such as "sustaining worker morale, facilitating personal growth and increasing sense of worth, promoting a sense of belonging related to the mission of the agency and developing a sense of security in job performance" (p. 11). Supportive supervision is extremely important in the human services, where high stress and worker burnout are serious personnel problems.

Kadushin (1985) states that the *educational component* of supervision "is concerned with teaching the worker what he needs to know in order to do his job and helping him to learn it. Every job description of the supervisor's position includes a listing of this function: 'instruct workers in acceptable social work techniques;' 'develop competence through individual and group conferences;' 'train and instruct staff in job performance' " (p. 139). In essence, the educational component relates to the transmission of knowledge, skills, attitudes, and values needed by the workers.

Several guidelines can help the social worker make appropriate and effective use of supervision.

1. Realize that your supervisor will expect you to
   - Be effective and get results consistent with the agency's mission, program, goals, and your job description.
   - Follow agency policy, procedure, and specific instruction.
   - Consult with your supervisor when you are unsure about how to proceed or when a course of action is raising unforseen issues or encountering unexpected problems.
   - Immediately inform your supervisor when you become aware of an ethical, legal, or procedural violation that could give rise to a formal complaint or in some way harm the agency or its clients.
   - Demonstrate an eagerness to learn the details of your job, to become more efficient and effective, and to accept constructive criticism and suggestions on how you could improve the quality of your work.
   - Take initiative and assume responsibility for work that needs to be done.
   - Work cooperatively with and be respectful of colleagues and engage in behaviors that improve staff morale.

- Maintain accurate and up-to-date records of your work with clients.

2. Expect your supervisors to:
- Provide needed on-the-job training.
- Keep you informed of changes in agency policy or procedure and any changes in your responsibilities.
- Explain the reasons behind agency policy and procedure.
- Provide encouragement and support when your work is particularly difficult.
- Evaluate your performance on a regular basis and offer specific suggestions on how it can be improved.
- Give you a clear warning when your performance falls below standards.

3. The social work student has a special set of responsibilities to himself or herself, the school, the practicum agency, and agency clients. Judah (1982) provides a list of these basic responsibilities.

Responsibilities to self:
- to identify learning needs and objectives;
- to be ethical in all activities;
- to fulfill as fully as possible all legitimate expectations of the learner in the field and to go beyond them as feasible;
- to apply self fully to learning and services—including realistic allotment of time to outside demands;
- willingness to recognize the needs of others in the field instruction partnership system and commitment to be helpful, if possible.

Responsibilities to school:
- to maintain open, honest, and sharing communication for achievement of system goals and maintenance goals, which includes problem solving in the field instruction partnership system;
- to complete all expected reports fully and on time;
- to provide feedback from agency in the form of case illustrations for classes and sharing of knowledge gained in the field; to question and comment on the usefulness of concepts and methods taught in class;
- to fulfill all educational requirements including spending the full time expected in the field as usefully as possible;
- to work diligently to solve problems arising out of inadequacies or misunderstanding in the field instruction system, including evaluation of the system and its functioning in relation to its goals;
- to work to improve ways in which the school functions with respect to field instruction through channels provided, such as committees, suggestions for improvements, and sharing in general;
- to responsibly budget time to allow for adequate attention to both class and field and other student responsibilities.

Responsibilities to field setting:
- to fully cooperate with field instructor and other partners in obligations of learning and reporting responsibilities including dictation, agendas for conference, identification of goals, problems, needs, and so on;

- to carry out service and other field activities in compliance with agency policy and practices;
- to help field instructor keep an *educational* focus, if this help is needed;
- to question and evaluate agency policies and practices and work responsibly for their improvement;
- to furnish all reports and other work required on time and fully, to devote the full amount of time expected in the field, and to be flexible when asked to change the specific hours worked for good reasons;
- to discover how one's own learning experiences may simultaneously promote one's growth as a professional and augment the agency's capacity to function;
- to enhance agency efforts, when possible, through extra service to clients, developments of new resources, public relations contacts, feedback, sharing new learning, and so on.

Responsibilities to clients:
- to practice social work in a disciplined manner and at the highest level of competence possible in view of time and skill limitations;
- to work to maintain and improve social work service, of one's own and others;
- to offer service promptly, courteously, and without prejudice, and in other ways to put the client's interests first, before one's own convenience;
- to respect the privacy of clients but also their right to opportunity to make use of service (outreach);
- to never exploit clients in one's own interest and to share with appropriate persons the instances in which the agency and school policies or requirements collide with a client's needs. (pp. 156–57)

4. What you get out of a job or learning experience reflects what you put into it. Most often, a satisfying work situation or a good learning experience happens because you make it happen.

Selected Bibliography

Austin, Michael. *Supervisory Management for the Human Services.* Englewood Cliffs, N.J.: Prentice-Hall, 1981.

Judah, Eleanor. "Responsibility of the Students in Field Instruction." In *Quality Field Instruction in Social Work,* edited by Bradford W. Sheafor and Lowell E. Jenkins. New York: Longman, 1982.

Kadushin, Alfred. *Supervision in Social Work.* 2nd ed. New York: Columbia University Press, 1985.

Middleman, Ruth R., and Gary B. Rhodes. *Competent Supervision: Making Imaginative Judgments.* Englewood Cliffs, N.J.: Prentice-Hall, 1985.

Munson, Carlton. *An Introduction to Clinical Social Work Supervision.* New York: Haworth, 1983.

Pecora, Peter, and Michael Austin. *Managing Human Services Personnel.* Newbury Park, Calif.: Sage, 1987.

Purpose: To organize and plan a speech or other oral presentation.

Discussion: Social workers make numerous presentations to the public and colleagues. It is important that we make every effort to inform the public about human needs, social services, and social work practice. For example, a single speech to a group of community or political leaders or key decision makers can have a powerful effect on the lives of clients if the speech moves the group to take some needed action. As a professional, the social worker is obligated to help move the profession ahead by sharing ideas and reports of practice successes and failures at professional conferences.

Preparation is the key to reducing whatever anxiety you may have about making a presentation. Broadly speaking, all presentations have three major components:

- *Preview.* Tell the audience what you will be talking about and how you will be approaching your topic.
- *Body of speech.* Present your information and develop your arguments.
- *Summary.* Review your major points and draw conclusions.

Many of the presentations made by a social worker are efforts to move an audience to take some specific action. Such a speech might include the following elements:

1. Opening remarks—identify yourself, if necessary, and describe the purpose and content of your presentation.
2. Identify the problem or issue.
3. Prove the existence of the problem with facts, figures, or case examples.
4. Describe the consequences of the problem to the people involved, the community, and the public at large.
5. Show how these consequences affect the audience and why they should also be concerned.
6. Pose the central question: Is there a solution?
7. Describe the solution to the problem and explain why this would be the most effective solution.
8. Explain why the audience should support the proposed solution.
9. Explain specifically what the audience can do to help.
10. Briefly summarize your key points, and thank the audience for their attention.

In order to enhance the quality of presentations at professional meetings, conference organizers often issue a "***call for papers***" and select only the best of those proposed. Individuals wanting to make a presentation at the conference are required to submit an abstract of their proposed presentation months in advance of the conference. All proposals are then reviewed by a committee, and those meeting certain criteria are selected for presentation. Fairly typical criteria are the following:

- Clearly identify the issue, problem, or concern to be presented.
- Make explicit the relevance and connection between the topic and the conference goals and objectives.
- Report only on completed studies or projects and include information on sample size, methodology, and findings.
- Specifically list the implications and/or recommendations that flow from the presentation and their relevance to practice.
- Reflect an awareness of other work done on the topic, citing relevant literature.
- Relate to the conference theme.

The following guidelines can be helpful in planning and making an oral presentation:

1. Be clear in your purpose. Why are you making the presentation? Is it to inform, to persuade (i.e., to win the listener over to your point of view), or to move the audience to some immediate action? Build your presentation—its content and style—around your purpose.

2. Carefully analyze your audience. Who will be in attendance? How large is the group? What do they already know about your topic? What do they want or need to know? What are their prevailing values and attitudes? Will they be receptive or resistant to your message? What kinds of information and arguments would they find most understandable and persuasive? What must you avoid doing to keep from offending the audience? Anticipate questions you may be asked and be prepared to answer them.

3. Consider the time of day and the length of the overall program when planning your presentation. How much time is available? Will the audience be alert or tired? How will your presentation fit in with what other speakers on the program will be discussing?

4. Plan to be as brief as possible. Details are best spelled out in the discussion that follows your presentation. Audiences want solid content, but the mind can only absorb what the seat can endure!

5. The best speakers are those who are enthusiastic about their topic. Enthusiasm will compensate for errors in organization, but no amount of planning can compensate for a speaker's lack of interest in his or her topic.

6. It is usually best to use 5×7 notecards. The cards should be numbered sequentially and contain legible large print. When making a presentation on a complex or technical topic, it may be necessary to read from a manuscript but this should be avoided or kept to a minimum. Once you have prepared your notes, practice your presentation and time it. People usually underestimate the amount of time they need to complete a speech.

7. Whenever possible, use visual cues that will help the audience follow the organization of your presentation. A handout that outlines the key points is often helpful. Another useful device is to put together key words (acronyms) that spell something. Visual aids presented through use of an overhead projector, charts and graphs, or a chalkboard help the audience track your presentation. If you are presenting statistical or numerical data, it is essential that you use visual aids or handouts.

8. Use a direct style of speech and vocabulary that your audience can understand. Avoid slang and jargon. If you must use technical terms, be sure to define them. Do not use initials (e.g., AFDC, IV-E, ICWA, etc.) unless you are sure your audience understands them.

9. Make sure you can correctly pronounce names of people, places, and other words you will be using. Write difficult-to-pronounce names phonetically on your notecards.

10. Examine your habits of speech for annoying words and phrases like "you know," "uh," and so on. By becoming more aware of their usage, you can begin to break these habits.

11. When it is time for your presentation, do not rush into your speech. After reaching the rostrum, take a few seconds to compose yourself and organize your notes. A few deep breaths may help you relax.

12. Begin your presentation by establishing a relationship with your audience. Establish rapport and be friendly and considerate. Never assume the audience understands why you are making a presentation. Clearly explain who you are and why you are speaking.

13. Present an aura of confidence by being well prepared and organized. Know what you want to say and how you want to say it. It is insulting to an audience to expect them to endure an unplanned and disorganized presentation. Never begin with something like, "Please excuse my lack of organization, but I have been so busy that ..." or "I'm not sure why I was asked to speak, but here goes." Such statements tell the audience to disregard what you are saying.

14. Don't overlook the importance of grooming and dress in the formation of a good first impression. Inappropriate clothing worn by a speaker can quickly evoke negative feelings or distract the audience.

15. Be sure to speak loud enough to be heard by all in the room, especially older persons who may have a hearing problem. Use a microphone when it is available; make sure that it is properly adjusted and that you remain close to it during your presentation.

Selected Bibliography

Prochnow, Herbert, and Herbert Prochnow, Jr. *The Speaker's Treasure Chest.* 4th ed. New York: Harper and Row, 1986.

Quick, John. *A Short Book on the Subject of Speaking.* New York: Washington Square Press, 1978.

Wohlmuth, Ed. *The Overnight Guide to Public Speaking.* Philadelphia: Running Press, 1983.

8.3	*Writing a Journal Article*

Purpose: To share one's knowledge with colleagues in order to strengthen the quality and effectiveness of social work practice.

Discussion: When a social worker develops or discovers something new, he or she is obligated to share that knowledge. The *Code of Ethics* is clear about this expectation: "The social worker should contribute to the knowledge base of social work and share research knowledge and practice wisdom with colleagues" (NASW 1980, Sec. 5.0.3). One method of sharing knowledge is through the publication of articles in professional journals. To prepare a publishable article, the writer should follow several distinct steps.

1. *Have a clear message.* Although you may have entirely new material based on an original idea or research data you have collected, most articles are based on updating or expanding existing information, the synthesis or combination of available knowledge, making a unique application of knowledge to practice activities, or simply expressing something already known in a form that makes it more accessible to the reader.

Since articles are limited in scope and length, the topic you intend to develop cannot be too complex. A good test of scope is to see whether you can state the primary ideas you want to communicate in one clear paragraph. If you cannot be this succinct, your topic is probably too broad. If your topic is highly complex, it may need to be broken into subparts and presented in more than one article.

Perhaps the most important single factor that can help you through the task of preparing an article is developing the right attitude. Believe that what you have to say can make a difference in the quality of practice of other social workers.

2. *Select an appropriate journal.* A few social work journals publish articles on a wide range of topics, but most specialize. A NASW guide to authors (Mendelsohn 1987) contains information about publishing requirements for 100 different journals. The following are some of the journals in which social workers publish. Please note that the placement of a particular journal under these headings is, in some cases, somewhat arbitrary.

General Subjects
Journal of Multicultural Social Work
Journal of Sociology & Social Welfare
New England Journal of Human Services

Social Service Review
Social Thought
Social Work

Fields of Practice
AFFILA-Journal of Women and Social Workers
Child and Adolescent Social Work Journal
Child and Youth Services
Child Welfare
Health and Social Work
Human Services in a Rural Environment
Journal of Gerontological Social Work
Journal of Social Work and Human Sexuality
Law and Social Work Quarterly
Public Welfare
Residential Treatment for Children and Youth
School Social Work Quarterly
Social Work in Education
Social Work in Health Care
Women in Social Work

International and Foreign
British Journal of Social Work
Canadian Journal of Social Work Education
Canadian Welfare
Indian Journal of Social Work
International Child Welfare
International Social Work
Journal of International and Comparative Social Welfare
Social Work Today
Social Worker-Travailleur Social

Methods of Practice
Administration in Social Work
Clinical Social Work Journal
Clinical Supervisor
Families and Society (formerly *Social Casework*)
Journal of Independent Social Work
Journal of Social Work Supervision
Journal for Specialists in Groupwork
Social Work with Groups

Research
Computers in Human Services
Journal of Social Service Research
Research in Social Work Practice
Social Work Research and Abstracts

Social Work Education and Journals Published by Schools of Social Work

Arete (University of South Carolina)
Iowa Journal of Social Work (University of Iowa)
Journal of Applied Social Sciences (Case Western Reserve)
Journal of Continuing Social Work Education
Journal of Social Service Research (Washington University, St. Louis)
Journal of Social Work Education
Journal of Teaching in Social Work
Smith College Studies in Social Work (Smith College)
Social Development Issues (University of Iowa)
Social Group Work Practice (University of Connecticut)
Tulane Studies in Social Welfare (Tulane University)

Each of the journals will periodically include a statement of its publishing requirements and provide information on preferred topics, length, style, and procedures for submitting articles. Increasingly, journals are requiring the use of the APA style (American Psychological Association 1983). Typically, the maximum length will be twelve to fifteen double-spaced pages.

3. *Picture your audience.* It is helpful to write to an individual, rather than an unknown audience. Select someone you know would be likely to read the article, and write to that person. Think about language that would communicate your ideas clearly to him or her, and use concepts with which you would expect that person to be familiar.

4. *Prepare an abstract.* Most journals require a seventy-five to one hundred word abstract to accompany the article. While it is often easier to write an abstract after the article is completed, preparing a first draft before writing the article can help you focus your attention on the most important points you want to address. The abstract should be clear, concise, and factual.

5. *Develop an outline.* How well your readers will be able to consume what you have to say is influenced by the organization of your article. Think through the logical connections between elements you want to include. Preparing an outline will help you achieve smooth and understandable transitions between the various parts of the article.

6. *Write the introduction.* The opening two or three paragraphs should tell what your article is about, explain why it is important, and suggest which social workers might be especially interested in this material. A good introduction also maintains the reader's attention and stimulates him or her to read the substantive material. Tying the subject to a current issue or including a short case related to the topic will help the reader see the benefit in reading the entire article.

For many writers, getting started is the most difficult part of writing. Don't let this initial frustration over the introduction stop you from writing completely. Some writers find it helpful to write a rough introduction with the intent of completely rewriting it later.

---

7. *Set the context or background.* While this is not necessary for every article, it is frequently important to let your reader know where this material fits into the scheme of social work. A short discussion of the context in which the material fits (e.g., practice theory, practice techniques, social welfare policy issues, social work education) helps the reader make the connection.

The reader also needs to know the context in which your material is placed. A literature review or even clarification of its relationship to a particular concept or school of thought helps provide this background information. Because of the relative brevity of articles, this contextual material cannot be extensive.

8. *The body of your article.* Concisely report the facts and observations you have to share. Back up your statements with alternative means of presenting the material (e.g., charts, figures, tables, and lists). If you use case examples, be sure that they are presented in a way that helps the reader generalize from that example to other case situations. Make the outline of your content clear to your readers through the frequent use of headings and subheadings. They make it possible for the reader to follow the flow of ideas or information. Articles are most readable when they contain short paragraphs with clearly focused content. Avoid gender-specific language and any terms that might reflect bias or stereotyping based on race, ethnicity, gender, age, handicapping conditions, or sexual preference.

Write clearly and simply. Avoid using professional jargon. Remember that as a writer, you should be committed to your *ideas* but not necessarily your *words*. Do not hesitate to rewrite them once they are on paper. They should always be subject to revision in order to make them more understandable to others. A NASW publication, *Some Principles of Good Writing* (1980), offers helpful advice for persons who wish to strengthen their written communication skills. (Also see Technique 7.2.)

9. *Prepare a summary and/or conclusion.* End your article with a short statement that draws together the key points you have addressed and presents the conclusions that you believe can be drawn from this material. If relevant to your topic, you may also point to additional research that is required to further develop the subject.

10. *Collect and format references.* Using the format appropriate for the journal you have selected, list the references that support the material you have presented. Endnotes or some type of reference list are most often used.

11. *Choose a good title.* The title you select will be the first clue the reader will have about your topic, so be sure that it clearly identifies your subject. A creative title can help to attract interest.

12. *Let it cool.* Avoid sending off your article as soon as it comes out of your typewriter or word processor. A week or two away from the material provides a fresh perspective and may yield alternative ideas for presenting your material or strengthening the way you express your ideas. It may also be helpful to use this time to get colleagues to review the work and offer comments. The person you selected to "write to" (item 3) is one obvious choice. Remember, however, that it is your article, and you must own the final result. When asking for comment, be clear that, while you want advice, you cannot be obligated to incorporate all suggestions offered. At the same time, this "cooling" period should not become an excuse for procrastination and excessive self-criticism. You may never be completely satisfied with your writing, but you simply must stop refining it at some point.

13. *Mail your manuscript and wait.* Send the required number of manuscript copies to the journal you have selected. Typically, the publisher will acknowledge receipt of the manuscript and send it to two or three reviewers to evaluate for possible publication. This part of the process may take several months.

The reviewers will usually be asked to give comments on the strengths and limitations of the article and how it meets the focus of that journal. They will conclude with a recommendation to reject, accept if revised in specific ways, or accept. Some journals will provide you with the reviewers' comments if the article is rejected. If that occurs, seriously consider those comments and either revise your article and sent it to another journal or drop your plan to publish this material.

If your article is accepted, you will work with professional editors who will offer suggestions for strengthening your presentation. You will have the opportunity to be sure that their editing does not misrepresent your content. This is normally done during a production period prior to publication. Depending on the backlog of the journal, it may take as much a year for the article to appear in print. When it is printed, most journals will provide you with several copies of the issue in which your article appears or offer reprints of the article.

When a journal publishes your material, you will most likely be required to assign the legal rights to this material to the publisher. It will then be necessary for the publisher to approve any subsequent reprinting or extensive quoting of the article in other books or articles, including your own.

Selected Bibliography

American Psychological Association. *Publication Manual of the American Psychological Association.* 3rd ed. Washington, D.C.: APA, 1983.

Mendelsohn, Henry N. *Author's Guide to Social Work Journals.* 2nd ed. Silver Spring, Md.: National Association of Social Workers, 1987.

National Association of Social Workers. *Code of Ethics,* Policy Statement 1. Silver Spring, Md.: NASW, 1980.

————. *Some Principles of Good Writing/The Library Search.* Silver Spring, Md.: NASW, 1980.

Turabian, Kate L. *A Manual for Writers of Term Papers, Theses, and Dissertations.* 5th ed. Chicago: University of Chicago Press, 1987.

8.4 *Building a Professional Library*

Purpose: To create a library of journals, books, and other materials needed to remain current with one's field of practice.

Discussion: In order to remain current on developments in his or her field of practice, the social worker must attend relevant conferences and workshops and read professional books and journals. In addition, intellectual stimulation can be an antidote for job burnout.

Books and journals are the least expensive means of obtaining new ideas but are usually not as personally satisfying as a good workshop. Every social worker should have easy access to at least two or three journals. One of these should be *Social Work* because it provides a selection of articles drawn from many fields of practice and frequently addresses professional and social policy issues of concern to all workers, regardless of practice setting. A subscription to *Social Work* and the monthly *NASW News* are two of the many benefits that come with membership in the National Association of Social Workers (NASW). (For information, write: NASW, 7981 Eastern Avenue, Silver Spring, MD 20910.)

If the social worker cannot afford the cost of more than one journal, he or she should consider a sharing arrangement with others. If each worker in a small group of social workers agreed to subscribe to a different journal and then exchange them within the group, the cost of having access to several journals would be sharply reduced. A similar book exchange will give the worker access to many more expensive hardbacks than he or she could afford to buy individually. For example, if four workers each agreed to purchase and share three professional books per year, the workers in the group would have access to a total of twelve per year.

Most social service agencies have some library resources. However, most of these libraries are small. A number of things can be done to build an agency library at a minimum of cost.

1. Request money for books and journals from those who control funds. A surprising number of agency supervisors and administrators never request library funds, which conveys a message that professional literature is not needed or wanted. Unfortunately, it also gives an impression that the staff does not care about learning better ways of providing service. If no one requests library funds, they most certainly will not be received. If requested, the needed funds may be secured.

2. A number of inexpensive social work-related publications can be obtained from the U.S. Government Printing Office. The GPO issues publication catalogs on a variety of topics, such as children and youth, social welfare and services, alcoholism, juvenile delinquency, rehabilitation, mental health, and minorities. (For catalogs, write: Superintendent of Documents, U.S. Government Printing Office, Washington, D.C. 20402.) U.S. senators and representatives can sometimes secure government publications free of charge for an agency or individual. They can also obtain them faster than an order sent to the Government Printing Office.

3. Sometimes, a request from a social agency to a local service club or concerned citizen will yield money for books or a journal subscription. An annual donation of from forty to sixty dollars will usually secure a yearly subscription to a professional journal.

City libraries usually are willing to obtain books suggested by local citizens. If an agency staff wants to see particular books or journals in the local library, a staff member should go to the library, present the rationale for requesting the publications, and provide the information (cost, publisher's address, etc.) needed for ordering. In most cases, library personnel will respond to reasonable requests because many social work topics—including adoption, family counseling and therapy, foster care, child abuse and neglect, and drug and alcohol abuse—are also of interest to the reading public. Workers also should check to see if nearby college or university libraries contain books and journals useful to agency staff.

Selected Bibliography

Lauffer, Armand. *Doing Continuing Education and Staff Development.* New York: McGraw-Hill, 1978.

8.5 Coping with Bureaucracy

Purpose: To handle the demands and frustrations associated with work within a large, complex organization.

Discussion: One of the most frustrating aspects of social work is dealing with bureaucracy. Being part of a bureaucracy is unavoidable for most social workers because most social work jobs exist within large organizations. To find satisfaction in their work, social workers must understand the organizational context of their work assignments and acquire skills needed to cope with what Knopf (1979) calls the "BS" (Bureaucratic System). The following guidelines suggest ways to cope with the frustrating aspects of bureaucracy.

1. A bureaucracy is neither all bad or all good. It is always a mix of positives and negatives. It is important to learn how to exploit the positives and work around the negatives. Study your organization. If you have an understanding of its history, legal base, formal and informal structure, funding, internal dynamics, office politics, official policy and procedures, and the like you will be better able to address job-related problems and concerns. Persons who have worked in the organization for many years are often a good source of information on "how it really works."

2. The modern bureaucracy is incapable of meeting the emotional and spiritual needs of its employees. So do not expect your agency to give meaning and purpose to life. Look elsewhere for ways of meeting those needs.

3. Maintain a sense of humor and perspective about your job and your place in the bureaucracy. Work hard and be a responsible employee, but don't take yourself or your organization too seriously. Your work and your agency are important but there are many other things that are also important. Do not assume responsibility for things over which you have no control, for that will only exaggerate your frustration.

4. Identify your personal and professional strengths and seek a niche in the bureaucracy where those strengths can be utilized and you can obtain a sense of job satisfaction. Think seriously before accepting a promotion or transfer that would take you away from the type of work you really enjoy. Remember that job satisfaction stems primarily from a feeling that you are capable of doing the job and do it well.

5. Although a bureaucracy can be changed, the rate of change is slow. Do work for needed change, but realize that many months and even years of effort may be required. Only frustration results if your expect to see change in a short time. Select your targets of change with great care; work for those changes that are actually possible. Do not fight many battles at one time; focus your limited energy on only one or two concerns. Don't try to make changes by yourself; rather, work as part of a group. A group has more influence than an individual.

6. When working for change within your bureaucracy, select your tactics with great care. Be a diplomat rather than a foot soldier. Aggressive tactics seldom work, and when they do, the change will usually occur after you have moved to another job or have been squeezed out of the organization.

7. Maintain direct service contact with agency clients, even as you rise to a supervisory or administrative level. This provides you with a constant reminder of the agency mission and what needs to be changed to improve service to clients.

Selected Bibliography

Horejsi, John, Thomas Walz, and Patrick Connolly. *Working in Welfare: Survival Through Positive Action.* Iowa City: University of Iowa School of Social Work, 1977.

Knopf, Ron. *Surviving the B.S. (Bureaucratic System).* Wilmington, N.C.: Mandala Press, 1979.

Pruger, Robert. "The Good Bureaucrat." *Social Work* 18 (July 1973): 26–32.

Russo, J. Robert. *Serving and Surviving as a Human-Service Worker.* Monterey, Calif.: Brooks/Cole, 1980.

8.6   *Stress Management*

Purpose: To cope effectively with the stress common to social work practice.

Discussion: Social work is a demanding and stressful profession. Basically, job-related stress can have three sources. First, there is the stress that is simply a part of a particular job or work environment. Everyone placed in a high-stress job will feel stressed—it comes with the turf. Second, there is stress caused primarily by a lack of coping skills. For example, a particular job may not be highly stressful for most people but will be for the individual who is poorly prepared for the job. Essentially, this is stress caused by a mismatch between the individual and his or her job requirements. Third, some individuals create their own stress.

For example, an individual may feel excessive stress because he or she has self-expectations that are unrealistically high or perhaps takes on an inordinate number of responsibilities.

Each social worker responds differently to the demands of the profession; some thrive, while others burn out. The term **burnout** refers to a state of physical or psychological exhaustion caused by an inability to cope with stress. Fortunately, it can be prevented or effectively controlled. Burnout is not inevitable in the helping professions. It has been suggested that all the attention given to the danger of burnout may give rise to a self-fulfilling prophecy. For example, Kane (1981) fears that "we seem to be socializing neophyte social workers to expect burnout simply because they care. . . . It seems that nowadays people are burned out before they are lit" (p. 2). Nevertheless, we need to be alert to the problem of stress. A personal stress management strategy should be an essential part of every social worker's professional life. The following guidelines suggest ways to handle stress:

1. The key to preventing negative stress reactions is to find your "place" or niche in the world of work. There must be a proper fit or match between you and the demands of your environment. Selye (1974) explains, "The best way to avoid harmful stress is to select an environment which is in line with your innate preferences, to find an activity which you like and respect" (p. 82). He further warns, "One of the major sources of distress arises from dissatisfaction with life, namely from disrespect for our accomplishments" (p. 75). This is, of course, why one worker thrives in a so-called high-stress job while another burns out.

2. Make an honest attempt to identify and recognize stress in your own life. This may be difficult because most people do not want to admit that stress is having a harmful effect. Listen to those who care about you for clues that you may be under more stress than you think. For example: "You're so crabby when you get home," "You're not as much fun as you used to be," "You never go anywhere with us anymore," and "You've looked so tired lately."

Signs of dangerous stress levels include general irritability, the urge to run and hide or cry, and anxiety. When you become aware of high stress, take precautions to lower the stress in your life, much as you take health precautions when you feel a cold coming on.

3. Examine the fit between your work activities and your values. Are you spending your time and energy on activities you consider important? Do you feel good about the choices you make? If, for example, you value family and friends, are you making choices that enable you to really enjoy them? On the other hand, if you find that life on the job is much more exciting than your personal or family life, that, too, must be faced with honesty. From her study of workaholics, Machlowitz (1980) concludes that such individuals "find time to do what they want to do and are exhilarated—not exhausted—by work. So when they say they 'don't have time' or they're 'too tired' they really mean they 'don't want to' " (p. 74).

4. Realize the importance of your own values, perceptions, and expectations in creating stress. As a social worker, you must feel good about your chosen profession and feel that you are successful and effective in what you do. If you do not, you will experience much distress and dissatisfaction. A hundred years before stress reactions were studies in the laboratory, an unknown author wisely stated, "In order that people may be happy in their work, these three things are needed: they must be fit for it, they must not do too much of it, and they must have a sense of success in it."

5. Take time to recognize the positives in both your personal and professional life. Do not focus exclusively on the negatives or what is lacking. And don't underestimate the genuine pleasure than can come from the simple everyday things in life.

6. Develop hobbies and outside interests, engaging in activities that are very different from what you do at work. Doing something different can often be as refreshing as a rest. At times, you may need an increase in positive forms of stress in your life because boredom itself is a stressor. Look for small ways to change your routines when life begins to feel stale.

7. Exercise, good nutrition, and a proper amount of sleep build up your natural defenses against the harmful effects of excessive stress. Reduce or eliminate the use of alcohol, nicotine, caffeine, and other drugs that are known to have long-term adverse effects on your body. Also, take advantage of the medical knowledge available by having regular physical checkups and come to terms with the treatable conditions that you may have, such as hypertension, diabetes, obesity, and depression. Information about your physical condition belongs to you, so do not hesitate to ask your doctor for details. In our sophisticated but fragmented health-care system, assuming responsibility for one's own health is essential.

8. Look for opportunities to take breaks during your work day. Keep the break activity simple, but enjoyable. For example, take a walk at lunch and notice the changing seasons, read something that makes you laugh, or watch children at play.

9. Take brief physical exercise breaks while doing intense desk work. Try isometric exercises, or climb a few flights of stairs. Talk a coworker into trying a new physical activity with you so you can encourage each other. Don't get competitive or take yourself too seriously. Just do it.

10. Time management is stress management. Lakein (1973) expresses the conviction that the payoff in satisfaction is well worth the effort of developing time management skills. "You'll probably find yourself thinking more about how you really want to use your time, working less hard, doing more of the things you've always wanted to do and enjoying your life a lot more" (p. 11). (See Technique 7.1 for additional information on time management.)

11. Remember that setting priorities is the first step in taking control in life. The next step is making your time and energy fit your priorities. The feeling of not being in control is recognized as a major source of chronic stress on the job. If you are unable to gain some sense of control at work, consult with an experienced worker who seems to enjoy what he or she does. What is he or she doing that you might try? If that doesn't help, get help from persons outside your agency. Unless you start making changes, the problem will only get worse.

12. Build a support group of friends or colleagues with whom you feel comfortable and are able to share your frustrations. Find enjoyable ways to spend time together—eat out, see a movie, take a walk, or travel together.

13. Recognize that perfection is not required in most work-related tasks. Realize that you and all other people have made mistakes and will continue to make them. But the world will not come to an end if you make one more mistake. Gently help yourself recover from a setback or mistake by thinking of previous accomplishments.

14. Like a long-distance runner, set your pace in life at a rate you can maintain and enjoy without wearing down. If you overextend yourself, you may rarely have the opportunity to savor the satisfaction of a well-won success. For most people, it is better to do a few things well than to do many things poorly or unreliably. Arrange your work activity so you accomplish at least one important thing each day. Knowing you reached a goal can produce a surprising amount of satisfaction.

15. If you are having serious personal problems, seek help early from trusted friends or appropriate professionals. The more serious the problems become without relief, the more areas of your life will be negatively impacted by them.

16. Listen for thoughts or sayings that have special meaning for you, soothing or lifting your spirit. For example, from *The Desiderata*: "Nurture strength of spirit to shield you in sudden misfortune. But do not distress yourself with dark imaginings. Many fears are born of fatigue and loneliness. Beyond wholesome discipline, be gentle with yourself" (Ehrmann 1948, 10).

17. Learn simple stress management techniques and begin making needed changes. But don't try to make large changes too quickly. Attempts to change dramatically in a short time are likely to fail. Small steps in the right direction will gradually add up. Apply to yourself the techniques you use with clients. When faced with a stressful interpersonal task, use techniques of roleplaying or behavioral rehearsal to reduce anxiety and build self-confidence. (See Techniques 12.5 and 12.7.)

18. As a technique for handling your fears, try exaggerating them all out of proportion. For example, if you fear being embarrassed, visualize yourself blushing to the point of turning beet red, sweating buckets, and shaking so hard your watch vibrates off your wrist. Exaggerating your fears to the point of being ludicrous may help you laugh at yourself and put your fear into perspective.

19. Use your professional problem-solving techniques on the stressors that are common to most work settings: poor physical working conditions, deadlines, heavy workloads and demands, interruptions, and interpersonal problems with coworkers and supervisors. These problems are real; as such, they require careful analysis in order to be modified. They will not go away without intervention. Do something about them!

Selected Bibliography

Edelwich, Jerry, and Archie Brodsky. *Burn-Out.* New York: Human Services Press, 1980.

Ehrmann, Max. *The Desiderata of Happiness.* Boulder, Colo.: Blue Mountain Press, 1948.

Kane, Rosalie. "Burnout May Be a Copout." *Health and Social Work* 6 (November 1981): 2–3.

Lakein, Alan. *How to Get Control of Your Time and Your Life.* New York: New American Library, 1973.

Machlowitz, Marilyn. *Workaholics.* New York: New American Library, 1980.

Muldary, Thomas. *Burnout and Health Professionals: Manifestations and Management.* Norwalk, Conn.: Appleton-Century-Crofts, 1983.

Selye, Hans. *Stress Without Distress.* New York: New American Library, 1974.

8.7	*Making Ethical Decisions*

Purpose: To think through and make decisions that are consistent with the principles of professional ethics.

Discussion: Many of the day-to-day decisions made by social workers involve ethical judgments and dilemmas. Basically, an ethical dilemma is a conflict between competing obligations. Few of the ethical problems faced by the worker lend themselves to simple answers. This book offers some very general guidance; we urge the worker to study social work ethics and frequently consult with peers and supervisors about ethical questions.

The NASW *Code of Ethics,* presented in Appendix 8.1, is an articulation of the basic value-based obligations of a professional social worker but such a document cannot resolve the dilemma that occurs when, in a specific case, two or more of the obligations are in conflict. Many ethical dilemmas involve unavoidable harm (i.e., every option will cause someone harm or distress). Increasingly, the ethical dilemmas faced by the social worker involve decisions on how best to allocate scarce resources in times of budget cutbacks and staff shortages. In all such cases, the decision to provide services to one client or client group results in withholding or limiting services available to others. Needless to say, these are very difficult decisions.

As a means of helping workers resolve ethical dilemmas, Loewenberg and Dolgoff (1988) provide a ranking of ethical principles and obligations; Obligation 1 has priority over Obligation 2, Obligation 2 has priority over Obligation 3, and so on:

> *Obligation 1*: A social worker should make professional decisions that guarantee the basic survival needs of individuals and/or of society. The protection of human life (whether the life of a client or of someone else) takes precedence over every other obligation. The means for protecting human life might include health services, food, shelter, income, and so on as appropriate in each situation.

> *Obligation 2*: A social worker should make practice decisions that foster a person's autonomy, independence, and freedom. Freedom, though highly important, does not override the right to life or survival of the person himself or of anyone else. A person does not have the right to decide to harm himself or herself or anyone else

on the grounds that the right to make such a decision is her or his autonomous right. When a person is about to make such a decision, the social worker is obligated to intervene, since Obligation 1 takes precedence.

Obligation 3: A social worker should make practice decisions that foster equality of opportunity and equality of access for all people.

Obligation 4: A social worker should make practice decisions that promote a better quality of life for all people.

Obligation 5: A social worker should make practice decisions that strengthen every person's right to privacy. Keeping confidential information inviolate is a direct derivative of this obligation.

Obligation 6: A social worker should make practice decisions that permit her (or him) to speak the truth and to fully disclose all relevant information.

Obligation 7: A social worker should make practice decisions that are in accord with the rules and regulations which she (or he) has voluntarily accepted.*

A first step toward resolving a dilemma is to examine it carefully. Questions based on those suggested by Loewenberg and Dolgoff (1988) and Pine (1987) can help the social worker analyze an ethical dilemma:

What ethical principles and obligations apply in this situation? Which ones are in conflict and why?

What additional information is needed to more fully understand this dilemma?

What aspects of the worker's or agency's intervention give rise to the dilemma (e.g., legal obligation, agency policy, questions of efficient use of limited resources, possible harm caused by intervention, etc.)?

What are the social worker's prima facie obligations in the case (e.g., legal mandates, job requirements, etc.)?

Who can or should resolve this dilemma? Is it rightfully a decision to be made by the client, by other family members, the worker, the agency administrator, or who? Should this responsibility be shifted to someone else?

Who stands to gain and who stands to lose as a result of making each possible decision? Are those who stand to gain or lose of equal or of unequal power (e.g., child vs. parent)? Do those with little power require special consideration or an advocate?

For each decision possible, what are the short-term and long-term consequences for the client, family, worker, agency, community, and so on?

When harm to someone cannot be avoided, what decision will cause the least harm or a type of harm with fewest long-term consequences? Who of those that might be harmed are least able to recover from the harm?

Will a particular resolution to this dilemma set an undesirable precedent for future decision making?

*Reproduced by permission of the publisher, F. E. Peacock Publishers, Inc., Itasca, Illinois. From F. Loewenberg and R. Dolgoff, *Ethical Decisions for Social Work Practice,* 3rd ed. 1988 copyright, pp. 122 and 123.

A growing number of agencies are forming an ethics committee to which the practitioner may bring ethical questions for discussion and consultation. Such committees usually undertake the ongoing study of ethics and guide the formulation of agency policy. They may also develop a ranking of specific ethical obligations pertinent to their services and clientele.

Selected Bibliography

Cory, Gerald, Marianne Cory, and Patrick Callanan. *Issues and Ethics in the Helping Professions.* 3rd ed. Pacific Grove, Calif.: Brooks/Cole, 1988.

Loewenberg, Frank, and Ralph Dolgoff. *Ethical Decisions for Social Work Practice.* 3rd ed. Itasca, Ill.: F. E. Peacock, 1988.

National Association of Social Workers. *Code of Ethics.* Silver Spring, Md.: NASW, 1980.

Pine, Barbara. "Strategies for More Ethical Decision Making in Child Welfare." *Child Welfare* 65, no. 4 (July–August 1987): 315–26.

Reamer, Fredrick. "Ethics Committees in Social Work." *Social Work* (May–June 1987): 188–92.

Wells, Carolyn, and M. Kathleeen Masch. *Social Work Ethics Day to Day: Guidelines for Professional Practice.* New York: Longman, 1986.

8.8 *Avoiding Malpractice Suits*

Purpose: To minimize the possibility of being named in a lawsuit alleging negligence.

Discussion: A growing number of social workers are being sued for malpractice or professional negligence. Because professionals operate on their own judgment, the consumers of professional services have a right to expect the practitioner to be competent and to adhere to the profession's standards of good practice and its ethical code. Brieland and Lemmon (1985) explain that "a social worker becomes liable for damages if injury or harm is inflicted on a client, if the client is treated improperly, or if the social worker neglects to do something that should have been done . . . " (p. 583). Besharov (1985) believes most social workers underestimate the extent of their liability. Also, social workers must realize they can be held liable even when they only contributed to a harmful action by another professional (e.g., providing a social assessment report to a psychiatrist who then makes a poor decision).

In general, it can be said that the plaintiff in a successful malpractice suit must prove four points:

1. The defendant (the social worker) was obligated to provide the plaintiff with a particular standard of care or professional conduct.
2. The worker was derelict because he or she breached that obligation by some act of commission or omission and the act had a foreseeable consequence.

3. The client suffered some injury or harm (physical, financial, emotional, etc.).
4. The worker's conduct was a direct or proximate cause of the client's injury or harm.

Stated differently, a social worker may be found negligent if (1) he or she fails to adhere to relevant standards of care or service, (2) he or she breaches a duty owed to the client, and (3) this breach of duty is the proximate cause of harm to the client. *Duty* refers to implicit or explicit promises or a contractual arrangement to deliver certain services or treatment. Whether a "breach of duty" has occurred is determined by measuring the action or omission against the performance of other social workers in similar practice settings. The client's injury must be one that would not have occurred "but for" the social worker's negligence. Despite this traditional "proximate cause" requirement, it should be noted that juries are increasingly finding liability "without fault" (i.e., finding providers of health and social services negligent even when they are not the proximate cause of the injury). A social worker can be found personally liable. In addition, the worker's employer or agency can be found liable. Most lawsuits will name both the social worker and the agency as defendants because the agency is assumed to be responsible for its employees and is, therefore, indirectly responsible for client injury.

A numbers of allegations may form the basis for malpractice suits against social workers. For example:

- Providing the transportation that involves a client in a vehicular accident causing bodily injury
- Violating a written or verbal contract or agreement
- Violating the client's right to privacy and/or breaching confidentiality
- Libeling, slandering, or defaming the client
- Violating the client's civil rights
- Failure to report suspected abuse or neglect; failure to protect a child or adult from abuse or neglect
- Failure of a protective services worker to properly investigate alleged abuse or neglect
- Failure to properly select or monitor a foster care or other placement
- Inappropriate placement or contributing to the inappropriate placement of a child or adult into foster care, an institution, the hospital, or jail
- Inappropriate or premature release of the client from foster care, hospital, an institution, or another protective setting (or contributing to the decision to release)
- Placement of or contributing to the placement of the client into a facility or foster home in which he or she is subsequently abused or neglected (i.e., failure to properly select foster parents or supervise a placement)
- Verbal or physical assault as part of a treatment
- Sexual abuse of and/or sexual involvement with the client
- Causing or contributing to the injury of the client by another member of a therapy group or other group activity
- Failure to prevent the client's suicide or contributing to client's suicide

- Failure to warn and/or protect the victim injured by a violent client
- Failure to inform the client of eligibility rules or regulations resulting in avoidable financial costs to the client
- Failure to consult with or refer the client to a specialist
- Failure to properly assess or diagnose the client's condition
- Practicing medicine without a license (e.g., suggesting changes in the client's use of prescribed medications)
- Misrepresenting one's professional training and qualifications
- Using a radical or untested approach, technique, or procedure
- Providing inaccurate information or advice to the client
- Providing birth control information or abortion counseling to a minor without consent of the parent
- Acting in a prejudicial manner in the selection of an adoptive home or in the licensing of a foster home, daycare facility, or the like
- Failure to be available to the client when needed (e.g., failure to provide professional coverage during the worker's vacation)
- Inappropriate or premature termination of treatment
- Causing conflict or alienation between a parent and child or a husband or wife
- Failure to properly supervise a child or handicapped person while the client is participating in an agency program
- Failure to supervise the work of others, including the work of volunteers, students, and consultants

It should be noted that a 1989 U.S. Supreme Court decision (*Joshua DeShaney* v. *Winnebago County Department of Social Services*) reduced the likelihood that child protection workers will be held liable for failure to protect a child from injuries inflicted by parents, so long as the child is not in the agency's custody.

Of course, there is a big difference between being named in a lawsuit alleging negligence and actually being found negligent by a jury. However, even if the suit is eventually dropped or dismissed, the worker and/or the agency will have incurred legal expenses during their defense. Besharov (1985) gives three pieces of advice to social workers who learn that they have been named in a negligence suit: (1) immediately make all appropriate notifications (i.e., notify agency superiors, insurance company, etc.); (2) do not alter case records or other documents (the "doctoring" of records can be easily detected, it will be used against you, and it may constitute a crime); and (3) get an attorney (find out if the agency will provide legal representation; if not, immediately get your own attorney and do not speak to anyone about the suit until you have legal counsel).

Legal experts explain that the key to avoiding a malpractice suit is adherence to reasonable, ordinary, and prudent practices. In order to defend against a negligence suit, the worker must show that his or her actions were fair, in good faith, and consistent with how other properly trained professionals would behave under similar circumstances. One of the best defenses is to be able to show that the client gave informed consent to the professional's intervention. This clearly demonstrates the need to document client involvement in all phases of problem identification and selection, assessment, case planning, and intervention. A number of additional guidelines will help the social worker avoid a malpractice suit or at least minimize damage.

1. Because of the growing number of social work malpractice suits, the social worker should consider malpractice insurance. (It can be purchased through the National Association of Social Workers by NASW members or directly from a number of insurance companies.)

2. Follow the *Code of Ethics* developed by the National Association of Social Workers. Also, adhere to your agency's policies and procedures, as well as state and federal laws and regulations affecting your agency's program.

3. Secure the training, education, and supervision needed to responsibly perform your job-related tasks and activities. Develop self-awareness and realize your personal and professional limitations. Obtain consultation immediately when you feel you are having unusual difficulties in your work with a client. Consult with your peers, supervisor, and/or attorney when faced with difficult ethical or legal issues.

4. Base your practice on a well-established practice theory or model. Keep your client fully informed of your goals, techniques and procedures, and any risks associated with the intervention. Maintain records that document your intervention and especially any circumstance that might have an adverse impact on the client. Be careful not to give your client a false sense of hope about what you will be able to do. Convey a realistic picture of what you and your agency's services can accomplish.

5. Inform clients of any circumstances that may affect confidentiality or any matter that may negatively affect the client or the client-worker relationship. Remember that confidentiality must be broken in order to report suspected child abuse or neglect, to warn others of your client's intention to physically harm them, and to alert others of your client's intention to commit suicide.

6. Follow-up on client complaints. Reach out to the client who has been angered by your actions and attempt to rebuild the relationship. If you work for a fee-charging agency, make sure that financial arrangements are handled in a completely open and businesslike manner.

7. Be completely professional in male-female relationships. A third party (potential witness) should be within earshot whenever a male worker interviews a female adult or child. Male workers in particular should be cautious about visiting a female client at her home.

8. Adhere to agency policy whenever a client presents you with a gift. As a general rule, inexpensive gifts valued at not more than a few dollars and food can be accepted, but a more expensive gift should not be accepted before consulting with your supervisor.

9. Be very cautious about giving any advice that could have a significant impact on the client's life (e.g., advising a client to get a divorce, how to invest money, etc.).

10. Before accepting a job with an agency, check into the agency's record of supporting and providing legal defense for employees who are named in a lawsuit.

11. Never agree to a tape-recorded interview with an attorney or other investigator before first consulting with your own attorney. (It is a common practice for attorneys to attempt to secure statements or information before you are aware that you are the target of a lawsuit.)

Selected Bibliography

Besharov, Douglas. *The Vulnerable Social Worker.* Washington, D.C.: NASW, 1985.
————, and Susan Besharov. "Teaching About Liability." *Social Work* 32, no. 6 (November 1987): 517–22.
Brieland, Donald, and John Lemmon. *Social Work and the Law.* 2nd ed. St. Paul: West, 1985.
Woody, R. H. *The Law and the Practice of Human Services.* San Francisco: Jossey-Bass, 1984.

8.9 Developing Self-Awareness

Purpose: To examine one's attitudes, personal habits, and interactional patterns to identify those that may obstruct work with clients.

Discussion: The social worker uses himself or herself as a tool or an instrument in the helping process. Just as a physician must be attentive to the quality and condition of medical instruments, the social worker must constantly examine the self to identify potential barriers to his or her effectiveness. Professional social workers have always emphasized the need to develop their self-awareness and self-knowledge. Siporin (1975) explains that worker self-awareness refers to "an accurate perception of one's own actions and feelings, and of the effects of one's behavior on others" (p. 78).

Many individuals are drawn to the helping professions (social work, nursing, medicine, counseling, etc.) because they believe the problems they have faced in life give them a special understanding or sensitivity to the problems of others. For example, many have grown up in alcoholic or otherwise dysfunctional families. Indeed, life's problems can be a powerful teacher and provide a degree of empathy that others do not have. However, this will be the case only to the degree that one has honestly examined those experiences and successfully worked through the residual feelings associated with them. If a professional denies or suppresses the emotions connected to painful life experiences and cannot come to peace with the past, efforts to help others will be plagued by misunderstanding, self-doubts, and feelings of failure.

Growing up in a dysfunctional family typically produces an individual who has low self-worth and a fear of strong emotions. According to Wegscheider

(1981 223–25), a professional helper with these characteristics will have serious problems in their work with clients:

- Because they fear emotion, they only give advice and try to find ready-made answers rather than lead the client through their pain to find answers for themselves.
- Because they are not comfortable with certain feelings, they avoid topics that their client needs to discuss.
- Because they are preoccupied with defending their own fragile self-worth and defending against their own suppressed emotion, they cannot fully attend to the client nor hear the client's subtle messages. At the other extreme, they are unable to control their own emotions and they react inappropriately to their client's feelings.
- Because they have such a strong need to be liked by clients, they are unable to confront a client when necessary and they tell the client what he or she wants to hear and not what needs to be said.
- Because of their low self-worth, they are terribly afraid of being seen as incompetent in their work and may hide behind a facade of false professionalism and the use of endless jargon and intellectualizing in an attempt to convince others of their competence.

Wegscheider (1981) further explains that the professional's "problem is not that he has some doubts about himself, but rather that he has not brought those doubts out into the open, looked at them, felt them fully no matter how painful they might be, then stayed in touch with them vigilantly so they would not contaminate the work with his clients" (p. 225). When a social worker becomes aware of some factor that interferes with client service, he or she must be willing to correct the problem or, if change is not possible, to seek a practice setting where the factor will not have a negative impact on clients. The following list outlines some of the factors that can interfere with the formation of a professional helping relationship and client service; use it as an aid in self-examination.

1. *Personal hang-ups and emotional problems.* To a considerable degree, our beliefs and behavior have been shaped by past experience. Most people carry a certain amount of emotional "baggage" into their adult lives, including unresolved parent-child conflicts, after-effects of traumatic events, and so on. Sometimes this "baggage" is carried to the workplace, where it can have a negative impact on clients. The following could have such an effect:

- Preoccupation with personal problems, resulting in an inability to give one's full attention to the client
- Inability to control one's emotions or exercise self-discipline when in an emotionally charged situation or when under the ordinary pressure associated with direct social work practice
- Inability to demonstrate warmth, empathy, and genuine caring for clients served by the agency
- Inability or unwillingness to work cooperatively with persons in positions of authority (e.g., judges, physicians, administrators, supervisors, etc.)
- Difficulty separating personal experience (e.g., having been a victim of child abuse, growing up with alcoholic parents, etc.) from the concerns and problems presented by clients

- Extreme defensiveness that prevents a critical examination of one's own performance as it relates to serving clients
- Avoiding certain clients or difficult tasks
- Personalization of client anger and frustrations (i.e., inability to maintain an appropriate level of objectivity)
- Imposing one's values, political beliefs, religious beliefs, life-style, or personal problems on clients
- Inability to respect the religious beliefs and cultural values of a client
- Alcohol or drug abuse
- Misuse or abuse of one's power or authority over clients
- Extreme level of shyness or nonassertiveness resulting in an inability to express one's opinions and engage in the give-and-take of client work, peer supervision, and team decision making

2. *Appearance, clothing, and grooming.* Research confirms the observation that people form impressions of others—especially the powerful first impression—on the basis of physical appearance. The social worker must pay attention to his or her clothing and grooming because it matters to clients and will affect how they respond to the worker. In particular, the worker must avoid an appearance that becomes a barrier to the client's utilization of an agency service. Of course, what is offensive to one client may be acceptable to another. For example, whether a client is attracted or offended by a particular style of dress depends on the age of a client. And, what is appropriate dress in one agency setting may be inappropriate in another. The staff in a particular setting must make decisions on what is acceptable. Many social agencies and most hospitals establish dress codes as a way of providing guidance to staff. When examining your appearance and its possible impact on clients, remember the following:
- Some unusual choices of clothing, hairstyle, makeup, perfume, or jewelry may offend clients served by the agency.
- Deficiencies in grooming and personal hygiene may offend clients.
- Uncovered infections, skin irritations, and similar conditions may distract the client or cause him or her worry and anxiety.

3. *Behaviors that devalue or degrade others.* Social work values dictate that every client should be treated with respect. The social worker must avoid behaviors that are disrespectful, including the following:
- Using words, phrases, or gestures that are in bad taste or known to offend clients and staff (e.g., cursing, sexual overtones, etc.)
- Telling sexist, off-color, or ethnic jokes
- Telling disrespectful and disparaging stories about clients
- Demonstrating prejudice against particular client groups
- Making sarcastic, insulting, cruel, or disrespectful comments about clients

4. *Distracting personal habits.* Most people have some undesirable mannerisms and habits that their friends and family have learned to accept. However, the social worker must be willing to modify habits that annoy clients, including:
- Fidgeting, pencil tapping, knuckle cracking, nail biting, and the like
- Scratching, pulling, or twisting hair

- Chewing gum or tobacco and smoking
- Scowling, frowning, or making other facial gestures that seem to express scorn, contempt, or bitterness

5. *Difficulties in cognitive functioning.* A social worker must be able to absorb information quickly and apply complex principles. A capacity for abstract thinking is essential. The following examples illustrate an insufficient level of cognitive functioning:

- Difficulty processing new information, drawing logical inferences, and solving problems
- Lack of reading speed and comprehension needed to understand records and reports, agency policy, and professional books and journals
- Cognitive deficits that interfere with attention, memory, impulse control, and judgment
- Difficulty identifying and explaining the assumptions and inferences behind one's professional judgments, conclusions, and decisions

6. *Difficulties in verbal communication.* The social worker's verbal communication must be understandable to clients and other professional persons. The following problems could hamper work with clients:

- Mumbling, speaking inaudibly, loud or penetrating voice tones, halting or hesitant speech, rapid speech
- Excessive nervous laughter, frequent clearing of throat, or other distracting mannerisms
- Frequent use of slang not understood by or offensive to clients
- Errors of grammar or awkward sentence construction that confuse clients
- Inability or unwillingness to adjust vocabulary to client's age or educational level
- Uncorrected vision or hearing problems

7. *Problems in written communication.* Because so much of the social worker's service to a client involves the exchange of information with other professionals, the worker must be able to communicate in writing. If letters, reports, and agency records are carelessly written or difficult to understand, those attempting to read them will conclude either that the worker does not care enough to communicate clearly or that the worker is incompetent. The worker's effectiveness is seriously damaged if the client or other professional persons form such negative impressions. Serious writing problems that merit correction include:

- Inability to prepare letters, reports, and records that are understandable to clients, agency staff, and other professionals.
- Problems recognizing and correcting errors of spelling, grammar, and syntax
- Difficulty selecting words that adequately express thought
- Inability to write at a speed sufficient to manage required paperwork

8. *Poor work habits.* Poor work habits may have a direct or indirect impact on the clients served by an agency. Some of the more commonly observed problems are:

- Being late for client appointments, team meetings, case conferences, and other scheduled events

- Missing deadlines for the completion of written reports that are important to clients or other agencies and professionals serving the client
- Incomplete or sloppy recordkeeping
- Lack of preparation for meetings with clients and other professionals
- Not following through on assignments or tasks
- Distracting other staff members or keeping them from their work
- Unwillingness to seek and utilize direction and guidance from the supervisor
- Blaming clients or others for one's own ineffectiveness; inability or unwillingness to acknowledge mistakes or limitations of knowledge and skill
- Lack of self-discipline in focusing attention on tasks to be accomplished
- Being more interested in diagnostic labels and theoretical issues than with clients as real people
- Unwillingness to follow established agency policies and procedures
- Behaviors occurring outside work hours that draw negative attention to the social worker and thereby lessen client and public respect for the social agency and/or the worker
- Unwillingness to share information and preoccupation with protection of professional or agency turf

Selected Bibliography

Lauffer, Armand. *Working in Social Work.* Newbury Park, Calif.: Sage, 1987.
Munson, Carlton. *An Introduction to Clinical Social Work Supervision.* New York: Haworth, 1983.
Siporin, Max. *Introduction to Social Work Practice.* New York: Macmillan, 1975.
Wegscheider, Sharon. *Another Change: Hope and Health for the Alcoholic Family.* Palo Alto, Calif.: Science and Behavior Book, Inc., 1981.

8.10 *Dealing with Sexual Harassment*

Purpose: To prevent or minimize sexual harassment in the academic setting or workplace.

Discussion: A long-standing problem that is beginning to be addressed openly in universities and social agencies is sexual harassment. According to the Equal Opportunity Guidelines (1980), unwelcome sexual advances, requests for sexual favors, and other verbal or physical conduct of a sexual nature can be defined as sexual harassment when:

1. Submission to such conduct is explicitly or implicitly made a term or condition of an individual's employment or participation in a education program or activity.
2. Submission to or rejection of such conduct by an individual is used as the basis for academic or employment decisions affecting that individual.

3. Such conduct has the purpose or effect of substantially interfering with an individual's academic or work performance or creating an intimidating, hostile, or offensive working or educational environment

In short, sexual harassment is the exploitation of a power relationship for sexual purposes. Sexual harassment can be found in most aspects of life. Social workers often need to help clients deal with harassment, as well as sometimes experiencing harassment themselves. Social workers, then, need to be knowledgeable about the prevalence and appropriate responses to incidents of sexual harassment.

Considerable attention has been given to identifying sexual harassment on college campuses, where the unequal faculty/student relationship creates a situation ripe for exploitation. Several studies conducted in universities indicate that from 10 to 35 percent of females experience some form of sexual harassment while in school, although only a small number are likely to report the incident (Paludi 1988). While sexual harassment is most frequently initiated by a male in a superior position to a female, at times, it is initiated by females. It includes both heterosexual and homosexual advances.

Research on sexual harassment in the workplace would suggest that it is present in social agencies, but this issue has received little attention in the social work literature. At the point where social work education and practice most directly interface—field instruction—the problem of sexual harassment also has gone largely unreported. One study of 138 respondents from a graduate school of social work and 253 respondents from three undergraduate social work departments indicated that 10 percent of the graduate students and 15 percent of the undergraduate students experienced at least one incident of sexual harassment during placement (Shank and Johnson 1986).

Two strategies are available for dealing with sexual harassment—organizational and individual. At the organizational level, it is advisable to address this problem before an incident occurs by creating an agency policy statement that clearly prohibits sexual harassment and identifies procedures for resolution. That statement should be published in the agency's personnel manual, and the agency director should periodically post or circulate the statement. Periodic training or discussions at staff meetings that sensitize all members to this issue help prevent harassment.

On the individual level, Largen (1980, 1–2) identifies steps one should take to protect himself or herself and exercise his or her legal rights.

1. First, try talking with the harasser. If you think that he or she can be reasoned with, try to do so. But be firm.

2. If reasoning does not work, take a sterner approach with the harasser. Confront him or her verbally and also in writing. Be specific about the act(s) that you feel are sexual harassment. Inform the harasser that sexual harassment is a violation of Title VII and/or your employer's policy, if applicable.

3. Keep a journal that documents each incident of sexual harassment, including dates, times, and descriptions of what happened. Also record the names of any witnesses, in case you need them later. Keep copies of anything written received from the harasser, along with copies of all written materials you compile in reference to the harassment.

4. Talk with coworkers, for two reasons:

a. You may find that other employees are being or have been sexually harassed by the same person. A group complaint to an employer will most likely offer more protection for all of you, based on the Federal Concerted Action Law, which protects two or more employees who take action to improve their working conditions.

b. You may find a coworker who is willing to be a witness for you, should one be needed. But expect that some coworkers will be afraid or reluctant to help. And if you do "make waves," expect some coworkers to resent it.

5. Keep any suggestive letters, cards, or memos you receive from the harasser. Note the date each item was received and how it came to you (mailed to your home, left on your desk, etc.). Confront the harasser in writing, acknowledging receipt of such items and your dislike of it.

6. If harassment continues, despite your verbal and written protests to the harasser, advise the appropriate officials at your place of employemnt in writing. If you are a federal employee, notify the Equal Employment Opportunity Commission (EEOC) Director and/or the Federal Women's Program Manager and make an appointment with the EEOC counselor. (A sex discrimination complaint must be filed with the EEOC within 180 days of the incident; some employees are required to file within 30 days.) If you are a union member, notify the union, too.

7. For protection and guidance, you may want to consult an attorney, particularly if your own efforts don't seem to be having any effect.

Because of potential legal action that can result from a sexual harassment complaint, it is important that written communication with the harasser clearly addresses the problem. Sandler (1983) identifies the format such a letter should follow; namely, it should include three parts:*

1. *What has happened, without evaluation, as seen by the writer.* Be as detailed and accurate as possible, providing dates (or approximate dates), places, and descriptions of the incidents. For example:

- "On [date of incident] when I met you for a conference about my work, you asked me to come to your house that evening and said it would 'help' my [evaluation]."
- "Several times this semester when I have talked to you after class, you put your arm around me and rubbed my back. Once you also tried to fondle my breast."
- "Last week at the department party you asked me to go to bed with you."

---

*Reprinted with permission by the Project on the Status and Education of Women, Association of American Colleges, 1818 R Street, NW, Washington, DC 20009. Copies of *Writing a A Letter to the Sexual Harasser* can be ordered from AAC/PSEW.

2. *How the writer feels about the events described in Part 1.* Express any feelings of dismay, misery, distrust, or revulsion, and include your opinions or thoughts about what happened. For example:

- "My stomach turns into knots when I come to class."
- "I cannot believe that you are able to evaluate my work fairly."
- "You have made me think about taking a job in another field."
- "It has become very difficult for me to concentrate on my work."

3. *What the writer wants to happen next.* This part is usually very short, since most writers just want the behavior to stop. For example:

- "I want our relationship to be purely professional from now on."
- "I don't ever want you to touch me again or make remarks about my sexuality."

Selected Bibliography

Equal Employment Opportunity Commission. "Guidelines on Discrimination Because of Sex, Title VII, Section 703." *Federal Register* 45 (11 April 1980): 2505.

Largen, Mary Ann. "What to Do if You're Sexually Harassed." Arlington, Va.: New Responses, 1980.

Paludi, Michelle, ed. *The Ivory Tower: Sexual Harassment in Academia.* Albany, N.Y.: SUNY Albany Press, 1988.

Sandler, Bernice R. "Writing a Letter to the Sexual Harasser: Another Way of Dealing with the Problem." Washington D.C.: Association of American Colleges, February 1983.

Shank, Barbara W., and Nancy Johnson. "Sexual Harassment: An Issue for Classroom and Field Educators." Paper presented at the annual program meeting of the Council on Social Work Education, March 1986, Miami, Florida.

I. The Social Worker's Conduct and Comportment as a Social Worker

   A. Propriety—The social worker should maintain high standards of personal conduct in the capacity or identity as social worker.

      1. The private conduct of the social worker is a personal matter to the same degree as is any other person's, except when such conduct compromises the fulfillment of professional responsibilities.

      2. The social worker should not participate in, condone, or be associated with dishonesty, fraud, deceit, or misrepresentation.

      3. The social worker should distinguish clearly between statements and actions made as a private individual and as a representative of the social work profession or an organization or group.

   B. Competence and Professional Development—The social worker should strive to become and remain proficient in professional practice and the performance of professional functions.

      1. The social worker should accept responsibility or employment only on the basis of existing competence or the intention to acquire the necessary competence.

      2. The social worker should not misrepresent professional qualifications, education, experience, or affiliations.

   C. Service—The social worker should regard as primary the service obligation of the social work profession.

      1. The social worker should retain ultimate responsibility for the quality and extent of the service that individual assumes, assigns, or performs.

      2. The social worker should act to prevent practices that are inhumane or descriminatory against any person or group of persons.

   D. Integrity—The social worker should act in accordance with the highest standards of professional integrity and impartiality.

      1. The social worker should be alert to and resist the influences and pressures that interfere with the exercise of professional discretion and impartial judgment required for the performance of professional functions.

      2. The social worker should not exploit professional relationships for personal gain.

   E. Scholarship and Research—The social worker engaged in study and research should be guided by the conventions of scholarly inquiry.

      1. The social worker engaged in research should consider carefully its possible consequences for human beings.

      2. The social worker engaged in research should ascertain that the consent of participants in the research is voluntary and informed, without any implied deprivation or penalty for refusal to participate, and with due regard for participants' privacy and dignity.

      3. The social worker engaged in research should protect participants from unwarranted physical or mental discomfort, distress, harm, danger, or deprivation.

4. The social worker who engages in the evaluation of services or cases should discuss them only for the professional purposes and only with persons directly and professionally concerned with them.
5. Information obtained about participants in research should be treated as confidential.
6. The social worker should take credit only for work actually done in connection with scholarly and research endeavors and credit contributions made by others.

II. The Social Worker's Ethical Responsibility to Clients
F. Primacy of Clients' Interests—The social worker's primary responsibility is to clients.
1. The social worker should serve clients with devotion, loyalty, determination, and the maximum application of professional skill and competence.
2. The social worker should not exploit relationships with clients for personal advantage, or solicit the clients of one's agency for private practice.
3. The social worker should not practice, condone, facilitate or collaborate with any form of discrimination on the basis of race, color, sex, sexual orientation, age, religion, national origin, marital status, political belief, mental or physical handicap, or any other preference or personal characteristic, condition or status.
4. The social worker should avoid relationships or commitments that conflict with the interests of clients.
5. The social worker should under no circumstances engage in sexual activities with clients.
6. The social worker should provide clients with accurate and complete information regarding the extent and nature of the services available to them.

7. The social worker should apprise clients of their risks, rights, opportunities, and obligations associated with social service to them.
8. The social worker should seek advice and counsel of colleagues and supervisors whenever such consultation is in the best interest of clients.
9. The social worker should terminate service to clients, and professional relationships with them, when such service and relationships are no longer required or no longer serve the clients' needs or interests.
10. The social worker should withdraw services precipitously only under unusual circumstances, giving careful consideration to all factors in the situation and taking care to minimize possible adverse effects.
11. The social worker who anticipates the termination or interruption of service to clients should notify clients promptly and seek the transfer, referral, or continuation of service in relation to the clients' needs and preferences.
G. Rights and Prerogatives of Clients—The social worker should make every effort to foster maximum self-determination on the part of clients.
1. When the social worker must act on behalf of a client who has been adjudged legally incompetent, the social worker should safeguard the interests and rights of that client.
2. When another individual has been legally authorized to act in behalf of a client, the social worker should deal with that person always with the client's best interest in mind.
3. The social worker should not engage in any action that violates or diminishes the civil or legal rights of clients.
H. Confidentiality and Privacy—The social worker should respect the privacy of

clients and hold in confidence all information obtained in the course of professional service.

    1. The social worker should share with others confidences revealed by clients, without their consent, only for compelling professional reasons.

    2. The social worker should inform clients fully about the limits of confidentiality in a given situation, the purposes for which information is obtained, and how it may be used.

    3. The social worker should afford clients reasonable access to any official social work records concerning them.

    4. When providing clients with access to records, the social worker should take due care to protect the confidences of others contained in those records.

    5. The social worker should obtain informed consent of clients before taping, recording, or permitting third party observation of their activities.

I. Fees—When setting fees, the social worker should ensure that they are fair, reasonable, considerate, and commensurate with the service performed and with due regard for the clients' ability to pay.

    1. The social worker should not divide a fee or accept or give anything of value for receiving or making a referral.

III. The Social Worker's Ethical Responsibility to Colleagues

    J. Respect, Fairness, and Courtesy—The social worker should treat colleagues with respect, courtesy, fairness, and good faith.

        1. The social worker should cooperate with colleagues to promote professional interests and concerns.

        2. The social worker should respect confidences shared by colleagues in the course of their professional relationships and transactions.

    3. The social worker should create and maintain conditions of practice that facilitate ethical and competent professional performance by colleagues.

    4. The social worker should treat with respect, and represent accurately and fairly, the qualifications, views, and findings of colleagues and use appropriate channels to express judgments on these matters.

    5. The social worker who replaces or is replaced by a colleague in professional practice should act with consideration for the interest, character, and reputation of that colleague.

    6. The social worker should not exploit a dispute between a colleague and employers to obtain a position or otherwise advance the social worker's interest.

    7. The social worker should seek arbitration or mediation when conflicts with colleagues require resolution for compelling professional reasons.

    8. The social worker should extend to colleagues of other professions the same respect and cooperation that is extended to social work colleagues.

    9. The social worker who serves as an employer, supervisor, or mentor to colleagues should make orderly and explicit arrangements regarding the conditions of their continuing professional relationship.

    10. The social worker who has the responsibility for employing and evaluating the performance of other staff members, should fulfill such responsibility in a fair, considerate, and equitable manner, on the basis of clearly enunciated criteria.

    11. The social worker who has the responsibility for evaluating the

performance of employees, supervisees, or students should share evaluations with them.

K. Dealing with Colleagues' Clients—The social worker has the responsibility to relate to the clients of colleagues with full professional consideration.

   1. The social worker should not solicit the clients of colleagues.

   2. The social worker should not assume professional responsibility for the clients of another agency or a colleague without appropriate communication with that agency or colleague.

   3. The social worker who serves the clients of colleagues, during a temporary absence or emergency, should serve those clients with the same consideration as that afforded any client.

IV. The Social Worker's Ethical Responsibility to Employers and Employing Organizations

L. Commitments to Employing Organization—The social worker should adhere to commitments made to the employing organization.

   1. The social worker should work to improve the employing agency's policies and procedures, and the efficiency and effectiveness of its services.

   2. The social worker should not accept employment or arrange student field placements in an organization which is currently under public sanction by NASW for violating personnel standards, or imposing limitations on or penalties for professional actions on behalf of clients.

   3. The social worker should act to prevent and eliminate discrimination in the employing organization's work assignments and in its employment policies and practices.

   4. The social worker should use with scrupulous regard, and only for the purpose for which they are intended, the resources of the employing organization.

V. The Social Worker's Ethical Responsibility to the Social Work Profession

M. Maintaining the Integrity of the Profession—The social worker should uphold and advance the values, ethics, knowledge, and mission of the profession.

   1. The social worker should protect and enhance the dignity and integrity of the profession and should be responsible and vigorous in discussion and criticism of the profession.

   2. The social worker should take action through appropriate channels against unethical conduct by any other member of the profession.

   3. The social worker should act to prevent the unauthorized and unqualified practice of social work.

   4. The social worker should make no misrepresentation in advertising as to qualifications, competence, service, or results to be achieved.

N. Community Service—The social worker should assist the profession in making social services available to the general public.

   1. The social worker should contribute time and professional expertise to activities that promote respect for the utility, the integrity, and the competence of the social work profession.

   2. The social worker should support the formulation, development, enactment and implementation of social policies of concern to the profession.

O. Development of Knowledge—The social worker should take responsibility for identifying, developing, and fully utilizing knowledge for professional practice.

   1. The social worker should base practice upon recognized knowledge relevant to social work.

2. The social worker should critically examine, and keep current with emerging knowledge relevant to social work.

3. The social worker should contribute to the knowledge base of social work and share research knowledge and practice wisdom with colleagues.

VI. The Social Worker's Ethical Responsibility to Society

P. Promoting the General Welfare—The social worker should promote the general welfare of society.

1. The social worker should act to prevent and eliminate discrimination against any person or group on the basis of race, color, sex, sexual orientation, age, religion, national origin, marital status, political belief, mental or physical handicap, or any other preference or personal characteristic, condition, or status.

2. The social worker should act to ensure that all persons have access to the resources, services, and opportunities which they require.

3. The social worker should act to expand choice and opportunity for all persons, with special regard for disadvantaged or oppressed groups and persons.

4. The social worker should promote conditions that encourage respect for the diversity of cultures which constitute American society.

5. The social worker should provide appropriate professional services in public emergencies.

6. The social worker should advocate changes in policy and legislation to improve social conditions and to promote social justice.

7. The social worker should encourage informed participation by the public in shaping social policies and institutions.

Techniques and Guidelines for Direct Service

Many social work supervisors have heard practicum students and new social workers ask questions like, "Well, I think I understand the basic theory and the general principles of working with people, but what specifically should I do when I see Mrs. Jones and her daughter this afternoon?" Obviously, these students and new workers have discovered that there is a difference between the knowing and the doing in social work practice. They sense the need for some specific direction on what to do when with the client.

Part III of this book addresses this need. As was explained in the Preface, the authors' decision to prepare a book that concentrates primarily on techniques and guidelines rather than on theory reflects their belief that many texts do an excellent job of presenting the theoretical frameworks of practice while few provide the concrete guidance so often requested by students and new workers. The chapters in this part correspond to the phases of the change process described in Chapter 5, "The Change Process in Social Work Practice."

Chapter 9, "Intake and Engagement," focuses on the initial contact with a client. Getting started with a new client is often a time of tension for both client and worker. On occasion, intake can be downright scary for the worker, if he or she must deal with an angry, involuntary client or one who is potentially violent. The social worker must be able to engage a wide variety of clients, clarify their presenting problems, and help them connect to the agency. If the agency cannot provide the needed service, the worker must be able to skillfully use the referral process in order to link the client to another resource.

Chapter 10, "Data Collection and Assessment," recognizes that, within a relatively brief period of time, the social worker must gather relevant information about the client and his or her problem or situation, draw inferences, and formulate working hypotheses on what approaches might prove helpful to the client. This chapter presents a wide selection of tools and techniques designed to facilitate data collection and client assessment. The usual training received by social workers gives little attention to such resources. Thus, this chapter is a rather unique contribution to worker knowledge.

Chapter 11, "Planning and Contracting," presents techniques and guidelines aimed at helping the worker and client arrive at agreed-upon intervention goals and objectives. The failure to formulate a plan is one of the most common errors made by human service professionals. A plan is necessary to give focus and direction to the interventive effort. To be useful, that plan must grow from honest and open exchanges—and sometimes disagreements—between client and worker.

Chapter 12, "Intervention and Monitoring," presents a sampling of direct practice techniques and a number of guidelines covering special client-worker situations, such as interviewing the child or the client who is mentally retarded. Within social work and other helping professions, there are hundreds of separate intervention techniques and procedures. Essentially, these are the "tools of the trade," the action or behavioral component of a professional's performance. Interestingly, they are not given a lot of attention in the typical social work classroom, perhaps because there are so many that it is hard to decide which are important for all students to learn. All too often, these techniques are either not learned at all or learned in a rather haphazard manner, over many years, from a supervisor, a fellow worker, or at an occasional workshop. The selections included in this chapter will alert the student and new social worker to the wide variety of techniques available for use in practice.

Chapter 13, "Evaluation and Termination," anticipates the practical problems associated with the evaluation of an intervention. Figuring out how to evaluate one's practice is a real struggle for most social workers. Few have either the time or agency support necessary to properly evaluate their work with clients. Yet, the worker has an ethical obligation to determine if he or she has been effective. Chapter 13 provides some relatively simple evaluation techniques that will help the worker examine his or her performance. Also included are guidelines for terminating the professional relationship that began at intake.

Intake and Engagement

9

Introduction

This chapter presents guidelines and techniques for use during the intake and engagement phase of the helping process. The intake period and, in particular, the first meeting between worker and client tend to be pattern setting. This is a time when first impressions are formed. If things get off to a good start, positive interaction is likely to follow. If things get off to a bad start, a significant barrier to the helping process has been erected. It is during intake that the person voluntarily seeking professional help decides whether to become a client. What happens in the first meeting strongly influences that decision and usually determines whether the client returns for a second interview or group session. In cases involving the involuntary client, what happens during the initial meeting will largely determine whether the social worker can eventually overcome the client's resistance to agency involvement.

For the student and inexperienced worker, the engagement of certain types of clients can be particularly difficult. For this reason, we offer guidelines for working with the involuntary client, the hard-to-reach client, the chemically dependent client, the manipulative client, and the dangerous client. Also included in this chapter is guidance on using the in-home interview, obtaining information from other agencies, making a referral, and using problem checklists as a tool for facilitating engagement.

During the intake and engagement phase, the social worker will be involved in most and possibly all of the following activities:

1. Greet for the first time and speak with the client in a way that is nonthreatening and puts the client at ease.
2. Demonstrate a genuine interest in the client and concern for his or her problem or situation.
3. Learn about the client's expectations of the agency and worker.
4. Identify any fears or misunderstandings the client may have about the social worker, the agency, or its services.

5. Explain what the worker and agency can and cannot do to address the client's concerns.
6. Explain pertinent eligibility requirements and any special procedures that must be followed or fees that must be paid in order to receive services.
7. Address the client's possible ambivalence about talking with the worker or receiving agency services.
8. Decide if the client's concerns can be addressed by the worker and agency or if a referral to another agency is necessary.
9. Assess the urgency of the client's needs or presenting problem and attend to the crisis or emergency, if one exists.
10. Explain the responsibilities that both the client and worker will assume during the helping process.
11. Explain in what way and to what degree the client will be able to exercise control over the helping process.
12. Explain to the client that he or she will need to provide the information (in some cases, very personal information) needed to assess the problem or situation, formulate short-term and long-term goals, and decide what type of intervention is likely to be most effective.
13. Secure the client's signed release of confidential information (if one is needed by the agency) and explain the principles of confidentiality that apply.
14. Complete required agency forms and paperwork associated with intake.
15. Reach tentative agreement on the minimum and, if possible, the maximum number of meetings that will probably be necessary.
16. Reach agreement on the time, place, and frequency of future meetings.

During intake and engagement, the social worker must be especially sensitive to the client's fear of the unknown and **resistance to change.** The need to make even small changes generates some degree of discomfort in all people. Change can be particularly threatening to clients with well-established, or rather rigid beliefs, attitudes, and behavioral patterns. Fear is at the heart of such resistance.

The client typically moves through four stages of *resistance* during the helping process: conflict, defensiveness, resolution, and integration. In the first stage, the client senses a need to make some change; he or she recognizes that there is a different and perhaps a better way of thinking, behaving, or coping with a problem, yet the client wishes to hold on to familiar beliefs, attitudes, and behaviors. Thus, the client experiences ambivalence or a conflict between the old and the new.

When a familiar pattern is threatened, it is normal to feel defensive. If the need to change is apparent to the client, he or she may fairly quickly overcome these feelings. But some clients strongly defend against new ideas and new ways that, if accepted, would force them to acknowledge that their usual ways were ineffective or inappropriate. Feeling threatened, they may hold even tighter to their familiar patterns. Or they may use rationalization to justify themselves. Some may attack the new ways or discredit the social worker. If they feel very threatened, they may withdraw from the helping relationship.

If the client feels understanding and support from the worker, feels some discomfort with their current situation, and feels some hopefulness about the possibility of actually making a change, he or she will decide to take a risk and make at least some small change. As part of this struggle, the client decides it is safe to let go of the old and embrace the new.

In the final stage, the client emerges from this struggle by integrating the new idea or new behavior into other patterns of thought and behavior. It is important to note, however, that this new pattern soon becomes a familiar one; and in the future, the client will resist any threat to this established pattern. In other words, this cycle of conflict, defensiveness, resolution, and integration must be repeated over and over again as the client grows, develops, and makes changes in life.

Selected Bibliography

Compton, Beulah, and Burt Galaway. *Social Work Processes.* 4th ed. Belmont, Calif.: Wadsworth, 1989.

Garvin, Charles, and Brett Seabury. *Interpersonal Practice in Social Work.* Englewood Cliffs, N.J.: Prentice-Hall, 1984.

Shulman, Lawrence. *The Skills of Helping: Individuals and Groups.* 2nd ed. Itasca, Ill.: F. E. Peacock, 1984.

9.1   *The First Telephone Contact*

Purpose: To engage the person contacting the agency by phone.

Discussion: The first contact between the worker and client is often by telephone. Most callers feel nervous; many are confused and uncertain about what to expect. Others have a distorted idea about what the agency can or will do for them. Thus, the worker must use the time on the telephone to lessen the caller's fears, secure at least a general understanding of what the caller expects from the agency, and, if appropriate, arrange for the first face-to-face interview. Several guidelines should be kept in mind.

1. Remember that, during a telephone conversation, you cannot read the client's nonverbal behavior. You will not always know if the caller is becoming confused or fearful in response to what you are saying. Keep your messages clear, simple, and nonthreatening.

2. Briefly explore and listen carefully to the caller's presenting concern so you can evaluate the appropriateness of the referral. Avoid gathering detailed information and avoid probing for feelings; that is best done during a face-to-face interview.

3. Avoid overwhelming the caller with extraneous information about your agency, its services, and procedures. Details are best handled in a face-to-face interview.

4. When arranging the first office visit, make sure the caller knows the exact location of your office and your full name. Some callers may need guidance on how to use public transportation to reach the agency. In some cases, a follow-up letter should be sent to the caller, repeating the time and place of the scheduled interview.

5. Be aware of the caller's relationships and roles (e.g., child, spouse, parent, etc.) and assess how family or household members will be impacted by the caller's decision to seek professional assistance. When taking a call from one member of a family or household, ask who else lives in the home and if they know about the caller's request for assistance. If the call is being kept secret from others, ask why secrecy is important. Determine if making the call places the caller in physical danger. Except in situations where secrecy is necessary to protect the caller, encourage the caller to seriously consider involving others (e.g., spouse) in at least the beginning phase of the helping process. Explain that the assessment of the problem will be more accurate and intervention more effective if all persons affected share their perceptions of the problem, their thoughts on what might be helpful, and their views on what changes are and are not possible. Explain that some agency services and interventions may be ineffective or even counterproductive unless family members or significant others also become clients. If it sounds as if others might be willing to participate, hold out for such a meeting. If the caller insists that others will not or should not participate, respect his or her wishes and set up a meeting with the caller alone. Later in the helping process you should again try to involve the client's significant others.

Selected Bibliography

Hartman, Ann, and Joan Laird. *Family Centered Social Work Practice.* New York: The Free Press, 1983.

Hepworth, Dean, and Jo Ann Larsen. *Direct Social Work Practice.* 2nd ed. Chicago: The Dorsey Press, 1986.

9.2 *The First Face-to-Face Meeting*

Purpose: To conduct the initial interview in a manner that lays foundation for a good working relationship.

Discussion: It is quite common to feel a bit nervous when meeting a client for the first time. It can be safely assumed that the client has similar feelings. It is during this first meeting that the worker and client size up each other and form initial impressions. In some cases the social worker will need to modify his or her usual patterns in order to address the special needs of persons in a hospital bed or a wheelchair, or if they have a visual, hearing, or speech impairment. Several guidelines can help the social worker get the interaction off to a good start.

1. Before beginning the first face-to-face session, anticipate what the client might be thinking and feeling. Be prepared to respond in an understanding way to the client's fears, ambivalence, confusion, or anger during a first meeting with a stranger whom the client may perceive as an authority figure.

2. Create a physical arrangement conducive to good communication. For a two-person meeting, chairs should face each other. A desk between the worker and client is a barrier to communication. Chairs for a family interview should be arranged in a circle. Make sure the room temperature is comfortable. Be aware of your own body language; how you are dressed, your posture, facial expressions, and gestures all send messages to the client. Try to send a message of respect, caring, and professionalism.

3. If the client requested the meeting, begin with some introductory remarks and possibly some small talk, but soon move on to the concerns that brought the client to the agency. If you, the worker, initiated the interview, begin by explaining who you are, who you represent, and why you need to speak to the person.

4. Explain the rules of confidentiality that will apply to your meeting, and inform the client if what he or she says cannot be held in complete confidence. For example, you might say, "Before we begin, I want to make certain you understand that I will be preparing a report for the court that is based on our meetings. So, what you tell me may end up in my report to the judge. Do you understand that?"

5. If you have only limited time to spend with a client, explain this at the beginning of the session so those things of highest priority will receive sufficient attention.

6. Give serious attention to what the client describes as his or her concerns, but realize that many clients will test your competency and trustworthiness before revealing the whole story or the real problem. Begin with whatever the client considers important and wants to talk about.

7. Do not jump to conclusions about the nature or cause of the client's presenting problem. Check out your assumptions and perceptions. Do not display surprise or disbelief in response to what the client tells you.

8. Do not rush the client. Respect his or her need to be silent and pause before speaking. Convey the message, "I will give you the time necessary to develop your thoughts and decide what you want to say."

9. Adapt your language and vocabulary to the client's capacity to understand. If you do not understand what the client is saying, ask for clarification or examples.

10. Use open-ended questions, unless you need specific data. Do not ask a question that you believe the client will be unwilling to answer. This may force the client to lie and that may obstruct the further development of a working relationship.

11. When you do not know the answer to a service-related question asked by the client, explain this in a nonapologetic manner and offer to find the answer for the client. Be careful not to make promises that you may not be able to keep.

12. Some notetaking during the intake phase is usually necessary and appropriate. Writing down pertinent client information can demonstrate concern for the client and a desire to remember important details. Notetaking can be distracting, however. If the client is bothered by notetaking, show him or her your notes and explain why they are needed. If the client still objects, cease taking notes. If you are completing an agency form, give the client a copy of the form to follow along as you talk.

13. Plan the next meeting with the client, if one is necessary. Before the interview ends, be sure the client has your name and phone number and you have his or her full name, address, and phone number.

The social worker will encounter a number of *clients who have significant physical or sensory disabilities.* The place and usual patterns of first meetings may need to be altered in order to address their special needs and limitations. A few guidelines should be kept in mind.

1. When interviewing a person in a wheelchair or hospital bed, sit or position yourself so that you directly face the client. Do not stand over him or her. Not only would this place the client in a psychologically inferior position but it may also force the client to strain his or her neck or body in order to look at you. If the client moves about in a wheelchair or by using crutches, a cane, or a walker, respect his or her wish to remain in control and move independently. Do not offer assistance unless it is needed, and respect the client's right to decline your assistance. Be patient if it takes him or her longer to complete tasks and movements. If you feel ill-at-ease, focus your attention on the interaction and away from the equipment or prosthesis.

2. When you meet with a blind person who is in an unfamiliar physical environment, you may need to provide information he or she needs to move about. When walking with a blind person using a cane, simply stay at his or her side and let the person maneuver. Never grab or move the individual, for this is both insulting and frightening. If the client wants your assistance, he or she will ask or reach out; respond by offering your elbow to hold and then walk about a half-step ahead. It is appropriate to alert the person to an unusual obstacle or danger he or she might not detect and to mention things like overhead obstructions, sharp turns, or stairs. If the person is using a seeing-eye dog, never touch, feed, or speak to the dog without first getting the owner's permission.

3. An individual with a hearing loss will easily confuse similar sounds and have difficulty accurately hearing the human voice, especially if there is background noise. Group conversations may be particularly troublesome. If possible, move to an area away from background noise. Since most hearing aids simply amplify sound, these limitations may exist even if the client is wearing an aid. If the client seems to be having difficulty, slow your pace slightly, speak as clearly as possible, but do not yell and do not exaggerate your sounds since this makes speech reading (lip reading) more difficult. To facilitate speech reading, be sure to position yourself so he or she can see your face and do not speak while looking away or down at papers. Do not position yourself in front of a window or a bright light, for this too interferes with speech reading. Also, a heavily mustached mouth may be difficult to read. Check often to see if the person is able to follow the conversation. Do not mistake simple nodding and smiling as a sign of comprehension, for this may be the person's response to embarrassment and reluctance to say they cannot understand. A person who is totally deaf is usually prepared to communicate in writing. Be aware that some deaf people use "hearing dogs"; these dogs usually wear an orange collar and leash. If the individual uses a sign language, find out what system he or she uses and secure the services of an interpreter who knows that system. Never mistake a hearing impairment or deafness as intellectual dullness.

4. Increasingly, governmental offices, hospitals, and other essential services are equipped with devices that can be used by persons who have difficulty communicating because of blindness, hearing loss, or speech impairments. A social worker likely to encounter clients with these limitations should become familiar with amplifiers, signaling devices, puff-blow devices, electronic artificial larynx devices, telebraille, TDD (telecommunications device for the deaf), and TTY (teletypewriter).

Selected Bibliography

Maluccio, Anthony. *Learning from Clients: Interpersonal Helping as Viewed by Clients and Social Workers.* New York: The Free Press, 1979.
Marziali, Elsa. "The First Session: An Interpersonal Encounter." *Social Casework* 69, no. 1 (January 1988): 23–27.

9.3	*Making a Referral*

Purpose: To link a client with an agency, program, or professional person that will provide the service needed by the client.

Discussion: An important social work activity is to link the client with the community resources, services, and opportunities that he or she needs, wants, and can use. Although many people view referral as a simple task, it is actually very complex. A number of studies indicate that many attempted referrals end in failure. For instance, Weissman (1976) reported that, in a given group of individuals referred to an agency for service, 32 percent had no contact with the agency to which they were referred and an additional 20 percent had no involvement with the agency beyond the initial contact. Since it appears that attempted referrals have at least a 50 percent failure rate, it must be concluded that many of those doing referral work lack the knowledge and skills needed to be effective or are attempting to make referrals that clients do not want or do not consider appropriate. By following these guidelines, the worker can increase the success rate of the referral process.

1. Be clear about the reason why referral is under consideration. Remember that a referral is an action intended to help a client solve a specific problem. Thus, before considering a referral, it is important to help the client identify and clarify the problem as he or she sees it. Only after the problem has been clearly defined can you hope to make an appropriate and effective referral. If the client is directed to an agency for help with what is, for the client, a low-priority concern, the referral will most likely fail. The client must agree that the problem for which you are making the referral is one on which he or she wants to work.

2. Before concluding that referral to another agency is necessary, make sure you have considered all sources of assistance available within your own agency. Because any attempted referral carries a risk of failure and may possibly add to the client's frustration, the social worker has an ethical obligation to first use the resources of an agency to which the client is already linked.

3. Referral is appropriate only when neither you nor your agency can provide the service needed and wanted by a client. Referral is also appropriate when you do not have the knowledge or skills needed to work with a particular client and when you have reason to believe your own values, attitudes, religious beliefs, or language will be a barrier to developing an effective helping relationship. Attempting to rid yourself of responsibility for dealing with a difficult client is never an acceptable reason for referral. "Passing the buck" or "dumping" a client on another agency is both unprofessional and unethical.

4. Be realistic about what other agencies and professionals have to offer your client. Some workers tend to overestimate the worth of yet untapped resources and undervalue the resource that the client is already using.

5. Make sure you know of all the agencies already involved with a client before considering a referral. Some problems are best handled through interagency case coordination and improved case management, rather than by expanding the number of agencies involved with the client. Professionals and other agencies already working with a client should be consulted prior to referring a client to yet another agency. The client's permission will usually be needed before this discussion can take place. Whenever necessary, obtain releases of information signed by the client prior to engaging in the referral process.

6. Before deciding on a referral to another agency, be sure to consider the client's friends, relatives, neighbors, natural helpers, and other informal resources as a source of assistance.

7. Whenever possible and appropriate, the client's family and other significant individuals should be involved in the decision making related to a referral. This will, of course, increase the number of persons who have opinions about the referral, which may bog down the process. However, it will avoid having others unexpectedly throw up obstacles to the process because they felt "left out." In the long run, full involvement increases the chance that the referral will link the client to a resource that will be useful.

8. Help the client tell his or her story about the agencies and resources he or she has used or rejected in the past. Also determine how the client approached and interacted with these resources; this will provide clues as to what needs to be done to facilitate the referral. A previous negative experience with an agency, a lack of time and energy, poor communication between client and agency, confusing agency policy and procedure, and a host of other factors can contribute to referral failure. Anticipate such possible barriers and take action to lay the groundwork for success.

9. Assume that the client is ambivalent about the referral. Although a part of the client may see the logic of using the services of another agency or professional, another part may be fearful. It is important to explore the client's ambivalence and help him or her express concerns and fears about using a particular resource.

10. The referral process is stressful and frustrating for many clients. They may encounter a harried agency receptionist, an overwhelmed intake worker, waiting lists, red tape, and illogical and confusing eligibility requirements. Thus, the client may need a great deal of emotional support during the referral process.

11. Acknowledge that the client has already invested emotion and energy in relating to you. A successful referral may mean terminating a satisfying and secure helping partnership. Be aware of these feelings and be prepared to deal with feelings of separation. (See Technique 13.9.)

12. Ordinarily, when telling a client about services available through another professional or agency, you should explain both the advantages and limitations of those services. However, with clients who are confused, fearful, or highly dysfunctional, it is best not to focus on the limitations. Doing so could create an added barrier to the client's use of a needed service. In some cases, it is even necessary to "sell" the idea of using a particular service. If the client asks for advice on whether to use a particular resource, you have an obligation to give your assessment of the services provided.

13. View the referral as the first step in a new helping process. It sets the stage for what will follow. If done well, the referral process itself will be an empowering and therapeutic experience for the client. Because the referral process involves the use of problem-solving skills such as problem definition, gathering information, and decision making, your involvement with the client during the referral process gives the client an opportunity to learn these skills and how to secure needed resources. Many clients need to be coached or taught how to approach an agency or apply for services.

14. Remember that all agencies and private practitioners have their own procedures, policies, and eligibility criteria. Do not expect them to suspend their ordinary procedures as a favor to you and/or your client. Be careful not to tell a client that he or she is eligible for a particular service unless you have the authority to make such eligibility decisions. Do not speak for another professional or agency.

---

15. Whenever possible, clients should make their own arrangements for the services they want. In some cases, however, the frightened, immature, or overwhelmed client will need help in setting up an appointment, securing transportation, arranging childcare and the like. As a general rule, the client should be expected to assume as much responsibility as possible, without, of course, placing the success of the referral in jeopardy. If a referral is really necessary, you should do whatever is necessary to establish the linkage. Sometimes you will need to accompany clients if they are confused or fearful about going to an agency. Family members, friends, or volunteers may be able to provide this moral support.

16. In order to make an effective referral, you must thoroughly understand existing community resources. Because much of social work practice involves linking people to needed resources, a social worker must invest the time and energy necessary to learn about available resources and keep up with the constant change that occurs within the community resource system. Just knowing that a resource exists is seldom sufficient. It is important for the worker to know someone on the agency staff who can be used as a contact point. Use interagency visits and NASW and other professional meetings as an opportunity to meet people working in the agencies to which you will be referring clients.

17. Make sure the client becomes linked to the resource. Weissman (1976) describes a number of techniques, which he calls **connection techniques,** that can increase the likelihood that a referral will be effective.

> *Writing out* the necessary facts: the name and address of the resource, how to get an appointment at the resource, how to get to the resource and a specific explanation of what the client may expect to occur once he arrives. . . .
>
> Providing the client with the name of a specific *person to contact* at the resource. . . .
>
> Providing the client with a brief *written statement* addressed to the resource, describing in precise terms the nature of the problem and what the client would like done. The client should be involved in the composition of this statement. . . .
>
> [Having the client call] the resource to make an appointment while he is in the worker's office. Alternately, the worker may place the call to ensure that the appropriate person is contacted, but the client then takes over the phone conversation. (p. 52)

With this last technique, it is important to remember that all too often the agency person on the other end of the phone does not really listen to the client and instead launches into a complex explanation of the service program, eligibility, and so on. Some instruction, support, and modeling for the client may be necessary to prepare the client to ask the right questions and to be assertive during the phone conversation. There are multiple advantages to this technique:

a. The client has support during the introductory contact.

b. The social worker can assist with drawing out needed information and clarification from both sides, serving to repeat and reinforce instructions given, as well as express immediate appreciation to the accepting agency.

c. The client and social worker share the experience. This can be especially valuable if the contact turns out to be disappointing, rude, abrupt, or inappropriate.

Many phone systems allow three-way conversations, so the social worker, client, and agency person can communicate together.

18. Even after the client has had a first interview with the other agency, take action to cement this connection. Weissman (1976) describes several **cementing techniques** designed to increase the chances that a client will continue with the agency beyond the first contact.

> *Checkback:* The client is asked to call the worker after the initial contact at the resource to summarize what has been accomplished so far.
>
> *Haunting:* The worker, with the client's approval, plans to contact the client by telephone after the initial contact at the resource and after each subsequent contact.
>
> *Sandwiching:* A planned interview with the client before he goes for the initial interview at the resource and immediately after the interview.
>
> *Alternating:* A planned series of interviews held intermittently during the period in which the client is involved in interviews at the resource. (p. 53)

These four cementing techniques will uncover any misunderstandings or problems the client may be having with the agency. If detected early, these problems can be corrected before they cause the client to withdraw from the agency.

20. Evaluate your referral work. It is important to do a follow-up evaluation on referrals to assess whether the client actually received what he or she wanted from the agency, if the client is making progress and, finally, if additional information is available to help guide the referral experience with other clients in the future.

Selected Bibliography

Abramson, Julie. "Six Steps to Effective Referrals." In *Agency-Based Social Work,* edited by Harold Weissman, Irwin Epstein, and Andrea Savage, pp. 65–71. Philadelphia: Temple University Press, 1983.

Matthews, R. Mark, and Stephen Fawcett. *Matching Clients and Services: Information and Referral.* Beverly Hills: Sage, 1981.

Weissman, Andrew. "Industrial Social Services: Linkage Technology." *Social Casework* 57 (January 1976): 50–54.

9.4   *Obtaining Information from Other Agencies*

Purpose: To secure needed information about your client from other agencies or professionals who have provided services to your client.

Discussion: It is often during the intake phase that the social worker decides it is important to obtain client information from records maintained by another

---

social agency or professional (e.g., medical records, reports of psychological or psychiatric examinations or treatment, etc.). Strictly speaking, those records belong to the client and should not be shown to anyone without the client's permission. Thus, if you desire to obtain record information, it is necessary first to secure your client's informed consent and written permission. (Parents control the release of information about their minor-aged children.) This permission statement is often called a **Consent for Release of Confidential Information.** Most agencies have developed a standard form for this purpose. Figure 9.1 is a sample form, based on the model developed by Wilson (1978, 237).

The client's permission must constitute an *informed consent.* Wilson (1978, 57) has identified several conditions that define informed consent.

1. The client must know what information is being requested, by whom, and for what purpose.
2. The client should have an opportunity to read the material to be released or, if necessary, have it read and explained in words he or she can understand.
3. The client should have an opportunity to correct any errors in the record before it is released.
4. The client should know whether the professional or agency that will receive the information is being given permission to pass it on to a third party. (The client must be given the opportunity to prohibit this transfer.)
5. The client must be informed of any negative consequences that might occur if he or she decides not to sign the consent.
6. The client must understand that by signing the consent form, he or she is granting a one-time only or a time-limited release of information. The client has a right to revoke consent if he or she should change his or her mind.*

Rules governing the handling of client information control both the sending and receiving of records. In keeping with the social work *Code of Ethics,* state and federal laws, and agency policy, the social worker cannot under ordinary circumstances release client information to any person outside his or her own agency without first obtaining the client's written permission. There are, however, some exceptions to this basic principle. For instance, a court order or a protective service agency investigator (i.e., investigation of child or elder abuse or neglect) may secure client records without the client's permission.

Selected Bibliography

Kagle, Jill. *Social Work Records.* Homewood, Ill.: The Dorsey Press, 1984.

Weger, Christine, and Richard Diehl. *The Counselor's Guide to Confidentiality.* Honolulu: Program Information Associates, 1986.

Wilson, Suanna. *Confidentiality in Social Work: Issues and Principles.* New York: The Free Press, 1978.

*Adapted with permission of The Free Press, a division of Macmillan, Inc. from *Confidentiality in Social Work: Issues and Principles* by Suanna J. Wilson. Copyright © 1978 by The Free Press.

Figure 9.1 Sample Release Form

The ABC Child Welfare Agency
Consent for Release of Confidential Information

(Name of social worker) of the ABC Child Welfare Agency requests permission from *(typed name of client)* to release certain confidential information about *(typed name of client)*. This information will be released to:

Name _____ Address _____

Organization _____ _____

Position _____ Phone _____

Material to be released _____

_____

_____

Purpose of the disclosure _____

_____

(Name of the individual receiving the data) of the *(name of the organization receiving the data)* must abide by the following limitations in his and his agency's use of the information received:

_____

_____

_____

My signature indicates that I know exactly what information is being disclosed and have had opportunity to correct or amend the data to make certain it is accurate and complete. I am also aware of all consequences that might occur as a result of signing this consent form or of my refusal to do so. I am aware that this consent can be revoked (in writing) at any time.

My signature also means that I have read this form and/or had it read to me and explained in language I can understand. All the blank spaces have been filled in except for signatures and dates.

This consent form expires on _____ unless revoked by me in writing prior to that date.
　　　　　　　　　　　　　　　　Date

_____ _____ _____
Client's Signature or "X"   Date Signed   Witness

_____ _____ _____
Client's Guardian   Date Signed   Witness

_____ _____ _____
ABC Child Welfare Agency Representative Date Signed

Distribution: ABC Child Welfare Agency files; *name of client; name of individual/agency receiving the data.*

Source: Based on Wilson (1978, 237). Reprinted with permission of The Free Press, a Division of Macmillan, Inc. from *Confidentiality in Social Work* by Suanna J. Wilson. Copyright © 1978 by The Free Press.

Purpose: To assist the client in identifying and explaining his or her problems or concerns.

Discussion: At the beginning of the intake phase, many clients have difficulty defining their problem. Some are reluctant to verbalize their thoughts because they feel ashamed or embarrassed; others cannot find the words to describe their concerns. The use of a problem checklist can make it easier for a client to acknowledge a problem and put it into words.

A problem checklist is simply a list of problems and concerns commonly reported by a particular client group. The list is compiled by a social worker who knows how people in certain situations typically think and feel. This list of concerns is given to the client, who considers each statement and checks off those that come close to describing how he or she is thinking or feeling. Providing the client with such a list, which includes some of his or her "secret" thoughts on paper, can prove reassuring to the client. It tells the client that he or she is not alone and not the first person to have a particular problem. The items in the checklist can open up a topic for discussion, uncover problems, and facilitate the exchange of information.

Frequently, clients are unaware of the services that can be provided by the social worker. If the social worker and client read through the problem checklist together, the client begins to understand how the social worker or agency can be of assistance. In this sense, the problem checklist serves as an educational tool. Also, the checklist can be used to provide focus and structure during an interview, which can be important in work with clients who are easily distracted. The problem checklist is most often used during the first face-to-face interview; however, it can be used as "homework" between the first and second meeting.

Figures 9.2 and 9.3 are examples of worker-designed problem checklists (Horejsi and Horejsi 1979). Figure 9.2 was designed to facilitate communication with teen-aged mothers, many of whom are reluctant to verbalize their worries. Some clients, like the new mother who is hospitalized for only one or two days after delivery of her baby, may be accessible to the hospital social worker for one brief contact; she may leave the hospital before the worker can see her for a second session. In such a case, a problem checklist can provide the focus needed to make the best possible use of very limited time. Figure 9.3 was developed as an intake tool for use with parents of handicapped children as a means of helping them talk about their concerns. These problem checklists should be viewed as samples or models. A social worker can look at the common patterns of feelings and problems of his or her clients and construct an individualized checklist to fit the needs of a particular setting and client group.

The major advantage of the problem checklist is that it helps clients conceptualize and report their concerns. The major disadvantage is that it does not give

Figure 9.2   Sample Problem Checklist

Concerns of Young Mothers: A Checklist

The birth of a baby is usually a time of great happiness and joy. But along with all the good feelings are concerns about the changes in lifestyle and responsibility that lie ahead. A new parent often feels uncertain and a bit scared about the responsibility of caring for a baby and raising a child. If we know about your concerns, we may be able to help you find ways to handle them.

Below is a list of worries and problems that have been expressed by other new mothers who have had babies in this hospital. Please read through this list and place a check (✔) by all of those statements that are similar to the concerns you now have. Your responses will be held in strict confidence.

1. ____ Have worries about paying hospital and doctor bills.

2. ____ Have worries about my baby's health and physical condition.

3. ____ Have worries about my own health and physical condition.

4. ____ Uncertain about how to feed and care for an infant at home.

5. ____ Uncertain where to turn when I have child care questions that are not directly related to health.

6. ____ Afraid I may become pregnant before I am ready to have another child.

7. ____ Worried about having enough money to care for my baby.

8. ____ Disappointed that my plans for the future have been changed by having a baby now.

9. ____ Worried about finishing school.

10. ____ Worried about getting or keeping a job with a baby to care for.

11. ____ Afraid when I feel resentment or anger toward my baby.

12. ____ Worried that my friends will not accept me and my baby.

13. ____ Worried about my relationship with the baby's father.

14. ____ Concerned that I do not feel love toward my baby.

15. ____ Feeling sad and depressed about my situation.

16. ____ Worried that I will be a burden to my own parents.

17. ____ Worried about living alone with my baby.

18. ____ Afraid my own parents and family will not accept me and my baby.

19. ____ Afraid I am going to lose my independence and freedom.

20. In the space below, please describe or list any other concerns not covered by the checklist.

_____

Thank you for completing this checklist. Now, please look over all of those items you have checked (✔) and draw a circle around the one or two that seem most important.

Source: Horejsi and Horejsi (1979).

Figure 9.3   Sample Problem Checklist

Parents' Concerns: A Checklist

Below is a list of problems and concerns frequently expressed by the parents of children with special problems or handicapping conditions. Please read through this list and place a check (✔) beside all of those that come close to describing your own concerns, worries, and feelings.

1. ____ Not knowing what to expect of my child. Not sure about my child's abilities.

2. ____ Worried about finding money to pay for medical care or special services needed by my child.

3. ____ Worried about the adequacy of the schools and the help my child will receive from school staff.

4. ____ Confused about what to do when I get conflicting information and advice from professionals.

5. ____ Worried about my ability to cope with the problems and stress.

6. ____ Worried about rejection by relatives, friends, and neighbors.

7. ____ Wondering about the basic causes of this problem and feeling like it was my (our) fault.

8. ____ Worried about another pregnancy and that my next child will have the same condition.

9. ____ Worried about our other children, their reaction and needs.

10. ____ Worried about my feelings of resentment toward my child.

11. ____ Worried about my child being dependent on us all his/her life.

12. ____ Worried about what will happen to my child after I am unable to care for him/her.

13. ____ Feeling like something is wrong with me because of my child's problems.

14. ____ Worried about my child's difficult and unusual behavior.

15. ____ Worried about the possibility of sexual abuse or exploitation of my child by others.

16. ____ Worried about how to help my child at home and how to provide appropriate training activities for my child.

17. ____ Other problems or concerns—explain: _____

_____

Now look over all of the above items you have checked and draw a circle around the two or three items that seem most important to you.

Source: Horejsi and Horejsi (1979).

attention to client strengths. The worker must counterbalance this rather negative focus with attention to client strengths and assets. Also, it must be remembered that many clients have reading problems, in which case the checklist can be used verbally as a structured interview technique.

Selected Bibliography

Horejsi, Charles. *Foster Family Care.* Springfield, Ill.: Charles Thomas, 1979.

Horejsi, Charles, and Gloria Horejsi. "Practice Oriented Social Assessment Tools." Paper presented at the Sixth Biennial National Association of Social Workers Professional Symposium, San Antonio, Texas, 1979.

9.6 | *The In-Home Interview*

Purpose: To engage and deliver services to the client who cannot or will not meet in an office setting and/or to secure a more accurate assessment by observing the client in his or her natural environment.

Discussion: The terms *in-home interview* or *home visit* refer to a meeting between social worker and client in the client's home. The in-home interview has become a lost art in many practice settings. In the early days of social work, home visiting was the modus operandi of the worker. In the late 1940s and the 1950s, when social work was working hard to attain professional status, the home visit was abandoned by many because it did not seem "professional" and did not fit the then popular office-based models of therapy. Of course the home visit has always been used heavily by social workers in child protection and public health agencies and by those providing services to the elderly. The home visit is an essential component in all outreach activities and of critical importance in work with the hard-to-reach client. (See Technique 9.8.) In recent years, the value of the in-home interview was rediscovered by family therapists and its use has increased. However, fear of high-crime neighborhoods is a limiting factor.

Despite its usefulness and necessity in so many cases, the in-home interview is a source of anxiety for many social workers. A number of guidelines can help the worker make proper use of this valuable diagnostic and treatment tool.

1. Understand the rationale for observing clients in their usual environment. Sherman and Fredman (1986) explain that

> information which is not readily presented in office visits may come across as the therapist interacts in a setting that is more natural to the family. Arranged home visits have the potential for decreasing family defensiveness and promoting the involvement of the entire family. It is a more natural setting for the family's functioning. It may also be possible that behavior change achieved in the home environment is both more adaptive to the family's reality and more likely to be retained. (p. 238)

The home visit is especially valuable in helping the worker develop empathy for the client and in understanding more fully how the environment impinges on the client.

2. Appreciate the depth of understanding that can be gained from an in-home interview. Ebeling and Hill (1983) explain that a person's home is his or her "sacred" space and a reflection of the individual's personality and life-style.

> Within the walls of a home, people experience the intimate moments of their lives. They sleep, wake up, bathe, eat, drink, make love, raise children. They fight, scream, and rejoice; they cry, laugh, and sing. They may experience the warmth of positive object relationships, the anguish of negative ones, or isolation and loneliness. . . .
>
> Their outer space reflects their inner space. The way the homes are decorated and furnished can reveal either the chosen life-style of the occupants or their economic position. It can also indicate depression, despair, and disorganization. (p. 64)

3. Do not confuse the in-home interview with a purely social or friendly visit. This technique, like all others, is to be used in a purposeful manner. When it is the social worker who requests an in-home interview, the client should be given a clear explanation as to how and why it will make the service more effective.

4. An in-home interview should be scheduled at a mutually convenient time. Unannounced visits should be avoided but may be necessary when the client does not have a phone or is unable to read a letter, or when prior attempts to reach the client have failed. If you must stop by a client's home unannounced, explain immediately your previous efforts to reach them and use the conversation to set up a scheduled home visit. (In many cases, the client will immediately invite you in.)

5. When you enter the home of a client, extend the same respect and courtesy you expect when someone enters your home. Ask where you are to be seated. Accept an appropriate offer of food or drink. Convey a genuine interest in family pictures and household furnishings that are an expression of the client's identity, interests, and culture. Ebeling and Hill (1983) remind us that it is essential that the social worker never show shock or disapproval as he or she enters the client's home—their sacred space: "No matter what the condition of the building, . . . regardless of the number of dogs, the darkness of the halls, or the odors of the stairways; no matter how barren or cluttered or 'hospital' clean; even no matter what signs of impusivity, violence, or sexual acting out are encountered" (p. 66).

6. Obtaining sufficient privacy is often a problem during a home visit—children may run in and out of the house, neighbors may stop by, the telephone may ring, and the TV may be blaring. This will be distracting to you but possibly not to your client. On the positive side, such distractions provide an accurate picture of the family's real-life functioning and their ecosystem. Significant distractions are best dealt with directly by expressing a need for privacy and for attention to the interview's purpose. When friends or neighbors are in the home, the client should be asked if it is permissible to discuss private matters in their presence. Some clients may invite their informal helpers and supportive friends to sit in on the interview and this choice should be respected.

7. If your client lives in a high-crime neighborhood, it is important to schedule the home visit for a time when the risks are at a minimum. Ask your client if you should take some special precautions and to describe the safest route.

Selected Bibliography

Ebeling, Nancy, and Deborah Hill, eds. *Child Abuse and Neglect.* Boston: John Wright, PSG, Inc., 1983.

Kagan, Richard, and Shirley Schlosberg. *Families in Perpetual Crisis.* New York: W. W. Norton, 1989.

Kaplan, Lisa. *Working with Multiproblem Families.* Lexington, Mass.: Lexington Books, 1986.

Sherman, Robert, and Norman Fredman. *Handbook of Structured Techniques in Marriage and Family Therapy.* New York: Brunner/Mazel, 1986.

9.7   *Engaging the Involuntary Client*

Purpose: To begin building a working relationship with a client who was forced into contact with a social worker and agency.

Discussion: The term **involuntary client** refers to an individual who is required or mandated to seek professional help. Many children, abusing or neglecting parents, prisoners, probationers, and psychiatric inpatients are involuntary clients. The coercive force bringing them into contact with the worker may be a legal authority such as a judge, probation officer, or child protection agency; a powerful family member; or an employer. Because they do not want to see a social worker, such clients are often resentful, angry, and sometimes belligerent. It is a challenge to engage the involuntary client in the helping process, but it can be done.

In most cases involving an involuntary client, the social worker will possess some degree of official authority. For example, social workers employed in child protection, probation, and parole are granted authority by law. Whereas the worker in a purely voluntary agency may suggest a course of action to a client, the worker in a correctional setting or court-related agency has the authority to impose a certain course of action. Many social workers are uncomfortable with such authority and avoid using it; others overuse or misuse legitimate authority. Workers who are in positions of legal authority must learn to use it in ways that are helpful to the client. In fact, a worker's compassionate and fair exercise of legitimate authority can be a therapeutic experience for clients who associate authority with abuse and exploitation.

Dale Hardman (1960), an experienced probation and parole officer, offers the following advice on the appropriate *use of authority:*

> I will make crystal clear, in defining my role, where my authority begins and ends, and I will consistently function within these limits. I will avoid veiled threats,

---

bluffing, or any behavior that might be so interpreted, since this clouds, rather than clarifies my limits. This rule will eliminate a vast amount of testing by the client. I will further clarify which decisions are mine to make and which the client must make.... Once I have made a decision, I will steadfastly resist all client efforts to alter my decision by threats, tantrums, seduction, illness, etc. I will just as steadfastly defend his right to make his decisions and stand by them. By the same token, if a client shows me rational evidence that I have made a hasty or unwise decision, I will alter it and will tell him so. Common terms which [clients] ... use to describe authority are "arbitrary, inconsistent, and unfair." For this reason I must demonstrate that authority can be considerate, consistent and fair. (p. 17)

Holder and Mohr (1980) remind new child-protection workers of the therapeutic use of authority with the following guidance:

1. Use your authority in a warm, personal, supportive manner and show an understanding of the parents' feelings about the problem.
2. Help the family to feel less fearful of authority by demonstrating a non-threatening and non-coercive attitude.
3. Help your client to see that you represent reasonable authority so that he can learn that other authority figures can also be reasonable.
4. Demonstrate your authority in a manner which indicates that you have no hidden agenda, i.e., be honest.
5. Clarify your protective service role and function. Do not retreat from your responsibility; make the family aware of your expectations.
6. Make the family aware of your knowledge that trauma is involved for children who must be separated from their parents.
7. Demonstrate your professional competence and ability to develop a helping relationship as you relate to the client....
8. Avoid a cold, impersonal approach to the family.
9. Avoid insensitivity to parental feelings since insensitivity may create anger, hostility and resistance and will make it difficult for you to establish a helping relationship.
10. Do not allow your behavior to convey to the parents that they are the "enemy" and that you're working "against" them.
11. Avoid excessive reliance on your legal authority. (pp. 49–50)

Also, consider these guidelines when working with the involuntary client:

1. Before meeting your client for the first time, be very clear as to what requirements are nonnegotiable for the involuntary client and what choices and options are available to the client. Also, anticipate how the client may be feeling about his or her loss of freedom.

2. When you first meet with your client, reveal the factual information you have about why the client is involved with your agency, and ask the client to correct any misunderstandings you may have about this information. Seek clarification from the referring source if there is a significant discrepancy between what the client has been told about why he or she must seek professional help and what you have been told by the referring person.

3. Provide a clear and completely honest explanation of both your role and responsibility and what you or your agency expect of the client.

4. Explain the rules of confidentiality that do and do not apply. For example, if you are expected to prepare a report to the court, the client has a right to know that what he or she tells you is not confidential.

5. Inform the client of any adverse consequences that may occur if he or she does not cooperate. However, respect the client's right to choose the consequences rather than your professional services. Remind the client who decides not to cooperate that he or she is, in effect, giving up the control he or she has to influence the outcome.

6. Assume that the client has negative feelings about being forced into contact with a social worker. Be prepared to encounter hostility, anger, and a number of defensive reactions, but do not take the client's reactions personally. (See Technique 6.7.) Foremost, you need to address the client's negativism. Do not ignore or avoid these feelings; deal with them directly. Use basic interviewing skills to help the client express negative feelings. Do not ask questions that could be construed as an attempt to trap the client or catch him or her in a lie. Demonstrate an empathetic understanding of what it is like to be forced to do something you do not choose to do.

7. Discuss the client's previous experience with professionals or the "system," along with any preconceived notions he or she has about social workers, counselors, or other professional helpers. Be aware of the client's cultural background or experience with discrimination and how this might add to his or her feeling of being overpowered by or alienated from social institutions. Provide the client with as much choice and self-determination as can be allowed within the legal constraints placed on him or her.

8. Consider trying to engage the client with what Rooney (1988) terms the "let's make a deal" strategy. In this approach, the worker agrees to do something that will lessen the client's discomfort (e.g., talk to the prosecuting attorney about reducing a criminal charge) or help the client get something he or she wants (something legal and legitimate) in exchange for the client's cooperation in the helping process.

9. Remember, there is no such thing as an unmotivated client. All clients are motivated—all have wants, needs, and preferences. When we label a client "unmotivated," we are simply acknowledging that what the client wants is different than what we want for the client. Successfully engaging the involuntary client requires that the worker tap into the client's own needs and wants and establish intervention goals that are at least partially consistent with the client's own inclinations rather than becoming an opposing force in the client's life. Some workers call this "going with the flow" or "moving with the motive." Work hard to identify something that both you and the client agree is a problem or a desirable course of action (e.g., getting off probation or not having to see a social worker anymore). Once there is an agreed-upon goal, you can more easily engage the client in problem solving aimed at making change. For example, you might say, "Well, we both want you to get off probation so you won't have to see me each week. What ideas do you have on how we can work together to reach that goal?"

10. Highlight the client's strengths and make frequent use of the reframing technique. (See Technique 12.11.) Use the problem search technique (see Technique 11.2) if you and the client cannot agree on the problems that need to be addressed.

11. With most clients, some degree of self-disclosure by the worker has the effect of breaking down client defensiveness. However, when working with a prison inmate population, sociopathic individuals, or persons who are skilled manipulators, you should not use self-disclosure or share personal thoughts and feelings in an effort to build a relationship. (See Technique 9.10.) The use of self-disclosure with these individuals will usually have unwanted consequences, as they have an uncanny ability to spot and exploit a helper's personal weakness. For similar reasons, you must never break or even bend agency rules as a favor to the client; even a minor concession quickly leads to further requests or a "blackmail" situation (e.g., "Look, if you won't do . . . for me, I'll tell your supervisor that you violated program rules when you allowed me to. . . . ").

12. Successful work with the involuntary client demands a high degree of motivation, self-awareness, and self-discipline by the worker. Unless the worker is aware of and able to control his or her feelings, he or she will not be effective with this client. Close supervision and peer review are critically important methods of developing these abilities.

Selected Bibliography

Hardman, Dale. "The Functions of the Probation Officer." *Federal Probation* 24 (September 1960): 3–10.

Holder, Wayne, and Cynthia Mohr. *Helping in Child Protective Services.* Denver: American Humane Association, 1980.

Oxley, Genevieve. "Promoting Competence in Involuntary Clients." In *Promoting Competence in Clients,* edited by Anthony Maluccio. New York: The Free Press, 1981.

Rooney, Ronald. "Socialization Strategies for Involuntary Clients." *Social Casework* 69 (March 1988): 131–40.

9.8   *Engaging the Hard-to-Reach Client*

Purpose: To build a working relationship with a client who is distrustful and reluctant to become involved.

Discussion: The term *hard-to-reach* is used here to describe a client with whom it is extremely difficult to build a relationship. Most of these clients are socially isolated, fearful, and distrustful. Many suffer from chronic mental illness and/or are extremely uncomfortable in interpersonal relations. The term *hard-to-reach* should not be confused with the term *involuntary client* (see Technique 9.7); some hard-to-reach clients are, in fact, voluntary, and many involuntary clients are actually quite easy to engage. In working with the hard-to-reach, the greatest challenge is to break through the client's distrust. Several guidelines should be followed.

1. You must be willing to use unconventional methods. The techniques that are most effective are usually not ones drawn from the traditional approaches to psychotherapy and counseling, nor ones used by conventional mental health and social service agencies. Homebuilders, a program operated by Behavioral Sciences Institute based in Federal Way, Washington, has a remarkable record of effective work with highly dysfunctional, multiproblem, and hard-to-reach families in imminent risk of having a child placed into foster care. Among the methods and principles that contribute to the success of the Homebuilders program are: (a) reaching out to families while they are in crisis; (b) responding to the family within twenty-four hours of referral; (c) using an intense time-limited intervention (a caseload of two families, intervention lasting four to five weeks); (d) being available to families twenty-four hours a day, seven days a week; (e) meeting with families in their home, not in an office setting; and (f) a willingness and ability to provide a wide variety of services (e.g., helping to clean the kitchen floor, meeting basic needs for food and shelter, case coordination, and applying the most sophisticated of psychotherapeutic techniques, such as individual and family therapy, assertiveness training, relocation, behavior management, etc.).

2. Remember that first impressions are extremely important to these clients. They are quick to form judgments; more often than not, they interpret situations in the most negative way possible. To be effective, you must be a warm, giving, and dependable person. In many ways, you must become a good parent figure to the client—loving but firm. That firmness and concern may express itself in the gentle setting of limits on what is and is not acceptable behavior. Use a liberal dose of self-disclosure to help the client see you as a real and genuine person.

3. Be prepared to tolerate a great deal of testing behavior, and be patient when progress is slow. Many hard-to-reach clients have been so beaten down by life that they feel helpless and hopeless about ever making a change in their situation.

4. Demonstrate your usefulness to the client in an immediate and concrete way. By doing something the client really wants, you neutralize some of the negative feelings. Home visits, sending birthday cards, sharing food, and other tangible expressions of concern are usually necessary. In their discussion of how to work with neglectful parents, many of whom are hard-to-reach, Polansky, DeSaix, and Sharlin (1972) explain that often these clients

> want to be given to, and will respond at first only on the basis of "what's in it for me?" Such concrete examples of caring as transportation to a medical clinic, financial assistance . . . are real and understandable to the [client]. . . . Nearly all successful workers agree that in the initial phases of treatment they do a great many things *for* the client, before she becomes able to do them *with* them. (p. 62)

Similarly, Hollis and Woods (1981) explain that reaching out to the client may take the form of "arranging for camp for the children, taking the children to busy clinics when the mother cannot do this herself, or even providing money for various household needs. These are, of course, important services in their own right, but they also symbolize to the client the worker's interest and concern" (p. 114).

5. By doing things for the client and by "feeding" the client's dependency needs, you provide assurance that you are "safe." More importantly, you demonstrate that you have something the client wants. By becoming useful to the client, you become attractive and thereby gain some psychological leverage. Unless you become attractive and a reinforcer, the client's distrust will keep him or her from entering into even a superficial relationship. Do not worry about creating over-dependency. That problem can be addressed later. Remember, your first objective is simply to build a human bond or connection.

6. Encourage frequent contacts. As a general rule, the more often two people interact, the more important they become to each other. Use frequent phone calls and brief letters to supplement face-to-face interviews. Also try to be available in times of crisis or emergency.

7. Be very tactful. The feelings of hard-to-reach clients are easily hurt and they are super sensitive to any hint of rejection. Do nothing that could be construed as criticism. If you accidentally do something that is hurtful to the client, discuss it immediately and repair the damaged relationship; if you do not, the client may withdraw from the relationship, once again convinced that no one can be trusted.

8. Place only minimal demands or expectations on the client until you have developed a meaningful relationship. This does not mean you should be completely permissive, however. You need to help the client understand that the two of you are to work on the client's problems and that you will not tolerate destructive or manipulative behavior.

9. Verbalize frequently the client's strengths and what is positive in his or her situation. Demonstrate openly that you really care for the client. Do not be afraid to touch or hug if the client accepts this close contact.

Selected Bibliography

Collins, Alice. *The Lonely and Afraid: Counseling the Hard-to-Reach.* Indianapolis: Odyssey Press, 1969.

Hollis, Florence, and Mary Woods. *Casework: A Psychosocial Therapy.* New York: Random House, 1981.

Horejsi, Charles. "The St. Paul Family-Centered Project Revisited: Exploring an Old Gold Mine." In *Treating Families in the Home,* edited by Marvin Bryce and June Lloyd. Springfield, Ill.: Charles C. Thomas, 1981.

Kinney, Jill, David Haapala, Charlotte Booth, and Shelley Leavitt. "The Homebuilders Model." In *Improving Practice Technology for Work with High Risk Families: Lessons from the Homebuilders Social Work Education Project,* edited by James Whittaker, Jill Kinney, Elizabeth Tracy, and Charlotte Booth. Seattle: University of Washington, School of Social Work, October 1988.

Polansky, Norman, Christine DeSaix, and Shlomo Sharlin. *Child Neglect: Understanding and Reaching the Parent.* New York: Child Welfare League of America, 1972.

Schlosberg, Shirley, and Richard Kagan. "Practice Strategies for Engaging Chronic Multi-problem Families." *Social Casework* 69, no. 1 (January 1988): 3–9.

9.9 Engaging the Client Who Is Chemically Dependent

Purpose: To engage the chemically dependent client in a way that increases the chances he or she will seek treatment.

Discussion: Many individuals receiving services from social agencies suffer directly or indirectly from the effects of alcoholism and drug abuse. The abuse of chemicals is interrelated with many other psychosocial problems, including marital discord, parent-child conflict, spouse abuse, child abuse and neglect, suicide, homicide, and financial problems. The use of chemicals is also related to criminal behavior and accidental injury, especially auto accidents. In addition, the use of alcohol and drugs by a pregnant woman can cause damage to the unborn child. Drug use also contributes to the spread of AIDS.

Most social workers consider the actively drinking alcoholic and the drug user to be "difficult" clients, in part because of the extreme denial, rationalization, and self-centeredness that is so much a part of the addictive process. A social worker's response to this client must be based on an understanding of how alcohol and drugs affect mind and body and on the realization that it is nearly impossible for an individual to break a dependency or addiction without specialized treatment.

A *chemical dependency* can be defined as a pathological relationship with a mood-altering substance that has life-damaging consequences. The dynamics of this relationship resemble those of a neurotic love affair, but in this case the love object is a chemical. The chemicals likely to be abused share a common characteristic—each has the capacity to alter a person's mood, temporarily; it makes the user feel good. Generally speaking, the chemicals most sought after are those with the most rapid onset of action. Onset of effect is related to chemical properties, dose, method of intake, and characteristics of the user. Each time it is used, its mood-altering effects reinforce usage, and over time this learning process results in what is termed *psychological addiction* or dependency. In addition, many drugs alter body chemistry, and this can lead to a *physical addiction* and such symptoms as craving and withdrawal. Central to the physical addiction process is the gradual development of *tolerance* (i.e., more and more of the chemical is necessary to create its desired mood-altering effect).

There are continual changes in the street language applied to illegal substances. Also, there are sometimes regional differences in terminology, popularity, and preferred methods of ingestion. Keeping up with these changes is made even more difficult by the fact that new chemical combinations appear frequently. Each new chemical combination is created for the purpose of producing more intense and long-lasting effects. Hence, each new drug is likely to be more addictive and more dangerous than those previously available. Provided here are brief descriptions of the legal and illegal substances most often abused and that are the basic ingredients for new combinations.

Alcohol

If one considers the number of individuals and families affected, the number of injuries and deaths caused by drunken driving, and the number of health problems either caused or exacerbated by drinking, the abuse of alcohol (a legal drug) is probably the number one drug problem in the United States. It is estimated that of every ten adults who drink at all, one has a serious drinking problem. Many individuals simultaneously abuse alcohol and one or more other drugs. Alcohol consumption by a pregnant woman can cause serious problems for the unborn child, including mental retardation, curvature of the spine, facial abnormalities, and other birth defects. The greater the consumption, the greater the impact on the fetus. Damage to the brain of the fetus by alcohol is one of the major causes of mental retardation. For every 1,000 newborns, 2 to 3 are now diagnosed as having full-blown *Fetal Alcohol Syndrome*—a cluster of physical and mental abnormalities. Additional newborns are also affected by alcohol but to a lesser degree.

Alcohol has the effect of depressing the functions of the central nervous system. Alcoholism is a chronic, progressive, and terminal illness. So long as the alcoholic continues to drink, it becomes worse. There is no cure; at best it can be controlled through complete abstinence. Experts generally agree that it is not possible for an alcoholic to ever become a social drinker. If the alcoholic tries to become only a social drinker, he or she slips back into a pattern of problem drinking.

In its early stage, alcoholism is difficult to recognize because its symptoms are subtle. However, you may observe that the person drinks a lot and that alcohol has a part in many of the person's activities. The incipient alcoholic can consume a great deal without showing the effects; researchers suggest this phenomena may be genetic in origin. At this early stage, the consumption of alcohol does not significantly interfere with job or family functioning and may be almost indistinguishable from the person who only occasionally drinks too much.

In the middle stage, the alcoholic is physically addicted. When his or her blood alcohol level is lowered, the alcoholic will experience withdrawal symptoms, including anxiety, agitation, and tremors. Family functioning and job are now affected. At this stage, it is common for family and friends to pressure the alcoholic to cut back. Concerned family members may reach out for help, but typically, the alcoholic denies there is a problem. He or she may quit for weeks or months at a time but eventually starts again. These short periods of abstinence convince the alcoholic that he or she can quit any time and that alcohol is not a problem.

In the later stage of alcoholism, the existence of a serious problem is apparent to all but the alcoholic. Although family, job, and health are all affected, the denial continues, at least until some major crisis occurs (e.g., an accident, loss of job, health problems, divorce, etc.).

The following list identifies a number of the *symptoms of alcoholism*. Usually, the alcoholic will display several of these.

- Inability to stop at one or two drinks
- Increased dependency on alcohol
- Blackouts (inability to remember what occurred during drinking bouts)
- Passing out when drinking
- Drinking alone
- Needing a drink the next morning
- Increase in the amount of alcohol consumed
- "Gulping" drinks
- Lateness and absenteeism at work
- Neglect or indifference to personal appearance
- Neglect of financial obligations in order to pay for alcohol
- Family quarrels and family tensions over drinking
- Lateness in returning home and a growing number of excuses (or perhaps offering no excuse at all)
- Changes in eating and sleeping habits
- Grandiose beliefs
- Hallucinations
- Persistent remorse
- Suspiciousness of family and friends
- Increased irritability
- Hostile and belligerent behavior when drinking
- Hand tremors and increased nervousness
- Falling, stumbling, or other unstable movement
- Hiding and protecting liquor supply
- Repeated unsuccessful attempts at abstaining from alcohol
- Angry denial that one has a drinking problem, usually accompanied with a strong "alibi system" to excuse or minimize drinking
- In its terminal phases, health problems affecting such vital organs as the brain, liver, and gastrointestinal system

Alcoholics Anonymous (AA) remains one of the most effective self-help recovery programs. The social worker can learn about AA and its twelve-step recovery program by attending "open" meetings and talking with members. AA members are usually willing to consult with professionals who are trying to decide how best to approach problems presented by an alcoholic client.

Stimulants

Nicotine, amphetamines, cocaine, and caffeine are all stimulants. Because of its relationship to cancer and heart and lung disease, the nicotine found in tobacco contributes to more deaths than all of the street drugs combined. Some people use stimulants ("uppers") to counteract the drowsiness or "down" feeling caused by sleeping pills and alcohol which depress the central nervous system.

This up/down cycle is extremely hard on the body. Generally speaking, the abuse of a stimulant is indicated by hyperactivity, nervousness and anxiety, dilated pupils, irritableness, and going for long periods without sleep or food.

Amphetamines and its many derivatives (e.g., benzedrine, dexedrine, and methedrine) manufactured by pharmaceutical companies are known on the street by such names as "speed," "uppers," "dexies," "bennies," and "crystal." These drugs are taken orally or by injection. Medically, the various amphetamines are used for treating narcolepsy, minimal brain dysfunction, and obesity. Some persons who develop amphetamine dependence started using this drug as an appetite suppressant. A number of amphetamines or amphetamine derivatives are manufactured illegally. "Crank" and "ice" are examples; both are methamphetamines. "Crank" can be snorted, swallowed, smoked, or injected; it produces an intense and long-lasting euphoria. The even more powerful "ice" is smoked and produces a high similar to that of crack cocaine but one that lasts from eight to twenty-four hours.

Users are attracted to the amphetamines because they produce euphoria. As with all drugs, the actual effects—including the adverse effects—are dose related. In general, amphetamines increase alertness, physical activity, heart and breathing rates, and blood pressure; dilate pupils; and decrease appetite. The user may experience a dry mouth, sweating, headache, blurred vision, dizziness, sleeplessness, and anxiety. Extremely high doses can cause people to flush or become pale and can cause rapid or irregular heartbeat, tremors, loss of coordination, and even physical collapse. A high dosage can cause an individual to become excited and talkative, and have a false sense of self-confidence and power. Regular users often feel restless, anxious, and moody.

Smoking "ice" causes schizophrenic-type behavior in many users. However, using large doses of any of the amphetamines over a long period of time also can result in an amphetamine psychosis: seeing, hearing, and feeling things that do not exist (hallucinations); having irrational thought or beliefs (delusions); and feeling as though people are out to get them (paranoia). Persons in this extremely suspicious state often exhibit bizarre and sometimes violent behavior. These symptoms usually disappear when they stop using the drug.

Long-term heavy use of amphetamines can lead to malnutrition, skin disorders, ulcers, weight loss, depression, and speech and thought disturbances. Kidney damage is also possible. An amphetamine injection creates a sudden increase in blood pressure that can cause bodily injury or death from stroke or heart failure. If taken during pregnancy, these drugs, especially "crank" and "ice," can do serious damage to the fetus.

The continued use of amphetamines is often prompted by efforts to avoid the "down" mood that occurs when the drug's effects wear off. When people stop using amphetamines abruptly, they may experience fatigue, long periods of sleep, irritability, hunger, and depression.

Cocaine

Cocaine, like the amphetamines, is a central nervous system stimulant. For years, cocaine hydrochloride has been used medically as a local anesthetic. Cocaine is obtained from cocoa trees, primarily in Peru, Colombia, and Bolivia. It is brought illegally to the United States in pure form as a fine white, crystalline powder. This powder is diluted to increase its bulk and street value. In this diluted form, it is only 15 to 25 percent cocaine and can be snorted through the nose. To increase potency and effect, the supplier can chemically extract the cocaine from the diluted powder, producing "crack" or "rock" cocaine that can be smoked. "Crack" is about 90 percent pure cocaine. Still another form of cocaine is cocoa paste, which is usually smoked; it can be especially dangerous because it contains contaminants such as kerosene, which can cause lung and brain damage.

When cocaine powder is "snorted," the euphoric effects begin within a few minutes, peak within fifteen to twenty minutes, and disappear within an hour. The user may have a sense of well-being and feel energetic, alert, and less hungry. Effects also include fixed and dilated pupils and increases in blood pressure, heart and breathing rates, and body temperature. Occasional snorting can cause a stuffy or runny nose; chronic snorting can ulcerate the mucous membrane of the nose. Some regular users report feelings of restlessness, irritability, anxiety, and sleeplessness. For some users, even low doses create psychological problems. Some who use high doses over a long period of time may become paranoid or experience a "cocaine psychosis," which might include hallucinations of touch, sight, taste, or smell. Some users take cocaine each day, but episodic use (e.g., on weekends) is common. "Binging" occurs when an individual takes numerous, high doses over a one- or two-day period; the binge ends when the supply is gone or the user collapses ("crashes") in physical exhaustion.

As compared to snorting powdered cocaine, the smoking of "crack" produces a shorter but a very intense "high." Smoking is the most direct and rapid way to transmit the chemical to the brain. Thus, it also increases the risks associated with using the drug (e.g., confusion, slurred speech, anxiety, hallucinations, and paranoid delusions). Whereas many users of cocaine powder develop an addiction over months or even years, "crack" smokers may become addicted in a much shorter period. Because "crack" addiction seems to create an unbreakable need for continuing use and because it is inexpensive, the typical pattern of use is that once a user begins an episode of use, he or she continues until the supply or money runs out or until physical exhaustion occurs. Within a day of the last use, intensive craving returns. Many "crack" users experience intense depression, which research suggests is related to the drug's effect on the brain. Children born to mothers who use "crack" during pregnancy suffer severe neurological damage.

Marijuana

Marijuana is the common name for a drug made from the plant *cannabis sativa.* The main psychoactive ingredient in marijuana is THC (delta-9-tetrahydrocannabinol). The amount of THC in the marijuana determines how strong its effects will be on the user. Hashish, or hash, is made by taking the resin from the leaves and flowers of the plant and pressing it into cakes; it may contain five to ten times more THC than crude marijuana. Marijuana and hash are usually smoked but are sometimes taken orally.

In the past, marijuana was regarded as a substance with a low addictive potential and unlikely to cause serious problems, but recent research and the clinical experience of drug treatment programs identify several adverse effects. Some individuals do become psychologically addicted. Heavy users may develop "amotivational syndrome," a general loss of interest in life's activities and an increase in passivity and sluggishness.

An individual "high" on marijuana or hashish will feel euphoric, may speak rapidly and loudly, and have dilated pupils. Some individuals experience sensory distortions. The drug can impair short-term memory, alter sense of time, and reduce ability to do things that require concentration, swift reactions, and coordination (e.g., driving a car or operating machinery). A possible reaction to marijuana is an acute panic reaction that is an extreme fear of "losing control." These symptoms disappear in a few hours.

PCP

PCP (phencyclidine), often called "angel dust," was developed as an anesthetic in the 1950s but later taken off the market for human use because it sometimes caused hallucinations. It continues to have use in veterinary medicine. PCP is available in a number of forms; it can be a pure, white crystal powder, a tablet, or a capsule. It can be swallowed, smoked, sniffed, or injected. PCP is sometimes sprinkled on marijuana and smoked. Although illegal, it is easily manufactured. It is sometimes sold as mescaline or THC, thus the user of those drugs may get PCP by mistake.

The sought-after effect of PCP is euphoria. For some users, small amounts act as a stimulant. For many users, PCP changes how they see their own bodies and things around them; movements and time are slowed. The effects of PCP are unpredictable and, for this reason, many "experimenters" abandon its use. Unfortunately, others become dependent. Negative effects include increased heart rate and blood pressure, flushing, sweating, dizziness, and numbness. When large doses are taken, effects include drowsiness, convulsions, coma, and sometimes death. PCP can produce violent or bizarre behavior. Regular use affects memory, perception, concentration, and judgment. Users may show signs of paranoia, fearfulness, and anxiety. When taking the drug, some users become aggressive; others withdraw and have difficulty communicating. A PCP-induced psychosis may last for days or weeks.

Hallucinogens

Hallucinogens, or psychedelics, are drugs that affect a person's perceptions, sensations, thinking, self-awareness, and emotions. Hallucinogens include such drugs as LSD, mescaline, psilocybin, and DMT. *LSD* is manufactured from lysergic acid, which is found in fungus that grows on grains. It is odorless, colorless, and tasteless. LSD is sold on the street in tablets, capsules, and occasionally in liquid form. It is usually taken by mouth but sometimes is injected. *DMT* is similar to LSD.

Mescaline comes from the peyote cactus. Although it is not as strong as LSD, its effects are similar. Mescaline is usually smoked or swallowed in the form of capsules or tablets. *Psilocybin* comes from certain mushrooms. It is sold in tablet or capsule form or the mushrooms themselves may be eaten.

The effects of psychedelics are unpredictable and depend on the dosage, the surroundings, and the user's personality, mood, and expectations. Usually, the user feels the first effects thirty to ninety minutes after taking it. He or she may feel several different emotions at once or swing rapidly from one emotion to another. The person's sense of time and self change. Sensations may seem to "cross over," giving the user the feeling of "hearing" colors and "seeing" sounds. For some users, these emotional changes are frightening and cause a "bad trip" that may last a few minutes or several hours, ranging from the mildly frightening to the terrifying and involving sensations of confusion, suspiciousness, anxiety, feelings of helplessness, and loss of control. Physical effects include dilated pupils, higher body temperature, increased heart rate and blood pressure, and often sweating, irregular breathing, and tremors. Some users may sit in a stupor, whereas others become agitated.

Taking a hallucinogen can unmask emotional problems. Flashbacks, in which the person experiences a drug's effects without having to take the drug again, can occur. Heavy users sometimes develop impaired memory, loss of attention span, confusion, and difficulty with abstract thinking.

Sedative Hypnotics

Sedative hypnotics are prescription drugs that depress the body's functions. These drugs are often referred to as tranquilizers, sleeping pills, or sedatives. Because they depress the central nervous system, they have a calming effect and promote sleep. An individual who has taken a dosage higher than prescribed may give the appearance of being drunk (e.g., staggering, slurred speech, dilated pupils, sleepiness, etc.) but not smell of alcohol. At high doses or when taken with alcohol (also a depressant), these drugs can cause unconsciousness and death.

Barbiturates and benzodiazepines are the two major categories of sedative hypnotics. Some well-known barbiturates are secobarbital (Seconal) and pentobarbital (Nembutal). Diazepam (Valium), chlordiazepoxide (Librium), and chlorazepate (Tranxene) are examples of benzodiazepines. A few sedative hypnotics do not fit in either category; they include methaqualone (Quaalude), etchlorvynol (Placidyl), chloral hydrate (Noctec), and mebrobamate (Miltown). All can be dangerous when not taken according to a physician's instructions.

The sedative-hypnotic drugs can cause both physical and psychological dependence. Regular use over a long period of time may result in tolerance. When regular large-dose users suddenly stop, they may develop withdrawal symptoms, ranging from restlessness, insomnia, and anxiety, to convulsions and death. Barbiturate overdose is a factor in nearly one-third of all reported drug-related deaths; these include suicides and accidental poisonings.

Babies born to mothers who abuse sedatives during their pregnancy may show withdrawal symptoms shortly after birth. Many sedative hypnotics pass through the placenta easily and may cause birth defects and behavioral problems in babies born to women who have abused these drugs during pregnancy.

Inhalants

Inhalants are chemicals that produce psychoactive vapors. Examples are model airplane glue, nail polish remover, lighter and cleaning fluids, and gasoline. Aerosols used as inhalants include paints, cookware coating agents, and hairsprays. Halothane, nitrous oxide (laughing gas), amyl nitrate, and butyl nitrite are also abused. Nearly all of the abused inhalants produce effects similar to anesthetics, which act to depress the body's functions. At low doses, users may feel slightly stimulated; some inhalants, like butyl nitrite, produce a "rush" or "high" lasting for a few seconds or a couple of minutes. Young people are likely to abuse inhalants, in part because these chemicals are readily available and inexpensive.

Possible negative effects include nausea, sneezing, coughing, nosebleeds, fatigue, bad breath, lack of coordination, and a loss of appetite. Solvents and aerosols decrease the heart and breathing rates and effect judgment. Deep breathing of the vapors may result in losing touch with one's surroundings, a loss of self-control, violent behavior, and unconsciousness. Inhalants can cause death from suffocation by displacing the oxygen in the lungs and also by depressing the central nervous system to a point that breathing stops. Long-term use can damage the liver, kidneys, blood, and bone marrow. Using inhalants while taking other drugs that also slow the body's functions, such as tranquilizers, sleeping pills, or alcohol, increases the risk of death.

Opiates

Opiates (narcotics), a group of drugs used medically to relieve pain, also have a high potential for abuse. Some opiates (opium, morphine, heroin, and codeine) come from the Asian poppy; others, such as meperidine (Demerol), are manufactured. Heroin accounts for 90 percent of the opiate abuse in the United States.

Opiates tend to relax the user. When opiates are injected, the user feels an immediate "rush." Indicators of opiate abuse include needle scars on the arms and the backs of hands, drowsiness, frequent scratching, red and watering eyes, sniffles, and a loss of appetite overall but an attraction to sugar and candies. In contrast to the effects of most other abused drugs that dilate the eye's pupils, the opiates constrict the pupils. When an opiate-dependent person stops taking the drug, withdrawal symptoms begin within four to six hours; symptoms include anxiety, diarrhea, abdominal cramps, chills, sweating, nausea, and runny nose and eyes. The intensity of these symptoms depends on how much was taken, how often, and for how long. Withdrawal symptoms for most opiates are stronger approximately twenty-four to seventy-two hours after they begin but subside within seven to ten days.

Most of the physical dangers of opiate abuse are caused by overdose; the use of unsterile needles, which spread AIDS and hepatitis; contamination of the drug by other chemicals; or combining the drug with other substances. Over time, opiate users may develop infections of the heart lining and valves, skin abscesses, and congested lungs. Babies born to a mother using an opiate often experience withdrawal symptoms and are at high risk of other health problems.

The social worker should follow a number of guidelines during the initial contact with the chemically dependent individual and his or her family.

1. Because the abuse of alcohol and other drugs is such a pervasive problem, assume that it will be a contributing cause to many of the individual and family problems you encounter in direct practice. The existence of a chemical dependency must be considered a possibility even when there has been no mention of the problem by the client and his or her family.

2. There is no great mystery surrounding the question of why people use drugs. Drugs and alcohol are attractive because they make people feel better, even if but for a short time. Curiosity and peer pressure also play a role in the initial stages. The powerful reinforcement provided by the chemical's mood-altering effects often leads to psychological dependence. No one starts using a drug with the intention of becoming dependent or addicted; in fact, all beginners believe they are invulnerable to addiction. There is a steady supply of both legal drugs (e.g., alcohol, nicotine) and illegal drugs because so much money can be made in this market.

3. Never underestimate the psychological power of alcohol and drugs. The addictive process can turn an otherwise kind and honest person into a self-centered individual who is willing to lie, cheat, and even injure loved ones in order to jealously protect and maintain his or her love relationship with a chemical. Typically, the abuser is adamant in denying any dependence on a drug and denies any connection between his or her current problems and the use of alcohol or a drug.

4. Be alert to signs of abuse. According to the DSM-III-R, the existence of a drug dependence (including alcohol) is probable when an individual exhibits at least three of the following:

a. Taking larger amounts or taking the drug for a longer period of time than was intended

b. Persistent desire to quit and/or one or more unsuccessful efforts to quit or reduce the amount taken

c. Much time spent in activities relating to securing, protecting, and taking the drug and recovering from the effects of its use

d. Frequent intoxication and withdrawal symptoms that interfere with performance of work, school, or family roles

e. Giving up previously important activities related to work, family, recreation, and so on in favor of drug use or drug-related activities

f. Continued use of drug even though the individual is aware its use is causing family, social, or health problems

g. Development of tolerance (i.e., more and more of drug is needed in order to attain desired mood-altering effect)

h. Presence of withdrawal symptoms and the use of the drug in order to relieve these symptoms

Other signs of drug abuse include:

- Unexplained changes in behavior and role performance at work, in school, or within the family
- Neglect of physical appearance, bodily hygiene, and dress
- Decreased physical and intellectual capacities (e.g., ability to concentrate, stay on track, think logically, etc.)

- Involvement in illegal activities (e.g., stealing, prostitution, etc.) when there has been no prior history of such activities
- Efforts to cover needle scars on arms
- Use of sunglasses to protect dilated eyes from bright light

5. Assess the degree to which your client's psychosocial functioning is impaired by his or her drug use. If it is a problem, referral to a treatment program is imperative. Consult with drug and alcoholism treatment specialists on how best to overcome the client's denial and resistance.

6. Be patient and nonjudgmental, but do not be afraid to be confrontive in your communications. You will not help the client by accepting his or her denials, alibis, rationalizations, or manipulations—all of which are part of the addictive process.

7. If you are a recovering alcoholic or drug abuser, share this fact with the client. Emphasize that you know from personal experience that controlling the problem is a difficult, day-by-day struggle, but that it is possible.

8. Do not lend the client money and do not become part of the enabling system that "covers" for the client by protecting him or her from the real-life consequences of chemical abuse.

9. If your client comes to an interview intoxicated, realize there is no point in trying to gather detailed psychosocial data or to engage the client in a counseling process. Explain in a polite but firm manner that you need accurate information to do your job and must, therefore, postpone the interview, rescheduling it for a time when the client is sober. Expect the client to become angry, but remain calm and firm.

10. If an intoxicated individual appears unexpectedly at your agency, secure only basic identifying information (name, age, address, etc.) and then give attention to the individual's physical condition. Be alert to the immediate life-threatening dangers of delirium tremens or drug overdose and the need for detoxification under medical supervision.

11. Encourage family members to make use of Al-Anon and Alateen groups, along with other resources such as COA (Children of Alcoholics), ACOA or ACA (Adult Children of Alcoholics), and programs that address the problem of codependency.

12. The assistance and support of the client's family and friends will probably be needed in the referral process. Thus, it is important to reach out to these individuals and engage them in the assessment, planning, and helping process. However, be alert to the possibility that they too may have a chemical abuse problem and/or may be contributing to your client's problem through enabling or codependency behaviors.

When appropriate, consult with family members and others deeply concerned for the chemically dependent person regarding use of a particular type of confrontation procedure (known as an "intervention") in which friends and family are helped to directly confront the chemically dependent individual regarding his or her behavior. This procedure is used to convince the person who is locked into the denial pattern that he or she has a major problem and that there will be serious and immediate consequences if he or she does not immediately enter treatment. If it is well planned and properly implemented, it can break through the denial and help the individual accept treatment. The intervention must be planned under the direction of a chemical dependency counselor who is skilled in using this procedure (Johnson 1986). The procedure requires detailed preparation and rehearsal by the persons who mean most to the client or those who exert power or control (e.g., spouse, children, employer, close friends, etc.). Each prepares a list of specific incidents of destructive drinking or drug-related behavior and vividly describes how he or she and the client are being hurt by the chemical abuse. It is important that these feelings be conveyed in a nonjudgmental and caring manner. During several practice sessions, each person reads his or her list and rehearses the presentation until he or she feels confident enough to directly face the chemically dependent person. Such rehearsals are critical to the success of the emotionally charged encounter. The group as a whole decides when to confront the chemically dependent person. It must be unannounced and arranged at a time when the individual will be as sober and lucid as possible. Those involved in the intervention insist that the individual listen and hear them out. The individual's usual denials and promises are not accepted, and no one comes to the person's rescue. Instead, everyone insists that the chemically dependent person must immediately—today—enter a treatment program. Prior to the confrontation, necessary arrangements are made so a treatment program is ready to accept the individual on the very day of the confrontation. Thus, all details (cost, insurance coverage, leave of absence from work, etc.) must have been worked out in advance.

13. Realize that the successful treatment of drug abuse problems usually involve three phases: (a) detoxification in a hospital or as an out-patient (i.e., supervised withdrawal from drug dependence, either with or without medication); (b) in-patient treatment within a highly structured therapeutic community where the client's denial system can be broken down and he or she begins to use counseling and self-help groups; and (c) out-patient, drug-free programs that provide counseling and self-help groups using the twelve-step approach. Following these three phases, the client enters the most difficult and the most important part of their recovery: the day-by-day and life-long struggle to rebuild his or her life and to remain drug free. To be successful, the chemically dependent person must take responsibility for his or her own recovery. The various twelve-step programs (e.g. Alcoholics Anonymous, Cocaine Anonymous, Narcotics Anonymous, etc.) have the best record of success in facilitating this long-term recovery process. These programs emphasize the development of one's spirituality and help the individual reorient his or her philosophy of living and life-style.

14. Because drugs alter mood, individuals with low self-esteem and feelings of powerlessness, loneliness, and emotional pain are especially prone to misuse drugs. Because they do not value themselves, they do not believe they are capable of changing their situation, so they look to things outside themselves (e.g., drugs) for relief from life's problems and pain. Effective recovery programs counteract these beliefs and help the individual develop self-esteem, learn problem-solving skills, rely on inner resources, and create drug-free relationships with others.

15. Be alert to problems caused by the misuse of other drugs and medications. For example, it is estimated that about one million individuals, mostly male, use *steroids* to boost their athletic strength and physical appearance; more than half of these people are under age eighteen. Steroids, which are inexpensive and easy to obtain, are not addictive like the other drugs discussed in this section, but they do pose a serious health problem. Steroids are attractive because they build muscles; however, they also cause tumors, high blood pressure, shrunken testicles, liver and kidney disorders, and erratic sleep disorders. In young users, steroids can retard growth. In some cases, their use leads to violent mood shifts, aggression, and violence.

Selected Bibliography

Alcoholics Anonymous. 3rd ed. New York: A. A. World Services, Inc., 1976.

American Psychiatric Association. *DSM-III-R.* Washington, D.C.: American Psychiatric Association, 1987.

Cermak, Timmen. *Diagnosing and Treating Co-Dependence.* Minneapolis: Johnson Institute Books, 1986.

Freeman, Edith. *Social Work Practice with Clients Who Have Alcohol Problems.* Springfield, Ill.: Charles C. Thomas, 1985.

Johnson, Vernon. *Intervention: How to Help Someone Who Doesn't Want Help.* Minneapolis: Johnson Institute Books, 1986.

Julien, Robert. *A Primer of Drug Action.* 5th ed. Salt Lake City: W. H. Freeman, 1988.

Kinney, Jean, and Gwen Leaton. *Loosening the Grip: A Handbook of Alcohol Information.* 3rd ed. St. Louis: Times Mirror/Mosby College Publishing, 1987.

Social Casework 70, no. 6 (June 1989). (Special issue on treating the alcoholic.)

9.10 *The Manipulative Client*

Purpose: To respond appropriately to the client who frequently manipulates other people.

Discussion: Most people, at least occasionally, attempt to manipulate others as a way of getting what they want. However, some individuals rely on manipulation and "conning" as a primary means of coping with life. These individuals can be very difficult clients, primarily because they are so skilled and subtle in "using" other people. Social workers who are unable to detect a manipulation may quickly find themselves in legal and ethical difficulties.

Some of the most practiced manipulators are persons labeled as "sociopaths," "psychopaths," or as having an "antisocial personality disorder." Many have a long history of criminal activity. They seem to be without a conscience, they habitually "con" others, and they seem unmoved by the distress they create or by a sense of loyalty or responsibility toward other people. For them, truth is whatever fits their purpose at the moment. Many grew up in environments where manipulation was the key to their physical and psychological survival; thus, it is useful for the social worker to view manipulation as the continuation of behavioral patterns that proved effective in the past. Included here are a few guidelines.

1. The manipulative client, like all clients, is deserving of respect. With this client, however, you need to be much more cautious, deliberate, and careful in your actions. You must be explicit in outlining your role, what you can and cannot do as a professional person, and your expectations of the client. You must demonstrate firmness and strength of conviction. Yochelson and Samenow (1985) remind us that the habitual manipulator is always behaving in ways that help him or her gain control of others.

> He tries to determine what others want to hear and feeds it to them. He finds and uses opportunities for digression and diversion. He discloses as it suits his purposes. He slants his version of events to make himself a victim and blames others for his plight in life. He tries whatever he thinks will impress the [change agent], enlist his sympathy and compassion, or convince him of a particular point of view. Failing this, he uses a variety of tactics to put [the change agent] on the defensive. These may be couched in highly intellectual terms as the criminal argues the meaning of a word, disputes a philosophic issue, and generalizes a point to absurdity. However, there are also open power plays as he intimidates, threatens, ridicules and erupts with angry reactions.
>
> The agent of change has no hope of being successful if he allows a criminal to set the conditions of a meeting. . . . The [agent of change] must stand firm. . . . [A professional] who is indecisive or lacks confidence does not instill confidence or respect in a criminal. Nor can [a professional] who is permissive later establish himself as a firm authority. Many criminals have had experience with permissive change agents and have exploited them. A person who is shy, timid, or reserved may do well in many endeavors, but he will fail to effect change in criminals. (p. 541)

2. Suspect a manipulation whenever your client takes an inordinate interest in your personal life or your feelings about your job. Be especially cautious when your client says such things as, "You are the only person that really understands me," "No one else has ever been as helpful as you," "You are the most caring person I have ever met," "If you could just do this one thing for me (often something illegal or unethical), I can get my life straightened out," "I have a wonderful opportunity to pull my life together—I just need a small loan," or "I need to tell you something but you must promise not to tell this to anyone else."

3. In order to avoid pitfalls, teamwork or close supervision is critical. If you suspect a manipulation, immediately consult with another professional and examine your actions and feelings. If you are part of a team, raise your concerns with other team members. Often you will find that the client is saying very different things to different team members. An elevated level of team communication and coordination is necessary to keep team members from being drawn into a manipulation where one member is played against another.

4. Be fair but unwavering in your expectations of these clients. Hold manipulative clients responsible for their behavior and do not rescue them for logical consequences of their choices. Before making a desirable change, they usually need first to experience the punishing consequences of their actions.

5. Many professionals who try to be nonjudgmental in their relationships with clients become judgmental when they encounter the manipulative client who knows how to "work the system"—meaning that the client can accurately predict how agencies, social workers, and other professionals will respond under certain circumstances. You can increase your tolerance for these clients and decrease your judgmentalness by remembering that manipulation is essentially a coping strategy. This client uses manipulation because it works or works better than anything else he or she knows how to do. Although there may be something particularly irritating about people who use deception and lies to manipulate the caring professionals in our health and social welfare programs, we need to remember that in other areas of society, being able to "work the system" is a mark of competence. For example, the lawyer, businessperson, or social worker who knows how to get the "system" to do what he or she wants is viewed as someone with great skill.

Selected Bibliography

Allen, Bud, and Diana Bosta. *Games Criminals Play.* Sacramento: Rae John Publishers, 1981.

Doren, Dennis. *Understanding and Treating the Psychopath.* New York: John Wiley, 1987.

Yochelson, Samuel, and Stanton Samenow. *The Criminal Personality.* Vol. II. Northvale, N.J.: Jason Aronson, 1985.

9.11 The Dangerous Client

Purpose: To respond to a potentially violent client in a manner that reduces the danger inherent in the situation.

Discussion: Social workers in correctional settings and child protective services, more than those in other fields of practice, are likely to encounter potentially violent persons. For example, the forced removal of a child from a parent almost always carries some risk of being physically threatened or assaulted. When interacting with an extremely angry and potentially violent person, the social worker should adhere to the following guidelines:

1. Never enter a situation known to be dangerous without first consulting with others about your plans. Consider the situation to be high risk whenever there is a history of previous family violence or possession or use of firearms or other lethal weapons, and when you are to meet an unfamiliar client in a nonpublic or isolated place. Do not hesitate to call for police assistance and protection.

2. A history of violent outbursts is the best predictor of future violence. An agency's recordkeeping system should utilize color coding or some other method of flagging the case record of a potentially dangerous client so that the social worker who meets the client for the first time can take appropriate precautions. Your agency should have an agreed upon emergency communication code so all staff will recognize a disguised request for assistance. For example, in a telephone message such as, "Hello, Bob. This is Jim. Would you please send a copy of our red resource book to my office," the phrase "red resource book" might be a code for "send the police to my office."

3. When making a home visit that could develop into a dangerous situation, always keep your office informed of your itinerary and check in by phone according to a prearranged time schedule. Before entering the home or building, take a few minutes to look around and think about your safety. Are you alone? Where are the escape routes? Do you hear a violent argument in progress? Never respond to an invitation to "come in" unless you see the person who is speaking and he or she has seen you. Make sure the person knows who you are and why you are there. (Being mistaken for someone else can be dangerous.)

4. For an office interview, position your furniture and yourself so you have easy access to the door or an escape route. Make sure that the client also has easy access to the door so he or she does not feel trapped.

5. When entering a room that contains a potentially violent person, move in slowly. Remain on the periphery until you can assess the situation. Be alert to many small things about the situation that feel or look unusual or out of place, for that can be a sign of danger. Intrusion may trigger violent behavior. Do not move into the person's space. Do not touch an angry person; do nothing that could be interpreted as a threat or intimidation. If possible, sit rather than stand, because sitting is a less aggressive stance. Also encourage the client to sit, as it usually has a calming effect.

6. Aggressiveness is often a reaction to being afraid. Do whatever you can to lessen the person's need to be afraid of you. Remain composed and speak in a gentle and soothing manner. Do not argue, lecture, accuse, or give advice. Demonstrate empathy for the person's feelings of frustration and anger. Use paraphrasing (see Technique 6.4) to ensure accurate understanding of his or her thoughts and feelings. If a mistake or inappropriate statement on your part caused the client's anger, admit the error and apologize. Use "I-messages" (see Technique 6.6) when expressing your concerns or explaining your intentions, role, and responsibility. Allow the angry client to ventilate; this can drain off some of the intensity.

7. Aggressiveness and anger also stem from a feeling of being controlled or trapped by others. To the greatest extent possible, increase the client's sense of control by offering him or her options and choices and by using language such as, "But, of course, it is up to you to decide what is best" or "Think about what we have discussed and decide which course of action you want to follow."

8. Be alert to signs of imminent attack, such as flaring nostrils, dilated pupils, pulsing veins, teeth grinding, fist clenching, and crouching of the upper body. Do not turn your back to angry or distraught persons or let them walk behind you. If the danger of the situation escalates, leave.

9. Maintain a neat, well-groomed appearance and an attitude of confidence that gives the impression you take your job seriously and are able to handle the situation. An angry person is more likely to attack someone who appears weak and afraid. On the other hand, do nothing that would be interpreted as a challenge.

10. When in the home of a potentially violent person, be alert to the fact that guns are usually kept in the bedroom, and be aware that the kitchen contains numerous potential weapons. If the person has threatened you and moves quickly to one of these rooms, leave immediately.

11. Do not attempt to disarm a person who has a weapon. Leave that to the police. If your client has a weapon, calmly explain that you intend no harm and slowly back away or otherwise try to extricate yourself from the situation.

12. If you work in a dangerous neighborhood or a dangerous practice setting, secure guidance from experienced peers, local merchants, and police on places to avoid and on how to protect yourself. Consider obtaining training in self-defense, but be sure to select an instructor who has had personal experience with violent persons. Remember, even excellent training does not adequately prepare you for the real thing. Never overestimate your ability to handle a situation or underestimate the paralyzing effect of fear.

Selected Bibliography

Bolton, Frank, and Susan Bolton. *Working with Violent Families.* Newbury Park, Calif.: Sage, 1987.

Bull, Ray, Bob Bustin, Phil Evans, and Denis Gahagan. *Psychology for Police Officers.* New York: Wiley, 1983.

Kaplan, Stephen, and Eugenie Wheeler. "Survival Skills for Working with Potentially Violent Clients." *Social Casework* 64 (June 1983): 339–46.

Schoborn, Karl. *Dealing with Violence: The Challenge Faced by Police and Other Peacekeepers.* Springfield, Ill.: Charles C. Thomas, 1975.

Data Collection and Assessment

10

Introduction

Data collection and assessment are essential steps in the problem-solving process. *Data collection* refers to the gathering of information; *assessment* refers to the intellectual activity of interpreting and giving conceptual order to those facts and observations. Both data collection and assessment are ongoing and continuing activities throughout the intervention. However, most of these activities are concentrated in the beginning stages of the helping process.

It is during the assessment process that the social worker draws heavily on the values, principles, conceptual frameworks, and theoretical formulations common to the social work profession. In addition, the worker draws on his or her practice experience and makes use of facts and theories of other disciplines such as psychology, sociology, medicine, law, political science, and economics.

Assessment is an activity directed toward understanding the client's problem or situation and developing a plan of action. It is a joint client-worker effort. Together, the client and worker try to make sense out of available information and use that understanding as a basis for deciding what can be done and how it can best be achieved. Broadly speaking, an assessment should answer the following questions: What is the problem? Who does it affect? Where does it occur? When does it occur? Why does it occur? How can it be solved or mitigated?

When assessing a client problem or situation, the social worker gives at least some attention to all dimensions of the *whole person:*

- *Volitional.* Personal choices and decisions, processes used to make a decision, impact of choices on others
- *Familial.* Interaction with family members, sense of belonging to a group of concerned people, sense of loyalty and obligation to relatives, one's personal history and traditions, and so on

- *Social.* Interaction with friends and peers; one's place in the community; one's roles, status, ethnic identity; one's use of various formal and informal resources to meet needs and solve problems
- *Spiritual.* One's view on the meaning and purpose of life; relationship with one's creator, views as to what is right and wrong, sense of responsibility for self and others
- *Emotional.* Subjective feelings or moods such as joy, love, sadness, anger, fear, shame, and so on; movement toward or away from persons
- *Intellectual.* Ideas, knowledge, and beliefs used to make decisions and to understand self and the world around us; ability to interpret what our senses tell us, and so on
- *Economic.* One's material resources and capacity to secure money and compete for desired goods and services
- *Physical.* One's energy, health, illness, pain, vision, hearing, mobility, and so on

A social worker's assessments and interventions are characterized by a focus on what has been called the **person-in-environment** configuration. This refers to the "fit," or "match," between the needs of the individual and the capacity of his or her social environment to meet those needs. DeHoyos (1989, 133) reminds us that this "match" is dynamic and is achieved through mutual interaction, exchange, negotiation, and compromise. We would add that in some cases, unfortunately, it is also achieved through coercion and violence, for sometimes the needs of one person are met at the expense of others.

Traditionally, social workers have been concerned about the ability of individuals, families, communities, and society as a whole to meet **basic human needs.** Such needs include the need for food, shelter, clothing, meaningful work, safety, belonging, self-esteem, affection, encouragement, self-actualization, and so on. A social work assessment must focus not only needs and whether they are unmet but also on how these needs are expressed and whether these needs and the expression of these needs are physically and psychologically normal. For example, a client may have a very strong need for a drug or perhaps a need to control or hurt others. These are needs of a sort but they are abnormal and destructive; thus, the social worker would try to change rather than meet such needs. The social worker must also consider whether the behaviors used by the client to meet his or her basic human needs are constructive and socially responsible. For example, one's need-meeting behaviors should not cause harm to others or violate norms and legitimate laws. During assessment, the social worker also examines the willingness and capacity of systems making up the client's environment (e.g., family, social network, employment, community, governmental agencies, etc.) to meet the client's needs. Thus, data collection and assessment give attention to:

- Basic human needs, especially those that remain unmet
- Whether the needs and their expression are normal
- Whether the client's usual ways of trying to meet needs are socially acceptable and socially responsible

- Sociobehavioral systems and processes that create obstacles as the client attempts to meet his or her needs
- Capacity of economic and governmental systems to provide the resources and opportunities necessary to facilitate an individual's need meeting efforts

Because an assessment can be only as good as the data on which it is based, the social worker must know how to gather accurate and usable data. Data are useful only when they can make a difference in practice; if the data cannot affect what the social worker actually does, then they probably should not have been gathered in the first place. There are several modes of data collection:

1. Direct verbal questioning of the client by the social worker
2. Direct written questioning of the client by the social worker
3. Projective or indirect verbal questioning of the client by the social worker
4. Projective or indirect written questioning of the client by the social worker
5. Observation of the client by the social worker in an analogue situation
6. Observation of the client by the social worker or other trained observer in the client's natural environment
7. Client self-monitoring and self-observation by means of a written recording tool or logs
8. Client self-monitoring by means of an electronic recording device
9. The use of existing written materials (e.g., case records)

Direct verbal questioning within the context of the face-to-face interview is the most common method of data collection used in social work. Direct written questioning may take the form of questionnaires, checklists, inventories, and the like. Not infrequently, these tools are used within the context of a face-to-face interview to supplement verbal questioning. Roleplaying is an example of projective verbal questioning. Self-administered written questioning is used in mailed surveys. The observation of a client in an analogue situation involves having the client perform certain tasks as part of a simulation. By observing the client in a situation analogous to real life, the social worker obtains valuable information on how well the client can perform a particular task. Since a client's behavior is strongly influenced by his or her environment, there are many advantages to observing the client in a natural setting (e.g., a home visit). Some workers become participant observers by sharing a meal with a client. Others may prefer only to observe, as is common in evaluations of a child's behavior problem. Behavioral approaches make frequent use of client self-monitoring as a method of collecting baseline data needed for planning an intervention. Much data can be found in existing written materials (case records, newspapers, committee reports, etc.). Since each approach to data collection has limitations, the social worker should use more than one method whenever possible. This increases the reliability and validity of data collection.

Most practicum students and new social workers receive training in verbal questioning (i.e., face-to-face interviewing) but are inadequately prepared to use other modes. Thus, this chapter presents several examples of direct written questioning and projective written questioning. The techniques presented make use of checklists, questionnaires to be filled out by the client, and vignettes to be discussed with the client. Some can be used during face-to-face interviews; others can be used to gather data by mail. Most are simple, inexpensive, and can be shared with and understood by clients. These data-collection tools should be viewed as examples and models. Several of those presented can be adapted to specific agencies and client groups. A set of guidelines for the development of data-gathering tools also appears in this chapter.

A *data-gathering tool* records raw data; an *assessment tool* goes one step further and incorporates some type of scaling or measurement procedure that informs the user about the probable meaning of the data. Most often, this involves comparing how the client responded to the instrument with the collective responses of others to whom the instrument was administered (e.g., standardized psychological tests). This chapter includes only a sampling of the assessment tools developed by social workers for use within the profession; there are dozens of others. In addition, several other assessment tools are presented; although not developed by social workers, they have been used frequently by social workers. In fact, literally hundreds of assessment instruments are potentially useful to the social worker. Psychologists have been particularly active in the development of such instruments.

Several of the instruments described here are what Levitt and Reid (1981) term *Rapid-Assessment Instruments* (*RAIs*). They explain that, in clinical social work,

> increasing emphasis is being placed on the use of short-term treatment and contractual agreements between workers and clients and hence the early diagnosis. These trends, in turn, have created the need for rapid assessment of client's conditions.... RAIs are short (no more than two pages), easy to administer ... and complete. Thus RAIs can easily be fitted into a typical clinical interview without interfering with the therapeutic process. (pp. 13–14)

Assessment tools and instruments should not be confused with *research instruments*. Instruments designed for research purposes may not be of use to the social work practitioner. A good research tool is not necessarily a good practice tool. Some research instruments are too complex or too time consuming to administer in direct service situations. Also, many research instruments yield little information that can be used in planning an intervention. The instruments that the practitioner finds most useful are those that are easily understood by the client, brief, and simple to administer. Moreover, the worker wants an instrument that can identify specific problems and guide the intervention.

Selected Bibliography

DeHoyos, Genevieve. "Person in Environment: A Tri-Level Practice Model." *Social Casework* 70, no. 3 (March 1989): 131–38.

Levitt, John, and William Reid. "Rapid-Assessment Instruments for Practice." *Social Work Research and Abstracts* 17 (Spring 1981): 13–19.

10.1 The Social Assessment Report

Purpose: To convey to other professionals a basic understanding of relevant social information about a particular client.

Discussion: A *social assessment report* (often called a *social history*) is frequently prepared by social workers in direct practice. As contrasted, for example, to a report prepared by a physician that focuses on physical functioning, the report prepared by a professional social worker focuses primarily on social functioning—the social, relational, or interactional aspects of the client's functioning and his or her situation. The word *social* refers to the interactions between and among people and between people and the significant systems of their social environment (e.g., family, school, job, hospital, etc.). Social workers are particularly concerned about the match (or lack thereof) between client needs and the resources (formal and informal) available to meet those needs. A good social assessment report will reflect this interactional focus.

Most reports contain two types of information: (1) the raw social data and (2) the worker's assessment or thoughts about the meaning of that data. Social data are the basic facts; the social assessment is a statement summarizing the worker's impressions and hypotheses that give added meaning to the data and their implications for social work intervention. The information presented in a report should lay a foundation for doing something with the client about his or her problem situation.

The organization, format, and content of a report will vary from agency to agency and reflect the agency's purpose and program. Also, the content will vary depending on the audience for which it is prepared: doctors, judges, psychologists, school personnel, interdisciplinary teams, and so on.

A good report is characterized by a number of qualities, which are outlined in the following list.

1. *Shortness.* The report should say no more than needs to be said to those who will use the report. Everyone is busy. Do not ask others to read more than is necessary.

2. *Simplicity.* Select the least complicated words and phrases. Avoid jargon, especially psychiatric labels, because such terms often mean different things to different people. Rather than use labels, describe and give examples of the behavior you want the reader to know about.

3. *Usefulness.* Keep the report's purpose in mind while you are preparing it. Ask yourself who will read the report and what they need to know. Do not include information merely because it is interesting and sensational.

4. *Organization.* Use numerous headings to break the information into topical categories. The following headings are often used:

- Identifying Information (name, date of birth, address, etc.)
- Reason for Social Work Involvement
- Statement of Problem
- Family Background
- Significant Others and Interpersonal Functioning
- Physical Functioning, Health Practices, and Health Problems
- Intellectual Functioning and Educational Background
- Emotional Functioning
- Problem-Solving Capacity
- Employment and Economic Situation
- Housing and Transportation
- Nutrition and Home Safety
- Impressions and Assessment
- Intervention Plan

The sample report presented in Figure 10.1 illustrates the use of topical headings.

5. *Confidentiality.* Respect the client's privacy. Assume that the client may want to read the report and has a right to do so. The Patients' Bill of Rights, the 1974 Federal Privacy Act, and ethical principles related to confidentiality and client access to records all suggest that a good social history report is one that has been or could be shared with the client/family. Think carefully before including information that you would not want the client or family (or their lawyer) to read.

6. *Objectivity.* Select words that express your observations and thoughts in an accurate and nonjudgmental manner. Beware of value-laden words and connotative meanings such as, for example, "Women's libber," "Chauvinist," "The client admits he doesn't attend church," and "He claims to have completed high school." Label your opinions and personal judgments as such and support your conclusions with data. Do not present an opinion as if it were a fact. The best way to do this is to place your conclusions, opinions, and hypotheses under a separate topical heading called "Worker's Opinion and Assessment."

When it is necessary to include highly personal information or draw conclusions that might offend the client/family, do so, if possible, by using the client's own words and quotation marks to convey information. Note the example below.

Correct Presentation: While I was talking with Jane, her father requested a glass of water. She responded in a loud voice and said, "Go to hell, you old fool."

Incorrect Presentation: It is apparent that Jane is a hostile and uncaring individual who is too self-centered and immature to cope with the demands of her elderly father.

7. *Relevance.* The information included in the report should have a clear connection to the client's presenting problem and/or the reason the social worker and agency are involved with the client.

Figure 10.1 Sample Social Assessment Report

Greystone Family Service Agency

Identifying Information

Date of Referral _____ Oct. 8, 1990 _____

Name _____ Shirley McCarthy _____ Case Record # _____ 5982 _____

D.O.B _____ July 6, 1970 _____ Sex __F__ Age __20__ Social Security # _____ 505-49-6712 _____

Address _____ 2109 B Street _____ Religion _____ Catholic _____

_____ Greystone, Montana 59807 _____

Phone _____ 555-1234 or work 555-3921 _____ Social Worker _____ Jane Green, BSW _____

Marital Status _____ Single _____ Report Prepared _____ 10/13/90 _____

Reason for Report
This report was prepared for agency staff use during peer supervision and for meeting with
Dr. Jones, the agency's psychiatric consultant. (The client is aware that a report is being prepared
for purpose of consultation.)

Reason for Social Work Involvement
Shirley was referred to this agency on October 8 by Dr. Smith, an emergency room physician at
City Hospital. She was treated there for having taken an unknown quantity of aspirin in an
apparent suicide attempt.

Source of Data
This report is based on two one-hour interviews with the client and a brief conversation with
Dr. Smith. I interviewed Shirley on October 9 and October 11.

Presenting Problem/Reason for Involvement with Client
Shirley is reacting with great anxiety and periods of depression related to the fact that she is
experiencing an unwanted pregnancy. The father is a former boyfirend with whom she has broken
off. She agreed to come to this agency in hopes of figuring out how she should deal with the
problem. She doesn't want her parents to find out about the pregnancy. She does not want an
abortion and does not want to care for a child. She says she has thought about adoption but
doesn't know much about what would be involved.

Family and Interpersonal Functioning
Shirley is the youngest of three children. Her brother, John, age 30, is a chemical engineer in
Austin, Texas. Her sister, Martha, age 28, is a pharmacist in Seattle. Shirley does not feel close to
either John or Martha and neither know of her pregnancy.

Shirley's parents have been married for about 33 years. They live in Spokane, Washington. Her
father, Thomas, is an engineer for an irrigation equipment company. Her mother, Mary, is a
registered nurse. Shirley does not want her parents to know about the pregnancy. "It would just kill
them if they found out."

The McCarthy family are life-long Catholics. All of the children attended Catholic grade and
high schools. At this time Shirley has little interest or involvement in the Church.

Shirley reports having few friends. She doesn't find it easy to get close to people.

Her former boyfriend, Bob (father of baby), was the first person she has dated more than a
couple of times. He was also the first man she really liked.

(Continued)

Figure 10.1 (Continued)

In college, she had trouble getting along with roommates in the dorm, so she finally got a small apartment so she could live alone.

Physical Functioning and Health Practices

According to Dr. Smith, Shirley is 5'8" tall and weighs 115 lbs. Dr. Smith reports that she is underweight but otherwise healthy. He does have concern about her willingness to obtain proper prenatal care during the pregnancy. Dr. Smith is concerned that this could be a "high-risk pregnancy" in that she could give birth to a premature or low-weight baby. Shirley does not have a regular doctor.

Shirley is probably 2½ months pregnant. Dr. Smith referred her to Dr. Johnson (an OB/GYN), but she did not go to the appointment.

Intellectual Functioning

Shirley completed two years of college at the University of Washington, where she was majoring in computer science. She received mostly A's in her computer courses and had an overall GPA of 3.8. Despite her good grades in high school and college, Shirley describes herself as "dumb."

She is attracted to subjects where there is a clear right and wrong answer. She does not like courses like philosophy, which seem "fuzzy" or "wishy-washy" to her.

During my interviews with her, I have been impressed with her good verbal ability. She has a good vocabulary and expresses herself very well.

Although she values precision and the data-based fields of study, she tends to make personal decisions impulsively. She says she "jumps into things without considering the consequences."

Emotional Functioning

Shirley describes herself as "moody." During my sessions, I have observed mood swings. She can move from sadness to enthusiasm in a matter of minutes. Even before the pregnancy, she had bouts of depression when she would sit in her room alone for hours at a time. In describing herself, Shirley uses the words "childish" and "immature." As long as she can remember, she has felt "younger" than others her age. She states she keeps her feelings to herself. She feels anger and sadness but tries to keep them from showing. In this sense, she is like her dad, who always keeps things to himself until he finally just blows up.

Problem-Solving Capacity

Shirley is bright and can be very thoughtful and analytical. This is an impressive quality. However, when dealing with everyday living, she seldom draws on this capacity. Rather, she lets things pile up until she is forced by circumstances to follow the course of action still open to her. She can think things through and decide what actions she "should" take, but she doesn't act. She attributes this to a life-long fear of making mistakes.

When faced with conflict, she is inclined to withdraw and avoid the problem. She is well aware of how this approach gets her into further difficulty, but she has not found a way to change it.

When I asked her about her suicide attempt, she was quick to assure me that she did not really want to kill herself and that it was a "stupid thing to do." She acknowledged a history of bouts with depression but said she had never before tried to hurt herself.

Economic Situation

Shirley's parents have paid her college tuition and some other expenses. Since high school she has worked summers. At present, she is working 30 hours per week at Greene's Department Store, earning $5 per hour. With this money, she maintains a small apartment and keeps her car running.

Figure 10.1 (Continued)

Aside from the college student health insurance, she has no coverage. She does not know if that policy covers pregnancy or if she must be back in school next term in order to use the plan.

Housing and Transportation
Shirley lives alone in a two-room apartment at 2109 B Street, Greystone, Montana. This is a rough part of town, so she is often afraid to be out alone after dark. She has a 1986 Toyota that runs well and provides reliable transportation.

Use of Community Resources
Other than her contacts with physicians and the hospital, Shirley is not now involved with other agencies or professionals. This is the first time she has ever had contact with a social agency. During our first session, she asked many questions about the agency and expressed confusion about why she had been referred here by Dr. Smith. I have the impression that it has been very difficult for her to reach for outside assistance.

Impressions and Assessment
This 20-year-old client is experiencing a great deal of inner conflict and depression because of an unwanted pregnancy. This resulted in a suicide attempt. In keeping with her tendency to avoid and deny, she has not been able to confront the problem directly. She has told no one else of the pregnancy, yet the father will probably have to be involved in any relinquishment and her parents' involvement may be needed for financial support. Prenatal care is needed, but it, too, has been avoided. Abortion is not an acceptable solution for her, and she is very ambivalent about adoption and how to manage her life while pregnant.

Intervention Plan
I will attempt to involve Shirley in a contract involving at least six sessions during which the focus will be helping her to sort out her feelings and move ahead on making plans and decisions that she can live with. The agency's "options counseling worksheet" will be used as a way of focusing our session. Major issues during the pregnancy include the involvement of the baby's father and her parents, financial plans, and medical care during the pregnancy. I also want to explore her problem with depression and the suicide attempt. After getting Shirley linked with a physician, I hope to work cooperatively with her doctor on the depression.

Shirley will need emotional support, some structure, and a gentle demand for work so she can overcome her tendency to avoid and deny, make some decisions, and take action.

Note: The names in this sample report are fictitious.

8. *Focus on Client Strengths.* Avoid preoccupation with psychopathology and family disorganization, personal weakness, and limitation. To the greatest extent possible, emphasize whatever strengths exist. Focus on what the client/family can do, not on what they cannot do. Successful intervention is built on client strength. Therefore, the social history and social assessment report must identify these strengths.

Selected Bibliography

Kagle, Jill. *Social Work Records.* Homewood, Ill.: Dorsey Press, 1984.
Wilson, Suanna. *Recording: Guidelines for Social Workers.* New York: The Free Press, 1976.

Purpose: To graphically depict a family and interactional data as an aid in the social assessment process.

Discussion: The genogram and ecomap are paper-and-pencil assessment tools. A *genogram* is a diagram very similar to a family tree. It can describe family relationships for two or three generations of a family (an attempt to depict more than three generations becomes very complex). The *ecomap* drawing places an individual or a family within its social context.

In addition to their value in assessment, the genogram and ecomap can significantly shorten the traditional narrative case recording. Family descriptions that might require two or three pages of narrative can often be reduced to a single page of genogram and ecomap diagrams. For example, a typical record or social history will focus on information such as:

- Age, sex, marital status, and household composition
- Family structure and relationships (e.g., biological children, stepchildren, parents, etc.)
- Job situation, employment, and responsibilities
- Social activities and interests (hobbies, recreational activities, etc.)
- Formal associations (church membership, participation in union, membership in service club, etc.)
- Sources of support and stress in social interactions (between people and between people and community systems)
- Utilization of community resources (Medicaid, economic assistance, public health, mental health, schools, Social Security, doctors, etc.)
- Informal resources and natural helpers (extended family, relatives, friends, neighbors, self-help groups)

All of these data can be "drawn" into a one-page ecomap.

Although the user of these diagrams can create his or her own symbols and abbreviations, certain symbols are commonly used, as shown on the next page. Words and notations—such as "m" for "married," "div" for "divorced," and "d" for "died"—may also be used in the family diagram and ecomap.

Figure 10.2 is a diagram of a reconstituted family, which appears within the dotted circle (boundary). It indicates that a man (age forty-five), his wife (age thirty-three), and three children (ages three, one, and ten) live in the household. The ten-year-old is from his mother's former marriage; the boy's biological father died in 1981. The forty-five-year-old husband was divorced from his former wife (age forty-two) in 1980. Also, we see that he has two daughters (ages twenty and eighteen) by this former wife and is now a grandfather, since his twenty-year-old daughter has a one-year-old daughter. The former wife is now married to a man who is age forty-four.

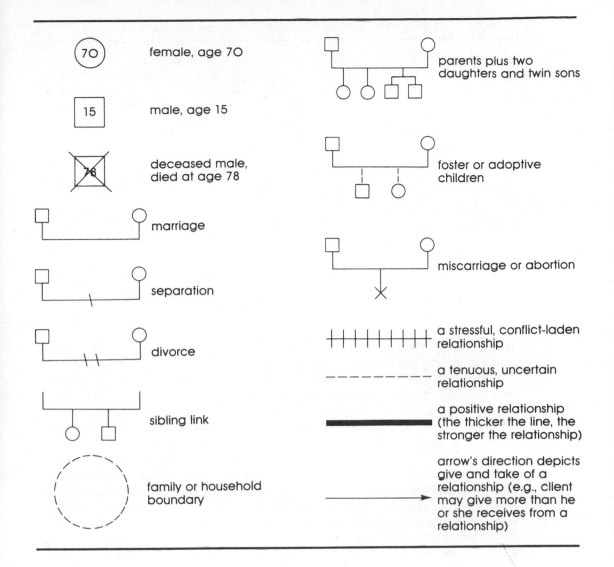

female, age 70

male, age 15

deceased male, died at age 78

marriage

separation

divorce

sibling link

family or household boundary

parents plus two daughters and twin sons

foster or adoptive children

miscarriage or abortion

a stressful, conflict-laden relationship

a tenuous, uncertain relationship

a positive relationship (the thicker the line, the stronger the relationship)

arrow's direction depicts give and take of a relationship (e.g., client may give more than he or she receives from a relationship)

An ecomap places the family or client of concern within their social context by using circles to represent significant organizations or factors impacting their lives. Various symbols or short phrases are used to describe the nature of these interactions. Figure 10.3 is an ecomap of Dick and Barb and their two children, John and June.

An ecomap is usually developed jointly by the social worker and client and helps both to view the family from a system's or ecological perspective. Ecomapping can be used by the worker to build a relationship and demonstrate a desire

Figure 10.2 Sample Genogram of a Reconstituted Family

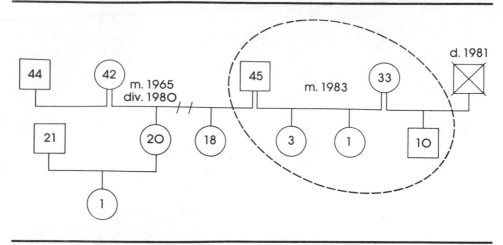

to learn about the client and his or her situation. It has been used in adoption and foster-care home studies and in marriage and family counseling. Many clients report that doing an ecomap helps them see their situation more clearly and sort out what they can do about their problems.

When examining an ecomap, the social worker should consider a number of basic questions: Does the family have an income adequate to cover basic needs such as food, shelter, transportation, and health care? Are family members employed? Do they enjoy their jobs? Does the family live in a neighborhood that is safe? Does the family interact with relatives, friends, and neighbors? Does the family participate in social, cultural, religious, and community activities? Are the family's values, beliefs, or life-style in conflict with those dominant in the neighborhood? Do the children have access to needed educational resources? Do they enjoy their school experience? Are some of the family members or the family as a whole experiencing high levels of stress? Answers to such questions yield important information for assessment and intervention.

Figure 10.3   Sample Ecomap

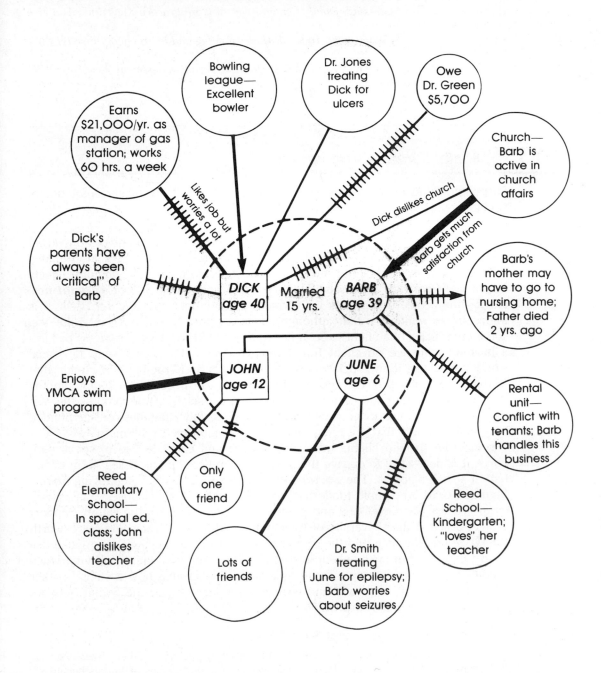

Selected Bibliography

Hartman, Ann, and Joan Laird. *Family-Centered Social Work Practice.* New York: The Free Press, 1983.

Holman, Adele. *Family Assessment: Tools for Understanding and Intervention.* Beverly Hills: Sage, 1983.

McGoldrick, Monica, and Randy Gerson. *Genograms in Family Assessment.* New York: W.W. Norton, 1985.

10.3 *Social Support Assessment*

Purpose: To identify persons to whom a client might turn for various types of social support.

Discussion: Gottlieb (1983) defines ***social support*** as "verbal and/or non-verbal information or advice, tangible aid, or action that is proffered by social intimates or inferred by their presence and has beneficial emotional or behavioral effects on the recipient" (p. 28). Social supports are a component of one's ***social network***—the people and groups with which one interacts on a regular basis. It is important to remember that although social supports are a positive influence, some other parts of a client's social network may add to his or her stress or have a harmful influence on client functioning. Many of the clients seen by social workers have few, if any, social supports. Whittaker and Tracy (1987) explain that "paradoxically, many of the families that are most in need of the social support that relatives, family and friends can provide are also the same families that are most isolated from relatives, family and friends. . . . Other families are surrounded by social networks that are themselves beset by multiple problems" (p. 1).

In order to help clients make appropriate and effective use of social supports, it is necessary to engage them in the identification and assessment of potential social supports. The ***Social Network Map*** and its accompanying ***Social Network Grid*** are simple tools that can be used for that purpose. This assessment process was developed and piloted by Tracy as part of the Family Support Project based at the University of Washington (Whittaker, Tracy, and Marckworth 1989). We find the map and the grid especially attractive because they make use of sort cards that draw the client into a gamelike visual and tactile activity. Tracy (undated) presents a sample script as a way of describing how a social worker might communicate with a client as they work together on the Social Network Map and the Social Network Grid.

> Step One: Developing a Social Network Map*
>
> Let's take a look at who is in your social network by putting together a network map. (Show network map—Figure 10.4.) We can use first names or initials because

*Reproduced with permission of Elizabeth Tracy.

Figure 10.4 Social Network Map

DATE: _____ / _____ / _____

RESPONDENT: _____

ID: _____

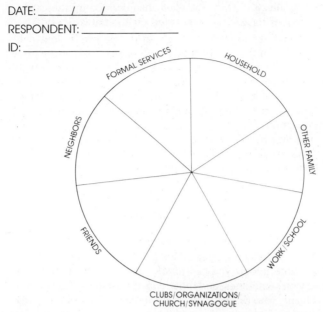

Family Support Project, University of Washington, School of Social Work and Behavioral Sciences Institute. James K. Whittaker, Principal Investigator; Elizabeth M. Tracy, Project Coordinator. Reproduced with permission of Elizabeth M. Tracy.

I'm not that interested in knowing the particular people and I wouldn't necessarily be contacting any of the people we talk about.

Think back to this past month, say since [date]. What people have been important to you? They may have been people you saw, talked with, or wrote letters to. This includes people who made you feel good, people who made you feel bad, and others who just played a part in your life. They may be people who had an influence on the way you made decisions during this time.

First, think of people in your *household*—that includes who?

Now going around the map, what *other family members* would you include in your network?

How about *people from work or school?*

People from clubs, organizations or religious groups? Who should we include here?

Other friends that haven't been listed in the other categories?

Neighbors? (*Note:* Local shopkeepers may be included here.)

Finally, list professional people or people from formal agencies (like DSHS) that you have contact with.

Look over your network. Are these the people you would consider part of your social network this past month? (Add or delete names as needed.)

Step Two: Completing the Social Network Grid (If there are more than 15 people in the network, ask the client to select the "top fifteen," and then ask the questions about only those network members. For each of the questions, use the appropriate sorting guide card. Once the client has divided up the cards, put the appropriate code number for each person listed on the network grid.)

Now, I'd like to learn more about the people in your network. I'm going to write their names on this network grid [see Figure 10.5], put a code number for the area of life, and then ask a few questions about the ways in which they help you. Let's also write their names on these slips of paper too; this will make answering the questions a lot easier. These are the questions I'll be asking (show list of social network questions), and we'll check off the names on this grid as we go through each question.

The first three questions have to do with the *types of support* people give you.

Who would be available to help you out in real *concrete* ways—for example, would give you a ride if you needed one, or would pitch in to help you with a big chore, or would look after your belongings for awhile if you were away? Divide your cards into three piles—those people you can hardly ever rely on for concrete help, those you can rely on sometimes, and those you'd almost always rely on for this type of help.

Now who would be available to give you *emotional support*—for example, to comfort you if you were upset, to be right there with you in a stressful situation, to listen to you talk about your feelings? Again, divide your cards into three piles—those people you can hardly ever rely on for emotional support, those you can rely on sometimes, and those you almost always can rely on for this type of help.

Finally, who do you rely on for *advice*—for example, who would give you information on how to do something, help you make a big decision, or teach you how to do something? Divide your cards into the three piles—hardly ever, sometimes, and almost always—for this type of support.

Look through your cards and this time select those people, if any, in your network that you feel are *critical* of you (or your lifestyle, or you as a parent). When I say "critical," I mean critical of you in a way that makes you feel bad or inadequate. Divide the cards into three piles—those people who are hardly ever critical of you, sometimes critical of you, and almost always critical of you. Again we'll put the code numbers next to their names.

Now look over your cards, and think about the *direction of help.* Divide your cards into three piles—those people where help goes both ways (you help them just as much as they help you), those where it's mostly you helping them, and those where it's mostly them helping you. OK, let's get their code numbers on the grid.

Now think about how *close* you are to the people in your network. Divide the cards into three piles—those people you are not very close to, those you are sort of close to, and those you are very close to—and then we'll put a code number for them.

Finally, just a few questions about *how often* you see people, and *how long* you've known the people in your network.

Divide the cards into four piles—people you see just a few times a year, people you see monthly, people you see weekly, and people you see daily. (*Note:* If you see someone twice or more than twice a week, count that as "daily.") OK, we'll put their numbers on the grid.

This is the last question. Divide the cards into three piles—those people you have known less than a year, from 1–5 years, and over 5 years.

Now we have a pretty complete picture of who is in your social network.

Figure 10.5 Social Network Grid

NAME	#	AREA OF LIFE 1. HOUSEHOLD 2. OTHER FAMILY 3. WORK/SCHOOL 4. ORGANIZATIONS 5. OTHER FRIENDS 6. NEIGHBORS 7. PROFESSIONALS 8. OTHER	CONCRETE SUPPORT 1. HARDLY EVER 2. SOMETIMES 3. ALMOST ALWAYS	EMOTIONAL SUPPORT 1. HARDLY EVER 2. SOMETIMES 3. ALMOST ALWAYS	INFORMATION/ADVICE 1. HARDLY EVER 2. SOMETIMES 3. ALMOST ALWAYS	CRITICAL 1. HARDLY EVER 2. SOMETIMES 3. ALMOST ALWAYS	DIRECTION OF HELP 1. GOES BOTH WAYS 2. YOU TO THEM 3. THEM TO YOU	CLOSENESS 1. NOT VERY CLOSE 2. SORT OF CLOSE 3. VERY CLOSE	HOW OFTEN SEEN 0. DOES NOT SEE 1. FEW TIMES/YR 2. MONTHLY 3. WEEKLY 4. DAILY	HOW LONG KNOWN 1. LESS THAN 1 YR. 2. FROM 1–5 YRS. 3. MORE THAN 5 YRS.
	01									
	02									
	03									
	04									
	05									
	06									
	07									
	08									
	09									
	10									
	11									
	12									
	13									
	14									
	15									
1–6		7	8	9	10	11	12	13	14	15

ID _____

RESPONDENT _____

University of Washington, School of Social Work and Behavioral Sciences Institute. James K. Whittaker, Principal Investigator; Elizabeth M. Tracy, Project Coordinator. Reproduced with permission of Elizabeth M. Tracy.

It is important to remember that the Social Support Map and the Social Network Grid do not objectively describe the client's support but rather reflect the client's perceptions and beliefs about his or her network and supports. It is quite possible that a client may exaggerate or underestimate the importance of some people and simply forget to name others.

Once the map and grid have been completed, the social worker engages the client in a discussion of how the client might reach out to and make use of identified social supports. Whether the supports are likely resources will depend, of course, on the nature of the client's problem or needs and the client's willingness to use them.

Selected Bibliography

Gottlieb, Benjamin. *Social Support Strategies: Guidelines for Mental Health Practice.* Beverly Hills: Sage, 1983.

Tracy, Elizabeth. *Social Support Assessment.* Seattle: University of Washington School of Social Work, Family Support Project (mimeograph, undated).

————, and James Whittaker. "The Evidence Base for Social Support Interventions in Child and Family Practice: Emerging Issues for Research and Practice." *Children and Youth Services Review* 9 (1987): 249–70.

————, and James Whittaker. "The Social Network Map: Assessing Social Support in Clinical Practice." *Families in Society* (in press).

Whittaker, James, and Elizabeth Tracy. "Supporting Families: linking Formal and Informal Helping in Family Preservation Services." *Permanency Report* 5, no. 1 (Winter 1987).

————, Elizabeth Tracy, and Peg Marckworth. *The Family Support Project: Identifying Informal Support Resources for High Risk Families.* Seattle: School of Social Work, University of Washington, 1989.

10.4   *Life History Grid*

Purpose: To graphically depict significant events in a client's life and/or the development of significant problems through time.

Discussion: The *life history grid,* described by Anderson and Brown (1980), is a method of graphically organizing and presenting data related to the various periods in a client's life. The grid is especially useful in work with children and adolescents, where an understanding of life experiences during a particular stage of development may shed light on current functioning. Data from a variety of sources (interview, agency records, hospital records, etc.) are brought together in a life grid.

Figure 10.6 is a grid prepared on David, a fourteen-year-old referred to a social worker because of behavior problems. When one examines David's life history grid, it becomes apparent that his problems have grown worse in reaction to his parents' escalating marital conflict and eventual divorce. Also, there appears to be a relationship between his asthma attacks and significant family changes.

Client: David

Figure 10.6 Sample Life History Grid

Year	Age	Location	Family	School	Health	Activities	Problems
1976	DOB: 3–23–76	Chicago, IL	Father 21, Mother 18	—	Normal birth	—	—
1977	1						
1978	2		Karen born				
1979	3	Billings, MT			Asthma, hospital, 3 days		
1980	4						
1981	5	Denver, CO	Donald born	K—Lewis & Clark School	Asthma, in hospital 3 times		
1982	6		Dad drinking a lot	I	Car accident, broken leg		Did not like school Frequently sick
1983	7	Butte, MT		II—new school			Lots of fights at school
1984	8		Dad fired from job	III		Cub Scouts	
1985	9		Mother takes job	IV	Asthma attack		Steals money from mother
1986	10			V	Appendectomy		Ran away from home
1987	11	Denver, CO	Parents separate and mother moves	VI—grades poor	Asthma attack/ hospital		Breaks classmate's nose in fight
1988	12			VII— truancy		Paper route	Alcohol & fighting
1989	13	Mother & kids move to Helena, MT	Parents divorce	VIII—new school			Hits teacher, suicide gesture
1990	14		Dad killed in car accident	Freshman at Big Sky HS		Tried out for football	Pot smoking, arrest for shoplifting, poor grades

Thus, we see that a life history grid can help a social worker formulate hypotheses about the causes of problem behavior and suggest focal points for intervention.

Selected Bibliography

Anderson, James, and Ralph Brown. "Life History Grid for Adolescents." *Social Work 25* (July 1980): 321–22.

10.5 | *Life Cycle Matrix*

Purpose: To graphically depict the developmental stage of all persons in a household.

Discussion: An assessment should consider the client's stage in the life cycle and the developmental tasks common to that stage. This is especially important in work with families because the various members are at different points in the life cycle. The use of a simple matrix can help the social worker organize his or her thoughts about the family members and the physical, psychological, social, and spiritual needs associated with a particular stage of life.

Figure 10.7 depicts a household made up of a father, mother, three children, and a grandmother. The importance of considering the developmental stage of each member of a household becomes apparent when it is acknowledged that certain tasks need to be accomplished and certain crises must be resolved during each stage. Within a family system, the developmental struggles of one member may interfere with the developmental tasks and crises faced by another family member.

Table 10.1 presents an overview of the life cycle intended to remind the social worker how developmental tasks change over time. The concept of develop-

Figure 10.7 Sample Life Cycle Matrix

Family Member	Developmental Stage								
	0–1	*2–4*	*5–7*	*8–12*	*13–17*	*18–22*	*23–34*	*35–60*	*61+*
Margaret (Grandmother)									X
John								X	
Mary								X	
John (Jr.)					X				
Jimmy			X						
Mary		X							

Table 10.1 The Life Cycle

Stage	Common Developmental Tasks	Developmental Crisis
Prenatal (conception to birth)	• in utero physical development	
Infant (birth–2 years)	• bonding and attachment • differentiation of emotions • maturation of nervous and motor systems • concept of object permanence • beginning understanding of causality	Basic trust versus mistrust of others
Toddler (2–4 years)	• fantasy and play • language • self-control • locomotion • use of symbols in thought	Basic sense of worth and autonomy versus shame and self-doubt
Early school age (5–7 years)	• group play • early gender identification • beginning moral standards • learning of classification, combination, and other basic intellectual skills	Taking initiative versus only reacting to or imitating others
Middle school age (8–12 years)	• cooperation with others • team play • same sex peer identification • introspection	Self-confidence and industry versus inferiority
Early adolescence (13–17 years)	• physical and sexual maturation • membership in peer group • boy-girl relationships • abstract thought processes • coping with strong emotions	Group identity versus sense of alienation
Late adolescence (18–22 years)	• dating and mate selection • sex role identity • internalization of moral principles • career choice • separation from parent	Individual identity versus role diffusion and confusion
Early adulthood (23–34 years)	• marriage • childbearing • work • developing lifestyle apart from parents	Intimacy versus isolation
Middle adulthood (35–60 years)	• childrearing • career development • management of home and financial resources	Expansion of life experience and concern for society versus stagnation and self-absorption
Late adulthood (61 + years)	• coping with physical change and health problems • acceptance of one's own life choices • redirection of energy after retirement • developing a perspective on one's death	Integrity versus despair

mental crisis reflects belief that psychosocial development proceeds by critical stages; each stage represents a turning point or a time to decide between hanging on to the old or letting go and moving on to a new way of thinking and behaving.

Selected Bibliography

Bloom, Martin. *Configurations of Human Behavior: Life Span Development in Social Environments.* New York: Macmillan, 1984.

——— . *Life Span Development: Bases for Preventive and Interventive Helping.* 2nd ed. New York: Macmillan, 1985.

Carter, Betty, and Monica McGoldrick. *The Changing Family Life Cycle.* 2nd ed. Boston: Allyn and Bacon, 1989.

Pillari, Vimala. *Human Behavior in the Social Environment.* Pacific Grove, Calif.: Brooks/ Cole, 1988.

Zastrow, Charles, and Karen Kirst-Ashman. *Understanding Human Behavior and the Social Environment.* Chicago: Nelson-Hall, 1987.

10.6   *Family Life Cycle*

Purpose: To identify developmental tasks and changes common to various stages in the life of a family.

Discussion: Just as an individual can be described in terms of his or her stage in the human life cycle (see Technique 10.5), it is possible to describe stages that occur throughout the life of a family unit. Although the stages of family development are less distinct and more variable than the stages of human development, such a conceptualization can help the worker view a family's functioning in a broader context, and better understand the family's strengths and problems.

Table 10.2 outlines the stages commonly observed within the nuclear family (i.e., married man and woman with their biological children) based on ones identified by Carter and McGoldrick (1989). Needless to say, the structure, functioning, and life cycle of many families vary significantly from that of the nuclear family; examples include extended family structures and the various types of single-parent families such as ones headed by an unmarried mother or father, divorced or widowed parents, and single adoptive parents.

Given the high rate of divorce in the United States, it is important for the social worker to understand how phases in the family life cycle are impacted by the dissolution of a marriage and by remarriage. Table 10.3, also developed by Carter and McGoldrick (1989), describes the family both prior to and after a divorce. A high percentage of those who divorce eventually remarry and start another family unit. A remarriage often gives rise to the so-called *blended family,* which is particularly complex because the two adults entering this new marriage may bring with them biological children and sometimes stepchildren from one or

Table 10.2 The Family Life Cycle

Family Life Cycle Stage	Emotional Process of Transition: Key Principles	Second-Order Changes in Family Status Required to Proceed Developmentally
1. Leaving home: Single young adults	Accepting emotional and financial responsibility for self	a. Differentiation of self in relation to family of origin b. Development of intimate peer relationships c. Establishment of self re work and financial independence
2. The joining of families through marriage: The new couple	Commitment to new system	a. Formation of marital system b. Realignment of relationships with extended families and friends to include spouse
3. Families with young children	Accepting new members into the system	a. Adjusting marital system to make space for child(ren) b. Joining in childrearing, financial, and household tasks c. Realignment of relationships with extended family to include parenting and grandparenting roles
4. Families with adolescents	Increasing flexibility of family boundaries to include children's independence and grandparents' frailties	a. Shifting of parent child relationships to permit adolescent to move in and out of system b. Refocus on midlife marital and career issues c. Beginning shift toward joint caring for older generation
5. Launching children and moving on	Accepting a multitude of exits from and entries into the family system	a. Renegotiation of marital system as a dyad b. Development of adult to adult relationships between grown children and their parents c. Realignment of relationships to include in-laws and grandchildren d. Dealing with disabilities and death of parents (grandparents)
6. Families in later life	Accepting the shifting of generational roles	a. Maintaining own and/or couple functioning and interests in face of physiological decline; exploration of new familial and social role options b. Support for a more central role of middle generation. c. Making room in the system for the wisdom and experience of the elderly, supporting the older generation without overfunctioning for them c. Dealing with loss of spouse, siblings, and other peers and preparation for own death. Life review and integration

Source: From Betty Carter and Monica McGoldrick, *The Changing Family Life Cycle: A Framework for Family Therapy,* 2nd ed. Copyright © 1989 by Allyn and Bacon. Reprinted by permission.

more previous marriages, and, subsequently, they may bear additional children. Multiple sets of grandparents, stepparents, and other relatives are significant figures in the dynamics and development of the blended family. The schema presented in Table 10.4, from Carter and McGoldrick (1989), presents important elements of the remarried family formation.

Table 10.3 Family Life Cycle and Divorce

Phase	Emotional Process of Transition Prerequisite Attitude	Developmental Issues
	Divorce	
1. The decision to divorce	Acceptance of inability to resolve marital tensions sufficiently to continue relationship	Acceptance of one's own part in the failure of the marriage
2. Planning the breakup of the system	Supporting viable arrangements for all parts of the system	a. Working cooperatively on problems of custody, visitation, and finances b. Dealing with extended family about the divorce
3. Separation	a. Willingness to continue cooperative coparental relationship and joint financial support of children b. Work on resolution of attachment to spouse	a. Mourning loss of intact family b. Restructuring marital and parent-child relationships and finances; adaptation to living apart c. Realignment of relationships with extended family; staying connected with spouse's extended family
4. The divorce	More work on emotional divorce: overcoming hurt, anger, guilt, etc.	a. Mourning loss of intact family: giving up fantasies of reunion b. Retrieval of hopes, dreams, expectations from the marriage c. Staying connected with extended families
	Postdivorce Family	
1. Single-parent (custodial household or primary residence)	Willingness to maintain financial responsibilities, continue parental contact with ex-spouse, and support contact of children with ex-spouse and his or her family	a. Making flexible visitation arrangements with ex-spouse and his family b. Rebuilding own financial resources c. Rebuilding own social network
2. Single-parent (noncustodial)	Willingness to maintain parental contact with ex-spouse and support custodial parent's relationship with children	a. Finding ways to continue effective parenting relationship with children b. Maintaining financial responsibilities to ex-spouse and children. c. Rebuilding own social network

Source: Betty Carter and Monica McGoldrick, *The Changing Family Life Cycle: A Framework for Family Therapy,* 2nd ed. Copyright © 1989 by Allyn and Bacon. Reprinted by permission.

The family life cycle is also impacted by environmental and situational factors. Colon (1980) explains that the cycle observed among both economically poor and dysfunctional families often has only three major stages: (1) the unattached young adult (who may actually be as young as age twelve); (2) families with children (a phase that covers most of the life span and often consists of a

Table 10.4 Remarried Family Formation

Steps	Prerequisite Attitude	Developmental Issues
1. Entering the new relationship	Recovery from loss of first marriage (adequate "emotional divorce")	Recommitment to marriage and to forming a family with readiness to deal with the complexity and ambiguity
2. Conceptualizing and planning new marriage and family	Accepting one's own fears and those of new spouse and children about remarriage and forming a stepfamily Accepting need for time and patience for adjustment to complexity and ambiguity of the following: 1. Multiple new roles 2. Boundaries: space, time, membership, and authority 3. Affective issues: guilt, loyalty conflicts, desire for mutuality, unresolvable past hurts	a. Work on openness in the new relationships to avoid pseudomutuality. b. Plan for maintenance of cooperative financial and coparental relationships with ex-spouses. c. Plan to help children deal with fears, loyalty conflicts, and membership in two systems. d. Realignment of relationships with extended family to include new spouse and children. e. Plan maintenance of connections for children with extended family of ex-spouse(s).
3. Remarriage and reconstruction of family	Final resolution of attachment to previous spouse and ideal of "intact" family; Acceptance of a different model of family with permeable boundaries	a. Restructuring family boundaries to allow for inclusion of new spouse—stepparent. b. Realignment of relationships and financial arrangements throughout subsystems to permit interweaving of several systems. c. Making room for relationships of all children with biological (noncustodial) parents, grandparents, and other extended family. d. Sharing memories and histories to enhance stepfamily integration.

Source: Betty Carter and Monica McGoldrick, *The Changing Family Life Cycle: A Framework for Family Therapy,* 2nd ed. Copyright © 1989 by Allyn and Bacon. Reprinted by permission. This table is a variation on a developmental scheme presented by J. W. Ransom, S. Schlesinger, and A. Derdeyn, "A Stepfamily in Formation," *American Journal of Orthopsychiatry* 49 (1979).

three- or four-generation household); and (3) a stage during which the grandmother retains a central role in the direct care of grandchildren and other young people in the household.

Selected Bibliography

Carter, Betty, and Monica McGoldrick. "The Changing Family Life Cycle." In *The Changing Family Life Cycle: A Framework for Family Therapy,* 2nd ed., edited by Betty Carter and Monica McGoldrick. Boston: Allyn and Bacon, 1989.

Colon, F. "The Family Life Cycle of the Multiproblem Poor Family." In *The Family Life Cycle: A Framework for Family Therapy,* edited by Elizabeth Carter and Monica McGoldrick. New York: Gardner Press, 1980.

Holman, Adele. *Family Assessment: Tools for Understanding and Intervention.* Beverly Hills: Sage, 1983.

10.7	*Client Strengths and Coping Strategies*

Purpose: To identify a client's strengths and usual methods of coping and problem solving.

Discussion: A social worker's assessment of a client and his or her situation should emphasize strengths rather than weaknesses and pathology. (See principle 11 in Chapter 4.) It should identify functional patterns of coping rather than focusing only on dysfunctional behaviors. In short, the assessment should focus mostly on what the client can do and will do, rather than on what the client cannot or will not do. This is not to suggest an approach that overlooks real limitations and pathology, but it means that the worker should search for strengths even in the most dysfunctional and chaotic of cases. The reasons for this emphasis is simple: A successful intervention plan must build on client strength. Numerous studies underscore this principle. If the worker focuses only on the client's problems and on what is going wrong, the client will feel even more hopeless and distraught.

Strengths can be identified by asking the clients questions such as: Despite your problems, what parts of your life are going well? Tell me about times when you have successfully handled problems similar to those you now face. What do you like about yourself? What do other people like about you? What do you do well? What would you not change about yourself or your situation? The worker can also observe strengths in the client's attitude and behavior. Additionally, it may be helpful for the social worker to consult the following list of *client strengths:*

- Recognizing the existence of a problem
- Acknowledging responsibility for one's actions
- Looking for and accepting information and guidance from others
- Willingness to assist and encourage others
- Willingness to take the risk involved in making changes
- Showing affection, compassion, and concern for others
- Seeking employment, holding a job, being a responsible employee
- Attempting to meet one's family and financial obligations
- Maintaining friendships and demonstrating loyalty and concern for family, relatives, and friends
- Exercising self-control
- Making plans and thoughtful decisions

- Being trustworthy, fair, and honest in dealing with others
- Having feelings of sorrow and guilt for having hurt others
- Demonstrating concern for and interest in improving one's neighborhood and community
- Seeking to understand others and their situations
- Accepting differences among people
- Willingness to keep trying despite hardship and setbacks
- Sharing joy and happiness with others
- Participating in social, community, or religious organizations
- Having and following one's dreams
- Willingness to forgive others
- Expressing one's point of view
- Standing up for one's own rights and the rights of others
- Attempting to protect others from harm
- Special aptitudes (e.g., mechanical, interpersonal, etc.)

We define a *coping strategy* as mostly conscious and voluntarily controlled thoughts and actions used by an individual to deal with emotional pain, interpersonal conflicts, and other personal problems or stressors. As compared to defense mechanisms (see Technique 10.8), a coping strategy does not involve a distortion of reality; it is a problem-solving rather than a problem-avoiding maneuver. Coping strategies serve two functions: to solve a problem (problem-focused coping) and to reduce the discomfort caused by stressors (emotion-focused coping). Generally, an individual must first deal with the emotion before he or she can move on to problem solving. However, emotion-focused and problem-focused coping frequently occur simultaneously. There is no agreed upon listing of coping strategies. Moreover, individuals vary widely in how they attempt to cope. For example, given a situation that causes much anxiety, some individuals might elect to withdraw and go off by themselves, others might visit friends or go to the gym for a brisk workout, and still others may pray. Other common coping strategies—some functional, some not so functional—include ignoring the problem, sleeping more, eating more, and overworking. Since each individual tends to habitually use certain coping strategies, the worker can get a pretty good idea of a person's usual coping patterns by asking specifically how he or she behaved and what he or she did in response to prior problems.

Coleman (1976, p. 124) believes that all people, regardless of culture, use certain "built in," emotion-focused coping strategies in their initial reactions to intense emotional pain:

- *Crying.* This is a common and normal means of alleviating tension and responding to loss. Crying seems to be a necessary part of successful "grief work."
- *Talking it out.* People who have undergone traumatic experiences need to describe and talk repeatedly about the experience. This means of alleviating tension is a natural form of desensitization so that they can eventually accept and tolerate the painful thoughts and feelings associated with the experience.

- *Laughing it off.* Joking about and viewing painful experiences with a sense of humor serves to release tension and place the matter in a broader perspective. In successful grieving, for example, there is often a good mix of crying and laughter among those who shared the death of a loved one.
- *Seeking support.* In times of stress, it is natural for children and adults to seek support, attention, and affection from others as a means of regaining one's emotional equilibrium.
- *Dreaming and nightmares.* This topic does not fit our definition of a coping strategy (i.e., conscious and voluntary) but it is a common reaction to highly traumatic experiences. Such dreams and nightmares are often repetitive and, like the desensitization process involved in "talking it out," the recurring dream forces the individual to grapple with the feelings and to integrate the experience mentally.

If a client has recently had a traumatic experience (e.g., rape, death of family member, etc.), a social worker should be alert to these coping mechanisms and, where possible, facilitate their use by the client. In work with clients who have moved beyond these initial reactions or have not had a recent traumatic experience, the social worker's assessment will need to give attention to the problem-focused coping strategies. Those described below are of a rather general nature, but they illustrate what the social worker is looking for during the assessment process. A client with good coping strategies will have the motivation, the capacity, and the opportunity to:

- Express thoughts and feelings in a clear, positive and, when necessary, assertive manner
- Ask questions and gather new information even when the new information challenges one's current beliefs
- Identify one's own social and emotional needs and learn socially acceptable means of meeting those needs
- Model one's own behavior after persons who behave in an effective and appropriate manner
- Recognize that one does have choices and can exert influence on one's own behavior, feelings, and life events
- "Cut one's losses" and withdraw from relationships or situations that are unhealthy or stressful and unchangeable
- Examine the spiritual dimension of life and draw on one's philosophical and religious beliefs for insight, strength, and direction
- Identify early signs that a problem is developing so action can be taken before the problem becomes more serious
- Take positive and appropriate steps—if only small steps—to solve problems, even when such actions are a source of fear and anxiety
- Engage in appropriate actions (e.g., physical workout) that release pent-up emotion
- Take care of one's body and maintain one's health
- Delay immediate gratification in order to stick with a plan that will attain a more distant but desired goal

- Use mental images of future actions or events to mentally rehearse how to handle expected difficulties
- Make fair and appropriate changes in one's daily activities of living so as not to interfere with the needs of others
- Ignore the unjustified criticism by others
- Remove one's self from situations that lead to self-defeating or harmful outcomes
- Seek out and use additional skills training and needed profession services

It will be noted that these various coping strategies listed above are essentially dimensions of the problem-solving process.

If the social worker's assessment reveals that a client lacks necessary coping strategies, the intervention plan should focus on helping the client learn specific *coping skills*. Of course, the skills needed will depend on the client's problem, situation, and goals. For example, an abusing parent may need to learn "parenting skills," an individual in need of a job will need to focus on "job-hunting skills," a married couple in conflict may need "communication skills," and a youth leaving the foster-care system will need to acquire "independent living" skills.

Selected Bibliography

Coleman, James. *Abnormal Psychology and Modern Life*. 5th ed. Glenview, Ill.: Scott, Foresman, 1976.

Curran, James, and Peter Monti, eds. *Social Skills Training: A Practical Handbook for Assessment and Treatment*. Washington Square: New York University Press, 1982.

Gambrill, Eileen. *Casework: A Competency-Based Approach*. Englewood Cliffs, N.J.: Prentice-Hall, 1983.

Hepworth, Dean, and Jo Ann Larsen. *Direct Social Work Practice*. 2nd ed. Homewood, Ill.: Dorsey Press, 1986.

10.8 Ego-Defense Mechanisms

Purpose: To identify a client's usual defense mechanisms in order to anticipate how the client will respond to conflicts and intervention tactics.

Discussion: Ego defenses, or defense mechanisms, are part of psychodynamic theory. Although this theoretical framework is not as popular as it once was, defense mechanism terminology continues to be used by many practitioners. Defense mechanisms frequently mentioned in the professional literature include denial, projection, repression, reaction-formation, rationalization displacement, intellectualization fantasy, and acting out. The DSM III-R (American Psychiatric Association 1987) defines *defense mechanisms* as "patterns of feelings, thoughts or behaviors that are relatively involuntary and arise in response to perceptions of psychic danger. They are designed to hide or alleviate the conflicts or stressors that give rise to anxiety" (p. 393). The terms *defense mechanisms* and *coping strategies* are often used interchangeably, but we find it useful to make a distinction based on the degree to which the response is under the client's conscious and voluntary control and whether self-deception and reality distortion is involved. (See Technique 10.7 for a discussion of coping strategies.) Coleman (1976) explains that "a person tends to be fairly consistent in the specific use of such mechanisms. While their reactions may serve useful defensive functions, they usually involve some measure of self-deception and reality distortion; . . . [and] are considered maladaptive when they become the predominant means of coping with stress" (p. 123).

There are very few of us who do not use defense mechanisms, singly or in combination, as we cope with anxiety, stress, and the problems of living. It is clear, however, that defensiveness impairs a person's ability to accurately perceive reality and get along with others. The rigid or inappropriate use of defenses is a barrier to realistic problem solving. High levels of defensiveness and distortions of reality are characteristic of disturbed personalities.

An individual who uses the ego defense of *denial* screens out certain realities by unconsciously refusing to acknowledge them. Denial is often used in combination with *rationalization,* which involves the justification of inappropriate behavior by manufacturing logical or socially acceptable reasons for the behavior. An example is the abusing parent who justifies physical abuse on the basis that "the only thing he understands is pain." Although clearly a distortion of the truth, a rationalization is not the same as a lie because the defensive pattern is so habitual that the person is not consciously and deliberately trying to fabricate a falsehood. Denial and rationalization are predominant defenses used by people who are chemically dependent.

In *projection,* others are seen as being responsible for one's own shortcomings or unacceptable behavior. For example, the child molester may believe that he was seduced by the young child and sees himself as the victim rather than the offender.

Repression refers to a mental process in which extremely threatening and painful thoughts or experiences are excluded from consciousness. This concept is used to explain certain forms of amnesia and conversion reactions. For example, it is not uncommon for a child to repress experiences of sexual abuse and not remember them until many years later.

Emotional insulation is a maneuver aimed at withholding an emotional investment in a desired but unlikely outcome. This defense creates a shield that protects the individual from loss or a recurrence of previous pain and disappointment. For example, a child who is moved frequently from foster home to foster home learns to use emotional insulation as a defense against the pain of separation and loss; unfortunately, such a child often carries this pattern into adulthood and is then unable to develop emotional attachments to a marriage partner or to his or her own children. This defense is closely related to the concept of "learned helplessness"—after a long period of frustration, many people simply give up and quit trying to escape their misery. These are the "broken" individuals who become passive recipients of whatever life brings them. Emotional insulation is commonly used by persons who have grown up in extreme deprivation and hopelessness.

Intellectualization involves the use of abstractions as a way of avoiding feelings and distancing one's self from emotional pain. The impact of disappointment is softened by theoretical explanations and platitudes. For example, the individual who is turned down for a much desired job may avoid feelings of disappointment by discussing our economic system and employment conditions.

Regression involves a retreat from one's present status or level of maturity to one that has fewer demands and stressors. For example, when a new child is born to a family, the five-year-old may begin behaving like an infant (e.g., wetting pants, sucking thumb) as a way of getting more attention and coping with fears of being overlooked by his or her parents. Regression is common among physically ill persons who are experiencing much fear or pain.

When using *reaction formation,* a person defends against troublesome thoughts, feelings, or impulses by rigidly adhering to exactly the opposite set of thoughts and behaviors. An example is an individual who discovers he is sexually attracted to children. In response, such a person becomes obsessed with the dangers of child sexual abuse and campaigns endlessly for prevention programs. Another example is the individual who is filled with anger and the desire to strike out at others but denies these feelings and rigidly holds to a philosophy of nonviolence that does not allow even the killing of a mosquito.

Displacement refers to transferring troublesome emotions (often hostility) and acting-out behaviors (e.g., violence) from the person(s) who arouses the emotion to another less threatening and less powerful person or thing. The classic example is the man who kicks his dog because he is angry with his boss.

When using *fantasy* as a defense, a person "day dreams" imaginary achievements and situations as a way of meeting personal needs or counteracting painful feelings of inadequacy. Serious problems develop when the person finds his or her reality so painful that much of the time is spent in a fantasy world. Excessive fantasy and the inability to distinguish between fantasy and reality are often symptoms of serious mental illness.

Acting out is not a defensive maneuver like the mechanisms described above, but it is a pattern of thought and behavior designed to alleviate stress and inner conflict. For example, an angry and frustrated individual may seek release from inner tension by attacking the person he or she views as the source of trouble. An example of another form of acting out is the battered wife who feels the tensions build and knows she will soon be beaten by her husband, so she proceeds to provoke him so she can "get it over with." Combat soldiers who can no longer handle the stress of waiting for an attack have been known to leave the safety of their foxhole and blindly charge the enemy.

Several *guidelines* can be offered to assist the social worker in assessing and responding to a client's defense mechanisms.

1. When using defense mechanism terminology, certain precautions are necessary. The patterns we call defenses are only hypothetical constructs inferred from the way people behave. At best, they are a useful shorthand language for describ-

---

ing behavior. Labeling a client's behavior as projection or rationalization, for example, in no way explains the behavior. You must look behind the surface behavior and identify the unmet needs and personal pain that causes the client to rely on the defense mechanism.

2. Because defenses are mostly learned and habitual, an individual tends to utilize those defenses he or she has used in the past. For example, if, in the past, an individual frequently used denial and rationalization, you can expect him or her to use those same defenses when again faced with anxiety or conflict.

3. People hold tightly to their defensive patterns. The more anxiety they experience, the more rigidly they use the defense. People do not easily give up these old habits of thought and behavior. It is usually only within a relationship characterized by empathy, warmth, and genuineness that a person can feel safe enough to at least temporarily "let down" his or her defenses and examine the underlying pain.

4. Sometimes it can be difficult to tell where a true description of a situation leaves off and rationalization begins. Behaviors that suggest rationalization by a client include: (a) groping for reasons to justify an action or belief, (b) inability to recognize inconsistencies in his or her own "story," and (c) unwillingness to even consider alternative explanations and becoming angry when one's "reasons" are questioned.

Selected Bibliography

American Psychiatric Association. *Diagnostic Statistical Manual of Mental Disorders, DSM-III-R.* 3rd ed., revised. Washington D.C.: American Psychiatric Association, 1987.

Bloom, Martin. *Configurations of Human Behavior: Life Span Development in Social Environments.* New York: Macmillan, 1984.

Coleman, James. *Abnormal Psychology and Modern Life.* 5th ed. Scott, Foresman, 1976.

Goldstein, Eda. "Ego Psychology." In *Social Work Treatment.* 3rd ed., edited by Francis Turner. New York: The Free Press, 1986.

10.9 *Assessing Problems in Role Performance*

Purpose: To clarify and describe the nature of a client's difficulty in performing role-related behaviors.

Discussion: As used here, a problem in role performance refers to a significant discrepancy between a client's behavior and that considered appropriate to one of his or her assigned roles (e.g., employee, parent, spouse, etc.). A number of concepts borrowed from role theories can help the social worker assess and describe role behavior. These concepts are especially useful because they bridge psychological and social perspectives on human behavior and deepen the understanding of social functioning.

The concept of **social role** derives from the observation that within a society's social structure and institutions, certain behaviors and norms are prescribed for certain relationships. For example, in the parent-child relationship, the parent is expected by society to provide the child with food, shelter, supervision, guidance, and so on. In a teacher-student relationship, the teacher is expected to teach, and the student is expected to learn that which the teacher judges to be important. The term *role,* borrowed from the world of theater, implies that a script, an actor, and an audience are components of interactional behavior.

Role expectation refers to the cluster of specific behaviors associated with a given role. Essentially, these expectations are societal norms or standards for a role. Sarbin and Allen (1968) explain, "Role expectations have a normative or evaluative character. . . . An individual is expected to behave in particular ways. . . . Approval or disapproval by other people is contingent on the nature and quality of one's role enactment. Role expectations . . . define the limits or range of tolerated behavior" (p. 501).

The term *role performance* (or role enactment) refers to a person's actual behavior, which may or may not conform to role expectations. *Role conception* (or subjective role) is an individual's beliefs about a role and how he or she expects to behave in that role. One's own expectation of self in a particular role may or may not conform to role expectations, as defined by other social systems and wider society. The term *role demands* refers to the specific knowledge, values, skills, physical and mental abilities, and other personal attributes necessary to perform a particular role successfully.

A number of terms are used to describe problems in role performance. *Interrole conflict* refers to an incompatibility or clash between two or more roles. For example, a mother may experience a conflict between her role as parent to a young child and her role as a corporate executive who is expected to make frequent out-of-town business trips. *Intrarole conflict* exists when a person is caught up in a situation where two or more sets of expectations are assigned to a single role. For example, a high-school boy may not be able to reconcile the role of student as defined by his teacher with how the role is defined by his peers. *Role incapacity* exists when, for some reason, an individual cannot adequately perform a role; possible reasons include physical or mental illness, lack of needed knowledge or skills, drug addiction, mental retardation, and so on. *Role rejection* occurs when an individual refuses to perform a role; an extreme example is when a parent abandons his or her child.

A problem of *role ambiguity* (or role confusion) exists when there are few clear expectations associated with a role—a condition most likely to occur in times of rapid social change. This is a problem because the individual is unsure of what is really expected and is unable to evaluate his or her own performance. *Self-role incongruence* exists when there is little overlap between the requirements of a role and the individual's personality. For example, an individual may occupy the role of a professional but not feel comfortable in that role. Another example is when an individual finds that his or her values, ethics, or life-style is at odds with the expectations of a role. The problem of *role overload* exists when a person occupies more roles than he or she can perform adequately. In reality, most individuals are unable or do not choose to conform to the expectations of all their social roles. Thus, most people live with some degree of *role strain,* a situation that necessitates making compromises and trade-offs, setting priorities, and using the various defense mechanisms and coping strategies to reconcile role demands with limited time, energy, and commitment.

Keeping these concepts in mind, a number of questions can help the social worker analyze role performance problems and make decisions concerning the type of intervention needed. The questions offered here are based, in part, on ones proposed by Mager and Pipe (1970) for the analysis of job-related performance problems.

1. *What is the nature and degree of the discrepancy between actual performance and role expectation?*
   - How does the client's behavior differ from that considered appropriate or "normal" for persons in this particular role?
   - What observations, events, or experiences have caused you and/or the client to conclude that a discrepancy exists?
   - Why are you and/or the client dissatisfied or concerned about the client's role performance? Why is this role important? What will happen if there no change in the client's role performance?
2. *Is the discrepancy caused by a lack of knowledge or skill?*
   - Does the client possess the knowledge or skill needed to perform this role?
   - Could the client adequately perform this role if he or she really had to or really wanted to? Could he or she do it if life depended on it?
3. *If the discrepancy is caused by a lack of knowledge and skill, how best can the problem be addressed?*
   - Was there a time when the client could perform this role? If so, what experience or condition has caused the client to lose the capacity or motivation to perform this role?
   - What can be done to help the client regain a capacity that has deteriorated?
   - Is the client now able to relearn the behaviors needed to perform the role?
   - What teaching methods or techniques will help the client learn the behaviors needed to perform this role?
4. *If the discrepancy is caused by a rejection or a lack of interest in the role, how can the problem be addressed?*
   - Does this role really matter to the client? Is it important to the client?
   - What roles or activities does the client consider more important?
   - Does the client see any benefits in performing this role?
   - Is the client rewarded or reinforced for the performance of this role? If not, how can rewards be increased?
   - Is the client punished by others or the social environment for attempting to perform this role? How can the client be helped to avoid this punishment?

Selected Bibliography

Mager, Robert, and Peter Pipe. *Analyzing Performance Problems.* Belmont, Calif.: Pitman Learning, 1970.

Perlman, Helen. *Persona: Social Role and Personality.* Chicago: University of Chicago Press, 1968.

Sarbin, Theodore, and Vernon Allen. "Role Theory." In *The Handbook of Social Psychology,* vol. 1, edited by Gordon Lindzey and Elliot Aronson. Reading, Mass.: Addison-Wesley, 1968.

10.10   *Observation of Family Dynamics*

Purpose: To identify the nature and structure of interactions among those persons making up a family system.

Discussion: Given the rather dramatic societal changes of recent decades, it is increasingly difficult to define the family. The Census Bureau defines a family as "two or more persons related by birth, marriage or adoption who reside in the same household." For purposes of planning and delivering social services, we prefer the definition by Karpel and Strauss (1983): "A group of persons related by biological ties and/or long-term expectations of loyalty, trust, and commitment, comprising at least two generations and generally inhabiting one household during the period of child rearing."

In addition to the *nuclear* and *extended family* structures, other variations in family form are common. These include *single-parent families* (i.e., one bioparent, adoptive parent, or foster parent, plus the children); *blended families* or stepparent families (i.e., two married adults plus each one's children from a prior marriage and possibly children born to them as a couple); and *functional families* (i.e., two or more unmarried adults—usually women—plus their children). There is also a growing number of families headed by what some call *skip-generation parents,* referring to grandparents taking primary responsibility for rearing their grandchildren. In part, this is due to the growing number of biological parents whose functioning is seriously impaired by addiction to drugs and alcohol.

As people become part of or join a new family, there is a tendency for them to repeat the behavioral patterns they learned as children in their *family of origin.* Moreover, when people live together for an extended period of time, their behavioral patterns become habitual. Once these patterns are established, there is a natural tendency for family members to try to preserve the status quo and hold on to that which is familiar, even when there are obvious problems in the family's functioning. The family is indeed a complex system and it is a challenging task to identify and assess its subtle and complex interactional patterns. This section presents questions that the social worker should keep in mind as he or she gathers information about a family's functioning and its relationship to the presenting problem.

How is family membership to be defined? Karpel and Strauss (1983) remind us that one can view membership in a number of ways. For example, who are members of the *biological family* (e.g., bio-parents, biological offspring)? Who are members of the *legal family* as defined by marriage, divorce, and adoption laws and court orders affecting child custody? What is the composition of the *functional family* (i.e., shared household, shared responsibility for child care, and tasks of daily living)? Who belongs to the *perceived family* (i.e., those who the members consider as currently being "in" or belonging to the family)? And finally, who belongs to the *family of long-term commitments,* as defined by an expectation of life-long loyalty, duty, and "being there for me" regardless of changes in household composition or legal definitions?

What facts and realities describe the family? What are the names, sex, and ages of the members? How is the family's functioning impacted by the developmental stages of its members (e.g., the presence of young children, teens, elderly)? How does the family's current functioning relate to the family life cycle? Does the family have a particular religious, ethnic, or cultural identity? In what neighborhood and community does the family live? How is the family affected by living in that particular neighborhood? What is the family's source of income? Are family members employed? Where? What circumstances surrounded the marriage or the formation of the family and the birth of the children? Is there a history of divorce, abandonment, or violence? Is the family significantly affected by a member's illness or disability?

How well are ordinary family functions performed? How does the family function as an economic unit (e.g., generate income, pay its bills, purchase necessities, etc.)? Does it successfully manage basic tasks for daily living (e.g., cooking, cleaning, laundry, etc.)? Does it serve as a place of rest and recuperation for its members (e.g., a place of respite and privacy)? Does the family provide appropriate socialization experiences for its children so they can learn the interpersonal and social skills they will need in adulthood? Does the family provide its members with a sense of identity and belonging? Does it provide nurturing, love, companionship, and intimacy? Do the children receive the encouragement and guidance needed to prepare for and succeed in school and work roles? Is the family able to transmit and reinforce values and beliefs necessary for a socially responsible and personally satisfying life?

What are the boundaries, subsystems, rules, and roles governing family interaction? Janzen and Harris (1986) identify four family subsystems: the *spouse subsystem* (i.e., two adults that usually involves a sexual relationship); the *parental subsystem* (i.e., those family members responsible for childrearing); the *sibling subsystem* and the *parent-child subsystem* (i.e., a special closeness between a particular parent and child). The rules, communication patterns, or behavioral patterns that regulate the inclusion or exclusion from these subsystems are termed *boundaries.* In a healthy family, these boundaries are fairly clear and in keeping with societal norms. By contrast, for example, in an incest family the child has been drawn into the spouse subsystem. In many cases of child physical abuse, a child moves into the parental subsystem and into a phenomenon called "role reversal," where the child nurtures and cares for the parent—often in an effort to keep the parent calm. When boundaries are unclear and defuse, members become intrusive and overly involved in the life of another family member. These relationships are often termed *enmeshed,* fused, or merged. The opposite condition is where the boundaries are so rigid that there is little or no meaningful interaction among family members or between the family's subsystems. Such families are said to have a *disengaged* pattern of relationships. A boundary also exists between the family and its social environment. The nature of that boundary determines whether the family will be *open* or *closed* to outside influences. Boundaries of an intergenerational nature exist within child-grandparent and extended family relationships.

When trying to understand a family, special attention must be given to its *role structure.* Roles are those patterns of thought and behavior that define who we are, how we behave toward others in the family, and, of course, how they behave toward us. Certain roles guide the daily tasks of living, such as who pays the bills and who cares for the children. It is often important for the social worker to try to determine how and why such tasks are assigned to certain family members. The role structure that develops in a family may be strongly influenced by the family's culture and religion. The roles one assumes or is assigned during the course of growing up in a family tend to be more permanent, less flexible, and less conscious than other social roles such as those of student, employee, social worker, or supervisor. Pet expressions for common family roles include "black sheep," "the happy one," "peace maker," "golden boy," "disciplinarian," "family worrier," "lone wolf," and "daddy's little girl." In professional literature, one finds references to the roles of "scapegoat," "identified patient," "infantalized child," "parentified child," "hero," "mascot," "lost child," "rescuer," and "mail carrier."

Essentially, *family rules* are explicit or implicit principles that maintain the family's organization or "systemness" and that govern interaction. Rules are reflected in the seating arrangement during meals and in family "regulations" such as "always clean the bathtub when finished." Most family rules are necessary and innocuous but some can appear silly to the outsider (e.g., "Don't take a trip in the car without first changing your underwear"). By contrast, it is the unspoken or hidden rules that contribute most to family dysfunction. Rules that suppress emotion, promote dishonesty, or generate feelings of shame are especially harmful; for example, "When Dad is drinking, never talk about his brother," or "Pretend you don't see Mom and Dad fighting," or "Only an evil person would ever feel anger toward a parent." In discussing the children in the alcoholic family, Black (1981) explains that these children usually grow up with the rules of "don't talk" (about the drinking or other real issues), "don't feel" (suppress all feelings), and "don't trust" (always be on guard and keep people at a distance). To understand family functioning, the social worker must identify the family rules but, more importantly, observe whether the rules can be openly discussed and changed and also what happens when rules are broken.

The boundaries, rules, and roles at work within a family can only be inferred after careful observation of the family. Some family members may be able to articulate family rules but most are so ingrained that they are never questioned.

How well does the individual fit within the family system? Although there is a great value in viewing the family from a systems perspective, it is important to remember that this dynamic system is made up of separate human beings, each having a unique genetic makeup, biology, personality, and life experience. Thus, social workers must be cognizant that each member has his or her own thoughts and feelings, hopes and expectations, obligations, talents, sense of identity, spirituality, coping strategies and ego defenses, special emotional needs, and physical or mental limitations. Workers must ask themselves whether there is a good match or a possible mismatch between this unique individual and the norms, values, and rules of his or her family system.

What are the moral and ethical dimensions of the family's functioning? Most authors of family therapy literature give scant attention to what Karpel and Strauss (1983) term the "ethical dimension" of family dynamics. This refers to issues such as obligation, loyalty, fairness, sacrifice, accountability, and entitlement that relate rather directly to a person's moral standards, religious beliefs, notions of good and evil, and spirituality. Even though most professionals are ill at ease when discussing these value-laden topics, one must remember that many of the conflicts among family members center on these issues.

How does the family make decisions? All families develop patterns or styles of decision making. In some families, all members can express opinions and participate in decision making. On the other extreme are the families in which one member makes all major decisions. Some practitioners learn about a family's decision making by meeting with the whole family and asking them to perform a task (e.g., plan a vacation or family outing) and then observing how and who makes the decisions.

What is the emotional mood of the family? Much like an individual, a family is often characterized by a prevailing mood. Is the family warm and caring? Optimistic? Hopeless and pessimistic? Depressed? Fun loving? Angry? Controlled?

How do family members handle "differentness"? Everyone is a unique individual but despite that uniqueness, everyone must learn to live with others. A common source of interpersonal difficulty is the inability to accept others as being different from oneself and/or the inability to accept oneself as being different from others. Thus, when studying the dynamics of a family, consider how each family member deals with the fact that he or she is different from others and how well he or she can accept the uniqueness of others in the family. There are four basic ways of handling differences:

1. *Eliminating others.* Attempts to deal with differentness by beating down or suppressing the individuality of others (e.g., finding fault with others, blaming, attacking, etc.)
2. *Eliminating self.* Handling differentness by suppressing one's own individuality and differentness (e.g., going along, agreeing, submitting to others regardless of one's true feelings., etc.)
3. *Avoiding issues.* Attempting to handle differentness by denying or avoiding those issues or topics that would reveal differences (e.g., keeping family communication on "safe" topics, changing the subject when threatening topics come up, etc.)
4. *Open and honest communication.* The most healthy method of dealing with differentness but one that requires family members to acknowledge the existence of differences and be prepared to resolve conflicts

How clearly do family members communicate their own expectations and needs? One's wants and needs may be verbalized so others are aware of them, or they may be felt but not verbalized. Even when someone is unwilling or unable to communicate his or her wants and needs, he or she often feels angry and disappointed because others do not understand or respond. All too often, a family member expects the others to be skilled at "mind reading." Needs and expectations can be met only after they are made known.

What communication patterns exist within the family? A pattern of verbal and nonverbal communication develops whenever two or more people interact on a regular basis; certain unwritten rules begin to guide interaction. The pattern reveals how each member regards himself or herself in relation to the others. There are many forms of workable communication patterns. What is functional for one family may not work for another. As with so many aspects of the family, culture and ethnicity have a strong impact on how family members communicate and on what works for the family. To decipher this pattern, the worker needs to observe: Who speaks to whom? Who speaks first? Who responds? Who listens to whom? Who speaks most? Least? Who speaks last? Who sits next to whom? Who physically moves away from other family members? Are messages directed to one person but meant for someone else? Are the messages clear? Do the words used say one thing but mean another? Are the family's communications characterized by evasiveness, denial, double messages, blaming, put downs, threats, hurtful jokes, interruptions, or defiance?

Do family members allow other members to get close emotionally? Everyone has a need for intimacy, yet at the same time, most people have some fear of closeness. Sometimes people avoid getting close to others because they fear that, if they reveal their vulnerabilities, others will take advantage of their weaknesses. Some people hide behind a facade because they fear others will not care for the "real" them. Even within a family, the members may keep others at a distance. Within a well-functioning family, members are able to safely reveal many of their inner thoughts and feelings but also maintain an appropriate level of privacy.

What are the interpersonal payoffs of "troublesome behavior"? To understand a family, the social worker must see beyond the so-called problem behavior and develop working hypotheses about why members of the family repeatedly engage in interactions that create so much distress and misery. Two interrelated themes of family interaction help to explain many problem and nonproblem behaviors: (1) the desire by a member for closeness versus his or her desire for distance and (2) the member's desire for belonging versus his or her desire for independence. People want intimacy but do not want to be oppressed by the closeness. People want to belong and be part of a family but do not want to be consumed or controlled by the need to be loyal and faithful to the family. When observing the family's struggle with a problem, the worker should constantly ask himself or herself, How does this behavior bring the family members closer emotionally or create a feeling of belonging? and How does this behavior promote a sense of separateness and independence?

Systems theory postulates the existence of forces that resist change and maintain a state of dynamic equilibrium. When the system's status quo is disrupted, it attempts to quickly reestablish stability. When other maneuvers do not work, the system may attempt to preserve itself and protect its systemness by scapegoating one family member. A related phenomenon, often termed *re-peopling*, refers to the family system's attempt to achieve stability by either adding or excluding a member. A request by parents to have their disruptive teenager placed in foster care and a couple's interest in adoption or becoming foster parents can at times be viewed a re-peopling maneuver.

Selected Bibliography

Black, Claudia. *It Will Never Happen To Me.* Denver; M.A.C., 1981.

Filsinger, Erik (ed.), *Marriage and Family Assessment: A Source Book for Family Therapy.* Beverly Hills: Sage, 1983.

Janzen, Curtis, and Oliver Harris. *Family Treatment in Social Work Practice.* 2nd ed. Itasca, Ill.: F. E. Peacock, 1986.

Karpel, Mark, and Eric Strauss. *Family Evaluation.* New York: Gardner Press, 1983.

Satir, Virginia. *Conjoint Family Therapy.* 3rd ed. Palo Alto, Calif.: Science and Behavior Books, 1983.

10.11   *Multiworker Family Assessment Interviews*

Purpose: To utilize more than one social worker in the assessment process in order to secure a more detailed understanding of how each family member views the family's problem.

Discussion: There are many advantages to using an approach that brings additional social workers into the assessment process. This is especially true when working with whole families. Kinney, Haapala, and Gast (1981) report that a multiworker model of assessment is particularly helpful when providing intensive family crisis services designed to prevent out-of-home placements.

A multiworker assessment interview is conducted after the social worker assigned to the case (i.e., the primary worker) has conducted an initial interview with the family. If this worker decides to use a multiworker assessment, it is explained to the family. Once the family agrees, secondary social workers are temporarily assigned to each family member (e.g., if there were four family members, four additional workers would be needed). Each secondary worker then spends an hour or so listening to their assigned family member's perspective on the family's problem and attempts to understand how that member sees himself or herself within the context of the family system. After these individual interviews are completed, the secondary social workers and the primary social worker meet for about an hour and share what they have learned about each family member. Meanwhile, the family members spend this time together without a social worker being present.

Next, all of the social workers and all of the family members meet together. Each secondary social worker sits next to his or her family member and speaks for that person; each speaks as if he or she were the family member and uses "I-messages" to describe his or her thoughts and feelings about the family's functioning. During this phase the family members are not to speak or respond to what is being said. If a family member does not like what is being said, he or she and the social worker can leave the room, discuss the difference, and then rejoin the group. After all of the social workers have spoken for the family members, the family members are asked to react to what they have heard.

The last part of this session is used to plan the next steps in the family's effort to secure help with their problem. After this multiworker assessment, the primary social worker continues to provide service.

Although this assessment process may take from three to five hours, it has important advantages.

1. A great deal of information is gathered and each family member's point of view is expressed and explored. The workers are often able to say things that the individual is afraid of saying, thus the issues are out in the open.
2. The family members usually leave this lengthy assessment session feeling they have been listened to and understood. Typically, the process yields a firmer commitment by the family members to work on the problem, a feeling of hopefulness, and ideas on how to make changes.
3. The process has the effect of creating several consultants who have firsthand knowledge of the family, which can be helpful to the primary social worker.

Selected Bibliography

Haapala, David, and Jill Kinney. "Homebuilder's Approach to the Training of In-Home Therapists." In *Home-Based Services for Children and Families,* edited by Sheila Maybanks and Marvin Bryce. Springfield, Ill.: Charles C. Thomas, 1979.

Kinney, Jill, David Haapala, and Elizabeth Gast. "Assessment of Families in Crisis." In *Treating Families in the Home,* edited by Marvin Bryce and June Lloyd. Springfield, Ill.: Charles C. Thomas, 1981.

10.12   *The ABC Model and the Behavior Matrix*

Purpose: To achieve greater precision in observation and the analysis of behavioral interactions.

Discussion: In recent years, many social workers have looked to learning theory, behavioral analysis, and behavior modification for techniques of helping clients learn new behaviors or eliminate problem behaviors. The influence of behavior-oriented approaches has done much to help practitioners be more focused and precise in data gathering and assessment. Two tools commonly used in behavioral analysis, the ABC model and the behavior matrix, are particularly useful to the social worker.

The ABC's of Behavior

In the **ABC model,** the letter *A* stands for *antecedent, B* for *behavior,* and *C* for *consequences.* For example, when assessing a problem behavior, such as a child's temper tantrum, the worker first clearly identifies and operationally defines the behavior under study. In this example, the tantrum is the *B* (i.e., target behavior) in the ABC model.

Next, the worker looks for the *A,* or the antecedent, which are the various situational factors or cues that lead up to or set up the behavior. In the tantrum example, it might be a particular action by the parent that sets the stage for the child's tantrum behavior; perhaps the parent begins to work in the kitchen or turns on the TV news.

Finally, the worker looks for the immediate consequences of the behavior, which is the *C* in the model. This may identify factors that reinforce or reward the behavior. For example, once the tantrum starts, the parent may try to comfort the child and, in the process, reinforce the tantrum behavior. By using the ABC model, the worker may be able to identify those factors than can be changed in order to reduce or eliminate a problem behavior.

Behavior Matrix

A second tool, actually an observational aid, is a three-cell matrix known as the **Behavior Matrix** (see Figure 10.8). After observing the interactions of an individual client, family, or small group, the worker records his or her observations in the appropriate cell. What emerges will be a picture of what positive behaviors should be reinforced, what negative behaviors should be extinguished, if possible, and what new positive behaviors will need to be learned by the client.

As an example, assume that the worker is attempting to help a developmentally disabled man learn to interact more appropriately when greeting other

Figure 10.8 Behavior Matrix

	Behavior Exists	Behavior Does Not Exist
Positive or Appropriate Behavior	1	2
Negative or Inappropriate Behavior	3	

adults. While observing and using the matrix, the worker sees that when introduced to another person, the client giggles, reaches for a handshake, and fails to look directly at the person he is greeting. The worker would record his or her observations as follows:

1. The giggle is an existing inappropriate behavior—enter comment in cell 3.
2. The handshake is an existing appropriate behavior—enter comment in cell 1.
3. Eye contact when shaking hands is a nonexisting appropriate behavior—enter comment in cell 2.

Having made such observations, the next step is to develop an appropriate intervention strategy. Table 10.5 matches recommended behavioral techniques to findings derived from the matrix. (See Technique 12.4, 12.5, and 12.6 for information on behavior techniques.)

Table 10.5 Behavioral Observations and Intervention Techniques

Observation	Possible Interventions
Desired behaviors do not occur at all	Instruction, modeling, prompting, shaping
Desired behaviors occur but infrequently	Additional reinforcement, shaping, behavioral rehearsal
Behaviors occur but not at appropriate times	Behavioral contracting, prompting, and other reminders
Desired behavior occurs so frequently as to be inappropriate	Reduce frequency of reinforcement, differential reinforcement, removal from reinforcing environment
Behaviors that occur are dangerous to self or others	Removal from reinforcing environment, reinforcement of an incompatible behavior

Selected Bibliography

Gambrill, Eileen. *Casework: A Competency-Based Approach.* Englewood Cliffs, N.J.: Prentice-Hall, 1983.

Gelfand, Donna, and Donald Hartmann. *Child Behavior Analysis and Therapy.* 2nd ed. New York: Pergamon Press, 1984.

Hudson, Barbara, and Geraldina MacDonald. *Behavioral Social Work.* Chicago: The Dorsey Press, 1986.

10.13   *Homemade Data-Gathering Tools*

Purpose: To create data-gathering questionnaires, checklists, vignettes, and other data-gathering tools for use with clients in a particular practice setting.

Discussion: The major advantage of commercially available data-collection tools is that they have proven to be useful to other professionals and exist in printed form. Their major disadvantages are that they must frequently be purchased from a publisher and some parts may not be appropriate for all clients. Moreover, some clients may be overwhelmed by a lengthy and detailed questionnaire but could accurately complete a simpler and shorter one. As an alternative to using copyrighted and commercially available tools, social workers should consider designing tools that would be useful with their clientele and agency setting.

Figure 10.9 is a sample of homemade questionnaire developed for use during initial interviews with couples seeking assistance with marital problems. Because it is short and takes only a few minutes to complete, clients do not find it burdensome. As with a problem checklist (see Technique 9.5), this type of questionnaire can be used to zero in on the client's primary concerns. The basic format used in this questionnaire has wide application. Items can be rewritten to focus on other relationships, such as parent-child or adult child-parent. Thus, the reader should use this sample questionnaire as a model for developing individualized data-gathering tools for his or her own practice.

The checklist is probably the most simple format for data gathering. It demands little of the client. With a little creativity, the worker can develop a checklist related to a specific set of client concerns. Figure 10.10 is an example of a checklist designed especially for the parents of children involuntarily placed in foster care by a child protection agency. It was developed by Horejsi, Bertsche, and Clark (1981) to help parents express their feelings about the removal of their child.

Information about a person's attitudes and values cannot be easily obtained through the use of direct verbal or written questioning. Projective or indirect methods are usually more effective. Think, for example, about the child welfare social worker responsible for deciding whether or not a couple should be

Figure 10.9 Model Homemade Questionnaire

Questionnaire on the Husband-Wife Relationship

Explanation: This is a questionnaire about how satisfied you are with what goes on between you and your spouse (between husband and wife). Your answer will help us identify possible sources of stress and worry. Place a check (✔) on the line under the phrase that best describes the degree of satisfaction you have in relation to the item. If an item does not apply to you, simply put NA next to the item.

	Very Satisfied	Mostly Satisfied	Mostly Dissatisfied	Very Dissatisfied
The way we make decisions	_____	_____	_____	_____
The way we divide up responsibility for child care	_____	_____	_____	_____
The way we handle money	_____	_____	_____	_____
The amount of money we earn	_____	_____	_____	_____
The way we resolve conflict	_____	_____	_____	_____
The way we divide up housework and other home-related jobs	_____	_____	_____	_____
The way we get along with our children	_____	_____	_____	_____
The way we discipline our children	_____	_____	_____	_____
The way we get along with in-laws and other relatives	_____	_____	_____	_____
The way we use our free time	_____	_____	_____	_____
The way we talk to each other	_____	_____	_____	_____
The way we care for our home	_____	_____	_____	_____
The amount of time we have together	_____	_____	_____	_____
The amount of alcohol used	_____	_____	_____	_____
The way we give each other emotional support	_____	_____	_____	_____
The amount of privacy we have	_____	_____	_____	_____
The way we handle birth control	_____	_____	_____	_____
The sexual part of our relationship	_____	_____	_____	_____
The way we plan for our future	_____	_____	_____	_____
The way we get along with the neighbors	_____	_____	_____	_____
The way we deal with moral or religious concerns	_____	_____	_____	_____
The way we handle anger and frustration	_____	_____	_____	_____

Please list here any other concerns you may have about your marital relationship: _____

_____

_____

(Continued)

Figure 10.9 (Continued)

What do you consider to be the major strength in your marriage?

_____

_____

What do you consider to be the one or two major problems in your marriage?

_____

_____

licensed as foster parents. In order to assess the couple's capacity for foster parenting, the worker needs to learn about their beliefs and attitudes surrounding child care. The worker could ask a direct question, like Do you believe in spanking a child who misbehaves? or How do you feel about children who wet the bed? Such pointed questions, however, tend to elicit rather superficial responses, which do not reveal the underlying attitudes that are so important in parenting.

An alternative approach is to use a series of carefully written vignettes as springboards for discussion and exploration. Basically, a vignette is a sketch or a brief description of a real-life problem or situation. It provides an indirect and less threatening method of gathering information and facilitates the expression of real feelings and personal viewpoints. Figure 10.11 presents two samples of vignettes, which were developed by Horejsi (1979) for use in the foster home study process. The vignette format can be used in many settings. Needless to say, the worker using this projective data-gathering tool needs to create vignettes that will elicit the type of information needed in order to better understand the client.

In general, social workers underutilize aids like questionnaires, checklists, and vignettes in their data collection with clients. The reader is encouraged to develop and experiment with these tools in his or her own practice. A number of guidelines will help those willing to give it a try.

1. Be clear about the purpose to be served by the tool, the reasons for using it, the type of information sought, and the type of client for whom it is being prepared.
2. The completion of the questionnaire should be a relatively easy task and not tax the client's physical or mental capacity. A simple, short, and focused questionnaire is more likely to be completed than a long one; thus, it is also more likely to yield reliable information.
3. Rather than attempt to develop an all-purpose questionnaire, it is better to design several, each with a specific purpose or focus, and then use them selectively.

Figure 10.10 Sample Homemade Checklist

Understanding the Parents' Feelings

Explanation: Below is a list of feelings that have been expressed by other parents who have had their children placed in foster care. Your feelings may be similar or they may be different from those of other parents who have had a similar experience. Please place a check (✔) by those statements that come close to expressing how you feel.

_____ I feel stunned and numb.

_____ I feel like this whole thing is a bad dream; I cannot believe this is really happening.

_____ I feel preoccupied with the thoughts of my child and the separation; I cannot seem to think of anything else.

_____ I feel shaky and nervous—as if a friend had suddenly died.

_____ I feel overwhelmed; I can't think clearly or do what I know I should do.

_____ I feel everyone blames me for what happened, even though it was not all my fault.

_____ I feel I was singled out unfairly and that I am being accused of being a "bad" parent.

_____ I feel like I have been railroaded and treated unfairly by the agency and the court.

_____ I feel like I cannot face my own child.

_____ I am afraid of what others think of me.

_____ I feel resentment toward everyone.

_____ I fear what I tell my social worker will be used against me.

_____ I feel afraid that I will never get my child back.

_____ I feel confused over why my child was placed in foster care.

_____ I feel that my other children will be placed in foster care.

_____ I feel depressed and sad.

_____ I feel alone and isolated; I feel everyone has abandoned me.

_____ I feel cut off from family and friends.

_____ I feel like running away and never coming back.

_____ I feel God is punishing me.

_____ I feel placement was necessary even though it was painful.

_____ Given time and help, I feel I can put things back together again.

_____ I am pretty sure of what I need to do in order to deal with this situation.

_____ I feel much better than I did when my child first went into foster care.

_____ I have mixed feelings about foster care—sometimes I want my child back and sometimes I think he/she is better off if we are not together.

Please describe here any feelings you have that do not appear on the above list.

_____

_____

Source: From Horejsi, Bertsche, and Clark, *Social Work Practice with Children in Foster Care* (1981), Appendix D, pp. 236–37. Courtesy of Charles C. Thomas, Publisher, Springfield, Illinois.

Figure 10.11 Sample Vignettes

The Brown Family: A Situation to Discuss
Mr. and Mrs. Brown are foster parents to Johnny, age five. Johnny is mentally retarded and has poor arm and hand coordination. Consequently, he has some trouble eating. Because today is Mrs. Brown's birthday, the Browns have decided to go out for an evening meal at a restaurant. While eating, Johnny drops food on the floor and is generally messy. In addition, he has a temper tantrum, cries, and throws food. This gets stares and disapproving looks from the other people in the restaurant.

    a. What do you think of this situation?
    b. How should this behavior be handled?

The Patterson Family: A Situation to Discuss
The Pattersons are very religious people. They have been foster parents to fifteen-year-old Alfred for the past five years. The Pattersons go to church services and participate in other church activities on a regular basis. It means a lot to them. Until a few months ago, Alfred went to church with them, even though he was raised in another religious denomination. Now Alfred refuses to go to church. He says that religion is foolishness and that he should not be forced to go to the Patterson's church when his parents belonged to a different one. The Pattersons feel that religion is central to their life, and they expect everyone living in their family to participate in religious activities.

    a. What do you think of this situation?
    b. How should a conflict of this type be handled?

Source: From Horejsi, *Foster Family Care* (1979), pp. 165–66. Courtesy of Charles C. Thomas, Publisher, Springfield, Illinois.

4. In general, the higher the client's level of education and motivation, the more likely he or she is to deal successfully with a written data-gathering tool. Remember that many people lack basic reading skills.

5. Open-ended questions are necessary when it is difficult to anticipate a client's responses. However, written responses to open-ended questions are often difficult to read and understand. Consequently, tools with many open-ended questions offer few advantages over the more time-consuming face-to-face interview.

6. The construction of precoded or close-ended questions (multiple choice, checklists, etc.) requires a good deal of knowledge about the kinds of responses clients are likely to give. However, a good close-ended question is easy on the client and can be read quickly by the worker.

7. When possible, the questionnaire items should follow a uniform format (i.e., each item has similar wording, grammar, and structure). This helps the client move easily from question to question and yields more reliable information because it minimizes the chance that the client will misunderstand a question.

8. The sequence of questions should follow a logical order. In general, the most sensitive or probing questions should appear toward the end of the questionnaire.

9. Each question or item should contain a single idea. Avoid two- or three-part questions. Questions should not reflect any bias of the worker or the agency. The language used should be simple, clear, and concise. Avoid professional jargon.

10. A pretest should be used to determine whether clients understand all of the questions, can complete it in a reasonable amount of time, and whether the data obtained are indeed useful.

11. Tools developed for use in multidisciplinary or interdisciplinary settings should be understandable to and useable by all members of the team.

12. Whenever possible, tools should be designed so that the data collected can be represented in a visual or graphic manner for quick review and rapid comprehension.

Selected Bibliography

Cautela, Joseph. *Behavior Analysis Forms for Clinical Intervention.* Vol. 1. Champaign, Ill.: Research Press, 1977.

——— . *Behavior Analysis Forms for Clinical Intervention.* Vol. 2. Champaign, Ill.: Research Press, 1981.

Horejsi, Charles. *Foster Family Care.* Springfield, Ill.: Charles C. Thomas, 1979.

——— . *Questionnaire on Husband-Wife Relationship.* Missoula: University of Montana, 1982.

Horejsi, Charles, Anne Bertsche, and Frank Clark. *Social Work Practice with Parents of Children in Foster Care: A Handbook.* Springfield, Ill.: Charles C. Thomas, 1981.

10.14 *Assessment of Adult Social Functioning (AASF)*

Purpose: To measure and record levels of adult social functioning.

Discussion: The *AASF (Assessment of Adult Social Functioning)* is an example of an instrument designed to assist social workers in data gathering, assessment, and case recording. According to MacNair (1981), the instrument "is designed to measure and record levels of social functioning in clients before and after services are provided to them" (p. 3).

Application of the AASF involves ranking the client on each of thirty-four items using a four-level index that ranges from a desirable level of functioning to one in which there are major problems. The instrument provides descriptive statements of client functioning to facilitate this ranking. Each item focuses on a type or an area of social functioning that may concern the practitioner and client. Only those items applicable to the client are rated.

The following is one of the six AASF items in Section 2, "Care of Self." This item, termed "Control of Time and Energy," and its four levels of functioning illustrate the rating and recording format used in the AASF.

AASF Item: Control of Time and Energy

Level		Now	Goals	Later
4	Sets clear conditions and bargains assertively concerning demands on personal time and energy.	4	P S	4
3	Sets unclear conditions in bargaining for use of personal time and energy.	3	P S	③
2	Allows demands on personal time and energy to be made without setting conditions.	②	ⓟ S	2
1	Reacts to demands on personal time and energy by withdrawing passively or aggressively.	1	P S	1

Note that under the *Now* column, the number "2" is circled, and alongside it the "P" is circled. This indicates that, at the start of intervention, the client was rated at level 2 for "control of time and energy" and this dimension of functioning was selected as a primary (P) target of intervention (the letter S refers to secondary). Also note that, after a period of intervention (i.e., later), the client was rated at level 3. The change of rating, if any, between the *Now* (before) and the *Later* (after) records the client's progress toward an intervention goal.

Although the instrument has the appearance of a scale, it is not a measurement scale in the true sense. The user should not attempt to summarize the rankings on the individual items. MacNair (1981) warns that "the instrument was not constructed with this intention in mind. In fact, both the number of items and the frequent use of 'not applicable' render any summary score misleading, if not useless" (p. 88). The AASF is an instrument for the practitioner; it is not a research tool.

Because we believe the individual items of the AASF serve to remind the social worker of the various dimensions of functioning that need to be considered in the social assessment process, we have included here a brief description of all 34 items. Our descriptions are paraphrased versions of those provided by MacNair (1981, 13–36) to depict the highest level of functioning. These essentially positive statements can also be viewed as client strengths and successful coping strategies. We believe many of these statements can be useful in the writing of intervention goals and the preparation of a service plan (see Techniques 11.4 and 11.5).

Client's Crisis Prevention and Management

1. *Response to Illness or Injury.* Client seeks out and uses appropriate treatment for illness or injury. Client's attitude and behavior serve to restore health.

2. *Recovery from Anxiety or Depression of a Crisis.* Relatively rapid rate of recovery from anxiety or depression brought on by crisis episode. Work and family's functioning continue without serious interruption.

3. *Coping with Loss or Separation.* Client carefully and purposely rebuilds alternate intimate relationships following a divorce, separation, or death of spouse or other significant person. Maintains satisfaction with self despite the loss.

4. *Safety or Legality of Behavior.* Client avoids behavior that could produce a crisis, arrest, or injury. Stays clear of daredevil high-risk activities, physical fighting, theft, property damage, malfeasance, and abuse of drugs and alcohol.

5. *Maintaining Balanced Budget.* Client balances income and expenditures and also has income adequate to purchase food, clothing, shelter, transportation, and other essentials.

6. *Job Stability.* Client shows commitment to job and achieves reputation as good and productive worker. Changes jobs only for reasons of career improvement.

Client's Care of Self

1. *Physical Care.* Client engages in health building, in nutritional and physical behaviors, including appropriate hygiene, diet, exercise, and sleep, and avoids misuse or abuse of medicines, harmful foods, drugs, and alcohol.

2. *Reductions of Anxiety or Depression.* Client is able to control anxiety, worry, and depression within normal limits. Personal satisfactions not reduced by anxiety or depression.

3. *Relationships That Are Encouraging.* Client selects companions who provide acceptance and encouragement and have qualities of warmth and genuineness. Avoids companions who are pervasively discouraging or manipulative.

4. *Control of Time and Energy.* Client is able to set priorities and reasonable limits on demands by others for client's time and energy. Has adequate time and energy to carry out essential responsibilities.

5. *Home Environment.* Home and neighborhood meet basic standards of safety and health.

6. *Career Choice.* Client chooses career that holds promise for earning needed income, promotions, and increasing responsibility and recognition. Career choice is good match between abilities and occupational requirements.

Client's Family Life

1. *Sexual Satisfaction.* Mutual and nonexploitative sexual activity is frequent enough and sufficiently enjoyable to satisfy self and partner.

2. *Partnership with Spouse.* Marital relationship is mutually satisfying and meets need for intimacy and emotional expressiveness.

3. *Attention to Children.* Relationship with children is accepting, supportive, and encouraging. Parent able to meet child's need for nurturing, guidance, and protection.

4. *Response of Children to Parent(s).* Children consider guidance, limits, and discipline by parents to be fair and reasonable.

5. *Family Encouragement for Public Life.* Spouses encourage each other and parents encourage children to participate in community, school, job, recreation, religious, civic, or other activities within the limits of energy and demands of other responsibilities necessary to maintain a healthy family life.

Client's Personal Satisfaction

1. *Self-Acceptance.* Client has positive self-image and an attitude of self-confidence. Has realistic picture of own strengths and limitations.
2. *Relationship with Friends.* Client communicates a feeling of belonging and a feeling of closeness to a variety of different people. Maintains satisfying interactions with friends, relatives, neighbors, and coworkers.
3. *Assertiveness.* Client can initiate interactions with others in social environment and influence them to cooperate and/or meet his or her own legitimate needs.
4. *Productivity.* Client is able to successfully complete tasks required on the job, in school, and at home.
5. *Learning.* Client is able to assess own learning needs, seek out instruction, and learn that which is needed for work, home, and school. Client is free of cognitive or sensory difficulties that impede learning process or can compensate for deficits.

Client's Adjustments to Disability

1. *Use of Prescribed Physical or Chemical Supports.* Client makes full and appropriate use of supports such as hearing aid, artificial limbs, medications, and so on.
2. *Control of Frustration.* Client's expressions of anger over disability do not offend family members, friends, relatives, and other helpers. Frustration is expressed in ways that reduce rather than increase tension. Client appreciates those trying to help him or her overcome frustration.
3. *Participation in Relationships.* Client with disability remains involved in intimate relationship and with family, relatives, and friends.
4. *Willingness to Talk about Disability.* Client willing and able to discuss disability and need for assistance without embarrassment or apology. Client lets others know what he or she can and cannot do.
5. *Participation in Occupation and Public Life.* Client is willing to learn and implement rehabilitation techniques that facilitate involvement in work activities and make possible a life-style as near normal as possible.
6. *Ability to Plan for Emergencies.* Client recognizes disability-related vulnerabilities and plans how to handle possible emergencies or accidents.

Client's Coping with Deviance or Addiction

(*Note:* As used here, the term *deviance* refers to such behaviors as delinquency, criminality, and abuse of others; *addiction* refers to abuse of alcohol and drugs, overeating, and other compulsive behaviors.)

1. *Control Over Deviance or Addiction.* Client has successfully overcome or controlled previous deviance or addiction and now maintains nondeviant life-style.

2. *Awareness of Deviance or Addiction.* Client recognizes nature of deviance or addiction and faces up to its personal and social consequences. Client is free of tendency to deny or rationalize.
3. *Relationships with Nondeviant Peers.* Client has overcome social barriers to meaningful relationships with nondeviant relatives, friends, and co-workers. Client interacts with wide variety of people and prior deviant behavior no longer limits range of associations.
4. *Participation in Nondeviant Leisure Activities.* Client participates in diverse social and leisure activities. Activities no longer limited by pursuit of deviance or addiction.
5. *Career Involvement.* Client pursues career and income completely free of hindrance by addiction or deviance.

Selected Bibliography

MacNair, Ray. *Assessment of Social Functioning: A Client Instrument for Practitioners.* Vol. 6, *Human Services Series.* Athens: Institute of Community and Area Development, University of Georgia, 1981.

10.15   *Assessment of Child and Adolescent Functioning (ACAF)*

Purpose: To measure and record levels of adolescent and child social functioning.

Discussion: The *ACAF (Assessment of Child and Adolescent Functioning),* developed by MacNair and McKinney (1983), is similar in purpose, format, and rating system to the Assessment of Adult Social Functioning (AASF), which is described in Technique 10.14. The ACAF consists of forty-five items divided over nine sections. As with the AASF, the worker ranks the client on each item using a four-level index.

The individual items of the ACAF serve as useful reminders of the many dimensions of functioning that should be considered when completing a social assessment of a child or adolescent. Thus, we present paraphrased versions of all forty-five items. Our statements are based on those offered by MacNair and McKinney (1983, 9–37) to describe an item's "level 4" rating (i.e., the highest and most positive level of child and adolescent functioning). These descriptions are useful starting points for the writing of intervention goals (see Technique 11.4) and for identifying client strengths (see Technique 10.7).

Child's Coping with Problem Behavior
1. *Awareness of Problem Behavior.* Child acknowledges that the behavior is a problem. Recognizes that problem is blocking positive interactions and neither underestimates nor exaggerates its effect.

2. *Self-Control Over Problem Behavior.* Child exercises control over the problem behavior or perhaps shows the behavior only at certain times and places and with certain people.
3. *Planning Actions That Eliminate Problem Behavior.* Child plans actions that will avoid any occurrence of the problem behavior. This action is clear and specific.
4. *Action That Replaces the Problem Behavior.* Child almost always chooses alternative actions that replace the problem behavior or avoids problem behavior.

Child's Crisis Prevention and Management
1. *Clarity of Emotional Responses.* Child clearly and accurately expresses the feelings suitable for the crisis event.
2. *Expression and Control of Emotions.* Child is able to express intense emotions without letting these emotions interfere with the activities of everyday living, such as responsibilities at home, school activities, and personal health habits.
3. *Learning from Experience.* Child confidently uses past crises experiences to deal with a current crisis event.
4. *Coping with Loss or Separation.* Child chooses suitable, helpful, and caring persons for support in experiences of loss and separation.
5. *Response to New Parent Figures.* Child accepts the emotional support and guidance offered by the new parent figures such as stepparents, guardians, or foster parents.

Child's Adjustment to Disabilities
1. *Use of Prescribed Physical or Chemical Supports.* Child shows correct applications of supports prescribed for a disability (e.g., hearing aid, artificial limb, or medicines) to achieve the greatest level of activity possible.
2. *Control of Frustration.* Child expresses frustrations in a manner that reduces tension and that does not negatively affect social interaction.
3. *Communication about Disabled Self.* Child lets others know clearly, consistently, and without embarrassment what he or she can and cannot do without help; seeks help when necessary.
4. *Adaptation to Disability.* Consistent with the limitations imposed by the disability, the child moves through the activities of daily living with relative ease. Learns new adaptive skills when necessary.
5. *Participation in Public Life.* Child is willing to learn about and participate in activities outside the home and school, such as shopping, recreation, entertainment, and community affairs.

Child's Family Life
1. *Response to Parental Expectations.* Child responds to reasonable parental expectations and accepts household and school work responsibilities. Almost always meets parents' reasonable expectations and appears to understand the reasons for those expectations.

2. *Sibling Relationships.* Child consistently maintains close supportive relationship with siblings; quarreling is not bitter or hostile.
3. *Activities with Family Group.* Child frequently joins in family's recreational, social, or spiritual activities, such as going to church, shopping, watching TV, and so on.
4. *Relationships with Extended Family.* Child regularly interacts and converses with extended family members such as grandparents, aunts, uncles, and cousins.

Child's Sexuality

1. *Acceptance of Sexuality.* Child consistently expresses contentment and comfort with biological, social, and psychological aspects of his or her own sexuality.
2. *Friendships with Opposite Sex.* Child consistently relates to members of the opposite sex in a way that contributes to meaningful friendships.
3. *Sexual Interest.* Child desires to know more about the biological facts pertaining to sex; accepts information about sex and expresses comfort with this information.
4. *Sexuality in Dating (Adolescent).* Adolescent perceives sexual activity in dating as a mutual, respectful activity. Respects dating partner and self and makes decisions about sexual activity accordingly. Sexual activity is kept within the limits of partner's and own sense of morality. No indication of compulsion or forced participation.
5. *Relationship with Parents Concerning Sexuality.* Child or adolescent frequently talks with parents about feelings, thoughts, and questions about sexual facts and experiences.

Child's School Life

1. *Academic Performance.* Child's performance is consistent with ability. (Evidence of ability includes observed responses to school work, responses to classroom exercises, intelligence shown in discussion, and standardized tests.)
2. *Response to Academic Activities.* Child is self-directed in pursuing activities and assignments.
3. *Relationship with Faculty.* Child communicates with authority figures (e.g., teachers, principals) concerning both academic and personal matters and desires to exchange ideas.
4. *Participation in School Social Life.* Child appears outgoing and self-directed; participates in both planned social activities and in the more spontaneous activities involving other students (i.e., sports, dances, clubs).
5. *Awareness of Career Possibilities.* Child knows future prospects in career choices and/or employment, according to age level. Expresses interest in career objectives.

Child's Neighborhood—Community Life

1. *Satisfaction with Neighborhood.* Child is content with the neighborhood's activities, residents, and physical environment.

2. *Stability of Commitment.* Child has strong neighborhood ties through parents and relatives as well as through cultural identification.
3. *Mutual Aid Relations in Neighborhood.* Child takes initiative to help neighbors; is willing to help and be helped by others in the neighborhood.
4. *Opportunities to Play.* Child looks for and initiates many fun things to do with friends and others in the community.
5. *Participation with Peers in Decision Making.* Child or adolescent joins with friends in peer network to lead, plan, and make decisions for activities within the neighborhood or community.
6. *Association with Adults in Community.* Child voluntarily communicates, relates, and interacts with adults in community.

Child's Care of Self
1. *Physical Care.* Child eats a balanced daily diet, gets adequate sleep, exercises regularly, and avoids practices such as smoking, using drugs and alcohol, overuse of medicines, and overeating.
2. *Reducing Anxiety or Depressions.* Child actively prevents or reduces the conditions triggering anxiety and depression; actively controls anxiety or depression through relaxation or another activity or by means of self-control. Anxiety or depression does not reduce personal satisfactions.
3. *Friendships That Are Encouraging.* Child selects friends who provide encouragement, acceptance, warmth, and help develop a positive self-image.
4. *Control of Personal Time and Energy.* Child sets reasonable limits on use of time and energy that avoids constant imposition or disruption by other children or adults.
5. *Balance of Work and Fun.* Child achieves a balance between work, school, and household requirements and other activities that provide recreation and enjoyment.
6. *Game Playing Related to Work (Child).* Child creatively plays housekeeper, doctor, carpenter, storekeeper, and so on, and thus develops an ability to imagine work roles; builds self-confidence in ability to perform adult roles.

Child's Personal Satisfaction
1. *Self-Acceptance.* Child accepts self openly and confidently; expresses feelings of self-worth.
2. *Friendships.* Child can make friends with many different kinds of people: male, female, old, young, passive, aggressive; members of other socioeconomic groups and races.
3. *Assertiveness.* Child handles himself or herself confidently and effectively in order to have needs met. Exercises personal rights without denying others their rights.
4. *Ability to Carry Responsibility.* Child completes tasks or responsibilities in various areas of life such as school, home, and neighborhood with no reminders or supervision.

5. *Learning Outside of School.* Child shows interest in learning new things and finds ways to pick up the necessary knowledge and skill.

Selected Bibliography

MacNair, Ray, and Elizabeth McKinney. *Assessment of Child and Adolescent Functioning: A Practitioner's Instrument for Assessing Clients.* Athens: Institute of Community and Area Development, University of Georgia, 1983.

10.16   *Clinical Measurement Package (CMP)*

Purpose: To measure various dimensions of client functioning.

Discussion: The *CMP (Clinical Measurement Package),* developed by Hudson and his co-workers, consists of nine separate scales designed to secure a measure of the client's attitude toward self, parents, spouse, family, or peers. Each scale is freestanding and need not be used in conjunction with others in the CMP. All are designed for use by the social work practitioner and can be appropriately used with most clients. The scales are:

- Generalized Contentment Scale (GCS)
- Index of Self-Esteem (ISE)
- Index of Marital Satisfaction (IMS)
- Index of Sexual Satisfaction (ISS)
- Child's Attitude toward Mother (CAM)
- Child's Attitude toward Father (CAF)
- Index of Parental Attitudes (IPA)
- Index of Family Relations (IFR)
- Index of Peer Relations (IPR)

According to Hudson (1981, 152), the Generalized Contentment Scale (GCS) was designed to measure nonpsychotic depression; the Index of Self-Esteem (ISE) measures the evaluative component of self-concept; the Index of Marital Satisfaction (IMS) measures the magnitude of a problem in the relationship between spouses or partners; and the Index of Sexual Satisfaction (ISS) measures the magnitude of a problem in the sexual component of a dyadic relationship.

Three separate scales focus on the parent-child relationship. The Child's Attitude toward Mother (CAM) and the Child's Attitude toward Father (CAF) are completed by the child (above age twelve) and measure the magnitude of problems in the parent-child relationship. The IPA, or Index of Parental Attitudes, is completed by the parent and measures the magnitude of problems in the parent-child relationship, as perceived by the parent.

The Index of Family Relations (IFR) measures the degree of stress and conflict within the family, as perceived by a particular family member. The Index of Peer Relations (IPR) measures the magnitude of a problem a client has in relation to some specified peer group.

Each of the CMP scales consists of twenty-five brief, simply written statements. For example, the first five items from the Index of Parental Attitudes (IPA) are as follows:*

1. My children get on my nerves.   _____
2. I get along well with my children.   _____
3. I feel that I can really trust my children.   _____
4. I dislike my children.   _____
5. My children are well behaved.   _____

To complete the scale, the client reads each statement and responds with one of five possible answers as a way of indicating the degree to which he or she is described by the statement. The five responses are: (1) rarely or none of the time, (2) a little of the time, (3) some of the time, (4) a good part of the time, and (5) most or all of the time. It takes only a few minutes for the client to complete the scale.

A score can be calculated in just a few minutes, and each CMP scale uses the same scoring procedure. Scores can range from 0 to 100; the higher the score, the more serious the problem. Hudson reports a clinical cutting score of 30. In other words, a score above 30 indicates the existence of a clinically significant problem. Hudson (1981) explains that the scales "should not be used with children under the age of 12 or with clients who may receive important rewards or punishments as a consequence of their scores on the scales, such as prisoners seeking parole or mental hospital patients seeking discharge" (p. 153).

Each of the nine scales has a reliability of at least 0.90. All have good face, content, construct, and discriminant validity. The scales were designed for repeated use with the same client in single-subject designs; thus, the CMP scales can be useful as a means of measuring the outcome of intervention. Their simplicity and ease of use make them attractive to social work practitioners. The scales have been widely used in the United States and Canada and are available in Chinese, French, German, and Spanish translations.

All nine are presented in Hudson (1985, 1982), Bloom and Fischer (1982), and Corcoran and Fischer (1987). The publication by Hudson (1982) offers the most complete discussion of the CMP and instructions for their use in practice. Recently the CMP scales plus others have been incorporated into a microcomputer program, *The Clinical Assessment System,* which performs scoring, record-keeping, and case management tasks.

Selected Bibliography

Bloom, Martin, and Joel Fischer. *Evaluating Practice: Guidelines for the Accountable Professional.* Englewood Cliffs, N.J.: Prentice-Hall, 1982.

*IPA items reproduced with permission from Hudson 1982.

Corcoran, Kevin, and Joel Fischer. *Measures for Clinical Practice: A Source Book.* New York: The Free Press, 1987.

Hudson, Walter. *The Clinical Measurement Package: A Field Manual.* Homewood, Ill.: The Dorsey Press, 1982.

———. "Indexes and Scales." In *Social Work Research and Evaluation.* 2nd ed., edited by Richard Grinnel. Itasca, Ill.: F. E. Peacock, 1985.

OUTP ST Software. *The Clinical Assessment System.* Park Forest, Ill.

10.17 Psycho-Social Screening Package (PSSP)

Purpose: To screen clients at intake for the purpose of identifying areas of functioning that are problems for the client.

Discussion: The *Psycho-Social Screening Package (PSSP)* was developed by Hudson (1982) as a method of efficiently collecting information from clients about a wide range of personal and interpersonal problems. It can be used solely as an intake screening tool, or it can be administered during both intake and again at the time of termination as a way of assessing the general status of the client and possible changes during intervention.

The PSSP is different in both purpose and structure from the CMP scales (see Technique 10.16). It contains twenty items, each of which relates to a different type of problem. Therefore, it can be used by the social worker to secure a "snapshot" view of many potential problems. The first twelve items of the PSSP relate to intrapersonal distress; the last eight focus on interpersonal or relationship problems. For example, items 1, 12, 15, and 18 of the PSSP are as follows:*

1. I feel depressed.
12. The quality of my work is poor.
15. There are problems in our family relationships.
18. My partner and I have problems with our sexual relationship.

The client answers each of the twenty items with one of six responses: (1) rarely or none of the time, (2) a little of the time, (3) some of the time, (4) a good part of the time, (5) most or all of the time, or (6) this item does not apply to my situation. Obviously, the worker is most interested in those items rated either 4 or 5 by the client.

Each item on the PSSP is scored and interpreted separately. In fact, Hudson warns against calculating a total score. Given the design of the PSSP, doing so would be inappropriate and misleading. Hudson (1982) explains, however, that it is possible to calculate a problem index score. "The best and safest way to obtain an overall index or score on the PSSP is to compute what is known as the problem index or PI score. That is done by summing only those items that are scored

*PSSP items reproduced with permission from Hudson 1982.

as three, four, or five and then dividing that sum by the number of such items" (p. 146).

An interesting feature of the PSSP is that nine of the items correspond to problem areas that can be assessed with a scale from the CMP. Thus, the social worker could follow the PSSP with the administration of one of the CMP scales in order to obtain an in-depth assessment of the problem area.

Selected Bibliography

Hudson, Walter. *The Clinical Measurement Package: A Field Manual.* Homewood, Ill.: The Dorsey Press, 1982.

10.18 *The Child Well-Being Scales (CWBS)*

Purpose: To measure the degree to which a child's physical, psychological, or social needs are being met.

Discussion: Magura and Moses (1986) explain that the *Child Well-Being Scales (CWBS)*

> are a set of standardized client outcome measures specifically designed to meet the needs of a program evaluation in child welfare services. The instrument measures a family's (or child's) position on 43 separate dimensions using fully anchored rating scales completed by social workers.... The scales focus on issues common to a broad range of child and family-oriented services, with particular emphasis on problems encountered in child protection. (p. 83)

The CWBS focuses on such dimensions as the adequacy of physical health care, quality and quantity of food available, amount of available living space in relation to family size and composition, interactional consequences of mental illness, amount and quality of attention given to children, supervision of teenagers, adequacy of temporary child care, management of disposable income, continuity of parenting, quality of interaction between parents, parental recognition of problems, appropriateness of behavioral demands placed on children, consistency of discipline, child's academic performance, protection of child from harm, and others. The CWBS is an "anchored scale," which means that it is one for which the user is given criteria for making a rating decision so as to reduce bias toward either optimistic or pessimistic ratings. For example, the criteria for a rating of "serious discord" within one dimension of the CWBS scales, the Parental Relations dimension, reads as follows:

- Parents seem to have more periods of arguments than of peace and harmony.
- Since contacts between parents tend to result in conflict, contacts on all except essential matters tend to be avoided. There is little tolerance and "grudges" are harbored for long periods of time.

- Parents may have a diminished emotional tie and may seek satisfaction outside the marital relationship. Children may not only be drawn into arguments, but may be the focus of arguments.
- Parents have talked about separation and one may have stayed away from home for several days on several occasions. But no legal separations or long periods of separation have occurred, and no legal action is pending. There may also be some hitting or slapping but no injuries have occurred. (Magura and Moses, 1986, 125)

Other criteria are given for the ratings of "severe," "moderated," and "no significant discord."

The CWBS is a valid and reliable instrument. Its scoring system incorporates "seriousness weights" that make it possible to compare and combine the ratings on the different scales. Ratings on individual scales can be combined into a total score ranging from 0 to 100. The lower the score, the more serious the child's and family's situation. A social worker who is familiar with the CWBS can complete the ratings in about twenty-five minutes.

Workers may find the detailed criteria of these anchored scales quite useful in their search for the wording and phrases that can be used in Goal Attainment Scaling (see Technique 13.3), Task Achievement Scaling (see Technique 13.2), and also in the formulation of intervention objectives. The CWBS, apart from its intended use, provides highly useful descriptions of the behaviors that distinguish functional and dysfunctional families.

Selected Bibliography

Magura, Stephen, and Beth Moses. *Outcome Measures for Child Welfare Services.* Washington, D.C.: Child Welfare League of America, 1986.

Seaberg, James. "Child Well-Being Scales: A Critique." *Social Work Research and Abstracts* (Fall 1988): 9–15.

10.19 *Assessing Mental Status*

Purpose: To determine if the client's thought and behavior indicate serious mental illness and the need for a psychiatric referral.

Discussion: Regardless of agency setting, the social worker will encounter clients who suffer from a major mental illness. Thus, it is important to be able to recognize certain signs and symptoms of mental illness so that the client will be promptly referred for a competent psychiatric and medical examination. It is important to remember that some mental disorders are caused by dramatic changes in the brain and nervous system (e.g., tumors, neurological diseases, etc.). In such cases, prompt referral for medical evaluation can mean the difference between life and death for the client.

Mental status exams follow various formats. For the most part, they consist of a set of simple questions aimed at gauging orientation to time and place, short- and long-term memory, and appropriateness of affect. Typical questions are: How old are you? In what year were you born? What did you have to eat at your last meal? Can you count backwards from ten? What is the name of the building we are in?

When a social worker is gathering information for purposes of assessing mental status, it is important to work the questions into the ordinary flow of conversation. Engaging the client in a description of his or her typical day—from awaking to bed time—provides a context for asking more pointed questions. If asked one question after another, the client may be offended, and if the client cannot answer the questions, he or she will feel embarrassed. Daiches (1983) describes eleven categories of information that should be considered in assessing mental status:

1. *General appearance and attitude* considers whether the client's basic appearance is appropriate and consistent with his or her age, social, and economic status. The client's dress, personal hygiene, speech, facial expressions, and motor activity provide important information about his or her self-perception and awareness of others. Marked inappropriateness in appearance may be associated with psychological disturbance, particularly if these characteristics have changed over a short period of time.

2. *Behavior* is concerned with the appropriateness of the client's conduct during the interview and with any reports of bizarre behavior by others or the client. Irrational behaviors, such as compulsions (repeated acts that the client feels compelled to do) and phobias (avoidance of places, persons, or objects because of unfounded fears) are characteristics of many disorders.

3. *Orientation to time and place* refers to whether the client is aware of who he or she is, where he or she is, and what time it is (year, month, date, and day). Disorientation is often associated with psychiatric conditions caused by organic dysfunction.

4. *Memory* deficits may be associated with psychiatric as well as physical disorders. Four types of memory may be assessed: immediate, short-term, recent, and remote.

- Immediate recall refers to the ability to recall things within seconds of their presentation.
- Short-term memory is generally defined as covering events transpiring within the last twenty-five minutes.
- Recent memory refers to the client's recollection of current events and situations occurring within the few weeks preceding the interview.
- Remote memory refers to events and situations transpiring before that period and to significant life events (e.g., marriage, first job, etc.).

Immediate and short-term recall are generally assessed by instructing the client to remember something (a word, number, or object) and then asking him or her to recall that item after the lapse of a few minutes. Recent memory can be tested by asking questions such as Where do you live? and How long have you lived there? Remote memory can be tested by asking Where were you born? Where did you go to school? and Who was president of the United States when you got married?

5. *Sensorium* refers to an individual's ability to utilize data from his sense organs (hearing, vision, touch, smelling, and taste) and more generally to his or her overall attentiveness and alertness to the surroundings. If a client cannot comprehend visual symbols (and has no visual impairment), touch, or ordinary conversation (and has no hearing impairment and can be presumed to understand the language) or otherwise demonstrates an inability to respond to sensory stimuli, he or she may possibly be affected by an organic brain disorder.

6. *Intellectual functioning* is screened by evaluating the client's abilities to read, write, and follow simple instructions, to do simple arithmetic, to think abstractly (e.g., How are an apple and orange alike?), and his or her awareness of common knowledge consistent with his or her level of education. Poor comprehension and deficits in abstract thinking and intellectual performance are commonly noted as symptoms of various psychological disorders.

Gauging educational attainment is important because low levels of intellectual functioning may be attributable to a lack of education. Poor levels of intellectual functioning among educated persons, however, may be indicative of organic or functional disorders. Intellectual deterioration is most apparent among individuals with central nervous system disorders but may also be evident in other disturbed individuals.

7. *Mood and affect* refer to the client's prevailing emotional state and the range of emotions displayed during the interview. Moods include such emotions as anger, irritability, elation, exhilaration, anxiety, fear, depression, sadness, apathy, and indifference. In assessing mood and affect, two questions are important.
- Is the client's emotional state a reasonable response to his or her situation? For example, it is important to determine whether a client's depression is the result of recent events (e.g., the death of a spouse).
- Does the client show emotions that correspond to the topic being discussed? A person's expression of mood will usually correspond to the subject matter being discussed. Inappropriate smiling or laughter when talking about sad events or rapid changes in emotional expression, such as laughing or crying without relevance to the conversation or circumstances, may be indicative of a more serious psychiatric disorder. Emotional lability can also have an organic origin (e.g., after a stroke).

8. *Perceptual distortions* may be exhibited by some psychologically impaired individuals. Two of the most significant perceptual problems that social workers are likely to encounter among their clients are illusions and hallucinations. Illusions are misinterpretations of actual stimuli. Hallucinations are perceptual experiences in the absence of external stimuli (e.g., hearing voices).

9. *Thought content* refers to the logic and consistency of an individual's general attitudes, ideas, and beliefs. Examples of thought content problems include delusional thinking (false beliefs that cannot be altered by logical arguments with the client) and obsessions (fixed or repetitive ideas that the client cannot get out of his or her mind).

10. *Insight* may be evaluated by focusing on whether or not the client understands that he or she has certain problems that have brought him or her to the attention of the worker or agency, that he or she understands what those problems are, and that he or she can describe some of the reasons for that problem. Ironically, the greater the severity of his or her mental problem, the more likely the client is to be unaware of existing problems that are of great concern to others.

11. *Judgment* refers to the individual's ability to make responsible and rational decisions in relation to obvious problems. It also refers to a client's mental capability to make decisions related to daily living, particularly as he or she relates to maintaining his or her physical well-being and survival.

Selected Bibliography

Daiches, Sol. *Risk Assessment: A Guide for Adult Protective Service Workers.* New York: The City of New York, Human Resources Administration, Project Focus, 1983.

Turner, Francis, ed. *Adult Psychopathology: A Social Work Perspective.* New York: The Free Press, 1984.

Waldinger, Robert. *Psychiatry for Medical Students.* Washington, D.C.: American Psychiatric Press, Inc., 1984.

10.20 Identifying Developmental Delays

Purpose: To identify a child's developmental problems.

Discussion: The social worker is often in a strategic position to observe preschool-aged children and conduct at least a cursory assessment of the child's physical and mental growth and development. Once children enter school, teachers will usually detect developmental delays. Children who are malnourished or chronically ill, many who are abused and neglected, and, of course, those who are mentally retarded will fall behind developmental norms. Early identification and intervention are of critical importance. Table 10.6 presents a listing of developmental milestones by Martin (1979, 32–33) that can be used in the assessment process. If a child is not able to accomplish two or three of the milestones for his or her age level, the child should be referred for an in-depth evaluation.

Table 10.6 Developmental Milestones*

Age	Motor	Mental	Language	Social
3–6 months	will bear weight on legs can roll over stomach to back engages hands in midline when pulled to sit, head is steady, doesn't fall back when on abdomen, can lift shoulders off mat when on abdomen, can lift head and look about will begin to reach for and grasp objects sits with support	looks at objects in hand looks after a toy which is dropped uses a 2-hand approach to grasp toys looks at objects as small as a raisin turns head to voice, follows with eyes	coos gurgles chuckles laughs aloud squeals has expressive noises	has a social smile will pat a bottle with both hands anticipates food on sight
6–9 months	rolls from back to stomach gets feet to mouth sits alone, unsupported, for extended period (over 1 minute) stands with hands held on back, can lift head up beginning attempts to crawl or creep when sitting, reaches forward to grasp without falling	bangs toys in play transfers objects from hand to hand reaches for a toy with one hand picks up a toy he/she drops is persistent in obtaining toys would pull a toy to self by attached string	responds to name vocalizes to social stimulus has single consonants, i.e., ba, ka, ma combines syllables, i.e., da-da, ba-ba likes to make sounds with toys imitates sounds	expects repetition of stimulus likes frolicky play discriminates strangers smiles to mirror image takes some solid food to mouth bites and chews toys beginning to enjoy peekaboo
9–12 months	crawls well can sit steadily for more than 10 minutes stands holding on to furniture can pull to sitting position walks, holding on to a hand or to furniture	will uncover a toy he/she sees covered up can grasp object small as raisin with thumb and one finger beginning to put things in and out of containers goes for an object with index finger outstretched likes to drop objects deliberately shows interest in pictures	understands no, or inflection of "no!" uses mama, or dada, first inappropriately, then with meaning by 12 months has at least one other word knows meaning of 1–3 words	cooperates in games will try to roll ball to another person plays patacake and peekaboo waves goodbye will offer toy without releasing it likes to interact in play with adult

(Continued)

275

Table 10.6 (Continued)

Age	Motor	Mental	Language	Social
12–18 months	by 18 months, walks well alone creeps up stairs can get to standing position alone can stoop and recover an object walking, pulls a pull-toy seats self on chair	looks at pictures in a book will scribble spontaneously with pencil or crayon uses spoon drinks from cup will follow one or two directions, i.e., take a ball to…	has 3–5 words will point to one body part will point to at least one picture uses jargon, i.e., unintelligible "foreign" language with inflection imitates some words	cooperates in dressing holds own bottle or cup finger feeds points or vocalizes to make desires known shows or offers a toy
18–24 months	can run, albeit stiffly walks up and down stairs with one hand held hurls a ball can kick a ball or object jumps with both feet stands on one foot with one hand held	can tower 2 or more one-inch blocks turns pages of a book, even if 2–3 at a time will try to imitate what an adult draws with pencil can point to 2–3 body parts	by two years, has at least 20 words by two years, is combining two words in a phrase jargon, which was elaborate by 18 months, is gone by 24 months verbalizes desires with words	uses spoon, spilling very little removes one piece of clothing imitates housework more and more handles a cup quite well
2–3 years	can walk up stairs without hand held can balance on one foot for one second can jump in place can walk on tiptoe can jump from the bottom step kicks ball forward can throw a ball	can tower 6 one-inch blocks can dump a raisin from a bottle to attain without hints can imitate a vertical line, possibly a horizontal line, with pencil can anticipate the need to urinate or defecate if worked with, can toilet self	uses 2–4 word phrases uses plurals names at least one picture talks incessantly vocabulary 100–300 words by 3 years uses some personal pronouns, i.e., I, me, mine points to several parts of a doll on request identifies over 5 parts of own body	puts on some clothing washes and dries hands has parallel play with peers can pour from a pitcher
3–4 years	rides a tricycle alternates feet when going up stairs can stand on one foot for 2–5 seconds can broad jump	can tower 8–10 one-inch blocks says full name can match colors has sense of round, square, and triangular shaped	can answer some questions knows rhymes and songs asks questions has understanding of on, under and behind	knows own sex beginning to play with other children unbuttons dresses with supervision

Age				
	uses scissors swings and climbs	figures and can match them copies a circle, line, cross with pencil can repeat 3 digits	vocabulary over 1000 words can match colors, and by 5 years, name 3–4 colors counts 3 objects with pointing 90% of speech intelligible can define words in terms of use can answer questions like, what do you do when you are cold… hungry… tired…?	can separate from mother easily dresses with little supervision buttons likes to play "dramatic" play, make-believe imaginative play with a doll
4–5 years	runs well and turns can hop on one foot 1–2 times beginning to skip stands on one leg for 10 seconds throws ball well overhand walks down stairs one foot to each step	can copy a cross with a pencil can pick the longer of two lines can copy a square with pencil		
5–6 years	skips on both feet alternately can catch a bounced ball can walk heel to toe on a line can hop on one foot for 10 feet	can copy a square or triangle from looking at a copy gives age knows morning from afternoon draws a person with a body, with 3–6 parts prints simple words	can repeat 4 digits asks questions about meaning of words counts 10 objects names coins can tell what some things are made of can define some words	no supervision necessary for dressing plays "dress-up" elaborate dramatic play does simple chores unattended at home

*If child is not accomplishing two or three of these milestones, consider developmental consultation.

Source: Harold Martin, Treatment for Abused and Neglected Children. Washington, D.C.: National Center on Child Abuse and Neglect, U.S. Department of Health Education and Welfare, DHEW Publication No. (OHDS) 79–30 199, U.S. Government Printing Office, 1979.

Selected Bibliography

Martin, Harold. *Treatment for Abused and Neglected Children*. Washington, D.C.: U.S. Department of Health Education and Welfare, DHEW publication No. (OHDS) 79-30 199, U.S. Government Printing Office, 1979.

Newman, Barbara, and Philip Newman. *Development Through Life: A Psychosocial Approach*. 4th ed. Chicago: The Dorsey Press, 1987.

10.21   *Psychological Testing*

Purpose: To make appropriate use of psychological testing in the assessment of client functioning.

Discussion: Not infrequently, the social worker will refer a client to a clinical psychologist for testing. Such testing can provide useful information on the client's intellectual capacity, patterns of motivation and coping behavior, self-concept, level of anxiety or depression, and general personality integration. It is important to remember that psychological tests are far from perfect tools; they focus on certain variables, while neglecting others that may be of importance. The value of testing depends heavily on the competence and experience of the psychologist who interprets the test data. Cronbach (1984), an authority on testing, reminds us that the value of test information should be judged by how much it improves decisions over the best possible decisions made without the test. A psychological test can provide some additional information on which to base a decision, but relying too heavily on test data, especially if it is a single test, is a common error made by those unfamiliar with the appropriate use of psychological tests.

Included here are brief descriptions of tests commonly encountered by the social worker. Several of these descriptions are based on information provided by the National Information Center for Handicapped Children and Youth (1985).

Infant Development Scales

- *The Brazelton Neonatal Behavioral Assessment Scale* tests an infant's (1) neurological intactness, (2) interactive behavior (including motoric control such as putting the thumb in the mouth and remaining calm and alert in response to stimuli such as a bell, a light, and pinprick), and (3) responsiveness to the examiner and need for stimulation.
- *The Bayley Scales of Infant Development* test mental abilities, including memory, learning, and problem-solving behavior; motor skills; and social behaviors, such as social orientation, fearfulness, and cooperation.
- *The Gesell Developmental Schedules* test for fine and gross motor behavior; language behavior; adaptive behavior, including eye-hand coordination, imitation, and object recovery; and personal-social behavior, including reaction to persons, initiative, independence, and play response.

- *The Denver Developmental Screening Test* is widely used and can be administered by a person with only limited training. As its name suggests, it is a screening tool, not a definitive test. It is used to discover possible developmental delays or problems in the four areas of personal/social, fine motor/adaptive, language, and gross motor skills that should be more carefully evaluated with other tests.

Intelligence Tests for Preschool- and School-Aged Children

- *The Stanford-Binet* can be used with both preschool- and school-aged children and is usually administered to children between the ages of two and eight. Examples of what is required include remembering where an object was hidden, building a four-block tower to match an existing tower, explaining the uses of common objects, and identifying pictured objects by name. One disadvantage of the Stanford-Binet is that it gives only an overall score, assessing general thinking and problem-solving ability, and does not provide subtest scores about particular strengths and weaknesses. Some items are culture specific, so the test is best suited for middle-class, English-speaking children; it may not provide a fair assessment of bilingual or bicultural children. Depending upon the child's age, the test requires vision, eye-hand coordination, hearing, and speech.
- *The Wechsler Scales* include separate forms for preschool- and school-aged children. The preschool form is called the *Wechsler Preschool and Primary Scale of Intelligence (WPPSI),* and the school-aged form is called the *Wechsler Intelligence Scale for Children—Revised (WISC—R).* The WISC—R is the test most likely to be used to assess the cognitive functioning of school-aged children. It has six verbal and six performance subtests.
- *The System of Multicultural Pluralistic Assessment (SOMPA),* a test based on the WISC—R, was designed to take into account a child's handicapping condition and sociocultural background and thus be nondiscriminatory.

Intelligence Tests for Adults

- *The Wechsler Adult Intelligence Scale—Revised (WAIS—R)* is usually considered to be the best general intelligence test for persons aged sixteen and older. Six subtests (information, digit span, vocabulary, arithmetic, comprehension, and similarities) make up its verbal scale, and five subtests (picture completion, picture arrangement, block design, object assemble, and digit symbol) make up the performance scale.

Special Abilities Test

- *The Bender Visual Motor Gestalt Test* is used to assess visual perceptual skills and eye-hand coordination. The client is given nine geometric figures, one at a time, and asked to copy each.
- *The Peabody Picture Vocabulary Test* assesses familiarity with vocabulary words without requiring the child to speak. The client is shown four pictures at a time and must point to the one that corresponds to the word the examiner says. The test was originally designed to be used with persons who are nonverbal, mentally retarded, and/or have cerebral palsy.

- *The Detroit Test of Learning Aptitude* measures auditory and visual memory and concentration.

Testing for Mental Retardation
An IQ score below 70 indicates that a client may be mentally retarded. However, a low IQ score by itself is not sufficient for diagnosis; the client's adaptive behavior must also be measured. *Adaptive behavior* refers to the person's ability to carry out everyday living skills, such as dressing, eating, washing, playing, functioning independently, and cooperating with others. Several instruments measure age-appropriate adaptive behavior: *The Vineland Social Maturity Scale, The American Association on Mental Deficiency's (AAMD) Adaptive Behavior Scales,* and *The Adaptive Behavior Inventory for Children.*

Personality Tests
Objective-type personality tests are pencil-and-paper tests designed to determine predominant personality traits or behaviors.

- *The Minnesota Multiphasic Personality Inventory (MMPI)* is probably the most often used objective personality test. It consists of 566 self-descriptive statements to which the client answers either true, false, or cannot say. Its ten subscales are physical complaints, depression, immaturity, conflict with authority, masculine or feminine interests, suspicion and hostility, anxiety, alienation and withdrawal, elevation mood and high energy, and introversion and shyness. It is used with persons sixteen years of age or older.
- *The Personality Inventory for Children (PIC)* is one of the few objective tests for younger children.

Projective tests provide a stimulus (e.g., inkblots, a set of pictures, or incomplete sentences) and ask the client to respond to the stimulus. These tests rest on the assumption that the client's responses will reveal his or her unique view of the world, including issues of concern and emotional needs. Another type of projective test provides instructions for the client to draw a picture, again with the idea that the drawing will reveal information about the inner self.

- *The Rorschach Test* was the first inkblot test and the one still most commonly used.
- *The Holtzman Inkblot Technique* is another projective test that may substitute for the Rorschach.

The most common picture-story tests are:

- *The Thematic Apperception Test (TAT)*
- *The Children's Apperception Test (CAT)*
- *The Michigan Picture Test*
- *The Tasks of Emotional Development Test*

- *The Blacky Pictures*
- *The Make-a-Picture-Story Test*

Referring a Client for Psychological Testing

1. Before deciding on a referral, be very clear about why you are seeking a psychological evaluation of your client.
2. When making a referral to a psychologist for testing, clearly explain how and why you and your agency are involved in providing service to this client, the case management decisions you face, and the type of information that would be helpful. Make a list of the questions you would like the psychologist to answer.
3. Provide the psychologist with information concerning the client's age, sex, education, occupation and employment history, ethnicity, and any special disabilities, such as hearing or visual problems or physical limitations. Also provide the results of any previous testing, including the dates of testing and the names of the tests used.
4. After consulting with the psychologist who will do the testing, prepare the client by giving him or her basic information on what to expect, where the testing will be done, and about how long it will take.
5. Have realistic expectations of psychological testing. In many cases, the results of testing will simply confirm the conclusions already reached by people who have observed the client for a matter of weeks or months.
6. Ask the psychologist to explain the limitations of the testing procedures used with your client, so you can decide how much faith you should place in the test results.

Selected Bibliography

Anastasi, A. *Psychological Testing.* 6th ed. New York: Macmillan, 1988.

Baily, Thelma, and Walter Baily. *Psychological Evaluations—An Aid to CPS Assessment.* Denver: American Humane Association, 1986.

Cronbach, L. J. *Essentials for Psychological Testing.* 4th ed. New York: Harper & Row, 1984.

National Information Center for Handicapped Children and Youth. "Psychological Testing of Children with Disabilities." *News Digest* (October 1985): 3–6.

10.22   *The DSM-III-R*

Purpose: To use proper terminology and classifications when exchanging information about a client's mental disorder.

Discussion: In order to communicate accurately with other professionals about a client's mental disorders and understand reports prepared by psychologists and psychiatrists, the social worker must be familiar with the ***Diagnostic and***

Statistical Manual for Mental Disorders (DSM-III-R), which is published by the American Psychiatric Association (1987). Also, an increasing number of social work settings look to third-party payments (e.g., Medicaid, Medicare, private health insurance, etc.) as a source of revenue. In order for an agency to submit a claim for such payments, the client must be assigned to a specific diagnostic category listed in this manual.

In the DSM-III-R system, over 200 disorders are classified within eighteen broad categories. Williams (1981) explains that, in the manual, each disorder

> is described in a systematic and comprehensive discussion outlining the disorder's essential features and associated features, including a description of the disorder's usual course, the individual's usual age at onset, most common complications, usual degree of impairment in social and occupational functioning, predisposing factors that place an individual at risk of developing the disorder, prevalence, sex ratio, differential diagnosis, and specific diagnostic criteria. (p. 101)

The eighteen categories are: (1) Disorders Usually First Evident in Infancy, Childhood or Adolescence; (2) Organic Mental Syndromes and Disorders; (3) Psychoactive Substance Use Disorders; (4) Schizophrenia; (5) Delusional Disorders; (6) Psychotic Disorders Not Elsewhere Classified; (7) Mood Disorders; (8) Anxiety Disorders; (9) Somatoform Disorders; (10) Dissociative Disorders; (11) Sexual Disorders; (12) Sleep Disorders; (13) Factitious Disorders; (14) Impulse Control Disorders Not Elsewhere Classified; (15) Adjustment Disorder; (16) Psychological Factors Affecting Physical Condition; (17) Personality Disorders; and (18) Conditions Not Attributable to a Mental Disorder That Are a Focus of Attention or Treatment.

With good reason, some social workers, like Kutchins and Kirk (1988), have reservations about the appropriateness of the DSM III-R for social work practice. Many are bothered by the labeling process inherent in using this system and by the emphasis on pathology rather than on client strengths.

At present, the National Association of Social Workers is sponsoring the development of a social work-oriented system known as *Person-in-Environment* (PIE) which describes and classifies problems of social functioning. PIE is not intended as a substitute for the DSM-III-R but rather is complementary. PIE's focus is on social role performance and environmental influences on behavior. Following tests of reliability and validity, PIE is expected to be available in the early 1990s.

Selected Bibliography

American Psychiatric Association. *Diagnostic Statistical Manual of Mental Disorders, DSM-III-R.* 3rd ed., revised. Washington, D.C.: American Psychiatric Association, 1987.

Karls, James, and Karin Wandrei. *Person-in-Environment (PIE).* California Chapter of the National Association of Social Workers, Revision 8 (June 1988).

Kutchins, Herb, and Stuart Kirk. "The Business of Diagnosis: DSM III and Clinical Practice." *Social Work* 33, no. 3 (May–June 1988): 215–20.

Williams, Janet. "DSM-III: A Comprehensive Approach to Diagnosis." *Social Work* 26 (March 1981): 101–06.

Purpose: To form an opinion about whether a client is at risk of suicide.

Discussion: Given the high rate of suicide among teenagers, young adults, and the elderly, the social worker will encounter clients who are at risk of taking their own lives. *Warning signs of suicide* include depression, preoccupation with death and pain, giving away prized possessions, personality change, sudden increase in the use of drugs and alcohol, and impulsive or reckless behavior. Clinical data indicate that most suicide victims have consulted with a physician within six months of their suicide. Although not all people who end their lives are clinically depressed, studies reveal that depression is often present. *Symptoms of depression* include lack of interest in activities, expressions of hopelessness, loss of appetite, withdrawal from others, early waking from sleep or erratic sleep patterns, irritability, and unexplained crying. Whereas depression in adults usually results in a retardation of activity, depression in children and youth is often expressed in agitation.

Legally and ethically, the social worker must make every reasonable effort to prevent a client's suicide. This includes providing counseling, staying with the person during times of high risk, and, if necessary, calling the police and arranging for involuntary hospitalization. If one has reason to believe that a client is at risk of suicide, draw on the experience of other professionals in making a decision on how best to proceed. The social worker must not allow himself or herself to be "hooked" by the suicidal client into a promise of complete confidentiality. Ordinary rules of confidentiality must be broken in order to prevent a death or a serious injury.

The following guidelines will help the worker in assessing suicide potential:

1. Take every message about suicide seriously. It is significant that the person is talking about harm to self rather than expressing frustration in other ways. It is a myth that people who talk about suicide will not kill themselves. However, the messages may be subtle; unfortunately, in some cases, it is not until after the death that their meaning becomes clear. In 10 to 20 percent of suicides, there are no real warnings.

2. Listen for indirect statements of suicidal intent such as: I won't be around much longer or There is nothing worth living for anymore or I can't stand it anymore. Be especially alert to such clues if the person has recently experienced a loss of an important relationship or a loss of status among peers, an episode of family violence, or is in the throes of adjusting to chronic pain, a life-threatening illness, or a serious physical limitation.

3. Keep in mind that suicidal persons are experiencing intense feelings of ambivalence—the desire to live and, at the same time, the desire to escape intense pain, even if by death. They do not really want to die but want desperately to get away from their pain. Thus, assume that a person talking about suicide is, in most cases, ambivalent and hoping for your assistance. Reach out and support that part of the person that is holding to life.

4. Ask simple and direct questions when communicating with the suicidal person. Do not be afraid to ask if he or she is thinking about suicide. Speaking openly about a person's wish to die will not increase the likelihood of suicide. Direct questioning tells the suicidal person that you are concerned and not afraid to talk straight. Also, direct questioning is a way of eliciting the information necessary to help the client. Examples of questions include: Are you thinking of killing yourself? Can you tell me why suicide seems like the answer? and Who else knows you are thinking about suicide?

5. Try to understand why life now seems so painful and futile to the individual. Always remember that suicide is seen by the person as a solution to a problem. It is of critical importance to identify the problem. Do not argue or become judgmental—the suicidal person already feels helpless and hopeless; making him or her feel even less worthwhile only adds to feelings of inadequacy.

6. Determine whether or not the person has chosen a specific suicide method (shooting, hanging, pills, etc.). Also determine if the person has access to the method he or she has chosen. The person who has selected a method and has access to it is at high risk.

7. Determine whether or not the person has worked out a specific suicide plan. Most persons who kill themselves have a plan; suicide is not usually an impulsive, unplanned action. Ask questions such as: Do you have a plan for killing yourself? How do you plan to get the gun you intend to use? Where do you plan to kill yourself? and What time of day or night do you plan to kill yourself? The more specific the person's plan, the higher the risk of suicide. Many suicidal persons have thought about their suicide plan, but most have not thought about an alternative or a "plan B." Thus, if you can interfere with or remove a key element of their plan, you can often thwart their suicide.

8. Determine how lethal the method is for the person. Highly lethal methods include shooting, jumping, hanging, drowning, carbon monoxide poisoning, car crash, or taking high doses of barbiturates, sleeping pills, or aspirin. Less lethal methods include wrist cutting, natural (cooking) gas, or taking tranquilizers and nonprescription drugs (excluding aspirin and Tylenol). The more lethal the method, the higher the risk and the greater the chance that a suicidal gesture will result in death.

9. Determine whether the person has attempted suicide in the past. Ask questions such as: Have you attempted suicide in the past? How did you try to kill yourself in your prior attempt? What kind of help did you receive? and Was it helpful? A history of previous attempts increases the risk.

10. Determine what has happened recently that causes the person to think more and more of suicide. For example, ask: What has happened that makes you feel so hopeless now? Determine what this event means to the person: Is his or her perception of the event realistic? Is the person too upset to understand the situation clearly? Will the event continue to trouble the individual or will things change in time? Ask: Why do you believe your situation will not improve? How might your situation be different six months from now?

11. Determine the person's ability to cope with stressful situations. Most suicidal persons have "tunnel vision"—they can think only about their pain and helplessness. It is important to help them identify and consider alternative methods of dealing with the pain they feel. How has the individual managed stressful situations in the past? Will any of these methods work in the present situation?

12. Determine whether or not the suicidal person has anyone to rely on during a time of crisis. Many of the people who commit suicide feel ignored or cut off from the significant people around them. The risk of suicide increases when a person is widowed, divorced, or separated. It is important to help significant others come to the support of the suicidal person.

13. Urge the client to consider alternatives to suicide. Identify other possible solutions to dealing with the pain the individual is experiencing but do not offer false hope that things will quickly or automatically improve. Ask the client to immediately enter counseling as an alternative to suicide. If necessary, ask him or her to agree not to commit suicide for a specific period (e.g., two weeks) or promise not to commit suicide before talking to you one more time. If a referral for counseling is made, you or someone else should accompany the client to the initial interview. Follow-up is necessary to ensure that the client is making use of the service.

14. It is important to realize that it may not be possible to prevent the suicide of a person who is genuinely committed to taking his or her own life. Counseling, close monitoring, and hospitalization may delay a suicide but such efforts will not always prevent a suicide.

Selected Bibliography

Hoff, Lee Ann. *People in Crisis: Understanding and Helping.* 3rd ed. Redwood, Calif.: Addison-Wesley, 1988.

Patros, Philip, and Tonia Shamoo. *Depression and Suicide in Children and Adolescents.* Boston: Allyn and Bacon, 1989.

Polly, Joan. *Preventing Teenage Suicide: The Living Alternative Handbook.* New York: Human Sciences Press, 1986.

Shneidman, Edwin. *Definition of Suicide.* New York: Wiley, 1985.

10.24   *Assessing a Child's Need for Protection*

Purpose: To identify an abused or neglected child and determine if the child is at great risk of further harm.

Discussion: Nearly every practicing social worker has some degree of involvement with cases of child abuse and neglect. State laws require social workers and other professionals to report suspected abuse or neglect. (Many states also mandate the reporting of elder abuse and neglect.) A cluster of physical and behavioral indicators usually suggest the existence of child abuse or neglect. These indicators are summarized in Table 10.7

Table 10.7 Physical and Behavioral Indicators of Child Abuse and Neglect

Physical Indicators	Behavioral Indicators
Physical abuse	
Unexplained bruises and welts:	Wary of touching an adult
—on face, lips, mouth	Apprehensive when other
—on torso, back, buttocks, thighs	children cry
—in various stages of healing	Behavioral extremes: aggressiveness
—clustered, forming regular patterns	or withdrawal
—reflecting shape of article used	Indiscriminately seeks affection
to inflict (electric cord, belt	Manipulative behavior to get
buckle)	attention
—on several different surface areas	Vacant or frozen stare
—regularly appear after absence,	Capable of only superficial
weekend, or vacation	relationships
Unexplained burns:	Frightened of parents
—cigar, cigarette burns, especially	Afraid to go home
on soles, palms, back, or buttocks	Reports injury by parents
—immersion burns (socklike, glove-	Reluctant to change clothing for
like, doughnut shaped, on but-	gym (hides bruises)
tocks or genitalia)	Wears clothing that will hide bruises
—patterned like electric burner,	Child does not look to parents for
iron, etc.	comfort or assistance
—rope burns on arms, legs, neck,	Parents slow or reluctant to seek
or torso	medical attention for child
Unexplained fractures:	Parents show particular dislike for or
—to skull, nose, facial structure	scapegoating of child
—in various stages of healing	Parents engage in doctor
—multiple or spiral fractures	"hopping"
Unexplained lacerations or	Illogical explanation of injury by
abrasions:	parents or child
—to mouth, lips, gums, eyes	
—to external genitalia	
Physical neglect	
Consistent hunger, poor hygiene,	Begging, stealing food
inappropriate dress	Extended stays at school (early
Consistent lack of supervision,	arrival and late departure) or
especially in dangerous activities	at public places
or for long periods	Constant fatigue, listlessness, or
Unattended physical problems or	falling asleep in class
medical needs and	Inappropriate seeking of affection
immunizations	Alcohol or drug abuse
Underweight, poor growth, failure	Delinquency (e.g., thefts)
to thrive	States there is no caretaker
Abdominal distention	Poor school attendance
Poor skin care, bald patches	Child shows unusual concern or
on scalp	responsibility for younger siblings

Table 10.7 (Continued)

Physical Indicators	Behavioral Indicators
Sexual abuse	
Difficulty in walking or sitting	Preoccupation with sex
Torn, stained, or bloody underclothing	Unwilling to change clothing for gym or participate in physical education class
Pain, swelling, or itching in genital area	Withdrawal, excessive fantasy, or infantile behavior
Bruises, bleeding, or scarring in external genitalia, vaginal, or anal areas	Bizarre, sophisticated, or unusual sexual behavior or knowledge
Vaginal/penile discharge	Sexual promiscuity, prostitution, and sexual abuse of other children
Fecal soiling or retention, poor sphincter tone	Poor peer relationships
Pregnancy, especially in younger girl or when father's identity is "uncertain"	Delinquent or runaway
	Early onset and use of drugs or alcohol
Recurring urinary infections	Unusually close relationship with adult that has secretive or sexual overtones
Venereal disease in young child	Extreme protectiveness of child by an adult
	Pattern of school absences justified by one parent
Emotional maltreatment	
Speech disorders	Habit disorders (sucking, biting, rocking, etc.)
Lags in physical development	Conduct disorders (antisocial destructive, etc.)
Failure-to-thrive	Neurotic traits (sleep disorders, inhibition of play)
Hyperactivity	Psychoneurotic reactions (hysteria, obsession, compulsion, phobias, hypochondria)
Self-mutilation	Behavior extremes:
	—compliant, passive
	—aggressive, demanding
	—inappropriately adultlike
	—inappropriately infantlike
	Development lags (mental or emotional)
	Depression and attempted suicide
	Lack of communication
	Excessive concern with authority issues and inordinate attention to details

Adapted in part from Jenkins, Salus, and Schultze 1979.

Once a case of abuse or neglect has been identified, the question of risk must be addressed. In other words, Is the child at high risk of serious harm and in need of immediate protection? As used here, *high risk* refers to the probability that the child is in great danger (i.e., threat to life and limb). Social workers employed in protective service agencies must make such risk assessments each day. In some cases, the removal of the child from his or her own home is necessary to protect the child. However, because the separation of parent and child is so traumatic to the child and so disruptive to the family, an out-of-home placement should be used only in those cases where the child is at high risk of serious harm and there is no alternative.

The Illinois Department of Children and Family Services has developed a tool for helping workers make this critical decision. The **Risk Assessment Matrix (RAM)** consists of thirteen factors that should be considered when forming a judgment about risk (see Table 10.8). Such a tool can never replace professional judgment, nor is it intended to. At best, it is an aid that reminds the worker of factors that have been found to be statistically related to the death or very serious injury of children in situations of abuse and neglect. (Many of these same factors should be considered when assessing risk in cases of elder abuse and neglect.)

Around the United States, a number of child protection agencies have either modified the Illinois RAM or created their own instrument. In addition to factors listed in the RAM, other risk assessment tools give special attention to the parent or caretaker's age, history of depression, drug or alcohol abuse, record of felonies (especially violent crimes), use of weapons, the number of prior reports for abuse or neglect, and the history of prior out-of-home placements.

Many recent attempts to construct risk assessment instruments make at least partial use of the *Family Risk Scales* developed by Magura, Moses, and Jones (1987), which attempt to identify those situations where there is high probability that an out-of-home placement will occur unless intervention reduces the risk. This instrument consists of twenty-six individual rating scales and utilizes a scoring system. Someone familiar with the scales needs about twenty minutes to complete the ratings.

Selected Bibliography

Bross, Donald, et al, eds. *The New Child Protection Team Handbook.* New York: Garland, 1988.

Jenkins, James L., Marsha K. Salus, and Gretchen L. Schultze. *Child Protection Services: A Guide for Workers.* Washington, D.C.: U.S. Department of Health, Education and Welfare, August, 1979. (DHEW Publication No. OHDS 79–30203).

Magura, Stephen, Beth Moses, and Mary Ann Jones. *Assessing Risk and Measuring Change in Families: The Family Risk Scales.* Washington, D.C.: Child Welfare League of America, 1987.

Stein, Theodore, and Tina Rzepnicki. *Decision-Making at Child Welfare Intake.* New York: Child Welfare League of America, 1983.

Tower, Cynthia. *Understanding Child Abuse and Neglect.* Boston: Allyn and Bacon, 1989.

Table 10.8 Risk Assessment Matrix

Factors	Low Risk	Intermediate Risk	High Risk
I. Child's age, physical and mental abilities	10 years and over; and/or cares for and protect self without or with limited adult assistance; no physical or mental handicaps/limitations	5 thru 9 years of age; and/or requires adult assistance to care for and protect self; emotionally withdrawn; minor physical illness/mental handicap; mild to moderately impaired development	Less than 5 years of age; and/or unable to care for or protect self without adult assistance; severe physical illness/mental handicap; over-active; is difficult or provocative; severely impaired development
II. Severity and/or frequency of abuse	No injury or minor injury; no medical attention required; no discernible effect on child; isolated incident	Minor physical injury or has an unexplained injury; requiring some form of medical treatment/diagnosis; ongoing history or pattern of punishment/discipline to the child	Child requires immediate medical treatment and/or hospitalization; abuse of a sibling that resulted in death or permanent dysfunction of organ/limbs; ongoing history or pattern of harsh punishment/discipline to the child; or child at severe risk of harm; or any sex abuse
III. Severity and/or frequency of neglect	No discernible effect on child; isolated incident	Caretaker suspected of failing to meet minimum medical, food and/or shelter needs of child; unconfirmed history or pattern of leaving child unsupervised	Caretaker is unwilling to meet minimal medical, food and/or shelter needs of child; confirmed history or pattern of leaving child unsupervised or unprotected for excessive periods of time; or child at severe risk of harm
IV. Location of injury	Bony body parts; knee, elbows, and buttocks	Torso	Head, face or genitals
V. Caretaker's physical, intellectual, or emotional abilities/control	No intellectual/physical limitations; realistic expectations of child; in full control of mental faculties	May be physically/emotionally handicapped; moderate intellectual limitations; past criminal/mental health record/history; poor reasoning abilities; needs planning assistance to protect child	Severely handicapped; poor conception of reality; unrealistic expectations/perceptions of child's behavior; severe intellectual limitations; incapacity due to alcohol/drug intoxication
VI. Caretaker's level of cooperation	Demonstrated willingness and ability to work with agency to resolve problem and protect child	Overly compliant with investigator; presence/ability of nonperpetrating adult to assure minimal cooperation with agency	Doesn't believe there is a problem; refuses to cooperate; uninterested or evasive
VII. Caretaker's parenting skills and/or knowledge	Caretaker exhibits appropriate parenting skills and knowledge pertaining to child rearing techniques or responsibilities	Inconsistent display of the necessary parenting skills and/or knowledge required to provide a minimal level of child care	Caretaker is unwilling/incapable of providing the necessary parenting skills and/or minimal knowledge needed to assure a minimal level of child care

(Continued)

Table 10.8 (Continued)

Factors	Low Risk	Intermediate Risk	High Risk
VIII. Perpetrator's access to child	Out of home, no access to child	In home, access to child is difficult; child is under constant supervision of other adult in the house	In home, complete access to child; uncertainty if other adult will deny access to child
IX. Presence of a paramour or parent substitute in the home	No paramour or parent substitute in the home; paramour/parent substitute in the home is viewed as supportive/stabilizing influence	Paramour or parent substitute is in the home on an infrequent basis and assumes only minimal caretaker responsibility for the child	Paramour or parent substitute resides with the family and is the alleged perpetrator
X. Previous history of abuse/neglect	No previous reported history of abuse/neglect	Previous substantiated report of abuse/neglect; no protective services provided to the child, family or perpetrator	Pending child abuse/neglect investigation; previous substantiated abuse/neglect report of a serious nature; multiple reports of abuse/neglect involving the child, family or perpetrator
XI. Environmental condition of the home	Home is relatively clean with no apparent safety or health hazards	Trash and garbage not disposed; water and/or electricity inoperative; infestation of ants, roaches or other vermin	Living in condemned and/or structurally unsound residence; exposed wiring and/or other potential fire/safety hazards present
XII. Strength of family support systems	Family, neighbors, or friends available and committed to help; membership in church, community, or social group	Family supportive but not in geographic area; some support from friends and neighbors; limited community services available	Caretaker/family has no relatives or friends available and is geographically isolated from community services; no phone or means of transportation available
XIII. Stresses/crises	Stable family; steady employment or income; means of transportation available; strong relationship with relatives	Pregnancy or recent birth of a child; insufficient income and/or food; inadequate home management skills/knowledge; relationship with relatives characterized by mutual hostility	Death of spouse; recent change in marital or relationship status; acute psychiatric episodes; spouse abuse/marital conflict; drugs/alcohol dependency; chaotic lifestyle

Source: Illinois Risk Assessment, reproduced by permission of the Illinois Department of Children and Family Services.

Purpose: To assist the social worker in assessing the client's behavior and functioning within a social context.

Discussion: For many years, Perlman's (1957) **4-Ps** (person, problem, place, and process) have proven useful to many social workers as a way of organizing their thoughts about a client, his or her situation, and the agency context of social work intervention. Doremus (1976) suggested the **4-Rs** (roles, reactions, relationships, and resources) as a way of conceptualizing assessment in health care settings. In addition, the authors offer the **4-Ms** (motivation, meanings, management, and monitoring) as further reminders of important elements in social work intervention. A blending of the 4-Ps, 4-Rs, and 4-Ms results in a twelve-item, easily remembered conceptual tool that helps a worker sift through available data, organize it, and begin formulating an intervention plan. As used here, the word *client* refers to an individual. However, the underlying ideas that make up the 4-P/4-R/4-M can be applied to work with other client systems, including couples, families, or small groups.

The 4-Ps
1. Problem
   - What is the nature of the client's problem (intensity, frequency, duration)?
   - How does the client define the problem as compared to how others (including the worker) define the problem?
   - Can the problem or situation be changed, solved, or ameliorated? What parts of the problem or situation can feasibly be addressed in a change effort?
   - How effective have previous agency efforts been in dealing with the client's problem or situation?
   - Is the problem or situation an emergency that requires a rapid response?
   - What will the consequences be if the worker or agency takes no action and does nothing for or with the client?
2. Person (Personality)
   - What aspects of the client's personality dynamics and behavioral patterns are relevant to the current problem or situation?
   - What aspects of the client's personality interfere with problem-solving efforts?
   - What is the relationship between the client's personality and his or her role performance, reactions to problem, relationships with significant others, and use of resources to cope with the problem or situation?
3. Place
   - What meaning does the client assign to his or her involvement with the agency (e.g., hopefulness, stigma, fear, humiliation, etc.)?

- Can the agency provide the services needed by the client? If not, is referral to another agency likely to be effective?
- Are agency programs, policies, or procedures contributing to the client's problem or situation?

4. Process
   - What type of helping process or approach is the client likely to find acceptable?
   - What approach is most likely to be effective?
   - How will the requirements of the helping process impact on the client's current role performance and relationships with significant others?

The 4-Rs

5. Roles
   - What roles and responsibilities does the client have in life (e.g., as a parent, spouse, employee, etc.)?
   - What do others (e.g., family, employers, etc.) expect of the client?
   - What capacities, behavioral patterns, and strengths has the client previously used to perform his or her roles, solve problems of role performance, and cope with the demands of roles?
   - How satisfied is the client with his or her role performance?
6. Reactions
   - What are the client's reactions (psychological, emotional, behavioral, physical, etc.) to the current problem or situation? How do these reactions compare to the client's usual or previous behavioral patterns? Is the client in a state of crisis?
7. Relationships
   - What people are significant in the client's life (family, peers, friends, relatives, etc.)?
   - How are they being impacted by the client's problem or situation?
   - What is the relationship between the behavior of significant others and the client's current problem or situation?
8. Resources
   - What formal and informal resources has the client used effectively in the past to cope with problems?
   - What additional resources are needed now to address the current problem or situation?
   - Does the client have access to these needed resources and is he or she willing and able to use them? Is the client eligible for needed formal resources?

The 4-Ms

9. Motivation
   - What does the client want to do about his or her problem or situation and how much does he or she want to do it?
   - What discomfort or aversive factors are pushing the client toward action?
   - What factors of hope and optimism are pulling the client toward action?
   - What can be done to increase client motivation?

10. Meanings
    - What meaning does the client assign to his or her life, situation, and problems? What ethnic, cultural, and religious beliefs and values are important to the client and relevant to the current problem or situation?
11. Management
    - How can the worker best use his or her limited time, energy, and resources to help the client deal with the problem or situation?
    - What overall plan or strategy will guide the worker's activity with the client?
    - How will work with this client affect the worker's other responsibilities?
12. Monitoring
    - How will the worker monitor his or her impact on the client and evaluate the effectiveness of the intervention?
    - How can the worker use peers, supervisors, or consultants to monitor and evaluate intervention?

Selected Bibliography

Doremus, Bertha. "The Four R's: Social Diagnosis in Health Care." *Health and Social Work* 1 (1976): 121–39.

Perlman, Helen. *Social Casework: A Problem Solving Process.* Chicago: University of Chicago Press, 1957.

Planning and Contracting   11

Introduction

Once the client and social worker have engaged in data gathering and agreed on an initial assessment of the client's problem or situation, they reach a stage in the problem-solving process called planning and contracting. During this stage, they must come to an agreement on intervention goals and objectives and formulate a plan to achieve those ends. This chapter presents selected techniques and guidelines for the planning and contracting phase of working with clients. In particular, it offers information on the selection of target problems, goals, and objectives; written service contracts; client needs lists; the use of informal resources; and the use of the small group as a resource.

As with all stages in the problem-solving process, joint decision making is emphasized during planning and contracting. It is during this stage that even subtle disagreements between worker and client on the nature of the problem and how to proceed will become evident. If there are disagreements, they must be discussed openly and resolved before proceeding.

The worker must remember that, in keeping with the social work principle of client self-determination, the client has the right to be fully informed about any intervention or professional decision that may impact his or her life. More specifically, Kuehn and Christopherson (1981, 54–55) explain that the client has:

1. The right to make decisions and have input in deciding intervention goals and approach
2. The right to know what general approach the worker proposes to use in intervention, the likelihood of success, and if there may be adverse consequences to the intervention
3. The right to know how long the intervention will last or about how long it will take to achieve the agreed upon objectives
4. The right to know how much time and money (if any) will be required of the client

5. The right to know of any consequences for terminating the intervention against the advice of the social worker or agency
6. The right to know what rules of confidentiality apply and to know who else (e.g., court, probation officer, parent, etc.) will have access to information about the client's participation and the effectiveness of the intervention
7. The right to know how the effectiveness of the intervention will be evaluated
8. The right to know of existing appeals or grievance procedures that can be used to challenge a decision made by a social worker or agency

The worker's decisions and activities during the planning and contracting phase must be guided by a genuine commitment to and respect for these client rights.

Selected Bibliography

Bloom, Bernard, and Shirley Asher, eds. *Psychiatric Patient Rights and Patient Advocacy.* New York: Human Sciences Press, 1982.

Kuehn, B. S., and E. R. Christopherson. "Preserving the Rights of Clients in Child Abuse and Neglect." In *Preservation of Client Rights,* edited by G. T. Hannah, W. P. Christian, and W. B. Clark. New York: The Free Press, 1981

11.1 *Selecting Target Problems and Goals*

Purpose: To select the target problems and goals that will give direction to the social work intervention.

Discussion: A goal is a desired end toward which an activity is directed. Broadly speaking, the goal of a social work intervention with a specific client is the desired end toward which that client and his or her social worker are working. This goal logically flows from the data-gathering and assessment phase.

Sometimes the social worker and client can quickly agree on the goal. This is likely when the client's need or problem is readily apparent. However, in many cases, the social worker and client will see things differently and they must struggle to clarify the nature of the problem and come to an agreement on what can and should be done about it. Often, the worker and client must also devote considerable time to the task of priority setting in order to decide which of the client's many problems should become target problems for intervention. Until those decisions are made, they cannot formulate a feasible intervention plan.

The principle of *client self-determination* dictates that the client has the right to select the problem to be worked on. There are also practical reasons related to client motivation for expecting the client—rather than the social worker—to select the target problems and intervention goals. Epstein (1980) observes, "There is no way in the world to stretch a client's motivation, to maneuver him into a commitment for a personal change he does not want, does not see, does not accept.... Clients, however, eagerly seek help and value help that makes sense to them, is useful in their daily lives, gets or keeps them out of trouble" (p. 177). Even in work with the nonvoluntary client, it is important to give the client as much choice as possible. In such cases, the worker or agency might mandate one but allow the client to select the second or third target problem.

Most clients have multiple problems. Both research and practice wisdom show that, in order to be effective, the helping process must concentrate available time and energy on just one, two, or three problems at a time. If priorities and a clear focus are not established, the helping effort flounders and usually ends in frustration for both client and worker. Writing from the perspective of the task-centered approach to social work practice, Epstein (1980, 189) provides guidance on how the worker and client can set *priorities* among the client's many problems:

1. List problems identified by the client (i.e., what the client sees as a problem and wants to change).

2. Next, list the worker's recommendations, if any. Also include any mandated problems, which are those identified by and imposed on the client by some legitimate authority such as a court or child protection agency.

3. Classify these many problems into logical groups or combinations so interrelationships and overlap can be identified.

4. Review each problem and grouping on the list, and have the client identify the two or three of highest priority.

5. The social worker then offers his or her opinion on which problems on the list are of highest priority.

6. Together, the worker and client discuss and finally judge the relative importance of each problem by considering the following:

- Which problems weigh most heavily on the client's situation?
- Which problems, if not corrected, will have the most adverse consequences for the client?
- Which problems, if corrected, would have the most positive consequences for the client?
- Which problems are of greatest interest or relevance to the client?
- Which problems can be changed with only a moderate investment of time, effort, and other resources?
- Which problems are essentially unchangeable or would demand an extraordinary or unrealistic amount to time and energy to change?

7. After considering these six questions, the three problems of highest priority are selected. As mentioned earlier, both experience and research suggest that it is usually counterproductive to try to address more than three problems at one time. Task-centered practitioners have termed this principle *"the rule of three."*

8. It is important for the social worker to remember that the client's problems and concerns will almost always affect or involve significant others (e.g., spouse, children, parents, close friends, employer, etc.). Unless these individuals, who are either part of the problem or part of the solution, are considered in the intervention planning, there is good chance that they will—knowingly or unknowingly—become an obstacle to the change process. In some cases, they may actively sabotage the client's attempt to make desired changes.

Selected Bibliography

Compton, Beulah, and Burt Galaway. *Social Work Processes.* 4th ed. Belmont, Calif.: Wadsworth, 1989.

Epstein, Laura. *Helping People: The Task-Centered Approach.* St. Louis: C. V. Mosby, 1980.

Garvin, Charles, and Brett Seabury. *Interpersonal Practice in Social Work: Processes and Procedures.* Englewood Cliffs, N.J.: Prentice-Hall, 1984.

11.2   *The Problem Search*

Purpose: To engage the reluctant client in a process designed to identify a problem on which he or she is willing to work.

Discussion: Not infrequently, the social worker encounters the nonvoluntary client who has been forced by either a court or a powerful family member to seek professional help. Typically, these clients deny the existence of a problem and resent having to speak with a social worker. With the court-ordered, nonvoluntary client, the client's involvement can sometimes be influenced with some pragmatic arguments such as, "Well, it looks like we are stuck with each other. Since we have to talk to each other, let's figure out what we can do together to get me and the probation department off your back." With a resistant adult client being pressured by other family members, there are only two options: terminate the contact or suggest the use of a problem search. The problem search can be viewed as a "mini contract" or an agreement to spend a couple of sessions trying to determine whether a problem exists and, if so, whether it should be addressed. According to Epstein (1980) and Reid (1978), the problem search procedure is used either when (1) the client has been referred by an authoritative agency or by his or her family but does not acknowledge the existence of a problem as defined by others or (2) when the client has requested a specific agency service but, in the worker's opinion, it is desirable to help the client expand that request or redefine the presenting problem. In this later situation, the social worker is concerned that the client's definition of the problem is not accurate or

---

realistic and/or that his or her request for a specific service will not resolve the problem. An example might be the father who requests foster care placement for his children because he and his wife are having serious marital problems.

Essentially, the problem search asks the client to participate in at least a couple of meetings to explore the situation in more depth and also to withhold judgment about the need for service and the worker's usefulness until after these meetings. Epstein (1980, 175) describes *five basic steps in the problem search*:

1. Explain the rationale and the advantages for spending a couple of sessions exploring the client's situation. Offer examples of how you might be able to help (e.g., "If we could spend some time talking about what is going on between you and your daughter, I may be able to offer some suggestions that would reduce the tension.").

2. Ask the client if he or she sees the value in scheduling a couple of exploratory interviews. Identify the specific reasons why they might be reluctant to do so (e.g., "What do you think of this idea? Are there reasons why this does not sound like a good idea?").

3. If the client agrees, proceed with the scheduling of two interviews. If the client is reluctant, make a strong recommendation and explain your concerns (e.g., "I will respect your decision on this, but I want you to know that I think it is very important that we meet together at least a couple of times. Let me explain why. I am worried that if you and your daughter do not learn to get along, she may run away or perhaps even kill herself.").

4. Begin the problem search process by focusing on not more than three high-priority concerns. Explain why you think they are important. Do not allow the interview to be sidetracked into less important matters. Realize that you have only a short time to demonstrate that you can be helpful to the client.

5. Because you have initiated the interviews and selected their focus, you will need to be more talkative, directive, and active than would be the case if the client was requesting assistance. Encourage the client to question your assumptions. If, at the end of the agreed upon problem search interviews, your client still sees no reason to be involved, respect his or her decision and terminate the contact.

Selected Bibliography

Epstein, Laura. *Helping People: The Task-Centered Approach.* St. Louis: C. V. Mosby, 1980.
Fortune, Anne, ed. *Task-Centered Practice with Families and Groups.* New York: Spring, 1985.
Reid, William. *The Task-Centered System.* New York: Columbia University Press, 1978.

11.3 Using Checklists in Goal Selection

Purpose: To assist the client in identifying and selecting intervention goals.

Discussion: Some clients have difficulty conceptualizing and articulating the goals they hope the social work intervention will achieve. In such cases, a check list may be useful. A worker familiar with the problems and concerns of a particular client group can easily construct a simple checklist and tailor it to the par

Figure 11.1 Sample Checklist

A List of Goals for Parents with Children in Foster Care

Explanation: Sometimes problems related to the parent's own behavior or problems between parent and child need to be solved before parents and child can be reunited. Having a clear goal in mind is one important step in successfully solving problems. Once there is agreement on a goal, it is possible to develop a plan of work toward the goal. Below is a list of goals that have been mentioned by many parents with children in foster care. Place a check (✔) by those goals that are close to ones that make sense for you and your situation. This checklist can help you and your social worker formulate a plan of action.

_____ Learn to talk to people about my concerns.

_____ Learn to like myself.

_____ Learn how to budget my money.

_____ Learn to prepare meals.

_____ Learn to take care of the house.

_____ Learn to find and make use of services such as daycare, employment counseling, legal services.

_____ Learn to cope with daily pressures and demands.

_____ Learn to show affection toward my children.

_____ Learn to make friends, mix, and feel comfortable with people.

_____ Learn skills needed to get a job.

_____ Learn how to have good visits with my child in foster care.

_____ Learn to get along with my spouse (husband/wife).

_____ Learn to control my anger and temper.

_____ Learn to talk with my child and make him/her feel secure.

_____ Learn ways of disciplining my child without using physical punishment.

_____ Learn how to talk and plan with the foster parents.

_____ Learn how to talk with my social worker and make use of the help he/she can provide.

_____ Learn to share my feelings and worries with other people, such as other parents who have had similar problems.

_____ Learn to find friends, neighbors, or groups that may understand my situation and help me deal with problems.

_____ Learn what to expect from children and find out what is "normal" behavior for my child.

_____ Learn to be more assertive and forceful in making my thoughts and feelings known to other people.

_____ Learn how to get along without alcohol or drugs.

_____ Learn how to deal with conflicts with my parents and relatives.

_____ Learn how to deal with emergency situations or times when I get overwhelmed.

_____ Learn to cope with strong emotions like guilt and sadness.

Source: From Horejsi, Bertsche, and Clark, *Social Work Practice with Children in Foster Care* (1981), p. 239. Courtesy of Charles C. Thomas, Publisher, Springfield, Illinois.

ticular type of client served and the practice setting. For example, Figure 11.1 is a goal checklist developed by Horejsi, Bertsche, and Clark (1981, 239) for use with parents of children who have been placed in foster care for reasons of abuse or neglect. This tool was designed to help these parents discuss and identify changes that needed to occur before the parent and child could be reunited.

Selected Bibliography

Horejsi, Charles, Ann Bertsche, and Frank Clark. *Social Work Practice with Parents of Children in Foster Care: A Handbook.* Springfield, Ill.: Charles C. Thomas, 1981.

11.4   *Formulating Intervention Objectives*

Purpose: To develop objectives that are measurable and relevant to the client's concerns.

Discussion: Although many people use the terms *goals* and *objectives* interchangeably, they do not have the same meaning. A statement of *goals* is usually broad and somewhat abstract (e.g., "to better cope with the demands of a handicapped child"). Not infrequently, a goal is a restatement of a problem in a way that suggests a solution. For example, if a family's lack of money creates stress that erupts in violence against children, a logical goal would be to increase that family's financial resources in order to reduce the stress and violence. An *objective* is more specific and concrete. According to Pipe (1975), the essential difference between a goal and an objective is that an objective is measurable, whereas a goal is not. It is helpful to think of an objective as one of many measurable steps that must be taken in order to reach a goal.

A key attribute of an effective intervention is an objective that is sharply defined. Unless objectives are clear, the helping process flounders and the evaluation of outcome is impossible. A good objective answers a five-part question:

1. Who . . .
2. will do what . . .
3. to what extent . . .
4. under what conditions . . .
5. by when?

The importance of properly formulated objectives becomes clear when poorly written objectives are compared with well-stated objectives.

Objectives Prepared by a Hospital Social Worker

Poor: "Improve responsiveness of social work staff to new referrals."

Good: "To conduct at least 80 percent of initial patient or family member interviews within four hours of receiving a referral from a doctor or nurse."

Objectives Prepared by an Administrator of a Big Brother/Big Sister Program

Poor: "Obtain more big brothers and big sisters for our children."

Good: "To recruit, train, and match 35 new volunteers before August 1."

Objectives Prepared by a Child Welfare Worker

Poor: "To enhance the development of parent-child relationships."

Good: "To encourage and facilitate parental visitation so that, by January 15, at least 70 percent of parents in my caseload visit their child in foster care at least once a month."

When developing an objective, it is important not to confuse *input* with *outcome*. This is a common error that results in something like, "Mr. Jones is to obtain counseling." Such a statement describes an input (counseling) but says nothing about the intended outcome. In this example, counseling is presented as an end, but in reality it is only a means to an end. What is the intended outcome of the counseling? What is the counseling to accomplish? A better objective would be, "Mr. Jones will obtain counseling focused on his physical abuse of his son and designed to help him learn to use 'time out' and positive reinforcement as alternatives to spanking and screaming as discipline."

In writing goals and objectives, ***positive language*** should be used. The words used should describe what the client will do, not what the client should stop doing (e.g., "learn and follow table manners" vs. "stop being so messy when eating").

In interpersonal helping, an objective agreed to by both client and worker should not take more than a few weeks to accomplish. Thus, an objective that would probably take a couple months to accomplish should be broken down into several smaller steps, treating each as a separate objective. Accomplishing these smaller objectives will sustain the client's motivation. Unless the client sees evidence that the time and energy invested in the helping process is succeeding, he or she may give up. If the client can perceive he or she is making concrete gains (i.e., reaching an objective), even if the steps are small, he or she will feel more hopeful and more motivated to continue.

In direct service work, an objective should be formulated in ***behavioral terms***; that is, the objective should be written using words that describe the client's observable actions. The following examples are poorly stated, nonbehavioral objectives:

"Client will work to improve self-esteem."
"Client will look for a job."
"Improve quality of child care."

Such objectives are vague and impossible to evaluate. The next examples are well-written objectives using behavioral language.

"To greet at least two people per day between June 1 and June 10 with the words 'Hi' or 'Hello' while smiling and making eye contact."

"To submit at least four completed job applications for janitorial work before July 1."

"To spend 15 uninterrupted minutes per day reading stories to Bobby while he sits on my lap."

It should be noted that the concept of *task,* as used by social workers favoring the task-centered approach, is both similar to and different from the concept of objectives, as presented here. Reid (1978) sees a task simply as a type of problem-solving activity, sometimes of a very general nature and sometimes highly specific, but always an activity that can be evaluated in terms of being achieved or completed. Epstein (1980) explains that there are two broad types of tasks: general and operational. A *general task*—somewhat like a goal—suggests the direction of an action but does not spell out exactly what is to be done. An example would be for a client to obtain appropriate child care. The term *operational task* refers to the specific actions to be undertaken. In order to obtain child care, for example, many separate actions would be necessary. Ordinarily, operational tasks flow from general tasks, much like objectives flow from goals. However, because the helping process is so complex and individualized, task-centered practitioners prefer the umbrella term *task* that covers goals, subgoals, objectives, and subobjectives while always emphasizing action and activity by the client and/or worker.

Regardless of whether meaningful distinctions can be made between such terms as *goal, objective,* and *task,* the point to remember is that an intervention must have a clear purpose and direction. What the social worker does and what the worker and client do together must always relate directly to this mutually agreed upon purpose.

While emphasizing the importance of formulating objectives that can guide intervention activities, we do not mean to suggest that this is a rigid, mechanical process or that an objective, once formulated, is not to be changed. To the contrary, a willingness to revise objectives to meet changing circumstances is also important. Objectives are intended to give direction, structure, and relevance to the helping process, but objectives should never stifle the humanness and individualization that are essential ingredients in effective helping.

In summary, a properly developed objective meets the following criteria:

1. It starts with the word *to,* followed by an action verb.
2. It specifies a single key result to be accomplished.
3. It specifies a target date for its accomplishment.
4. It is as specific and quantitative as possible and, hence, measurable and verifiable.
5. It is readily understandable by the client and others who will be contributing to or participating in the intervention.
6. It is realistic and attainable but still represents a significant challenge.
7. It is willingly agreed to by both client and worker without pressure or coercion.

8. It is consistent with agency policies and procedures and with the social work *Code of Ethics.*

Selected Bibliography

Epstein, Laura. *Helping People: The Task-Centered Approach.* St. Louis: C. V. Mosby, 1980.
Mager, Robert. *Preparing Instructional Objectives.* Belmont, Calif.: Fearon, 1972.
Pipe, Peter. *Objectives—Tool for Change.* Belmont, Calif.: Fearon, 1975.
Reid, William. *The Task-Centered System.* New York: Columbia University Press, 1978.

11.5   *Written Service Contracts*

Purpose: To provide direction and focus during intervention.

Discussion: Increasingly, social workers are using written service contracts (or agreements) in their work with clients. A contract spells out the plan that the client and worker have formulated on how to reach the goal(s) of intervention. Maluccio and Marlo (1974) explain that the **contract** is an "explicit agreement between worker and the client concerning the target problems, the goals, and the strategies of social work intervention, and the roles and tasks of the participants. Its major features are mutual agreement, differential participation in the intervention process, reciprocal accountability, and explicitness" (p. 30). The American Public Welfare Association (1979) defines a *service agreement* as "a written document which specifies the behavioral objectives of service and describes, in concrete terms, the actions that will be taken within established time frames to facilitate accomplishment of the objectives. The agreement is signed by all those involved in the service planning process, as appropriate.... The agreement constitutes a non-legally binding commitment to pursue mutually agreed-upon goals" (p. 82).

While the authors prefer the term *service contract,* other practitioners or agencies may use the terms *service agreement, case plan, treatment plan,* or *intervention plan* when referring to this document. Often, these terms are used interchangeably. However, service contracts should not be confused with *behavioral contracts* (see Technique 12.6). The two have similarities but also important differences. A behavioral contract is much more specific in focus than a service contract and covers a shorter period of time, often a matter of days or at most a week or two. The period covered by a service contract may be several months, although it is ordinarily renegotiated and rewritten after six months.

A written service contract should answer the following questions:

1. What is the desired outcome of the worker's and/or agency's service to the client?

2. What is to be done by the client? By when?
3. What is to be done by the client's significant others (family, friends, neighbors, etc.)? By when?
4. What is to be done by the worker? By when?
5. What is to be done by other agency staff? By when?
6. What services are to be obtained from other agencies? By when?
7. What events will trigger a reassessment of the client's situation and/or a revision of the service contract?

Consider the following guidelines on the utilization of written service contracts.

1. Be clear about your agency's policy and legal requirements related to the use of written service contracts. While verbal contracts or agreements are common, workers in some fields such as child welfare and developmental disabilities will find that written plans are required by law and agency policy. For example, Public Law 96-272 requires that a written case plan be developed for every child placed in foster care. Section 475 of that federal law states:

> The term "case plan" means a written document which includes at least the following: A description of the type of home or institution in which a child is to be placed, including a discussion of the appropriateness of the placement and how the agency which is responsible for the child plans to carry out the judicial determination made with respect to the child in accordance with section 472(a)(1); and a plan for assuring that the child receives proper care and that services are provided to the parents, child, and foster parents in order to improve the conditions in the parents' home, facilitate return of the child to his own home or the permanent placement of the child, and address the needs of the child while in foster care, including a discussion of the appropriateness of the services that have been provided to the child under the plan.

The following statement, taken from a Montana state agency manual concerning the handling of certain cases of child abuse and neglect, is fairly typical of agency policy on written service contracts:

> The tasks of identification, assessment and formulation of treatment recommendations rest primarily with the social worker working with the family. The results of these formulations are set forth in the written treatment plan to advise the parents and the court of the problems identified and the course of action recommended to remedy these problems. The treatment plan should contain the following elements:
> - Identification of the problems or conditions which resulted in the abuse or neglect.
> - Treatment goals for the family which address the needs identified and which, when attained, will assure the adequate level of care for the child that is necessary for the successful reunification of the family.
> - Specific treatment objectives, or tasks, which outline in detail the series of steps which must be taken by each member of the household to reach the treatment goals. These objectives should clearly define the separate roles and responsibilities of all of the parties involved in the treatment process. Objectives should clearly state the actions which are necessary, and the time period in

which the objective should be accomplished. The objectives should be reasonably attainable and designed to fit the capabilities and existing circumstances of the family involved.

2. Understand both the advantages and disadvantages of using contracts. Maluccio and Marlow (1974) explained that a contract "can facilitate worker-client interaction, establish mutual concerns, clarify the purposes and conditions of giving and receiving service, delineate roles and tasks, order priorities, allocate time constructively for attaining goals, and assess progress on an ongoing basis" (p. 30). Reid and Epstein (1977) pointed out that service contracts are especially important in social work with nonvoluntary clients.

> Contracting, as do most things in social treatment, works best when the client has an active interest in getting help and some notion of what he wants to accomplish. Unfortunately many if not most of the clients of social work do not fall into this category. Forming contracts becomes far more difficult when the client is reluctant to accept the services of a social worker or is uncertain about the nature of his problems or the kind of help he wants. Although contracts are hard to develop with such clients, we would argue that they are even more important with this group.... Most important, use of contracts with the unmotivated or uncertain client provides some assurance that he will not be treated "behind his back" for conditions that have not been made clear to him. (p. 9)

An obvious disadvantage is the time it takes to prepare a written service contract. In fact, this may be one of the major reasons why they are not used more often. Epstein (1980) has identified a number of problems associated with written contracts, including an uncertain legal status, the possibility of concentrating on trivial objectives and the avoidance of serious problems that require risk taking in order to achieve success, and the potential danger of vulnerable or powerless clients agreeing to a contract primarily out of fear of being punished. Despite these potential problems, Epstein (1980) concludes that, "for the most part in the bulk of ordinary practice, contracts can and should be used.... The practice has some obvious merits. [But] written contracts... should not be viewed as a panacea" (p. 195)

3. The contract should be phrased in simple, clear language, so that the client can read it and know exactly what it says. The wording should not confuse or intimidate. The use of vague language confuses the client and results in a lack of direction in the helping process. Avoid legal or social work jargon; make an effort to substitute plain, everyday terms whenever possible. It may be necessary to prepare the contract in the client's first language (e.g., Spanish) if he or she has a poor understanding of English. In cases where the client cannot read, the worker should consider recording the agreement on a cassette tape, in addition to preparing a written statement.

4. A contract should reflect a consensus between the social worker and client. By definition, a contract expresses a mutual understanding and agreement. It specifies what the client will do *and* what the worker/agency will do. A contract must never be one-sided and list only requirements that the worker or agency imposes on the client.

5. Develop the contract only after a thorough social assessment, during which the client and worker study and agree on the problems to be tackled. The terms of the contract should be consistent with the abilities of the client and the capacities of the worker and agency.

6. A contract should be success oriented. Specifically, it should be developed in a way that makes success highly probable, without, of course, sacrificing relevance. If the worker believes that the client will be unable to meet the terms of a particular contract, that alone is an indication that the contract has been poorly conceptualized.

7. The goals and objectives identified in the agreement must be realistic and worth achieving from the client's viewpoint. Since the purpose of the contract is to bring about needed change, it must focus on behaviors or situations that can, in fact, be changed. Avoid wasting time and energy on things that are beyond anyone's control.

8. Be explicit about goals and objectives. A goal is a desired future condition; it is a statement of intent. Goals tend to be broad yet specific enough to provide direction for intervention. An objective breaks down the goal into a number of action steps, which are stated in a manner that permits the evaluation of progress. (Additional information on goals and objectives is presented in Techniques 11.1 and 11.4.) In selecting goals and objectives, logical sequences must be considered. New behaviors may need to be learned in a particular sequence, and some problems must be tackled one phase at a time. For example, the client who wants a job must first learn how to complete an application.

9. The time period covered by the contract must be adjusted to the client's capacity. This is especially important when dealing with a client who is very troubled or who operates at a low level of social functioning. Basically, the more troubled and limited the client, the shorter the time period and the fewer the number of goals and objectives that should be included in the agreement.

10. Do not avoid or delay making a decision on whether you and your agency can provide a needed, relevant, and effective service to a client. When this issue is ignored or the decision is avoided, time, energy, and resources are often spent on situations that are unlikely to benefit from the service.

11. Do not invest time and energy doing things for clients that they can do for themselves. This happens when a worker is overly eager to be helpful, the client presents himself or herself as being passive and helpless, and the worker overlooks or underestimates client strengths. Also, the busy social worker may find it easier to do things for the client, rather than teach or encourage the client to do for himself or herself.

12. Do not get sidetracked by negative diagnostic labels. All too often, workers uncritically accept and draw erroneous inferences from a label applied to the client by another professional (e.g., "schizophrenic," "mentally retarded," "inadequate personality," "unmotivated"). If the worker neglects to study the client's actual behavior, he or she may overlook strengths and capacity for change.

13. A contract, once written, should not be viewed as being rigid or immutable. Provisions of the contract should be modified as necessary to keep up with the realities of the situation and the needs of the client. This flexibility is important in maintaining the trust of the client.

Selected Bibliography

American Public Welfare Association. *Standards for Foster Family Services Systems for Public Agencies.* Washington, D.C.: American Public Welfare Association, 1979.

Epstein, Laura. *Helping People: The Task-Centered Approach.* St. Louis: C. V. Mosby, 1980.

Maluccio, Anthony, and Wilma Marlow. "The Case for the Contract." *Social Work* 19 (January 1974): 28–36.

Reid, William, and Laura Epstein. *Task Centered Practice.* New York: Columbia University Press, 1977.

Seabury, Brett. "The Contract: Uses, Abuses and Limitations." *Social Work* 21 (January 1976): 16–21.

——— . "Negotiating Sound Contracts with Clients." *Public Welfare* 37 (Spring 1979): 33–38.

11.6 *Client Needs List*

Purpose: To remind the worker and client of concerns and needs that should be addressed in a service contract or case plan.

Discussion: A *needs list* is a tool used to guide the case-planning and case-management activities related to a certain category of clients. Basically, it is a checklist that reminds all involved of concerns that should be addressed when formulating a service plan for a particular client. Such lists are most often used in work with clients who are highly dependent on the services of social agencies and other human services organizations. Examples include the frail elderly, the developmentally disabled, children in foster care, and the chronically mentally ill.

A needs list is especially useful when the case planning is done by a multidisciplinary and/or multiagency team because potential interagency and interprofessional problems must be anticipated and resolved if the plan is to succeed. Those involved in formulating a service plan—including the client—must decide how the needs can best be met and who will be responsible for seeing that they are met.

Figure 11.2 is an example of a needs list used in work with developmentally disabled adults capable of functioning in an independent living situation. Note that the needs on the list are concrete expressions of fundamental human needs, such as the five categories identified by A. H. Maslow (1970, 35–58):

- *Physical and life-sustaining needs.* The need for food, water, air, warmth, sexual gratification, elimination of bodily wastes, and so on
- *Physical safety.* The need for protection from physical attack and disease

Figure 11.2 Sample Needs List

Needs List for Independent Living

1. Housing suitable for client's level of mobility and physical limitations (consider stairs, wheelchair accessibility, etc.)
2. Safe heating and electrical system and useable toilet facilities
3. Home furnishings (chairs, tables, TV, radio, etc.)
4. Bed, blankets, sheets, etc.
5. Clothing for all seasons of the year
6. Food, food storage, stove
7. Telephone or other means of requesting assistance
8. Items needed for food preparation (e.g., utensils, pots, pans)
9. Items needed to maintain personal hygiene (razor, soap, sanitary napkins, etc.)
10. Financial resources/money management system
11. Transportation
12. Medical and dental care
13. Medication and monitoring of dosage, if needed
14. Social contacts and recreational activities
15. Concern and interest shown by family, friends, and neighbors
16. Protection from harm or exploitation
17. Appropriate level of supervision
18. Training (job-related, community, survival skills, etc.)
19. Employment or work-related activity
20. Adaptive aids (e.g., eyeglasses, hearing aids, leg braces, etc.)
21. Therapy and other special treatments (e.g., physical therapy, speech therapy, etc.)
22. Maintenance of cultural and ethnic heritage
23. Participation in spiritual or religious activities
24. Legal assistance

- *Love.* The need to be cherished, supported, and aided by others
- *Self-esteem.* The need to have a sense of personal worth and value, to respect and value one's self
- *Self-realization.* The need to be creative and productive and to attain worthwhile objectives.

Some social workers and case-planning teams may prefer to use a client needs list that is more oriented toward client skills. Figure 11.3 contains excerpts from a list by Leavitt (1983) used in formulating a service plan for a client who is seriously mentally ill but capable of living in a community. This type of list could be used both to assess a client's readiness to live independently and to clarify which agency or professional is responsible for teaching essential skills to the client.

Figure 11.3 Sample Needs List with Skill Orientation

Safety Skills
- Ability to recognize unsafe behavior—improper disposal of cigarettes and matches, smoking in bed
- Ability to prevent unsafe behavior in self or others
- Capacity to respond to unsafe conditions through appropriate reporting and simple action—use of fire extinguisher, telephone to police, etc.
- Capacity to recognize felonious behavior or plans and not participate—stealing, rape, arson, forgery
- Capacity to get help in case of attack or molestation

Skills of Illness Management
- Appropriate use and understanding of medication
- Recognition of developing symptoms and signs of illness
- Capacity for self-referral
- Capacity to participate in psychosocial therapies

Money Management Skills
- Recognize and count currency, make change
- Negotiate the purchase of items
- Account for purchases
- Maintain simple records of income
- Maintain simple record of expenses
- Make periodic payments on time and within budget
- Compare values—shop

Transportation Skills
- Capacity to determine orientation in progressively complex physical environment—building, neighborhood, town
- Map reading (optional)
- Capacity to lay a course between two points
- Capacity to follow directions for travel
- Capacity to give directions for transportation to another person
- Capacity to utilize public transportation
- Capacity to drive

Source: Leavitt 1983 (pp. 32–33).

Selected Bibliography

Bertsche, Ann, and Charles Horejsi. "Coordination of Client Services." *Social Work* 25 (March 1980): 94–98.

Leavitt, Stephen. "Case Management: A Remedy for Problems of Community Care." *Case Management in Mental Health Services,* edited by Charlotte Sanborn. New York: Haworth Press, 1983.

Maslow, Abraham H. *Motivation and Personality.* New York: Harper & Row, 1970.

Steinberg, Raymond, and Genevieve Carter. *Case Management and the Elderly.* Lexington, Mass.: Lexington Books, 1983.

Weil, Marie, James Karls, and Associates. *Case Management in Human Service Practice.* San Francisco: Jossey-Bass, 1985.

Purpose:　To assist the client in identifying and utilizing informal resources.

Discussion:　Whenever possible, the intervention plan should draw on helping resources that are available within the client's social network, such as the extended family, friends, neighbors, church groups, and service organizations. Such resources are often termed *informal* as contrasted to *formal resources,* such as social agencies, hospitals, and trained professionals. Informal resources can provide emotional support, material assistance (e.g., money, loans, food, housing), physical care (e.g., child care, supervision of frail elderly persons living in their own home), information and referral, and the mediation of interpersonal conflict.

Self-help groups, such as AA and Parents Anonymous, are usually considered to be informal resources, even though they are part of a national organization and may use professionals as advisors. Another important informal resource is the *natural helper,* an individual who has often resided in the community for a long time and is known for his or her ability to help others. An example is the "neighborhood Mom" to whom children gravitate for nurturing, advice, and friendship. Other natural helpers include respected elders, religious leaders, and healers. Another informal resource—one often overlooked by professionals—is other agency clients. Clients can often be of help to each other; however, in some cases, they can also exacerbate each other's problems.

Although informal resources are the oldest and most common form of interpersonal helping, some professionals are reluctant to encourage or assist their clients in using these resources. Bertsche, Clark, and Iversen (1982, 11–12) identify a number of reasons why professionals underutilize informal resources.

- Traditional education and training in social work and the other helping professions have not given much attention to informal resources. Consequently, social workers perceive professional helpers and formal services as inherently more valuable and more effective than nonprofessionals, regardless of the client's problem or situation.

- Informal helping is often an "invisible" activity. Unless the social worker grew up in a particular neighborhood or community, he or she will have little awareness of the informal network and how to gain access to it.

- Until recently, informal resources have not been studied and researched. Consequently, many social workers are unaware of their value and effectiveness for some clients and some types of problems.

- The use of informal resources demands greater personal involvement from the social worker and more time in identifying appropriate resources (e.g., in assessing their dependability).

- It has often been assumed that clients make use of informal resources, as a matter of course. Thus, it was believed that agency clients did not need to be encouraged to explore and make use of informal resources.

- It has been assumed that the client's involvement with a formal resource was a clear indicator that informal resources did not exist for the client or that the client had chosen not to use them.
- The use of informal resources has been judged inappropriate because of the professional's need to protect client confidentiality.

Many people prefer to use informal resources over the formal ones, for several reasons.

- No stigma is attached to receiving help from an informal resource.
- Informal helping is available twenty-four hours a day, seven days a week and at no cost.
- You do not have to be categorized, labeled, diagnosed, or otherwise meet eligibility requirements in order to secure needed help.
- Informal helping involves a reciprocal relationship—the give and take among two equals or peers—rather than the expert/client relationship that is part of a professional helping process.

When considering the use of informal resources, the social worker should keep the following guidelines in mind:

1. There are sound theoretical and practical reasons for using informal resources. During the past twenty years, social workers in a wide variety of settings (child welfare, mental health, health care, etc.) have demonstrated a growing interest in informal resources, which is consistent with systems theory, the ecological perspective, and the emphasis on empowerment. The goal of practice is always to help the client better cope with problems in social functioning. The resources used—whether formal, informal, or a mix of both—are simply the means to that end.

2. When working with a client during the assessment and planning phases, the client's social network should always be viewed as a potential source of assistance. The client's relationship—past and present—with relatives, friends, neighbors, churches, and service organizations should be explored in an attempt to identify possible informal resources that are relevant to the client's current situation. If identified, the advantages and disadvantages of attempting to use the resource need to be discussed. Often, clients need guidance on how best to reach out to the resource, establish a relationship, and handle the expectation of reciprocity (i.e., the expectation that you, as a receiver of help, will stand ready to help others in the future). In the final analysis, it is the client who decides which resources he or she will attempt to utilize.

3. Informal resources must never be viewed as a panacea or an inexpensive answer to complex human problems. They are not. Nor should the professional feel threatened by the client's use of or preference for informal resources. The attention given to informal resources does not devalue formal or professional services. Both are needed and important. One should support and supplement the other.

4. The use of informal resources may be culturally appropriate for your client. For example, the Native American client typically values mutual assistance within the extended family, the clan, and the tribe. For members of many ethnic groups, the emphasis in any helping process should be on reinforcing interdependence, not promoting independence.

5. The ethical and legal codes concerning confidentiality need not be a barrier to the use of informal resources. Most often, the client first approaches the informal resource. Thus, the client is in control of what he or she chooses to reveal. In cases where the social worker needs to talk with an informal resource, he or she must, of course, first secure the client's permission, just as is done when the worker communicates with another agency.

6. Do not attempt to "professionalize" informal resources. Generally, they work best when they are left alone and not tampered with by professionals. Efforts to train informal resources have sometimes disrupted a natural helping process.

7. Learn about self-help groups available in your community. You may wish to seek information from the National Self-Help Clearinghouse, 25 W. 43rd Street, Room 620, New York, NY 10036 (telephone: 212/642-2944).

Selected Bibliography

Bertsche, Jon, Frank Clark, and Martha Iversen. *Using Informal Resources in Child Protective Services.* Missoula: University of Montana, Department of Social Work, 1982.

Gitterman, Alex, and Lawrence Shulman, eds. *Mutual Aid Groups and the Life Cycle.* Itasca, Ill.: F. E. Peacock, 1986.

Pancoast, Diane, Paul Parker, and Charles Froland. *Rediscovering Self-Help.* Beverly Hills: Sage, 1983.

Powell, Thomas. *Self Help Organizations and Professional Practice.* Silver Spring, Md.: National Association of Social Workers, 1987.

11.8   *The Small Group as a Resource*

Purpose: To develop groups that can be a resource to clients.

Discussion: Small groups are an invaluable resource to clients. They can provide a sense of belonging and support, information and new perspectives, an awareness that others have similar problems and concerns, models for learning new behaviors, and an opportunity to be helpful to others. Despite these many advantages, workers in many practice settings do not make groups available to their clients. One reason is that most clients go to a direct service agency expecting a one-to-one helping relationship rather than group participation. Given that expectation, workers may assume that groups are inappropriate. Another reason is the difficulty of bringing several people together at a mutually convenient time and place. There is also an erroneous belief that group members must all have the same problem or concern; such a belief makes it nearly impossible to ever find enough participants for a group. Some workers avoid groups because they are fearful that they will not be able to handle group issues and dynamics.

When individuals come together for several meetings, the group will move through various **stages of group development.** According to Garland, Jones, and Kolodny (1976), the stages are pre-affiliation, power and control, intimacy, differentiation, and separation. It is during the *pre-affiliation stage* that members size each other up, consider what they have in common, and decide whether they want to belong to the group. Unless the members feel they have something in common and share the same goals for the group, they will resist further involvement. During this stage, members tend to be dependent on the leader for direction.

During the *power and control stage,* members "test" each other and the leader and come to a decision of where they fit in the group. They may challenge each other for position and leadership. Also, members tend to challenge the designated group leader. At this time a number of informal rules develop to govern what is and is not acceptable behavior within the group.

As the members get to know each other, they gradually let down their defenses and the group enters the *intimacy stage.* Members recognize and value what they have in common. Next, the group moves to the stage of *differentiation* wherein differences of opinion and behavior are exhibited but respected and valued. Members begin to understand that each has a life beyond the group and may behave quite differently outside the group. As the life of the group approaches its ending, it enters the *separation stage* and each member must struggle with the loss of meaningful relationships.

For those who want to make a group experience available to their clients, we offer the following guidance:

1. Before deciding to form a group, be clear as to its purpose and why it will be of benefit to your clients. Your answers to all other questions about starting and using a group relate directly to the question of purpose and hoped for benefits.

2. Decide what is an appropriate group size. Size depends on such factors as the age of the clients, concerns to be addressed, your experience as a leader or facilitator, and, of course, purpose. You will want the group to be small enough so all members have a sense of belonging and a chance to participate, but large enough to provide a variety of personalities and a minimum of pressure on those who tend to be quiet or are fearful of intense interaction. You will also need to consider the developmental abilities of the members. For preadolescents, a group of only three or four is often workable. For adolescents, a group of from six to ten is preferred. Most adults seem comfortable in a group of about eight. You must also anticipate the inevitable problem of nonattendance and dropouts. When you begin the group, it must be large enough to continue to function when some members miss a meeting and others decide to end their participation.

3. Decide which clients are to be offered the group experience. Probably the most important criterion for selecting members is determining who can benefit.

Some group leaders have definite beliefs about the mix of personalities they want in the group (e.g., having an outgoing, verbal person to offset the quietness of a shy person). Some leaders may want to eliminate from consideration those who are reputed to be aggressive or uncooperative. It is our belief that in a great many practice settings, the leader does not have the luxury of using a selection process based on such criteria. We also believe the use of rigid criteria is unrealistic and sometimes unfair since it is seldom possible to predict with certainty how an individual will behave in a group. The worker should simply select for membership those that have a need for a group experience, share some common concerns with other members, have at least a basic capacity to enter into relationships, and whose behavior is somewhat close to normal limits. Persons exhibiting extremely bizarre or truly dangerous behavior should be eliminated from consideration for group membership. Once in the group, a voluntary member should be free to drop out if he or she feels uncomfortable or that the group will not meet his or her needs.

4. Decide on the frequency and the length of the meetings. For most adults, a meeting lasting 1½ to 2 hours is about right. Because of their more limited attention span, shorter but more frequent meetings are usually best for children and adolescents. The practice setting will usually dictate the frequency of meetings. In an institutional setting, daily meetings are often possible and desirable. When members are drawn from the community it may not be feasible to meet more often than biweekly or monthly.

5. Decide when and where the group will meet. A meeting space should be quiet, private, comfortable, and large enough for people to move around and accommodate a circle of chairs. The decision of when to meet must consider each member's work and family responsibilities and other matters of personal convenience. There is never a right time for all members and it is usually necessary to select the time that is agreeable to the majority and, of course, the leader.

6. Before you begin, decide the approximate number of times the group will meet. This is, of course, tied to purpose. An information sharing or training group might meet only once or twice, whereas a support or therapy group might meet weekly for several months or even longer. Consider setting a limit such as three, five, or ten meetings, with the understanding that at the end of that period, you and the group will discuss whether the group should continue for a longer period.

7. Decide whether the group will be open or closed to new members. This is usually a decision for the group, but the decision needs to be made during the initial meeting. Adding new members to the group has the advantage of maintaining group size as some members drop out. Also, new members may bring fresh perspectives. However, the frequent introduction of new members is a barrier to the development of group cohesion and it may limit the depth of discussion.

8. Decide if the group is only for voluntary clients, involuntary clients, or both. Obviously, there are many advantages to limiting the membership to persons who want to attend. Although involuntary members can be forced (e.g., by court order) to attend, they cannot be forced to interact in a meaningful and productive manner. Nevertheless, the successful utilization of group methods in correctional programs, as well as chemical dependency and child abuse treatment programs, demonstrates that groups made up of involuntary clients are feasible and effective. However, the leader of such groups must be strong and skilled in confronting resistant and manipulative behavior.

The addition of involuntary members to a voluntary group will usually work if the group has been functioning quite well and the involuntary member is willing to cooperate to at least a minimal degree. On the other hand, it is not likely to work if the group is not functioning well and/or the involuntary member is highly resistant and disruptive. When adding an involuntary member, it is best to wait until the group has reached the intimacy stage. An addition should be avoided during the power and control stage.

9. When extending an invitation to join a group, be prepared to explain how the group will be of benefit, what will happen during the meetings, when and where the group will meet, and the atmosphere you hope to create (e.g., informal, fun, learning, supportive, etc.). Also, be prepared to offer other information that might raise interest and reduce fears about participating in a group.

10. As the group moves through the usual stages of development, assess the functioning of each group member and consider the use of various communication skills to deal with identified problems. The answers to the following questions will help the worker in this assessment: Is the member in agreement with the group's purpose and format? Is the member personally involved—sharing feelings, opinions, and experiences? Does the member attend on a regular basis and participate in discussion or activities? Does the member seem to enjoy being with other members? Does the member engage in a good mix of confrontation and support of others? How might the group's activities be modified to address the problems or concerns identified?

11. Be prepared to establish rules—possibly written—to govern the behavior of group members. Depending on the nature of the group and its members, such rules may or may not be necessary. Possible rules include:

- Members are expected to attend all meetings.
- Members are expected to maintain confidentiality.
- Members cannot smoke or do drugs during the meeting.
- Members are not allowed to remain for the meeting if they arrive under the influence of alcohol or drugs.
- Minor-aged members must have parents' written consent to participate.
- Members are to avoid any dating or sexual relationships with other members.
- Members who use or threaten violence or engage in sexual harassment will be excluded.

12. Select activities (programs) for each meeting. These activities should be consistent with the group's overall purpose and encourage the type of activity needed, considering the group's stage of development (e.g., introductions, ice breakers, refreshments, structured discussion, free and open discussion, roleplay, guest speaker, etc.).

13. Anticipate how you can best handle the numerous practical problems associated with a meeting, such as: room is too hot, too cold, too large, or too small; leader must miss a meeting; members who arrive late; members who bring friends; will you have refreshments and if so, who pays; conflict between smokers and nonsmokers; who will remind members of next meeting; and so on.

Selected Bibliography

Cory, Gerald, Marianne Cory, Patrick Callanan, and J. Michael Russell. *Group Techniques.* Revised ed. Pacific Grove, Calif.: Brooks/Cole, 1988.

Garland, James, Hubert Jones, and Ralph Kolodny. "A Model for Stages of Development in Social Work Groups." *In Explorations in Group Work,* edited by Saul Bernstein. Boston: Charles River Books, 1976.

Garvin, Charles. *Contemporary Group Work.* Englewood Cliffs, N.J.: Prentice-Hall, 1987.

Gitterman, Alex, and Lawrence Shulman, eds. *Mutual Aid Groups and the Life Cycle.* Itasca, Ill.: F. E. Peacock, 1986.

Middleman, Ruth. *The Non-Verbal Method in Working With Groups.* New York: Association Press, 1968.

Rose, Sheldon, and Jeffrey Edleson. *Working with Children and Adolescents in Groups.* San Francisco: Jossey-Bass, 1988.

Zastrow, Charles. *Social Work with Groups.* 2nd ed. Chicago: Nelson-Hall Publishers, 1989.

Intervention and Monitoring

Introduction

This chapter describes a number of intervention techniques and guidelines that will prove helpful to the direct service social worker. Many can be adapted for use with either individuals, families, or small groups. (Techniques and guidelines focusing primarily on work with organizations and communities are described in Chapters 14 and 15.) It should be noted that several of the techniques included here are elaborations of the basic communication skills presented in Chapter 6. Also, such activities as the referral process (described in Chapter 9) and the problem search (explained in Chapter 11) could logically be classified as interventions.

The techniques in this chapter have been drawn from several theoretical orientations. This is consistent with the authors' belief that the social worker must look to many sources for techniques that can be applied in the diverse situations encountered in practice. The fields of behavior modification and behavioral therapy are especially rich sources of clearly described techniques. But, as Fischer and Gochros (1975) explain, behavior modification cannot be the sole approach to intervention.

> Many of the goals and activities of social work practice are outside the boundaries of behavior modification as an intervention strategy.... For instance, mobilizing, modifying, and providing material services and resources is a major area of social work activity. Assisting individuals to make decisions—within the context of a nurturing interpersonal relationship—is perhaps one of the unique and best developed areas of social work practice and is a major component of most social work helping. (pp. xvii–xviii)

Similarly, Reid (1978) observes that behavioral techniques

> are designed to alter specific behaviors. Many of the problems dealt with by social workers cannot be readily reduced to behaviors to be modified. Thus in problems involving lack of resources, difficulties with organizations, troublesome environments, decision making, novel situations and crisis events, it may not be possible (or feasible) to single out particular behaviors on the part of others to be changed. (p. 105)

Regardless of what specific techniques are used to help the client, certain basic principles and guidelines should assist in the worker's intervention.

1. Helping is not the sterile application of just the right technique. Rather, it is a very human struggle. Be willing to participate in that struggle with your client.
2. Remember that your job is to facilitate problem solving by your client. You are to help your client search for the struggle toward a solution with which he or she can live. In a great many cases, the solution the client chooses will not be the one you would choose for yourself.
3. Problem solving is not solution giving by a professional. To the contrary, problem solving is mostly a search and a process of considering options and making decisions; each client must struggle with problems in his or her own unique way. The solution to a client's problem must grow out of his or her own values, belief system, and usual methods of coping with life.
4. A client is only motivated to change that which he or she perceives to be a real problem. The individual is motivated to work on a problem only when he or she feels hopeful that a solution is possible. No matter what you want for the client, it is only what the client wants that makes change possible. The social worker's goals for a client can be realized only after they become the client's own goals.
5. Remember that your client's behavior is always purposeful. Even dysfunctional behavior serves a purpose by meeting a need or mitigating some conflict or other problems—often a problem you know nothing about. If you can figure out that purpose, you have found a key to understanding. Always look beyond and behind your client's surface behavior.
6. View your client holistically and in context. People do not live in a vacuum. Everything affects everything else. Life is complex; do not act as if it were simple, completely logical, or completely controllable. Help your client take control of those things he or she can control and give up efforts to control those things over which her or she has no control.
7. Emphasize empathy. View the world, life, and living through your client's eyes. Remember, his or her world is not your world, nor does it have to be. Realize that your client is probably doing the best he or she knows how. If given your client's life's experiences and current circumstances, you could be doing much worse.
8. Always demonstrate genuine respect and caring for the client, even if his or her behavior is abrasive, obnoxious, or repulsive. Don't be afraid to let your client know you care—if you don't care, then be afraid for yourself.
9. Remember that it is not your responsibility nor right to judge or punish a client in any way for his or her problems or troublesome behavior. Most of your clients have already received an abundance of disapproval from others. Disapproval from you will only dampen communication and soon destroy your relationship. Seek to accept and understand. Because acceptance and understanding are in such short supply, they will have great value to your client.

10. Do not moralize or preach. You do not need to argue the "rightness" of your choices in life. If your moral character is indeed worthy of emulation, your client will be influenced by your behavior and your explanations will not be necessary.
11. Reach for and explore your client's feelings. Do not be afraid of emotion. Struggling with confusing and conflicting feelings is what helping is all about. When emotions are high, they must be dealt with before problem solving can proceed. If feelings scare you, work with things, not people.
12. Maintain confidentiality. Respecting your client's desire for privacy is critical to the establishment of trust. Trust is an essential ingredient in the helping process.
13. Expect a client who is struggling with serious psychosocial problems to feel frustrated and overwhelmed. His or her anger may be directed toward you, even when you are not the true source of the frustration. When this happens, do not take it personally or react defensively.
14. Develop self-awareness and self-discipline. Don't allow your problems to distort the helping process. Meet your emotional needs and handle your personal problems outside your professional relationships. Your client already has a fair share of life's problems. Don't ask him or her to worry about yours.
15.. Listen much more than you talk. What your client has to say is much more important and helpful than what you have to say to your client. Keep your own message short, simple, and clear. Leave the jargon in your textbooks and at professional conferences.
16. Do not take the side of one person or another in your client's interpersonal conflicts. If you do, be prepared to lose. Do take the side of reality, social responsibility, and human decency.
17. Search for your client's strengths and for positives in the situation. Build on those strengths. Give more attention to what your client can do, rather than to what he or she is unable to do.
18. Don't be overwhelmed or defeated by labels others have attached to your client. Take all labels and diagnostic statements with a grain of salt.
19. Believe in the possibilities of change. Remain hopeful—especially when your client is feeling hopeless. Expect him or her to work toward agreed upon goals; do not be afraid to challenge and confront the client when reasonable progress is not being made.
20. A client should participate as much as possible in the professional and agency decisions that impact his or her life. Keep your client informed of what you are doing on his or her behalf.
21. To the greatest extent possible, a client should be helped and encouraged to make use of the informal resources that exist within his or her own social network (e.g., family, friends, neighbors, natural helpers, etc.).
22. Avoid creating unnecessary client dependence; a client should be encouraged to make his or her own decisions, even when those decisions move the client in a direction you would not choose for yourself. Plan and conduct interventions so the client can learn problem-solving skills that will

be useful in the future. The help you provide should prepare and empower your client to cope without your assistance.

23. Recognize your limitations, but do not underestimate your abilities. Refer your client to another professional only when he or she has needs that are beyond the scope of your agency's program or your own skills and training. Make use of a supervisor, consultant, or knowledgeable peer when confronted with a situation you do not know how to handle.

24. Do not defend or justify an agency procedure or policy that is illogical or unfair. Doing so only makes you look foolish and insensitive. It is best simply to acknowledge that the policy or procedure in question makes little sense but that it is a reality that cannot now be changed and, therefore, must be followed. This does not suggest that the client is expected to adjust to injustice; rather, it acknowledges that there are many policies and procedures that neither the client nor the direct services worker has the power to change.

25. Always remember that human beings are incredibly resilient and adaptive. They can put up with a great deal of pain and discomfort if they understand why it is necessary in order to reach a goal they desire. Never underestimate a person's ability to endure difficulties in order to obtain what he or she truly values.

Selected Bibliography

Fischer, Joel, and Harvey Gochros. *Planned Behavior Change: Behavior Modification in Social Work*. New York: The Free Press, 1975.

Gambrill, Eileen. *Critical Thinking in Clinical Practice*. San Francisco: Jossey-Bass, 1990.

Reid, William. *The Task-Centered System*. New York: Columbia University Press, 1978.

Whittaker, James, and Elizabeth Tracy. *Social Treatment*. 2nd ed. New York: Aldine de Gruyter, 1989.

12.1 *Planning an Interview*

Purpose: To formulate a tentative plan for an interview or contact with a client.

Discussion: One of the most common errors made by new workers is to go into a session without a clear purpose. Just as there should be an overall intervention plan, there should be a plan for each contact the worker has with the client. Of course, this plan must be tentative and flexible in order to respond to client concerns that could not be anticipated. The following questions can help the worker formulate such a plan:

1. What are the overall goals and objectives of the intervention with this client? How will my next contact relate to these goals and objectives?

2. What needs to be accomplished during the interview? What decisions need to be reached during the interview? Who needs to be present?

3. Should the next contact be a face-to-face or a telephone interview? One-on-one, family, or group session?

4. Will other professionals and/or concerned individuals participate in the interview (e.g., a family conference in a medical setting)? What objectives do these other participants have and how might differences in expectations be resolved?

5. How much time do I have to devote to the interview? How much time can the client devote to the interview?

6. Where and when will the interview take place? What arrangements are necessary prior to the interview (e.g., scheduling interviewing room, transportation, child care for client's children)?

7. What specific techniques might be used during the interview to achieve specific tasks and work toward intervention goals and objectives?

8. What factors related to the client's cultural, ethnic, or religious beliefs and social and family network need to be considered in preparing for the interview?

9. What factors related to the client's current emotional or psychological state (e.g., anger, fear, confusion, depression, etc.) need to be considered in preparing for the interview?

10. What factors related to the client's current physical functioning (e.g., mobility, pain, discomfort, hearing problems, effects of medication, etc.) need to be considered in preparing for the interview?

11. What documentation on this contact is necessary for the agency record?

Selected Bibliography

Epstein, Laura. *Talking and Listening: A Guide to the Helping Interview*. St. Louis: Times Mirror/Mosby, 1985.

Kadushin, Alfred. *The Social Work Interview*. 2nd ed. New York: Columbia University Press, 1983.

Schubert, Margaret. *Interviewing in Social Work Practice*. New York: Council on Social Work Education, 1971.

12.2　Giving Information and Advice

Purpose:　To enhance the client's problem-solving capacity by providing needed information and guidance.

Discussion:　*Information giving* refers to providing a client with information he or she needs to make a decision or carry out a task. Shulman (1981) prefers the term *providing data* and considers it to be a fundamental social work skill. As used here, the term *advice giving* refers to worker statements that recommend or suggest what a client should do. In information giving, the client feels free to use the information as he or she sees fit; in advice giving, the client clearly senses the social worker's preference.

One of the common errors made by inexperienced social workers is to give advice when the client has not asked for it. This is an understandable error because often the worker has known other clients with similar problems or has had personal experience with the problem now faced by the client, and, naturally, the worker wants the client to benefit from those experiences. However, there are many pitfalls in advice giving, and the worker needs to be very careful in using this technique. Follow these guidelines for **advice giving:**

1. Before giving advice to a client, reflect on how you feel when someone gives you advice. Also remember that most people do not usually follow advice, even when they have requested it. On those rare occurrences when someone does follow advice, it was usually offered by a person he or she has known for a long time and trusts completely.

2. Whether or not the giving of advice is appropriate depends largely on the purpose of the worker-client interaction. If it is a counseling-therapy relationship, advice is rarely appropriate. If the purpose relates to referral, brokering, or advocacy, advice giving may be appropriate.

3. Do not offer advice unless you have determined that the client genuinely wants your opinions and suggestions. Wait until you thoroughly understand your client's situation. Never give advice on a topic outside your area of training and expertise.

4. When you do give advice, present it in a way that says, "This is what I would do" or "This is what others have done." But leave the responsibility for deciding what to do to the client. Always explain the reasoning or rationale behind the guidance you offer.

5. Consider the issue of legal liability if you advise a client and he or she later suffers an adverse personal or financial consequence as a result of your recommendation. For example, beware of advising a client who asks questions such as: Do you think I should get a divorce? Do you think I should quit my job and look for another? Do you think it would be OK if I cut down on my medicine?

6. Be alert to the dangers of giving advice to a manipulative client, who may then hold you responsible if things do not turn out well (e.g., "I did what you said and it didn't work, so it's your fault"). Also be alert to the danger of encouraging dependency in a client who can and should take responsibility for decision making.

Recall the distinction we have made between *giving advice* and *giving information*. When **providing information** to a client, keep these guidelines in mind:

1. Complicated, multistep instructions (e.g., how to get to another agency or how to apply for public assistance) may need to be written down. Also write out names, addresses, and phone numbers needed by the client.

2. Use pronouns (e.g., *it, this, that, those, them*) with caution. For example, the statement, "Fill out the form and take it to the person at the desk over there" could be very confusing to someone who does not know what the "form," "it," "person," or "over there" mean specifically. It is best to use the exact word rather than a pronoun, or provide sufficient description so there can be no mistake about what or who you are referring to.

3. Speak distinctly. Avoid talking fast or using words the client may not understand. Remember that poor grammar and awkwardly constructed sentences result in confusion and misinterpretation.

4. Provide information or directions in a logical, organized, step-by-step fashion. If you are haphazard in your presentation, the client will become confused. Give the client time to think about what you are saying, and invite him or her to ask questions to clarify any uncertainty.

5. Never assume that the client understands what you have said. Anticipate and look for nonverbal signs of misunderstanding. Ask the client to repeat the key points of what you have said so you know he or she understands completely.

6. Carefully consider the client's previous experience and current state of mind when giving information. Adapt what you say to his or her educational background, level of intelligence, command of the language, fears, and the like. If it is likely that the client will misunderstand, make sure that you give the same information to the client's significant others.

Selected Bibliography

Haley, Jay. *Problem Solving Therapy*. 2nd ed. San Francisco: Jossey-Bass, 1987.
Hollis, Florence, and Mary Woods. *Casework: A Psychosocial Therapy*. 3rd ed. New York: Random House, 1981.
Shulman, Lawrence. *The Skills of Helping: Individuals and Groups*. 2nd ed. Itasca, Ill.: F. E. Peacock, 1981.

12.3   *Encouragement, Reassurance, and Universalization*

Purpose: To enhance the client's problem-solving capacity by providing supportive and encouraging statements.

Discussion: The interrelated techniques of encouragement, reassurance, and universalization are basic to work with clients, regardless of practice setting. Reid (1978, 325) explains that *encouragement* often takes the form of supportive statements that express praise or approval of the client's behavior, attitude, or feelings; it is a means of recognizing and supporting client strengths. Hollis and Woods (1981) explain that encouragement "takes place when the worker expresses confidence in the client's abilities, recognizes achievements, shows pleasure in success" (p. 113). It is important for the worker using encouragement to send a clear, targeted message that relates directly to the client's behavior or performance. Here are two examples:

- "You're doing a great job completing your homework assignment."
- "On the basis of what you have done so far on this job, I think you are capable of handling this new responsibility."

A vague overgeneralization like "You're a wonderful person" is seldom perceived as genuine encouragement because the client knows it is an exaggeration. At best, the client accepts such a global statement as a gesture of politeness; at worst, he or she takes it as a put-down. By always tying words of encouragement to specific client behavior, the worker will avoid the danger of sounding phony.

The term *reassurance* refers to expressions of confidence in the client's capabilities. It is often used when the client is doubtful about his or her decisions, thoughts, or feelings when they are, in fact, sound, realistic, and socially acceptable. Reassurance, like advice, is called for at times, but the worker must be aware of its pitfalls. Inexperienced workers often misuse reassurance when they become uncomfortable with the client's emotion. Hollis and Woods (1981) warn that reassurance "must be used with delicacy and discrimination. Yielding to the temptation to overuse reassurance in an attempt to build up a relationship or because the worker cannot endure the client's anxiety may merely leave the client with the feeling that the worker does not fully comprehend the reasons for guilt or anxiety, or that the worker is deficient in moral discrimination and therefore is not a person whose judgement matters" (p. 111).

Universalization is a form of reassurance that consists of statements explaining to the client that his or her thoughts, feelings, or behavior are the same or very similar to those of other people in similar situations. An example is: "I have known a lot of people who had to place their parent in a nursing home and they described the same feelings you are telling me about." This technique is intended to counteract the client's feelings of being different, deviant, or separate from others.

Selected Bibliography

Hollis, Florence, and Mary Woods. *Casework: A Psychosocial Therapy*. 3rd ed. New York: Random House, 1981.

Reid, William. *The Task-Centered System*. New York: Columbia University Press, 1978.

12.4 Reinforcement and Related Behavioral Techniques

Purpose: To modify the frequency, intensity, or duration of a specific behavior.

Discussion: Behavioral techniques are some of the most powerful available to the social worker when the intervention objective is to help the client learn a new behavior or alter an existing one. They are especially useful when dealing with child behavior problems. The social worker usually employs behavioral techniques when trying either to strengthen (increase) or weaken (decrease) a particular target behavior. The term *target behavior* refers to an operationally defined and measurable behavior that is the focus of the intervention. The *strength* of a target behavior can be described in terms of its frequency, intensity, or duration.

Reinforcement is a technique rooted in operant learning theory. By definition, **reinforcement** is any event or activity that increases the likelihood that a target behavior will occur more frequently than in the past. Thus, a reinforcer is anything that strengthens a target behavior. There are two forms of reinforcement: positive and negative. **Positive reinforcement** involves adding, presenting, or giving something to the client (such as attention, objects of value, or privileges) that has the effect of increasing the target behavior. Ordinarily, a positive reinforcer is a pleasurable event or an obvious reward, but sometimes even a painful event can prove to be a positive reinforcer. Thus, only by observing the effects of what you believe is a reinforcer can you know for sure that it is a reinforcer. For this reason, it is important to establish a *baseline measurement* that describes the frequency, intensity, or duration of the target behavior prior to intervention. As a general rule, what a person does when he or she does not have to do something else is an indicator of what is positively reinforcing for that person (e.g., how a person spends extra time and money).

There are two kinds of positive reinforcers: primary and secondary. *Primary reinforcers* are inherently rewarding and almost universally reinforcing. Examples include food, water, sex, warmth, and so on. *Secondary reinforcers* are learned, usually as a result of having been associated with primary reinforcers. Examples include money, tokens, and new clothes. Social reinforcers—such as praise, attention, and hugs—are usually considered to be secondary reinforcers, but there is some evidence that they are universally reinforcing.

Both positive and negative reinforcement increase the frequency, intensity, or duration of a target behavior. **Negative reinforcement** involves subtracting or removing some condition that is aversive or unpleasant to the client, which has the effect of increasing the target behavior. Negative reinforcement is often confused with punishment, but they are not the same. Punishment decreases the target behavior, whereas negative reinforcement strengthens the behavior.

As a technique of behavior change, **punishment** involves the presentation of a painful or unpleasant stimulus that has the effect of suppressing a target behavior or reducing its strength. For ethical and legal reasons, the social worker must avoid the use of punishment. Most agencies and treatment programs prohibit the use of punishment for one or more of the following reasons:

1. Often, the results of punishment are short term. When the threat of punishment is not present, the target behavior often recurs.
2. The use of punishment provides a poor behavioral model for the client.
3. Punishment can be excessive or reach truly dangerous levels when administered by an angry or frustrated person.
4. Punishment may also suppress desirable behavior and make the client afraid to respond.
5. The use of physical punishment may make the worker vulnerable to a civil lawsuit or criminal charges (e.g., assault).

A behavior that is not reinforced tends to decrease in frequency, duration, or intensity. The term *extinction* describes the planned withdrawal of whatever reinforces a target behavior so as to eliminate or reduce the frequency of that behavior.

There are two basic **reinforcement schedules**: continuous and intermittent. *Continuous reinforcement* constitutes providing a reinforcer each time the desired target behavior occurs. In *intermittent reinforcement*, the target behavior is not rewarded every time it occurs. Continuous reinforcement is almost always used in the first stages of a program designed to teach a new behavior because it allows faster learning than intermittent reinforcement. However, a behavior that has been continuously reinforced is comparatively easy to extinguish. To make the newly learned behavior resistant to extinction, continuous reinforcement should be replaced by intermittent reinforcement.

A behavior that is maintained by a completely *random reinforcement schedule* (e.g., slot machine, bingo, fishing, etc.) or learned during a time of high emotion or personal crisis is highly resistant to change and difficult to extinguish.

When one behavior is described as being incompatible with another, it means that a person cannot perform both behaviors concurrently. For example, a child cannot play basketball and watch TV at the same time. A highly useful procedure in planned behavior change is to recognize such an incompatibility and ignore an unwanted target behavior while at the same time reinforcing an incompatible desired behavior and encourage a new desired behavior. This technique is often called **differential reinforcement**.

The techniques of chaining, prompting, fading, and shaping are especially useful when the objective is to help a client learn a new behavior. These techniques are frequently used in training programs for the mentally retarded, in speech therapy, and in certain aspects of physical rehabilitation.

Chaining refers to a procedure that breaks down a complex behavior (e.g., dressing) into many separate steps or components and teaches only one of these steps at a time. As new components are learned, they are "chained," or linked, to the ones already learned. The number of steps needed to teach a particular behavior will depend on the complexity of the behavior and the capacity of the client. There are two types of chaining: forward and backward.

In *forward chaining*, the first step in a behavior chain is taught first. For example, in teaching a client to put on his trousers, the client would first be taught how to pick up and hold his pants. All subsequent steps are taught in order of their "natural sequence." This sequence may be determined by observing several people perform the behavior and noting the most common sequence of steps.

In *backward chaining*, the last step in the chain is taught first. Thus, all of the steps in the sequence would be done for the client except the one being taught. For example, in dressing training, the first step to be taught would be "pulls pants up to the waist." One advantage of backward chaining is that the last step in the chain is always the one that is reinforced. Thus the client is always reinforced at the very end of the behavior chain (e.g., when he has finished putting on his pants). For some self-help skills, such as hand and face washing, backward chaining is not feasible.

The term **prompting** describes any form of assistance given by the worker to help the client perform a specific behavior. A prompt may be a verbal cue or instruction, a gesture or other nonverbal cue, or physically moving or guiding the client through the behavior. Prompting should be used only when necessary.

Fading is the process of gradually withdrawing prompts and decreasing the frequency of reinforcement as the client begins to learn the desired behavior. In the first steps of a training program, the worker will use continuous reinforcement and frequent prompting to help establish the new behavior. Later, when the client begins to perform the target behavior, the worker will gradually "fade out" or decrease the frequency of the reinforcement and prompting.

Shaping is a technique of building a new behavior by reinforcing close approximations of the desired response. For example, a speech therapist teaching a child to say "cookie" may reward the child when he says "gowk." Perhaps later, the child is reinforced for saying "gook-koo" and still later, "gookie." Finally, after many days or weeks of reinforcing the child for closer and closer approximations of the desired sound, the child is able to say "cookie."

Much of what one learns—especially one's social or interactional behavior—is learned by observing others and subsequently repeating or imitating their behavior. This learning process is termed **modeling**. Needless to say, both functional and dysfunctional behaviors are learned this way. A social worker can enhance the learning of functional behavior by keeping several principles in mind.

- Individual A is most likely to imitate the behavior of individual B if he or she views B as having some valued status (e.g., power, prestige, attractiveness, etc.) and if he or she observes B being rewarded for the behavior.
- In addition, A must in some way identify with B and feel similar. If A views B as being completely different, A may conclude there is no chance he or she could actually perform the behavior and/or that there was little or no chance that it would be rewarded.
- A is most likely to learn B's behavior if he or she has an opportunity to perform or practice the behavior soon after observing it and is then rewarded for the behavior.

Under ordinary conditions, licensed foster parents and child care staff working in hospitals, treatment centers, and group homes are prohibited from using any form of physical punishment. The procedure termed **time out** is an alternative to physical discipline. Its purpose is to reduce or eliminate a problem behavior by temporarily removing the child from an environment that is reinforcing the unwanted behavior. Consider this set of instructions given to a foster parent who is learning methods of nonviolent child care for use with a ten-year-old foster child.

1. Find an area in your home that can be used for time out. If your child kicks, throws things, or has tantrums, be sure to choose an area that has few breakable objects. You might use the child's bedroom or other quiet area that is well lighted and ventilated.

2. Identify the behaviors that will always result in time out (i.e., clearly define the target behavior). For example, you may decide to use time out whenever the child hits other children or screams at you.

3. Each time a target behavior occurs, use the time-out procedure immediately. Walk up to the child, explain what rule was broken, and tell him or her what must now happen. For example, "Johnny, whenever you hit your sister, you must go on time out." Accompany the child to the time-out area; don't look at or talk to him or her on the way. If the child resists, take him or her there as quickly as possible.

4. Leave the child in the time-out area for a preselected period of time. As a rule of thumb, use the formula of one minute per year of the child's age. At the end of the time period or when the child is quiet and behaving well, go to the door and ask if he or she is ready to come out and behave correctly. For example, if Johnny threw toys, ask him, "Are you ready to come out and put your toys away?" If he hit his sister, ask him, "Are you ready to come out and be friendly to your sister?"

5. If the child answers this question "yes," have him or her come out and correct the earlier behavior. Reinforce the correct behavior with praise. For example, say, "I like the way you are picking up your toys."

6. If the child does not answer "yes" or screams, cries, throws a tantrum, or displays other undesirable behavior, walk away from the door and wait until he or she is again quiet and behaving appropriately. Then go back and repeat the question.

7. At first, you may have to question the child several times before he or she is ready to come out and correct the bad behavior. Don't be discouraged—just continue to follow these rules. If you follow the rules carefully, chances are that the child will soon learn to follow them, too.

8. Try to arrange a special activity, privilege, or treat at the end of each day that the child does not have to be taken to the time-out area, and tell the child that the reward is for his or her good behavior.

Selected Bibliography

Gambrill, Eileen. *Behavior Modification Handbook of Assessment, Intervention and Evaluation.* San Francisco: Jossey-Bass, 1977.

———. *Casework: A Competency Based Approach.* Englewood Cliffs, N.J.: Prentice-Hall, 1983.

Hudson, Barbara, and Geraldine MacDonald. *Behavior Social Work.* Chicago: The Dorsey Press, 1986.

Pinkston, Elsie, John Levitt, Glenn Green, Nick Linsk, and Tina Rzepnicki. *Effective Social Work Practice.* San Francisco: Jossey-Bass, 1982.

Schinke, Steven, ed. *Behavioral Methods in Social Welfare.* New York: Aldine, 1981.

Thyer, Bruce, and Walter Hudson, eds. *Progress in Behavioral Social Work.* New York: Haworth, 1987.

12.5 Behavioral Rehearsal

Purpose: To assist the client in learning a new behavior to better cope with a particular situation.

Discussion: *Behavioral rehearsal* is a technique drawn from behavioral therapy that teaches a client how to handle a specific interpersonal exchange for which he or she feels unprepared. As implied by its name, the client rehearses or practices a specific behavior to be performed in an upcoming situation. Behavioral rehearsal helps reduce anxiety and builds the client's self-confidence about being able to handle the situation. Essentially, it is a form of roleplaying that makes heavy use of modeling and coaching. Like other forms of roleplay, behavioral rehearsal provides the client with an opportunity to try out new behaviors in a protected environment and without risk of failure. For example, the technique can be used to prepare a client for a job interview (e.g., the social worker takes the role of the employer and conducts a simulated job interview.) As the client practices the behavior, the worker provides feedback and offers suggestions and alternative ways of behaving. The worker may demonstrate or model the behavior, so it can be imitated by the client. Whether used during a one-to-one interview or during a group session, the steps are basically the same:

1. The client identifies the problem or concern and then describes or demonstrates how he or she would usually behave in that situation.
2. The worker (and/or group members) makes suggestions on how the situation might be handled more effectively.
3. The client is given an opportunity to provide additional information about the problem or concern and also to ask the worker (or group members) to further explain the suggestions.
4. A roleplay is used to demonstrate the behavioral changes suggested to the client. The worker (or group members) will usually take the role of the client. However, the client may enact the behavior if he or she feels ready and understands the changes being suggested.
5. After the roleplay, the worker (or members) first identifies the positive aspects of the performance, then makes additional suggestions for improvement. If necessary, the roleplay is repeated to further illustrate the preferred way of behaving.
6. When the client understands how he or she ought to behave, he or she practices the behavior until satisfied with the performance.
7. Homework outside the session can be used to further the client's learning of the new behavior.

The major limitation of behavioral rehearsal is that the client may successfully learn what to do in the presence of the worker but may not be able to generalize it to the real world. Sometimes the real situation poses problems that cannot be anticipated during a practice session.

Selected Bibliography

Curran, James, and Peter Monti, eds. *Social Skills Training*. New York: The Guilford Press, 1982.

Garvin, Charles. *Contemporary Group Work*. 2nd ed. Englewood Cliffs, N.J.: Prentice-Hall, 1987.

12.6   *Behavioral Contracting*

Purpose: To increase the client's motivation to modify a behavior.

Discussion: A ***behavioral contract*** is an agreement designed to bring about a behavioral change, usually by providing a reward for a desired behavior. DeRisi and Butz (1975) explain that behavior contracting "is a technique used to structure behavioral counseling by making each of the necessary elements of the process so clear and explicit that they may be written into an agreement for behavior change that is understandable and acceptable to everyone involved. It is also an exchange of positive reinforcement . . . between two or more persons" (pp. 1–2). The agreement may be between the social worker and the client, or the worker may help two or more clients (e.g., a husband and wife, parent and child) negotiate their own behavioral contract. Any target behavior is suitable for contracting, as long as it can be clearly described and is agreed to by everyone affected by the contract. Target behaviors should be described in positive terms. In other words, the contract should describe what the client *will* do, rather than what he or she *will not* do.

A behavioral contract can follow one or two forms: a contingency contract or a reciprocal behavioral contract. In a ***contingency contract***, one person sets up a consequence associated with the behavior of another. For example, a group home manager may agree to take a resident to a movie if the resident cleans his or her room five days in a row. By contrast, the ***reciprocal behavior contract*** is an agreement between the members of a dyad (e.g., husband-wife, parent-child), in which each agrees to reward the other for a specific desired behavior. For example, a husband agrees to take his wife to a movie of her choice if she will take the car to the repair shop, and she agrees to cook his favorite meal if he will clean the house.

Alexander and Parsons (1982) offer a number of guidelines for selecting the tasks that will become part of a family's reciprocal behavioral contract.

1. Design the task to provide an immediate sense of relief or pleasure for each person involved. Although family members may occasionally be asked to do something for the long-term good, in general a task will be effective if each person either enjoys doing it or receives immediate pleasure or relief as soon as it is accomplished.
2. Be sure everyone agrees that the task assigned can be accomplished and will result in mutual payoffs. Even if the therapist believes the family members can

accomplish the task, if one or more family members believe it is impossible, they probably will not do it. . . .

3. Have all family members explain the task assignment before they leave the session. . . . Therapists must constantly remind themselves that family members and therapists not only may assign dramatically different meanings to the same word or phrase but also may assume different specific behaviors are necessary to carry out specific tasks. . . .

4. Keep the task simple enough to ensure success. . . . Successful completion of tasks allows the family to experience new ways of behaving and to sense that intervention is in fact helpful not just painful. . . .

5. Develop tasks that allow people to set and attain personal as well as group goals. Too many therapists fall into the trap of developing tasks that help the entire family and forget that altruism becomes difficult if individuals aren't also allowed to pursue their personal goals.

6. Believe in approximation. . . . Most families have taken quite a bit of time to develop the maladaptive relationships they bring to the therapist. It is unrealistic to expect that they can produce major changes without having made minor changes first.

7. Keep track of the task. Family members must get the idea that the therapist takes these tasks seriously. Family members can become quite lax in maintaining newly developed interaction styles. . . . When this failure occurs, family members and therapists can become discouraged and even resentful and aggressive toward one another.

8. Create tasks for spectators. Even when a task must be completed by only one person, interdependence and mutual support will be enhanced if spectators also have a formal role, even if it is only a monitoring function. (pp. 83–84)*

Gambrill (1977, 1983) provides numerous examples of contingency contracting, including applications in marital counseling, parent-child conflicts, and the treatment of drug and alcohol abuse. Variations of behavioral contracting, often termed *point systems* or *token economies*, are frequently used in group homes and residential treatment facilities.

When using a contingency contract, the reinforcement (rewards) for compliance, along with any adverse consequences for noncompliance, should be clearly described and understood by all. Whenever noncompliance can have serious consequences for a client (e.g., when used in a probation or child protective services agency), the contract should be written so as to minimize misunderstanding. In other situations, a verbal agreement may suffice. The contingency contract, like the reciprocal contract, should be developed in a way that increases the likelihood of success because success sustains motivation.

Selected Bibliography

Alexander, James, and Bruce Parsons. *Functional Family Therapy*. Monterey, Calif.: Brooks/ Cole, 1982.

DeRisi, William, and George Butz. *Writing Behavioral Contracts.* Champaign, Ill.: Research Press, 1975.

Gambrill, Eileen. *Behavior Modification Handbook of Assessments, Intervention and Evaluation.* San Francisco: Jossey-Bass, 1977.

―――. *Casework: A Competency Based Approach.* Englewood Cliffs, N.J.: Prentice-Hall, 1983.

12.7   *Role Reversal*

Purpose: To assist the client in understanding the behavior and/or feelings of a significant other.

Discussion: This technique is especially useful during family interviews focusing on interpersonal conflict. It is designed to help one person understand how another feels about or perceives the situation. The social worker may elect to use role reversal when two clients, such as husband and wife or parent and child, are in conflict, and when it is apparent that one or both of the clients has little awareness of how the other feels. The best time to use role reversal is when two people have reached an impasse and keep repeating the same dialogue or when one is "stuck" on a particular perception.

Johnson and Matross (1975) explain that, during a role reversal,

> the client takes the role of another person and presents the viewpoint of that person as if the client were he. To initiate the use of role reversal the helper identifies another person involved in the client's problems. This can be a current person (such as his wife) or a past person (such as his father when the client was 10 years old).... Once the person has been identified, the helper asks the client to present the position and attitudes of the other person. In doing so the client is to present the position and attitudes as if he were that person. Sometimes it is helpful for the client to switch back and forth between his position and viewpoint and the viewpoint and position of another significant person; in such a case having the client switch chairs as he switches viewpoints helps the process. Sometimes it is possible to have the person being role played observe and comment on the accuracy of the representation. Other times it is possible to have another person [e.g., the worker] to play the role of the other person and then periodically have the client and the other role player switch roles. (pp. 63–64)

The worker might initiate the role reversal by saying something like, "Would you mind reversing roles to see how it feels being the other person? Let's start by switching chairs. Try to assume the posture of the role you are taking." It can also be helpful to recall a typical line of the repetitious dialogue and ask them to start with that. For example, "Joe, I want you to start playing Susan's part in this conflict and begin with the line 'Joe, you don't care about me.' " It is important to have the participants actually switch chairs to help structure the reversal; if the clients do not change chairs, they often become confused as to which role they are playing. The worker should explain, "In this chair, you are yourself. In that chair, you are Joe."

When working with couples and families, the role reversal technique may be adapted for use as homework, asking the couple or family members to take an hour at home prior to the next session and reverse roles. It also allows the individual to experience how his or her own behavior, as dramatized by another, affects others. It can provide insight and maybe even a little humor if the clients are instructed not to take the task too seriously.

Selected Bibliography

Johnson, David, and Ronald Matross. "Attitude Modification Methods." In *Helping People Change*, edited by Frederick Kanfer and Arnold Goldstein. New York: Pergamon Press, 1975.

Ohlsen, Merle. *Marriage Counseling in Groups*. Champaign, Ill.: Research Press, 1979.

Sherman, Robert, and Norman Fredman. *Handbook of Structured Techniques in Marriage and Family Therapy*. New York: Brunner/Mazel, 1986.

12.8   *Managing Self-Talk*

Purpose: To assist the client to manage emotional reactions by modifying distorted interpretations of reality.

Discussion: Social work places much emphasis on viewing the client within an environmental context. The profession is particularly concerned about how the realities of life and external influences affect one's social functioning. However, in many situations, the client is more influenced by his or her interpretation of reality than by objective reality itself.

The term ***self-talk*** refers to the messages that we give ourselves. What we "say" to ourselves reflects our unique interpretation of what has happened and what we have experienced. Social workers who adhere to the theoretical assumptions of cognitive therapy emphasize that our self-talk evokes emotional reactions, which, in turn, give rise to behaviors. Emery (1981) explains the basic principle of cognitive therapy:

> How you evaluate or think about your experiences determines how you react emotionally. If you think you've lost something, you'll feel sad; if you think you're in danger, you'll feel anxious; if you think others have treated you wrongly, you'll feel angry. Recent research has found that people with emotional disorders systematically distort their experiences. The direction and type of cognitive distortion determines the nature of the emotional disorder. (p. 23)

Wodarski and Harris (1987) explain that cognitive theorists identify four types of distortions in thinking:

> *Arbitrary inference* is the process of drawing a conclusion when evidence is lacking or is contrary to the conclusion.
>
> *Overgeneralization* is the process of making an unjustified generalization on the basis of a single incident.

Magnification is the propensity to exaggerate the meaning or significance of a particular event.

Cognitive deficiency is the disregard of an important aspect of a life situation. (p. 481)

Many dysfunctional emotional reactions and problem behaviors are the result of unclear thinking or faulty beliefs about how we or others should or ought to behave. McMullin (1986, 55–56) lists numerous examples of irrational thoughts that create problems for clients. These include beliefs such as: "Home is safe. Thus, the farther away from home I travel, the greater the danger"; "I must fit in with everybody else's values and behavior, otherwise I will be totally alone and rejected by everyone"; "I must try as hard as I can in everything I attempt"; and "I can't be assertive because I don't want to be arrogant and egotistical."

By helping a client learn to think more precisely, the worker can help him or her control troublesome emotions and behave more effectively. This is, of course, more difficult than it sounds. Patterns of thinking are habits, which means they are not easily changed and are themselves a barrier to change.

The social worker can use a five-step approach to help a client modify distortions in self-talk.

1. Identify what you are feeling and thinking right now.

2. Get in touch with your self-talk. Pay attention to extremes in thinking, as suggested by the use of words such as *never, can't, always, everybody, completely,* and so on.

3. Examine the objective reality of your situation. Once the facts have been identified, relax, take a deep breath, and repeat them out loud three times.

4. Notice that, when you hold to the facts and avoid using inaccurate words, you begin to feel differently and things do not seem as bad as before.

5. Keeping the facts of your situation clearly in mind, consider what you can do about it.

This five-step method is illustrated below in a dialogue between a social worker and a college student who has just learned that he failed a math exam.

Client: "I cannot believe I am so stupid. I had a B average in math and got an F on the last test. I might as well leave school and get a job as a dishwasher. I am a complete failure. I don't deserve to be in school."

Worker: "Wait a minute! You have said before you wanted to learn how to stop putting yourself down. Let's try something. Start by telling me again what you are feeling and thinking right now."

Client: "Well, I just can't pass math tests. I'm stupid. I am embarrassed and I hate myself. I am never going to get through college. My parents are going to kill me for this. This is the worst possible thing that could have happened. My future is down the drain. Everything is just awful."

Worker: "Let's take a look at that kind of self-talk. Try to recognize what you are saying to yourself; notice your extreme language. Let's take a look at the way things are in reality. Is it true you cannot pass math tests?"

Client:	"Well, not really. I passed all of them before this one and I still have a B average in college."
Worker:	"Are your parents really going to kill you?"
Client:	"Well, no, but they will be disappointed."
Worker:	"Is failing a test really the worst possible thing that could happen to you?"
Client:	"Well, no, but it seems pretty awful right now."
Worker:	"Does failing this test really mean you have no future?"
Client:	"Well, I still have a future. I know what you are saying, and I agree that I am overreacting. But I don't know how to put a lid on those thoughts and feelings."
Worker:	"Do this for me. Repeat outloud the truth—the reality—of your situation, which is as follows: I flunked one math test. My parents will be unhappy. I have a B average in college. I can remain in college. My life is not over."
Client:	(repeats above)
Worker:	"Now take a couple of deep breaths and relax. Now say that outloud again, three times."
Client:	(client follows instruction)
Worker:	"How do you feel when you change your self-talk?"
Client:	"Well, I guess it isn't as bad as I thought. I feel less upset than before."
Worker:	"Our emotions react to what we tell ourselves about our experiences. If your self-talk is distorted, your emotions are going to be more extreme and more negative than they need to be. You can use this technique yourself when your feelings start to get out of control. Certainly, your situation is not as bad as it seemed when you were telling yourself all those awful things. But you still have to make some plans on how to prepare for your next math test. Now let's talk about that."

Selected Bibliography

Emery, Gary. *A New Beginning: How You Can Change You Life Through Cognitive Therapy.* New York: Simon & Schuster, 1981.

McMullin, Rian. *Handbook of Cognitive Therapy Techniques.* New York: W. W. Norton, 1986.

Wodarski, John, and Pamela Harris. "Adolescent Suicide: A Review of Influences and the Means of Prevention." *Social Work* 32 (November–December 1987):477–83.

12.9   *The Empty Chair*

Purpose: To help the client understand his or her feelings toward self or a significant other.

Discussion: The *empty-chair technique*, sometimes called the double-chair technique, is borrowed from Gestalt therapy. It is usually used to clarify the issues involved in an interpersonal conflict. It helps the client view the conflict from a different angle and gain insight into why he or she is feeling and behaving in a certain way. Some skilled practitioners are able to use the technique to clarify intrapersonal conflict.

The social worker may elect to employ this technique after recognizing a specific conflict that needs to be explored with the client. To get started, the worker pulls up an empty chair and places it opposite the client. The chair "becomes" the person or situation with which the client is in conflict. The client is asked to speak to the chair, explaining his or her perceptions and feelings. The client is then asked to sit on the chair (assuming the role of that person or situation) and respond to what was just said. The client may move back and forth several times throughout this dialogue. The worker uses other interviewing techniques to explore the exchange as it unfolds.

As an example of application, consider Mary, a forty-year-old woman, who has exhaustingly high housekeeping standards. Even though she does not enjoy housework, she spends many hours each day cleaning all rooms in her house, including her children's rooms and the garage. When asked how she became so devoted to cleaning and housework, Mary says that her mother greatly emphasized the importance of housework. The worker pulls up an empty chair and asks Mary to sit on it, assume the role of her mother, and tell Mary about the importance of doing housework. In the role of her mother, Mary explains that cleanliness is next to Godliness, that the oldest child should take care of the younger ones, and that a good wife is devoted to her home. Then, the worker has Mary switch chairs, become herself, and respond to what her "mother" had to say. Her first response is, "Yes, ma'am." Further exploration reveals that this response covers much hostility. What Mary really wants to say aloud is, "No, I don't want to do it. I am tired of working all the time. I am tired of doing things for other people." The worker then uses the empty chair to represent Mary's husband and invites Mary to express her feelings to him. During the course of this dialogue, Mary may realize that, as an adult, she now has some choices that she did not have as a child. Moreover, she realizes that she has never told her husband how she feels.

The technique can be adapted to many situations. In the hands of a skilled social worker, it can be very powerful. It can be combined effectively with behavioral rehearsal and role reversal techniques.

Selected Bibliography

Corey, Gerald. *Theory and Practice of Counseling and Psychotherapy*. 3rd ed. Monterey, Calif.: Brooks/Cole, 1986.

Fagan, Joen, and Irma Shepherd. *Gestalt Therapy Now: Theory, Techniques, Applications*. Ben Lomond, Calif.: Science and Behavior Books, 1970.

Sherman, Robert, and Norman Fredman. *Handbook of Structured Techniques in Marriage and Family Therapy*. New York: Brunner/Mazel, 1986.

Purpose: To increase the client's self-awareness, especially in regard to self-imposed barriers to change.

Discussion: Egan (1975) has described confrontation as "a responsible unmasking of the discrepancies, distortions, games and smoke screens the client uses to hide both from self understanding and from constructive behavioral change" (p. 158). In his more recent writings, Egan (1990) concludes that the word *challenge* is now preferred to the word *confrontation*. He defines a challenge as "an invitation to examine internal and external behavior if it is found to be self defeating, harmful to others, or both and to change the behavior" (p. 184).

A challenge or confrontation is initiated by the social worker. Thus, its focus will depend on the worker's professional judgment as to what changes are essential for a client and what stands in the way of those changes. Most often the challenge will focus on the client's avoidance or self-deception, such as failure to acknowledge or "own" an obvious problem; rationalizations, evasions, distortions, and game playing; unwillingness to recognize consequences of one's behavior; discrepancies between what the client says and what he or she does; unwillingness to take steps to correct a problem or deal with an important issue.

For a challenge to be effective, it must be done with concern for the client's feelings and perceptions. The worker must avoid using this technique when angry or frustrated with the client. Egan (1975) explains that the motive of the professional "should be to help the client, not to be right, not to punish, to get back at the client, or to put him in his place" (p. 166). Highly defensive clients will usually reject its message by rationalizing, verbally attacking the worker or minimizing the importance of the situation. If challenged, depressed clients may withdraw from the relationship. Several guidelines need to be considered in the use of this technique.

1. Do not challenge when you are feeling angry or frustrated. Unless you have a genuine concern for the client, its use may be little more than an expression of frustration or a desire to punish a difficult client.

2. Do not challenge or confront a client if you cannot or do not intend to become more deeply involved. Once offered, it is the responsibility of the worker to help the client deal nondefensively with the message, to understand it and to consider what it means for future choices and behavior. Unless you have the time to help the client make use of this information, do not use this technique.

3. A confrontation or challenge offered by someone for whom the client has no positive feelings will have no beneficial impact whatsoever. It will be effective only if the client feels care and respect from the social worker and if the client has similar feelings toward the worker. If those feelings are not there, the information will be discounted.

4. Couple the challenging message with positive observations about the client. In other words, present the message within a context of recognizing and supporting the client's strengths.

5. Make sure your message is descriptive and nonjudgmental. Be prepared to give a detailed description of the client's self-destructive or negative behavior, and provide concrete examples of how this behavior creates problems. Vague, general statements are often misunderstood. Moreover, judgmental statements tend to trigger anger, whereas descriptive statements provide information that can be used in problem-solving efforts.

6. Present the observations or data on which your inferences are based. For example, an observation should be stated directly: "I saw you..." or "You told me...." An inference is the conclusion based on your observations. Because an inference is really an opinion, it should be stated tentatively: "Because of what I have seen you do, it seems to me that..." or "I sense that...." For example, if the confrontation focuses on self-defeating behavior, present descriptions of the behavior before explaining how the behavior is counterproductive for the client and make sure the client understands the distinction between your observations and your inferences.

7. Use "I-messages" throughout the challenge. They generate much less resistance than "You-messages."

Selected Bibliography

Cormier, William, and L. Sherilyn Cormier. *Interviewing Strategies for Helpers*. Monterey, Calif.: Brooks/Cole, 1985.
Egan, Gerald. *The Skilled Helper*. Monterey, Calif.: Brooks/Cole, 1975.
————. *The Skilled Helper*. 4th ed. Monterey, Calif.: Brooks/Cole, 1990.
Hepworth, Dean, and Jo Ann Larsen. *Direct Social Work Practice*. 2nd ed. Homewood, Ill.: The Dorsey Press, 1986.

12.11   *Reframing*

Purpose: To assist the client in viewing the behavior of significant others from a different perspective and in a more positive light.

Discussion: *Reframing,* sometimes called *relabeling* or *redefining,* is a technique used to help a client modify the meaning he or she assigns to a particular event or behavior. Its purpose is to gently persuade a client that the event or behavior can be viewed in a different and more positive light. In other words, it is designed to alter a client's perspective.

Reframing is especially useful in work with persons having interpersonal conflicts, such as a couple or family. Its use encourages family members to reexamine their definitions of the problem and their beliefs about why others are behaving as they do. It promotes interpersonal understanding and helps each person feel more favorable about the other. When a person perceives things in a new way, he or she usually feels and behaves differently.

The following example illustrates a social worker's use of reframing.

Foster parent: I get so upset with Mary (foster child). So often she blows up and gets angry with me. But I haven't done anything to make her angry!

Social worker: That must be frustrating—to know you do not deserve to be the target of her anger. As you know, Mary is an angry child because of the severe abuse she experienced. But, in one way of looking at it, Mary is paying you a big compliment. When she gets angry in your presence she is demonstrating that she feels safe with you and trusts that you will not retaliate and hurt her.

An alternative to the social worker providing the client with a new meaning is to encourage the client to "brainstorm" several different interpretations. For example, the worker might begin by explaining that there is a difference between the factual reality of a particular life experience and the "story" an individual tells himself or herself about that experience. The client will usually agree that five people will most likely tell five slightly different stories about the same experience. Using that agreement as a foundation, the worker can encourage the client to come up with additional "stories" (interpretations) that could be told about the particular behavior being discussed. After thinking up several alternative perceptions, the client will usually soften his or her position and at least acknowledge that there may indeed be a different way to interpret the behavior of others. The process of reframing recognizes the wisdom of the first century philosopher Epictetus, who said, "It is not the things themselves which trouble us, but the opinions that we have about these things."

Selected Bibliography

Minuchin, Salvador, and H. Charles Fishman. *Family Therapy Techniques.* Cambridge, Mass.: Harvard University Press, 1981.

Watzlawick, Paul, John Weakland, and Richard Fisch. *Change: Principles of Problem Formulation and Problem Resolution.* New York: W. W. Norton, 1974.

12.12 Family Sculpting

Purpose: To help a client or family system understand their own feelings and behavior and those of other family members by acting out significant family events.

Discussion: *Family sculpting* is a technique designed to help a client (within a group session) or a client family reenact and thus relive some important aspects of their family's behavior. It is a tool for assessment as well as treatment. The term *sculpting* is an artistic analogy that describes how one of the family members physically arranges or molds the family in a way that conveys a certain meaning, much like a sculptor working with clay.

The social worker begins by explaining the technique to the family. Baron and Feeney (1976) offer a sample explanation.

> "We're going to do something a little different today that will help us learn what's happening in the family. First of all, it involves everyone getting up out of their seats (worker stands as an example). Now we need someone who will make a family sculpture. What I mean is, I want someone, without talking, to arrange the family into a picture which if I were walking through the park would tell me something about who you are. Who's close to whom, who is far away, might be a way to start. The rest of the family has to let the sculptor sculpt. That means being as much like clay as possible. Some sculptors have sculpted the parents with Mom standing on Dad ruling the roost. Others show us kids who are still sitting on Momma's lap even though they are teenagers. You get the idea. Who wants to try it?" (p. 82)

After such an explanation, someone will usually volunteer to do the first sculpture. In the beginning, this family member may need support and encouragement from the worker. The worker watches to make sure that the sculptor really sculpts and does not just verbalize instructions. Verbalizing can result in arguments and keeps members from touching. Playful touching and a bit of silliness are some of the positive aspects of this technique.

Hartman (1984) offers the following guidance, once a family member has begun the sculpting:

> It may be suggested that the sculptor imagine the family at home in the evenings. Where will each person be? What will they be doing? Chairs and other props may be used. Placement of the members should include not only where they are in relationship to other members but also where they are looking and how their bodies are positioned.
>
> As the sculpture develops, family members may object because they see themselves in the family system in a different way. For example, if a child placed dad in the corner behind the newspaper he might not like that picture of himself, nor what his son or daughter is communicating through the sculpture. It is important, however, to allow the sculptor to finish without interruption and to assure other family members that they will be able to sculpt the family later in the way they see it if they so wish.
>
> The worker should give the sculptor support and help as needed, encouraging him or her to take whatever time is needed and asking enabling questions like, "Do you want mom to be looking in any particular direction?" or "Is that the way you want it? Are there any changes you want to make?"
>
> After the sculptor has completed the sculpture to his or her satisfaction, and taken his or her place in the tableau, the worker assumes the role of monitor and while the actors maintain their positions asks each member how they are experiencing their place in the sculpture. This invitation surfaces disagreements on the part of the family members as to how they see the family. It surfaces how they are feeling about current family structure and may expose points of stress and tension. (p. 24)*

*Reprinted by special permission of CWLA from *Working with Adoptive Families: Beyond Placement,* 1984.

In a variation of the family sculpture, the sculpting member gives each person a sentence to say, something typical of their relationship. This further reflects how the sculptor sees himself or herself in the family.

This is a flexible technique. The instructions for a family sculpture can be done within the context of the family's past or present. It can also vary from visualizing the ideal to portraying the most feared circumstances. And the technique can be used as part of a group therapy session. In this latter application, the sculptor chooses group members to play the roles of the sculptor's family, including the sculptor. Once the sculptor is developed, the worker asks the client to assume his or her own role and everyone discusses their feelings and perceptions.

Selected Bibliography

Baron, Roger, and Floyd Feeney. *Juvenile Diversion Through Family Counseling.* Washington, D.C.: National Institute of Law Enforcement and Criminal Justice, U.S. Government Printing Office, 1976.

Hartman, Ann. *Working with Adoptive Families: Beyond Placement.* New York: Child Welfare League of America, 1984.

Hartman, Ann, and Joan Laird. *Family Centered Social Work Practice.* New York: The Free Press, 1983.

12.13 *Homework Assignments*

Purpose: To assist the client in learning a new behavior by assigning specific tasks and activities to be worked on between counseling sessions.

Discussion: Learning a new skill or developing a new behavioral pattern is essential to the solution of many problems in social functioning. Moreover, the new skill and/or behavior needs to be practiced in the client's natural environment, not just during sessions with the social worker. The purpose of homework is to facilitate such learning.

The term ***homework*** refers to assignments given to the client that are to be carried out by the client between sessions. Needless to say, homework should be directly related to the client-worker contract and the objectives of intervention. The worker and client should jointly select and plan homework. It is important that the homework make sense to the client. For example, given a client whose problem revolves around low self-esteem and an inability to interact comfortably with others, a homework assignment might be to strike up at least two conversations per day while riding to and from work on the bus.

When using homework assignments, the worker should give the client a precise set of instructions. Often, these need to be written. A worker can prepare the written instructions before the session. If possible, they should be written on NCR (no carbon required) paper or duplicated so both the client and the worker will have a copy.

Shelton and Ackerman (1974) explain that homework instructions contain one or more of the following:

1. *A do statement.* "Read, practice, observe, say, count . . . some kind of homework."
2. *A quantity statement.* "Talk three times about . . . ; spend thirty minutes three times . . . ; give four compliments per day . . . ; write a list of at least ten . . . "
3. *A record statement.* "Count and record the number of compliments; each time he hits, mark a _____ on the chart; whenever that thought comes to you, write a _____ on the . . . "
4. *A bring statement.* "Bring . . . your list; the chart; the cards; your spouse . . . to the next appointment."
5. *A contingency statement.* "Call for your next appointment after you have done . . . ; for each activity you attend, one dollar will be deducted . . . ; each minute spent doing _____ will earn you _____; one-tenth of your penalty deposit will be forfeited for each assignment not completed." (p. 16).

Homework is not appropriate for all clients. As a technique, it works best with an intervention approach that emphasizes client training and skill building. The use of homework presumes that the client is willing to accept direction from the worker and willing to practice new behaviors outside sessions with the social worker. Thus, a client must be willing and able to work independently.

Selected Bibliography

Hudson, Barbara, and Geraldine MacDonald. *Behavioural Social Work.* Chicago: The Dorsey Press, 1986.

Reid, William. *Family Problem Solving.* New York: Columbia University Press, 1985.

Shelton, John, and J. Mark Ackerman. *Homework in Counseling and Psychotherapy.* Springfield, Ill.: Charles C. Thomas, 1974.

Shelton, John, and Rona Levy. *Behavioral Assignments and Treatment Compliance.* Champaign, Ill.: Research Press, 1981.

12.14 Envelope Budgeting

Purpose: To assist the client in money management.

Discussion: Many of the clients served by social workers are economically poor. They find it difficult to stretch a very limited income to cover the bare essentials. Most of their money transactions are in cash; few have checking accounts. *Envelope budgeting* can be taught to clients who need a simple approach to cash management. This technique provides some structure and a means of monitoring cash outflow but has the flexibility needed to handle emergencies.

The first step in setting up this budgeting system is for the client to identify the key categories of expenditure: rent, food, clothing, transportation, household supplies, and so on. The next step is to determine how many dollars need to be spent for each category during a particular spending cycle, such as a one- or two-week period. An envelope is prepared and labeled for each category, and all of the envelopes are kept together in a box. In the "food envelope," for example, the client places the money allotted for food.

As money is removed from an envelope and spent, the client has a tangible measure of cash outflow and the balance that remains. The client is encouraged to resist the temptation to shift money from one category to another, but this may sometimes be necessary. When the client obtains additional income, cash is again placed in the envelopes for the new spending cycle.

This simple money management technique is especially useful with clients who have limited arithmetic skills, such as adults who are mentally retarded. The technique can also be used with clients who have only counting skills. Subtraction and addition skills are helpful but not essential. This budgeting technique helps people plan and monitor expenditures but it is not a permanent solution for clients who are overwhelmed by debt or have expenditures that far exceed their income. In such cases, more complex approaches—such as consumer credit counseling, debt consolidation, or even bankruptcy—may be necessary.

Selected Bibliography

Family Economics Research Group. *A Guide to Budgeting for the Young Couple.* U.S. Department of Agriculture Home and Garden Bulletin, No. 98. Washington, D.C.: U.S. Government Printing Office, October 1979.

Feldman, Frances. *The Family in Today's Money World.* 2nd ed. New York: Family Service Association of America, 1976.

12.15   *Managing Personal Debt*

Purpose: To assist the client in addressing bills and personal debt.

Discussion: The client with too many bills and too little money usually experiences much stress. There is no easy way to climb out of debt, but the client can do a number of things to get control of the problem. Offer the following guidance to a client who has serious financial problems:

1. If at all possible, avoid purchasing new items on credit until existing debts are paid. Accumulating additional debts makes the problem worse and even more difficult to control. The overuse of credit cards and revolving credit accounts are common sources of debt.

2. Eliminate revolving credit accounts at stores so you are not tempted to buy something every time you go to the store. Also avoid using credit cards except for identification. If the overuse of credit cards is responsible for your financial problems, destroy them and use only cash. If you must continue to use credit cards, buy only what you know you can pay for within thirty days and thereby avoid charges for interest.

3. Make a careful analysis of what you owe. Begin by making four columns on a piece of paper. In column 1, list all of the items for which you are billed on a regular basis (usually monthly), such as loan and credit card bills, utilities, rent or house payments, car payments, dental and medical, phone, insurance, and the like. In column 2, list the expected monthly payment for each item in column 1. In column 3, list the amount actually paid each month. In column 4, total the amount owed for all items. Begin your analysis by marking all items for which interest is charged; these items should be come high-priority targets for payment because added charges for interest constantly add to the debt problem. If you must skip payments or reduce the amount paid, do so on items that do not involve interest charges. Also, prioritize the interest-related bills according to the amount still owed; concentrate on paying off those on which the least amount is owed, which will eliminate all credit charges associated with that bill and free up money for other bills. Completely paying off a bill also provides a feeling of making progress on debt reduction and this record of progress can be used to argue for payment extensions because it demonstrates your willingness and ability to pay bills.

4. If you cannot pay a bill, do not avoid the problem. Do not expect old debts or past due payments to be forgotten or forgiven. A missed payment must still be paid and paid with interest. Never miss a payment without first explaining the problem to your creditor. If the creditor understands your situation and believes you intend to pay, the creditor may be willing to make some adjustment. Be sure to describe the actions you are taking to solve your financial problems. Some lenders and businesses have emergency plans that can provide temporary relief. They might be able to rewrite your loan at a lower rate of interest or spread the loan over a larger time period, both of which will lower the monthly payment.

5. Do not avoid bill collectors. A frank discussion may result in an acceptable solution. Remember that collection agencies do not really want your possessions because then they have to go through the trouble of selling them. Moreover, they do not want to do anything that will cause you to lose what little income you do have. What they really want is money. If you can demonstrate a genuine desire to pay and do pay even a little each month, a creditor will sometimes find this acceptable. If you avoid bill collectors or show no effort to pay the bill, they seldom hesitate to do whatever is legal to recover something of value and make your life uncomfortable.

6. Sell those possessions you do not need. Garage sales, flea markets, auctions, and pawn shops are ways of selling unneeded items and securing some additional money. Consider selling your car unless it is needed for work-related transportation. Getting rid of a car is especially important if you are buying it on installments. A car loan creates a vicious cycle of debt because by the time it is finally paid off, the car must often be replaced. Look seriously for a less expensive means of transportation.

7. Make use of credit-counseling resources, but before using a particular program, be sure to find out: (a) who sponsors the program; (b) what, if any, charges are involved; and (c) how the program operates. If possible, use the services offered by nonprofit agencies. Do not confuse credit-counseling services available for little or no cost with the for-profit businesses that do debt pooling and debt adjustment for a high fee. A good consumer credit-counseling program can reduce your stress and worry, help you develop the self-discipline needed to handle bills and debt, and help you avoid bankruptcy.

8. When other less drastic methods fail to impact the debt problem, loan consolidation or bankruptcy must be considered. The following descriptions of these approaches are based on Goetting (1985). When utilizing a *consolidation loan* strategy, you take out a new loan and immediately pay off all bills. The single payment on this new loan is designed to be smaller than the total of the other monthly payments, and it is easier to keep track of payments on just one loan. However, a consolidation loan stretches your payments over a longer period of time. You must still pay the whole amount before you are debt free, and the longer time involved means you will pay more interest. Another disadvantage of a consolidation loan is that it is easy to forget how much is owed overall, and you may be tempted to take on new credit obligations because the new loan payments seem small in comparison to your previous bills.

9. *Bankruptcy* may be necessary in cases of extreme financial difficulty when creditors are unwilling to renegotiate debts, when a consolidation loan cannot be obtained, and when informal loans cannot be obtained from family or friends. For individuals and married couples, the Federal Bankruptcy Act provides two types of bankruptcy. The most common type of bankruptcy is a Chapter 7—*straight bankruptcy* or liquidation proceeding. After a petition is filed with the U.S. District Court, a bankruptcy judge notifies the people to whom you own money (creditors) of their rights to file a claim against you and to question you on the witness stand. Creditors have an opportunity to object to your not having to pay what you owe. If there are no objections, the bankruptcy judge will grant what is called a "discharge in bankruptcy," which relieves you from legal liability for the payment of all debts owed at the time of bankruptcy. All of your possessions, with the exception of those exempt by state or federal law, are turned over to a trustee to be sold. The proceeds from the sale of your possessions are distributed to the creditors who filed claims. The remaining debt is legally erased. Debts such as child support or alimony, taxes, unlisted debts, and/or debts obtained under false pretenses cannot be discharged.

Another bankruptcy option, called a Chapter 13, or *wage earner plan,* allows you to keep your possessions while paying off your debts. You develop a plan for repaying your debts over a period of three years (sometimes five years) and if your plan is approved by the judge, your creditors must stop all collection efforts. They must also stop charging you interest and late charges on most types of debts. Each payday, a fixed amount of your wages is turned over to a court-appointed trustee, who then gives it to creditors. Creditors will usually agree to this plan because they are more likely to be paid under this arrangement than under straight bankruptcy.

Bankruptcy is a complex legal process and has a number of negative consequences. For example, a bankruptcy remains on your credit report for ten years and jeopardizes your credit rating. A person considering bankruptcy should seek the advice of an attorney and/or a credit-counseling agency. Information on the bankruptcy process can be obtained from the Administrative Office of the U.S. Courts, Division of Bankruptcy, Washington, D.C. 20544.

Selected Bibliography

Goetting, Marsha. *Debt Free by ??: Do It Yourself Money Control Program.* Bozeman, Mont.: U.S. Department of Agriculture Cooperative Extension Service, July 1985 (Bulletin 1261).

Goetting, Marsha, Anne Wiprud, and Mary Maifeld. *Taking Control During a Financial Crisis.* Bozeman, Mont.: U.S. Department of Agriculture Cooperative Extension Service, September 1986 (Bulletin 1342).

Porter, Sylvia. *New Money Book for the 80s.* New York: Hearst Corporation, 1980.

12.16   *Decision-Making Worksheets*

Purpose: To assist the client in considering alternatives and making a decision.

Discussion: Helping clients make difficult decisions is an important social work activity. A social worker familiar with key issues and common feelings surrounding a particular decision can facilitate the client's decision making by constructing a ***decision-making worksheet,*** which provides direction during the decision-making process and focuses the client's attention on factors that need to be considered prior to arriving at a decision.

Figure 12.1 contains excerpts from a decision-making worksheet designed for use with pregnant teenagers considering whether to relinquish their babies for adoption. As can be seen from this sample, a worksheet is simply a format for raising questions and helping the client analyze his or her situation. Obviously, skilled interviewing could accomplish the same thing, but the worksheet can provide added structure. In addition, a well-written document can be used as a homework assignment between sessions.

Figure 12.1 Sample Decision-Making Worksheet

Planning for My Baby

I. Questions about my relationship with my baby's father.
   A. Can I count on him for financial support?
   B. Can I count on him for emotional support?
   C. Has my relationship with him changed since I got pregnant?
   (and so on)

II. Questions about my relationship with my parents.
   A. What do my parents want me to do?
   B. Can I go against their wishes?
   C. If my mother helps take care of my baby, is it possible the baby will become "her baby?"
   (and so on)

III. Questions about my life after having the baby.
   A. If I keep the baby, how will this affect future dating, marriage, and children?
   B. If I give my baby up for adoption, how will this affect my future dating, marriage, and children?
   (and so on)

IV. A daydream exercise.
   A. If I could pick the ideal time for having a baby, when would it be? Where would I be? What would the baby's father be like?
   B. How does the above ideal situation compare with my real situation?
   (and so on)

V. Picturing myself.
   A. Draw a picture of yourself one year ago. Around your picture, indicate in words or pictures the things that were important to you then. What were your activities, how did you use your time? What were your goals and aspirations one year ago?
   B. Think about yourself now. Change the above picture of yourself one year ago to fit things today. Cross out those activities in which you are no longer involved. Have your goals and aspirations changed?
   C. Draw a picture of yourself one year from now. Again, around your picture, write in those things that you will be involved in one year from now. How will you spend your time? In one year, what will be your goals and aspirations?
   (and so on)

Source: Lutheran Social Services, pp. 1–2, 4–5.

Selected Bibliography

Lutheran Social Services. "Decision-Making Plans for the Baby." Missoula, Mont.: Lutheran Social Services. Mimeo.

Roles, Patricia. *Facing Teenage Pregnancy: A Handbook for the Pregnant Teen.* New York: Child Welfare League of America, 1984.

————. *Saying Goodbye to a Baby: A Book about Loss and Grief in Adoption.* New York: Child Welfare League of America, 1988.

Winkler, Robin, Dirk Brown, Margaret vonKeppel, and Amy Blanchard. *Clinical Practice in Adoption.* New York: Pergamon Press, 1988.

Purpose: To assist the client in problem-solving efforts by making a clear distinction between the problem to be solved and possible solutions.

Discussion: When helping a client solve a problem, it is often necessary to distinguish between the problem and the means of solving that problem. For example, a client may request a worker's assistance on figuring out how she can get money to buy a car because she needs to get to and from a new job. In this case, the client has confused means and ends. The client's real problem is a lack of transportation, not the lack of a car. Buying a car is only one of several means of securing needed transporation; others might include public transportation, paying a private car owner for a ride, walking, or taking a taxi.

A simple listing may help the client keep the ends and means separate. The following list was developed during an interview with a young single mother who had requested foster care placement for her child because she could not care for the child while holding a job.

End	Means
Child care while mother works in order to secure money to support self and child.	Licensed daycare center
	Paid babysitter
	Informal babysitting exchange with friend
	Babysitting (relative)
	Change jobs or hours of work
	AFDC

As can be seen, once the client's presenting problem was redefined as a need for child care, rather than a need for placement, several new options emerged as a means of solving the problem.

Selected Bibliography

Kaufman, Roger. *Identifying and Solving Problems.* La Jolla, Calif.: University Associates, 1976.
Maple, Frank. *Shared Decision Making.* Beverly Hills: Sage, 1977.
Priestley, Philip, James McGuire, David Flegg, Valerie Hemsley, and David Welham. *Social Skills and Personal Problem Solving: A Handbook of Methods.* London: Travistock Publication, 1978.

12.18   *Brainstorming*

Purpose: To help a client identify several possible solutions to a problem.

Discussion: Problem solving includes the important step of identifying all possible alternatives or solutions. Too often, some potential solutions are overlooked or not seriously considered because they do not fit preconceived notions or expectations. Habits of thought and rigidity of thinking can limit creativity in problem solving. The technique of ***brainstorming*** is designed to overcome this limitation. It can be applied to any problem for which there may be a range of solutions. The objective of brainstorming is to free persons temporarily from self-criticism and the criticism of others in order to generate creative and imaginative solutions to a specific problem. However, it should not be used until the problem has been clearly defined. Only confusion will result when the technique is applied to a vaguely stated problem.

A successful brainstorming session will identify a wide variety of solutions. Many may be unrealistic, but it is only after all possible alternatives have been identified that the participants are permitted to evaluate the proposed solutions in search of those that are feasible.

A worker setting up a brainstorming session will give the participants several instructions:

1. Participants are encouraged to develop a large number of solutions. The goal is to obtain a quantity of solutions—quality will be determined later.
2. Participants are encouraged to be freewheeling in their thinking. Even wild ideas are welcomed and accepted without judgment.
3. Participants are encouraged to combine and elaborate on the solutions that are offered.
4. Participants cannot criticize or evaluate one another's proposed solutions.

During the brainstorming session, a recorder writes down all of the ideas as fast as they come up. If possible, do this on a blackboard or flipchart so the visual record stimulates further ideas. The leader of the brainstorming session should quickly stop any criticism of ideas, whether verbal or implied by tone of voice or nonverbal gesture. Also, the group leader needs to keep the participants focused on the problem or issue under consideration. A brainstorming session, plus the evaluation of each proposed solution (fifty might be generated in a single session), could take several hours. Thus, brainstorming should not be used if adequate time is not available.

Brainstorming is most often used in work with groups or committees, but many workers adapt its principles for use in one-on-one counseling sessions. Although brainstorming is most often used when a group is in search of a problem's solution; it can be used in other phases of the problem-solving process, such as: What information do we need? Where or how can we get this information? How will we evaluate proposed solutions?

Selected Bibliography

Johnson, David, and Frank Johnson. *Joining Together: Group Theory and Group Skills.* Englewood Cliffs, N.J.: Prentice-Hall, 1975.

Zastrow, Charles. *Social Work with Groups.* 2nd ed. Chicago: Nelson-Hall Publishers, 1989.

Purpose: To help the client make a decision when there are four or more options.

Discussion: The *priorities-weighting grid* is a decision-making tool that can help an individual, family, or small group make a difficult decision by systematically examining each option in relation to every other option. It is useful when those who need to make a decision have numerous options but cannot see that any one choice is better than another. Essentially, this technique moves the client through a series of forced choices; from this process, the preferred option will emerge.

This technique can be used with a client during an interview, or taught to clients so they can use it at home to make personal and family decisions. The grid can focus on decisions as diverse as prioritizing one's personal values or something as mundane as deciding which of five used cars to buy. In this latter example, choices would have to be made between the relative importance of price, condition, size, and so on. The grid is not an effective tool if a choice is to be made between only two or three options.

Figure 12.2 is a sample priorities-weighting grid. Directions for completing the grid are on the next page.

Figure 12.2 Sample Priorities-Weighting Grid

Priorities	Priorities Grid	Options/Alternatives
1.	1 1 1 1 1 1 1 1 1 1 _____	1. _____
	2 3 4 5 6 7 8 9 10	
2.	2 2 2 2 2 2 2 2 2 _____	2. _____
	3 4 5 6 7 8 9 10	
3.	3 3 3 3 3 3 3 3 _____	3. _____
	4 5 6 7 8 9 10	
4.	4 4 4 4 4 4 4 _____	4. _____
	5 6 7 8 9 10	
5.	5 5 5 5 5 5 _____	5. _____
	6 7 8 9 10	
6.	6 6 6 6 6 _____	6. _____
	7 8 9 10	
7.	7 7 7 7 _____	7. _____
	8 9 10	
8.	8 8 8 _____	8. _____
	9 10	
9.	9 9 _____	9. _____
	10	
10.	_____	10. _____

1. List the options you are considering down the right side of the page. Assign each a number; order is not important.
2. Compare option 1 with option 2, circling your preference on the grid. Next, compare option 1 with option 3; again, circle your preferred option on the grid.
3. When you are finished comparing option 1 with every option listed, proceed in the same manner comparing option 2 with 3, then 4, and so on through the list.
4. When finished, count the number of times you circled each number. Remember to count both horizontally and vertically.
5. Finally, list your options in the priorities column on the left side of the paper according to their score: highest number as 1, lowest as 10. In the case of a tie score, examine the grid and determine which option you chose when you compared the two.

Selected Bibliography

Carkhuff, Robert. *The Art of Problem-Solving*. Amherst, Mass.: Human Resource Development Press, 1973.

12.20   *Decision-Making Matrix*

Purpose: To help the client make a decision when there are just two or three options.

Discussion: Many of the problems faced by clients revolve around decision making. For example, a sixty-year-old woman must decide whether to place her eighty-three-year-old mother in a nursing home or try once again to care for her at home. Another example might be a young unmarried mother must decide between keeping her child or relinquishing it for adoption. Decision making is troublesome for most people; it can be especially difficult for the client who has multiple problems and is under much stress. Many individuals either avoid making decisions or they make decisions impulsively without considering the advantages and disadvantages of each option.

A simple *decision-making matrix* can help a client think through the pros and cons of each option and arrive at a decision. The matrix has three columns: (1) Alternative, (2) Cost, and (3) Result/Benefit. In the Alternative column, the client lists the two or three options being considered. Then, across from each alternative, in the Cost and Result/Benefit columns, the client describes both the drawbacks (costs) and the advantages (results/benefits) associated with each option. Finally, after all the pros and cons have been outlined on the matrix, the client compares each option and makes a decision.

Figure 12.3 Sample Decision-Making Matrix

Alternative	Cost	Result/Benefit
1. Return to John	a. Abuse would probably continue b. Children are fearful c. Would have to face same hard decisions in the future d. I could get seriously hurt or killed e. Medical costs	a. Preserve family b. Hard decision is delayed until later c. Would have place to live and money d. John says he cares for me
2. Leave John and end the marriage	a. Fear of the unknown—(I need to be with somebody) b. Trauma of divorce for me and kids c. Would have less money to live on d. Might be forced on AFDC e. Legal costs f. Custody battle over children	a. Abuse, pain, and fear would end b. Decision would have been made and I could try to put my life together c. Children would be less nervous and upset d. I could find out if I can function on my own e. Opportunity for fresh start

Figure 12.3 is an example of a matrix completed by a social worker and a battered wife client during an interview focusing on the decision of whether the client should return to her husband or end her marriage.

Selected Bibliography

Kaufman, Roger. *Identifying and Solving Problems.* La Jolla, Calif.: University Associates, 1976.

12.21 Indirect Discussion of Self in Small Groups

Purpose: To make it easier for group participants to discuss personal concerns.

Discussion: This technique is designed to stimulate and structure small-group discussion of the participants' problems and concerns while at the same time protecting the individual client's privacy. It allows clients to discuss matters that they would not ordinarily share with others. Moreover, this technique can engage a reluctant client in group discussion. Essentially, the technique calls for each participant to respond to a set of questions by writing answers on 3 × 5 cards.

The unsigned cards are collected, shuffled, and randomly passed out to the group members. The members then discuss and analyze the responses, problems, or concerns found on the cards.

To begin the process, each participant is given three 3 × 5 cards and told to draw a postage-size square in the upper right-hand corner. In this square, each card is labeled A, B, or C. The participant will use each card to write a response to a specific question: question A, question B, question C. Instruct the participants not to put their names on the cards. And before they write, tell them exactly how the cards will be collected, shuffled, and then redistributed randomly for discussion. Warn participants against writing a response in a way that might reveal their identity. However, encourage the group to be honest in answering the questions, since the identity of the person writing the card will be protected.

The social worker using the technique preselects the questions. The following is a sample set of stem sentences used in a group session with physically abusing parents.:

On Card A: (complete the statement) "Before a hitting episode, I feel ... "
On Card B: (complete the statement) "The thing I feel most after a hitting episode is ... "
On Card C: (complete the statement) "One thing I could do to decrease the hitting episodes is ... "

The technique is also useful in training sessions. The next sample is a set of stem sentences used in a training session for foster parents and social workers concerned with improving their work with the biological parents of children in foster care:

On Card A: (complete the statement) "In my work with biological parents, I find it most difficult to ... "
On Card B: (complete the statement) "I know I shouldn't have this negative feeling toward biological parents, but I feel ... "
On Card C: (complete the statement) "The thing that would help me most to improve my work with biological parents is ... "

After all of the participants have finished writing their responses, collect the cards in sequence: first, all of the A cards, then the Bs, then the C cards. Shuffle each stack separately. Then pass out all of the A cards randomly, then the Bs, then the Cs. This procedure ensures that each participant receives a response to each of the three questions or stem sentences.

The next step is to have small groups of three or four members, if part of a large group, study and discuss the cards they have been given. They might be asked to summarize what the cards seem to be saying. For example, the foster parents might be asked to study the cards and answer the following:

1. Identify the frustrations and difficulties experienced by foster parents in their work with biological parents.
2. Identify the possible causes of these difficulties.
3. Identify methods of improving relationships with biological parents.

After a small group has studied their cards, participants are encouraged to trade their cards with other small groups in order to obtain even more data. Typically, the participants discover that most of them share common worries, problems, and feelings. This can be reassuring. Use of the technique helps counteract feelings of isolation and the belief that "no one else feels like I do."

The technique works best in groups larger than about fifteen, but it can be adapted for use in smaller groups and even with families. When used with a small group, the social worker should also submit a set of cards. Sometimes, the worker can help things along by writing responses that are sure to attract the attention of group members.

Selected Bibliography

Horejsi, Charles. *Values and Attitudes in Child Welfare: A Training Manual.* Missoula, Mont.: University of Montana, Department of Social Work, 1982.

12.22   *Resolving Interpersonal Conflict*

Purpose: To assist people in resolving conflicts and disagreements.

Discussion: The social worker is frequently in the position of trying to help clients resolve conflicts (e.g., between parent and teenager, husband and wife, etc.) and sometimes in the position of trying to help two professionals resolve a conflict. An important first step in helping others resolve a conflict is to realize that the dynamics of the conflict may be complex and that the conflict is often about issues no one is mentioning. People often fight over a minor issue because they are afraid to face the real one. If true resolution is to take place, the real issue must be identified.

Bisno (1988, 31) alerts us to various motives behind a conflict by identifying six types of conflict: those characterized by a clash of opposing interests or commitments; those created in order to achieve some hidden purpose; those related to errors of attribution and unknowingly misdirected to the wrong party or wrong issue; those deliberately directed to the wrong party or wrong issue in order to avoid the real issue; those based on misperceptions, misunderstandings, and poor communications; and, finally, those created for the purpose of expressing hostility or other strong emotion.

A worker trying to mediate a conflict could keep several other guidelines in mind.

1. Do not take sides. Be fair and respect the views and feelings of everyone involved. Remind the parties in conflict of the things they share and already agree on, such as certain values, concern for a third party, desire to avoid further pain, and so on.

2. Appeal for a demonstration of mutual respect and a willingness to at least listen and try to understand differences in perception and needs. Attempt to get those in conflict to agree that during the discussion, they will avoid issuing threats, name calling, moralizing, attacking sensitive spots, or bringing up past hurts and disagreements that are unrelated to the current conflict.

3. Urge those in conflict to ask themselves four questions before they speak:
- Do I want to resolve this conflict or am I really after some other hidden goal that I am afraid to talk about?
- Is what I am going to say true, or is it an exaggeration or only a partial truth that will invite an angry response?
- Is what I am going to say relevant and pertinent to the issue we are discussing?
- Is what I am going to say constructive—something that will move us closer to mutual understanding?

4. Help those in conflict to clearly identify and define the problems and issues. But urge them to avoid taking a definite stand on what they want as a solution, for doing so simply sets the stage for a struggle of wills. Ask each person to state briefly his or her concerns and needs as clearly as possible. Ask the others to repeat what they have heard. If they have not understood, repeat this process. The objective here is to help each person understand what the other is really saying and to gain empathy for each other's perspective and feelings.

5. Use techniques of reflection, clarification, paraphrase, and summarization to assist each to express his or her point of view, needs, and concerns (see Chapter 6). Until these differences are made explicit, there will be no movement toward a solution. Help each to use "I-messages" in expressing his or her side in the conflict.

6. Once the issues are on the table and there is some degree of mutual understanding, use the concept of brainstorming to identify several potential solutions. Look for solutions or compromises that provide some benefits to both sides.

7. Throughout the discussion, constantly recognize and reinforce efforts to control anger, to understand the other party, and to honestly express needs and concerns—even if these are only feeble efforts.

Selected Bibliography

Bisno, Herb. *Managing Conflict.* Newbury Park, Calif.: Sage, 1988.
Folberg, Jay, and Alison Taylor. *Mediation: A Comprehensive Guide to Resolving Conflicts Without Litigation.* San Francisco: Jossey-Bass, 1986.
Stuart, Richard. *Helping Couples Change.* New York: The Guilford Press, 1980.

12.23 *Feelings List*

Purpose: To assist a client in the identification and expression of feelings.

Discussion: Many of the clients seen by social workers are persons who grew up in dysfunctional families (e.g., alcoholic, abusive, etc.) where they learned to suppress their feelings; often they were severely punished for expressing emotion or for asking the "wrong" questions. Many other clients were exposed to a childrearing pattern that allowed the expression of feelings but at the same time invalidated these feelings; for example, as when a mother tells her angry child, "You're not really angry, you're just tired." As these individuals grow older, they carry with them a tendency to suppress, misinterpret, or mistrust their own emotions and feelings. Many are unsure of their true feelings; many cannot distinguish one emotion from another and can speak of feelings in only broad terms such as *sad, glad, upset,* or *OK.*

Simplistic as it sounds, a written list of feeling words can help a client identify and express feelings during interview. As the client struggles to identify and sort out feelings, he or she is encouraged to review the list as an aid in finding the words needed to describe and express feelings. Below are sample feeling words drawn from lists used by Porter (1986), Wegscheider (1981), Black (1981), and Mayer (1983).

controlled	embarrassed	attached	abandoned
excited	courageous	worthless	serene
concerned	tender	secure	curious
manipulated	tough	lost	ashamed
hateful	sarcastic	protected	guilty
desperate	competitive	isolated	vulnerable
joyful	confident	relieved	apathetic
disloyal	fearful	detached	warm
attractive	assertive	defensive	unfeeling

Wegscheider (1981) offers several suggestions on how to use a feelings list:

Even . . . an incomplete list serves as a starting point from which we can begin to discriminate between some of the often mistaken pairs—differentiating between, say, shame and either embarrassment or guilt; between hurt and either hate or anger; between excitement, tension, and anxiety. I find the list works equally well with individuals and with groups, either peer groups or families. . . .

Here again I find some elementary teaching is helpful. I explain that everyone has feelings; they are part of being human. Though sometimes unpleasant, they are neither good or bad; they just are. It is what we do in response to them that is good or bad. We need to know clearly what we are feeling so we can act in a way that is healthy for ourselves and others. We also need to be able to share our feelings freely because they are our common denominator, the one place where people can truly connect. (p. 172)

If you believe the use of a "feelings list" would be helpful to your clients, we suggest that you select words that will be meaningful to persons served by your agency. Your client's age, life experience, culture, and educational level need to be considered when compiling a list.

Selected Bibliography

Black, Claudia. *It will Never Happen to Me.* Denver: MAC Publishing, 1981.

Mayer Adele. *Incest: A Treatment Manual for Therapy with Victims, Spouses and Offenders.* Homes Beach, Fla.: Learning Publications, 1983.

Porter, Eugene. *Treating the Young Male Victim of Sexual Assault.* Syracuse, N.Y.: Safer Society Press, 1986.

Wegscheider, Sharon. *Another Chance: Hope and Health for the Alcoholic Family.* Palo Alto, Calif.: Science and Behavior Book, 1981.

12.24 Client Advocacy

Purpose: To secure services that the client is entitled to but unable to obtain on his or her own.

Discussion: When the social worker assumes the role of client advocate, he or she speaks, argues, manipulates, bargains, and negotiates on behalf of the client. At the direct service level, an advocacy stance may be necessary in order to secure benefits or services that the client is entitled to but, for one reason or another, is unable to obtain. As compared to other tactics for securing services (e.g., referral/brokering, mediation), advocacy is essentially a confrontation. Because the worker's advocacy may threaten another professional or agency, the risks must be carefully considered. Remember these guidelines:

1. Make sure your client wants you to become his or her advocate. Do not engage in advocacy unless you have an explicit agreement with your client and he or she understands both the potential benefits and risks. To the greatest extent possible, involve your client in all decisions concerning the actions you will take. If possible, help your client to argue the case rather than speaking on his or her behalf.

2. Realize that your advocacy can damage your relationship or your agency's relationship with another agency or professional and that this damaged relationship may create problems in the future when you need their cooperation to serve other clients. Do not use advocacy until you have tried approaches (e.g., negotiation, brokering, etc.) with fewer risks.

3. Your willingness to assume the role of client advocate should arise from a desire to help your client, and never from a motive of dislike for another professional or agency or a desire for self-aggrandizement.

4. Before you engage in a confrontational tactic, be sure you understand the facts of the matter. Do not base your decisions on hearsay or on one-sided descriptions of why your client was denied service. Realize that many clients do not understand the explanations given by agency representatives and that often they are confused by complex eligibility requirements. Get the facts before you decide how to proceed.

5. Successful advocacy requires a high level of interpersonal skill and empathy. You need to be able to put yourself in the shoes of those you are confronting. Try to understand the feelings and position of the opposing party. Communicate your concerns in a factual and nonabrasive manner, but speak in a tone that conveys that you feel strongly about the matter. Face-to-face meetings are almost always more effective than phone calls and letters.

6. Before you speak with a representative of the agency or organization that denied services to your client, write down exactly what you intend to say and the questions you will ask. Begin your conversation with a courteous request for an explanation of why your client was not able to secure desired services. Write down the answers. If the answers you receive are significantly different from your prior understanding, discuss the matter with your client and seek clarification. Keep a detailed record of who you talked to, their position, their responses, and the time and date of the communication.

7. Do not assume that you know the inner workings of another agency or its policies, procedures, or eligibility requirements unless you have recently worked in that agency. Appreciate the real limitations and complexities that exist within human service agencies. Respect the other agency's chain of command (e.g., do not ask to speak with a supervisor until you have spoken to the line worker; do not ask to speak with an administrator until you have spoken with the supervisor).

8. If the information you have gathered indicates that the agency should be able to serve the client—or wants to but cannot because of a technicality or an unreasonable policy—ask the representative for information on how the decision can be appealed and who else you should speak to about the matter. Consider asking if the top administrator, board members, or a legislative committee should be informed of the difficulty faced by your client or perhaps consulted on how the matter can be resolved. Consider using a measured expression of anger to demonstrate your resolve.

9. When pursuing an appeals process, prepare detailed documentation of the client's need and what was done, step by step, to try to secure needed services. List names, dates, and content of all communication. Include copies of all letters sent and received.

Selected Bibliography

Mailick, Mildred, and Ardythe Ashley. "Politics of Interprofessional Collaboration: Challenge to Advocacy." *Social Casework* 62 (March 1981): 131–37.

Sunley, Robert. *Advocating Today: A Human Service Practitioner's Handbook.* New York: Family Service Association of America, 1983.

Weissman, Harold, Irwin Epstein, and Andrea Savage. *Agency-Based Social Work: Neglected Aspects of Clinical Practice.* Philadelphia: Temple University Press, 1983.

12.25   *Cross-Cultural Helping*

Purpose: To become sensitive to the importance of culture in the helping process.

Discussion: The social worker will interact with many individuals who have cultural or ethnic backgrounds quite different than the one that most strongly influenced the development of his or her own values, beliefs, and behavioral patterns. *Culture* refers to the learned patterns of thought and behavior that are passed from generation to generation. Cultures differ in terms of language, religion, world view, values, art, custom, manner of emotional expression, and the rhythms and patterns of everyday life. Cultures are dynamic; some change slowly and some change rapidly. A culture is like a fabric with each fiber reinforcing the others. One fiber or element of a culture cannot be removed without affecting the overall strength and integrity of the fabric. Moreover, a new "fiber" (e.g., TV, a new language, automobile, drug use) cannot be inserted into the fabric without distorting and displacing the other fibers. So it is with a culture. Once the culture has been altered by technology or other factors, it is never the same and it can never return to a prior state of development.

Related to the concept of culture is *ethnicity,* which Hraba (1979) defines as "self-conscious collectives of people who, on the basis of common origin or a separate subculture, maintain a distinction between themselves and outsiders" (p. 27). One's sense of identity, loyalty, and belonging to a particular ethnic group is closely tied to national origin, language, religion, and skin color. Some ethnic groups, especially those clearly identified by skin color, face pervasive oppression and discrimination. The essence of racism and prejudice is the tendency to form judgments solely on the basis of a person's color or ethnic background. Like many others, U.S. society is racist in its prevailing attitudes and beliefs; the social worker who has grown up in such an environment must make a deliberate effort to overcome the effects of that socialization. Ridding oneself of prejudice is a life-long struggle. Certain behaviors are often observed among professional helpers who retain prejudice and racist attitudes:

- Offering stereotypic explanations for human behavior, especially the behavior of persons of a specific ethnic or racial group
- Using the same helping strategies for all clients who are members of a particular ethnic group
- Dismissing the importance of cultural background in a person's life or, on the other extreme, believing that cultural background explains most everything
- Avoiding discussions of race and culture, or, on the other extreme, talking about them continually

Solomon (1976) identifies several characteristics of the nonracist practitioner. For example:

ability to perceive in any behavior, other's or one's own, alternative explanations of that behavior, particularly those alternatives which the self might most strongly reject as false. . . .

ability to feel warmth, genuine concern and empathy for people regardless of their race, color or ethnic background. . . .

ability to confront the client. . . . There are many practitioners who find confrontation of issues that may have racial connotations to be so threatening that the issues are denied or avoided. Thus, the client is denied an opportunity to learn something about himself and how he relates to others (pp. 301–11)

The opposite of racism and prejudice is the capacity to individualize the client while recognizing that cultural background does make a difference in how people view themselves and others, along with what they feel is or is not valuable, right and wrong, proper and improper. Social workers must be able to accept another's perceptions while keeping their own.

It is especially important that the worker be open to learning about the client's culture yet understand that one can achieve only a superficial knowledge of another person's culture that is not his or her own. Every attempt to describe a culture involves the use of generalizations. Even when a member of a particular ethnic group attempts to describe the beliefs, values, and behaviors common to that group, he or she is forced by the limitations of language to use generalizations and, of course, all general statements about a group (e.g., the white middle class, the blind, Blacks, Democrats) give rise to the dangers of stereotyping and overgeneralization. Hartman (1985) believes it is critically important for social workers to seek to understand the culture of their clients, especially if members of a minority, but warns that when

> drawing a profile of any minority group's members, it is essential to remember that we are viewing central tendencies, that particular characteristics are likely but not necessarily present. Social workers can and must learn about these central tendencies and can be sensitized to watch for and respond to particular characteristics. But, at the same time, they must always remember that any individual member of a group may *not* have a certain characteristic. (p. 105)

Because most social agencies and social programs are created by decision makers representing most strongly the beliefs and values of majority groups in society, the social workers employed by these programs may be viewed with fear or suspicion by clients who are members of a minority group. Whittaker and Tracy (1989) explain that a major obstacle in working with a member of an ethnic minority is the "differing expectations as to what constitutes 'help,' making it extremely difficult to select appropriate and effective intervention methods" (p. 158). Whittaker and Tracy warn that some of the most popular and commonly used techniques may not be effective when working cross-culturally. For example:

> Self-disclosure may be particularly difficult between dominant-culture workers and discriminated minority groups, since it presumes a degree of trust which may not exist initially.
>
> Short-term, task-oriented styles of social work may be ineffectual with clients who feel that extended periods of time "just talking" is an appropriate way to enter a relationship. . . .
>
> Reflection, reaching for feeling, or asking for insights may appear inappropriate or intrusive.
>
> Some ethnic groups, for example Asian-Pacific Americans, may view help-seeking as a shame-inducing process and will be extremely reticent to disclose personal problems. . . .
>
> Many ethnic minority (e.g., Puerto Rican, Hispanic) groups expect a more active helping relationship with the worker offering advice and tangible assistance.
>
> Techniques that rely on intrapersonal solutions versus social resolutions may be less appealing.

Cognitive behavioral or rational emotive techniques ... [e.g., managing self-talk, imagery, challenging irrational beliefs, etc.] may run counter to important cultural values and beliefs. (pp. 158–59)

In work with all clients, but especially with clients of a different cultural background, the social worker is advised to expect and respect differences and find delight and excitement in the variety to be found among human beings. Miller (1982) provides several guidelines for transcultural interactions:

- Consider all clients as individuals first, as members of a minority status [second] and as members of a specific ethnic group [third].
- Never assume that a person's ethnic identity tells you anything about his or her cultural values or patterns of behavior.
- Treat all "facts" you have ever heard or read about cultural values and traits as hypotheses, to be tested anew with each client. ...
- Remember that all minority group people in this society are bicultural, at least. The percentage may be 90–10 in either direction, but they still have had the task of integrating two value systems that are often in conflict. The conflicts involved in being bicultural may override any specific cultural content.
- Some aspects of a client's cultural history, values and lifestyle are relevant to your work with the client. Others may be simply interesting to you as a professional. Do not prejudge what areas are relevant. (p. 182)

Other guidelines are as follows:

1. Self-awareness is of critical importance. Constantly examine your own beliefs and attitudes and be alert to the possibility that you are making judgments based on bias or stereotype.

2. Realize that overlooking client strengths, misreading nonverbal communication, and misunderstanding family dynamics are among the most common errors made in cross-cultural helping. Because of the difficulty in reading nonverbal cues cross-culturally, the worker should move slowly when reaching for feelings and putting the client's feelings into words. The overlooking of strengths results when the worker does not fully appreciate the situation—especially the contextural and systemic aspects—with which the client is trying to cope. A worker is most likely to misunderstand client behaviors motivated by beliefs related to religion and spirituality, family obligations, and sex roles if those beliefs are at variance to his or her own.

3. Be alert to the fact that in many ethnic families, certain members are the key decision makers and other family members will hesitate to make an important decision without consulting that key member. For example, in many Hispanic families the husband has considerable authority and his wife and even his adult children may feel obligated to obtain his approval before taking a course of action. Also, within the extended families common to the Native-American tribal cultures, certain individuals perform the role of advisor and other family members will delay making a decision until they have obtained his or her advice on the matter. Thus, when working with a client from an ethnic group, it is well to ask if he or she wants to invite others to the interview or somehow involve them in the decision making. Not infrequently, clients will simply bring these respected individuals to important meetings.

4. Because members of many ethnic minority groups have suffered from racism and prejudice, it is to be expected that they will be somewhat distrustful of professionals and agencies that represent and reflect the dominant forces in society. They will enter a helping relationship with caution as they size up the social worker. Lum (1986) explains,

> At first, . . . [the client] may be aloof, reserved or superficially pleasant. He or she shows no overt interest in or curiosity about the worker. Then the client checks out the helper by asking about his or her personal life, background, opinions and values. These probes are intended not only to evaluate the worker but also become acquainted and to establish a personal relationship. (pp. 82–83)

The worker needs to respond to these probes with honest, nonevasive answers. Because visiting people in their own home is usually seen as an indication of caring and respect, the in-home interview may help the worker build trust (see Technique 9.6).

5. Ask your clients to explain relevant aspects of their beliefs and culture and ask for their advice in how you might adapt your methods to their values and traditions. Do not be afraid to say that you do not understand their beliefs and customs. If you genuinely care for the clients and demonstrate concern for their situation, most clients will explain what it is about their culture that you need to understand. It often helps to use a bit of self-effacing humor (i.e., laughing at your own ignorance) when asking questions about a set of beliefs or customs that you do not understand. This display of humility makes you less threatening.

6. If you believe cultural or ethnic factors might be relevant in your work with a particular client or family, consult with a person familiar with that ethnic group.

7. Learn about the values and beliefs of an ethnic group by attending celebrations, ceremonies, and other social and religious events sponsored by the group. Contact leaders in the ethnic community and express your desire to learn. Because they value their ethnicity, they will usually offer their assistance if they perceive your interest to be genuine.

8. Be alert to the fact that societal or systemic problems (poverty, unemployment, poor housing, lack of access to health care, etc.) bring ethnic minorities to agencies more often than do psychological problems. Thus, the provision of concrete services and the roles of broker, advocate, and mediator are of special importance.

Selected Bibliography

Devore, Wynetta, and Elfriede Schlesinger. *Ethnic Sensitive Social Work Practice.* 2nd ed. Columbus, Ohio: Merrill, 1987.

Hartman, Ann. "Summing Up." In *Empowering the Black Family.* Ann Arbor: University of Michigan, National Child Welfare Training Center, 1985.

Ho, Man Keung. *Family Therapy with Ethnic Minorities.* Newbury Park, Calif.: Sage, 1987.

Hraba, Joseph. *American Ethnicity.* Itasca, Ill.: F. E. Peacock, 1979.

Jacobs, Carolyn, and Dorcas Bowles, eds. *Ethnicity and Race Critical Concepts in Social Work.* Silver Spring, Md.: National Association of Social Workers, 1987.

Logan, Sadye, Edith Freeman, and Ruth McRoy. *Social Work Practice with Black Families.* White Plains, N.Y.: Longman, 1989.

Lum, Doman. *Social Work Practice and People of Color: A Process-State Approach.* Monterey, Calif.: Brooks/Cole, 1986.

Miller, Nancy. "Social Work Services to Urban Indians." In *Cultural Awareness in the Human Services,* edited by James Green. Englewood Cliffs, N.J.: Prentice-Hall, 1982.

Solomon, Barbara. *Black Empowerment: Social Work in Oppressed Communities.* New York: Columbia University Press, 1976.

Whittaker, James, and Elizabeth Tracy. *Social Treatment.* 2nd ed. New York: Aldine De Gruyter, 1989.

12.26   *The Client in Crisis*

Purpose: To assist the client in coping with a personal crisis.

Discussion: The social worker will encounter many individuals who are in a state of crisis. Although the word *crisis* is widely used, it has a specific meaning within the mental health field. Dixon (1987) defines a crisis as "a functionally debilitating emotional state resulting from the individual's reaction to some event perceived to be so dangerous that it leaves him or her feeling helpless and unable to cope effectively by usual methods" (p. 11). Among the events that can precipitate a crisis are the death of a loved one, loss of a job, martial separation, birth of a handicapped child, serious illness or accident, house fire, rape or mugging, or other traumatic event. A crisis is a subjective reaction. Thus, an event that precipitates a crisis in one individual may be handled fairly well by another.

A crisis is a time of both danger and opportunity. It is a dangerous time because if the crisis is not resolved constructively, it can set in motion a downward spiral that leads to a level of functioning lower than that which existed prior to the crisis. On the other hand, a crisis can be an opportunity to learn new coping skills and make life changes that actually elevate one's level of functioning. A crisis is said to be *time limited;* within a matter of weeks, the person comes to some level of adjustment or emotional steady state. And, as suggested, that adjustment may be either positive or negative, depending, in part, on how others respond to the person during the crisis.

It is important to distinguish a personal crisis as described above, from a particular coping pattern that Kagan and Schlosberg (1989) term "perpetual crisis" or "crisis oriented." They explain that

> living in a crisis-oriented family is like riding a roller coaster 24 hours a day: terrifying, energizing and addicting. . . . Real, rather than perpetual crisis, puts us into acute grief. . . . For families in 'perpetual crisis' the grief process is blocked. . . .

> Crisis becomes a way of life. . . . Instead of becoming vulnerable and facing change, crisis-oriented families protect themselves from facing difficult issues. (pp. 2–3)

Thus, a perpetual crisis is more a life-style than a reaction to some threatening event.

The following practice guidelines apply to a person in a real crisis but not to persons in "perpetual crisis."

1. Realize that this state of disorganization will diminish over time; with or without professional help, the crisis (as defined above) will be over within about four to six weeks. The purpose of crisis intervention is to prevent the development of more serious and longstanding problems and help the client resolve the crisis in a positive way.

2. Listen actively and offer emotional support. A person in crisis is in a heightened state of either anxiety or depression and also feels a sense of failure because he or she is unable to cope. The client is probably preoccupied with the precipitating event and will have difficulty focusing attention on anything else. Before the client can consider alternatives, make decisions, or plan ways for resolving problems, he or she will need much emotional support from the worker and significant others. This support may range from simply acknowledging the existence of the problem to offering strong verbal reassurance (e.g., "You did the right thing in leaving your house and coming to our shelter for battered women").

3. Involve others in the helping process. People in crisis are often most receptive to assistance provided by those whom they know and trust (e.g., family, friends, employer, minister, neighbors, etc.). Encourage the client to reach out to others, or, with his or her permission, contact these significant others yourself and enlist their help on behalf of the client.

4. Allow the client to express emotion. Be aware of the intense anxiety felt by the individual, especially during the first stages of a crisis. Calmly allow the client to cry or express feelings of fear or anger while you continue to provide emotional support and acceptance. The client's strong feelings will lessen with time.

5. Communicate hope and optimism. A hopeful attitude is an essential element in responding to a person in crisis. If you can sincerely communicate a belief in the client's ability to cope, he or she will be less fearful and will gradually begin to regain self-confidence.

6. Be actively involved. To most people in crisis, their own problems are of utmost importance. They have tunnel vision and can think of little else. Consequently, they are not able to analyze their situation. You will need to ask questions and actively examine the details of their situation.

7. Use partialization. The person in crisis feels as if he or she is facing a giant and completely unmanageable problem. By breaking the problem down into several smaller ones, to be addressed one at a time, the client will feel more hopeful about regaining control.

8. Provide factual information. Often, a crisis arises because the person has misconceptions about his or her situation or because intense feelings have distorted his or her perception of reality (e.g., "I just know that I'm going to lose my job" or "This goes to prove that no company is going to hire someone who's in a wheelchair like me"). Provide factual information related to the person's concern (e.g., "No, it is not because you are in a wheelchair that you weren't hired; there are laws against discrimination of that kind"). When appropriate, give honest feedback needed to correct misunderstandings (e.g., "Mr. Jones told me that you weren't hired because you were belligerent and sarcastic during the interview").

9. A person in crisis has difficulty making decisions and anticipating the consequences of his or her actions. Thus, you may need to provide highly specific advice and directions as to what the person needs to do or what will probably happen if he or she takes a certain course of action. It is especially important to help the client anticipate the consequences of destructive behaviors (e.g., "If you lose control and again beat your child, we will have to protect her; she will be placed in a foster home").

10. Encourage and reinforce adaptive behavior. Help the individual identify what kinds of coping behaviors worked in the past; encourage the client to take similar actions to address their current problem. An important part of crisis intervention is to encourage clients to take action so they begin to regain a faith and trust in their own capabilities.

11. Consider using a behavioral contract (see Technique 12.6) as a means of providing the client with structure and direction. This helps the client mobilize inner resources, and it also sends the message that you have confidence in his or her ability to take the steps needed to get through the crisis.

Selected Bibliography

Dixon, Samuel. *Working with People in Crisis.* 2nd ed. Columbus, Ohio: Merrill, 1987.

Kagan, Richard, and Shirley Schlosberg. *Families in Perpetual Crisis.* New York: W. W. Norton, 1989.

Parad, Howard, and Libbie Parad. *Crisis Intervention—Book 2.* Milwaukee: Family Service America, 1989.

Slaikeu, Karl. *Crisis Intervention: A Handbook for Practice and Research.* 2nd ed. Boston: Allyn and Bacon, 1990.

12.27 The Child as Client

Purpose: To adapt basic social work techniques and approaches to the special needs of the child under age twelve.

Discussion: Because children are not simply miniature adults and because how they think and feel is strongly influenced by their developmental stage and their limited life experience, basic communication and interviewing techniques (Chapter 6) need to be adapted for use with children. Also, some new skills, such as the use of play, need to be added to the worker's repertoire. A number of guidelines should be considered when working with children.

Planning the Interview

1. When planning an interview with a child, determine the child's age and probable level of development, and anticipate how this will affect the child's capacity to understand and use language. But realize that there will be much variation among the children at a particular age.

2. Be clear about why you are meeting with the child and what you need to accomplish during the meeting. Plan several alternative methods to accomplish your goal. Anticipate what might go wrong (e.g., child will not talk, child cries, child will not leave parent, etc.) and plan how you will handle such situations.

3. Prior to the interview, assemble the play materials that may be needed. Depending on the child's age, provide "open-ended" art materials (e.g., paints, markers, clay, water toys) as well as materials that can be used to portray themes (e.g., dolls, puppets, blocks or Legos for building, toy cars and trucks, toy animals, doll house, etc.). For older children, consider card or board games, puzzles, or simple electronic games. Because play is normal activity for children, it is also a child's natural method of communication.

4. Plan to hold the interview in a space that is familiar and comfortable for the child but that affords privacy. As an alternative, consider an accessible community space that allows some privacy (e.g., a spot in a park, walk in the schoolyard).

Introducing Yourself and Getting Started

5. When first meeting a child, explain who you are and how you want to be addressed (e.g., "My name is John Smith. Please call me John. My job is to help children who are having problems at home."). Place yourself at the child's physical level, (e.g., sit or squat so you do not tower over the child). Initiate some friendly interaction by showing an interest in items the child may be wearing or carrying, or ask about school, favorite games, or TV shows. If the child refuses to interact, engage in a parallel activity and gradually initiate conversation about the activity. For example, if the child does not talk but begins playing with a doll, pick up a doll and engage in similar play.

6. If the child appears frightened, attempt to normalize the situation (e.g., "If I was in your place, I would feel scared talking to a new person. You are acting brave by just coming here."). It may be necessary to allay the child's fear that he or she is in trouble and that the interview is some kind of punishment.

7. If the child is at least six or seven years of age, ask what he or she knows about the purpose of the interview. This will reveal what the child is expecting. Then, in language he or she understands, explain why you want to speak with the child. Ask if he or she had talked to anyone else about this meeting and what others have said about the meeting, or discuss what instructions the child was given.

8. Do not attempt to disguise a professional interview as recreation; this may confuse the child about who you are and your role. Also be cognizant that only very limited confidentiality can be provided to a child. Do not promise that you can keep secrets, but describe what you can do to keep the child protected and safe, as well as what might happen after the child shares information with you.

Gathering Information from a Child

9. Children between ages three and six are eager to please adults and easily and strongly influenced by an adult's leading questions; thus, you must be careful not to put words in their mouths or suggest what they are to say. Also, because they are influenced more by the context of the message (i.e., who said it and how, when and where it was said) than by the literal meaning of the words, you must be very concrete in your communication. Three- to six-year-olds are very sensitive to an adult's reactions to what they say. Thus, it is important to present an accepting, warm, empathetic attitude or else they may judge that you disapprove of what they are saying and cease talking.

10. If the child is below about age six, most of the information you gather will be from observations of the child's play and interactions with you and others. At this young age, a child will sometimes act out his or her thoughts and feelings. Clues that something is troubling a child may be gleaned from observations, if you have the opportunity to observe the child in a variety of settings.

11. Use dolls or pictures to set up a situation relevant to the purpose of the interview and then ask the child to complete the story or describe how the dolls or characters in the picture feel and what they are thinking about. Children under about age six will often project their own thoughts and feelings onto the dolls or pictures. You may need to initiate the storytelling about the dolls or pictures but once they are attentive, you can ask them to continue the story. The techniques of active listening do not work with children below age six or seven.

12. If the child is older than about age six, he or she will be better able to use words to express thoughts and feelings and capable of responding to questions— if your questions are simple and age appropriate. Remember that children of this age frequently need assistance to describe their thoughts and feelings. For example, you may need to ask: What happened next? Then what did you do? How did you feel? However, children find it difficult to respond to "why" questions. Children will not be willing to talk at length about some past event if their attention is captured by something in the present. They may describe only once or with just a few statements what they think or feel, and then they are ready to move on to a different topic or activity. Encouraging them to stay with the original topic will often be unsuccessful. You may initiate a return to the original topic at a later time. Children will often become noncommittal (e.g., not answering, shrugging) when they are uncomfortable or unsure how to explain what they are thinking or feeling. Thus, it is important to facilitate the child's expression of thoughts and feelings without being so directive that the child withdraws or becomes uncomfortable when trying to put thoughts, feelings, and events in words. You can use play to help a child express himself or herself nonverbally. As a general rule, the less structured the play material, the better.

13. The nine- or ten-year-old is able to describe others using concepts of personality traits and attitudes. Because children this age can think conceptually, they pay more attention to the words and content of a message, rather than just the context or who said it and how it was said. Also, they are able to detect phony or insincere messages and become suspicious when they observe incongruency.

Story completions, dolls, and drawing are usually still necessary interviewing techniques for children between ages seven and ten; however, many children older than age nine will respond thoughtfully to an interviewer's questions if the interviewer is nonthreatening and unhurried. Children find it easier to talk about themselves if they can do so while playing a simple card game or a board game (e.g., checkers) that does not require a great deal of concentration. "Puppet-to-puppet" interaction will often elicit involvement and communication. Talking on play telephones is often successful. Sentence completions (e.g., When at home, I am afraid that . . .) are also useful. Many children of this age respond well to humor if it is not very subtle.

Interpreting Information Obtained from a Child

14. Children between the ages of about three and six will be very subjective, concrete, and egocentric in their thinking and communication. For example, they assume an event that makes them happy will have the same effect on all other people. They tend to report their feelings in a global manner and their thinking is characterized by an "all or nothing" pattern. For example, things are either good or bad; the child is unable to understand or describe mixed feelings or ambivalence. However, the child may describe a situation or person at one time as "mean" or "awful," and then later describe the same situation or person as "nice" or "fun." Thinking in absolutes causes them to categorize both themselves and others as either good or bad, smart or dumb, and the like. Children of this age describe themselves and others in terms of external characteristics (e.g., age, hair color, grade in school, etc.); they do not mention personality traits except in global terms such as "she is pretty" or "he is a bad person."

15. Beginning at about age six, children's thought processes begin to be more objective and logical. Gradually, they acquire the ability to imagine themselves in the role or the situation of another person, and they also understand that each individual thinks and feels differently. However, even seven-year-olds may still believe that they are totally responsible for how others, especially parents, feel and behave. It is not until about ages nine or ten that children truly understand that many different factors cause the behavior and emotions they observe in others.

16. By about age ten, children no longer think in absolutes and can view themselves as a mix of characteristics and abilities (e.g., someone who is good at some things but not others or good sometimes and bad at other times). It is at this age that they understand it is possible and normal to feel simultaneously opposing emotions. Also, at about age nine or ten, children have the ability to reflect on their own thoughts and actions (e.g., "I think Johnny thinks I like him") and can figure out how others will probably react in a particular situation or will react to certain information. Moreover, children can now manipulate words and information in order to influence how others will respond.

17. Not infrequently, social workers find themselves in situations where they must form a judgment about whether a child is telling the truth. Four- to six-year-olds will tell a simple lie (e.g., "I didn't break the cup") in order to avoid punishment, but they do not have the cognitive abilities to fabricate a complex story such as one having several interrelated elements, actions, or actors. At this young age, they have what some call a "script memory." For example, they can remember distinct events (e.g., a birthday party) and rituals (e.g., going to bed), but they tend not to accurately remember events that are not part of their routines. In trying to describe something that happened, they can often recall central actors or central events but not the connecting details, such as what happened before and after and how one action led to another. In addition, children of this age frequently exaggerate events or boast when describing their abilities and experiences. However, when asked, "Is that pretend or real?" or "Is that an 'I wish' story or is it true?" they generally can articulate what was "real" and what was "exaggeration."

18. Children between the ages of seven and eleven value honesty and fairness and generally avoid telling a lie. It is rare for them to fabricate. However, they do have the cognitive abilities to add or withhold information, disguise their thoughts, and use deception as a means of avoiding punishment or getting what they want. Children in this age group tend to embellish the truth in order to tell an exciting story. Nine-, ten-, and eleven-year-olds are very eager to please adults and are inclined to say what they believe adults want to hear. Children between ages seven and eleven have good memory of central actors and events and good free recall (i.e., able to recall and describe without the aid of detailed questioning by an interviewer).

19. As a general rule, the younger the child, the less likely he or she is to fabricate a falsehood—there may be misunderstanding or confusion but not a deliberate lie. In cases where a child self-reports sexual abuse, false reports are extremely rare among children below age twelve, and also quite rare among teenagers; the latest studies find only from 1 to 2 percent false reports.

20. Most young children will incorporate their thoughts, feelings, and recent experiences into their play (e.g., a child who had dawdled while dressing and was late for preschool may recreate this event by having dolls "hurry and get ready" so they're "not late for school"). However, it must be remembered that children also incorporate into their play themes from TV programs, from stories, from incidents that their friends report, and from events they have observed outside their home. It may be difficult to pinpoint the source of children's play themes.

21. Themes of violence are common in the stories told by normal, nonabused, young children. For example, among three-year-olds, about 66 percent of girls and 90 percent of boys include act of violence and destruction in the stories they tell to other children and adults. Thus, talk by a child about violence is not, by itself, an indicator of physical abuse.

22. Sometimes a parent or parent figure will coach a child on what he or she should tell a social worker. This is fairly common in situations related to child custody evaluations and child abuse. Certain behaviors indicate that a child is reciting a fabricated story in order to please or protect a parent: either a great deal of inconsistency regarding the major elements of the story or extreme consistency regarding major events but with no detail; flat affect (i.e., absence of anxiety, fear, guilt, shame, anger, etc.); use of adult phrases and terminology; the only emotion expressed is anger (i.e., suggests motive of revenge); and visual perception only (i.e., child is unable to describe smell, sounds, touch associated with the situation they describe). If a parent has coached a child, the parent is usually threatened by the social worker's suggestion of a private interview with the child.

23. Young children do not use clocks or calendars to measure time. In fact, preschool children do not grasp the concept of time and grade school-aged children typically use events such as nap time, lunch time, Christmas, start of school, and events as markers of time. For these reasons, you should not assume that a child can accurately describe when certain events happened.

24. Remember that children are very responsive and reactive to parents and parent figures. It is important to view the child's behavior within the context of his or her family system and relationships with significant others. The child's behavior is often a barometer of the family functioning; behavioral problems often reflect conflicts within the family.

25. Realize that during an interview, you will get only a sample of the child's behavior. The child may behave quite differently in other situations or with other people. The farther removed the child is from his or her normal social and family context, the more cautious you must be in drawing conclusions about the child's usual behavioral patterns. For example, the child who appears anxious during an office interview may simply be fearful because he or she is in an unfamiliar environment.

Other Considerations

26. Allow the child to set the pace of the interview. Follow his or her lead. Children, especially young children, have a short attention span and are easily distracted. Allow the child to move around and explore the room. Excessive squirming and a lack of attention probably indicate that the child is tired and that the interview should probably end.

27. The vocabulary you use should be appropriate to the age of the child. For example, with a twelve-year-old, you can use words and expressions similar to those used with adults. But with a four-year-old child, your expressions must be very simple and concrete.

28. Because young children are more responsive to the context than to words, it is usually helpful to make heavy use of nonverbal messages (e.g., facial expressions, touch, gestures, etc.) in your communication. However, do not kiss or caress the child. This makes children uncomfortable, and it opens the door to a misinterpretation of your intentions by others and a possible accusation of sexual abuse. Touch can be especially confusing and threatening to a child who has been sexually abused.

29. Answer a child's question honestly, directly, and correctly (e.g., "I believe you will be in foster care until the school term ends"). Do not use euphemisms and do not beat around the bush. Use no more words than are necessary. Avoid giving elaborate explanations to a child's simple and straightforward question. Promises must not be made lightly. If you may not be able to keep a promise to a child, do not make it! When giving information, try to give it in small doses.

30. When behavior-control rules are necessary during an interview, explain the rules, along with any consequences for breaking them (e.g., "You are not permitted to hit me; if you do hit me, I will put away the toys and today's meeting will end").

31. Give children a choice, if possible, but do not give the impression they have a wide choice if they do not. This point is illustrated in the following statements:

> *Incorrect:* "Well, Jimmy, what would you like to do? We can do whatever you like."
>
> *Correct:* "Jimmy, today you can use the finger paints or the crayons. Which do you want to use?"

Offer choices among alternatives that you can accept.

32. Outings, treats, or gifts should be used judiciously. Although they are an extension of normal adult-child interaction and may be helpful in building a relationship, they can be overdone and misused. Be careful that your desire to give to the child is not viewed as competition with his or her own parents.

33. Do not express displeasure or criticism of the child's parents. Regardless of the parents' behavior, they are very important to the child, and he or she usually feels protective of them. For example, a child will usually defend his or her parents even if they have been abusive. Be objective, concrete, and nonjudgmental in talking about the parent-child relationship and the parents' behavior (e.g., "Your dad does have a problem with alcohol. He gets drunk at least once a week. Because he cannot seem to stop drinking, he is not able to be the kind of parent he wants to be").

34. A series of interviews should usually have structure and a routine, depending on each child's needs. For example, some children like interviews that have definite beginning and ending rituals. Others, however, may want relief from structure and need freedom—to roam at will and do whatever they feel like doing.

The Child in Out-of-Home Placement

Many of the children known professionally to social workers are in out-of-home placement (i.e., foster family care, group homes, institutional care, etc.). The guidelines below will help the worker address the special concerns of the child in placement:

35. Realize that placement is always disruptive and emotionally traumatic to a child. Many children blame themselves for the family problems that led to the placement. Consequently, many children view placement as a punishment for real or imagined wrongdoings.

36. Be sensitive to the pain involved in the separation and loss experiences that are so much a part of foster care and other placements. Relationship losses—especially a series of losses—have adverse and long-lasting effects on a child. Thus, it is critically important to minimize the number of separations and losses,

---

or, when they are unavoidable, to minimize their impact. As a rule, the more gradual the separation, the less damaging it is. If a child must be separated from someone to which he or she is emotionally attached, the move should be as gradual as possible, thus giving the child an opportunity to prepare and adjust. A certain amount of ritual (e.g., going-away party, gift, etc.) helps the child make the transition by symbolically ending one relationship and beginning another. Without such a ritual, the child usually feels as if he or she was simply given away or rejected. A transition ritual gives the child permission to let go of one relationship and begin a new one.

37. Some children make a fairly good adjustment to placement, but, as a rule, they have many unresolved emotional conflicts locked inside. The child in placement usually feels insecure and uncertain about why he or she is in placement. Thus, assume that the child has many unasked questions about his or her past, present, and future; make it easy for the child to ask these questions. Be factual and honest when talking about his or her current situation and possible changes in the future. If a child does not understand why he or she is separated from his or her parents, the child will usually create an elaborate fantasy that explains the situation. It is better for the child to struggle with an unpleasant reality than adjust to a pleasant fantasy.

38. Because foster children feel so unsure about their future, you must be prepared to become a dependable and predictable figure in their lives. Contacts must be on a regular basis. If you must miss an appointment, explain the reason directly to the child. The foster child is especially sensitive to any hint of rejection.

39. When speaking with foster parents, adoptive parents, or group care staff, be truthful about the child's current situation and history. Efforts to conceal the child's life experience in an attempt to protect the child or because you fear others will not understand, almost always backfire. Invariably, negative information about the child's life experience will be revealed or somehow demonstrated by the child's behavior.

40. Remember that the child's biological parents are part of his or her identity. No matter how badly they may have treated the child, they are of great importance to the child. Never judge or in any way criticize the child's parents; if and when you do, you are in effect, ridiculing the child. Do everything possible to maintain frequent contacts and visits between the child in placement and his or her parents, siblings, and other close relatives. In the long run, frequent visitation is helpful to the child, even if the visits are at times disruptive.

41. Help the child develop a "cover story" that he or she can use to explain being in placement to friends, teachers, and others. Donley (1975) offers the following advice on the matter:

> I believe that a child must have a clear, understandable, acceptable explanation of his circumstances.... He will be asked questions about himself and it is essential that he should have a socially acceptable and logical explanation for who he is and where he is and why he is in this situation (e.g., why he is in placement). Unskilled workers do not appreciate how essential this is and do not help the child develop a "cover story" for public consumption. Without it the child is left to his own devices and frequently falls into fabrication.... Fabrication, once found out, will very

quickly give the child a reputation in the neighborhood for being a spinner of tall tales, or at worst, a liar. (p. 22)

Selected Bibliography

Amacher, Ethel, and Virginia Eaddy. *Play Techniques in Interviewing Children*. Knoxville: Office of Continuing Social Work Education, University of Tennessee, 1983.

Crompton, Margaret. *Respecting Children: Social Work with Young People*. Beverly Hills: Sage, 1980.

Donley, Kay. *Opening New Doors*. London: Association of British Adoption Agencies, 1975.

Garbarino, James, and Frances Stott. *What Children Can Tell Us: Eliciting, Interpreting and Evaluating Information from Children*. San Francisco: Jossey-Bass, 1989.

Jones, David, and Mary McQuinton. *Interviewing the Sexually Abused Child*. Denver: C. Henry Kempe National Center for the Prevention and Treatment of Child Abuse, 1986.

LeVine, Elaine, and Alvin Sallee. *Listen to Our Children: Clinical Theory and Practice*. Dubuque, Iowa: Kendall/Hunt, 1986.

Skafte, Dianne. *Child Custody Evaluations: A Practical Guide*. Beverly Hills: Sage, 1985.

12.28 *The Adolescent as Client*

Purpose: To adapt basic social work techniques and approaches to the needs of the adolescent.

Discussion: The developmental period between ages twelve and eighteen is stormy for many youths. It is a time of firsts—physical and sexual maturity, withdrawal from the protection of parents, and an emersion in relationships outside the family. Many parents experience serious conflicts with their adolescent children. Most of these conflicts revolve around issues of authority and control. Parents typically worry that their children will get into drugs, irresponsible sex, illegal activity, or become injured by recklessness. Some parents feel so stressed and angry that they physically abuse their adolescents or kick them out of the home.

Adolescents are overloading the social service system and most agencies are ill equipped to deal with the complex and pressing needs of adolescents. Problems most likely to bring the adolescent to the attention of a social worker include running away, delinquency, pregnancy, drug abuse, threat of suicide, family conflict, and the need for foster care or residential treatment. We offer a number of guidelines for those working with adolescents.

1. Despite the frustration you may feel, always remember that adolescents are resilient and have great capacity to grow and change. An effective intervention can prevent serious problems and have a positive, life-long impact. Do not overlook the rewards of working with adolescents. Because these are lively, inquisitive, and questioning clients, working with adolescents can be stimulating and genuinely fun. Because they are in a time of rapid change, there is joy in watching them learn and mature.

---

2. Remember that adolescents are typically idealistic, painfully self-conscious, in conflict with their parents over authority issues, fiercely attached to peers, preoccupied with bodily changes, trying to maintain control over sexual desires, seeking popularity and conformity within their peer group, and desperately trying to develop a sense of identity apart from their family. It is critically important that these typical behaviors during this stage in life not be labeled as negative or abnormal.

3. The helping relationships and environments we create for adolescents must provide fair and appropriate models of adult behavior, set realistic limits on their behavior, and allow the adolescents to openly discuss whatever they want. They have an intense need to be heard. However, you must listen for the underlying meaning rather than to the words used because the words themselves may be offensive and shocking. Listen nonjudgmentally and encourage them to talk about their life—as they experience it—about their needs and about what they want in the future.

4. Adolescents will test the limits of controls put in place by an adult, so expect to be challenged. Before you create a rule, be sure that it is really necessary, can be enforced, and it is worth fighting over. Inform adolescents of rules and the consequences for violating a rule. Be fair and consistent in enforcing rules and imposing consequences.

5. Because of their high energy level, interaction with adolescents should allow and even encourage movement and activity. If possible, avoid office interviews and try talking with your adolescent clients while walking, shooting baskets, working out, or riding in a car. Movement makes it easier for them to talk and express feelings.

6. Because the peer group is so important during adolescence, group approaches (group discussion, psychodrama, group counseling and therapy, and structured group activities) can be useful. Most adolescents are more accepting of a group-related intervention than a one-to-one interview. Behavioral contracting (see Technique 12.6) works fairly well with adolescents.

7. Keep parents informed and involved in your work with their child while providing the adolescent with as much confidentiality as is legally permissible. Continually distinguish between the adolescent's personal problems, problems that belong to his or her parents, and problems that arise primarily from interaction between the adolescent and his or her parents. By helping parents recall and talk about their own adolescence, you can often increase their tolerance and understanding of their teenager.

8. Because of the rebellion and alienation from adults that is common to this developmental period, adolescents in need of out-of-home care do not usually do well in foster family care; most adjust better to a group home or other group care facility where they can live with age peers. A group home must provide structure and a predictable environment so that adolescents know the limits of acceptable behavior.

9. With adolescent clients—more than with any other clients—it is important to be yourself and to be genuine. Adolescents are sensitive to any hint of phoniness or artificiality in others, even though they themselves often pretend to be someone they are not. It is nearly impossible to keep up with the latest adolescent slang, so don't try to talk like an adolescent. Imitating adolescent talk is likely to make you appear phoney.

10. Be alert to the fact that when we work with adolescents, our own unresolved adolescent struggles often rise to the surface and we may project them onto our clients. Our own unresolved authority issues and parent-child conflicts are especially likely to be reactivated by the adolescent client.

11. Generally, adolescents do not seek professional help. Usually, they are involuntary clients. Given the authority struggle that is common to this developmental phase, this is especially difficult for adolescents. Silence is their usual means of resisting adult intrusion. Also, adolescents challenge adult authority by being rude, contradictory, and using abusive language.

12. Because adolescents' emotions are so intense and so characterized by ambivalence, they usually cannot verbalize how they are feeling. Allow them to express feelings but do not push them toward such expressions since this invites further resistance.

13. Most adolescents are preoccupied with the here and now. They tend not to emphasize planning nor do they think much about the distant future. Gently encourage adolescents to examine their current decisions and actions in terms of their impact on future decisions, opportunities, and goals. When adolescents' thinking is unrealistic, it is usually best to tell them so and explain why in a respectful but firm manner.

Selected Bibliography

Aldgate, Jane, Anthony Maluccio, and Christine Reeves. *Adolescents in Foster Families.* Chicago: Lyceum Books, 1989.

Dangerfield, David, and Michael Shaffer. *Aggressive Adolescents.* Tulare, Calif.: Professional Training Associates, 1978.

Herbert, Martin. *Working with Children and Their Families.* Chicago: Lyceum Books, 1989.

Maier, Henry. *Developmental Group Care of Children and Youth.* New York: Haworth, 1987.

Wodarski, John. *Social Work Practice with Children and Adolescents.* Springfield, Ill.: Charles C. Thomas, 1987.

12.29 The Life Book

Purpose: To help a child, especially an older child, in a foster care or adoption placement develop a sense of identity and understand his or her experiences with separation and placement.

Discussion: The *life book* is both a therapeutic tool and a personalized record of a child's life experience. Backhaus (1984) explains that a Life Book is an individually made book covering the child's life from birth to present, written in the child's own words. It generally includes a narrative describing what has happened to the child, when, and why, as well as what the child's feelings are about what has happened. The book may also incorporate photos, drawings, report cards, awards and certificates, letters from previous foster or adoptive parents and birth parents, a birth certificate, a genogram, and anything else a particular child might want to include. It is current practice to assemble a Life Book for older children who are being adopted as part of their preparation. Life Books . . . can be invaluable for those being adopted, living in foster or residential care, or returning to birth parents. (p. 551)

The life book is especially useful in helping a child:

1. Develop a sense of continuity and identity
2. Understand past separations and placements and reduce confusion and misconceptions about these and other disruptive experiences
3. Avoid the unhealthy use of fantasy and denial in trying to cope with painful life experiences
4. Remember significant people and childhood events
5. Maintain in one place a record of important personal data (i.e., birth and medical information, pictures of family and significant others, school records, etc.)

The life book is an ongoing technique. The worker involves the child in the creation of the book and uses it as a tool for discussing the child's life experience and his or her feelings about those experiences.

Selected Bibliography

American Foster Care Resources. *The Book About Me.* King George, Va.: American Foster Care Resources, 1984.

Aust, Patricia. "Using the Life Story Book in Treatment of Children in Placement." *Child Welfare* 60 (September 1981): 535–60.

Backhaus, Kristiana. "Life Books: Tool for Working with Children in Placement." *Social Work* 29 (November-December 1984): 551–54.

12.30   *The Elderly Client*

Purpose: To adapt social work techniques and approaches to the special needs of the elderly.

Discussion: By the year 2000, about 13 percent of the U.S. population will be age sixty-five or older. By the year 2030, this percentage will grow to about 21 percent. Social workers must give increasing attention to the needs of older people, especially those in their seventies, eighties, and nineties. A number of guidelines will help the worker serving the elderly client.

1. Most elderly people actively struggle to maintain their independence. As a person ages, he or she experiences many losses (e.g., death of loved ones, loss of health, etc.); becoming staunchly independent is a normal coping mechanism. Consequently, elderly clients may be resistant or ambivalent about receiving services they perceive as limiting their freedom. To the greatest extent possible, enable elderly clients to retain control, make choices, and maintain independence.

2. Allow and even encourage the client to reminisce. The past means a lot to an elderly person. Thinking and talking about the past is a normal activity for the elderly—it is not a sign of deteriorating mental abilities. Listen carefully to the reminiscence; it will reveal much about the client's values, feelings, and current concerns.

3. As individuals grow older and closer to death, they think more about their life's achievements and disappointments. Typically, their religious beliefs and spirituality take on added importance as they review their life and assess its meaning and purpose. They may desire to communicate what they have learned from life. Look for opportunities that allow the elderly to teach what they have learned.

4. During their later years, elderly persons typically become intensely aware of their unique relationship to children and grandchildren. It may be of great importance for them to stay in contact with offspring or reactivate relationships that have deteriorated. Some older persons may want to reach out to estranged offspring and patch up differences or make amends for the harm they caused. Do everything possible to facilitate intergenerational family communication.

5. If the elderly client is much older than you, the two of you probably have very different mores, values, and attitudes. For example, "taking charity" is especially difficult for older people, and they usually find it harder than younger persons to accept counseling and psychotherapy. Many elderly are concerned about the cost of services. Early in your contact, clarify any financial implications. Many clients will simply reject services rather than inquire about the cost or reveal their inability to pay.

6. A good way to break the ice and get the relationship off to a good start is to show an interest in the furnishings in the elderly client's room or home, such as family pictures, unique pieces of furniture, homemade items, and the like.

7. In the beginning, always focus on the client's most obvious and concrete needs, which are the ones he or she can most easily discuss. Like most other clients, the elderly person understands and can easily talk about needs like transportation, housing, medical care, and home maintenance, but finds it difficult to express feelings of fear and loneliness to a stranger.

8. Most elderly people suffer from some degree of vision and hearing loss (see Technique 9.2). Thus, it is important to speak clearly and concisely and repeat the message as often as necessary. Your nonverbal communication is especially important as a means of compensating for the client's auditory deficit. Also, the pace of an interview will usually be slower with an elderly person, and the client's lack of energy may limit the length of the interview. For both physical and psychological reasons, an interview in the client's home is usually more comfortable than an office interview. Elderly clients may be especially bothered by unusual clothing or hairstyles worn by a worker.

9. Given the impact of racism, discrimination, and prejudice on people, you must be especially sensitive when interacting with the elderly person who is a member of a racial or ethnic minority. Lowy (1985) offers a number of suggestions for social workers:

- Respect the elder's interactional style. This may mean spending more time in initial interviews so that the client has "sufficient time to look them over."
- Bureaucratic coolness in interpersonal exchange is likely to antagonize some minority elders, while addressing a Black elder by his or her first name may be regarded as demeaning and disrespectful rather than informal and friendly. Workers must be sensitive to the fact that their presence in initial contacts will be evaluated by the client in terms of his or her prior experience with authority and power, and may reflect experience with discrimination and oppression. . . .
- [Recognize] the importance of working with minority aged within their own homes, which serves as a leveling factor in the relationship and allows the worker to observe how environmental and familial variables affect the client. . . .
- In general, minority elderly prefer intimate types of service provision (i.e., needs met by self or family). However, care must be taken not to assume that this is the case for any individual client for . . . ethnicity alone is not a good predictor of service preferences. It must be considered together with age, level of education, cohort effects and "family member living status." (pp. 230–231)

The values common to a particular ethnic group may make life either more or less difficult for the aging person. For example, Devore and Schlesinger (1987) remind us that elderly of certain ethnic groups (e.g., Chicano, Chinese, Native American) usually occupy a position of respect and influence within families, and the importance of hard work as a value within an ethnic group (e.g., Slavic-American) may cause the nonworking elderly person to feel particularly unworthy and unimportant.

10. Be alert to indicators of elder abuse and neglect (especially self-neglect), such as bruises, cuts, burns, or untreated injuries that are explained in a vague or defensive manner; improper clothing for the weather; wandering outside at odd hours or into areas where they may be exposed to danger; mail, newspapers, or other deliveries piled up and you know the person is home; unusual activity or no signs of movement from their homes; unpleasant odors associated with hygiene or housekeeping; person does not recognize you or does not know where he or she is or the day or time; person has means to meet basic needs but is facing an eviction, utility shutoff, or has many unpaid bills; or person is dependent on a stressed, chemically dependent or mentally ill caregiver and basic needs are not being met.

Selected Bibliography

Beaver, Marion, and Don Miller. *Clinical Social Work Practice With the Elderly.* Homewood, Ill.: The Dorsey Press, 1985.

Brink, T. L., ed. *Clinical Gerontology: A Guide to Assessment and Intervention.* New York: Haworth, 1986.

Devore, Wynetta, and Elfriede Schlesinger. *Ethnic-Sensitive Social Work Practice.* 2nd ed. Columbus, Ohio: Merrill, 1987.

Getzel, George, and M. Joanna Mellor, eds. *Gerontological Social Work Practice in the Community.* New York: Haworth, 1985.

Lowy, Louis. *Social Work With the Aging.* 2nd ed. New York: Longman, 1985.

12.31 *The Client with Mental Retardation*

Purpose: To adapt basic social work techniques and approaches to the special needs of the client who is mentally retarded.

Discussion: Roughly 3 percent of the U.S. population is mentally retarded. Of those, about 80 percent are in the mild to moderate range and 20 percent are at the severe and profound levels. Most mentally retarded persons are never institutionalized. In fact, most have jobs (albeit low-paying ones) and many marry and have children. The term *developmental disabilities* encompasses mental retardation and certain related and often overlapping conditions, such as cerebral palsy, epilepsy, autism, dyslexia, and other neurological problems that are evident at birth or during childhood (hence, the word *developmental*). The person who is mentally retarded or developmentally disabled lives in a society that emphasizes intelligence, education, competition, and attractiveness. Consequently, many have experiences a lifetime of rejection and failure. Although society shows much concern for the mentally handicapped child, it tends to reject and avoid the mentally handicapped adult.

Proctor (1984) explains that "the extent to which interventive approaches need to be different for retarded clients depends upon both the clients' level of intellectual disability and the outcomes sought." The following guidelines will aid the social worker serving the client who is mentally retarded.

1. Individualize the client; discard any preconceived notions or stereotypes concerning persons who are mentally retarded. Realize that they have the same physical, psychological, social, and spiritual needs as any other human being. Unfortunately, they encounter extraordinary frustration in trying to meet these needs. Because of the frustration and rejection they experience, many clients with mental retardation also develop an overlay of emotional problems.

2. Adapt your approach to the abilities and limitations of the client (e.g., intellectual level, language difficulties, coordination problems, etc.). As much as possible, all clients should participate in making decisions that impact on their lives. In the case of the profoundly retarded individual, little or no meaningful participation can be expected and most of the social work activity will involve contacts with family and other professionals. On the other hand, the person who is mildly retarded can and should be an active participant in the social work process.

3. Since verbal skills and abstract thinking are not among the strengths of persons who are mentally retarded, you must develop alternatives to verbal interviewing and counseling. Be familiar with behavioral techniques and related teaching methodologies. Nonverbal group work techniques, roleplaying, modeling, and the creative arts are also useful. (This is not to say that verbal techniques cannot be effective with some clients.)

4. Because so many of the client's problems are caused or aggravated by the attitudes and behavior of others, you must be prepared to formulate an intervention plan that gives much attention to persons in the client's environment (e.g., family, neighbors, teachers, landlord, employer, etc.). The practice roles of advocate, case manager, broker, and mediator are especially important.

5. Because the client's attention span may be short, the length of interviews will need to be adjusted accordingly. Because the client's memory may be impaired, each contact and communication should be planned as a discrete event or experience rather than as a continuation of previous conversations. When you give explanations and directions, you may need to repeat them or use examples. Your language must be clear, straightforward, and simple, but never childish.

6. In your interactions with the client, do nothing to reinforce inappropriate behavior. For example, hugging is not conventional greeting behavior among strangers. Rather than allow yourself to be hugged, initiate a handshake.

7. Be especially careful about demeaning behavior, such as referring to an adult mentally retarded person as a "kid." Address a retarded adult just as you would any other adult. Use "Mr." or "Miss," unless you know each other well enough to use first names.

8. Learn more about mental retardation. Realize, for example, that there are more than 200 known causes for the many types of mental retardation and that specific behavioral patterns and medical disorders are associated with certain forms of retardation. Such knowledge is critical in the formulation of intervention plans and in working as a team with other disciplines, such as psychology, physical therapy, occupational therapy, medicine, and speech therapy.

9. The principles of normalization should guide the development and delivery of services and the formulation of client habitation plans. These are complex principles but invaluable to professionals working with persons who have a disability. Normalization is misunderstood by many professionals. Wolfensberger (1972) defines normalization as "utilization of means which are as culturally normative as possible in order to establish and/or maintain personal behaviors and characteristics which are as culturally normative as possible" (p. 28). The phrase "culturally normative" equates with "typical" or "conventional." Normalization does not mean being "normal." Rather, normalization attempts to decrease deviance (i.e., differences that are devalued and socially created). Normalization does not mean that the person with a handicap is placed in situations that generate unusual frustration or impossible competition just because such situations are typical for the "average" person. However, it does attempt to remove all forms of overprotection and recognizes that individual growth and development involves a degree of risk taking.

Selected Bibliography

Baroff, George. *Mental Retardation: Nature, Cause and Management.* 2nd ed. New York: Wiley, 1986.

Gallagher, James, and Peter Vietze, eds. *Families of Handicapped Persons.* Baltimore: Paul H. Brooks Publishing, 1986.

Horejsi, Charles. "Applications of the Normalization Principles in Human Services." *Journal of Social Work Education* 15 (Winter 1979): 44–50.

Proctor, Enola. "Social Work with Retarded Adults." In *Adult Psychopathology: A Social Work Perspective,* edited by Francis Turner. New York: The Free Press, 1984.

Wikler, Lynn, and Maryanne Keenan, eds. *Developmental Disabilities.* Silver Spring, Md.: NASW, 1983.

Wolfensberger, Wolf. *The Principle of Normalization in Human Services.* Toronto: National Institute on Mental Retardation, 1972.

12.32   *The Client on Psychotropic Medication*

Purpose: To provide appropriate guidance to the client taking psychotropic medication.

Discussion: Years ago, mental hospitals were filled with individuals who could not live with their families or in the community because of the severity of their symptoms. The use of psychotropic drugs now allows most of these individuals to function outside a hospital.

The social worker will encounter many clients who take medication to control psychiatric symptoms. These medications fall into discrete groups, each of which alleviates a particular set of symptoms. The major groups are antipsychotic, antidepressant, antianxiety, antimanic, psychomotor stimulants, and sedative-hypnotics. Each medication has a chemical name, a generic or general name (e.g., amitriptyline), and a registered trade or brand name (e.g., Elavil). Each has a specific target symptom, contraindications, potency, and potential side effects. The selection of a specific medication is based on the patient's medical history, physical exam, laboratory tests, use and abuse of other medications, alcohol or street drugs, and, of course, the disorder or symptoms being treated. Physicians generally advise against the taking of psychotropic medications during pregnancy.

When an individual is hospitalized and/or experiencing disabling symptoms, he or she may be started on a quick-acting medication or given a fairly large dose. Most people do not need to take the same dosage after leaving the hospital or after the severe symptoms subside, and a physician may want to reduce the dosage or switch to a medication that is slower acting but has other advantages.

Usually, it is desirable for physicians to reduce the dosage but reductions are best done gradually—a process that may take weeks or months. Even when on a "maintenance dose," some people find that their symptoms worsen from time to time. This may be due to stress, biochemical changes, or some other factors.

Some patients are frightened when their doctor suggests they take less medication because they fear a return of symptoms. On the other hand, some individuals are very resistive to the use of medication because they fear real or imagined side effects or because it is perceived as a loss of control or a blow to their self-esteem.

All of the antipsychotic medications can have side effects that include sedation; weight gain; spasms of eye, face, neck, and back muscles; blurred vision; shuffling gait; and tremors. These effects are dose-related and diminish if the amount taken is reduced. Tardive dyskinesia is a troublesome side effect seen most often in patients who have been taking antipsychotic medications for many years. Symptoms include involuntary movement, lip smacking and sucking, jaw and tongue movement, and a blunting of normal emotional responses. In some individuals, these symptoms persist long after the drug that caused them has been withdrawn.

Side effects associated with other drug groups include dry mouth, weight gain, drowsiness, oversensitivity to the sun, and menstrual cycle disturbance. Children and the elderly are particularly vulnerable to side effects. A psychotropic medication may exacerbate nonpsychiatric medical problems such as hypertension, liver disease, epilepsy, and glaucoma. Despite these troublesome side effects, it must be remembered that symptom control is of critical importance to persons suffering from a major mental illness. There is a benefit-risk balance with all medications. In general, a physician will reduce the side effects by prescribing the lowest dosage that produces the desired effects, discontinuing a problematic medication and trying another, avoiding the simultaneous use of two medications that have a similar effect, and, whenever possible, treating only one symptom at a time.

When working with a client using psychotropic medications, several guidelines should be kept in mind.

1. The decision to prescribe a medication is a complex medical judgment to be made only by a competent physician, preferably a psychiatrist. For ethical and legal reasons, you must never give medication instructions outside the physician's directions.

2. Encourage your client to maintain regular contact with a physician so the effects of the drug can be monitored and dosage can be properly regulated. If you observe what appears to be unusual or unexpected side effects, but your client is unwilling to see a physician, get the name and dosage of the medication and consult with a physician. Also, inform the physician if your client is no longer taking a medication as prescribed.

3. Make sure your client and your client's family and friends understand the dangers of modifying the prescribed daily dosage and of exchanging medications with others. Also, alert your client to the dangers of using alcohol or street drugs while taking any medication. If your client takes more than one medication, an adverse drug interaction could occur. This happens when the two drugs mixed together have an effect very different than when each is taken alone. Side effects can also occur when the client mixes a psychotropic medication with nonprescription drugs like a cold medicine. Some foods (e.g., aged cheese) may cause adverse reactions when eaten by a person on certain medications.

4. As in the case of other forms of medical treatment, an adult has a right to refuse to take psychotropic medications. Exceptions are when a court has declared that the individual is legally incompetent to make that decision and/or when his or her behavior constitutes an imminent threat to self or others. Because the decision to reject a needed medication can have tragic results when disabling or psychotic symptoms recur, you should do everything possible to inform the patient and his or her family and close friends of the possible adverse consequences. In the final analysis, however, the decision of a legally competent adult must be respected.

Selected Bibliography

Gerhart, Ursula. "Psychotropic Medications." In *Encyclopedia of Social Work,* 18th ed., edited by Anne Minahan. Silver Spring, Md.: National Association of Social Workers, 1987, pp. 405–409.

Hyman, Steven, and George Arana. *Handbook of Psychiatric Drug Therapy.* Boston: Little, Brown, 1987.

U.S. Pharmacopoeial Convention, Inc. *Advice for the Patient.* Vol. 2, 5th ed. Rockville, Md.: U.S. Pharmacopoeial Convention, Inc., 1985.

Evaluation and Termination 13

Introduction

As conceptualized in this book, the problem-solving process ends with a final evaluation of the intervention and the termination of the professional relationship between client and social worker. This chapter focuses on those ending activities, providing several relatively simple evaluation techniques and guidelines for termination of service.

Broadly speaking, the evaluation process assesses whether intervention was effective and efficient. *Effectiveness* refers to whether the objectives were reached; *efficiency* refers to the ratio between the resources applied and the outcome. Ideally, an intervention is both effective and efficient. However, an intervention may be effective but not efficient, as in a case where much time and effort and many resources are necessary to achieve an objective. Needless to say, an intervention that does not achieve its goals and objectives is neither effective nor efficient.

Social workers and social agencies are concerned with two types of evaluation: social treatment evaluation and program evaluation. **Social treatment evaluation** attempts to assess the effectiveness and efficiency of an intervention with a specific client or a particular family or small group. By contrast, **program evaluation** attempts to assess the effectiveness and efficiency of a program serving a large number of clients or perhaps even a whole community. The beginning-level worker is usually concerned with measuring the effectiveness of direct service activities but not likely to have responsibility for program evaluation. Thus, this chapter focuses primarily on techniques that can be used to assess effectiveness of direct practice activities. Basic information on program evaluation is included in Chapter 14.

The single-subject design is especially useful when intervention focuses on a discrete behavior that is fairly easy to measure in terms of frequency, intensity, or duration. However, many common social work activities and interventions—such as referral, brokering, coordinating services, and advocating—do not lend themselves to the type of measurement and the baselining used in the single-subject approach. As an alternative, the techniques of goal-achievement scaling and task-achievement scaling can be used to evaluate such interventions, as well as others. Self-anchored and rating scales are additional ways of individualizing the measurements used in an evaluation of client change. The goal checklist described in this chapter can be used to combine certain case planning and evaluation activities and reduce the time needed to complete evaluation-related paperwork. Sometimes, the use of a post-intervention survey of client satisfaction is the only feasible way of gathering information about the probable impact of intervention. Thus, we include information on using client satisfaction questionnaires. We also include a description of peer review that can be used to examine the process of intervention even in the absence of client outcome data.

The social worker should always begin an intervention with a clear description of the goals and objectives. Without such specificity, it is impossible to decide later whether or not the intervention was successful. Simply stated, unless objectives are stated before the intervention begins, it will be impossible to determine the effect of the intervention. (See Chapter 11 for guidlelines on developing intervention objectives.)

Evaluation always involves some type of measurement. We cannot overemphasize the importance of trying to observe and measure those things that are relevant and central to the provision of service to clients. All too often, those conducting an evaluation tend to view that which is most easily measured as important, rather than trying to measure that which is really important to clients and to practice and service delivery.

Bloom and Fischer (1982) remind us that our measurement procedures should meet certain criteria:

1. *Reliable.* Your measure must be consistent, giving similar results when it is used under similar conditions.
2. *Valid.* To the extent possible, ensure that your measure really measures what it's supposed to.
3. *Useful.* Will the measure be relatively easy to implement, will it supply practical, useful information, and will the data actually be *used*?
4. *Direct.* . . . Try to select a measure that most accurately reflects (or actually is) the real problem. The closer the measure approximates the real problem, the more useful it will be. . . .
5. *Nonreactive.* Try to use measures that will do as little as possible to affect changes in the problem simply by the very act of measurement.
6. *Sensitive to change.* . . . Try to make sure that the measure you select will show changes if the changes do come about.
7. *Appropriate for single system designs.* . . . Will the measure be applicable when used on a repeated basis to collect data? If the measure is too long or complicated or takes too much time to use, then it may be useful only as a pre- and post-test and not for administration on a regular basis. (pp. 220–21)

Related to evaluation is the issue of termination. A key element of effective practice is the ability to lead the client through a smooth and satisfying termination of the helping relationship. Ending such a relationship at the appropriate time and with a positive outcome for the client requires considerable skill and careful planning. The social worker who is sensitive to issues surrounding termination helps the client leave the relationship with positive feelings and the ability to sustain gains made during the period of service.

Selected Bibliography

Bloom, Martin, and Joel Fischer. *Evaluating Practice*. Englewood Cliffs, N.J.: Prentice-Hall, 1982.

Blythe, Betty, and Tony Tripodi. *Measurement in Direct Practice*. Newbury, Calif.: Sage, 1989.

Monette, Duane, Thomas Sullivan, and Cornell DeJong. *Applied Social Research: Tool for the Human Services*. New York: Holt, Rinehart & Winston, 1986.

Reid, William, and Audrey Smith. *Research in Social Work*. 2nd ed. New York: Columbia University Press, 1989.

Rossi, Peter, and Howard Freeman. *Evaluation: A Systematic Approach*. 4th ed. Newbury, Calif.: Sage, 1989.

13.1 *Single-Subject Designs (SSD)*

Purpose: To evaluate the impact of an intervention by using a baseline and subsequent measurements of change.

Discussion: The study of a single case for the purpose of advancing social work knowledge and evaluating practice is as old as social work itself and as new as the application in the late 1950s of within-subject research methodology. Attention to this new technology has spread rapidly in social work since the mid-1970s, spurred on by the intensified call for accountability by funding sources, consumers, and the profession itself.

Bloom and Fischer (1982) point out that "this new practice/research technology actually has been described by several different terms: intensive or idiographic research, single N or $N = 1$ research, single subject research or single subject design, single case-study design, time series research or design, single organism research, single case experimental design, and ... single system designs" (p. 7). There are more than a dozen variations of the single-subject design. Some are very complex and rigorous and useful only to the researcher; the simpler ones can easily be used by the beginning-level worker in many direct service situations. A description of all the variations is beyond the scope of this book. Thus, only the basic elements of the design and the least complex of the variations will be addressed here.

The phrase ***single-subject*** denotes a focus of attention on a single client— usually a single individual but possibly a family or small group. Also, the term single-subject distinguishes this approach from the more traditional multiple-subject or experimental/group designs. In the single-subject design the client becomes his or her own control group. An individualized baseline—one relevant and meaningful in terms of the client's unique problem, situation, and goals—is used as the benchmark from which change is monitored and measured over the course of intervention. The establishment of one or more baseline measures is an essential activity, regardless of what particular version of the single-subject design is used.

The term ***target behavior*** refers to the behavior that the intervention intends to change. Any measurable aspect of a client's problem or situation can become the target. When selecting the target behavior, Polster and Lynch (1985) suggest that

> since it may not always be possible to measure all aspects of the desired change, the target behaviors selected must be representative of the changes which must occur to indicate successful accomplishment of the intervention goals. The target behavior must also be one which the worker, other cooperative persons (collaterals) in the environment, or the individual (subject) have opportunities to measure. Behaviors which are covert and leave no reliable evidence of having occurred, or which occur in places or at times when no one is available to record them, are not suitable as target behaviors unless the behavior leaves an observable product which can be recorded. (p. 384)

A ***baseline*** is usually established by observing the frequency, intensity, or duration of the target behavior over a period of days or weeks. When time does not permit an observation prior to intervention, it may be possible to retrospectively establish a baseline with information gathered from interviews with the client focusing on previous patterns of behavior; from interviews with the client's family or significant others; or from agency records, police reports, school reports, and the like.

The term ***multiple baseline*** refers to the use of more than one baseline as a means of measuring change. For example, in work with a child having trouble in school, one baseline might focus on frequency of school attendance, a second on grades received on weekly assignments, and a third on a teacher's weekly rating of the student's level of cooperation in the classroom. Unless the target problem is highly specific, multiple baselines are usually necessary in order to capture the impact of an intervention. In some cases, the client's score on a rating scale such as those in the Clinical Measurement Package (see Technique 10.16) can be used as a baseline. Changes in the client's score on repeated administrations suggest the impact of intervention.

The various versions of the single-subject design are identified by a set of initials. The letter *A* refers to the baseline. The letter *B* refers to the intervention. Thus, an *AB* single-subject design refers to the establishment of a baseline followed by intervention. The measured change from the baseline is attributed to the impact of intervention.

The *ABA* version removes the intervention (*B*) after a period of time to test the impact of the intervention. If there is a return to the original baseline, it is assumed that the change was caused by the intervention and not other factors in the client's life.

The *ABAB* design goes one step further, adding a fourth stage to the ABA by restarting an intervention. If there is again a change from the second baseline, the worker can be quite sure that his or her intervention is responsible for the change.

The *BAB* variation begins immediately with an intervention, eventually with-draws the intervention in order to establish a baseline, and then restarts the intervention. This particular design is used when it is not feasible to establish a baseline before beginning an intervention.

Another useful version of the single-subject design is termed the multiple-element design or the *ABCD* design, which is used to evaluate the impact of a series of different interventions, one following the other. For example, after the establishment of the baseline (*A*), the first intervention (*B*) is tried for several weeks; then a second intervention (*C*) is implemented and subsequently, a third intervention (*D*). This design makes it possible to compare the relative effective-ness of several different interventions on a particular target behavior.

A simple graph can be used to record the results of intervention. While sta-tistical procedures are available to evaluate single-subject data, the visual inspec-tion of a graph will be adequate in most cases. Figure 13.1 is a graph showing the baseline (*A*), the intervention (*B*), a removal of the intervention (*A*), and then a return to the intervention (*B*). This is, of course, an example of an *ABAB* design. In this case, the presenting problem was marital conflict expressing itself in fre-quent verbal arguments. The husband and wife sought professional assistance

Figure 13.1 Graph of Intervention Results

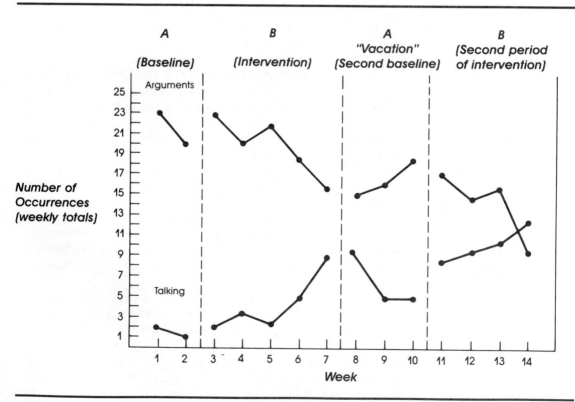

because they wanted to learn how to "talk more and argue less." Note that two weeks prior to the start of the first intervention period, the clients were asked to make daily records of the number of times they argued (shouting, name calling, etc.) and the number of times they talked calmly with each other for at least a three-minute period. Only the weekly totals are shown on the graph. The intervention, consisting of a weekly joint interview and a weekly small group discussion with three other client couples, was aimed at reducing the number of arguments and increasing the amount of time they spent in calm and amiable conversation. After five weeks of intervention, the couple was asked to take a three-week "vacation" from treatment. After that, the second five-week period of intervention began. A visual inspection of the graph shows that the first five-week intervention did reduce the frequency of arguments and increased the couple's talking together. When the intervention stopped, the couple talked less and argued more. The second period of intervention again moved the couple in the direction of positive change.

Selected Bibliography

Bloom, Martin, and Joel Fischer. *Evaluating Practice: Guidelines for the Accountable Professional.* Englewood Cliffs, N.J.: Prentice-Hall, 1982.

Levy, Rona. "Single Subject Research Designs." In *Encyclopedia of Social Work,* edited by Anne Minahan. Silver Spring, Md.: NASW, 1987.

Polster, Richard, and Mary Ann Lynch. "Single-Subject Designs." In *Social Work Research and Evaluation,* 2nd ed. edited by Richard Grinnell. Itasca, Ill.: F. E. Peacock, 1985.

Thomas, Edwin. "Problems and Issues in Single Case Experiments." In *Handbook of Clinical Social Work Practice,* edited by Aaron Rosenblatt ad Diana Waldfogel. San Francisco: Jossey-Bass, 1983.

13.2   *Task Achievement Scaling (TAS)*

Purpose: To determine the degree to which the client and/or worker completed agreed-upon intervention tasks.

Discussion: *Task Achievement Scaling (TAS)* is a simple and flexible evaluation tool. It is especially useful when the social work intervention is such that it does not lend itself to the use of baselining or single-subject designs. Examples include the referral of a client to an agency, obtaining needed information for a client, arranging transportation or daycare, or securing housing for a client. Also, TAS can be used in brief service situations, such as when a client and worker meet only one or two times.

The TAS procedure was developed for use in task-centered practice and research. In *task-centered practice,* work toward the client's goal is broken down into many separate actions or tasks. A task is usually something that is to be accomplished by the client or the worker in a matter of days or, at most, in a couple of weeks. The tasks are selected by mutual agreement. Each task must make sense to the client, be feasible, and be directly related to the client's problem or goal. Usually, not more than two or three tasks are worked on at any one time.

The structure provided by this approach facilitates the problem-solving process. In task-centered work, a session typically begins with a review of what has been accomplished since the last session. The two or three tasks that the client and worker have previously selected for accomplishment are discussed in detail. Successful task achievement is reinforced by the worker. If there is little progress, the reasons are examined and modifications are made in task planning and implementation prior to the next session.

Task Achievement Scaling refers to rating the degree to which the agreed upon task has, in fact, been achieved. Ideally, the rating is done by both worker and client. But in many cases, only the worker will do the rating for purposes of professional accountability and recordkeeping. Reid and Epstein (1972, 1977) have utilized a four-point rating scale (i.e., the TAS) in their practice and research to record progress on each task: (4) completely achieved; (3) substantially achieved, action is still necessary; (2) partially achieved, considerable work remains to be done; and (1) minimally achieved or not achieved. Where appropriate, a fifth rating—(No) for "No opportunity to work on task"—can be used.

Reid and Epstein (1977) describe the task achievement scale as follows:

(4) *Completely achieved.* This rating applies to tasks that are fully accomplished, e.g., a job has been found, a homemaker secured, financial assistance obtained. It may also be used for tasks that are fully accomplished "for all practical purposes:" if a couple's task was to reduce quarreling a rating of (4) could be given if they reached a point where hostile interchanges occurred infrequently, no longer presented a problem, and they saw no need for further work on the task.

(3) *Substantially achieved.* The task is largely accomplished though further action may need to be taken before full accomplishment is realized. Thus, if the task is to improve work performance, significant improvement would merit a rating of (3) even though further improvement would be possible and desirable.

(2) *Partially achieved.* Demonstrable progress has been made on the task but considerable work remains to be done. For example, if the task is to obtain a job, a rating of (2) could be given if the client has been actively looking for work and found a job he could take (and might) but was reluctant to. Or this rating would be appropriate for a couple who had made some headway on a shared task of finding things of mutual interest to do together even though they and the caseworker may be dissatisfied with their progress. Specific evidence of task accomplishment is required, however. . . .

(1) *Minimally achieved* (or not achieved). This rating is used for tasks on which no progress has been made or on which progress has been insignificant or uncertain. If a client's task were to locate and enter a suitable vocational training program, a rating of (1) would be given if the client were unable to locate a program, even though much effort had gone into searching for one.

(No) *No opportunity* to work on task. For example, client cannot carry out task in classroom because school is closed by teachers' strike. (p. 289)

Note that only results are rated, not good intentions, effort, or motivation.

The TAS is typically used to evaluate session-by-session progress. However, a slight elaboration of the Reid and Epstein four-point scale permits a summarization of task ratings and the calculation of a percentage figure that can serve as a crude end-of-service outcome measure. To do this, use this five-point rating scale:

(4)   Completely achieved
(3)   Substantially achieved
(2)   Partially achieved
(1).   Minimally achieved
(0)   No progress

By summing the final rating on each task and then dividing this sum by the highest sum possible, a percentage of success is determined. For example, if, over a series of six sessions, a total of seven separate tasks were agreed upon and targeted for accomplishment, the maximum score possible would be 28 (7 tasks $\times$ 4 = 28). A summary score of 28 would indicate that all seven tasks were completely achieved. If, however, the seven individual task ratings were actually 4, 4, 3, 3, 3, 2, and 1, the summed score would be only 20. As the final step, divide 20 by 28 and arrive at an end-of-service outcome of 71 percent. In other words, the client achieved 71 percent of all that was agreed upon, planned, and translated into tasks.

The appealing feature of TAS is its simplicity and the fact that it can be used when more rigorous procedures are not feasible because of insufficient time or data. Moreover, it does not intrude upon the helping process. Needless to say, it has real limitations as an evaluation tool; but when no other tool can be utilized, the TAS does yield a crude measure of effectiveness. More importantly, it measures those activities that the client has identified as being important.

Selected Bibliography

Fortune, Anne. *Task-Centered Practice with Families and Groups.* New York: Springer, 1985.

Reid, William. *The Task Centered System.* New York: Columbia University Press, 1978.

Reid, William, and Laura Epstein. *Task Centered Casework.* New York: Columbia University Press, 1972.

Reid William, and Laura Epstein, eds. *Task Centered Practice.* New York: Columbia University Press, 1977.

13.3   *Goal Attainment Scaling (GAS)*

Purpose: To measure the degree to which the client has reached individualized goals.

Discussion: *Goal Attainment Scaling (GAS)* is a procedure that permits an evaluation of an intervention, even when the objectives and goals of the intervention are unique to a particular client. GAS has been utilized in mental health centers, drug abuse programs, probation and parole, and a number of other human service settings.

An application of GAS begins during the contracting and goal-setting phases of an intervention. Goals are selected and written onto a form called a "Goal Attainment Follow-Up Guide." The format of the guide is the same for all clients, but the scale content is individualized. The guide consists of a succession of scales, each of which represents a series of possible client outcomes—both positive and negative—related to an agreed upon area of client functioning, such as interpersonal relations, employment, parenting, and so on. Each area becomes the focus of a separate scale.

Figure 13.2 presents a completed Goal Attainment Follow-Up Guide focusing on five individualized areas of a client's functioning (education, suicide, manipulation, drug abuse, and dependency on agency). For each of the five areas, a five-point outcome scale has been constructed. The possible outcomes described range from the "most unfavorable" (-2) on one extreme, to "most favorable" or "best anticipated" $(+2)$ on the other extreme.

There are three steps in constructing a goal attainment follow-up guide:

1. *Identify the major areas of functioning in which intervention is expected to have an impact.* For example, typical goal areas in mental health settings include alcohol, depression, education, interpersonal relationships, suicide, and work performance. Usually, the number of areas should not exceed four or five.

2. *Assign a number to each goal area to indicate its importance in comparison with other goal areas toward which the client is preparing to work.* These numbers weigh the outcome on the individual scales, so the final score reflects the relative value of the results achieved. For example, if "drug abuse" is viewed as two times more important than "family relationship," the drug abuse goal area could be assigned a weight of 20 and the family relationship area a weight of 10. Thus, when the summary Goal Attainment Score is computed for the client, the outcome in the drug abuse goal area would have twice as much influence on the final score as the outcome in the family relationship goal area.

3. *Specify five levels of possible outcome in relation to each goal area.* These outcomes should be progressive. The lowest is the "most unfavorable outcome thought likely"; next is "less than expected success." The third or middle level is "expected level of success." The top levels are "more than expected success" and "best anticipated success." Statements of potential outcome are tailored to the needs, capabilities, and aspirations of the individual client. The outcome statements should be specific (so expectations are clear), observable (so there is little confusion as to the level of outcome that actually occurs), and realistic (so the scale is relevant to the client's situation). Once a scale has been constructed, a

Material on GAS was adapted from Hagedorn et al., National Institute on Mental Health, *A Working Manual of Simple Program Evaluation Techniques for Community Mental Health Centers* (Washington, D.C.: U.S. Government Printing Office, 1976), DHEW Pub. No. (ADM) 79–404, pp. 223–30.

Figure 13.2 Sample Five-Scale Follow-Up Guide

Crisis Intervention Center (CIC)
Goal Attainment Follow-up Guide

Client: Jan Smith
Level at Intake: ✓

Worker: Jim Green
Level at Follow-up: X

Guide developed: 9/23/86

Date of follow-up: 1/16/87

Check whether scale has been mutually negotiated between patient and CIC

Scale Headings and Scale Weights

	Scale 1: Education ($w_1 = 20$)	Scale 2: Suicide ($w_2 = 30$)	Scale 3: Manipulation ($w_3 = 25$)	Scale 4: Drug Abuse ($w_4 = 30$)	Scale 5: Dependency on CIC ($w_5 = 10$)
	Yes X No ___	Yes ___ No X	Yes ___ No X	Yes X No ___	Yes X No ___
Scale Attainment Levels					
a. (−2) Most unfavorable treatment outcome thought likely	Patient has made no attempt to enroll in high school.	Patient has committed suicide.	Patient makes rounds of community service agencies demanding medication and refuses other forms of treatment.	Patient reports addiction to "hard narcotics" (heroin, morphine).	Patient has contacted CIC by telephone or in person at least seven times since her first visit.
b. (−1) Less than expected success with treatment	Patient has enrolled in high school, but at time of follow-up has dropped out.	Patient has acted on at least one suicidal impulse since her first contact with the CIC but has not succeeded.	Patient no longer visits CIC with demands for medication but continues with other community agencies and still refuses other forms of treatment.	Patient has used "hard narcotics" but is not addicted and/or uses hallucinogens (LSD, pot) more than four times a month.	Patient has contacted CIC 5–6 times since intake.

Figure 13.2 (Continued)

Check whether scale has been mutually negotiated between patient and CIC

Scale Headings and Scale Weights

	Scale 1: Education ($w_1 = 20$) Yes X No ___	Scale 2: Suicide ($w_2 = 30$) Yes ___ No X	Scale 3: Manipulation ($w_3 = 25$) Yes ___ No X	Scale 4: Drug Abuse ($w_4 = 30$) Yes X No ___	Scale 5: Dependency on CIC ($w_5 = 10$) Yes X No ___
Scale Attainment Levels					
c. Expected level of treatment success (0)	Patient has enrolled and is in school at follow-up, but is attending class sporadically (misses an average of more than a third of her classes during a week). X	Patient reports she has had at least four suicidal impulses since her first contact with the CIC but has not acted on any of them. X	Patient no longer attempts to manipulate for drugs at community service agencies but will not accept another form of treatment.	Patient has not used "hard narcotics" during follow-up period and uses hallucinogens between 1–4 times a month.	Patient has contacted CIC 3–4 times since intake.
d. More than expected success with treatment (+1)	Patient has enrolled, is in school at follow-up, and is attending classes consistently but has no vocational goals. X	Patient reports she has had no suicidal impulses since her first contact with the CIC.	Patient accepts nonmedication treatment at some community agency. X	Patient uses hallucinogens less than once a month. X	Patient has contacted CIC 1–2 times since intake.
e. Best anticipated success with treatment (+2)	Patient has enrolled, is in school at follow-up, is attending classes consistently, and has some vocational goals.	Patient reports she has had no suicidal impulses since her first contact with the CIC.	Patient accepts nonmedication treatment and by own report shows signs of improvement.	At time of follow-up, patient is not using any illegal drugs.	Patient has not contacted CIC since intake. X

Source: Hagedorn et al. 1976, p. 224.

check (✔) is placed in the cell that best describes the client at the time the follow-up guide was constructed (i.e., when intervention began). This serves as the baseline measure.

These three steps create the GAS Guide. Experience suggests that it takes a minimum of twenty to thirty minutes to complete the follow-up guide.

The evaluation of an intervention using the GAS Guide requires the use of a follow-up interview after the intervention to determine the client's level of functioning on each scale. These evaluation interviews may occur at intervals during intervention (e.g., every six weeks) and at termination or shortly after the intervention has terminated. Follow-up interviews may be in person or by telephone. It takes approximately forty minutes to conduct the follow-up interview and complete the scoring.

Scoring requires determining the level on each scale that best describes the client at the time of follow-up and placing an X in the appropriate cell. From a scored follow-up guide, it is possible to calculate two numerical measures of treatment efficacy: (1) a summary Goal Attainment Score and (2) a Goal Attainment Change Score. The task of calculating these measures is a problem for many users of GAS because it involves the use of a rather complex formula.

A summary Goal Attainment Score is generated by transforming the scores on the individual scales of a goal attainment follow-up guide into a single numerical value. This value is a global index of the degree to which goals have been met. The recommended means of obtaining a Goal Attainment Score is a formula reported by Kiresuk and Sherman (1968). This formula produces a statistic that is essentially an average of attainment on all scales, corrected for the number of scales, the "weight" (relative importance) of the scales, and the intercorrelation of the scales.

A Goal Attainment Change Score indicates the amount of difference in a client's status before and after intervention; it is determined by subtracting the summary Goal Attainment Score calculated at the time the follow-up guide was constructed from the score calculated at the time of follow-up. A negative score indicates deterioration; a score near zero indicates little or no change; a positive score indicates progress.

As a possible alternative to the calculation of one or both of these scores, the worker may prepare a statement of outcome by simply writing a few sentences that describe the client's change on the scales (e.g., Ms. Smith moved from −2 to +1 in the area of education on her GAS follow-up guide). However, the use of a calculated numerical score would be necessary in program evaluation where the data on many clients must be combined.

The evaluator who has the necessary time can obtain valuable information about program results from a study of GAS follow-up guides, including:

1. The types of problems chosen as a target of intervention and their relative frequency
2. The types of problems on which particular workers or the agency as a whole make the most or least amount of progress

3. The types of problems worked on relative to particular client groups (e.g., most common targets of intervention among clients over age sixty-five)

Selected Bibliography

Hagedorn, Homer, Kenneth Beck, Stephen Neubert, and Stanley Werlin (National Institute of Mental Health). *A Working Manual of Simple Program Evaluation Techniques for Community Mental Health Centers.* Washington, D.C.: Government Printing Office, 1976, DHEW Publ. No. (ADM) 79–404.

Kiresuk, Thomas J., and Geoffrey Garwick. "Basic Goal Attainment Scaling Procedures." In *Social Work Processes,* rev. ed., edited by Beulah Compton and Burt Galaway. Homewood, Ill.: Dorsey Press, 1979 (pp. 412–21).

Kiresuk, Thomas J., and Sander H. Lund. "Process and Outcome Measurement Using Goal Attainment Scaling." In *Program Evaluation: Alcohol, Drug Abuse, and Mental Health Services,* edited by Jack Zusman and Cecil R. Wurster. Lexington, Mass.: Lexington Books, 1975.

Kiresuk, Thomas J., and Robert E. Sherman. "Goal Attainment Scaling: A General Method for Evaluating Comprehensive Community Mental Health Programs." *Community Mental Health Journal* 4 (1968): 445–53.

Seaberg, James, and David Gillespie. "Goal Attainment Scaling: A Critique." *Social Work Research and Abstracts* 13 (Summer 1977): 4–8.

13.4 *Goal Checklist*

Purpose: To measure the client's movement toward goals between intake and termination.

Discussion: The *Goal Checklist* developed by Fraser, Pecora, and Haapala (1988) was developed for use in child welfare and family services settings. It is an example of an evaluation tool that utilizes a list or a "menu" of agency-relevant goals from which the social worker and client select those that are to give direction to the intervention. After the intervention is complete, the goals are rated in a manner similar to task achievement scaling. The use of a goal checklist is possible within settings where the intervention goals are similar for most clients serviced by the agency.

Since the goals are not unique to each client and are printed on the evaluation form, this tool demands less time to complete than either the TAS and GAS. Also, it lends itself to the compilation of agency statistics about the types of client problems addressed and the degree to which goals were reached. The major advantages of the Goal Checklist are that it is simple and quick to use. Its major disadvantages are that the goals are rather global and it does not utilize a baseline. Because the format used is quite versatile and because it can serve as a model for ones that could be developed in other practice settings, we present it, in its entirety, as Figure 13.3.

Figure 13.3 Goal Checklist

Client/Family   Worker   Date

INSTRUCTIONS:

Complete within 1–2 weeks of Intake:
STEP 1: Indicate the family's treatment goals by checking (at left) those goals that apply to this case. Check only those goals that will be a significant part of your intervention. One indicator of this is that the problem area or goal will be reflected elsewhere in your case reports. For example, only rate goal #01 (establish trust) if this is to be a major focus of intervention. If there are goals that do not fit under an existing category, use #17 ("other") to describe these goals.

Complete at termination (case closing):
STEP 2: Indicate which of the goals you checked were the two most important goals by circling (at right) the "I" under the "Two Most Important Goals" column.
STEP 3: For all the goals you checked, rate the level of goal achievement by circling the number under the rating scale most appropriate for each goal.

GOAL	RATING SCALES					Two Most Important Goals
	No Progress		About Half Achieved	Totally Achieved		
___01. Establish trust and functional working relationship with clients. (e.g., significant family members see the value of working with the therapist, client hostility toward counseling reduced, clients finally agree to try/do something)	1	2	3	4	5	I ___
___02. Increase communication skills. (e.g., use of I-messages, active listening, problem-solving and family meetings, avoiding labels and blaming)	1	2	3	4	5	I ___
___03. Increase parenting skills. (e.g., use of positive consequences, consistency, behavioral charting and contracting, setting appropriate limits, giving clear expectations, reducing physical punishment, awareness of developmental stages.)	1	2	3	4	5	I ___
___04. Increase anger management and conflict resolution skills. (e.g., negotiating areas of conflict, problem-solving, assertiveness, taking "no" for	1	2	3	4	5	I ___

(Continued)

Figure 13.3 Goal Checklist (Continued)

GOAL	RATING SCALES					Two Most Important Goals
	No Progress		About Half Achieved		Totally Achieved	
__04. *(Continued)* an answer; reduced "backtalk," hitting, yelling, swearing, property damage)						
__05. Improve school performance and/or attendance. (e.g., school allows child to return, child attends regularly, child on time to school, homework done, gets along with schoolmates and teachers)	1	2	3	4	5	I __
__06. Increase self-esteem. (e.g., client sees positives about self, client uses affirmations.	1	2	3	4	5	I __
__07. Decrease anxiety, worry, or fear. (e.g., decrease feelings of fear, worry panic; ruminates less, feels more relaxed)	1	2	3	4	5	I __
__08. Decrease depression and/or suicidal thoughts or behaviors. (e.g., client feels less hopeless and helpless, feels in control of his life; engages in pleasant events, reduced talk about depression or self-destruction.)	1	2	3	4	5	I __
__09. Increase compliance with house rules. (e.g., chores, smoking, bedtime, curfew, dating)	1	2	3	4	5	I __
__10. Decrease running away. (e.g., stays out overnight or longer only with permission)	1	2	3	4	5	I __
__11. Improve household physical conditions. (e.g., clean house, adequate food, pest control, laundry done)	1	2	3	4	5	I __
__12. Increase social support network. (e.g., involved with friends, relatives, neighbors, church, clubs)	1	2	3	4	5	I __
__13. Increase use of community resources. (e.g., SSI, AFDS, food banks, counseling, medical, daycare, bus system)	1	2	3	4	5	I __
__14. Decrease delinquent or illegal behavior. (e.g., stealing, prostitution, gang activities, assault, destruction	1	2	3	4	5	I __

GOAL	RATING SCALES				
	No Progress	About Half Achieved	Totally Achieved		Two Most Important Goals
of property, sex offenses— regardless of whether client has been officially charged with these behaviors)					
___15. Decrease drug and/or alcohol use.	1	2	3	4	5	I __
___16. Increase appropriate sexual behavior. (e.g., birth control, choice of partners, avoiding victimization)	1	2	3	4	5	I __
___17. Other (please specify):	1	2	3	4	5	I __

Source: Fraser, M. W., Pecora, P. J., & Haapala, D. A. (1988). *Families in Crisis: Findings from the Family-Based Intensive Treatment Project.* (Volume II). Salt Lake City, UT: University of Utah Graduate School of Social Work, Social Research Institute; and Federal Way, WA: Behavioral Sciences Institute. Reprinted with permission.

Selected Bibliography

Fraser, M. W., P. J. Pecora, and D. A. Haapala. *Families in Crisis: Findings from the Family-Based Intensive Treatment Project* (Volume II). Salt Lake City: University of Utah Graduate School of Social Work, Social Research Institute; and Federal Way, Wash. Behavioral Science Institute, 1988.

13.5 Self-Anchored and Individualized Rating Scales

Purpose: To measure the intensity of a client's problem.

Discussion: The **self-anchored scale** and the **individualized rating scales** are relatively simple and flexible procedures that can be used when an intervention is focusing on a client problem for which the use of a standardized instrument is not available or feasible. Bloom (1975) and Bloom and Fischer (1982) describe these two types of scales as "do it yourself scales" and the "all purpose measurement procedure." The scales are similar in construction, but the self-anchored scale is completed by the client, whereas the rating scale is completed by someone other than the client. Corcoran and Fischer (1987) explain the basic procedure for developing such scales:

> Once the problem area is defined, you present to the client a picture of a social or psychological thermometer, with one end being the most intense end of the problem

and the other the least intense. Then you select the number of points for the scale. We usually recommend 0–10 or 1–9, although if the client has difficulty in discriminating among that many points, you can collapse the scale to 1–7 or 1–5 points. Make sure you are clear with the client that they are equal intervals, so that the difference between 1 and 2 on the scale is no greater than the difference between 5 and 6. Finally, you and the client attempt to anchor the scale points using as much concrete detail to define each point as possible. (p. 30)

More detailed instructions are found in Bloom and Fischer (1982, 166–80).

The self-anchored scale is especially useful because it can be used to measure the intensity of feelings and inner conflicts. Who but the client can possibly measure the intensity of his or her own pain, guilt, or anxiety? Below is an example of a nine-point, self-anchored scale measuring the intensity of a mother's anger toward her handicapped child named Karen.

1···············2···············3···············4···············5···············6···············7···············8···············9

| No awareness of anger. Enjoy time with Karen. | Moderate feelings of anger. Some bitterness and resentment. | Intense anger. Want to strike out and hurt Karen. Have feelings of hatred. Want her to die. |

A rating scale, because it is completed by others, must be of a more behavioral nature. A seven-point rating scale measuring this mother's anger might look like this:

1···············2···············3···············4···············5···············6···············7

| Mother smiles at Karen. Holds her gently. | Mother speaks sharply. Handles Karen in rough manner. Mother frequently frowns and scowls. | Mother yells and screams at Karen. Threatens or hits child. |

Selected Bibliography

Bloom, Martin. *The Paradox of Helping.* New York: Wiley, 1975.

Bloom, Martin, and Joel Fischer. *Evaluating Practice: Guidelines for the Accountable Professional.* Englewood Cliffs, N.J.: Prentice-Hall, 1982.

Corcoran, Kevin, and Joel Fischer. *Measures for Clinical Practice: A Source Book.* New York: The Free Press, 1987.

13.6   *Differential Impact Scoring (DIS)*

Purpose: To obtain client's perceptions on changes that have occurred since intervention began and differentiate changes attributed to intervention from those attributed to other factors.

Discussion: When a client is receiving services from more than one professional and more than one agency, how do we determine which intervention is having or has had an impact? And, how do we account for changes in the client's life circumstances that may cause either an improvement or a worsening of the client's situation but that have nothing to do with the interventions? A limitation in our usual attempts to secure a "before-and-after" measure is that the identified change, whether positive or negative, may have resulted from influences other than the worker's or the agency's intervention. In such cases, it would be inappropriate for an agency either to claim credit for positive change or to assume responsibility for negative changes. The ABA and ABAB single subject designs (see Technique 13.1) attempt to address this problem, but for practical and ethical reasons it is not always feasible to stop and then later restart an intervention as a way of deterimining which of several interventions might be having an impact.

The procedure we call **_Differential Impact Scoring (DIS)_** is a crude but practical method of separating out the impact of a specific intervention from other factors and interventions that also influence the client. A major limitation of DIS is that it depends on self-reported data and measures only the client's perceptions or opinions. Perceptions voiced by a client may or may not be an accurate description of what really happened and why.

The example of DIS presented below is drawn from a study (Horejsi, 1972) of a lay volunteer program's impact on the functioning of youths on probation, as perceived by the parents of those youths; we believe its basic format and scoring procedure can be adapted for use in many other settings. During the months of contact with the lay volunteer, these adolescent clients also had regular contact with their probation officer, and many of the youths and their families were simultaneously receiving services from mental health, social service and health care agencies, school programs, and other professionals. In an attempt to determine if the volunteers were having any impact on these youths, respondents (i.e., the parents) were asked thirty-seven questions about whether they had observed changes in their child's school attendance, grades, money management, choice of friends, control of anger, communication with family, and so on. (Two sample questions are shown in Figure 13.4.) If the respondent expressed the belief that a change (either "better" or "worse") had occurred, a follow-up question asked whether the respondent believed the volunteer had anything to do with the perceived change; possible responses were "great deal," "quite a bit," "only a little," and "nothing." This thirty-seven-item scale can be administered in about thirty minutes.

An *item score* ranging from $+10$ to -10 was obtained by a multiplication procedure. For example, an individual item score of zero would result if a parent stated that his or her child's school attendance had either "improved" ($+2$) or "gotten worse" (-2) and that the volunteer had "nothing" (0) to do with this change. An item score of plus six ($+6$), for example, would result if the parent stated that his or her child's school attendance had "improved" ($+2$) and that the volunteer had "quite a bit" (3) to do with the change (i.e., $2 \times 3 = 6$). All possible item scores are shown in Figure 13.5.

Figure 13.4   Sample Questions from Interview Schedule

Item 16.   *What about the frequency with which you and (youth's name) have disagreements or arguments? Has this improved, remained the same, or gotten worse?*

A_____ improved   B_____ remained the same   C_____ worse

(If either improved or worse) In your opinion, to what extent did the volunteer have something to do with (this improvement) (this change for the worse)?

1_____ volunteer had a great deal to do with the change

2_____ volunteer had quite a bit to do with the change

3_____ volunteer had only a little bit to do with the change

4_____ volunteer had nothing to do with the change

Item 24.   Do you think things have improved, remained the same, or gotten worse in regard to how often (youth's name) *gets into arguments or fights* with other kids?

A_____ improved   B_____ remained the same   C_____ worse

(If either improved or worse) In your opinion, to what extend did the volunteer have something to do with (this improvement) (this change for the worse)?

1_____ volunteer had a great deal to do with the change

2_____ volunteer had quite a bit to do with the change

3_____ volunteer had only a little bit to do with the change

4_____ volunteer had nothing to do with the change.

A *summary score* for each youth was obtained by summing all thirty-seven item scores. A high positive summary score resulted when a parent reported many improvements and attributed most of them to the volunteer's intervention. A low positive score resulted when a parent perceived few improvements that could be attributed to the volunteer's influence. A negative summary score

Figure 13.5   Possible DIS Item Scores

Parent's Evaluation of Child's Functioning	Parent's Perception of Volunteer's Contribution to Change	Individual Item Score
Improved (+2)	"great deal" (5)	$2 \times 5 = 10$
Improved (+2)	"quite a bit" (3)	$2 \times 3 = 6$
Improved (+2)	"only a little" (1)	$2 \times 1 = 2$
Improved (+2)	"nothing" (0)	$2 \times 0 = 0$
Remained the same (0)	—	0
Worse (−2)	"nothing" (0)	$-2 \times 0 = 0$
Worse (−2)	"only a little" (1)	$-2 \times 1 = -2$
Worse (−2)	"quite a bit" (3)	$-2 \times 3 = -6$
Worse (−2)	"great deal" (5)	$-2 \times 5 = -10$

indicated that negative changes had occurred and the parents believed that the volunteer's intervention had caused the deterioration. Theoretically, summary scores could range from a high of 370 ($2 \times 5 \times 37$) to a low of -370 ($-2 \times 5 \times 37$).

It should be noted that the respondent's choices of "improved," "remained the same," and "worse" could be expanded to, for example, "much improved" ($+3$), "improved some" ($+1$), "the same" (0), "somewhat worse" (-1), and "much worse" (-3). We find, however, that many clients have difficulty making more precise distinctions when confronted with numerous choices. It is best to keep evaluation procedures as simple as possible so as not to confuse the respondents.

As suggested above, the DIS is at best a crude measure, but it can prove useful when other approaches are not feasible. Magura and Moses (1986) use a somewhat related approach in their attempt to determine what interventions had an impact on the client. Their *Parent Outcome Interview* is an instrument designed to obtain the client's perceptions of agency services in child welfare cases. In addition to asking respondents whether a change had occurred (i.e., better or worse), a series of open-ended follow-up questions probed for the reasons why the services were or were not effective and, if effective, how the improvement in functioning took place. Such an evaluation approach requires additional interview time with the respondents (i.e., the Parent Outcome Interview required two hours to administer) but yields a much more detailed understanding of which interventions are effective and why they are or are not working.

Selected Bibliography

Horejsi, Charles. "Attitudes of Parents Toward Juvenile Court Volunteers." *Federal Probation* (June 1972): 13–18.

Horejsi, Charles. "Juvenile Probationers' Behavior and Attitudes Rating Scale." In *Tests and Measurements in Child Development: Handbook II,* edited by Orval Johnson. San Francisco: Jossey-Bass, 1976, pp. 1092–93.

Magura, Stephen, and Beth Moses. *Outcome Measures for Child Welfare Services.* Washington, D.C.: Child Welfare League of America, 1986.

13.7   *Client Satisfaction Questionnaire (CSQ)*

Purpose: To determine the client's satisfaction with the services he or she has received.

Discussion: A *Client Satisfaction Questionnaire (CSQ)* is a simple and inexpensive method of soliciting a client's opinions about the services he or she has received. A major limitation of a CSQ is that it records only the client's perceptions of what happened as a result of intervention. Certainly, reality may differ

Material in this section was adapted, in part, from Hagedorn et al., National Institute on Mental Health, *A Working Manual on Simple Program Evaluation Techniques for Community Mental Health Centers* (Washington, D.C.: U.S. Government Printing Office, 1976), DHEW Pub. No. (ADM) 79–404, pp. 230–37.

from perception, and perception may change over time. Another limitation is the tendency of a CSQ to yield data biased in the direction of positive responses, particularly if administered by mail. Dissatisfied clients are less likely than satisfied ones to return the questionnaire.

A short CSQ has the advantage of being easy to complete. A lengthy, detailed questionnaire will, of course, collect more information but may result in lower rate of completion. A CSQ, coupled with in-depth interviewing (by phone or face to face), is needed to secure detailed information on specific service variables related to the client's satisfaction and dissatisfaction.

Most often, a CSQ is administered at the point of service termination or shortly thereafter. Some agencies routinely administer a CSQ after three to five interviews (and periodically thereafter if the client receives services for a longer period), at the point of termination, and perhaps two months following termination.

A brief "generic" CSQ is presented in Figure 13.6. Figure 13.7 presents a portion of a more detailed CSQ used in a shelter for abused women; it illustrates an alternative arrangement of questions and asks the client to respond on a four-point scale, ranging from "strongly disagree" to "strongly agree." Such a numerical scale facilitates the tabulation of data and makes possible the calculation of averages. Other examples of CSQ can be found in Reid and Epstein (1977) and in Beck and Jones (1977). Follow these four steps in using a CSQ:

1. *Decide what population of clients to sample.* The sample could be representative of agency clientele in general, of clients who have received a particular type of service, or of clients who make up a particular demographic group (e.g., clients over age sixty). A basic knowledge of sampling methods is required in order to draw a sample that is representative. Criteria for CSQ distribution should be determined by the evaluator and relate to statistical requirements, administrative convenience, and what the evaluation is intended to accomplish.

2. *Design the questionnaire.* Remember to keep it as simple and brief as possible and to avoid professional jargon and technical terminology. In addition to questions intended to elicit opinions about services received, the agency may want to gather certain client and demographic information in order to determine if satisfaction with or complaints about services are related to factors such as the client's ethnicity, age, socioeconomic status, type of service received, and the like. However, a CSQ asking for such information tends to weaken assurances of anonymity and confidentiality. (See Technique 10.13 for additional information on developing a questionnaire.)

3. *Administer the questionnaire.* This step can often be carried out by clerical staff, volunteers, or social service aides; however, those administering the questionnaire must be trained in its use in order to increase reliability. The assurance of confidentiality to respondents is very important. A mailed CSQ can provide the client with anonymity but does presume that the client can read. If the target population consists of former clients, the questionnaire can be either mailed or administered by phone. If it includes clients who are still in regular contact with the agency, the questionnaire can usually be administered to them by a receptionist. The greatest amount of work in administering the questionnaire will probably

Figure 13.6   Sample Client Satisfaction Questionnaire

Evaluating Your Experience
at ABC Agency

Thank you for taking a few minutes to evaluate the service you have received at our agency. Your answers to this brief questionnaire will help us to improve our services. Feel free to offer comments.

Instructions: For each question below, check (✔) your answer.

1. How do you feel about the way you were treated by the receptionist?
   _____ very dissatisfied   _____ mostly satisfied
   _____ dissatisfied   _____ very satisfied
   _____ no feelings one way or the other
   Comments _____

2. How do you feel about the length of time you had to wait before our agency dealt with your problem or situation?
   _____ unhappy or dissatisfied   _____ pleased or satisfied
   _____ no feelings one way or the other
   Comments _____

3. Did you accomplish what you expected to achieve when you came to this agency?
   _____ yes, completely   _____ no real progress
   _____ mostly, yes   _____ worse off now than before
   _____ I changed my mind about what I expected (please explain) _____
   Comments _____

4. Do you feel your situation/problem(s) has changed since you became involved with this agency?
   _____ things are now much worse   _____ things are somewhat better
   _____ things are somewhat worse   _____ things are much better
   _____ no change, one way or the other
   Comments _____

5. Which of the following statements comes closest to your feeling about the impact of this agency's services on your situation or problem?
   _____ agency made things much worse
   _____ agency made things somewhat worse
   _____ agency had no impact, one way or the other
   _____ agency made things somewhat better
   _____ agency made things much better
   Comment _____

6. How do you feel about the social worker who dealt with your problem or situation?
   _____ very dissatisfied   _____ satisfied
   _____ dissatisfied   _____ very satisfied
   _____ no feelings one way or another
   Comments _____

7. If a friend needed services from an agency like ours, would you recommend our agency?
   _____ never   _____ probably yes
   _____ probably not   _____ definitely yes
   Comments _____

8. Overall, how do you feel about your experience with our agency?
   _____ very dissatisfied   _____ very satisfied
   _____ dissatisfied   _____ satisfied
   Comments _____

(Continued)

Figure 13.6 (Continued)

9. It is helpful for us to know something about the person who completed this questionnaire.
Please check:

_____ male   _____ parent of agency client
_____ female   _____ spouse of agency client
_____ client

be in following up on those clients who fail to return the questionnaire within a specified period of time; these clients will have to be called or sent a letter to obtain a reasonable return rate. If the questionnaire responses are to be anonymous, there will obviously be problems in follow-up; therefore, a guarantee of confidentiality without the added assurance of anonymity may be preferable. Statistical techniques can be applied to decide whether there are significant differences between those who return the questionnaire immediately and those who require urging.

4. *Tabulate and analyze the questionnaire data.* Manual tabulation is possible for short questionnaires. Computer processing is desirable for long questionnaires and when a large number must be tabulated.

Figure 13.7 Evaluation of Shelter Services

Your comments will help us improve future services to women and children. Your answers are confidential and will in no way affect future contact we may have with you. Thank you for your cooperation.

Please circle the number that best represents your opinion of services you received.

Basic Needs	*Strongly Disagree*	*Mostly Disagree*	*Mostly Agree*	*Strongly Agree*
1. I felt safe from my abuser while in the shelter.	1	2	3	4
2. My room assignment was adequate for my family.	1	2	3	4
3. The shelter was clean.	1	2	3	4
4. My family had enough food.	1	2	3	4
5. The meals were nutritious.	1	2	3	4
6. The food tasted good.	1	2	3	4
7. I had access to enough personal care items (diapers, shampoo, toothpaste, etc.)	1	2	3	4
8. I had access to adequate clothing.	1	2	3	4
9. I had access to necessary medical care.	1	2	3	4
10. Transportation was available when I needed it.	1	2	3	4

Selected Bibliography

Beck, Dorothy Fahs, and Mary Ann Jones. *How to Conduct a Client Follow-up Study.* New York: Family Service Association of America, 1977.

Epstein, Irwin, and Tony Tripodi. *Research Techniques for Clinical Social Workers.* New York: Columbia University Press. 1980.

———. *Research Techniques for Program Planning, Monitoring and Evaluating.* New York: Columbia University Press, 1977.

Hagedorn, Homer, Kenneth Beck, Stephen Neubert, and Stanley Werlin (National Institute of Mental Health). *A Working Manual of Simple Program Evaluation Techniques for Community Mental Health Centers.* Washington, D.C.: Government Printing Office, 1976, DHEW Pub. No. (ADM) 79–404.

Reid, William, and Laura Epstein, eds. *Task Centered Practice.* New York: Columbia University Press, 1977.

13.8   *Peer Review*

Purpose: To evaluate the quality of a social worker's practice by comparing his or her intervention against a set of principles and standards.

Discussion: The process of ***peer review*** refers to a periodic examination of a social worker's performance by a fellow worker who understands the agency's clientele, policies, procedures, and goals. Essentially, peer review is a form of quality control in which a sampling of a worker's cases are examined by one's colleagues. Some settings, like hospitals, are required to establish peer review systems by accrediting organizations or regulatory agencies.

The first step in developing a peer review procedure is for the social workers to agree on a set of principles or criteria that reflect good practice in their particular setting. In order to keep the process relatively simple, the number of criteria should probably not exceed ten. Those participating in the peer review will also need to agree on the procedure for selecting cases to be reviewed. The random selection of cases from a worker's active case file is a common approach. Peer review sessions should be regularly scheduled (e.g., monthly); a single session should be limited to about one-half hour. A system of rotation ensures that each worker has a chance to conduct a peer review on all other workers in his or her unit or department. This can be a valuable learning opportunity because it reveals differences in how workers approach intervention. Results of the peer review should be recorded on a form. A recurring problem found in the performance of an individual worker may require remediation. And a recurring problem among all of the workers may signal a system problem and the need to examine policy and procedure.

Figure 13.8 presents an example of peer review policy and procedure for a five-worker unit within a child welfare agency. Many variations are possible.

Figure 13.8 Sample Peer Review Policy and Review Form

Policy: Each social worker will participate in an ongoing cycle of peer review and consultation. The supervisor will be responsible for developing the peer review schedule. Each month, each social worker will have two cases reviewed by a peer and will also review two cases of another worker. One of the cases to be reviewed will be selected by the worker being reviewed and one case will be drawn at random from the worker's active caseload. The reviewer will complete the peer review form and submit it to the supervisor.

On a quarterly basis, the supervisor will analyze the peer review reports, identify common performance problems, and meet with staff to jointly formulate a plan to address common performance problems.

Schedule

Reviewer	November	December	January	February
Greta	Mary	Larry	Ruth	Jim
Jim	Greta	Mary	Larry	Ruth
Ruth	Jim	Greta	Mary	Larry
Larry	Ruth	Jim	Greta	Mary
Mary	Larry	Ruth	Jim	Greta

Monthly Peer Review Form

Date _____ Social Worker _____ Reviewer _____

Case name and number _____

	Yes	No	NA

1. Client problem(s) clearly stated in record.
2. Client/family members involved in treatment planning.
3. Written treatment plan in record.
4. Intervention methods are appropriate for clients' problems.
5. Frequency and duration of client contact is appropriate for problem.
6. Treatment planning, worker's action, and approach used reflect concern for permanency planning.
7. Appropriate and effective use made of community resources.
8. Progress toward goals is evident.
9. Case recording is clear, concise, and descriptive.
10. Required agency forms completed and included in record.

Other comments: _____

_____

_____

_____

Selected Bibliography

Carter, Reginald. *The Accountable Agency.* Beverly Hills: Sage, 1983.

Jackson, Josephine. "Clinical Social Work and Peer Review." *Social Work* 32 (May–June 1987): 213–20.

Munson, Carlton. *An Introduction to Clinical Social Work Supervision.* New York: Haworth, 1983.

13.9   *Termination of Service*

Purpose: To terminate the professional relationship between social worker and client in a timely and responsible manner.

Discussion: The "closing of a case" or the termination of services to a client should be viewed as an essential and planned component of the helping process. When deciding if termination is appropriate, the following factors should be considered:

- Have the intervention objectives been reached?
- Has an agreed upon time limit to service provision been reached?
- Is the problem or situation that brought the client to the agency sufficiently resolved so the client can now function at an acceptable level and not be at risk of being harmed by self or others?
- Has the worker and/or agency made a reasonable investment of time, energy, and skill without measurable results?
- Has the client and/or worker reached a point where one or both do not anticipate benefit from future contacts?
- Has the client become inappropriately dependent on the worker or agency?
- Would the client be more appropriately served by another agency or professional?

In some situations, a transfer of the client to another worker within the agency is necessary. This, too, is a type of termination. An intraagency transfer is necessary:

- When the worker will no longer be available to serve the client (e.g., worker moving to another job, etc.)
- When the client will be better served by another agency staff member
- When a conflict between the worker and client cannot be resolved and is interfering with service provision or client progress
- When, for some reason, the worker simply does not like the client and cannot develop or demonstrate necessary empathy and warmth
- When there is a serious and insurmountable gap in mutual understanding and communication caused by difference in values, religious beliefs, langauge, or cultural background

Ideally, termination is a mutual decision by worker and client that occurs when the service objectives have been reached. Many situations are far from ideal, however. All too often, the client decides to end the relationship before reaching the agreed upon objectives, and sometimes circumstances dictate that the worker decide unilaterally to terminate. Examples of the latter include times when:

- The client is considered to be a physical danger to the worker or continually harasses the worker
- The client files a lawsuit or an official complaint against the worker
- The client violates, without good cause, a financial agreement regarding the payment of fees for service

The social worker has a professional obligation to make a termination or transfer as positive an experience as possible. Several guidelines can aid in this process.

1. The worker should do everything possible to keep termination from being abrupt or unexpected. Termination should be discussed during the contracting phase of the helping process (see Chapter 11). The client should be reminded from the beginning that intervention is goal oriented and time limited. The client will be gradually prepared for termination if the intervention includes, as it should, an ongoing monitoring of progress.

2. In a case where the adult client wants to terminate but the social worker thinks they should continue, the worker should explain these reasons to the client and also explain any possible consequences of terminating. If the client still wishes to terminate, his or her decision should be respected. It should be noted that usually a child or adolescent client does not have the authority to decide the termination of services; in cases involving a minor, the minor's parent or guardian make the decision.

3. The termination of a service provided under court order requires special consideration. The Colorado Chapter of NASW (1989) offers the following guidance:

> The social worker must determine whether all terms of the order have been met before terminating service. There may be cases in which the client seeks termination against the recommendation of the social worker and in violation of the court orders. In these cases, the social worker is obligated to fully inform the client of the possible consequences of the action, to tell the client that termination will be reported to the court, and to advise the client to discuss the matter with his or her attorney. (p. 9)

4. Special attention must be given to any termination prompted by an administrative decision to cut back on the services provided, to restrict case transfers within the agency, or to modify a client service contract once the worker who has serviced the client leaves or changes positions within the agency. The social worker also faces an ethical dilemma when a third-party payer (e.g., an insurance company, Medicaid, etc.) decides to end financial reimbursement for the services needed by a client. For such situations, the Colorado Chapter of NASW (1989) provides the following guidance: "The social worker should be directed in these and other dilemmas by his or her primary responsibility to the client. When the social worker judges that the client is jeopardized by agency policy or administrative decision, he or she should first advocate in behalf of the client within the agency. If the conflict cannot be resolved within the agency, assistance may be sought from NASW" (p. 9).

5. The social worker must anticipate how the termination might affect other persons in the client's family and social network. In situations where a termination may place the client or others at risk of harm, it may be appropriate to notify others of the proposed or planned termination. This notification must, of course, be done in ways consistent with the law and ethics concerning confidentiality and the release of client information.

6. In some cases, termination can be difficult because of a social worker's own psychological needs. A worker with emotional problems may want to be needed and appreciated so strongly that he or she maintains regular contact with a client even when there is no professional reason for doing so. This reflects a lack of self-awareness and is, of course, professionally irresponsible.

7. As termination approaches, it is desirable to gradually decrease the frequency of contact. If the client is quite dependent on the worker, this weaning process should be accompanied by efforts to connect the client with natural helpers and informal resources within his or her neighborhood or social network.

8. The feelings of loss and anger that often accompany the ending of any important relationship should be broached by the worker, even if not mentioned by the client.

9. The scheduling of a follow-up interview or telephone contact several weeks after official termination may be reassuring to the client who fears separation. Also, the client should be informed that he or she can return to the agency if the need arises.

Selected Bibliography

Colorado Chapter of NASW. "Practice Standard Guidelines: Termination of Services for Adult Clients." *The Integrator: Chapter Newsletter* (April/May 1989).

Hepworth, Dean, and Jo Ann Larsen. *Direct Social Work Practice.* 2nd ed. Homewood, Ill.: The Dorsey Press, 1986.

Stream, Herbert. *Therapeutic Principles in Practice.* Beverly Hills: Sage, 1985.

Techniques and Guidelines for Indirect Practice IV.

Most entry-level social work positions primarily involve working with clients on a face-to-face basis. That activity requires skills in working with individuals, families, and small groups. Part III of this book identified techniques and guidelines that facilitate that direct service practice. Part IV is also intended for the new social worker but the focus has shifted to techniques and guidelines that are supportive of the indirect service activities of the social worker.

Effective social work practice requires considerable effort in behalf of clients. While most clients are only nominally aware of these indirect service activities, they nevertheless are important if positive results are to be achieved. The social worker who has mastered some or all of these techniques will be a valuable agency staff member and a significant contributor to the community.

Chapter 14, "The Organizational Context of Practice," anticipates that virtually all new social workers will be employed by some form of social agency and that their practice will be strongly influenced by the goals, rules, procedures, service delivery approaches, and resources of that agency. At times, it is necessary for the social worker to influence the board members or other decision makers for the agency in order to strengthen its operation. To do this, the social worker needs tools to assess the service requirements of clients or potential clients and to create a more appropriate environment within the agency in which to provide services. Recognizing that the quality of staff is the key to an effective agency, it is also evident that staff selection, staff and volunteer training, staff performance, and evaluation practices have a profound impact on the ability of the agency to achieve its goals. Knowledge and skill in these day-to-day personnel and other management matters such as planning, budgeting, and obtaining support from the community are important preparation for the new social worker.

Chapter 15, "The Community Context of Practice," recognizes that social work practice and the social agency do not exist in a vacuum. Both should be considered part of a human service network within a community. Thus, the social worker must study and understand the dynamics of the community in which he or she practices. The use of techniques for making a community assessment can facilitate the new social worker's orientation to the community and understanding of its needs. When possible, the social worker is obligated to improve that community to make it better for all people. The new social worker will most likely be able to influence community life through work with various groups and committees. If one is skilled in moving community groups to action, he or she becomes more effective as a social worker. Once community groups have assessed problems and arrived at conclusions regarding legislative or other community decisions needed to correct problems, the worker's ability to influence the community decision makers becomes a valuable skill for social work practice.

The reader is reminded that this book is not intended for the social worker who is working in a specialized aspect of practice. The material in Chapter 14, for example, does not contain the in-depth knowledge and techniques required of a social worker serving primarily in an administrative role in a social agency. Similarly, Chapter 15 includes techniques that might be used by the direct service worker and omits the more sophisticated planning tools required of the social worker who works primarily at the community level.

The Organizational Context of Practice $\quad$ 14

Introduction

Most social workers are employed in complex organizations, such as social agencies, schools, and hospitals. Therefore, they must be skilled in organizational maintenance and change if they are to succeed in using their practice competencies fully. Pruger (1973, 25–36), for example, has identified that social workers serve in three distinct capacities when they work in an agency: helper, organizer, and bureaucrat. In each capacity, the social worker and his or her practice is affected directly by the agency's structure, governing policies, funding base, and the administrative procedures that guide day-to-day operations.

In the capacity of helper, the social worker strives to make agency procedures and services appropriate to the needs of the client and potential client. Since the life stresses on people constantly change, the provision of human services must also be continually reviewed and adapted to changing conditions. For example, eligibility requirements must be revised, assistance levels changed, and fee schedules updated.

A second place the social worker interfaces with the agency in the capacity of helper is in the ongoing effort to make agency procedures compatible with good social work practice. As Finch (1976) predicts, "The success of social workers in organizational settings will increasingly hinge on their ability to recognize the ways in which organizational structure affects the delivery of services. The effective worker will be skillful at modifying the organization's patterns to remove impediments to practice" (p. 375). Thus, every frontline social worker must understand the politics of social agencies and be prepared to engage in organizational change (Gummer 1990).

In the capacity of organizer, the social worker is responsible for making the agency run efficiently and effectively. In performing the roles of workload manager, staff developer, and administrator (see Chapter 3), the social worker directs attention to planning, budgeting, accountability, public relations, and staff development activities. In this capacity, influencing organizational behavior becomes a central part of the social worker's practice and provides a special opportunity to make the organization responsible for offering high-quality services.

Finally, distasteful as the label may be, the social worker must serve in the capacity of a bureaucrat. Social workers must live with bureaucratic rules and abide by bureaucratic regulations. For example, a schedule must be followed, reports must be completed, and policies and procedures must be honored.

In all three capacities—helper, organizer, and bureaucrat—the social worker is confronted by the challenge of attempting to be both professionally effective and personally fulfilled within the constraints of the agency. In all probability, neither will be fully achieved. As with many things in life, a compromise must be made among the elements of a work situation. Harrison (1987, 52) suggests that a "quality work life" requires a balance of (1) job security, (2) fairness and adequacy of pay, (3) working conditions, (4) interpersonal relations, and (5) meaningfulness and challenge of work. If these factors do not meet at least minimal levels, the social worker must make an effort to change the agency—or seek employment elsewhere. This chapter is devoted to identifying some of the essential techniques and guidelines that social workers need to achieve and maintain a quality work life.

Selected Bibliography

Finch, Wilber A., Jr. "Social Workers Versus Bureaucracy." *Social Work* 21 (September 1976): 370–75.

Gummer, Burton. *The Politics of Social Administration: Managing Organizational Politics in Social Agencies.* Englewood Cliffs, N.J.: Prentice-Hall, 1990.

Harrison, Michael I. *Diagnosing Organizations: Methods, Models, and Processes.* Beverly Hills: Sage, 1987.

Pruger, Robert. "The Good Bureaucrat." *Social Work* 18 (July 1973): 26–32.

14.1 *Learning about Your Agency*

Purpose: To learn about an agency's purpose, structure, and procedures.

Discussion: Most social workers are employed by either a private or a public agency. A *public agency* (whether at the county, state, or federal level) is one established by legislation adopted by elected officials and funded with tax monies. By contrast, the *private or voluntary agency* exists as a nonprofit corporation (a legal entity) that is supported primarily with voluntary contributions. It must be noted, however, that many private agencies enter into purchase-of-service contracts with public agencies and, at times, compete successfully for grant funds. Thus, private agencies often make use of public monies in their operation.

The creation and development of a social agency is best understood as a response to a perceived need or problem. However, it is usually the perceptions of elected officials and powerful community leaders that determine agency purpose. Professional social workers may have some input that shapes an agency's goals, but most often, they are not the final decision makers.

An agency's purpose, structure, funding base, and operational procedures have a far-reaching impact on the social worker's practice, and, of course, on the consumers of service. These organizational variables determine the nature of the services provided and specify who is eligible to receive those services.

In order to perform in a professionally responsible manner, the social worker must understand how the agency functions and why it works that way. The guidelines that follow will help you get to know an agency.

If your agency is a private, nonprofit agency:

1. Read the agency's bylaws.
2. Study the agency's organizational chart. Figure out where you and your immediate supervisor fit into the chain of command.
3. Examine the agency's budget. Pay special attention to the sources of income because the agency must be responsive to these sources if it is to remain solvent.
4. Study the agency's manual of policies and procedures.
5. Talk to social workers and other professionals outside the agency in order to ascertain how the agency is perceived in the community.

If your agency is a public agency:

1. Read the law(s) that established the agency.
2. Read the law(s) that describes the programs the agency is to administer (e.g., child abuse and neglect laws).
3. Read the agency's administrative rules that apply most directly to your area of service.
4. Study the agency's manual of policies and procedures. Pay special attention to how the manual is organized and how changes are incorporated into existing manual materials.
5. Study the organizational chart and figure out how your department, your immediate supervisor, and you fit into the chain of command.
6. Study the personnel rules and procedures that apply in the agency. These will be quite specific in a state or federal agency and have a powerful impact on the nature and content of your performance evaluation.

Selected Bibliography

Gruber, Murray, ed. *Management Systems in the Human Services*. Philadelphia: Temple University Press, 1981.
Patti, Rino. *Social Welfare Administration*. Englewood Cliffs, N.J.: Prentice-Hall, 1983.
Weissman, Harold, *Overcoming Mismanagement in the Human Services Professions*. San Francisco: Jossey-Bass, 1983.

Purpose: To establish the formal goals of a human service agency.

Discussion: Social agencies must stake their claim to specific areas of service provision. It is important for agencies to clearly state the particular goals they intend to achieve, the services they will provide, and their procedures for operation. Only then can the public be accurately informed about the nature of the agency, can clients have a clear idea of what services to expect, can unplanned duplication and overlap of services be minimized, and can staff members effectively coordinate their work.

The goals, as well as the structure (see Technique 14.5), established by a social agency have a significant influence on the social worker and the services provided. Rothman, Erlich, and Teresa (1981) make this point: "The collective welfare of practitioners' clients and constituents is profoundly affected by the organizational structures and goals of social agencies. Changing an organization's goals thus becomes a key task for many practitioners, and failure to accomplish this objective is frequently a great hinderance to effective practice" (51).*

Like people, organizations resist change. When a social worker considers it important to alter agency goals, it may take considerable effort to accomplish that change. Rothman, Erlich, and Teresa (1981, 56) propose a strategy for changing an organization's goals that involves altering the structure of influence by either (1) increasing the power of groups already functioning in the organization or (2) introducing new groups into the organization that can minimize the impact of established decision makers that are resistant to change. They suggest that, in a social worker's initial effort at facilitating change, he or she should select a situation or problem that involves change of a limited scope. It might relate to a specific program, activity, or unit of the agency and should be achievable in a three-month period. Subsequent efforts might deal with more complex goal changes, but it is advisable to begin at the level suggested here.

Rothman, Erlich, and Teresa (1981, 73) suggest that finding answers to the following questions will be useful for the social worker engaged in this change effort:*

1. What type of goal is involved among the multiple organizational goals? Has this goal been in flux historically? Can the direction of change be capitalized on? (Rothman, Erlich, and Teresa [1981, 54–55] identify six types of goals that might be addressed: societal goals, output goals, investor goals, system goals, product goals, and derived goals.)

2. What locus of organizational operation is instrumental in maintaining or changing this goal: the board, the executive staff, the operating staff, members, clients, and so on?

3. Are other individuals or groups in the agency in tune with your desired goals? Are they situated close to the primary locus of influence or at another locus?

4. How can the power or influence of these groups be strengthened? Is a shift from one locus to another necessary? How can the power or influence of the people in the current critical locus be reduced, either prior to or simultaneously with a shift of influence to the new group?

5. If there are no such internal groups, are there external groups of this type? Can they be moved into relevant positions of influence within the organization?

6. How can the reaction of current power holders be neutralized or minimized during the transition process?

7. How can the influence of the new group be stabilized or institutionalized?

8. When the transference of influence has been achieved, have the desired changes in goal orientation been realized?

Selected Bibliography

Gummer, Burton. *The Politics of Social Administration: Managing Organizational Politics in Social Agencies.* Englewood Cliffs, N.J.: Prentice-Hall, 1990.

Hasenfeld, Yeheskel. *Human Service Organizations.* Englewood, Cliffs, N.J.: Prentice-Hall, 1983.

Rothman, Jack, John L. Erlich, and Joseph G. Teresa. *Changing Organizations and Community Programs.* Beverly Hills: Sage, 1981.

14.3 Establishing and Changing Agency Bylaws

Purpose: To create and maintain appropriate bylaws and governance procedures for a private or voluntary social agency.

Discussion: The formal expression of an agency's goals and operating procedures is found in its bylaws. When an agency is created, the bylaws spell out its mission and decision-making structure. The bylaws establish the parameters within which the social worker operates, which both permit and constrain practice. Although the original bylaws may capture the original intent of the founders, agencies must change over time to keep pace with the changing community needs and new concepts of service provision. The responsibility for stimulating a needed change in the goals and procedures of an agency often falls first to the staff, with the board and/or a broader membership group subsequently amending the bylaws to reflect the proposed changes.

The social worker should be familiar with how the agency's bylaws specify the mission and dictate the process to be followed for making any changes in organizational goals. For the agency to work most effectively, the bylaws must be periodically reviewed with feedback from the staff serving as a primary informant on needed revision.

Key elements the social worker might expect to find included in a set of bylaws are:

1. Statement of agency purpose
2. Description of membership requirements and voting privileges
3. Functions of the board of directors and executive committee
   a. procedures of election and tenure of service
   b. responsibilities and authority
   c. minimum number of meetings per year
   d. cause and methods of removal
   e. filling vacancies
   f. indemnification
   g. employment of staff (executive director)
4. Functions of officers
   a. procedures for election and tenure of service
   b. responsibilities and authority
5. Functions of executive director
   a. roles and responsibilities
   b. reporting procedures
6. Committees and meetings
   a. methods of appointment and membership requirements
   b. responsibilities
   c. quorums
   d. annual meetings
   e. procedures for calling special meetings
7. Other items
   a. statement of fiscal year
   b. required financial and service reports
   c. parliamentary authority (Robert's Rules)
   d. amendments to bylaws

Selected Bibliography

Azarnoff, Roy S., and Jerome S. Seliger. *Delivering Human Services.* Englewood Cliffs, N.J.: Prentice-Hall, 1982.

Kettner, Peter M., John M. Daley, and Ann Weaver Nichols. *Initiating Change in Organizations and Communities: A Macro Practice Model.* Monterey, Calif.: Brooks/Cole, 1985.

Trecker, Harleigh B. *Boards of Human Service Agencies: Challenges and Responsibilities in the 80's.* New York: Federation of Protestant Welfare Agencies, 1981.

Purpose: To understand the authority and responsibilities of governing boards and advisory boards in the operation of human service organizations.

Discussion: Virtually every social agency has a governing board (typically called a board of directors or board of trustees) or an advisory board. In theory, boards represent the community's interests in the services provided by the social agency and often perform functions that enhance the agency's ability to offer its services. Azarnoff and Seliger (1982, 123), however, note that "governing boards and advisory councils are among the most frequently misused forms of consumer and citizen involvement in agencies providing human services." Since boards play a central role in making the social agency a positive environment in which services are provided, it is important that social workers (whether serving in administrative or other roles) work effectively with boards to assure that their contributions to agency functioning are appropriately utilized.

In private or nonprofit social agencies, the board is the body that is legally sanctioned to manage the organization. In reality, a governing board oversees the operation of the organization, and staff are hired to manage the day-to-day operations and perform the services the agency was established to offer. Gelman (1983, 83) notes that, legally, the board is responsible for the total management of a nonprofit corporation. But in reality, boards cannot be present to manage the day-to-day operations and an executive director is employed to carry out this function.

When a governing board shares its authority with the executive director, who subsequently shares that authority with other staff members, it is important that the lines of responsibility be clearly drawn. A governing board typically is responsible for the following functions:

1. *Policy making.* The governing board is legally charged with formulating the general objectives, operating policies, and programs of the agency. It should periodically review and revise the agency bylaws to assure that the operation of the agency conforms to the established goals and procedures.

2. *Planning.* As a link between community interests and agency, the board should engage in long-range planning that helps the agency project community needs and evolve programs appropriate to its mission.

3. *Funding.* A governing board is legally responsible for procuring the funds needed to operate the organization, budgeting the use of those resources, establishing procedures for the allocation of those funds, and overseeing fiscal operation of the organization. The board, then, can be expected to engage in preparing and/or approving budgets and grant applications and in representing the agency in appeals for funds from foundations, public fund allocation committees, and other funding agencies such as the United Way.

4. *Staffing.* In discharging the authority to operate the agency, the board hires an administrator (i.e., executive director) to manage the day-to-day operation of the organization. Within the hiring guidelines and personnel procedures established by the board, the administrator assures that qualified staff provide the agency's services.

5. *Facilities.* The board is responsible for assuring that the organization has appropriate housing for the operation of the established programs. If a capital campaign is required to secure needed space for program activities, for example, the board should play a major role in this activity.

6. *Community interpretation.* The board is a critical liaison with the general community. It not only interprets community needs to the agency but also helps the community learn about the agency's programs and services. The board typically serves in the capacity of planning the agency's public relations activities.

7. *Evaluaton.* Ultimately, the governing board must be accountable for all aspects of agency operation. Therefore, it must assess the effectiveness of the services provided and periodically evaluate the efficiency of the agency's operations.

In a public agency, by contrast, the advisory board (also called an advisory council or advisory committee) has no legal authority or responsibility for the operation of the organization. It is established either because the public officials responsible for the operation of the organization desire citizen input and/or because public law requires the maintenance of an advisory body as a channel for citizen participation. As the name implies, an advisory board offers advice, but that advice may or may not be heeded by administrative staff—at times a point of confusion if board and staff alike are not clear about the differences between governance and advisory functions. Azarnoff and Seliger (1982, 124) identify the following as typical responsibilities of an advisory board:

1. *Recommend policies and practices to the board of directors and the project or executive director.* Consultation from an advisory board serves an important function in informing decisions. While usually the advisory function is found in public agencies, it can also serve the private agency regarding specific issues or programs.

2. *Evaluate agency services and recommend improvements.* Where staff are oftentimes too close to the services to offer an objective view of service provision or when the credibility of the staff to accurately assess the agency's functioning is in question, advisory committees perform a valuable function.

3. *Assist in determining the needs of consumers.* As representatives of the community, advisory boards are in a good position to represent the interests of the agency's clientele or potential clientele. For this reason, among others, it is important that agency client's or people familiar with client needs serve on advisory committees.

4. *Publicize agency activities.* Like the governing board, the advisory committee can inform the public of the agency's programs and methods of service delivery.

Selected Bibliography

Azarnoff, Roy S., and Jerome S. Seliger. *Delivering Human Services.* Englewood Cliffs, N.J.: Prentice-Hall, 1982.

Conrad, William R., Jr., and William E. Glenn. *The Effective Voluntary Board of Directors: What It Is and How It Works.* Rev. Ed. Athens, Ohio: Swallow Press, 1983.

Gelman, Sheldon R. "The Board of Directors and Agency Accountability." *Social Casework* 3 (February 1983): 83–91.

Independent Community Consultants. *The Nonprofit Board Book.* West Memphis, Ark.: Independent Community Consultants, 1989.

14.5   *Models of Agency Structure*

Purpose: To identify alternative means of structuring staff roles and responsibilities to achieve efficient and effective service provision.

Discussion: Like agency goal statements, the organizational structure of an agency has a significant impact on the ability of the social worker to provide effective services. Structure can be expected to vary according to the unique attributes and special orientation of each agency. For example, public agencies are constrained by the laws that establish and sanction their operation, dependent on a budget allocation from an external legislative body, and governed by a politically elected or appointed board. Consequently, structure must be developed that is responsive to the requirements of these external forces. Private agencies, by contrast, typically have a voluntary board, elected by its membership, that is more aware of the internal operation of the agency. In this situation, the structures that guide staff performance need not be as formal and operating procedures can be more flexible.

Whether the agency is public or private, the board must secure a person to manage the operation of the agency. This director will be responsible for the agency's internal structure and operating procedures. Allowing for the limitations to structural innovation that may be externally imposed, the director is normally the key person making decisions regarding the agency's operating procedures. For the social worker interested in influencing the director's decisions about the agency's operating structure, it is useful to recognize a range of models that are used in social agencies.

Bureaucratic Model

Human service organizations have tended to follow the traditional hierarchical bureaucratic approach: two to four people (assistant directors) report to the director, three to five supervisors report to each assistant director, and several workers report to each supervisor.

While this approach has been reasonably successful in at least some types of industry,* rigid adherence to the bureaucratic approach has not worked well in social agencies, where professional autonomy is required and collegial consultation, rather than administrative supervision, more appropriately reflects the professional model of practice.

Collegial Model

At the other end of the structure continuum is the collegial approach in which each person in the organization enjoys equal status. The individual practitioner is completely responsible for his or her own behavior and practice decisions. Under this approach, responsibility to others in the organization is addressed only when individual actions affect the group as a whole.

While fitting the professional model, the collegial approach lacks efficiency when large numbers of practitioners are involved and makes it difficult to provide the documentation of service provision that is increasingly demanded as public accountability.

Project-Team Model

One structure that falls between the bureaucratic and collegial approaches is the project-team approach, which provides for groups of staff to be organized around specific tasks (e.g., serving victims of spouse abuse). While one member may be designated as team leader or coordinator, the team members enjoy equal status. Kettner, Daley, and Nichols (1985) note that, in some cases, members of an agency board and other volunteers may participate with staff as members of a project team (p. 159).

The advantage of the project-team model is that it offers the flexibility required to bring small groups of workers from various parts of the agency together to address a specific need. The structure allows for staff specialization in the service area and, therefore, more in-depth service to clients. However, the high degree of flexibility tends to blur the traditional lines of accountability and requires new approaches for monitoring the services quality.

Mixed-Matrix Model

Another intermediate structure is the mixed-matrix approach, in which the bureaucratic approach is augmented by teams performing specific functions. Kettner, Daley, and Nichols (1985) illustrate this approach, noting that, to carry out a contract, for example, an agency with an adoption unit as part of its bureaucratic structure might establish a team to recruit and approve adoptive homes. The supervisor of the adoption unit might serve as liaison between the unit and the team, but the team could be composed of persons assigned to other units in the agency or temporarily hired to perform specific tasks related to that contract (pp. 159–60).

A strength of the mixed-matrix model is that it maintains the traditional lines of agency authority; thus, the usual procedures of accountability are not dis-

*Peters and Waterman question this conclusion in their best-seller, *In Search of Excellence* (1982).

rupted. Yet, the flexibility of mixing staff from various units to perform specific functions or carry out time-limited tasks allows the best talent to focus on the topic—regardless of the unit to which those workers are administratively assigned. This approach is most closely aligned with the successful models used in business and industry as described by Peters and Waterman (1982).

Selected Bibliography

Kettner, Peter, John M. Daley, and Ann Weaver Nichols. *Initiating Changes in Organizations and Communities.* Monterey, Calif.: Brooks/Cole, 1985.

Middleman, Ruth R., and Gary B. Rhodes. *Competent Supervision: Making Imaginative Judgement.* Englewood Cliffs, N.J.: Prentice-Hall, 1985.

Peters, Thomas J., and Robert H. Waterman, Jr. *In Search of Excellence: Lessons from America's Best-Run Companies.* New York: Harper & Row, 1982.

14.6 *Staff Recruitment and Selection*

Purpose: To conduct a fair and effective search for agency staff.

Discusssion: The quality of staff is the most critical feature in the provision of human services. The skill or ability of the staff to provide the agency's services is the key to success. At the same time, social work values require that a search is open, fair, and does not discriminate on the basis of race, national origin, gender, age, handicap, or sexual preference. It is important, therefore, that social workers lead or effectively participate in recruiting and selecting new staff. It is also useful for the new social worker to understand how searches are conducted in order to successfully apply for available positions.

The Search Committee

One of the most critical elements of a good search is the membership of the search committee. If the members of this committee all reflect a particular viewpoint (such as being all majority group members, all males, etc.), it is more likely that the person selected for the position will also represent that viewpoint. Thus, the membership should include a mix of persons in terms of ethnic background, age, and gender. It should also reflect a range of perceptions of the agency, including staff, board, and clientele. Usually, a committee of four or five persons is sufficient; it is small enough to be efficient yet large enough to represent a range of perspectives.

Contents of a Position Announcement

The search committee (often with input from other staff and board members) must prepare a position announcement. This announcement should be prepared very carefully, as it must serve to attract qualified applicants and, at the same time, become the basis on which applicants can be evaluated in an affirmative action search. At a minimum, a position announcement should contain:

1. *A description of the major tasks of the position.* In most cases, this can be adapted from the job description the agency has developed for this position. Any changes in that description should be identified *before* the position announcement is finalized. Applicants are expected to prepare a cover letter that specifically identifies their preparation for this job.

2. *A statement of legitimate requirements for the position.* In order to avoid discriminating against potential applicants, and particularly against population groups that have less access to advanced education, it is important that the qualifications are appropriate to the work to be performed. For example, a M.S.W. degree should not be required when a B.S.W. is sufficient for the work to be conducted; five years of practice experience should not be required of an entry-level position; and so on. The National Association of Social Workers (Teare et al. 1984, 12–14) has carefully examined court decisions that indicate an agency can be held liable if positions are overclassified and results in a mix of applicants that underrepresents minorities, for example, in the expected population distribution. It is important to carefully identify those characteristics that are *required* and distinguish them from those that are *preferred.*

3. *The closing date for applications.* Provide enough time between the date the announcement is published and the closing date to allow potential candidates to learn of the opening, prepare application materials, get permission from potential references, and permit the mail to reach the search committee. A minimum of four weeks is suggested.

4. *A description of how to apply.* Clearly identify the materials that will constitute a completed application. Usually, this will include a resumé, names and addresses of three to five persons who could be contacted as references (or letters of reference supplied with the application), and sometimes an application form. Include the name, address, and phone number of the person responsible for the search or a person who can be contacted for answers to questions an applicant might have.

5. *The salary range and starting date.* If these factors are known, include them, as they help to screen persons who would not consider the position based on these factors. Such self-screening saves time and energy for both the applicant and the selection committee.

Advertising

It is also important to advertise the position widely. The most commonly used sources are the local newspaper, the *NASW News* (national), and the state chapter or local program unit of NASW's newsletter. It may also be productive to circulate a flyer to local social agencies and especially to contact any coalitions of minority social workers that exist in the community or region. In addition, the committee, board, and staff should identify and encourage applications from qualified persons with whom they are familiar. While it takes only one strong applicant to conclude a successful search, the chances are vastly improved when selection can be made from a pool of strong candidates.

Paper Screening

When the closing date has passed, the completed applications are reviewed by the committee. This "paper screening" involves independently reading the candidates' files and evaluating each according to the criteria identified in the position announcement. Prior to examining individual files, the committee should develop an evaluation form that will be used by each member to score the applications. This form should list the required and preferred characteristics and sometimes numerical weights to represent the importance of a specific characteristic for the job. In addition, a narrative statement of impressions of the candidate should be recorded to serve as a basis for committee discussion and as documentation in case the search process is challenged by an unsuccessful candidate.

When this review of applications is completed, the committee is then prepared to meet, compare evaluations, discuss differences in perception, eliminate unacceptable candidates from consideration, and develop a priority list to invite for interviews. It is a professional courtesy to let applicants that are not placed on the priority list know that they are no longer under consideration.

Interviewing

Usually, three to five candidates are interviewed for a position, although the priority list may include back-up candidates. The interviews should be carefully planned and hosted by members of the committee. However, other members of the staff and board should participate in the interviews. A list of questions to be asked of all candidates should be prepared by the committee in order to provide a fair comparison between the finalists. All persons involved in interviews should be warned against asking inappropriate personal questions about a candidate's marital status, plans for having children, child care arrangements, sexual preference, and other such topics. It should be assumed that professionals will make appropriate provision for their personal lives and keep that separate from professional responsibilities. The interview should be a time of give and take between the candidate and the agency. It is important to remember that not only is the agency determining if the candidate is suitable for the job, but the candidate is also making a decision about accepting the position, should it be offered.

Selection

Following the interviews, feedback from the various participants should be collected and reviewed by the committee. At this point, the committee should be prepared to conclude the search and recommend one or more persons (preferably in rank order) to the executive director or other person responsible for hiring. The committee's frank evaluation of the candidates' strengths and limitations should be shared with this person. The job can then be offered and negotiated. When the position is filled, all persons left from the priority list should be informed of the decision and thanked for their interest. Records of the search should be maintained for a minimum of three years.

Selected Bibliography

Scigliano, Virginia Stoutamire. "The Search Committee: Don't Call Us, We'll Call You." *The Journal of the College and University Personnel Association* 30 (Fall 1979): 36–40.

Teare, Robert J., Thomas P. Gauthier, Catherine Higgs, and Herbert S. Feild. *Classification Validation Processes for Social Service Positions: Overview.* Vol. 1. Silver Spring, Md.: NASW, 1984.

Purpose: To secure employment as a social worker in a human service organization.

Discussion: Once a social worker has completed professional education, the next task is to secure employment. A national study of baccalaureate social work (B.S.W.) graduates (Teare, Shank, and Sheafor 1990) indicates that 86.0 percent find jobs within the first year after graduating (another 5.7 percent immediately enter graduate programs) with 71.4 percent of the graduates' first jobs in social work. Over time, 84.3 percent of all B.S.W. graduates are employed in social work positions. Although current national data on employment patterns of new M.S.W. social workers are not available, it is likely that an even higher percentage move directly into social work jobs and that at some time nearly all are employed as social workers.

Finding and securing a job in social work takes time and effort. When hiring staff to provide human services to vulnerable clientele, social agencies are necessarily careful in their selection process (see Technique 14.6). It is important for the social worker who is seeking a job to present himself or herself in a manner that ensures the best chance of being selected for a position.

The first step in finding employment is to discover the job openings. In most communities several sources of information might be examined. Agencies with good affirmative action plans will advertise their positions. The classified advertisements in local newspaper and/or the *NASW News* should be read on a regular basis. The personnel departments of city, county, or state agencies will normally post all job openings on agency bulletin boards and most of these positions will also be advertised in the newspaper. The local United Way staff will frequently be aware of job openings in its member agencies, which may be a valuable resource for identifying available positions in the private agencies. Finally, informal networks among professionals develop in every community (see Technique 14.8) and are an excellent source of information about jobs that are open and those that may soon become available.

Once an open position is located, an application for that job must be prepared. The application typically has two parts, a cover letter and a professional resumé. The cover letter should focus on the particular job being applied for and should stress the applicant's qualifications for that position. It should be no more than one page in length and must be carefully written with no spelling, punctuation, or grammatical errors. The letter should clearly indicate that it and the resumé represent an application for the position, describe why the applicant is particularly interested in that job, and discuss qualifications for the position. The cover letter is not the place to discuss salary expectations or reasons for leaving past jobs. Indicate that a list of references will be provided on request (unless the job announcement indicates that these references should be supplied as part of the application). Be sure to obtain advance permission from the people named as references. The letter should be upbeat and positive about the position for which one is applying.

The professional resumé is more generic than an application letter and might be used when applying for several positions. It is an organized summary of one's professional qualifications. Its purpose is to present the applicant's background in a manner that will convince the employer to invite him or her for an interview. There is no prescribed format or style for a resumé. Rather, use a creative approach to attract the attention of members of a screening committee who may be selecting a few finalists from a large number of applications. However, avoid being cute or clever. Often photocopy shops provide layout consultation, have laser printers available, and can recommend good quality paper, making it relatively inexpensive to prepare an attractive resumé. In addition, many colleges or universities have an office that provides workshops and consultation to students in preparing job applications.

At a minimum, the following information should be included in a resumé. Other items may be added at one's discretion.

- *Personal data.* Include your name, address, and phone number. If you have a number where you can be reached during working hours, be sure to include that to facilitate scheduling an interview.
- *Education.* Give name of your degree(s), your major, the colleges or universities you attended, and graduation dates. List all schools you have attended (listing in reverse order) and possibly add grade-point average, honors, special projects, or any special skills or training that might be relevant to a social work job (e.g., computer, foreign language).
- *Experience.* List employment in reverse order (i.e., beginning with your current or most recent job), giving the job title, name of organization, dates of employment, and job duties. It is also helpful to list any volunteer experience that might have contributed to your social work commitment and competencies.
- *Activities and interests.* Identify your professional interests as well as those that extend beyond social work. Note membership in professional organizations, your participation in various clubs or organizations and any offices held, and any hobbies or special interests.
- *References.* A statement such as "References Available Upon Request" is usually best to place on a resumé. If a job announcement calls for providing references, they should be listed in the cover letter. This flexibility allows for selecting the most appropriate references for each position. In general, the persons selected as references should be able to comment on your professional skills and might include a faculty member, a field instructor, and/or job supervisors or persons who supervised volunteer experiences. Remember that in many instances an agency will contact the references by telephone rather than by letter.
- *Other information.* It may be desirable to add other information such as publications, travel experiences, and unique experiences that contribute to the applicant's competence as a social worker.

If the application is successful, the applicant will be invited to an interview at the social agency. Typically, the interview process will involve appearing before a panel of interviewers, although there will usually be some one-to-one discussions as well. Preparation for the interview is essential. First, research the agency thoroughly. Know the services it offers, its target clientele, and something about its structure and goals. This information might be obtained by stopping by the agency in advance to pick up informational materials, by talking with the receptionist about the agency, or by discussing the agency with clients and/or other social workers in the community. Second, be ready with some good questions about the agency and the job. Remember that an interview is a two-way street—both the applicant and the agency are deciding if there is a good match between one's skills and interests and the requirements of the job. Third, dress professionally and be as relaxed as possible during the interview process.

Finally, if offered the position, be sure to know exactly what will be expected on the job, and negotiate the salary or other benefits with the employer. NASW (1990, 18) recommends that before accepting a new position, one should (1) obtain a letter of appointment, stating salary, duties, and other pertinent information; and (2) review the agency's personnel manual and be sure the provisions are understood. Clarifying these matters before employment can prevent problems that may otherwise arise at a later date.

Selected Bibliography

Germann, Richard, and Peter Arnold. *Job and Career Building.* Berkley, Calif.: Ten Speed Press, 1980.

National Association of Social Workers. "NASW Advertising Policies." *NASW News* 35, (June 1990).

Teare, Robert J., Barbara W. Shank, and Bradford W. Sheafor. "The National Undergraduate Practitioner Survey: Practice Content and Implications for Education and Certification." Council on Social Work Education Annual Program Meeting, Reno, 1990.

14.8 Building Support Networks

Purpose: To develop a support system that enhances the professional life of the social worker.

Discussion: At least partially as a response to the structured relationships found in bureaucratic organizations, staff members have increasingly found it useful to build informal networks among colleagues, both within one's employing agency and among social workers in other human service agencies (Heus and Pincus 1986, 78). These networks improve the quality of services to clients and strengthen interagency and interprofessional linkage. Increasingly, as Gladen, Mathers, and Stewart (1989) report, "provider support networks" have become an important resource for personal survival in social agencies.

Networks not only provide a source of support and consultation for the social worker, they also offer reinforcement when agency standards differ from professional expectations and thus help to reduce job-related stress that develops when a person feels isolated from professional colleagues. One study of professional networks (Gladen, Mathers, and Stewart 1989, 15) found very high utilization of networks by human service professionals and an indication that networks were perceived as being even more effective for dealing with work-related professional stress than for stresses generated from one's personal life.

Building a support network requires a conscious effort to identify and maintain relationships with several colleagues who can be readily contacted when consultation and/or support is needed. However, a network is not a formal group that meets regularly. Networks are based on one-to-one relationships, making the membership of any one social worker's network likely to be different from that of any other social worker. Networks, then, are quite flexible and new members may be added and others dropped if found not to be constructive.

The key to network building is to consciously identify and cultivate respected and supportive colleagues within one's agency and from other human service organizations for the purpose of having an "on-call" professional support group. Recognizing that these relationships are reciprocal, building a support network also requires a commitment to be "on call" when needed by the other person.

Selected Bibliography

Gladen, Donna, Cecelia Mathers, and Deborah Stewart. "Perception of Networks by Human Service Providers." Unpublished master's research paper. Department of Social Work, Colorado State University, 1989.

Heus, Michael, and Allen Pincus. *The Creative Generalist: A Guide to Social Work Practice.* Barneveld, Wisc.: Micamar, 1986.

Whittaker, James K., and James Garbarino. *Social Support Networks: Informal Helping in the Human Services.* New York: Aldine de Gruyter, 1983.

14.9 Effective Staff Meetings

Purpose: To engage in meetings of the staff of a social agency that efficiently use time and promote intraagency communication.

Discussion: An important factor in the successful operation of a social agency is the quality of the communication among the staff. Although information can readily be communicated in writing or through electronic communication systems, research by Barretta-Herman (1989) suggests that agency staff tend to resist these forms of communication in favor of face-to-face interaction. Thus, in human service organizations the staff meeting has become the primary means of communicating important agency information, discussing issues of policy or operating procedures and exchanging knowledge related to practice. The ability of the social worker to understand the dynamics of staff meetings and effectively participate in these exchanges is a key to effective practice.

As the primary forum for formal interaction among staff members, it is essential that staff meetings have clear objectives, be carefully planned with sufficient background material to prepare the staff to discuss the agenda items, and be operated in an efficient but democratic fashion that is open for discussion and interchange among the participants. However, the meeting must be more than a discussion. It must address issues of staff concern and end with a clear plan to follow up on any actions taken or agreements reached by the staff members.

Barretta-Herman's (1990) analysis of staff meetings in human service organizations indicates that the most successful meetings occur:

- When they fulfill their objectives as defined jointly by management and practitioners as a major key in the communication system of the agency
- When they provide a forum for active discussion, creative problem solving and participation of its members
- When the structure of the meeting ensures decisions taken are followed through (p. 5)

For additional information on groups, see Techniques 11.8, 12.18, 15.5, and 15.10.

Selected Bibliography

Barretta-Herman, Angeline. "Computer Utilization in the Social Services." *New Zealand Journal of Social Work* 7 (Fall 1989).
———. "The Effective Social Service Staff Meeting." *Business Communication: New Zealand Perspectives.* Auckland: Software Technology, 1990.

14.10 Selecting and Training Volunteers

Purpose: To screen and prepare volunteers to effectively provide human services as caregivers in the community and as an adjunct to the agency staff.

Discussion: Throughout history, volunteers have played an important role in the provision of human services. The utilization of people who want to help can be an important means of maximizing scarce agency resources. At the same time, volunteers who are not carefully selected and prepared for these service responsibilities can be ineffective or damaging to clients. Social workers often have the responsibility to recruit, screen, place, train, and monitor the work of volunteers.

Screening
One of the most difficult tasks is to screen volunteers. Maintaining goodwill for the agency with the potential volunteer must be balanced against the protection of clients. The social workers should carefully describe the role of volunteers in the agency, identify the skills needed, and make clear the expectations of volunteers if they are to serve. Several questions should be asked to assess a potential volunteer.

- What previous volunteer experiences have you had?
- What do you see as your strengths in helping people?
- What do you see as your limitations in helping people?
- Why are you interested in volunteering in this agency?
- What activities would be most interesting to you? Least interesting?
- Can you commit to a set time to work here each week?
- What are your thoughts about maintaining the confidentiality of information you might gain while volunteering here?
- What do you expect to gain personally from this experience?

Job Description

The social worker's assessment skills are required to determine if an individual should be used as a volunteer and, if so, in what capacity. Many agencies prepare job descriptions for volunteer activities that make explicit the requirements for each volunteer position. Gaby and Gaby (1979, 296) suggest that such a job description include:

- The purpose of the job
- The area of responsibility
- Typical tasks
- The duration of the position
- The name or title of person(s) to whom the volunteer would be responsible
- Training requirements
- Time needed (per week, etc.)

Training

Volunteers must be trained for the work they are assigned. They must also be oriented to the agency and its expectations of volunteers, reminded of the importance of confidentiality, and prepared for the specific tasks they are to perform. Part of this orientation can be conducted with groups of volunteers. In these sessions, it is helpful to use case examples and allow the volunteers to share ideas and interact with staff and other volunteers around this material. In addition, the volunteer must be prepared for the specific activities he or she will perform. The staff member to whom the volunteer is responsible when providing that service is usually the best person to provide the training. Demonstrations of how the activity should be performed and ongoing coaching are necessary to assure a successful volunteer experience.

Support and Monitoring

Once the volunteers are selected and prepared, it is important that the social worker continue to work with them to help them use their capacities as fully as possible and to monitor their performance to assure that clients are receiving the quality of service anticipated. Volunteer caregiving has traditionally been approached as a supplement to the services the professionals provide. Following this approach, volunteers would be assigned specific duties and tasks that support professional tasks provided by the social worker or, in other cases, to provide nonclinical interaction with clients, such as personal care, friendly conversation, transportation, or other forms of general help.

More recently, the use of volunteers has expanded to supplement and strengthen the services an agency offers its clients by creating a cooperative treatment approach between professionals and volunteers. Many times, this involves working with the primary day-to-day caregivers of clients who are ill or handicapped. Through this collaborative effort between professionals and volunteers, the client is able to remain in his or her own home, enjoying greater independence and a more satisfying life. In addition, this volunteer-supported home care is far less expensive than the cost of hospital, nursing home, or other form of institutionalized care.

Miller (1985, 413) notes that, in the latter form of volunteer caregiving, the professionals should view their role as facilitating and complementing the caregiving that naturally takes place. However, "professional caregiving should not abdicate its role of making sure needs are met." Miller goes on to identify the following policy changes or direct practice activities that should be considered in support of this volunteer caregiving:

1. provide financial aid and income tax credits for support networks that are the major caregivers for dependents, aged, and mentally or physically handicapped children;
2. provide flexible work schedules to allow support network members to share in providing emotional and physical support;
3. provide day care and health programs for dependents who need care during weekdays, and to give caregivers temporary relief from their role;
4. include support network members in case planning and provide supportive services to network members so that they can continue in their role as caregivers;
5. assist in developing support networks when they are absent or assist in strengthening weak networks;
6. provide relevant information on professional services to support network members so that they can act out linkage functions with professional caregivers; and
7. eliminate regulations for income maintenance programs such as Supplemental Security Income and Medicaid that restrict or penalize the involvement of support networks, family, and "responsible others" in providing care. (p. 413)

Selected Bibliography

Gaby, Patricia V., and Daniel M. Gaby. *Nonprofit Organizations Handbook: A Guide to Fund Raising, Grants, Lobbying, Membership Building, Publicity and Public Relations.* Englewood Cliffs, N.J.: Prentice-Hall, 1979.

Miller, Pamela A. "Professional Use of Lay Resources." *Social Work* 30 (September-October 1985): 409–16.

Navarre, Ralph G. *Professional Administration of Volunteer Programs.* Madison, Wisc.: "N"-Way Publishing, 1986.

14.11 Needs Assessment

Purpose: To provide data on the utilization of and/or need for specific human services offered in a community or region, or to an identified population group.

Discussion: Although the perspective of the agency board and staff is an important source of information for determining agency goals and services, it is also important that decisions be based on a formal evaluation of the need for these services. Agencies should periodically conduct needs assessments, thus making the social worker with knowledge of this process a valuable contributor to the agency.

The Minnesota State Planning Agency (Franczyk 1977) observes that the term *needs assessment* usually refers to "the process of identifying the incidence, prevalence and nature of certain conditions within a community or target group. The ultimate purpose is to assess the adequacy of existing services and resources in addressing those conditions. The extent to which those conditions are not adequately addressed denotes a need for different services or resources" (p. 4).

When conducting a needs assessment, two judgments must be made by those conducting the analysis and those who will use the findings (e.g., agency board, city council, United Way). First, there should be agreement about what constitutes a need. Second, there must be a willingness to take action if an unmet need is identified. It is not a good use of time or resources to conduct a needs assessment if there is not a recognition in advance that if needs are discovered some corrective action is both possible and probable.

Methods and Steps of a Needs Assessment

Several methods may be used to gather needs assessment data:

1. Community forums attended by concerned and interested members of the community
2. Caseload counts (i.e., counts of persons utilizing various services)
3. Opinions expressed by experts or other professionals having relevant knowledge or experience
4. Opinion and attitude surveys
5. Social indicators (e.g., suicide rates, poverty rates, divorce rates, etc.)

The Minnesota State Planning Agency (Franczyk 1977) identifies six steps in the needs assessment process.

Step 1. *Selecting units and topics for analysis.* This step involves the identification of target groups (populations at risk) and/or the geographical area about which information is to be gathered. These target groups and geographical areas are known as the units of analysis. The kinds of information desired about each of these units are the topics of analysis.

Step 2. *Selection of one or more methods for gathering data.* On one level, a choice must be made between establishing an ongoing, agency based, informational system and implementing a short-term data collection project. On another level, the advantages of using existing data must be weighed against the costs of generating new data.

Step 3. *Gathering data/generating information.* Information about the needs of the specific units of analysis is generated from the aggregation and analysis of the individual bits of data collected.

Step 4. *Identifying unacceptable social or human conditions.* Having formulated a composite picture of the conditions experienced by the units of analysis, certain conditions are judged to be in violation of acceptable standards.

Step 5. *Comparing observed conditions to existing services.* Step five involves the gathering of information about the availability, adequacy and effectiveness of existing services in meeting identified needs.

Step 6. *Recommending changes in existing services.* The product of a well done needs assessment should be a confirmation of existing services as adequate or recommendations for change to cope with the observed inadequacy. (p. 6)

Guidelines for Conducting a Needs Assessment

The following guidelines should be kept in mind when conducting needs assessment:

1. It is essential to have a clear understanding of the policy issues and administrative concerns that prompted the decision maker to recommend the use of a needs assessment. In other words, what problems do the decision makers hope to solve through the use of a needs assessment?

2. The goals and objectives of the needs assessment must be clear before it is possible to select appropriate methods of data collection and analysis. All too often, those planning a needs assessment jump ahead to the question of What questions should we ask the people we are going to interview? before they are clear on exactly what kind of data they can and will use in the planning of new services or the modification of existing services.

3. It is helpful to know how other communities or agencies have approached the task, but it is usually a mistake to borrow someone else's objectives and methodology. Those who are in a position to use the data should decide what approach would be useful and work best in their community. Such decisions should not be made by outside consultants or by persons or agencies that have a vested interest in seeing the assessment yield certain findings.

4. In planning a needs assessment, it is important to remember that, for several reasons, certain needs will not have been met. For example:

- No services are available in the community.
- Existing services are not accessible because of transportation problems, eligibility criteria, and the like.
- Persons in need are not aware that services exist.
- Existing services are not integrated to provide a continuity of service to multiproblem individuals and families.
- Existing programs do not have adequate resources to provide quality service.
- Existing services are unacceptable to residents of a particular community. For example, they may be perceived as degrading, threatening, or in conflict with existing ethnic, religious, or cultural norms and values.

5. A needs assessment should not only identify unmet service needs but also shed light on the quantity, quality, and direction of existing services. For example:

- *Quantity.* Does the level of service meet the need? This involves some assessment of the number of persons in need of service compared with the capacity of providers to serve those persons.
- *Quality.* Are the services effective? Do they accomplish what they are intended to do? Do they work?

- *Direction.* Are the approaches used in service delivery appropriate or possibly out of touch with the real needs of clients? Does the philosophy that gave rise to existing programs coincide with the generally accepted philosophy espoused by experts in the field?

6. Do not attempt a needs assessment until there is evidence that the agency(s) and community possess the administrative and political readiness to use the data once it is gathered. If they are not ready, the report will simply gather dust on a shelf.

Selected Bibliography

Franczyk, James J. *Needs Assessment: A Guide for Human Service Agencies.* St Paul: Minnesota State Planning Agency, January 1977.

McKillip, Jack. *Need Analysis: Tools for the Human Services and Education.* Beverly Hills: Sage, 1987.

Nuber, Keith A., William T. Atkins, James A. Jacobson, and Nicholas A. Reuterman. *Needs Assessment.* Beverly Hills: Sage, 1980.

United Way of America. *Needs Assessment: The State of the Art.* Alexandria, Va.: United Way of America, 1982.

14.12   *Project Planning and Evaluation*

Purpose: To plan, coordinate, and schedule project activities efficiently.

Discussion: The introduction of a new service or special project into the day-to-day operation of a social agency can be a disruptive experience unless it is carefully planned and integrated into the life of the organization. Efficient planning of new program activities involves selecting the most effective strategy for accomplishing objectives, scheduling activities to maximize efficiency, and carefully planning the manner in which tasks are completed so as not to disrupt other parts of the agency.

Strategy Selection

Achieving the objectives of a new program activity usually involves selecting from a number of alternatives. Craig (1978) identifies five evaluative criteria that might be used to compare alternative strategies that have been identified.

1. *Appropriateness.* Is it "right' for you to use this kind of strategy? This question includes whether or not the strategy is appropriate to the organization's overall purpose and also whether the strategy is appropriate for anyone to use at all. . . .

2. *Adequacy.* Given the size of the problem, will this strategy make enough of a difference to make it worth doing? . . .

3. *Effectiveness.* How successful will this strategy be in reaching the stated objective? . . .

4. *Efficiency.* How costly is the strategy compared to the benefits obtained? Are the benefits obtained worth the money and the other resources used? Do we get the most for our money? . . .

5. *Side effects.* What good and bad side effects might occur as a result of the strategy? . . . (pp. 50–51)*

Charting each alternative and assessing them according to these five criteria provides a clear picture of the choices that might be made and the advantages and losses of each. Table 14.1 is an example of a chart that might be developed to compare several alternative approaches to an organizational activity (Craig 1978).

Table 14.1 Example of an Alternative Comparison Chart

Objective: Process for recruiting and promoting minorities and women that has the support of employee unions and minority/women's groups.

Strategy	Appropriate Yes/No/Maybe	Adequacy Hi/Med/Low	Effectiveness Hi/Med/Low	Efficiency Hi/Med/Low	Side Effects Good/Bad
A. Develop task force of employees and advocates to write Affirmative Action plan.	Maybe	Hi	Hi	Med (probable benefits high, so is cost)	Good—precedent for better decision-making process. Bad—too much citizen involvement; time-consuming.
B. Ask for suggestions first, then circulate plan, ask for comments.	Yes	Med	Med	Hi (probable benefits high, cost not so high)	Good—precedent for more input in decision-making. Bad—hostility if we don't adopt their comments.
C. Write plan, then circulate for comments.	Yes	Low	Low	Med (probable benefits low, but so is cost)	Good—avoid direct confrontation. Bad—plan may not have real support.
D. Copy plan from another city where it was implemented without conflict.	Maybe	Low	Low	Low (low cost, but low benefit too)	Good—maybe no one would know we'd done a plan. Bad—plan might never be used.

Source: Craig 1978, p. 52. A Learning Concepts Publication, distributed by University Associates, San Diego.

*A Learning Concepts Publication, distributed by University Associates, San Diego.

Scheduling

A variety of techniques have been developed to help schedule activities. One frequently used scheduling tool is the **Gantt chart.** This chart provides a visual means of depicting the relationship between the activities required for a project and the time frame for completing each. The activities are listed down the left column and the periods of work on each activity charted by month or week across the top of the page (see Figure 14.1). The usefulness of a Gantt chart is that it helps to identify the sequencing required for the entire project and helps to keep track of the completion dates for specific activities.

Figure 14.1 Sample Gantt Chart

Activity	J	F	M	A	M	J	J	A	S	O	N	D
1. Collect literature on parent-effectiveness training.	▬	▬										
2. Secure permission to initiate parent-effectiveness training group from supervisor.			▬									
3. Interpret parent-effectiveness training in staff meeting.				▬								
4. Request all workers in unit to nominate families for parent-effectiveness training.					▬							
5. Send letters to nominated families, inviting them to participate and asking for preference on which night to meet.						▬						
6. Set meeting times, reserve room, and notify families of first meeting.							▬					
7. Make daycare plans for children of the participants.								▬				
8. Prepare presentations and materials for parent-effectiveness training sessions.									▬	▬		
9. Hold twelve weekly meetings with participants.									▬	▬		
10. Assess the value of the sessions to the participants.											▬	
11. Report results to supervisor and other staff members.												▬

A second useful planning tool is the Program/Project Evaluation Technique or **PERT chart** that was developed by the Sperry Rand Corporation. It provides a more sophisticated graphic representation of the sequence and timing of the various activities that must occur and the tasks to be accomplished as the process moves from start to finish. It is a map of the work to be accomplished.

Two features of the PERT process are especially useful. First, the tools for charting events are helpful in sorting out the proper sequencing of events. Figure 14.2 provides a section of a PERT chart that might be developed for a project designed to assess the effectiveness of services provided by an agency. A series of circles are coded to identify each activity or event (e.g., F, G1, G2) and connected with arrows to reflect the necessary order and sequence of events that might be used in presenting a particularly complex PERT chart.

Second, the PERT process provides a useful formula for developing a time-line for completing the work. The expected time in number of days of work activity required for each task is based on three estimates. The project team uses its best judgment to identify an optimistic estimate of the time required for this activity (a), an estimate of the most likely amount of time required (m), and a pessimistic time estimate (b). The final estimate is based on adding $a + 4m + b$ and dividing by 6. With these estimates of the time required for each activity, it is the possible to start with the completion date for the project and work backwards to determine the dates by which each of the activities must be completed.

Figure 14.2 Sample PERT Chart

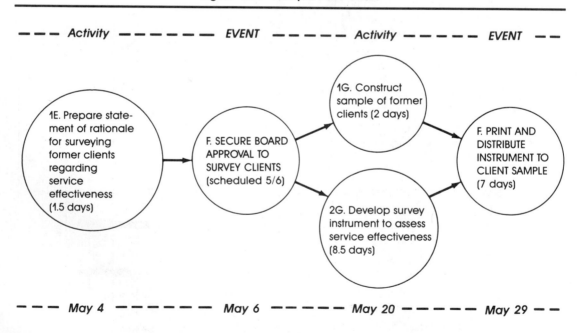

- - - Activity - - - - - - EVENT - - - - - Activity - - - - - EVENT - -

1G. Construct sample of former clients (2 days)

1E. Prepare statement of rationale for surveying former clients regarding service effectiveness (1.5 days)

F. SECURE BOARD APPROVAL TO SURVEY CLIENTS (scheduled 5/6)

F. PRINT AND DISTRIBUTE INSTRUMENT TO CLIENT SAMPLE (7 days)

2G. Develop survey instrument to assess service effectiveness (8.5 days)

- - - May 4 - - - - - - May 6 - - - - - May 20 - - - - - May 29 - -

Task Planning

A final step in completing a special project is to identify and carry out the activities required to implement the strategy that has been selected. This activity involves clearly identifying the tasks to be completed, the rationale for engaging in this activity, noting when it must be completed and who should be involved, and specifying the time or other resources required for completing the task. Table 14.2 is an example of a chart that might be developed for this purpose (Craig 1978).

Selected Bibliography

Brody, Ralph. *Problem Solving: Concepts and Methods for Community Organization.* New York: Human Services Press, 1982.

Table 14.2 Example of a Task Planning Sheet

Staff Member: Personnel Manager
Strategy: Form task force to develop Affirmative Action Plan
Activity: Get agreement of members to serve on task force

Tasks	Why?	When?	Who?	Resources?
1. List key groups and potential task force members.	Make sure all possibilities are considered.	Jan. 3	Self	3 hrs.
2. Go over list with department director and agree on whom to approach.	Get director's perspective and approval.	Jan. 4	Self and director	2 hrs.
3. Review overall strategy with department director.	Make sure we're on same wavelength, confirm commitment to strategy.	Jan. 4	Self, director, and key clerical staff	same meeting as #2
4. Arrange meetings with some potential members for preliminary discussion.	Person-to-person, informal approach most likely to succeed.	Jan. 15–12	Self and director	6 hrs.
5. Etc.				

Source: Craig 1978, p. 80. A Learning Concepts Publication, distributed by University Associates, San Diego.

Craig, Dorothy. *Hip Pocket Guide to Planning and Evaluation.* San Diego: University Associates, 1978.

Drezner, Stephen M., and William B. McCurdy. *A Planning Guide for Voluntary Human Service Delivery Agencies.* New York: Family Service Association of America, 1979.

14.13   *Preparing a Budget*

Purpose: To prepare an estimate of income and expenditures for an agency or a special project during a designated period of time.

Discussion: A budget is an important financial planning tool. It states the anticipated sources of income and expected uses of those resources during a fiscal year. The budget is a central part of the organization's planning, as it indicates what services it can afford to provide. Approval of a budget by a board of directors serves as sanction for the executive director to spend the agency's resources within the limits of the estimates contained in the budget. Thus, it frequently is both a planning tool and the basis of spending authority.

A budget should be the most accurate estimate possible. In a stable organization, the budget should be built on past experience with allowance for anticipated changes in income and expenditures or new programming. In an era of declining support for human services, funding for new programs must come through curtailment of certain programs or more efficient use of existing resources. Since most human service agencies are highly labor intensive, the personnel aspects of the budget become the most critical point to consider in regard to reallocation of resources.

Three types of budgeting are typical of human service agencies: (1) line-item budgeting, (2) incremental budgeting, and (3) program budgeting. Each should be tied to the ultimate purpose of maximizing the use of resources to achieve the goals and objectives of the organization. The constant tug experienced between efficiency (cost per unit of service) and effectiveness (ability to achieve service goals) must be addressed as part of the budgeting process.

Line-Item Budgeting

This type of budget is the most commonly used in social agencies. It simply requires that the various income and spending categories be identified and the amount of money anticipated in each category be stated (see Figure 14.3). The accounting system of the agency is usually organized around these categories, making it possible to readily obtain a historical picture of the income and expenditures that will serve as the basis for projecting the future. Since a budget is a planning device, it must be prepared in advance of the year in which it will be in effect, which makes it impossible to know exactly the expenditures of the most recent year. Thus, partial-year data and the current approved budget become essential elements in building a budget.

Figure 14.3 Sample Line-item Budget

Categories	Last Actual Year	Year-to Date	Current Budget	Proposed Budget
Income				
Beginning Balance	6,375	10,648	6,000	32
Contracts for Service	17,358	7,156	15,000	18,000
Contributions	5,392	938	5,000	5,000
Grants	5,000	2,500	5,000	–0–
Gifts and Bequests	14,321	7,106	10,000	10,000
Investment Income	4,987	2,386	5,000	5,000
Membership Dues	2,510	1,050	2,500	2,500
Program Service Fees	48,746	24,657	50,000	55,000
Sales	–0–	–0–	–0–	–0–
United Way Allocation	20,000	10,000	20,000	29,000
Total Income	124,689	66,443	118,500	124,532
Expense				
Salaries	67,518	35,447	70,894	74,439
Employee Benefits	4,756	2,557	5,114	5,265
Payroll Taxes	2,171	1,180	2,360	2,385
Consultation Fees	10,000	4,120	10,000	11,000
Professional Development	2,500	1,195	2,500	2,500
Total Personnel	86,945	44,499	90,868	95,589
Supplies and Equipment	8,938	6,053	9,000	9,500
Telephone	3,063	1,600	3,200	3,200
Printing	984	407	600	600
Occupancy	12,000	6,300	12,600	13,200
Travel	570	287	600	600
Membership Dues	1,000	1,000	1,000	1,000
Miscellaneous	541	295	600	600
Total Operating Expenses	27,096	15,942	27,600	28,700
Total Expenses	114,041	60,411	118,468	124,289
Ending Balance	10,648	6,020	32	243

The line-item budget must then be backed up by an audit report verifying the last year's actual income and expenditures and listing the amounts of any other assets, endowment, or building fund reserves that are excluded from the operating budget, as well as identifying the agency's liabilities.

Incremental Budgeting

Based on estimates of increases or decreases in revenue, a series of budget projections might be built on the basis of the current line-item budget. That is, using a "what if?" approach, a budget might be developed to reflect the impact of five and ten percent budget reductions, no change in revenue, or five and ten percent revenue increases. An incremental budget is particularly helpful in reflecting the impact of inflation and identifying the service implications of either increases and decreases. Such a budget is often useful in identifying the cost of adjusting an organization's current program to provide new services.

Program Budgeting

A final type of budget used by social agencies is the program or functional budget. Again, this is based on a line-item budget and adds the feature of attributing the total cost in each income and expense category to the various aspects of agency operation. This approach makes it possible to estimate the income and expenditures related to any function of the agency, thus providing a clear picture of the cost-effectiveness of that function. Attributing the income or expenses to particular program areas calls for careful estimates (e.g., the amount of executive director's time devoted to fundraising) and an accurate identification of the purposes for which income is generated (e.g., fees for a particular service).

Preparing a program budget involves using the total from the "Proposed Budget" column (see Figure 14.3) of the line-item budget and projecting a distribution of those items according to both the operational support services (i.e., management, fundraising) and each of the various service programs of the agency.

Selected Bibliography

Budgeting: A Guide for United Ways and Not-for-Profit Human Service Organizations. Alexandria, Va.: United Way of America, 1975

Hildreth, W. Bartley, and Rodger P. Hildreth. "Budgeting and Fiscal Management." In *Handbook of Human Services Administration,* edited by Jack Rabin and Marcia B. Steinhauer. New York: Marcel Dekker, 1988.

Knighton, Art, and Nancy Heidelman. "Managing Human Service Organizations with Limited Resources." *Social Work* 20 (November–December 1984): 531–35.

14.14   *The "5-Ps" for Marketing Human Services*

Purpose: To interest the public in participating in or supporting the work of a human service organization.

Discussion: The use of marketing concepts in the human services is relatively new. O'Conner (1982) indicates that the first journal articles to address the marketing of nonprofit organizations did not appear until 1975. Since then, there has been growing attention to the application of the marketing concepts used in selling commercial products to develop support for organizations concerned with health and human services. In reality, human service organizations are in competition with other community interests for resources and must be prepared to use marketing techniques to secure the resources they need.

Most social workers are not used to thinking about their agency's services as a product to be sold, but doing so helps workers better understand how to attract funding, needed volunteers, and clients that can benefit from services. Marketing ideas can help an agency attract skilled board members, foster parents, big brothers and big sisters, and other human and material resources essential to agency operation and service delivery.

Adapting concepts from business, Horejsi (1989) suggests that five concepts—the 5 P's—should be considered when developing a human services marketing strategy. He also suggests that it helps to understand the dynamics of the marketing process if social workers think about all the factors that influence their own decisions when they consider buying an automobile or some other major purchase.

Product

Successful salespeople are enthusiastic about their product and they can explain its advantages, as compared to the other products, that might attract the potential customer's interest. Thus, social agency personnel must truly believe in the worth of their product (service). They must be able to honestly explain its worth and advantages in simple language and, if possible, back up their beliefs with data drawn from independent evaluations.

If social workers and other agency personnel really believe in their services, their conviction will be communicated in their verbal statements and nonverbal behavior. If, for some reason, the agency's "product" is not "selling" well (e.g., not attracting support or clients), it is time to figure out why and modify or improve the service so it becomes more attractive.

Potential Buyer

In order to attract supporters and clients to a service program, its personnel may need to conduct some type of market survey. What are the characteristics of those who now buy your product? What are the attractive features of your product? Who has purchased your product in the past? If you have lost customers to other products, why are those products now more attractive than yours? The answers to such questions help an agency better understand its potential supporters and consumers and help target marketing efforts toward those groups most likely to respond.

For purposes of marketing, it is important to remember that there is no such thing as a "general public." There are, however, subgroups of people who share common interests and values. It is important to determine which subgroups are most likely to be interested in a particular program. Demographic factors such as age, religion, ethnic background, income, and education may have a bearing on which subgroups can be attracted to which agency. An agency should not waste time trying to attract those unlikely to ever develop interest in supporting or using its services.

Place

Once the attention of the target audience has been attracted, the agency needs a place to meet the group and further explain the value of its product. In the human service field, this "place of business" is typically the social agency. Whether or not potential buyers decide to contribute or use an agency's services will depend, in part, on their first impressions of the agency's building and offices, its personnel, and its program. First impressions are exceedingly powerful. They will be shaped by the agency's reputation for providing quality services, and for treating clients with respect, courtesy, and fairness. They will expect a comfortable atmosphere in which to meet and interact with staff. If an agency can create a positive public image, it has taken a large step toward attracting both supporters and consumers.

Price

In the marketplace, "price" is measured in terms of dollars (i.e., how much a customer has to pay to get the wanted product). In the human services, price is more appropriately viewed as what an agency supporter or a consumer must give up (i.e., pay) in order to support or utilize the services. If financial supporters or volunteers give their money and time, they are not able to give those dollars or their time to some other worthy cause. Thus, they want to know that their gifts are appreciated and will make a real difference in someone's life. Or perhaps they want to make sure their association with the agency will provide some benefit, such as interesting training, job-related experience, or a feeling of being useful.

It is important to be completely honest about price. For example, in an effort to recruit foster parents, a child welfare agency needs to be accurate in describing the "price" to be paid by the foster parent in terms of time, frustration, worry, and probably some out-of-pocket expenses. If one is not honest, the buyer will later feel cheated and become justifiably angry.

Promotion

Working with the media (see Techniques 14.16, 14.17, and 14.18) is an effective way to reach a large number of people with a simple message about an agency. Stories in newspapers and on TV can make people aware of a particular agency and its needs, but they are not usually effective in bringing people to the decision that they will support it with their time or money. The same can be said for presentations and public appearances at service clubs, schools, public meetings, and so on; they help, but it takes something more to get a real commitment. When it comes to making that final decision of whether to support an agency, face-to-face interaction with agency personnel is of critical importance.

As in business, a satisfied "customer" is the best advertisement an agency can have; on the other hand, a dissatisfied customer can do a lot of damage to an agency's image and reputation. As a general rule, presentations by satisfied customers (e.g., long-time financial supporter, enthusiastic volunteers, clients pleased with agency services, etc.) are more persuasive than presentations by agency staff.

Selected Bibliography

Horejsi, Charles R. "Foster Home Recruitment: A Marketing Perspective." Unpublished document. Missoula: Department of Social Work, University of Montana, 1989.

Lee, Joel M. "An Introduction to Health Care Marketing." In *Handbook of Human Services Administration,* edited by Jack Rabin and Marcia B. Steinhauer. New York: Marcel Dekker, 1988.

O'Conner, C. P. "Why Marketing Isn't Working in the Health Care Arena." *Health Care Marketing* 2 (January 1982): 3–36.

Rubright, Robert, and Dan MacDonald. *Marketing Health and Human Services.* Rockville, Md.: Aspen Systems, 1981.

14.15   *Fundraising for a Social Agency*

Purpose: To secure funds from the community to support a special project or the ongoing work of a social agency.

Discussion: Raising funds for human service agencies is a difficult and time-consuming activity. Many organizations—including large federated campaigns such as the United Way and voluntary health-related organizations such as the American Cancer Society—are dependent on financial support from local communities. The small agency or inexperienced social worker may find it necessary to compete with these experienced and sophisticated fundraising agencies for the interest and money of potential contributors.

Fundraising for the ongoing work of a social agency should employ methods that can be repeated each year with the income and expenses built into the agency budget.

For most social agencies, however, a major fundraising campaign is an occasional event in which funds for a building, furnishing a room, or supporting a special program activity are solicited. The costs of such efforts in dollars spent on preparation of advertising, pledge cards, and the like must be clearly identified, along with a recognition of the loss to other program activities if staff time is diverted to this fundraising.

When considering involvement in a fundraising effort, it is important to recognize the complexity of the task. It takes time, energy, and know-how to successfully raise funds. It is estimated that it will take a minimum of three months to plan and raise funds from individuals and local businesses (e.g., through canvasing and direct mail); three to six months to raise money from local foundations, service clubs, and unions; and at least six to eighteen months to raise funds from national foundations, United Way, and financial institutions (Community Resource Center, no date). That investment of time and energy usually means that at least some other responsibilities in the agency must be set aside in order to free time for fundraising. Thus, the social worker needs to make a judgment that he or she has a good chance of success before embarking on a fundraising effort.

Guiding Principles
The Community Resource Center (no date) suggests several principles that may be useful for the social worker who is considering fundraising.

---

1. Fundraising is a very personal activity. In reality, people give money to other people, not to an organization or a cause.

2. Diversify your organization's funding base. Do not build your organization on a single source of funds.

3. Writing a proposal may *not* be the right answer. In and of itself, a proposal is not an effective way of securing funds. A grant is never a stable foundation on which to build a program.

4. In fundraising, it is critical to plan ahead—allow twelve to eighteen months. The most difficult time to get dollars is when you need them.

5. Build networks. Get to know "key" people in *one* corporation/foundation/church and have them help you gain credibility with others in that organization.

6. Basically, success in fundraising is running a good program and letting other people know about it.

7. Look for money at the local level first. Persons at the local level are most likely to have a vested interest in seeing your program succeed.

8. It is important to research the values and priorities of potential funding sources and match their priorities with yours.

9. When asking for money always be specific in terms of dollar amount, why it is needed, and exactly how it will be used.

10. Get volunteers, board of directors, and your finance committee involved. They will have credibility in the community and their involvement increases their ownership of the fundraising effort.

11. If an individual cannot make a cash donation, explore if an in-kind donation is possible (e.g., time, used equipment, expertise).

12. Remember that "them that ask, get." If you don't ask, you won't get.

13. Get expert advice if you are unsure of how to proceed in your fundraising effort.

Elements of a Campaign

These general steps should be followed for best results in a fundraising campaign (Gaby and Gaby 1979, 61–69):*

1. *Develop the plan.* Be sure that the purpose for which the funds are raised is consistent with the goals of the agency and that the time, effort, and expense are justified. Also, be realistic about the potential money that can be raised and the requirements for raising that amount of money. Set a tentative goal that will result in enough revenue to pay the expenses and carry out the program activity for which the funds are raised. Determine the approach to be used and identify the committees, solicitors, and other personnel that will be needed. Develop a budget and a written plan for this activity (see Figure 14.2).

*Excerpts in Technique 14.15 from the book *Nonprofit Organization Handbook* by Patricia V. Gaby and Daniel M. Gaby. © 1979 by Prentice-Hall, Inc., Englewood Cliffs, N.J. Reprinted by permission of the publisher, Prentice-Hall, Inc.

2. *Secure a chairperson.* A fundraising campaign requires a volunteer chairperson who has a high level of credibility in the community and can give time to lead the campaign. The chairperson is recruited before other volunteers. That person should then participate in designing the remainder of the campaign plan, recruiting the necessary personnel, and serving as primary spokesperson for the effort.

3. *Recruit and prepare the workers.* People must be asked to work in a fundraising campaign; they rarely volunteer. The campaign chair, agency board members, or other key people should be selected to recruit others to participate in this activity. Volunteers must be carefully prepared for the task and be given written materials to help them interpret the need for contributions. The staff should play the central role in preparing these materials.

Some workers may not be comfortable asking for money and can better serve other important roles in making the campaign run smoothly, such as monitoring the success of solicitors, preparing reports, and organizing materials. Always remember to praise and thank those who work on a campaign. Individual and collective meetings with persons working on the campaign are important for solving problems and motivating workers to make their contacts.

4. *Develop an organizational structure.* In addition to the campaign chair, it is usually helpful to have a campaign committee and a special gifts committee that can target selected persons for support. Since public awareness of the effort is essential, a committee especially qualified to work with the media should be established early. A general rule is to involve a large number of people in soliciting funds or selling the tickets, giving each fewer contacts to make. A large part of the funds raised should come from those who are soliciting others. Thus, the pyramid approach of team captains and groups of workers has a proven success rate.

5. *Develop materials and forms.* Fisher (1978, 81) indicates that it is important to begin a fundraising effort by developing and pretesting a "question and answer sheet covering all aspects of your organization with special emphasis on the exact need for the fund raising campaign." From this material, it is then possible to generate material for media releases, brochures, speech copy, and so on. Other materials that might be developed are posters, exhibits, a letterhead, banners, slide shows, and bumper stickers.

Careful records must be kept. Develop forms that will make it possible to track the activities of the campaign, know who has and has not been contacted from the prospect list and by whom, record the success of the contact, and note any problems that may occur. These records are essential for both the accountability of the fundraising effort and the basis for proper recognition and thanks at the end of the campaign.

6. *Consider professional fundraising help.* Large fundraising efforts can be very disruptive to an agency and create a negative image if improperly conducted. Gaby and Gaby (1978) suggest professional help when:

- you have had successive disappointments without such help;
- you don't have people with enough training to direct a fund-raising appeal;
- you need additional help that you cannot get from within your own organization;
- you are running a capital campaign and your goal is over $100,000. (p. 67)

Suggestions for person who might serve as consultants might be obtained from religious, educational, or human services agencies in your community or by contacting the American Association of Fund-Raising Counsel, Inc., 500 Fifth Avenue, New York, NY 10036.

Selected Bibliography

Community Resource Center. "Some Principles of Philanthropy." Unpublished materials. Denver: Community Resource Center, not dated.

Fischer, John. *How to Manage a Nonprofit Organization.* Toronto: Management and Fund Raising Centre, 1978.

Gaby, Patricia V., and Daniel M. Gaby. *Nonprofit Organizations Handbook: A Guide to Fund Raising, Grants, Lobbying, Membership Building, Publicity and Public Relations.* Englewood Cliffs, N.J.: Prentice-Hall, 1979.

Lauffer, Armand. *Getting the Resources You Need.* Beverly Hills: Sage, 1982.

Lord, James Gregory. *The Raising of Money.* Cleveland: Third Sector Press, 1987.

14.16 Dealing with the Media

Purpose: To inform the public and generate support for the services offered by your agency.

Discussion: The public has a right to know about the social programs and agencies supported by taxes or voluntary contributions. All too often, the public hears only negative information about these services or the people who use them. Social workers have a responsibility to help the public fully understand the impact of human services on the quality of life for all persons. Social workers can make a valuable contribution to their agencies by developing the skills to work effectively with the media in providing this information.

General Advice

"It's Time to Tell": A Media Handbook for Human Services Personnel (Church 1981, 12–14) provides a number of suggestions for those working with newspaper, radio, and television media.

1. Rather than wait for the media to come to you for information or a story, be assertive and reach out to the media. Don't wait until a bad story provokes your response. Instead, work at creating positive opportunities to explain your agency and its program.

2. Develop contacts among the media people in your community. Create a contact file on media professionals and develop a working relationship with them. Remember that if they know and trust you and you help them, the reporters and photographers can mean the difference between your agency or program getting covered and getting good coverage. Keep them informed of what is going on in your agency. All that you share with them may not become news, but more will if you keep them informed.

3. Make sure you are authorized to speak for your agency. If more than one person from the agency is authorized to deal with the media, make sure that the efforts are coordinated.

4. Make it easy for the media to contact you by providing all reporters who cover your agency with your home and office telephone numbers and the name and numbers of someone else to call if you are not available.

5. Know the deadlines of the newspapers, radio, television news shows.

6. Be fair. When you release a story, make sure that all media organizations get your news release or phone call as close to the same time as you can manage.

7. When you give an exclusive story, know that you have just given that reporter information you will not give another newsperson. You have given him or her information—plus the privilege to be the first person to print or broadcast that information.

8. If your story does not run, there may be many good reasons. It could have been thrown out at the last minute for something of more value newswise. Reporters seldom have time to answer repeated requests to justify the reason a story is not used. But it's all right to ask if there was something wrong with the story—something that could be corrected in future stories.

9. Handle errors in stories carefully. Unless a serious error has been made, no comment is usually necessary. When a comment is in order, go to the reporter who made the error and handle the correction in private. Explain the facts, and indicate any damage that has or might be caused by the error. Control your emotions and hold your discussion to the facts of the error.

10. Express your appreciation every time you submit material, whether it is used or not. Everyone likes to be appreciated for efforts, as well as actual successes. Don't forget to send a media professional's boss a copy of your thank-you letter. At least once a year, thank the reporter's boss for the investment of his or her resources in your program.

The Press Kit

A useful tool for establishing and maintaining relationships with either the print or soft media is to prepare a press kit for distribution to media editors and reporters. A press kit is simply a 9½" × 12" two-pocket folder that contains information that interprets the agency and suggests stories for the media. The folder should be colorful or in some way attract the attention of the reporter when it is in a file or on the reporter's desk. A cover letter should be included that draws the attention of the reporter to the contents of the press kit.

Meltsner (no date, 4) suggests the following materials as the minimum for inclusion in a press kit.

- *Agency information.* This may be a brochure, annual report, or a brief description of the agency's goals, programs, and clientele.
- *Calling card.* A business card should contain the agency contact person's name, address, and telephone number. This should be displayed prominently, perhaps by stapling it to the pocket of the folder.

- *Campaign or public relations effort information.* If you have a particular goal for this public relations effort, such as raising funds for a specific program or recruiting volunteers to work with troubled children, explain this special effort with a brochure about the project or a short information sheet.
- *At least one backgrounder.* A backgrounder is a sheet that familiarizes the reader with concepts, terms, and data that might be useful in preparing a story about the agency. What is mental health? What kind of problems are addressed in family counseling? What happens in a therapy group? What is developmental disability?
- *A fact sheet or news release.* Depending on what you want the media to cover, you may include a fact sheet that contains basic who, what, where, when, and how information that allows the reporter to create his or her own story. A news release is a one- to three-page story that can be printed as is or reduced or expanded into the reporter's own story. If possible, include a black-and-white photograph with a caption to help the reporter visualize the situation you are addressing.
- *A public service announcement.* A thirty-second spot makes a direct appeal for your project.
- *At least one reprint.* To suggest ideas for a story, include previously published articles about the agency or the project.

Selected Bibliography

Brawley, Edward A. *Mass Media in Human Services.* Beverly Hills: Sage, 1983.

Church, Don. *"It's Time to Tell": A Media Handbook for Human Services Personnel.* Washington, D.C.: U.S. Department of Health and Human Services, 1981.

Meltsner, Susan. "Public Relations Tools for Human Service Providers: The Press Kit." Unpublished materials, not dated.

14.17   *Preparing a Newspaper Release*

Purpose: To prepare materials for a news or feature story in the print media.

Discussion: When preparing a newspaper release, you will improve the chances of it being used if you prepare it in a form familiar to the reporter and if it requires a minimum amount of editing. The following guidelines are commonly accepted for preparing a press release (Gaby and Gaby 1979, 224–25).*

1. Use legal-size paper ($8\frac{1}{2}'' \times 14''$).

2. Always type the release, making sure it is neat, clean, and double-spaced, with wide margins so the editor has room to write.

*Excerpts in Technique 14.17 from the book *Nonprofit Organization Handbook* by Patricia V. Gaby and Daniel M. Gaby. © 1979 by Prentice-Hall, Inc., Englewood Cliffs, N.J. Reprinted by permission of the publisher, Prentice-Hall, Inc.

3. At the top of the page, put:

    a. the organization's name and address

    b. your name or the name of the contact person

    c. the phone number where you or the contact person can be reached

    d. the release date (FOR IMMEDIATE RELEASE or FOR RELEASE: *specific date*)

4. Just below the identifying information, place a HEADLINE in all caps.

5. The opening paragraph should begin with a dateline in all caps: TOPEKA, KAN.—March 22, 1991. Summarize the central theme in one or two sentences, including the important Who, What, Where, When, and Why information.

Include the more detailed information in subsequent paragraphs, remembering that editors will often shorten a story by cutting from the end. Say the most important things first.

6. Make the style simple and logical. Stay on the subject, and use short sentences and paragraphs. Use quotes liberally to liven up the prose. Photographs (glossy prints) can also add to the appeal of your story.

7. All abbreviations must be understood, so use the full name before using initials. Spell out numbers from one to ten, using numerals from 11 and up.

8. If the release runs longer than one page, insert (MORE) in parentheses at the bottom of the page; at the top of page two, type 22; at the top of page three, type 333; and so on.

9. At the end, type ---30--- or ### to signal the reporter that the release has concluded.

Selected Bibliography

Gaby, Patricia V., and Daniel M. Gaby. *Nonprofit Organization Handbook: A Guide to Fund Raising, Grants, Lobbying, Membership Building, Publicity and Public Relations.* Englewood Cliffs, N.J.: Prentice-Hall, 1979.

Maddalena, Lucille. *A Communications Manual for Nonprofit Organizations.* New York: American Management Association, 1981.

14.18   *Preparing for Radio or TV News*

Purpose: To prepare for a radio or television news broadcast.

Discussion: Coverage about a human service agency or program on a television news broadcast or on radio can reach a large segment of the public. The human interest flavor of the stories originating from social agencies is especially amenable to the audio and visual images of radio and television. The social worker attempting to utilize these forms of media should know how to prepare materials to get a story broadcast and how to prepare himself or herself for an interview on radio or television.

Gaby and Gaby (1979)* suggest the following guidelines for getting a story televised. The guidelines also are readily translated to work with radio stations.

- Contact the assignment editor, not the political reporter. The assignment editor is the one who makes the decision about what and who is to be covered by the crews.
- When you write a statement for the broadcast media, limit it to 60 seconds and be sure to hit just the highlights . . . two paragraphs would be about the limit.
- If you hope to get a camera crew out to cover the event, schedule it between 10 A.M. and 2:30 P.M. If your schedule it any later, you'll miss it, because they have to get the film back to the station for processing in time for the 6:00 news. . . .
- Try to avoid scheduling events nights and weekends if you particularly want TV coverage. The stations are usually shorthanded during those off times and chances of getting coverage are not as good.
- Try for a location of events as close to the station as possible. Again, your chances of getting coverage are better if the trip is fast and convenient for the crew.
- If the TV station doesn't show up to cover the event, consider filming it yourself. Just because the station didn't get there doesn't mean it might not use your film (if it is of acceptable quality) along with the script for the audio. (p. 232)

Selected Bibliography

Gaby, Patricia V., and Daniel M. Gaby. *Nonprofit Organization Handbook: A Guide to Fund Raising, Grants, Lobbying, Membership Building, Publicity and Public Relations.* Englewood Cliffs, N.J.: Prentice-Hall, 1979.

Jones, Clarence. *How to Speak TV, Print and Radio: A Self-Defense Manual When You're the News.* 3rd. ed. Tampa, Fla.: Video Consultants, 1990.

14.19   *Developing Grant Applications*

Purpose: To prepare a proposal to a governmental agency or private foundation for a grant to support a new program activity, a demonstration project, or research effort.

Discussion: The ongoing resources available to a social agency frequently are fully committed for operating the existing programs of an agency, and the incremental increases that might be obtained each year are eaten up by inflation. The opportunity to test program innovations or conduct research on some aspect of the agency's program requires either discontinuation of some part of the program or seeking grant funds from an external source. Discontinuation of a program is rare, as it is often not possible to justify the elimination of a service to a client population or to transfer the staff providing that service into a new and

*Excerpts in Technique 14.18 from the book *Nonprofit Organization Handbook* by Patricia V. Gaby and Daniel M. Gaby. © 1979 by Prentice-Hall, Inc., Englewood Cliffs, N.J. Reprinted by permission of the publisher, Prentice-Hall, Inc.

untested activity. For these reasons, human service agencies often fail to experiment with new and improved forms of service delivery.

Sources of Funds
In response to these difficulties in funding innovative program proposals, both governmental agencies and private foundations have established grant programs. For the social worker, the ability to successfully prepare a proposal for grant support is a valuable tool for improving the quality of services to clients.

The single most important factor in a successful grant application is the idea or innovation to be demonstrated or tested. It must be carefully thought out and have the potential of meeting a need or improving the quality of an existing service. In addition, the person or persons developing the grant application must be committed to the idea. It takes time and energy, usually in addition to ongoing assignments, and has a low success rate. Yet, it is often the only way to improve services.

Government Grants. Once the idea is clearly developed, possible funding sources must be explored. The largest amount of money is available through agencies of the federal government. Most government grants relate to areas that governmental agencies have defined in relation to their priorities. The public is notified of these priorities through Requests for Proposals (RFPs); the applications are reviewed and awarded on a competitive basis. Some discretionary funds are also available to allow for innovative program ideas that are not currently among the priorities. It is helpful to discuss your ideas with the person who administers the funds in your area of interest (e.g., aging, child welfare, alcoholism) in the regional or national office of that federal agency before investing too much time and energy in developing a proposal.

Two published sources of information are particularly useful regarding grant possibilities from the federal government. The *Catalog of Federal Domestic Assistance* is an essential sourcebook published each year with a supplement that updates after six months. It contains a comprehensive listing and description of federal programs. Programs are cross-referenced by function (e.g., housing, health), by subject (e.g., drug abuse, economic development), and by the federal agency in which the program is administered. The description of each program includes valuable information such as uses and restrictions on the funds, eligibility requirements, and the application and award process.

A second valuable source is the *Federal Register.* This document is published every government working day and contains notices, rules and regulations, guidelines, and proposed rules and regulations for every federal grant-giving agency.

Both the *Catalog of Federal Domestic Assistance* and *Federal Register* are usually available through public libraries, university libraries, or the research and grant administration office of most universities. Copies can be obtained from the Superintendent of Documents, Government Printing Office, Washington, D.C. 20402.

Private Foundations. Another potential resource for support of innovative program ideas is the private foundation. Most foundations develop specialized areas of interest, and some make resources available only for programs located in a specific geographic region. Perhaps the most helpful published source for identifying possible foundation resources is *The Foundation Directory.* Once again, local libraries or universities are likely to have this publication.

Foundations usually are open to an informal inquiry. Make an exploratory telephone call or submit a one-page letter that succinctly states your idea; most likely, you will learn quickly whether the foundation is interested in reviewing a formal proposal. If a foundation is not interested in your proposal, the staff can be helpful in referring you to another foundation that may be interested.

Guidelines for Developing a Proposal

When the government agency or foundation to which you will apply for grant support has been identified, the proposal should be prepared according to the format and guidelines required by that source. The supposedly all-purpose grant application has little chance of success. The "Ten Commandments of Realistic Foundation Solicitation" (source unknown) provide useful guidelines for both government and foundation proposals.

1. *Do your homework.* Make a careful study of the foundation before submitting any proposal, paying special attention to its correct address, names of personnel, annual reports, newsletter, history, nature of grants, special interests, geographic limitations, officers, recent grants, and so on.

2. *Be pragmatic.* Do not attempt to be clever or cute in your approach. Follow the procedures and policies indicated by the foundation, as well as the format, if one is specified.

3. *Make informal inquiries.* Save time for yourself and the foundation by informally inquiring about the possibility of foundation interest in the proposal.

4. *Be brief, direct, and clear.* Assume that the recipient of your foundation inquiry is busy, impatient, skeptical, not especially interested in your problems, and faced with many more requests than he or she can even read thoroughly, let alone grant.

5. *Use all resources.* Exploit the specialized resources of the *Foundation Directory, Foundation News,* public and private research facilities and directories, newsletters, and other similar resources of up-to-date information on trends, interests, new grants, and policy and personnel changes.

6. *Prepare solid proposals.* Following any guidelines foundations may issue, prepare proposals that present the essential information needed by the foundation to make a decision. You may want to answer these questions:

    a. What do you want to do, how much will it cost to do it, and how much time will it take?

    b. How does the proposed project relate to the foundation's interest?

c. What difference will the project make to your agency, clients, discipline, the state, the nation, the world?

d. What has already been done in the area of your project?

e. How do you plan to do it?

f. How will the results be evaluated?

g. Why should you, rather than someone else, do this project?

7. *Don't waste the foundation's time.* Recognize that foundations are understaffed and generally overwhelmed with requests. Do not make a nuisance of yourself by requesting unnecessary personal interviews, telephone calls, correspondence, and work on decisions.

8. *Cultivate foundation personnel.* Fundraising, even with foundations, is primarily a person-to-person business. Use every opportunity to become known to foundation personnel, including trustees and field representatives.

9. *Practice accountability.* The acceptance of a foundation grant carries with it the responsibility of reporting results and giving appropriate credit for the foundation's role in the project. Stewardship is very important.

10. *Be a good salesperson for your project or cause.* An informed, enthusiastic, and committed agency representative often will make a difference between an affirmative and negative attitude on the part of the foundation officer, who in turn must sell his or her board, committee, or colleagues on the project.

Proposal Contents. A formal grant proposal should carefully follow the outline required by the funding source. In general, the following components are expected:

1. *Cover page.* Include the project title, principal investigators, name of agency, dates for project activity, total budget request, and signatures of authorized agency personnel approving application.

2. *Abstract.* Prepare a short statement of the objectives and procedures to be used, methods of evaluation, and plan for dissemination results.

3. *Statement of problem and objectives.* Indicate the rational for this project and prepare a clear statement of objectives in measurable terms.

4. *Methodology, procedures, and activities to be followed.* Describe the design and approach of the project, who will be served, the administrative structure for the project, and lay out a clear plan of action with phases and dates for activity detailed.

5. *Evaluation methods.* Describe how the results of the activity will be assessed.

6. *Dissemination of results.* Indicate how the results of the project will be disseminated so that others can benefit from the knowledge gained from this activity.

7. *Personnel and facilities.* Describe the staff required to carry out the project, include resumés of key personnel who will be assigned to this activity, and indicate how new staff will be selected. Also, describe any special equipment required, and indicate how the agency will make space available to accommodate project activities.

8. *Budget.* Provide a detailed budget of the anticipated costs of the project. Indicate what will be required from the funding source and what will be contributed by the agency or other sources. Many funding sources require that matching funds from local sources be identified as a requirement for funding. In some instances, a cash match is required, but in others, in-kind contributions (e.g., staff time or office space) are acceptable.

Reasons for Rejection. Finally, keep in mind the reasons that grant proposals are most frequently unsuccessful. Reviewers most commonly mark down proposals for the following reasons:

1. The proposal is either too trivial or beyond the scope of the investigator or agency.

2. The need for the proposed project is not properly documented and/or the objectives are not clearly stated and relevant to the need.

3. The reviewer is not convinced that the proposed plan would achieve the desired results due to the competence of the staff, quality of the plan, or the support of the requesting agency.

4. There is not adequate commitment by the agency and/or community to continuing the service if the project proves successful.

5. The proposal is not realistic in estimates of the funds, personnel, or equipment required to successfully carry out the project.

6. The evaluation procedure is inappropriate or inadequately presented.

7. The proposal is poorly written.

8. The budget is not adequately developed, the required matching money is not evident, or the request is beyond the resources of the funding agency.

9. The proposal fails to follow the guidelines or meet the deadline for submitting a proposal to this governmental unit or foundation.

Selected Bibliography

Annual Register of Grant Support. Chicago: Marquis Professional Publications, most recent edition.

Catalog of Federal Domestic Assistance. Washington, D.C.: U.S. Government Printing Office, most recent edition.

Federal Register. Washington, D.C.: U.S. Government Printing Office, published daily.

Foundations Directory. New York: The Foundation Center, most recent edition.

Foundation Fundamentals: A Guide to Grant Seekers. 3rd ed. New York: The Foundation Center, 1986.

Locke, Lawrence F., Waneen Wyrick Spirduso, and Stephen J. Silverman. *Proposals that Work.* 2nd ed. Beverly Hills: Sage, 1987.

Purpose: To identify characteristics and procedures for evaluating the performance of social workers.

Discussion: An important factor in the growth and development of the new social worker is regular formal evaluation conducted by a competent senior social worker. While much informal evaluation occurs within a supervisory process, formal performance evaluation involves a periodic examination of the overall activity of the worker and creates an opportunity to identify aspects of one's practice performance that should be targeted for improvement. Such evaluation is an essential tool for helping the new worker get clear feedback about the quality of his or her performance.

At the same time, performance evaluation is an administrative tool often used as part of the agency's assessment of the worker's performance and may have either positive or negative consequences for the worker. It may lead to decisions to promote, increase salary, or grant other rewards; or it may lead to negative decisions such as placing the worker on probation or terminating employment. The worker and supervisor should be aware that this dual purpose (professional development and administrative decision making) can potentially minimize the usefulness of this evaluation process if not carefully conducted.

Three factors are essential for productive performance evaluation.

1. *People.* The supervisor or other person serving as evaluator must be highly competent. That person must know what constitutes good practice and be able to identify and appreciate the strengths of the worker; yet he or she must also understand that new social workers should be expected to have uneven abilities. A trusting relationship between the worker and evaluator is essential. That trust must center around the desire to help the worker develop his or her fullest potential as a social worker. While negative administrative outcomes may eventually determine that such development will not occur within that particular agency, the evaluation process will be most productive if it centers on the worker's competencies.

2. *Criteria.* The criteria on which the evaluation will be based must be made clear *before* the period of evaluation is begun. One of the most unproductive and anxiety-producing factors that can interfere with an evaluation process is the failure to have clear criteria on which to base the evaluation. The following outline of appropriate areas for assessment for the evaluation of a direct service position is suggested by Kadushin (1985):

Sample Content Areas for Worker Evaluation
   I. Ability to establish and maintain meaningful, effective, and appropriately professional relationships with client system
      A. Attitudes as manifested in appropriate behavior toward client
      B. Objective, disciplined use of self in relationships in behalf of client
      C. Adherence to professionally accepted values in client contact

II. Social work process—knowledge and skills
   A. Social study (data-gathering) skills
   B. Diagnosis (data assessment) skills
   C. Treatment (intervention) skills
   D. Interviewing skills
   E. Recording skills
III. Orientation to agency administration—objectives, policies, procedures
IV. Relationship to, and use of, supervision
   A. Administrative aspects
   B. Interpersonal aspects
V. Staff and community relationships
VI. Management of work requirements and workload
VII. Professionally related attributes and attitudes (self-evaluation)

Establishing measurable criteria for each area of worker evaluation is difficult. In 1981, the Veteran's Administration mandated the development of performance standards for its professional and nonprofessional staff. Since that time, considerable effort has been devoted to specifying appropriate standards to measure work performance of social workers in VA medical centers. Harkness and Mulinski (1988) report an example of one set of standards that serve as the basis for evaluating a social worker's performance in relation to (1) direct patient care, (2) documentation of activities, (3) quality of professional relationships, and (4) conduct of professional responsibilities. Criteria are then developed to assess the degree to which a worker successfully meets the standards.

3. *Process.* The assessment of the worker's performance on these facts may take the form of a narrative statement, be translated to a series of evaluative scales, or both. In any case, it is to the benefit of both the worker and the agency that these are placed in the context of a process in which they are written and carefully reviewed, discussed, revised, signed by both the worker and supervisor with notation regarding any disagreements, and placed in the worker's permanent record. From discussion of the evaluation materials, the worker and supervisor can establish goals, adjust assignments, and plan professional developmental activities that will strengthen the worker's performance by the time the next evaluation occurs. Supervisory conferences during the period between formal performance evaluations can then focus on the specific services being provided by the worker and on progress toward the new developmental goals. Including this material in the worker's record documents the evaluation (which then serves as part of the agency's public accountability) and, at the same time, helps the worker defend against possible arbitrary personnel actions.

Selected Bibliography

Brennan, E. Clifford. "Evaluation of Field Teaching and Learning." In *Quality Field Instruction in Social Work: Program Development and Maintenance,* edited by Bradford W. Sheafor and Lowell E. Jenkins. New York: Longman, 1982.

Harkness, Laurie, and Paul Mulinski. "Performance Standards for Social Workers." *Social Work* 33 (July–August 1988): 339–44.

Kadushin, Alfred. *Supervision in Social Work.* 2nd. ed. New York: Columbia University Press, 1985.

Rock, Barry D. "Goal and Outcome in Social Work Practice." *Social Work* 32 (September–October 1987): 393–98.

14.21   Program Evaluation

Purpose: To determine how well a social agency's program is meeting its objectives.

Discussion: A social program is a planned sequence of activities designed to achieve desired individual or social change. Hence, program evaluation refers to the systematic examination of a program to determine whether and/or how it is achieving its goals and objectives. Program evaluation may involve the assessment of the performance of several individual workers (see Technique 14.20) but takes a broader view that incorporates all aspects of a specific program. Tripodi, Fellin, and Epstein (1978) explain that a program evaluation focuses on three dimensions: *program effort* (i.e., descriptions of the type and quantity of activities, numbers of people served, staffing patterns, etc.); *program effectiveness* (determination of whether program objectives are being attained); and *program efficiency* (assessment of the cost of achieving the objectives).

Because program administrators and staff have a vested interest in the program, evaluations are usually designed and conducted by consultants from outside the agency. That introduces more objectivity into the process but requires that the agency staff be able to precisely explain what they are trying to accomplish, how, and why. That is difficult for many practitioners.

For those who participate in the program evaluation process designed by others or who hope to evaluate one or more of their own programs, the following guidelines are useful.

1. *Identify the users of the evaluation data and report* (e.g., administrators, practitioners, program planners, legislators, fundraisers, etc.). What do they really want and need from this evaluation? What type of information can they understand and use? Is it reasonable to believe that evaluation results will affect the continuation, modification, or termination of the program? Do not begin a program evaluation effort unless the results can and will make a real difference in terms of the program's operation and the services provided.

2. *Decide if an evaluation is feasible.* Do you have the necessary time, money, and skill available? Do you have access to experts in program evaluation? Are the data you need actually available? Are all key staff members committed to the idea of evaluation? Is the program stable enough to undergo a careful examination? Has the program been in operation long enough to make an evaluation worthwhile?

3. *State the goals and objectives of the program.* Securing clear statements of the program goals and objectives is at once the most difficult and most critical step in making an evaluation. Objectives must be measurable; if they are not, it is not possible to conduct an evaluation. You cannot evaluate a program or intervention until you know precisely what it is trying to accomplish. Moreover, its intervention activities must be logically connected to its goals and objectives and must focus on factors or forces over which it has control. Never place your program in a position of being responsible for something beyond the influence of its intervention activities.

4. *Describe the program's interventions that you intend to evaluate.* Clearly describe the units of intervention or the services. For example, to describe when an intervention activity is happening, you might ask, When does it begin and end? Does the worker decide when an intervention has occurred or does the client or someone else? Can you distinguish an intervention from other client-staff interactions? Can you decide when a service has been used? For example, if a client attended only two of five scheduled sessions of a parenting class, has he or she received parent training?

5. *Select measurable indicators of change.* Once you are clear as to the specific attitudes, behaviors, or conditions your program is trying to change, and you are clear as to the interventions used to bring about those changes, you need to select indicators of change that can be detected and measured. Make sure these indicators are ones that can be reasonably attributed to your program's intervention. Also, decide if it is reasonable to believe that the desired effects of the intervention will occur within the time frame you are using. If you cannot wait to measure long-term benefits, you must choose indicators that reflect more immediate changes.

6. *Select appropriate and feasible data collection and measurement tools and/or instruments.* Developing a valid and reliable instrument is a complex, time-consuming, and expensive process, so try to use available instruments. Examine evaluations done on similar programs and use instruments that others have found useful. Sources for identifying useful instruments for program evaluation include Buros (1986), Corcoran and Fischer (1987), Feldman and Sherman (1987), Hudson (1982), and Magura and Moses (1986).

7. *Plan how you will collect, tabulate, and analyze the data.* Do not collect more data than you can manage and use. Make sure the data you want are actually available. For example, if you plan to gather data from case files, are you sure all of them contain the information you need? If you think the data are stored in the computer system, can you get it out? Can the information you seek be obtained without a release from the client? If your evaluation design involves contacting former service consumers, will you be able to locate them?

8. *Interpret the results of your evaluation.* The final product of your effort is to report the results so that appropriate recognition of the quality of services can be achieved and/or changes in the program can be made. Caution should be used in making this interpretation. Factors other than the nature of the intervention may account for a program's success or failure. For example, successful programs often have a deeply committed and motivated person in a leadership position. These individuals "make" the program work despite obstacles. Such leadership factors may have as much to do with a successful outcome as program design or intervention method. On the other extreme are factors like low staff morale that produce poor outcomes despite a well-conceived program.

Selected Bibliography

Buros, O. K., ed. *Mental Measurements Yearbook.* 8th ed., Vols. 1 and 2. Lincoln: University of Nebraska Press, 1986.

Corcoran, Kevin, and Joel Fischer. *Measures for Clinical Practice.* New York: The Free Press, 1987.

Feldman, Norman, and Robert Sherman. *Handbook of Measurements for Marriage and Family Therapy.* New York: Brunner/Mazel, 1987.

Hudson, Walter. *The Clinical Measurement Package.* Homewood, Ill.: The Dorsey Press, 1982.

Magura, Stephen, and Beth Moses. *Outcome Measures for Child Welfare Services.* Washington, D.C.: Child Welfare League of America, 1986.

Rutman, Leonard, and George Mowbray. *Understanding Program Evaluation.* Beverly Hills: Sage, 1983.

Schalock, Robert L., and Craig V. C. Thornton. *Program Evaluation: A Field Guide for Administrators.* New York: Plenum Press, 1988.

Tripodi, Tony, Phillip Fellin, and Irwin Epstein. *Differential Social Program Evaluation.* Itasca, Ill.: F. E. Peacock, 1978.

Weiss, Heather B., and Francine H. Jacobs. *Evaluating Family Programs.* Hawthrone, N.Y.: Aldine de Gruyter, 1988.

14.22 *Agency Evaluation*

Purpose: To identify data that should be collected to assess the ongoing performance of a social agency in order to make it more efficient in delivering human services.

Discussion: Social agencies are expected to demonstrate that they are efficient and effective in the provision of human services. Agency boards, legislative bodies, and other funding sources increasingly demand that agencies evaluate their services and document their goals efficiently. Social workers are also interested in performance indicators that might stimulate the organizational changes necessary to improve their opportunity to provide high-quality services. Thus, it is useful to be familiar with such indicators of agency performance.

The performance of an entire agency includes the quality of services provided by individual workers (see Technique 14.20) and the success of each program (see Technique 14.21) offered by the agency. However, in an agency, the whole is more than the sum of its parts. It is important to assess periodically how all aspects of the organization fit together to achieve the goals (see Technique 14.3) of that agency.

Methods of Data Collection

Baumheir (1978) notes that the methods of data collection used for the evaluation of human service agencies are quite varied, including "professional reviews, site visits, performance monitoring, descriptive assessments, systems analysis, and various applications of program standards and fiscal accountability" (p. 87). Such measurement, however, can become expensive and divert resources that might more appropriately be spent on agency services. Thus, it becomes critical that the purpose of an agency evaluation be clearly identified.

Baumheir (1978) has generated the following list of factors that social agencies might select to evaluate the programs they provide.

1. *Acceptability.* Do sponsors, constituents, and consumers find the programs desirable?

2. *Humaneness.* Are programs offered in a fair and humane manner?

3. *Appropriateness.* Are programs designed in a manner that fits with the values and needs of the community?

4. *Viability.* Will the agency and program gain political and economic support?

5. *Exposure.* Does a program reach its intended audience?

6. *Responsiveness.* Does the agency and/or program respond to public needs and concerns?

7. *Accountability.* Are the resources properly accounted for and wisely used? Do they follow the laws and compliance requirements of funding sources?

8. *Impact.* Does the program have the intended outcome of resolving human problems? Does it have unintended consequences?

9. *Contextual criteria.* How does the program fit into the community and interact with other resources to meet human needs? How is it influenced by these environmental factors?

10. *Relevance.* Do the programs adequately address the problem under consideration?

11. *Marketability.* Are clients willing to buy or use the services?

12. *Productivity.* Is the program efficient in using resources to provide its services?

13. *Utility.* Is the program sufficiently responsive to the problem under consideration?

14. *Satisfaction.* Are clients and the public satisfied with the results (effectiveness) and the efficiency of operation?

15. *Timeliness.* Are the services provided at the time they are needed?

16. *Normative.* Do the services meet the community standards and expectations for quality services?

Agency Performance Indicators

To assess agency performance, it is necessary first to determine which factors are to be assessed and which administrative or program areas are affected; next, data regarding the appropriate indicators for this analysis must be collected. For the social worker engaged in this activity, the selection of indicators often proves to be a complex task. For example, one such study regarding public welfare agencies, the Human Service Management Indicator Project, identified 500 possible indicators. These were screened to seventy-five data sets that "represented significant organizational performance areas, were factors over which managers had some control, and included areas where the data were likely to be easily available" (Neves, Wolf, and Benton 1986, 135). Some of these indicators helped to set the work of the agency into the context of the environment in which the services were delivered, others were data for analysis of management decisions, and still others were concerned with specific programs being offered. The selected management indicators included:

- *Demographics*
    Population of jurisdiction
    Per capita income
    Unemployment rate
- *Finance*
    Local revenues
    Personnel costs and fringe benefits and purchase of service
    Objects of expenditure
- *Space Utilization*
- *Personnel*
    Turnover
    Full time equivalent (FTE) in particular programs
    Mix of staff (administrative, clerical, program)
    Absenteeism
    Vacancies
    Use of volunteers
    Utilization of clerical staff
- *Intake*
    Waiting time for appointments
    Time to complete applications
    Workload and productivity
- *Child Abuse and Neglect Investigation*
    Number of referrals to department
    Abused and neglected children sent to substitute care
    Disposition of investigation
- *Substitute Care*
    Substitute care caseload
    Length of continuous time in care
- *Child Day Care*
    Costs of care
    Reasons for care
    Percentage of children in day care centers
- *AFDC*
    AFDC approvals
    AFDC participation
    AFDC cases referred for fraud investigation

- *Food Stamps*
  Food stamp staffing
  Food stamp cases referred for fraud investigation (Neves, Wolf, and Benton 1986, 136)

While these indicators were selected for a specific type of human service agency, they are illustrative of the data sets that other social workers might consider developing for their own agency performance evaluations.

Selected Bibliography

Baumheir, Edward C. "Evaluation of Human Services Programs." In *Human Services Management: Priorities for Research,* edited by Michael J. Murphy and Thomas Glynn. Washington, D.C.: International City Management Association, 1978 (as cited by Myron E. Weiner, *Human Services Management: Analysis and Applications.* Homewood, Ill.: The Dorsey Press, 1982, pp. 275–76).

Elkin, Robert. "Paying the Piper and Calling the Tune: Accountability in the Human Services." *Administration in Social Work* 9 (Summer 1985): 1–13.

Harrison, Michael I. *Diagnosing Organizations: Methods, Models, and Processes.* Beverly Hills: Sage, 1987.

Neves, Carole M. P., James F. Wolf, and Bill B. Benton. "The Use of Management Indicators in Monitoring and Performance of Human Service Agencies." In *Performance and Credibility: Developing Excellence in Public and Nonprofit Organizations.* edited by Joseph S. Whorley, Mark A. Abramson, and Christopher Bellavita. Lexington, Mass.: Lexington Books, 1986.

Rossi, Peter H., and Howard E. Freeman. *Evaluation: A Systematic Approach.* 4th ed. Beverly Hills: Sage, 1989.

14.23   *Factors Affecting Organizational Change*

Purpose: To identify conditions that, when present in an organization, are conducive to the implementation of proposals for change generating from organizational analysis.

Discussion: The collection of data and preparation of formal agency performance evaluations does not assure positive organizational change. The agency must be ready to change and the decision makers must be willing to make the hard decisions that will accomplish change. It is helpful for the social worker to recognize the conditions conducive to organizational change. Warhheit, Bell, and Schwab (1977) analyzed the research findings on organizational change and suggest that change is most likely when the following conditions are present:

1. Organizations are more likely to implement research findings when the scope of their domain is not reduced, i.e., when their relationship to the wider environment is not lessened or curtailed as a result of the changes.

2. Organizations are more likely to change their goals and structures when their resources are enhanced by the changes, i.e., when their funds, facilities, autonomy, and power are increased as a result of the changes.

3. Organizations are more likely to accept or produce changes when they do not dramatically rearrange the power and resource allocations within the organization itself.

4. Organizations are more likely to accept or produce changes in their structures when these changes are consistent with their history, ideology, and mandates.

5. Organizations are more likely to attempt changes when the changes are perceived as being economically, practically, and politically feasible.

6. Organizations are more likely to initiate changes when the alternatives to no change pose a threat to their domain and/or their resources.

7. Organizations are more likely to consider changes when the consequences of failure arising from the changes are not serious or irreversible.

8. Organizations are more likely to attempt changes when other similar organizations have successfully modified their programs using the same approaches to effect beneficial changes.

9. Organizations are more likely to adopt changes when there is a strong consensus among administrative and program staff regarding the proposed modifications.

10. Organizations are more likely to attempt changes when the needs for change have been so powerfully demonstrated to the organization and the community that they cannot be ignored. (pp. 56–67)

Selected Bibliography

Warheit, George., Roger A. Bell, and John J. Schwab. *Needs Assessment Approaches: Concepts and Methods.* Washington, D.C.: U.S. Department of Health, Education, and Welfare, 1977.

The Community Context of Practice 15

Introduction

The commitment of social workers to simultaneously address both the person and the person's environment places them in the position of needing knowledge, techniques, and guidelines for working with the range of human service agencies in a community. At the same time, social workers must be concerned with the fact that many other aspects of the community and the larger society impact the quality of life for all people but especially for the more vulnerable members of the population.

People do not necessarily divide up their lives in the same fashion that social agencies divide their areas of responsibility. Thus, a family may need to receive services from several agencies and several social workers at the same time. The ability of the social worker to coordinate his or her work with the work of other professionals becomes an important part of the indirect service activity of the social worker. At other times, the social worker can only improve conditions for people by working for change at the community level, including the local, state, or national levels. These practice activities could range from working on a committee to develop a strong housing code, to lobbying, or even to testifying before a local, state, or national legislative body.

For the new social worker, bringing about community change may seem well beyond the scope of beginning professional practice. That may be partially true. Unless the social worker has had specialized educational preparation and experience in community work, many of the more technical and sophisticated techniques used in community planning activities should not be attempted. Those more advanced techniques are not included in this book, as it is intended for the generalist social worker who has not had such specialized preparation.

However, much community work takes place on a daily basis as the social worker carries out the responsibilities of serving clients and connecting them with community resources. The unique perspective of the social worker results in an important understanding of how the policies and procedures of human service organizations or of governmental policy decisions affect individual clients. Effective social workers are frequently asked to bring this perspective to committees, task forces, and planning groups that are created to help communities better meet the needs of their residents.

This chapter is limited to guidelines and techniques that can increase the effectiveness of the social worker in these change activities. For example, the primary arena for interorganizational and community change is the small work group or the committee. Skill in parliamentary procedures and the ability to move groups in desired directions can have an important influence on the broader community. At other times, it is important to persuade larger groups such as a city council or county commission to act or to lobby state or national legislators for a particular position. If these actions are to be effective, they must be underpinned by a thorough background knowledge of the community and careful assessment and planning regarding this particular situation.

15.1   *Learning about Your Community*

Purpose: To develop a community assessment to help understand the context in which human services are delivered.

Discussion: To serve effectively and make contributions to community decisions, it is important for the social worker to know about the community in which he or she is working. To acquire this information, the new social worker or experienced social worker moving to a new community should make a thorough assessment of that community.

Usually, general information based on census data, economic development forecasts, and community planning projects is already compiled and available at the public library, Chamber of Commerce, United Way, and government offices (e.g., especially the offices of the city and county planning departments). Supplemental data that are especially useful for the social worker might be obtained by reading historical accounts of the development of the community, interviewing long-time residents, and following the events reported in the local newspaper. From these latter sources, it is particularly important to record the names of key figures in the community who are potentially important decision makers in the community change process.

The following outline will help the social worker develop a profile of the community. It is based on community study outlines developed by Devore and Schlesinger (1987), Warren (1955), and Warren and Warren (1984).

- *Basic Information*
  - Name(s) of community (e.g., Southside, Watts)
  - Location (i.e., neighborhood, city, county, state)
  - Type of local government

- *Population*
  - Size and mobility
  - Age and sex distributions (e.g., number of preschoolers, children in grade school, teenagers, persons over age sixty-five)
  - Country of birth of significant groupings
  - Types of households (e.g., married couples, single parents)
  - Minority and ethnic groups
  - Religious affiliations and traditions
- *Sense of Identity and Belonging*
  - Do residents have a sense of identification with and loyalty and belonging to the community?
  - Major reasons people want to live or remain in the area
- *History of the Area*
  - When and why was area settled or developed?
  - Background of those who first settled and developed area
  - Change in population and its makeup over time
  - Major events that shaped the area's development and the attitudes of residents
  - Prevailing values and beliefs
- *Educational Level*
  - Median educational level for adult population
  - Median educational level for adult women
  - Median educational level for major minority and ethnic groups
  - School dropout rates
- *Local Economics and Business*
  - Percentage of labor force employed and unemployed
  - Major industries and products
  - Major employers and corporations
  - Are major businesses locally owned or controlled by persons outside the community?
  - Degree of unionization
  - Skills required by major employers
  - Common working hours
  - Forecasts of future economic growth and job opportunity
- *Income*
  - Median income of men
  - Median income of women
  - Median income of minority groups
  - Number of persons/families below the official poverty line
  - Number of persons/families receiving public assistance
- *Housing*
  - Common types of housing (e.g., private homes, apartments, public housing)
  - Percentage of dwellings occupied and vacant
  - Percentage of dwellings overcrowded or substandard

- *Geography and Environmental Influences*

    Effect of climate, mountains, valleys, rivers, lakes, and the like on transportation patterns, economic development, and population distribution

    Effect of highways, railroads, truck routes, and other man-made barriers on neighborhoods, social interaction, and service delivery

    Effect of environmental factors on current and future development (e.g., water supply, pollution, sewage treatment, sources of electricity and energy, distance from markets)

- *Information Sources*

    Sources to which various segments of community look for information

    TV and radio stations and newspapers in community

    Leaders and spokespersons for various segments of community, including minority and ethnic groups

- *Educational Facilities and Programs*

    Types of grade schools and high schools (e.g., public, private, neighborhood, magnet)

    Do schools have bilingual programs?

    Do schools have sufficient specialized programs and services for children with handicapping conditions?

    Are schools sensitive to problems and strengths of persons from minority and ethnic groups?

    Are minority and ethnic groups adequately represented on school staffs, school boards, and so on?

    What college-level, vocational, and job-training programs are available?

- *Local Politics*

    Form and structure of local government

    Relative power of political parties

    Voter participation

    Current issues and controversy

    Types of taxes used to generate public funds

- *Health and Welfare Service System*

    Major providers of health services (e.g., hospitals, public health facilities, private clinics)

    Major providers of social services and their primary sources of funding

    Self-help and informal helping networks

    Comprehensiveness and coordination of services

    Availability, accessibility, and flexibility of services

    Are providers sensitive to special needs or concerns of minority and ethnic groups? Are staff members bilingual? Are all clients treated with dignity?

- *Major Problems and Concerns of the Community*

    What are major social problems (e.g., inadequate housing, inadequate public transportation, lack of jobs, drugs, crime, poverty)?

    What efforts are underway to address these concerns?

    Major gaps among existing social, health care, and educational services

---

Selected Bibliography

Devore, Wynetta, and Elfriede G. Schlesinger. *Ethnic-Sensitive Social Work Practice.* 2nd ed. St. Louis: C. V. Mosby, 1987.

Warren, Rochelle, and Donald Warren. "How to Diagnose a Neighborhood." In *Tactics and Techniques of Community Practice,* 2nd ed., edited by Fred Cox, John Erlich, Jack Rothman, and John Tropman. Itasca, Ill.: F. E. Peacock, 1984.

Warren, Roland L. "The Good Community—What Would It Be?" *Journal of Community Development Society* 1 (Spring 1970):14–23.

———. *Studying Your Community.* New York: Russell Sage Foundation, 1955.

15.2   *Developing Professional Cooperation*

Purpose: To develop and nurture interagency and interprofessional relationships.

Discussion: In most cases, no one professional and no one agency can provide all of the services needed by a client. Thus, if a client is to be served properly, interprofessional and interagency cooperation is necessary. Teamwork and cooperative behavior grows from a proper mix of values, attitudes, and interpersonal skills. For example, Motz and Schultz (1988, 37) have observed that effective members on interagency child protection teams have the following characteristics: (1) assertiveness, (2) ability to listen and openness to differing ideas, (3) willingness to support other team members, (4) ability to offer criticism in a constructive manner, (5) strong commitment to the team approach, and (6) consistent attendance at team meetings.

The following guidelines encourage cooperation and teamwork:

1. Realize that genuine cooperation is something that must be nurtured. It does not happen by accident. Be prepared to invest time and effort in creating and reinforcing cooperative behavior.

2. Clarify the role and responsibilities of those with whom you are working. Make sure everyone is clear about what they can and cannot expect of each other. Consider developing written interagency agreements that will address such relationships (see Techniques 15.3 and 15.4). Be aware of any prior interagency agreements that define interaction and expectations (e.g., contracts, letters of agreement, purchase of service agreements, informal agreements between agency executives and/or line staff).

3. Use reinforcement—including thanks, recognition, and praise—to encourage cooperative behavior. Also, take a real interest in the professionals with whom you frequently work. Learn about their personal and professional interests, aspirations, and so on. Share your personal thoughts and feelings, as well. Where appropriate, invite them to office parties and informal social gatherings as a way of deepening relationships and promoting goodwill along with congenial professional relationships. Do not engage in gossip, backbiting, or any activity that may diminish respect for other professionals or agencies.

4. Be willing to address directly and openly those conflicts or hidden agendas that disrupt team effort. Efforts to suppress conflict by denial, avoidance, capitulation, or domination only postpone the conflict and sometimes make the problem more troublesome. In and of itself, conflict is not bad; it can have important benefits. Conflict that arises from thoughtful difference of opinion is healthy. Conflict that stems from prejudice, displaced hostility, or thoughtless loyalty to actions of the past is disruptive and must be addressed if it stands in the way of service delivery. When it is necessary to express a difference of opinion or deal with a conflict within the groups, use "I-messages" (see Technique 6.6) and other communication skills that convey your message in a clear, straightforward, nonthreatening manner. Also, remind the group of its goal: helping the client. Try to resolve interprofessional and interagency conflicts by focusing on shared values and by using negotiating skills.

5. Remember that even under the best circumstances, teamwork can be demanding and stressful. This is especially true when the team is attempting to make difficult, value-laden decisions and to formulate plans concerning highly dysfunctional individuals and families. If the team is unable to communicate clearly and resolve its own conflicts, it may end up behaving much like the dysfunctional families it is trying to serve.

6. Realize that some of those with whom you must work may not be committed to teamwork. Some may try to manipulate others for reasons unrelated to client service. When this is evident, be firm but diplomatic in expressing the need for cooperation and putting the good of the client or client system before other considerations.

7. When functioning as part of a team, encourage the selection of a leader or chairperson who is nondefensive, supportive of others, and respected by others in the group.

8. Concern for client confidentiality is a reason commonly given for not working closely with other agencies and professionals. Sometimes this issue is more imagined than real. Clients can be asked to sign a release of information, thus removing this barrier. If professionals or agencies want to work together but are hesitant to do so because of the confidentiality issue, they should ask their agency's legal consultant to research the matter and recommend a workable procedure.

Selected Bibliography

Garner, Howard. *Helping Others Through Teamwork.* New York: Child Welfare League of America, 1988

Motz, Janet, and Michael Schultz. "Rural Child Protection Teams." In *The New Child Protection Team Handbook,* edited by Donald Bross et al. New York: Garland, 1988.

Rossi, Robert, Kevin Gilmartin, and Charles Dayton. *Agencies Working Together: A Guide to Coordination and Planning.* Beverly Hills: Sage, 1982.

Purpose: To improve services to clients through cooperative arrangements and clarification of procedures, roles, and responsibilities that facilitate interagency cooperation.

Discussion: Social work is often the pivotal profession in the effort to coordinate the interactions among agencies. The social worker must be skilled at helping agencies develop formal and informal mechanisms to make this interaction occur smoothly.

Informally, much agency interaction occurs when social workers are involved in interagency teams, case conferences, human service planning activities, or participants in NASW chapter meetings where discussion of problems affecting agency coordination inevitably occurs. The social worker who is new to a community should quickly attempt to participate in these activities and build this informal network for service coordination.

Even when agencies are interested in collaboration, it is often difficult to establish formal mechanisms that allow them to maintain meaningful working relationships. It is useful for the social worker to recognize that agencies have used a number of formalized activities to both enhance their services and structure linkage with other agencies. Lauffer (1978, 188–205) suggests the following possibilities:

1. *Administrative approaches: Fiscal integration*
   a. Purchase of service
   b. Joint budgeting
   c. Joint funding
2. *Administrative support services*
   a. Conducting studies
   b. Information processing, dissemination, and exchange
   c. Recordkeeping
   d. Grants management and technical assistance
   e. Publicity and public relations
   f. Procedural integration
   g. Joint program or project evaluation
   h. Central program evaluation
   i. Standards and guidelines
3. *Administrative and programmatic linkages involving agency personnel*
   a. Loaner staff
   b. Outstationing
   c. Liaison teams and joint use of staff
   d. Staff training and development
   e. Screening, employment counseling, and placement
   f. Volunteer bureaus
   g. Ombudsmen

4. *Programmatic linkages through development of centralized services*
   a. Information and outreach
   b. Intake
   c. Diagnosis
   d. Referral
   e. Transportation
   f. Follow-up
   g. Grievance machinery
5. *Programmatic coordination through service integration*
   a. Case management
   b. Ad hoc case coordination
   c. Case conferences
   d. Joint program development
   e. Joint projects

Selected Bibliography

Lauffer, Armand. *Social Planning at the Community Level.* Englewood Cliffs, N.J.: Prentice-Hall, 1978.

Neugeboren, Bernard. *Organization, Policy, and Practice in the Human Services.* New York: Longman, 1985.

15.4 *Using Protocol Statements*

Purpose: To improve service to clients through the use of protocol statements that specify the responsibilities of each agency involved in the case.

Discussion: When two or more agencies are involved in a particular case or other practice activity, it is critical to the well-being of the client that each clearly understands its own responsibilities and those of others involved. Increasingly, agencies formalize such relationships by using protocol statements. A protocol is a concise, written description of the steps to be taken by a professional or agency in a situation where mistakes or omissions can have serious negative consequences. Levy (1980) explains the use of protocols by hospital social workers as follows:

> The protocols are designed to ensure consistent and complete provision and documentation of social work services. Separate protocols have been developed for the specific types of social work problems encountered at the medical center. Each protocol lists the necessary steps in social work intervention for a particular problem. Both the appropriate intervention process and the necessary documentation are indicated by the protocol; that is, the social worker is to perform each activity listed and also document those activities for which documentation is required. (p. 21)

The following excerpts are from a thirteen-step protocol developed by Bertsche, Francetich, and Horejsi (1985) for use in a state child protective services agency during the investigative phase of child sexual abuse cases. The key actors in this example are Child Protective Services (CPS), law enforcement, and the County Attorney's Office (prosecutor). Because criminal prosecution of the offender is common in sexual abuse cases, it is critical that these three agencies understand who is responsible for specific activities and to know the preferred sequence of these activities.

Protocol: Child Sexual Abuse Investigation

1. *Receive Referral* (i.e., report of alleged abuse)
   - CPS social worker speaks with referral source if possible. Obtain specifics (i.e., location of alleged incident, quotations from child). Make collateral contacts such as: individuals with knowledge of the sexual abuse as mentioned by referral source; school; doctors or other medical information sources; and the police department to discover if the offender named has a past arrest record for sexual molestation.
   - Contact County Attorney and advise of referral and that it will be investigated. If County Attorney is not available, a message left with the secretary.

2. *Interview with Child*
   CPS worker conducts interview with the child but obtains only enough information to determine that, most likely, abuse has occurred. Interview will be conducted in a manner appropriate to the developmental level of the child.

3. *Assessment*
   Based on information gathered from the child in Step 2, worker assesses need for:
   - Emergency placement.
   - Medical exam (non-offending parent may arrange this if parent believes and is supportive of child).
   - Action concerning other siblings in the home.

4. *County Attorney/CPS Consultation*
   CPS worker advises the County Attorney of action taken thus far. In conjunction with County Attorney, CPS worker arranges formal interview using one of the following:
   - Social worker and mental health therapist.
   - Social worker and law enforcement.
   - Any combination determined to be most appropriate.

5. *Formal Interview*
   (In some instances the non-offending parent is interviewed first, and if supportive of child, is present at the formal interview but seated behind child.)
   - The interview is conducted in the manner determined most appropriate by the social worker and County Attorney. Emphasis should be on making this interview as non-threatening and non-traumatic for child as possible.
   - A tape recorder supported by written notes will suffice, if video equipment is not available. There should be two methods of recording used in case one malfunctions. Once taken, the report (tape, film, notes, etc.) forms evidence and needs to be appropriately protected. (Usually the Sheriff's Office or Police Department maintains the tapes.)

6. *Interview with Non-Offending Parent(s)*
   In this interview the worker assesses the non-offending parent's ability to protect

the child from further abuse, the level of support for the child, and the need for out-of-home placement. If alleged offender is present, he/she is told that the referral will be made to law enforcement. (pp. 2.1–2.3)

The other steps in this thirteen-step protocol are (7) "Request for Legal Action Via Civil Court (when appropriate)," (8) "Separation of Alleged Offender from Child," (9) "Interview with Offender," (10) "Follow-Up," (11) "Prosecution," (12) "Ongoing Casework," and (13) "Treatment Plan."

Selected Bibliography

Bertsche, Jon, Sherry Francetich, and Charles Horejsi. *Protocol Notebook for Child Welfare Workers.* Missoula: University of Montana, Department of Social Work, 1985.

Horejsi, Charles, Jon Bertsche, Sherry Francetich, Bill Collins, and Russell Francetich. "Protocols in Child Welfare." *Child Welfare* 66 (September/October 1987): 423–31.

Levy, Louis. "An Intergrated Data Management System for Social Service." *Quality Review Bulletin* 6 (October 1980): 20–25.

Schmitt, Barton, ed. *The Child Protection Team Handbook: A Multi-disciplinary Approach to Managing Child Abuse and Neglect.* New York: Garland STPM Press, 1978.

15.5 Leading Small-Group Meetings

Purpose: To schedule and conduct efficient and productive committee and group meetings.

Discussion: Social workers spend considerable time participating in groups: agency staff meetings (see Technique 14.9), interagency team meetings, and various agency and community committees and task forces. Group action has become an important factor in the decision-making process for organizations working to meet community needs. Toseland, Rivas, and Chapman (1984) reached two important conclusions from their study of task group decision making: "The reliance of agencies on groups for making decisions regarding agency policies, practices, and business is warranted. [And] even if group leaders or group members do not act on the decision made by a group in which they participated, they are likely to make a better independent decision because they participated in a group" (pp. 343–44).

While group consideration of issues may have inherent benefits, without proper planning and direction, group meetings can waste much valuable time and reduce the opportunity for making significant community or organizational change.

As the leader of a small group, the social worker is responsible for making the meeting as productive and efficient as possible. Barker et al. (1979), Brilhart (1978), and Bertcher (1979) identify a number of principles and guidelines that should be followed by the worker when he or she is in a leadership position.

1. *Prepare for the meeting by engaging in the following activities:*
   a. Clearly identify the purpose of the meeting. *Never have a meeting unless there is a real need for one.*
   b. Decide who should participate.
   c. Identify objectives for the meeting and anticipate what the participants will and should expect. You may want to involve them in the planning.
   d. Decide the best time and place for the meeting, and determine how participants will be notified of the purpose, agenda, time, and place of the meeting.
   e. Decide how much time will be required for the meeting and construct a realistic agenda. Plan to address high-priority items first.
   f. Decide what physical arrangements are necessary (e.g., room reservations, seating arrangements, audiovisual equipment, refreshments).
   g. Decide if a written report will be needed and, if so, who will prepare it and how it will be distributed.
   h. Decide if a follow-up meeting will be needed.

2. *Get the discussion off to a good start.*
   a. Make sure that all members are introduced to each other. This might be done with an icebreaker activity or a coffee hour. Use nametags if members do not already know each other.
   b. Explain the purpose of the discussion and its relevance to the participants.
   c. Distribute materials needed for the discussion (e.g., fact sheets, outlines, case examples).
   d. Create an atmosphere that helps the participants feel unthreatened and responsible for contributing to the discussion.

3. *Keep the discussion orderly, efficient, and productive.*
   a. Make sure the goal is understood by all and that it is a goal that makes sense to the group. Keep the participants oriented toward that goal. For example, occasionally ask, "Are we still on target for reaching our objectives?"
   b. Be alert to extended departures from the topic. If the group is drifting away from the topic, call this to everyone's attention. Ask if the digression means that there is disagreement on the goal or if it is an indication that the group is ready to move on to another topic.
   c. If there is much repetition in the discussion, ask if the group has exhausted the subject at hand. If so, help them get started on a new topic.
   d. Be the group's timekeeper. Keep the group informed of the time limits so high-priority topics will get the attention they deserve.
   e. Bring the discussion to a conclusion, which might include:
      - a summary of progress made by the group
      - comments about planning and preparation for another meeting
      - assignments for follow-up and implementation
      - commendations when appropriate
      - request an evaluation of the meeting in order to improve future ones.

4. *Give all members an equal opportunity to participate.*

a. Explain in your opening remarks that the role of the group leader primarily will be that of coordinator to ensure that all members have an opportunity to be heard.

b. Address your comments and questions to the group as a whole, rather than to specific individuals, unless specific information is needed from a particular person.

c. Make sure that all members have a chance to participate. While no one should be forced to speak, neither should anyone be prevented from speaking.

d. Scan the group every minute or two. Look for indications that a member wants to speak. If this is seen and the member has been quiet, bring that person into the discussion by asking if he or she would like to add something to the discussion.

e. If the group contains members who dominate the discussion, try to control them for the benefit of the group. A number of techniques can be used. A good general rule is to begin with a more subtle approach and become directive only if necessary. Some possible ways to deal with such members are:

- When possible, seat the talkative members where they are more easily overlooked by other members.
- When a question is asked of the group, meet the eyes of those members who have spoken infrequently and avoid eye contact with the dominant talkers.
- When a frequent talker has made a point, cut in with something like, "How do the rest of you feel about that idea?"
- Adopt a rule that each person can make but one statement per topic.
- In private, ask the excessive talkers to help in getting the quiet members to speak more often.
- Point out the problem and ask others to contribute more. For instance, "We have heard a lot from John and Mary, but what do the rest of you think about . . . ?"

f. If asked by a member to express a personal opinion about a controversial issue, try to bounce the question back to the group, unless members already have expressed their opinions. Say, "Well, let's see how others feel about this first." If you must express a personal opinion, do so in an open and honest manner that will not inhibit others from speaking on the topic.

g. Don't comment after each member has spoken; it is too easy to get into a "wheel" pattern of communication, with the leader becoming the hub of the wheel.

h. React to what members say with acceptance and without judgment, showing only that a point is understood or that it needs clarification. If evaluation seems necessary, invite it from others with a question such as, "Does that fit with your perception on the matter?"

i. Use nonverbal communication to promote discussion. Nods and gestures can be used to encourage participation, especially from the quiet members.

---

5. *Promote cooperation and harmony in a small group.*

a. Be alert to the possibility of hidden agendas, and call them to the attention of the group. The group usually can solve a problem of conflicting purposes if it is brought into the open for discussion.

b. Emphasize the importance of the mutual sharing of ideas and experiences and the need for clear communication.

c. Use the word *we* often to stress the group's unity of purpose.

d. Keep conflicts focused on facts and issues. Stop any attacks on a member's personality.

e. Do not let the discussion become so serious that the members do not have some fun. Humor can reduce tension. Effective discussion is characterized by a constant shifting between the serious and the playful.

6. *Use questioning techniques to maintain attention on a topic and stimulate analytical thinking.*

a. Use open-ended questions rather than closed-ended ones, which can be answered with a yes or no.

b. Questions should be understandable to all. Vague or obtuse questions frustrate the members.

c. Questions should be asked in a natural and conversational tone of voice.

d. Questions should usually be addressed to the group as a whole, rather than to a particular individual. This motivates everyone to think and respond.

e. Questions occasionally should be asked of persons who are not giving their attention to the discussion. This usually stimulates the individual and the whole group to redirect its attention to the topic.

f. Questions should be asked in a manner that indicates the leader's confidence in the person's ability to respond.

g. Questions should be selected to maintain the focus on the topic under discussion. Avoid questions that would cause the group to leave its task and go off on a tangent.

7. *Encourage critical thinking.*

a. Ask for more detail and specification. Dig for the rationale and assumptions behind an opinion or a belief. Help those offering opinions to furnish evidence for the positions they take.

b. See that the evidence offered for a position is tested and not accepted at face value.

c. Assign one or two members of the group to challenge ideas and play "devil's advocate" so that differences are aired openly.

Selected Bibliography

Barker, Larry, Donald Cegala, Robert Kibler, and Kathy Wahlers. *Groups in Process.* Englewood Cliffs, N.J.: Prentice-Hall, 1979.

Bertcher, Harvey. *Group Participation Techniques for Leaders and Members.* Beverly Hills: Sage, 1979.

Brilhart, John. *Effective Group Discussion.* 3rd ed. Dubuque, Iowa: W. C. Brown, 1978.

Toseland, Ronald W., Robert F. Rivas, and Dennis Chapman. "An Evaluation of Decision-Making Methods in Task Groups." *Social Work* 29 (July–August 1984): 339–46.

15.6   *Chairing a Committee*

Purpose: To effectively serve as chair of a committee and lead that group to successful action.

Discussion: The committee is a particular type of small group for which the social worker might assume leadership responsibility. As chairperson of a committee, the social worker should make use of the guidelines for working with small groups (see Technique 15.5). In addition, chairing a committee requires the use of a formal task-oriented approach that can be facilitated by the selective use of Techniques 15.7, 15.8, and 15.9.

People are usually willing to serve on committees if they find that their time is used efficiently and that the effort will have productive results. Reflecting the other side of this matter, Dyer (1977) surveyed 200 university personnel serving on various committees and identified the following factors that made them *dislike* serving on committees:

1. *Poor leadership.* The leader fails to keep the discussions on the subject, [fails] to monitor and direct to keep things moving in the appropriate direction, and [fails] to engage in those activities that are stimulating and motivating to the members.

2. *Goals are unclear.* Members are not really sure what they are trying to accomplish.

3. *Assignments are not taken seriously by committee members.* There is an apparent lack of commitment.

4. *There is a lack of clear focus on the committee's assignment*—e.g.,"What are we supposed to be doing today?"

5. *Recommendations of the committee are often ignored by top management.* Management must be responsive to the committee.

6. *Waste of time.* Unproductive discussions of problems with no conclusions, actions or decisions made.

7. *Lack of follow-through with assignments on the part of committee members.*

8. *Domination by one person or clique.* Some talk and push for their positions too much, while others are reluctant to get involved.

9. *Lack of preparation by committee members, including the chair of the meeting.* Agenda not prepared, materials and things that really need to be there are not available. Someone has not done the necessary homework.

10. *No action taken.* The committee spends valuable time without coming up with specific items resulting in some kind of action.

11. *Members have hidden agendas—personal axes to grind.* They get into discussions that distract the committee from its goal. (pp. 74–75)

An essential skill for both the chairperson and the members of a committee is familiarity with the use of parliamentary procedures. For almost a century,

Figure 15.1 Parliamentary Motions: Order of Precedence

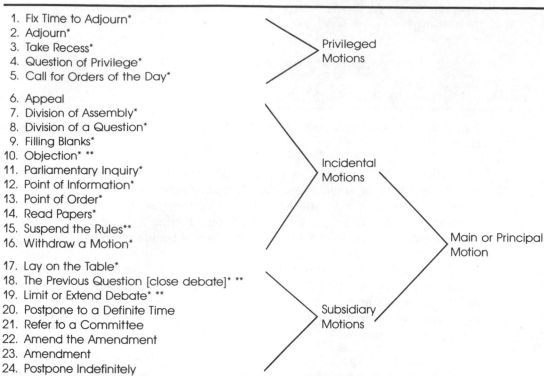

1. Fix Time to Adjourn*
2. Adjourn*
3. Take Recess*
4. Question of Privilege*
5. Call for Orders of the Day*

Privileged Motions

6. Appeal
7. Division of Assembly*
8. Division of a Question*
9. Filling Blanks*
10. Objection* **
11. Parliamentary Inquiry*
12. Point of Information*
13. Point of Order*
14. Read Papers*
15. Suspend the Rules**
16. Withdraw a Motion*

Incidental Motions

17. Lay on the Table*
18. The Previous Question [close debate]* **
19. Limit or Extend Debate* **
20. Postpone to a Definite Time
21. Refer to a Committee
22. Amend the Amendment
23. Amendment
24. Postpone Indefinitely

Subsidiary Motions

Main or Principal Motion

* Motion is not debatable.
** Motion requires two-thirds approval vote.

Robert's Rules of Order (Robert 1967) has been the accepted expression of the procedures that should be followed in formal committee proceedings. Although not very interesting reading, a copy of this publication or another guide to parliamentary procedures should be on every social worker's bookshelf. Figure 15.1 provides a useful summary of these rules of order.

As explained in the footnote of Figure 15.1, a single asterisk (*) denotes those motions that are not debatable; two asterisks (**) denotes those that require a two-thirds vote of the committee or assembly for approval. After action has been taken on the main or principal motion, for example, it is possible to move for a "division of the assembly" (undebatable) or to "suspend the rules" (two-thirds vote required).

Selected Bibliography

Dyer, William G. *Team Building: Issues and Alternates.* Reading, Mass.: Addison-Wesley, 1977.

Garfield, James O. *Parliamentary Procedure at a Glance.* Rev. Ed. New York: Hawthorne/
    Dutton, 1971.
Robert, Henry M. *Robert's Rules of Order.* New York: Pyramid Books, 1967.

15.7   *Negotiating Committee Purpose and Procedures*

Purpose: To assist a committee in setting clear goals and operating procedures.

Discussion: One means of helping a committee avoid some of the pitfalls that lead to unproductive meetings is to engage the members in setting committee goals and operating procedures. Whether the committee is new or one that has continued over an extended period of time, it is useful for the chairperson or other members to periodically review and renegotiate the objectives and methods of operation so that all members can fully participate in the work. Dyer (1977, 76–81) identifies several steps that should be followed in building a productive committee.

1. *Develop a realistic priority level.* It is important to give committee members a chance to discuss why they are serving on the committee, clarify the relative importance of this work in the context of their total responsibilities, and indicate the amount of time they are able to commit to this activity. Sharing these matters helps establish the pace at which the committee can operate and allows the chair to identify persons who can carry major responsibilities.

2. *Share expectations.* Each person should be asked to identify his or her greatest concerns about working on this committee, how he or she sees it functioning, and what actions are necessary to ensure positive outcomes.

3. *Clarify goals.* The committee members should collectively discuss and write down a statement that they agree represents the group's *core mission.* Subgoals can then be developed to reflect the intermediate or short-range objectives necessary to accomplish this mission. Each decision and action should be examined for its contribution to the mission or subgoals that have been established.

4. *Formulate operating guidelines.* The committee members should then establish procedures for their operation. Answers to the following questions will provide clear guidance for the chair and allow members to know how to proceed:
    a. How will we make decisions?
    b. What will be our basic method of work?
    c. How do we make sure everyone gets a chance to discuss issues or raise concerns?
    d. How will we resolve differences?
    e. How will we ensure that we complete our work?
    f. How will we change things that are not producing results?

In addition, it should be recognized that the formality with which a committee operates often depends on its size, the existing relationships among the members, and the speed with which it needs to make decisions. The purpose of some committees is best served by a very open dialogue that explores topics in depth before action is taken. For others, the work is more task-oriented, with subcommittees considering the issues and preparing reports of their deliberations on which the full committee will act.

Selected Bibliography

Dyer, William G. *Team Building: Issues and Alternates.* Reading, Mass.: Addison-Wesley, 1977.

Shindler-Rainman, Eva, and Ronald Lippitt. *Taking Your Meeting Out of the Doldrums.* Columbus, Ohio: The Association of Professional Directors, 1975.

Tropman, John. *Effective Meetings: Improving Group Decision-Making.* Beverly Hills: Sage, 1980.

15.8   *Nominal Group Technique (NGT)*

Purpose: To help consensus-oriented groups arrive at decisions.

Discussion: Committees that depend on a consensus approach sometimes get stuck in reaching a decision. One technique that helps bring issues into the open and move the group toward consensus is the ***Nominal Group Technique (NGT).*** It is particularly suited for groups of approximately six to nine people. The authors of this approach—Delbecq, Van de Ven, and Gustafson (1975, 14)—summarize the main elements of the NGT process:

1. A solitary generation of ideas in writing
2. Round-robin feedback from group members to record each idea in a terse phrase on a flipchart
3. The discussion of each recorded idea for clarification and evaluation
4. Individual voting and priority ideas with a group decision being mathematically derived through rank ordering or rating

This approach can be used with small groups addressing direct service issues, such as identifying and sharing experiences about a practice problem or condition. For this application it might take as much as 1½ hours to complete the process. The NGT is also useful for working with task groups dealing with organizational or community problems. Lauffer (1982, 74) indicates that its application as a team planning tool to activities ranging from task analysis to the development of an action plan might take up to nine hours. The difference is largely in the scope of the problems to be identified and the complexity of the issues to be discussed.

Some specific guidelines for the social worker using the shorter form of the Nominal Group Technique (Zimmerman and Morgan 1975, 53–54; Brilhart 1978, 221–22) are as follows:

1. The chair acts as facilitator and does not vote.
2. The issue is stated on a flipchart.
3. The pros and cons are freely discussed for ten minutes.

4. Each person is asked to spend five to fifteen minutes working silently, writing down ideas or solutions on a piece of paper. The chair polls each committee member for one idea or solution.

5. Each idea or solution is listed on the chart and numbered. The chair then polls each member for a second idea or solution and repeats this process until the lists have been exhausted.

6. Ten more minutes are allowed for clarification of the ideas or solutions presented—not for defense of the position.

7. All members vote on a secret ballot, ranking their top five choices 1, 2, 3, 4, 5. By adding the scores for each idea or solution, the lowest scores will reflect the most favored positions by the committee.

8. Have a full evaluation discussion of the several items at the top of the list. Encourage critical thinking, invite disagreement, and seek careful analysis of the items.

9. If a clear consensus is not reached, revote and then discuss the items again. This can be repeated until a synthesis of ideas is developed or there is clear support for one idea.

The NGT encourages active involvement by all committee members as they consider and write down their ideas. Too often, in a group process, a few members carry the discussion and others do not actively and creatively think about the issues from their own perspective. The interactive presentation of the issues allows all committee members an opportunity to express themselves and respond to the ideas from both the verbal and less-verbal members.

Selected Bibliography

Brilhart, John. *Effective Group Discussion.* 3rd ed. Dubuque, Iowa: W. C. Brown, 1978.
Delbecq, André L., Andrew H. Van de Ven, and David H. Gustafson. *Group Techniques for Program Planning: A Guide to Nominal Group and Delphi Processes.* Glenview, Ill.: Scott, Foresman, 1975.
Zimmerman, Lynn Nybell, and Joyce Morgan. *Staff Development and Training: Convenor's Guide.* Ann Arbor: University of Michigan, School of Social Work, 1975.

15.9 *RISK Technique*

Purpose: To facilitate committee or group members expressing their fears or concerns about an issue or proposed action.

Discussion: At times, committees (and especially staff committees) are faced with issues that involve a perceived risk or that are a source of fear. When new policies are adopted by a board, when new legislation is passed that affects a social program and/or the resources available, or when administrators establish a change in routine, it often creates the need to identify the facts and issues in the situation and set aside rumors and fantasized outcomes. In these situations, the **RISK technique** can be particularly useful.

To use this technique, the leader must take a nondefensive posture and communicate an interest in having the group members express *all* fears, issues, concerns, complaints, and anticipated problems. By maintaining this approach, the leader, who typically would be a supervisor or middle manager in an organization, encourages members of the group to express their views and to nonemotionally listen and understand one anothers' fears. Brilhart (1978) identifies the following steps in using this procedure:

1. Present in detail the proposed change of procedure or policy to the group.
2. Explain the purpose and procedures to be followed in the RISK technique.
3. Invite and post all "risks," fears, problems, doubts, concerns, etc. The leader should allow no evaluation and make none himself, verbal or nonverbal, much as in brainstorming. The leader or other members of the group may clarify or simplify a member's risk statement, but never modify its intent. It is essential that the wording of the "risk" as posted be fully acceptable to the presenter. Allow plenty of time. Often the most significant items, the most threatening and disturbing to members, do not come until late in the session, often after periods of silence. The leader should keep encouraging the members to think of more risks. Members will be feeling out the leader and each other to determine if it is safe to express these, or if they might be in some way ridiculed or retaliated against.
4. After the initial meeting, reproduce and circulate the list to all participants, inviting any additions that may have been thought of in the interim.
5. At the next meeting of the group, add any further risks mentioned.
6. Then, have the group decide if each risk is serious and substantive. No risk should now be considered as the property of its presenter, but of the entire group. Often the discussants can resolve many of each other's fears, doubts, and concerns at this point as they share experiences, ideas, and points of view. All such items should now be removed from the list.
7. Remaining risks are now processed into an agenda.... Some can be resolved by obtaining information, but the problems remaining can now be dealt with one at a time in problem-solving discussions, solutions being worked out by the group. (p. 225)*

Selected Bibliography

Brilhart, John. *Effective Group Discussion.* 3rd ed. Dubuque, Iowa: W. C. Brown, 1978.

15.10 *Problem Solving by a Large Group*

Purpose: To help a large group of people arrive at a decision.

Discussion: At times, it is necessary for a social worker to initiate problem-solving activity within a large group of people. The technique described here is

*From Brilhart, John K., *Effective Group Discussion* 3rd ed. © 1978 Wm. C. Brown Publishers, Dubuque, Iowa. All Rights Reserved. Reprinted by permission.

intended to elicit ideas from all members and provide an opportunity for participation, even when as many as thirty or more people are involved.

The technique begins with the group leader explaining the purpose of the meeting: for example, "We need to come up with a method of collecting information from the agencies in town on trends in the number of homeless people applying for help." The following steps should then be followed:

1. *Each individual is asked to think privately about the problem and possible solutions.* Members are asked to make written notes on their thoughts.

2. *Dyads are formed.* Each person in the dyad is instructed to interview his or her partner and to try to understand that person's perspective on the problem and proposed solutions. The dyads work for ten minutes.

3. *Quartets are formed.* For fifteen minutes, each group of four people discusses the problem and possible solutions. Each quartet records the key points of its deliberation on a large piece of paper, which is hung on the wall for all to see.

4. *Each individual studies the papers for ten minutes.*

5. *The whole group reassembles and shares their analysis of the problem and proposed solutions.* This final step sets the stage for the prioritizing of proposed solutions to be explored in more depth.

Selected Bibliography

Brody, Ralph. *Problem Solving: Concepts and Methods for Community Organization.* New York: Human Services Press, 1982.

Kahn, Si. *Organizing: A Guide for Grassroots Leaders.* New York: McGraw-Hill, 1982.

15.11 Class Advocacy

Purpose: To advance the cause of a group in order to establish a right or entitlement to a resource or opportunity.

Discussion: The term *class advocacy* refers to actions on behalf of a whole group or class of people. This is in contrast to *case advocacy* (see Technique 12.24), in which the advocacy is on behalf of a specific individual. Class advocacy is also briefly described as a function of the social change agent role in Chapter 3.

Because class advocacy seeks change in law and public policy at either the local, state, or national level, it is essentially a political process aimed at influencing the decisions of elected officials and high-level administrators. It entails building coalitions with other groups and organizations that share concerns about a social issue. The social worker participates as a member of an organization, rather than as an individual practitioner.

Since the goal is to bring about a change, resistance and opposition should be expected. Class advocacy involves conflict, sometimes bitter conflict. Those

---

with power can and will use their power to resist change. There is always some risk in class advocacy. When a person sets out to alter the status quo, there is a good chance that he or she will ruffle some feathers, lose some friends, create some enemies, or get labeled as a troublemaker. Not everyone is comfortable with this type of advocacy. Further, class advocacy is not an appropriate function for every organization. Every individual and every organization must examine the pros and cons of taking on an advocacy role and decide whether it fits with the purpose of the organization.

For those who become engaged in class advocacy, the following guidelines may increase the chances of success.

1. Realize that you and your organization can make a difference. You can bring about needed changes in laws, policies, and programs. Change is not impossible. It is frequently hard—but not impossible.

2. Remember that you cannot do it alone. Individual social workers will need to join with others. A group has more power than an individual. Also, your organization needs to join with other organizations that share your concerns. Several organizations, working together, have more power than a single organization working alone.

3. Working with other organizations will mean that your own organization will have to make some compromises and perhaps do things differently than it prefers. In the long run, however, your organization will accomplish more as part of a coalition than it will by working alone.

4. Many improvements are needed in our human service systems. Since you cannot do everything that needs to be done, you must decide which concern has the highest priority. Choose your cause very carefully. If your organization takes on several causes at one time, you may be spread too thin. It is better to make real gains in just one area than to make minimal gains or fail completely in a dozen.

5. It is also important to choose a cause where success is possible. Be realistic! Don't waste your organization's time and energy on a lost cause. That will only result in frustration. As in other aspects of life, a successful experience generates hope and a feeling that other successes are possible. If the members of an organization can see even small successes, they will be more willing to invest themselves in future advocacy efforts and be more motivated to work on other needed changes in the system.

6. Anticipate the many problems that will arise and plan for their solution. Sunley (1983, 154–56) identifies a few of the common problems that advocates for change might experience.

- Advocates do not have sufficient time and proposed actions fall behind schedule.
- Advocates and supporters begin to have doubts and second thoughts about actions after they are underway.
- Advocates are thrown off course or demoralized by the delaying tactics used by opponents of change.

- Advocacy efforts founder because the purpose lacks clarity and the persons involved do not share common goals.
- Factional disputes and power struggles develop within the action system.
- Dissatisfied, undisciplined, or uncooperative individuals create personnel and morale problems among advocates.

7. Successful advocacy is built on a foundation of careful analysis and planning. It is important to define what you see as a problem and carefully study the problem—before you make a decision on what to do about it. Don't launch an effort to change something until you know exactly what has to be changed, why it has to be changed, and what will be involved in bringing about the change.

8. Before you take action, carefully assess what achieving your goal will require in the way of time, energy, money, and other resources. Do you have the resources? If not, it is best to scale down your goals or wait until later when you are better organized and more capable of reaching your goal.

9. There is always resistance to change. Analysis of the situation to be changed should include understanding why there is resistance. The advocate needs to know how opponents think and feel when asked to change. You need to be able to put yourself in your opponent's shoes (i.e., you must have empathy). If you can do that, you are in a good position to figure out how best to approach the matter.

10. If you only feel anger for those that oppose you—if you feel they are stupid or simply being stubborn—that is a good indication that you have not done your homework and that you do not really understand the problem. It also means that your advocacy effort is likely to fail. People always have reasons for opposing change. You may not agree with their reasons, but you must understand them if you are to figure out a way to successfully overcome that resistance.

11. Successful advocacy requires a good deal of self-discipline. It is important to think before you act. That applies to both individuals and organizations. As indicated previously, class advocacy requires that you build coalitions and work cooperatively with other groups and organizations. Those coalitions are built on mutual trust and mutual self-interest. One of the most serious errors an organization can make in advocacy is to act impulsively. If that happens, the other organizations in the coalition may pull back or be reluctant to cooperate with your organization because they fear that your recklessness will cause damage to their organization or to the coalition. Also, if you or your organization acts impulsively, those that oppose you can more easily discredit your organization. When dealing with legislators it is especially important that your organization appear responsible and trustworthy.

12. Advocacy involves the use of power. You may not have as much power as you want, but don't overlook the power you do have. Essentially, power is the ability to make others behave the way you want them to behave (see Technique 15.14). Think of power as a resource that can be used or "spent" for a particular purpose. There are different kinds of power. It is important to study your own organization and its membership in order to discover the type of power that you do possess.

Among the types of power you have in your organization is the power that comes from knowledge and expertise. For example, if you are advocating on behalf of children, you have detailed information about children and troubled families, and you know how the system works or does not work for the benefit of children and families. Information, if carefully assembled and presented, can have a powerful impact on legislators, agency administrators, and the public.

No doubt some members of your organization are highly respected in the community. They are held in high esteem by the public because of their past achievements. They have credibility that gives them a type of power. Individuals who are respected can have a significant influence on legislators and administrators. You need to encourage and help those respected individuals to become spokespersons for your organization.

Don't forget that personal commitment, time, and energy are also types of power. Much can be accomplished just by sticking with a task and seeing it through to the end.

Organizational solidarity is also a type of power. If legislators and decision makers can see that members are solidly behind their organization, they will pay attention to what the organization's leaders have to say.

Within your organization are members who are natural leaders. They tend to be charismatic and articulate. They can excite people and get them to work together on a cause. Charisma is a rare quality, but it is definitely a type of power. Identify those individuals in your organization and let them speak for your organization's cause.

13. There are times when advocacy must take the form of a lawsuit. Many changes and reforms would never have happened without lawsuits and court decisions (Morales and Sheafor 1989). For example, within the past twenty years, most of the reforms in the areas of mental health and mental retardation grew out of lawsuits. An organization committed to advocacy will, at times, need to encourage and support lawsuits that have potential for bringing about a needed change.

14. Class advocacy calls for a considerable investment of time, energy, and, of course, money. Thus fundraising is an essential component of successful class advocacy (see Technique 14.15).

15. Most people in the United States depend on television to tell them what is important, but many at least skim the newspaper for information. If you want to get your message across, if you want the public to understand and support your cause, you need to learn how to make use of television and newspapers (see Techniques 14.16, 14.17, and 14.18). If you have someone in your organization who knows about advertising and the use of media, make use of that person. If you don't know anyone with that knowledge, approach an advertising agency or perhaps a school of journalism and ask if they would be willing to donate some of their time and help you get your message on TV or in the newspapers.

Selected Bibliography

Mahaffey, Maryann, and John Hanks, eds. *Practical Politics: Social Work and Political Responsibility.* Silver Spring, Md.: National Association of Social Workers, 1982.

Morales, Armando, and Bradford W. Sheafor. *Social Work: A Profession of Many Faces.* 5th ed. Boston: Allyn and Bacon, 1989.

Rubin, Herbert, and Irene Rubin. *Community Organizing and Development.* Columbus, Ohio: Merrill, 1986.

Sunley, Robert. *Advocating Today: A Human Service Practitioner's Handbook.* New York: Family Service Association of America, 1983.

15.12   *Social Policy Analysis*

Purpose: To make a thorough and accurate assessment of social policy and program issues in order to guide community change activities.

Discussion: The analysis of public social policy issues can be a difficult and time-consuming task. Several good models that can guide such an analysis exist within the social work literature. Depending on the social worker's role and preparation for making an analysis, it is possible to approach this important task in greater or lesser depth. Social workers who are not engaged in full-time community change activity usually do not have the time or resources available to apply the more complex models.

Whether working with a complex or more simplified policy analysis model, it is important to be conscientious about using accurate data and cautious in drawing conclusions. More ground is lost by not having adequate support for one's conclusions when challenged than by the limitations of the assessment model used.

Chambers (1986, 7–168) has developed an approach to public policy analysis that is relatively simple and straightforward. As such, it is especially helpful in identifying the key questions that should be addressed by the occasional policy analyst.

1. *Social problem analysis.* The first step in the analysis of a social policy or program is to have a clear understanding of the social problem that created the situation requiring such a policy. To assess this problem, it is useful to undertake the following activities:

a. *Identify how the problem is defined and locate estimates of its magnitude.* For example, what definition of poverty, mental illness, or unemployment is commonly used? Are there other definitions that might more appropriately be used? How many people experience this problem as it is defined? What particular subpopulations are most likely to face this problem?

b. *Determine the causes and consequences of the problem.* What social factors have caused this problem? What has been the result? Are there multiple causes? Are there multiple consequences from a single cause?

c. *Identify the ideological beliefs or basic principles that are embedded in the description of the problem.* The definition of a problem is highly influenced by beliefs about "what ought to be," or values. Is there a difference of opinion about the seriousness of the problem? What population groups hold varying views about the nature of this problem?

d. *Identify the gainers and losers in relation to the problem.* Who gains from the existence of the problem? What do they gain and how much? Who loses? What do they lose and how much? How serious are the negative consequences on the lives of the losers?

2. *Social policy and program analysis.* Once the problem is understood, the second step is to assess the social policy and/or program that is being considered as a means of offering relief to the victims the problem. The following activities are useful for this analysis:

a. *Search out the relevant program and policy history.* Is this a new problem? Why is it being raised now? What is different from past efforts to deal with the problem? Have conditions, values, or both changed to make this matter relevant now?

b. *Identify the key elements or operating characteristics of the proposed policy or program.* What are the goals and objectives of the proposal? Who would be eligible to benefit from the plan? What benefits or services would be delivered if this proposal gains approval? What administrative structure would be required and how would it work? How would the program be financed and how much money would be required? Are there any undesirable consequences from interactions among the characteristics listed above?

3. *Draw conclusions.* After the information identified above has been collected, it is necessary to judge the merits of the policy or program under analysis. Ultimately, it is the weight of the evidence matched with one's beliefs about what the quality of life should be for members of the society that results in a recommendation favoring or opposing the proposal—or suggesting modification. Answers to the following questions might be considered in arriving at your conclusions about this program or policy proposal:

- It is appropriate for addressing the problem identified?
- Does the remedy proposed adequately deal with the causes as well as the consequences of the problem?
- Will it yield an outcome different from others attempted in the past?
- Would the costs associated with the proposed remedy justify the possible outcomes?
- Are there better remedies that might be proposed?

With a solid analysis of the policy or program proposal in hand, the social worker is prepared to influence the legislation that would impact the social problem under consideration. At times, the social worker will work through committees or other groups to affect these decisions; on other occasions, it is more appropriate to contact a legislator directly and express a position on the proposal.

Selected Bibliography

Chambers, Donald E. *Social Policy and Social Programs: A Method for the Practical Public Policy Analyst.* New York: Macmillan, 1986.

DiNitto, Diane, and Thomas Dye. *Social Welfare Politics and Public Policy.* Englewood Cliffs, N.J.: Prentice-Hall, 1983.

Martin, George T., Jr. *Social Policy in the Welfare State.* Englewood Cliffs, N.J.: Prentice-Hall, 1990.

Pierce, Dean. *Policy for the Social Work Practitioner.* New York: Longman, 1984.

15.13   *Force Field Analysis (FFA)*

Purpose: To identify the forces, and the relative power of each force, that affect a social problem or issue.

Discussion: *Force Field Analysis (FFA)* is a tool that organizes data about the various forces that may affect a change effort. Although this technique is most commonly used by social workers engaged in organizational and community change, the basic concepts of FFA can also be applied in social work with individuals, families, and small groups. This analysis can assist the social worker in formulating strategies to overcome the forces working against the desired change. Brager and Holloway (1978) explain that "in analyzing a field of forces a wide range of variables is identified which have a probability of influencing the preferences of significant organizational participants with respect to the desired change. . . . By means of force-field analysis, a practitioner can identify the range of driving and restraining forces critical to his goal and assess the intervention necessary to move them in the desired directions" (p. 108).

Lauffer (1982, 129–31) recommends that the following steps be followed in using the FFA technique:*

1. Describe the problem or the situation you want to change.

2. Specify your goals or objectives (e.g., to win the city council's endorsement of a new low-income housing program).

3. Identify and list all of the restraining forces that are working against the achievement of your goal (e.g., real estate developers, mortgage and lending businesses).

4. Identify and list all driving forces that are working in the direction of achieving the goal (e.g., Mayor, Council of Churches).

*Armand Lauffer, *Assessment Tools for Practitioners, Managers, and Trainers.* Copyright © 1982 by Sage Publications. Reprinted by permission of Sage Publications, Inc.

5. Estimate (high, low, uncertain) the *potency* (strength), *consistency* (stability over time), and *amenability* to change or influence each of the restraining and driving forces you identified in steps 3 and 4.

6. Having identified those restraining forces amenable to influence, identify the *actors* (persons and organizations) most likely to influence each force. Develop a strategy for mobilizing and using that source of influence.

7. Having identified the driving forces amenable to influence, identify the actor (person or organization) most able to sustain and reinforce that force and counteract any effort by the opposition to weaken this driving force.

In his description of FFA, Lauffer (1982) suggests the use of a Force Field Balance Sheet to graphically represent this analysis (see Figure 15.2).

In using the FFA balance sheet, it is important to clearly and briefly specify the problem or need being addressed and to identify the goal or objective being addressed. One to five (or more) restraining/driving forces are identified, and

Figure 15.2   Force Field Balance Sheet

The Problem Situation or Need:

The Goal or Objective:

Restraining Forces (against change)   *Driving Forces (for change)*

(H = High, L = Low, U = Uncertain)   (H L U)

Potency   Consistency   Amenability   Actors

Critical and Facilitating Actors

A. _____   D. _____
B. _____   E. _____
C. _____   X. <u>Me, our group</u>
                      <u>or organization</u>

Actors   Amenability   Consistency   Potency

Source: Armand Lauffer, *Assessment Tools for Practitioners, Managers, and Trainers.* Copyright © 1982 by Sage Publications. Reprinted by permission of Sage Publications, Inc.

each is assessed according to the strength (high/low/uncertain) of force in relation to:

Potency = strength of the force
Consistency = stability of the force over a period of time
Amenability = ability of the force to change or influence

In addition, the key people or organizations regarding this matter are identified below; their code letters are identified with each driving force. The result is a one-page assessment of the situation.

Once the balance sheet has been completed, it is possible to estimate the likelihood of success and to make a judgment concerning the merits of continuing the effort. Are the chances of success worth investing time and resources on this matter? If you decide to continue, use the balance sheet to guide your planning. Lauffer (1982, 131) suggests that, for each working force, you write down "everything you need to do to unlock or expand it if it is a driving force, or to nullify or reduce it if it is a restraining force." By isolating the critical issues and actors on both sides of the issue, you will be prepared to begin the process of developing a strategy to influence the appropriate decision makers.

Selected Bibliography

Brager, George, and Stephen Holloway. *Changing Human Service Organizations*. New York: The Free Press, 1978.

Lauffer, Armand. *Assessment Tools for Practitioners, Managers, and Trainers*. Beverly Hills: Sage, 1982.

15.14   *Analyzing Community Decision Making*

Purpose: To assess the factors that influence the actions of legislators and other community decision makers.

Discussion: As social workers seek to influence the decisions that affect the quality of human services in a community, they must eventually develop a strategy for convincing the persons in authority of the merits of that action. While ideally, the decisions would be made on the merits of the proposal, in reality, decision makers weigh external pressures and various personal considerations in making decisions.

Research on community decision making and community power structures does not yield a consistent picture of the forces that lead to these decisions. However, several generalizations can be made regarding variables that at least partially explain why some communities tend to center the decision making in a small, elite group of people while others are more pluralistic and involve a broader spectrum of the community. Trounstine and Christensen (1982, 40–47) conclude that the following patterns are most likely to be found:

1. *Size.* Large cities tend to be pluralistic. They are likely to become more diverse and competitive as they grow, resulting in a greater range of people involved in making decisions.

2. *Population diversity.* Communities that have more varied and complex class and ethnic structures develop more special interest groups and more community organizations that compete for power and resources. Therefore, there are more challenges to any dominant elite group and a tendency to increase pluralism in decision making.

3. *Economic diversity.* More diversified communities in terms of varied sources of employment, high levels of industrialization, and the presence of absentee-owned industry (as opposed to local people owning the major industries) all tend to make communities more pluralistic.

4. *Structure of local government.* Reformed governments (i.e., cities with council-manager format, nonpartisan-at-large elections) tend to be more elitist than those partisan governments with representatives elected by districts. Further, the greater the competition or balance among political groups, the more likely the community will have a pluralistic decision-making structure.

The trend in the United States is toward a decline in communities that could support an elite decision-making structure, which makes it possible for social workers (who are rarely part of elite groups) to have greater influence over community change. Becoming skillful at assessing the various forces that influence decision makers and discovering ways to direct those forces is important to successful change activity.

The literature on influencing community decision makers identifies three factors that should be assessed in determining a strategy.

1. Decision makers are responsive to the personal characteristics of the people who seek to influence their decisions.
2. Decision makers are impacted by the institutional base (e.g., control of money, jobs, information and votes) from which that person speaks. The person who can combine these personal and institutional sources of influence can be especially effective in influencing decisions.
3. Decision makers are also influenced by their own personal judgment of the matter and their assessment of the personal gains and losses from acting on the various options (Dahl 1960, 39–40).

Using a method like the Force Field Analysis technique discussed earlier, the social worker should carefully assess the strength of these factors and seek to counterbalance those that do not support the desired position. Figure 15.3 identifies the influence factors that should be considered.

Figured 15.3   Factors Influencing Community Decision Makers

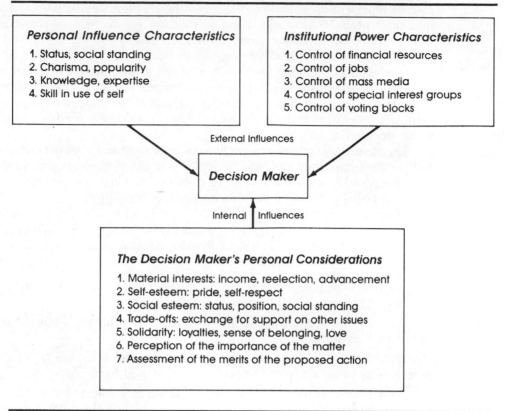

Personal Influence Characteristics	**Institutional Power Characteristics**
1. Status, social standing	1. Control of financial resources
2. Charisma, popularity	2. Control of jobs
3. Knowledge, expertise	3. Control of mass media
4. Skill in use of self	4. Control of special interest groups
	5. Control of voting blocks

External Influences

Decision Maker

Internal Influences

The Decision Maker's Personal Considerations

1. Material interests: income, reelection, advancement
2. Self-esteem: pride, self-respect
3. Social esteem: status, position, social standing
4. Trade-offs: exchange for support on other issues
5. Solidarity: loyalties, sense of belonging, love
6. Perception of the importance of the matter
7. Assessment of the merits of the proposed action

Selected Bibliography

Dahl, Robert. "The Analysis of Influence in Local Communities." In *Social Science and Community Action,* edited by Charles R. Adrian. East Lansing: Michigan State University 1960.

Lineberry, Robert, and Ira Sharkansky. *Urban Politics and Public Policy.* 2nd ed. New York: Harper & Row, 1978.

Trounstine, Philip J., and Terry Christensen. *Movers and Shakers: The Study of Community Power.* New York: St. Martin's Press, 1982.

15.15   *Persuading Community Decision Makers*

Purpose: To influence the actions of legislators and other community decision makers in relation to human service issues.

Discussion: Decisions that are made at the local, state, and national levels by elected representatives and other public officials have substantial impact on the quality of peoples' lives and, more specifically, on the human services. Social workers have an important perspective that should be considered when these decisions are being made. That perspective comes from social work's role at the interface of people and the world around them, giving the social worker a unique view of how public social policy helps or hinders the most vulnerable members of the population. Armed with a careful analysis of the issue and a sound assessment of the decision makers involved, the social worker is prepared to intervene in the decision-making process.

Legislators and other decision makers do not usually seek out social workers to hear their important opinions on legislation affecting social programs. Therefore, the social worker must take the initiative to persuade decision makers of the most socially desirable position on pending legislation.

Summaries of the research findings on social influence and persuasive communication—such as those by Bettinghaus (1980), King (1975), Smith (1982), and Pincus and Minahan (1973)—yield several general principles that the social worker should keep in mind.

1. An individual is most likely to be persuaded by someone he or she perceives as having intelligence, self-esteem, and self-confidence.

2. An individual is most likely to be persuaded by someone he or she perceives as having high status.

3. An individual is most likely to be persuaded by someone he or she likes, perceives as being similar to himself or herself, and finds attractive.

4. An individual is most likely to be persuaded by someone he or she perceives as being powerful, whether that power is real or imagined. As a general rule, older individuals, men, and individuals holding positions or having titles that imply power are perceived as having power.

5. An individual who is authoritarian and dogmatic is most likely to be persuaded by those he or she perceives as being authoritative.

6. An individual is most likely to be persuaded by someone who can provide rewards or punishment.

7. An individual is most likely to be persuaded by an individual with whom future interaction is anticipated.

8. An individual is most likely to be persuaded by someone from whom they desire social acceptance.

9. An individual is most likely to be influenced by someone he or she perceives as being competent and trustworthy.

10. An individual who has high anxiety, a strong need for approval, and a strong need for affiliation with others is more easily persuaded than a person not displaying these characteristics.

11. An individual is most likely to be influenced when he or she feels uncertain, confused, and insecure.

Since social workers are not usually in positions of influence themselves, they frequently must work through others who are in a better position to be heard by decision makers. At other times, however, it is possible for the new social worker to cultivate trusting and respectful personal relationships with the decision maker. To build the respect of a legislator, legislative aide, or other public official, the social worker must present sound and responsible positions. These positions might be communicated in writing, through personal contact, or both.

Selected Bibliography

Bettinghaus, Edwin. *Persuasive Communication.* 3rd ed. New York: Holt, Rinehart & Winston, 1980.

King, Stephen. *Communication and Social Influence.* Menlo Park, Calif.: Addison-Wesley, 1975.

Pincus, Allen, and Anne Minahan. *Social Work Practice: Model and Method.* Itasca, Ill.: F. E. Peacock, 1973.

Smith, Mary. *Persuasion and Human Action.* Belmont, Calif.: Wadsworth, 1982.

15.16   *Visiting a Policy Maker*

Purpose: To plan and carry out a visit to the office of a legislator or other policy maker in an effort to influence his or her decision on a social policy matter.

Discussion: Most local, state, and federal legislators and other key decision makers spend their time in a very restricted environment; they speak primarily with their staff members, lobbyists, and colleagues. Hence, many policy makers welcome the opportunity to hear the positions of their constituency on significant issues—even though they cannot possibly agree with the position of each person they represent. An effective way to influence the thinking of these individuals, then, is to visit them at city hall, the courthouse, or the capitol—or to visit them when the legislative body is in recess and state and federal legislators have returned home.

A few guidelines are useful in planning visits to legislators, as well as other decision makers (Gaby and Gaby 1979, 174–75):*

1. *Schedule the meeting in advance.* It is for your own benefit, as well as the legislator's, to have an appointment. Without an appointment made well in advance, you have little chance of meeting with a busy decision maker or of that person having time to talk with you in any depth.

*Excerpts in Technique 15.16 from the book *Nonprofit Organization Handbook* by Patricia V. Gaby and Daniel M. Gaby. © 1979 by Prentice-Hall, Inc., Englewood Cliffs, N.J. Reprinted by permission of the publisher, Prentice-Hall, Inc.

2. *Be on time.* You may have to wait for the legislator to complete other responsibilities before meeting with you, but when you are there on time, you establish your claim on that person. If the legislature is in session, a limited amount of time each day is usually set aside for such appointments. It is important to be present when your appointment is scheduled.

3. *Be positive.* Begin on a friendly note. Find a reason to praise the decision maker for some action, remind him or her of a campaign promise that relates to your issue (if appropriate), and thank him or her for being willing to take time to hear your position.

4. *Get to the point quickly.* Have your presentation planned. While you want to be informal in your conversation, you still want to pack in a lot of information and get to your point in a brief period. Too much small talk or a roundabout approach to the topic may prohibit you from getting to the substantive issues.

5. *Be specific about what you are asking.* Be very sure that the person knows what you want him or her to do. Are you simply offering information? Do you want him or her to propose an amendment to a piece of legislation? Do you want him or her to vote a particular way?

6. *Don't be afraid to express your conviction.* Let the legislator know that, as a social worker, you are in a unique position to recognize the implications of this decision. While it may be counterproductive to be too abrasive, you should leave no doubt in the legislator's mind that you believe in what you are proposing. You should not waste your time on issues that don't really matter, and the legislator should understand that you feel the matter is important.

7. *Leave something in writing.* Leave a statement that reflects your position and provides the facts you have presented for placement in the file on this matter. Or write a note thanking that person for spending the time to hear your viewpoint and include this summary information. Be sure that your name, address, and telephone number are on the material so you can be contacted to clarify points or provide information on related matters.

Selected Bibliography

Gaby, Patricia V., and Daniel M. Gaby. *Nonprofit Organizations Handbook: A Guide to Fundraising, Grants, Lobbying, Membership Building, Publicity, and Public Relations.* Englewood Cliffs, N.J.: Prentice-Hall, 1979.

Smith, Virginia W. "How Interest Groups Influence Legislators." *Social Work* 24 (May 1979): 234–39.

15.17   *Writing to a Policy Maker*

Purpose: To influence a legislator or other policy maker through written communication.

Discussion: Although face-to-face contact is perhaps the most effective way to influence a legislator or other decision maker, many times, that is simply not possible because of constraints of time, distance, resources, or the availability of the decision maker. Letters, telegrams, and telephone calls, when properly timed, have also been demonstrated to be effective in influencing decisions. The addresses and telephone numbers of your city, county, state, or federal legislators (e.g., commissioners, council members, senators, representatives) will usually be listed at least once each week in your local newspaper, making it relatively easy to identify them. Locating other officials may require more research. Also, when writing someone on a social policy matter, it is important to use the correct spelling of the name, the proper title, and the accurate address.

The following guidelines (Gaby and Gaby 1979, 175–76) should be observed when writing a legislator or other decision maker:*

1. *Be brief.* After making a thorough analysis of the policy matter, limit your written communication to one page.

2. *Include only one topic per letter.* Legislators are dealing simultaneously with a number of issues, and the temptation is to comment on several matters. The best way to gain the attention of the decision maker, however, is to limit each letter to a single topic so that the letter can be maintained with the correspondence regarding that topic for review when it is time to cast a vote.

3. *Start on a positive note.* Try to praise the person for some action, speech, or public statement. In particular, try to indicate that a thoughtful vote on this matter is consistent with campaign promises or other public statements and/or the record compiled as a legislator.

4. *Identify the specific bill or issue you are addressing.* Be sure there is no misunderstanding about which matter concerns you so your letter will be reviewed when action is being considered.

5. *Give facts.* Borrow a number of facts from your policy analysis (e.g., how many people would be affected negatively by the legislation, what impact that has on older people, how a particular neighborhood might be impacted).

6. *Write in simple style.* You are dealing with busy people who cannot take time to read material that does not get to the point quickly. Clear and direct language will suggest that you know your topic.

7. *Seek a response.* Ask a question or propose an alternative that will encourage a response. When someone has had to consider your ideas thoroughly enough to prepare a response to your letter, you will have had a good hearing.

8. *Time your letter carefully.* Try to get your letter to the decision maker when the arguments are being formulated. Once his or her mind is made up, it is too late.

*Excerpts in Technique 15.17 from the book *Nonprofit Organization Handbook* by Patricia V. Gaby and Daniel M. Gaby. © 1979 by Prentice-Hall, Inc., Englewood Cliffs, N.J. Reprinted by permission of the publisher, Prentice-Hall, Inc.

9. *Follow up after the vote.* Let the policy maker know that you are watching. Offer praise if he or she votes your position or regret if he or she votes the other way. If you follow up, you will more likely be remembered on the next issue.

Selected Bibliography

Gaby, Patricia V., and Daniel M. Gaby. *Nonprofit Organizations Handbook: A Guide to Fundraising, Grants, Lobbying, Membership Building, Publicity, and Public Relations.* Englewood Cliffs, N.J.: Prentice-Hall, 1979.

Smith, Virginia W. "How Interest Groups Influence Legislators." *Social Work* 24 (May 1979): 234–39.

15.18 Initiating Social Legislation

Purpose: To influence public policy decisions by working proactively to introduce and support the passage of social legislation.

Discussion: As discussed earlier in this chapter, the social worker often reacts to social policy proposals and seeks to influence the actions of policy makers. However, on occasion, the social worker should initiate efforts to have social legislation considered and approved by legislative bodies. This involves identifying the factors that should be included in the legislation, writing or working with the appropriate legislative officer to draft a bill, seeking sponsors, giving testimony, and other activities required to get the proposal heard by the appropriate legislative body.

At one time or another, most social workers become involved in a proactive effort to initiate and pass a specific piece of legislation. Dear and Patti (1981) have formulated seven principles or tactical guidelines for such an effort at the state level of government. They indicate that these guidelines can be "used by part-time, single-issue advocates who make an occasional foray into the legislative arena to promote a bill of immediate interest to their agency or a client constituency" (p. 289).

1. Introduce the bill early in the session or ideally, before the session has begun.
2. It is advisable to have more than one legislator sponsor a bill.
3. The advocate of social legislation should seek to obtain the sponsorship of the majority party.... It is even more beneficial to obtain meaningful bi-partisan sponsorship with the primary sponsor a member of the ... majority.
4. Whenever possible, the advocate should obtain the support of the Governor and the relevant state agencies.
5. The advocate should seek influential legislators as sponsors of proposed legislation, provided that they are willing to exercise their influence in promoting the bill.
6. The advocate should press for open committee hearings on the bill and, when such hearings are held, attempt to arrange for testimony in behalf of the bill by expert witnesses.
7. The advocate should use the amendatory process as a strategy for promoting a favorable outcome for the bill. (pp. 290–94).

Selected Bibliography

Dear, Ronald, and Rino Patti. "Legislative Advocacy: Seven Specific Tactics." *Social Work* 26 (July 1981): 289–96.

Mahaffey, Maryann, and John Hanks, eds. *Practical Politics: Social Work and Political Responsibility.* Silver Spring, Md.: NASW, 1982.

15.19   *Giving Legislative Testimony*

Purpose: To provide expert testimony that informs legislators in regard to a specific piece of social legislation.

Discussion: An important activity in the process of promoting a piece of legislation is to give testimony to a legislative committee. These committees perform the primary analysis of the merits of a proposed legislative action. Moreover, members of committees dealing with bills in a particular area (i.e., health and welfare, budgets) are considered by other legislators to have special expertise in these matters; thus, their understanding of and views on the issues takes on special importance. Legislative testimony is one means of informing the committee members of one's position.

Kleinkauf (1981, 298–302) identifies the following phases required for preparing and giving effective legislative testimony:

1. *Researching the bill.* First, carefully research the substance of the bill. Four steps should be followed in this activity:

a. Review the existing statutes that the bill seeks to amend, revise, supplement, or delete.

b. Gather factual data that will refute or support key points in the bill.

c. Anticipate the costs associated with implementing this bill.

d. Find the position being taken on the bill by governmental departments or other organizations that might be affected by its passage or be charged with its implementation.

Also become familiar with the procedural issues related to this bill. For example:

- Has it had a previous history? If so, why was it not approved?
- How does the current version differ from those previously considered?
- Who favored or opposed the previous version?
- What process is being followed to move it through the legislative body this time?
- Where are we now in that process?

2. *Analyzing the committee.* As in other efforts to influence actions, next, you must assess the decision makers. Lobbyists from groups that are supportive of your position (e.g., NASW or the League of Women Voters) can help provide information about the committee members' constituencies, special interests, backgrounds, and voting records.

You will also need to find out about the dynamics within the committee.

- How do the members line up by party affiliation?
- Who influences other committee members?
- Who is likely to be active in questioning persons giving testimony?
- What rules does the committee have about how much time will be allowed for testimony?
- Are there friends on the committee who could be primed to make supportive statements?

3. *Preparing testimony.* Testimony is most effective when it is both oral and written. If a social worker is testifying as a representative of a committee or an organization, it is best to have a position paper on the issue that expresses the general position of that group. That position paper should be limited to one typewritten, double-spaced page that could be left for the committee members.

The oral testimony should be prepared to highlight specific items and open discussion about specific language in the bill that would accomplish the goals set out in the position paper. The person giving the testimony should have prepared additional factual data that can be given orally in support of the position.

4. *Testifying.* Above all, be prepared. Dress appropriately, and remain calm. Be straightforward and brief. Also be responsive to questions. Make sure to state that you appreciate the opportunity to testify.

5. *Dealing with questions.* Be prepared to deal with questions from the committee. Expect that some will come from members hostile to the position you are presenting. Kleinkauf (1981, 302) cautions: "Never attempt to fake an answer if you are not sure of one. If you do not know something, say so, and avoid the temptation to claim more expertise than you actually have." Roleplaying this part of the presentation with knowledgeable colleagues can help prepare you for dealing with questions from the committee.

6. *Following up.* If you promised to provide additional information as part of your testimony or in the question period, be sure to provide that material. Follow the bill through the legislature (possibly to other committees), recognizing that additional testimony may be required, amendments may be made, a substitute bill may be presented, or a compromise may be negotiated with the other house of the legislature. When the bill is finally signed into law, you should also monitor its implementation to be sure that its intent is actually being achieved.

Selected Bibliography

Kleinkauf, Cecilia. "A Guide to Giving Legislative Testimony." *Social Work* 26 (July 1981): 297–303.

Appendix

A Cross-Referencing of Selected Techniques and Guidelines to Client Systems and Special Situations

Chapter	The Individual as Client	The Family as Client	People Having Special Needs or Requiring Unique Responses
6	All of Chapter 6	All of Chapter 6	All of Chapter 6
7	7.7 7.8 7.9 7.10	7.7 7.8 7.9 7.10	
8	8.7 8.8 8.9 8.10	8.7 8.8 8.9	
9	All of Chapter 9	All of Chapter 9	9.2 9.8 9.6 9.9 9.7 9.10
10	10.1 10.7 10.13 10.18 10.23 10.2 10.8 10.14 10.19 10.24 10.3 10.9 10.15 10.20 10.25 10.4 10.10 10.16 10.21 10.5 10.12 10.17 10.22	10.6 10.11 10.16 10.7 10.12 10.17 10.8 10.13 10.18 10.9 10.14 10.19 10.10 10.15	10.19 10.20 10.21 10.23 10.24
11	All of Chapter 11	All of Chapter 11	11.7 11.8
12	All of Chapter 12	All of Chapter 12	12.24 12.29 12.25 12.30 12.26 12.31 12.27 12.32 12.28
13	All of Chapter 13	All of Chapter 13	
14			
15	15.13	15.3 15.5 15.13	

Note: Selected readings in this book as classified under specific client systems encountered in practice and under some special circumstances requiring an adaptation of generic skills.

Therapeutic and Self-Help Groups	Committees and Task-Oriented Groups	Agency Administration and Operation	Organizations and Communities	Professional Development/ Career Enhancement
All of Chapter 6	All of Chapter 6	All of Chapter 6	All of Chapter 6	
		All of Chapter 7		
8.8 8.9		All of Chapter 8		8.2 8.3 8.4 8.9
All of Chapter 9		9.3 9.4		
10.1 10.9 10.16 10.2 10.12 10.17 10.3 10.13 10.18 10.7 10.14 10.22 10.8 10.15 10.25	10.13	10.13		
All of Chapter 11	11.8	11.4 11.7 11.5 11.8	11.1 11.7 11.4 11.8	
All of Chapter 12	12.18 12.22 12.19 12.23 12.20 12.25 12.21	12.17 12.22 12.18 12.24 12.19 12.20 12.21	12.17 12.24 12.18 12.19 12.20 12.22	
All of Chapter 13	13.2 13.3 13.8	13.1 13.7 13.2 13.8 13.3	13.2 13.3	
		All of Chapter 14	14.1 14.5 14.2 14.10 14.3 14.23	14.7 14.8 14.20
15.5	15.5 15.8 15.6 15.9 15.7 15.10		All of Chapter 15	

Author Index

Cohen, Nathan E., 54, 62
Coleman, James, 237–238, 239, 240, 242
Collins, Alice, 194
Collins, Bill, 477
Colon, F., 234–235, 236
Colorado Chapter of NASW, 411
Community Resource Center, 447, 450
Compton, Beulah, 173, 297
Connaway, Ronda, S., 35, 48
Connolly, Patrick, 146
Conrad, William R., Jr., 423
Corcoran, Kevin, 268, 269, 399–400, 462, 463
Corey, Gerald, 336
Cormier, L. Sherilyn, 84, 86, 100, 102, 105, 107, 338
Cormier, William, 84, 86, 100, 102, 105, 107, 338
Cory, Gerald, 152, 316
Cory, Marianne, 152, 316
Council on Social Work Education, 11, 13, 21, 32, 87, 93, 98
Craig, Dorothy, 437–438, 441, 442
Crews, Frederick, 114
Crompton, Margaret, 373
Cronbach, L. J., 278, 281
Curran, James, 239, 330

Dahl, Robert, 496, 497
Daiches, Sol, 274
Daley, John M., 77, 78, 420, 424, 425
Dangerfield, David, 375
Dayton, Charles, 473
Dear, Ronald, 502, 503
DeHoyos, Genevieve, 25, 32, 212, 214
DeJong, Cornell, 386
Delbecq, Andre L., 484, 485
DeRisi, William, 330, 332
DeSaix, Christine, 193, 195
Devore, Wynetta, 362, 378, 379, 469, 472
Diehl, Richard, 182
Dillard, John, 102, 103
DiNitto, Diane, 493
Dixon, Samuel, 363, 365
Dolgoff, Ralph, 30, 33, 150–151, 152
Donley, Kay, 372–373
Doremus, Bertha, 291, 293
Doren, Dennis, 208
Douglas, Auriel, 114

Downs, Susan, 127, 130
Drezner, Stephen M., 442
Dunham, Arthur, 53, 55, 56, 58, 62
Dwyer, Margaret, 126–127
Dye, Thomas, 493
Dyer, William G., 481, 482, 483, 484

Eaddy, Virginia, 373
Ebeling, Nancy, 188, 189
Edelwich, Jerry, 149
Edinburg, Golda, 132
Edleson, Jeffrey, 316
Egan, Gerald, 337, 338
Ehrmann, Max, 149, 150
Elkin, Robert, 466
Emery, Gary, 333, 335
Emmons, Michael, 120
Epstein, Irwin, 39, 45–46, 48, 358, 407, 461, 463
Epstein, Laura, 69, 73, 76, 78, 296, 297, 298, 302, 303, 305, 307, 321, 390–391, 404, 407
Equal Opportunity Guidelines, 160, 163
Erlich, John L., 418–419
Evans, Phil, 210

Fagan, Joen, 336
Family Economics Research Group, 343
Fawcett, Stephen, 181
Fear, David, 115, 116
Feeney, Floyd, 340, 341
Feild, Herbert S., 426, 427
Feldman, Frances, 343
Feldman, Norman, 462, 463
Fellin, Phillip, 461, 463
Ferner, Jack, 112
Filsinger, Erik, 250
Finch, Wilber A., Jr., 415, 416
Fisch, Richard, 339
Fischer, Joel, 15–16, 32, 84–85, 86, 268, 269, 317, 320, 385, 386, 389, 399–400, 462, 463
Fisher, John, 449, 450
Fishman, H. Charles, 339
Flegg, David, 348
Follberg, Jay, 355
Fortune, Anne, 298, 391
Francetich, Russell, 477
Francetich, Sherry, 476–477
Franczyk, James J., 435–436, 437
Fraser, M. W., 396–399
Fredman, Norman, 187, 189, 333, 336

Freedberg, Sharon, 62
Freeman, Edith, 206, 363
Freeman, Howard E., 386, 466
Frey, Louise, 132
Friedlander, Walter E., 51, 56–57, 62
Froland, Charles, 312

Gaby, Daniel M., 433, 434, 448–449, 450, 452–453, 454, 499–500, 501–502
Gaby, Patricia V., 433, 434, 448–449, 450, 452–453, 454, 499–500, 501–502
Gahagan, Denis, 210
Galaway, Burt, 173, 297
Gallagher, James, 381
Gambrill, Eileen, 239, 254, 320, 328, 331, 332
Garbarino, James, 373, 431
Garfield, James O., 483
Garland, James, 313, 316
Garner, Howard, 473
Garvin, Charles D., 53, 63, 173, 297, 330
Garvin, James, 316
Garwick, Geoffrey, 396
Gast, Elizabeth, 251, 252
Gauthier, Thomas P., 37, 41, 44, 46, 48, 426, 427
Gehrig, Clyde C., 57–58, 62
Gelfand, Bernard, 18, 33
Gelfand, Donna, 254
Gelman, Sheldon R., 421, 423
Gentry, Martha E., 35, 48
Gerhart, Ursula, 383
Germain, Carel B., 26, 33
Germann, Richard, 430
Gerson, Randy, 224
Getzel, George, 379
Gillespie, David, 396
Gilmartin, Kevin, 473
Gitterman, Alex, 26, 33, 312, 316
Gladen, Donna, 430, 431
Glasser, Paul H., 53, 63
Glenn, William E., 423
Gochros, Harvey, 317, 320
Goetting, Marsha, 345, 346
Goldstein, Arnold, 83, 84, 86
Goldstein, Eda, 242
Goldstein, Howard, 55, 63, 69, 78
Gordon, Thomas, 104
Gottlieb, Benjamin, 224, 228
Green, Glenn, 328
Grossman, Lee, 112

Maifeld, Mary, 346
Mailick, Mildred, 358
Maluccio, Anthony, 85–86, 87, 177, 303, 305, 307, 375
Maple, Frank, 348
Marckworth, Peg, 224, 228
Marlow, Wilma, 303, 305, 307
Martin, George T., Jr., 493
Martin, Harold, 274–277, 278
Marziali, Elsa, 177
Masch, M. Kathleen, 152
Maslow, Abraham H., 307–308, 309
Mathers, Cecelia, 430, 431
Matross, Ronald, 332, 333
Matthews, R. Mark, 181
Mayer, Adele, 356, 357
Meenaghan, Thomas M., 71, 78
Mellor, M. Joanna, 379
Meltsner, Susan, 451, 452
Mendelsohn, Henry N., 139, 143
Middleman, Ruth R., 135, 316, 425
Miller, Don, 378
Miller, Nancy, 361, 363
Miller, Pamela A., 434
Minahan, Anne, 11–12, 13, 33, 74, 75, 78, 498, 499
Minuchin, Salvador, 339
Mohr, Cynthia, 190, 192
Monette, Duane, 386
Monti, Peter, 239, 330
Morain, Mary, 82, 83
Morales, Armando, 33, 490, 491
Morgan, Joyce, 484, 485
Moses, Beth, 270, 271, 288, 403, 462, 463
Motz, Janet, 472, 473
Mowbray, George, 463
Moy, Caryl, 83
Muldary, Thomas, 150
Mulinski, Paul, 460, 461
Munson, Carlton, 135, 160, 409

National Association for Retarded Citizens, 60, 63
National Association of Social Workers, 21, 29–30, 33, 37, 38, 39, 42, 43, 45, 46, 48, 139, 142, 143, 150, 152, 164–168, 410–411, 430
National Information Center for Handicapped Children and Youth, 278, 281
Navarre, Ralph G., 434
Neubert, Stephen, 392–394, 396, 403, 407

Neugeboren, Bernard, 475
Neves, Carole M. P., 465–466
Newman, Barbara, 278
Newman, Philip, 278
Nichols, Ann Weaver, 77, 78, 420, 424, 425
Noller, R., 33
Nuber, Keith A., 437
Nunnally, Elam, 83

O'Conner, C. P., 444, 447
Ohlsen, Merle, 333
OUTP ST Software, 269
Oxley, Genevieve, 192

Paludi, Michelle, 161, 163
Pancoast, Diane, 312
Parad, Howard, 365
Parad, Libbie, 365
Parker, Paul, 312
Parnes, S. J., 17, 33
Parsons, Bruce, 330–331
Patros, Philip, 285
Patti, Rino, 417, 502, 503
Pearsall, Thomas, 114, 116
Pecora, Peter, 135, 396–399
Perlman, Helen Harris, 33, 66, 78, 245, 291, 293
Peters, Thomas J., 424, 425
Pierce, Dean, 493
Pillari, Vimala, 232
Pincus, Allen, 17, 33, 430, 431, 498, 499
Pinderhughes, Elaine, 132
Pinderhughes, Gary, 132
Pine, Barbara, 151, 152
Pinkston, Elsie, 328
Pipe, Peter, 244, 300, 303
Polansky, Norman, 193, 195
Polly, Joan, 285
Polster, Richard, 387, 389
Porter, Eugene, 356, 357
Porter, Sylvia, 346
Powell, Thomas, 312
Powers, Gerald T., 71, 78
Priestley, Philip, 348
Prochnow, Herbert, 138
Prochnow, Herbert, Jr., 138
Proctor, Enola, 379
Project on the Status and Education of Women, 162
Pruger, Robert, 146, 415, 416

Quick, John, 139

Rapp, Charles, 63
Rawley, Callman, 50, 55, 63
Reamer, Fredrick, 152
Reeves, Christine, 375
Reid, William, 214, 215, 297, 298, 302, 303, 305, 307, 317, 320, 323, 324, 342, 386, 390–391, 404, 407
Reilly, Robert, 102, 103
Reuterman, Nicholas A., 437
Rhodes, Gary B., 135, 425
Rich, Christine, 39–40, 48
Richmond, Mary E., 66, 78
Rivas, Robert F., 477, 481
Robert, Henry M., 482, 483
Rock, Barry D., 461
Rogers, Carl R., 16, 33
Roles, Patricia, 347
Rooney, Ronald, 107, 191, 192
Rose, Sheldon, 316
Roseland, Ronald W., 481
Rosenberg, Donna, 130
Rossi, Peter, 386, 466
Rossi, Robert, 473
Rothman, Jack, 418–419
Rubin, Herbert, 491
Rubin, Irene, 491
Rubright, Robert, 447
Russell, J. Michael, 316
Russo, J. Robert, 146
Rutman, Leonard, 463
Rzepnicki, Tina, 290, 328

Sallee, Alvin, 373
Salus, Marsha K., 287, 290
Samenow, Stanton, 207, 208
Sandler, Bernice R., 162, 163
Sarbin, Theodore, 243, 245
Satir, Virginia, 66, 78, 250
Savage, Andrea, 39, 45–46, 48, 358
Schacter, Burt, 33
Schalock, Robert L., 463
Schinke, Steven, 328
Schlesinger, Elfriede, 362, 378, 379, 469, 472
Schlosberg, Shirley, 104, 107, 189, 195, 363–364, 365
Schmitt, Barton, 126, 477
Schneiderman, Leonard, 44, 48
Schoborn, Karl, 210
Schubert, Margaret, 321
Schultz, Michael, 472, 473
Schultze, Gretchen L., 287, 290
Schwab, John J., 466–467

Subject Index

National Association of Social Workers, 12, 21, 29, 30, 37, 39, 42, 43, 45, 46, 47, 155, 164–168, 282, 426, 474. *See also* Code of Ethics

National Self-Help Clearing-house, 312

Natural helper, 310

Needs assessment:
of agency, 434–437
of client, 307–309

Negative reinforcement, definition of, 325

Negativism, client, 191

Neighborhood of child client, 265–266

Networking, 36. *See also* Support networks for social worker

Newspaper release. *See* Media and social agencies

Nominal Group Technique (NGT), 484–485

Nonverbal communication, 99–100, 377

Nonvoluntary client, 297, 305

Normalization:
definition of, 380–381
philosophy, 60

Notetaking, 176

Nuclear family, 245

Objective, definition of, 300

Objectivity:
definition of, 85
of social worker, 51–52

Open-ended questions, 102, 175, 258

Oral presentations by social worker, 136–138

Organizational context, 415–467
agency operations, 416–425
budgeting, 442–444
change, 466–467
evaluation of agency, 463–466
evaluation of program, 461–463
evaluation of social worker, 459–461
fundraising, 447–450
grant applications, 454–458
marketing, 444–447
media, 446, 450–454
needs assessment, 434–437
project activities, 437–442
staff selection, 425–430, 432–433

Organizations, power in, 489–490

Out-of-home placement of child client, 371–373

Paperwork, 111

Paraphrasing client's response, 101, 209

Parent Outcome Interview, 403

Parents Anonymous, 310

Partializing client's concerns, 93

Participation of client, 56–57

Patients' Bill of Rights, 216

Peabody Picture Vocabulary Test, 279

Peer review for social worker, 407–409

Performance evaluation, 459–461

Person-in-Environment configuration, 212, 282

Personal debt, 343–346

Personal growth of social worker, 131–168. *See also* Professional development

Personal habits of social worker, 156–160

Personal satisfaction of client, 262, 266–267

Personal style of social worker, 51

Personality Inventory for Children (PIC), 280

Personality tests, 280

Personnel management. *See* Staff development

PERT chart, example, 440

Phase, definition of, 66

Physical disabilities of client, 176–177

Planning for change process, 71–72, 294–316
goal selection, checklist, 298–300
informal resources, 310–316
intervention objectives, 300–303
problem search, 297–298
service contract, 303–309
target problems, selection, 295–297

Point systems, 331

Policy makers:
persuading, 497–502
writing to, 500–502

Position announcement, 425–426

Positive language, 301

Positive reinforcement, definition of, 325

Positivism, 84

Power in organizations, 489–490

Practice models, 74

Practice principles of social work, 5–9, 22, 49–63

Practice research, 38–39

Preintake, 67–68

Prejudice of social worker, 358–359

Prescription drugs, 381–383

Press kit for media, 451–452

Prevention levels, 75

Primary prevention, 37

Principle, definition of, 49

Priorities-weighting grid, 350–351

Prioritizing:
problems, 296–297
tasks, 109, 148

Private agency, 416

Problem checklist as aid for client, 184–187

Problem solving:
helping client learn skills, 58–59
imagination and, 17–18
by large group, 486–487

Problem-Oriented Recording (POR), 122–124

Process:
definition of, 66
recording of, 126–127

Procrastination, 110

Professional background of social worker, 7–8

Professional cooperation, 472–477

Professional development of social worker, 52–53, 131–168
bureaucracy, 145–146
ethics, 150–152, 164–168
harassment, 160–163
negligence, 152–156
objectivity, 51–52
professional library, 143–145
roles, 34–48
self-awareness, 156–160
stress management, 146–149
supervision, 132–135

Professional resumé, 429

Professionalization of social work, 9–10, 28–30, 34–48, 85

Program budgeting for agency, 444

Program evaluation, 384, 461–463

Project activities, 437–442

Project on the Status and Education of Women, 162

Project-team model in social agency, 424

Projection, 240
Projective tests, 280
Prompting technique, 327
Protection, child's need, 285–290
Protocol statements, 475–477
Psychological testing, 278–281
Psycho-Social Screening Package (PSSP), 269–270
Psychosocial assessment and diagnosis, 38
Public agency, definition of, 416
Purpose of agency, 416–417

Quality assurance monitoring, 41
Questioning, 102–103, 213–214

Racist attitudes of social worker, 358–359
Radio news. *See* Media and social agencies
Random reinforcement schedule, 326
Rapid-Assessment Instruments (RAIs), 214
Rationalization, 240
Reaction formation, 241
Reassurance, 324
Reciprocal behavior contract, 330
Reconstituted family, 220
Referrals, 36, 69, 177–181
connection techniques, 180–181
Reflection of feelings of client, 101
Reframing technique, 97, 338–339
Regression, 241
Reinforcement, 324–328
schedules, 326
Relationship with client, 15–16, 83–86
Report writing, 112–114
Repression, 240
Requests for Proposals (RFPs), 455
Research instruments, 214
Resistance to change, 172, 489
Resource assessment, 35–36, 39–40, 41
Respect of client, 54–55, 158, 318, 361
Rights of client, 294–295
Risk Assessment Matrix (RAM), 290
RISK technique, 485–486
Robert's Rules of Order, 482
Role performance of client, 242–244
Role reversal, 332–333

Roleplaying, 329, 332–333, 336, 339–341
Roles of social worker. *See* Professional roles of social worker
Rorschach Test, 280

Safety of social worker, 107, 189, 208–210
Sanction of social work, 12
School life of child client, 265
Scientific aspects of social work, 21–31
Self-anchored scale, 399–400
Self-awareness of social worker, 156–160
Self-care, client, 261, 266
Self-determination of client, 57–58, 295–296
Self-disclosure by social worker, 192
Self-neglect, 378
Self-talk, 333–335
Sensory disabilities of client, 176–177
Service contract, 303–307
Service system linkage, 36
Sexual harassment, 160–163
Sexuality of child, 265
Shaping technique, 327
Silence, communication during, 90, 106
Single-parent family, 245
Single-subject designs (SSD), 386–389
Skip-generation family, 245
Small groups:
discussion of self, 352–354
meetings of social workers, 477–481
as resource, 312–316
SOAP format, 122, 124–125
Social agencies. *See* Agencies
Social and adaptive skills, teaching to client, 36–37
Social assessment report, 215–219
sample, 217–219
Social change agent, as a role, 44–46
Social conditions, 24–25
Social history of client. *See* Social assessment report
Social legislation, initiating, 502–503
Social Network Grid and Map, 224–228
Social policy analysis, 491–493

Social programs, 27–28
Social roles of client, 242–244
Social support assessment, 224–228
Social treatment:
of client, 38
evaluation, 384
Social work:
definition of, 1
practice, principles of, 53–62
practice models, 31
as a profession, 28–30
purpose of, 10–11
scope of, 11–12
Social Work, 144
Social work contract, definition of, 73
Social Work Dictionary, 34, 36, 38, 43, 45
Social worker:
personal characteristics, 7, 51
principles of, 50–53
professional background, 7–8
roles and functions, 34–48
style, 30–31
Some Principles of Good Writing, 142
Special abilities test, 279–280
Speech, making a, 136–138
Sperry Rand Corporation, 440
Stabilizing care, ongoing, 38
Staff:
development, 42–43
meetings, 431–432
recruitment and selection, 425–430
Stanford-Binet, 279
Strengths of client, 92–93, 192, 219, 236–239, 319
Stress management, 146–149
Structuring, definition of, 85
Suicide risk, 283–285
Summarization technique in communication, 101
Supervision of social workers, 132–135
Support networks for social worker, 430–431
System of Multicultural Pluralistic Assessment (SOMPA), 279

Target behavior, 387
definition of, 324
Target problems, 295–297
Task Achievement Scaling, (TAS), 389–391

Task-centered approach, 302, 389–391
Task planning, projects, 441
Tasks of Emotional Development Test, 280
Telecommunications device (TDD), 177
Telephone communications, 117–119
with client, 173–174
Teletypewriter (TTY), 177
Television news. *See* Media and social agencies
Termination of service, 76–77, 384–386, 409–411
Testifying in court, 127–130
Thematic Apperception Test (TAT), 280
Theoretical orientations of social work, 22, 25–27
Tickler file, 110
Time management, 41, 108–112, 148

Time out, 327–328
"To-do" lists, 109
Token economics, 331
Tone of voice, 99
Training volunteers, 433
Transferability, 58–59
Transference, 95
Treatment plan. *See* Service contract

Universalization, 324

Value systems in social work, 20–21, 53–54
Veteran's Administration, 460
Videotape recordings, 127
Vineland Social Maturity Scale, 280
Vision loss of client, 377
Vision of social worker, communicating to client, 55–56
Voluntary agency, definition of, 416
Volunteers, selecting and training, 432–433

Warmth with clients, 16, 84
Webster's Dictionary, 22
Wechsler Adult Intelligence Scale—Revised (WAIS—R), 279
Wechsler Scales, 279
Whole-person orientation in social work practice, 54, 211–212, 318
"Why" questions, 103
Work habits, 159–160
Workload management, 40–41, 108–130
controlling, 119–120
letter writing, 115–116
narrative records, 120–127
report writing, 112–114
time management, 108–112
Writing journal articles, 139–143
Written communication, 159
letters, 115–116
to policy makers, 500–502
reports, 112–114